S0-ACG-407

Handbook of
Business Strategy

Second Edition

Editor

HAROLD E. GLASS
C & G Consultants, Inc.

WARREN, GORHAM & LAMONT
Boston • New York

Copyright © 1991 by

WARREN, GORHAM & LAMONT, INC.
210 SOUTH STREET
BOSTON, MASSACHUSETTS 02111

—————

ALL RIGHTS RESERVED

No part of this book may be reproduced in any form, by photo-
stat, microfilm, xerography, or any other means, or incorporated
into any information retrieval system, electronic or mechanical,
without the written permission of the copyright owner.

ISBN 0-7913-0698-4

Library of Congress Catalog Card No. 90-071266

PRINTED IN THE UNITED STATES OF AMERICA

Contributing Authors

Andy Beaulieu (Chapter 18)
The Hay Group

Joseph Wayne Brockbank (Chapter 2)
University of Michigan

Sayan Chatterjee (Chapter 13)
Case Western Reserve University

Robert H. Clement (Chapter 1)
C & G Consultants, Inc.

Michael Cooper (Chapter 10)
Opinion Research

Kevin Cuthbert (Chapter 26)
Research for Management

David G. deRoulet (Chapter 22)
Cleveland Consulting Associates

Denis H. Detzel (Chapter 29)
Research for Management

James W. Down (Chapter 12)
Temple Barker & Sloane, Inc.

Alan L. Farkas (Chapter 8)
Farkas Berkowitz & Co.

Martin R. Frankel (Chapter 11)
Bernard Baruch College, CUNY

David H. Gaylin (Chapter 12)
Temple Barker & Sloane, Inc.

Joseph H. Gekoski (Chapter 5)
Strategic Management Group, Inc.

Andrew Geller (Chapter 18)
The Hay Group

Harold E. Glass (Chapter 1)
C & G Consultants, Inc.

Donald C. Hambrick (Chapter 19)
Columbia University

Lee Hawley (Chapter 18)
  The Hay Group

Walter R. Holman (Chapter 8)
  Farkas Berkowitz & Co.

Ira Kay (Chapter 25)
  The Hay Group

David A. Kudon (Chapter 11)
  Abbott Laboratories

Marvin B. Lieberman (Chapter 21)
  John E. Anderson Graduate School of Management, UCLA

Peter Lorange (Chapter 23)
  Norwegian School of Management
  The Wharton School, University of Pennsylvania

Michael Lubatkin (Chapter 14)
  University of Connecticut

George Manderlink (Chapter 18)
  The Hay Group

Susan Schwartz McDonald (Chapter 17)
  Booz-Allen & Hamilton, Inc.

Walter Mardis (Chapter 3)
  The Hay Group

Carolyn L. Middlebrooks (Chapter 26)
  Research for Management

David B. Montgomery (Chapter 21)
  Stanford University

Thomas A. Moore, Jr. (Chapter 27)
  First Michigan Bank Corporation

Brian Morgan (Chapter 10)
  Opinion Research

David M. Ondersma (Chapter 27)
  First Michigan Bank Corporation

Ronald G. Quintero (Chapter 7)
  R. G. Quintero & Co.

William R. Sandberg (Chapter 6)
  University of South Carolina

Sidney Schoeffler (Chapter 4)
  Mantis, Inc.

David M. Schweiger (Chapter 6)
University of South Carolina

David C. Shanks (Chapter 9)
Arthur D. Little, Inc.

Lyle Spencer (Chapter 28)
McBer & Co.

Leslie L. Spero (Chapter 5)
Strategic Management Group, Inc.

James C. Spira (Chapter 22)
Cleveland Consulting Associates

David Ulrich (Chapter 2)
University of Michigan

James P. Walsh (Chapter 15)
Dartmouth College

Janet Weiss (Chapter 20)
University of Michigan

Roderick E. White (Chapter 24)
The University of Western Ontario

Gordon Wyner (Chapter 16)
M/A/R/C Inc.

Steven Zlotowski (Chapter 5)
Strategic Management Group, Inc.

Preface

MANAGERS TODAY ARE BESET by increased competition, rapidly changing products and markets, and new societal and employee expectations. As a result, the need for effective planning has become greater, even as the size of the corporate planning staff has decreased. Effective planning has become too important to be viewed as the province of planners alone. The second edition of *Handbook of Business Strategy* is intended to help planning and line managers improve the effectiveness of their strategic planning. In particular, this handbook addresses three key questions:

- What tools and concepts should we know?
- What do we know that actually works?
- How do we most productively implement what we plan?

The needs of managers have changed significantly since the first edition. For example, there is a new awareness among many managers that their companies must create shareholder value if they are to be successful and remain independent. Many of the standard tools and concepts of strategic planning, such as the role of market share, are undergoing major transformations. At the same time, there is growing recognition that companies must create value at the business unit level by identifying sustainable sources of competitive advantage. For instance, in many businesses the customer is gaining renewed importance, as demonstrated by such now-familiar phrases as "customer orientation," "market focus," and "product and service quality."

The wave of mergers and acquisitions has also left its mark on industry. Fueled by the availability of debt instruments such as high-yield, or junk, bonds and the increasingly international nature of competition, unprecedented mergers, buyouts, and acquisitions have taken place in numerous corporations. Many business observers have noted the lack of success among these restructurings, whether measured by stock market evaluation, changes in operating performance, or the eventual reselling of the acquired assets. Companies bought today are quickly sold tomorrow, with little apparent gain in financial value. However, businesses must be managed, not simply acquired, milked, and then divested.

Probably no area of change has been greater in strategic planning than the emphasis on linking strategy development with implementation. Management appears unwilling any longer to support large planning staffs that are divorced from operating management. Elaborate strategic planning processes are giving way to more focused efforts that tie together the plans themselves with the implementation needs of line management.

The second edition of this handbook addresses these changing needs in twenty-nine chapters that are organized into five part divisions:

- Part I: Elements of Effective Planning
- Part II: Tools for Strategic Planning
- Part III: Corporate Development: Mergers and Acquisitions
- Part IV: Formulating Business Unit and Corporate Strategy
- Part V: Strategy Implementation

To reflect the changing needs of managers today, the second edition emphasizes three themes. The first theme focuses on the new key concepts and techniques that planners and line managers should understand in today's strategic-planning environment. For example, how can managers create strategic unity? How can shareholder value best be defined? These new key concepts and tools receive particular attention in Parts I, II, and III.

The second theme concerns empirical evidence about which strategic-planning processes and techniques are most effective and which are not. The second edition systematically explains the existing empirical evidence in order to provide insight about what has actually proven to work. Parts II and III stress specific planning processes and techniques that have been used successfully in a wide range of business settings. Parts IV and V present extensive evidence of what types of strategic activities have yielded the best results.

The third theme stresses how to successfully implement management plans. Part V in particular demonstrates how management processes, organizational structure, employee development, and corporate culture can be used effectively as tools for implementation.

I would like to thank the thoughtful people at Warren, Gorham & Lamont for their assistance throughout the entire development of this handbook. Catherine Dillon provided invaluable guidance in getting the project under way. Louise Hockett's steady hand helped the book through its final stages. In addition, I would like to thank the management of BG Enterprises for working so hard under such a demanding editor.

HAROLD E. GLASS

King of Prussia, Pennsylvania
July 1990

Contents

PART I

Elements of Effective Strategy

1

Strategic Planning and Effective Implementation

HAROLD E. GLASS

ROBERT H. CLEMENT

C&G Consultants, Inc.

INTRODUCTION

Strategic planning can make a difference, particularly when it has a long-term focus and is used as a management tool, rather than simply being an exercise in forms completion. Company after company has learned that superior planning does not necessarily translate into superior performance. A good plan is a critical first step. But superior performance requires that the plan be successfully implemented. In particular it is useful to link planning with implementation in four key areas: organizational structure, human resources, management processes, and business culture. Whether a company is seeking to increase market share, diversify, or retrench, it needs to consider implementation planning throughout the strategic planning process. This chapter demonstrates the link between strategic planning and implementation by examining the characteristics and the implementation planning practices of companies that have increased their market shares. It concludes with a case study of an implementation planning framework used by one company to translate strategy into practice and negative cash balances into positive cash balances.

STRATEGIC PLANNING

Years ago, strategic planning became very popular in business, and corporate planning staffs grew quite large, often numbering scores of people. Elaborate procedures sprang up to capture data on all aspects of business unit performance, which top management was to use to review and evaluate business performance against the plan.

In 1970s and 1980s, criticism steadily mounted against many of the concepts and methods of strategic planning. For many managers dealing with all the detail and oversight, strategic planning turned into a tedious, bothersome exercise in forms completion. Managements eventually ruled on the usefulness of large planning staffs and of strategic planning by systematically reducing the size of these staffs in corporation after corporation and by simplifying the planning process itself.

Eventually, serious questions arose as to whether strategic planning had any value at all. While strategic planning was at its height in the United States, American industry experienced dramatic losses in competitiveness in industry after industry. Stories in both the popular and business press have told of corporate inflexibility and sluggishness, poor productivity growth, uncompetitive cost structures, and disappointing levels of innovation. In some cases, unfair rules of international competition, poor school systems, or inappropriate government actions have been blamed. Senior managements have also come under attack for being too self-serving and overly cautious, as did business schools and the investment community for imbuing corporate management with overly financial, short-term objectives. Many have viewed strategic planning itself as the culprit behind American industry's shortcomings. Managers overanalyzed situations at the expense of decision making. According to Peters and Waterman, the managements in excellent companies avoid living in an ivory tower and combine analysis with a bias for action.[1]

However, much of the discussion about strategic planning has been misguided. Research in the late 1980s has demonstrated the value of strategic planning when it is linked with effective implementation of the plans. Management can no longer plan one set of strategies, yet organize and run the company according to another set, and still expect to achieve success. A well-conceived strategy is successful only to the extent that it is effectively carried out.

The Problems With Strategic Planning

Oppressive Paperwork and Intrusive Staff. Critics of strategic planning charged that it often degenerated into little more than expensive, time-consuming collection and completion of elaborate forms. Corporate staff might return the plans to a business unit for no other reason than that they lacked supporting detail.

Worse yet, line management feared the intervention of planning staffs in the operation of the business unit itself. Corporate planning functions saw themselves as the chief planners, rather than as resource and support for corporate and business unit management. Consequently, planners easily justified their intervention in line management activities. In contrast, today senior line managers are viewed as the chief planners, with planning staffs there to support them.

Planning Concepts With Limited Validity. Perhaps even worse than intrusive staff and oppressive paperwork, many key concepts of strategic planning fell out of favor as more and more managers questioned their usefulness and validity. Analytical concepts such as the reduction of earnings volatility through diversification and portfolio theory provided limited guidance and, in fact, tended to divert attention away from the importance of understanding customers, markets, and competitors. Competitive advantage is established by meeting customer needs more effectively than the competitors can. But many managers found that the key strategic planning concepts took management's attention away from this business fundamental.

A case in point is portfolio theory or planning, which became a fundamental building block during the formative years of strategic planning. Port-

---

[1] Thomas J. Peters and Robert Waterman, Jr., *In Search of Excellence* (New York: Harper and Row, 1982).

folio planning schemes all shared the common assumption that a business's stage of life more or less dictated its strategic direction. As a business matured, for example, it was to be milked for cash, starved for investment, and eventually divested. Two messages emerged for management: Diversify, and concentrate management efforts on growth businesses. However, the overwhelming evidence is that (1) diversification does not lead to improved business performance, and (2) significant amounts of money can be made from the effective management of mature, and even declining, businesses.

Most critically, however, portfolio planning provided management with no guidance on how to manage the business. Portfolio theory had management concentrating on financial concepts such as reducing the volatility of revenue streams rather than on the creation and implementation of superior strategies for dealing with markets, products, customers, and competitors. In other words, the customer was forgotten as industry failed to develop, market, and service quality products. However, the frustration with strategic planning has brought managers "back to basics." A renewed emphasis on quality as a determinant of success in the marketplace is being witnessed. Product and service quality have become king.

The Dubious Value of Strategic Planning. In addition to the costs in time and money involved in strategic planning, many senior managers began to examine whether strategic planning actually increased company performance. Academics as well looked at the evidence for the increased business performance associated with strategic planning.

Planning was a central tenet of academic and consulting lore, and initial empirical studies pointed to a positive relationship between planning and performance. However, later work raised major questions about the validity of the findings. In the early 1980s, J. S. Armstrong reviewed many of these early studies to determine whether or not planning paid off. He concluded that at best, the results were mixed. Many of the major claims put forward in the studies that Armstrong examined did not hold up. Moreover, Armstrong's evaluations of later studies also did not uncover a positive relationship between strategic planning and improved business performance.[2]

The Importance of Strategic Planning

Conclusions to the contrary notwithstanding, there is work that points to the positive effects of strategic planning on company performance.[3] A 1987

---

[2] J.S. Armstrong, "The Value of Formal Planning for Strategic Decisions: Review of Empirical Research," *Sloan Management Review* vol. 3, no. 3 (1982).

[3] This unpublished research was done by the authors of this chapter in conjunction with Dr. Michael R. Cooper, now chief executive officer of the Opinion Research Corporation of Princeton, New Jersey.

study by the firm of Research for Management surveyed over 20,000 managers at all levels from fifty-six companies, representing a wide range of industries. A number of questions in the survey addressed the nature and value of strategic planning. The responses came predominantly from the recipients and users of the strategic plans—the plans' best judges.

Figure 1-1 presents results from the study. The percentages indicate the number of managers reporting satisfaction with the strategic planning being done in their respective companies. Responses are divided into two categories: those from organizations that had achieved above-average profitability, when compared to industry peers, and those from organizations that had not. Almost all managers reported that their companies use some type of planning, but managers from higher-performing companies give a significantly more positive evaluation of the usefulness of planning in their companies. This is true for both manufacturing and service companies, although the difference is more pronounced among manufacturing companies.

Managers evaluated the strategic plans themselves on a number of dimensions, such as formality, completeness, and long-range orientation (see Figure 1-2). Although managers from higher-performing companies tended to rate all the dimensions more highly than did managers in poorer-performing companies, the responses on two dimensions particularly stood out. Managers in more successful companies emphasized both the goal clar-

FIGURE 1-1

Managers' Evaluation of the Value of Strategic Planning

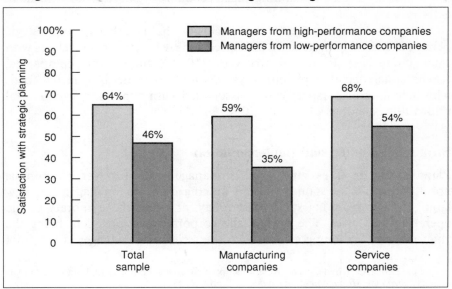

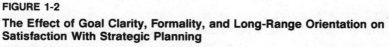

FIGURE 1-2

The Effect of Goal Clarity, Formality, and Long-Range Orientation on Satisfaction With Strategic Planning

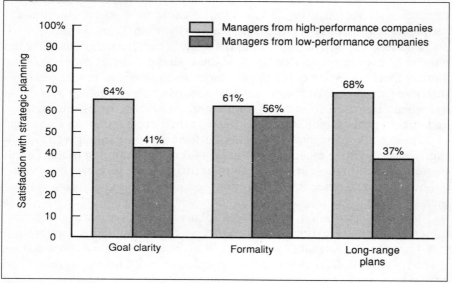

ity provided by senior management through the strategic plan and the long-range nature of the plan. Plan formality made little difference. Thus, it is the nature of strategic planning that accounts for success, not the mere activity.

Rhyne's research supports the conclusion that it is the type of strategic planning, rather than the mere presence of the activity, that correlates with financial success. From his survey of 210 "Fortune 1000" companies, Rhyne concluded that planning systems that combine an external focus with a long-term perspective are associated with superior ten-year total return to stockholders.[4]

Strategic Planning and Implementation

Planning can be an essential tool for management. However, planning is not a substitute for sound decision making by senior management. Few large strategic planning staffs exist today, at either the corporate or the operating unit level. The days of the corporate vice president being the chief planner are long gone. Instead, the senior line manager is the chief

---

[4] Lawrence C. Rhyne, "The Relationship of Strategic Planning to Financial Performance," *Strategic Management Journal* vol. 7, no. 5 (1986).

planner in successful companies, and the planning process is a tool used to anticipate and address the strategic challenges facing the company.

Successful planning is a long-term process with an external focus. As Porter asserts, it concentrates on identifying sustainable sources of competitive advantage.[5] Management should no longer waste time questioning the utility of strategic planning. Instead, management must move on to understanding how and when strategic planning is most effectively implemented. The fundamental problem for many corporations today is that strategic plans are developed with little or no thought given to how they will be implemented. A sustainable competitive advantage is one that can be both identified and implemented.

What follows is an examination of how certain companies successfully implemented one particular strategic goal—increased market share. Companies that increase market share approach their organizations in distinctive ways. Through working with organization structures, people, management processes, and culture, these companies are able to implement their strategic plans.

INCREASING MARKET SHARE

Numerous studies have shown the link between market share and profitability, but few attempts have been made to understand what successful businesses actually do to increase market share. What, if any, organizational characteristics distinguish businesses that have improved their market position from those that have not? Do the cultures of these businesses differ? Are the backgrounds of their key managers different? What can other companies planning similar strategies learn about successful implementation?

Businesses with a pattern of market share growth are managed differently than businesses that are not gaining ground. The implementation practices of gainers and losers are different.[6]

Attention was first focused on market share when another study, conducted by Buzzell, Gale, and Sultan, concluded that market share was the single most important determinant of profitability. This seminal study, conducted in 1975, made use of the Profit Impact of Market Strategies (PIMS) data base. The authors asserted that on average, a difference of 10

---

[5] Michael E. Porter, *Competitive Advantage: Creating Sustaining Superior Performance* (New York: The Free Press, 1985).

[6] The authors of this chapter participated in a multiyear study primarily funded by the Hay Group, Philadelphia, Pennsylvania, 1985–1989. The unpublished data from this discontinued study were supplemented by the authors of this chapter by additional data collected during the winter of 1990.

percentage points in market share is accompanied by a difference of 5 points in return on investment (ROI).[7]

The importance of this overall finding was not lost on management. As Kress and Switzer put it, the "effects of this research rippled through business and academic circles, as managers, undergraduate business students, and MBAs were taught the gospel of 'profitability through market share.' "[8] When Buzzeli and Gale updated their original research ten years later, they found market share and profitability were still strongly related, with a net effect of 3½ points of ROI for every 10 points of market share.

The most important reason for the link between market share and profitability, the researchers assert, is that organizations with larger market shares enjoy greater economies of scale. Their unit costs are simply lower than the unit costs of competitors with smaller market shares. Buzzell and Gale indicate that these cost advantages are substantial and are directly reflected in higher profit margins. In addition, their studies show that market leaders generally benefit from stronger perceptions of product quality and are able to maintain higher prices for their products. As a result, market leaders have a more favorable capital structure, as reflected in the ratio of investment to sales. Their operating ratios—measured in terms of pretax profits to sales—are far more attractive. Capacity utilization also is usually highest among market leaders.[9]

Since the original study by Buzzell, Gale, and Sultan in 1975, many management experts have contended that the importance of market share has been overemphasized. Their primary criticisms have been that:

- The data bases used (particularly the PIMS data base) have not included a number of important variables such as organization and competitor behavior.
- Businesses with smaller market shares can also demonstrate superior profitability in certain circumstances.
- The general relationship between market share and profitability is spurious and is actually a function of other underlying variables such as management skills.
- There is no straight-line relationship between market share and profitability. The lowest profitability may often be found for those businesses "stuck in the middle."

---

[7] R. D. Buzzell, B. T. Gale, and R. G. M. Sultan, "Market Share—Key to Profitability," *Harvard Business Review* vol. 63, no. 1 (Jan.–Feb. 1975), pp. 97–106.

[8] George Kress and Deborah Switzer, "Market Share: How Important Is It?," *Handbook of Business Strategy: 1988/1989 Yearbook* (Boston, New York: Warren, Gorham and Lamont, 1989).

[9] R. D. Buzzell and B. T. Gale, *The PIMS Principles: Linking Strategy to Performance* (New York: The Free Press, 1987).

Later reviews of studies that used data bases other than PIMS, however, have led to the conclusion that market share leadership is associated with profitability. Certainly, the impact of market share may vary by type of business or industry. Moreover, as Porter has pointed out, market share is not really the cause of profitability; it is the result of management actions.[10] Highly focused, low- and medium-market share companies can be profitable. Still, high market share and above-average profitability do go together in industry after industry. The question, then, is no longer whether market share is related to profitability but, instead, what businesses that want to increase market share can to do achieve this goal, and in particular, what these businesses can learn from companies that have successfully increased market share.

IMPLEMENTING A STRATEGIC PLAN: FROM PAPER TO PROFIT

Developing a strategy to increase market share or to achieve any other goal without adequate consideration of the implementation issues involved in executing that strategy is a virtual guarantee of failure. Regardless of how management wishes to enlarge market share — by improving product quality or service, lowering prices, or increasing marketing and selling efforts — it must address the key implementation planning areas in order for the strategy to have a full chance of success. That is, management must conceive the strategy in the context of the structure, people, processes, and culture required for that strategy's successful execution.

Choosing a Workable Strategy

Finding the right approach to expanding market share is a real challenge. For instance, regulatory or legal constraints may hinder a market leader's ability to grow. The long-distance telecommunications market, where the Federal Communications Commission's actions over the last ten years has prevented a share increase for the market leader, AT&T, is an example of the interference of such constraints.

The costs of attacking market leaders may be so high as to prevent market followers from launching large-scale strategies for share growth. Philip Morris, for example, finally gave up on its very expensive, and ultimately unsuccessful, campaign to increase 7-UP's share of the soft drink market.

---

[10] Michael E. Porter, *Competitive Strategy: Techniques for Analyzing Industries and Competitors* (New York: The Free Press, 1989), Chapter 2.

Another approach to increasing market share is price competition. This strategy may be tempting, but it is rarely successful. Because market followers usually do not enjoy cost advantages, price cutting can quickly become counterproductive. Market leaders can easily respond with comparable price cuts that they are in a better position to absorb and accommodate because their cost structures are lower. The airline industry, for example, has frequently experienced price wars, usually started by one of the smaller, struggling airlines. The market leaders respond almost immediately by lowering their fares, with little change in market standing resulting from the fare reductions.

In general, the most workable and successful strategies involve attempts to gain market share through innovation or improved service and product quality.

Matching Organizational Structure and Strategy

A business's organizational structure can also have a significant impact on the success of a strategy to increase market share. Our study showed that a market-focused organizational structure gives a company a competitive edge in its attempt to increase market share. Such a structure keeps the organization closer to the customer and enhances the organization's ability to anticipate and respond to customer needs. In the study, businesses with a market-focused structure reported three-year market share increases of 8 percent compared to a increase of 2 percent for functionally organized businesses (see Figure 1-3).

Market responsiveness is especially important in rapidly changing markets. Particularly noteworthy, then, is the study's finding that market share differences are even greater for businesses in more turbulent markets. Turbulent markets are those characterized by particularly large changes in a business unit's environment, such as accelerated rates of new product introduction, market instability, or inflation. The differences between functional and market-focused businesses are also pronounced for the largest business units in the study—units that might be expected to be somewhat slower to react to market needs.

A flatter organization, with fewer management levels, is yet another way to remain close to customers and foster more rapid decision making. Customer proximity and speedy decision making are needed if a business is to enlarge its market share.

A study using some of the OASIS data predicted the number of management levels likely to be found in sales and marketing organizations on the basis of the size and the sales of the various business units. The study found that businesses with flatter sales and marketing organizations were best able to increase market share. The reported market share increase was largest when the actual number of layers was fewer than or equal to the

FIGURE 1-3

The Effect of a Market-Focused Organization on Market Share Growth

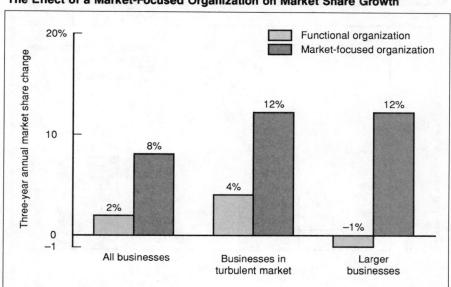

number predicted by the model. In contrast, when the actual number of layers exceeded the predicted number of levels, reported market share increase was less.[11]

Matching People to Strategy

Competitors' actions, shifting customer preferences, and the availability of financial and human resources are all important determinants of a business's success. But probably no variable is more important than the management skills that exist within the organization. And nowhere is this more obvious than in organizations that have achieved market share increases.

For instance, units where the top manager has had previous marketing or sales experience are able to obtain markedly greater increases than units where the top manager has not had such experience (see Figure 1-4). The difference is especially strong for businesses in turbulent markets, where market share positioning is critical.

Infusing new ideas throughout the organization is usually essential to bringing about a substantial change in market share in most organizations. New ideas may be required for product development, product introduc-

---

[11] The results of this earlier analysis were summarized in an internal Hay Group document, "OASIS Research: Working Draft" (1989).

FIGURE 1-4

The Effect of Top Manager Marketing and Sales Experience on Market Share Growth

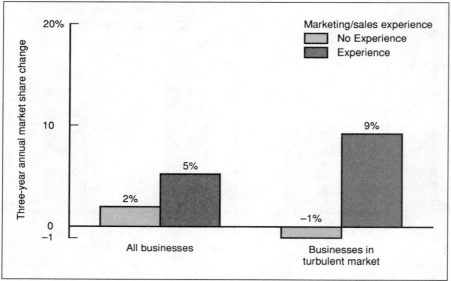

tion, product positioning, and product selling. Market share change is clearly associated with the presence of a higher percentage of managers hired from outside the business unit (see Figure 1-5). These outsiders bring new ways to look at old problems and to identify and address new problems.

Managing the Process

Market share increases can come about through a rededication to improved product quality or service. In the early and mid-1980s, for example, Ford Motor Company began an effort to improve the quality of its new automobiles. Not only were capital expenditures increased to bring new types of equipment on line, but Ford management and employees instituted a series of employee-oriented programs to increase product quality. Working conditions were changed to foster employee commitment, and employee involvement in product quality control was also increased. At the same time, incentive programs were introduced that rewarded superior product quality.

New product sales often fuel market share changes. But as numerous studies have shown, few tasks are more challenging than getting successful

FIGURE 1-5

The Effect of Managers Hired From Outside on Market Share Growth

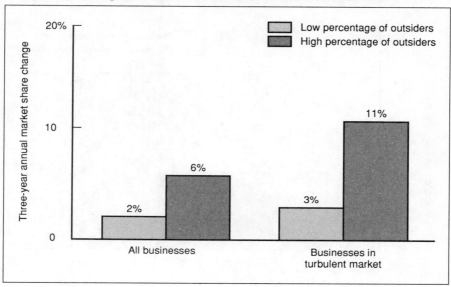

new products to market. Problems arise in determining unfulfilled customer needs, communicating those needs to product developers, bringing the new products out of the labs, conducting successful product launches, or providing adequate sales support. Figure 1-6 shows that companies that can carry out these processes and get successful new products to market have a greater chance to increase market share than companies that cannot.

Creating the Right Culture

Corporate culture is among the most elusive concepts in business today. Even though it may be hard to define "culture," it is now generally recognized that each business reflects a set of attitudes and values that guide the behavior of people in that organization.

The OASIS study asked the top three levels of management in each business to complete a questionnaire about their business's corporate culture. The results clearly illustrate that the cultures in businesses that experience market share growth are distinctive. These companies have cultures that emphasize:

- An achievement orientation
- A freedom for management action

FIGURE 1-6

The Effect of Successful New Product Introductions on Market Share Growth

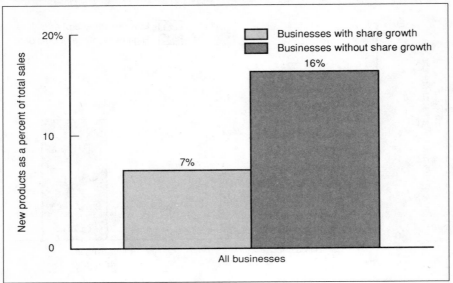

- An uninhibiting set of management processes
- A risk orientation
- A dynamic and entrepreneurial environment

A dominant cultural characteristic in these organizations is their demonstrated flexibility, i.e., their ability to anticipate and respond to changes in the marketplace. Managers in these businesses report that they are more risk-oriented and willing to stick out their necks to ensure that their businesses respond to their markets. For example, one pharmaceutical company was able to establish dominant market share, although its anti-ulcer drug was, in the eyes of many, not particularly distinctive medically. Prevailing industry wisdom was that a product without distinctly superior medical properties could not overtake an established blockbuster drug with years of patent protection remaining. However, management believed that innovative marketing could help their product's ultimate success. In no sense was management willing to risk the safety of their drug. But decreases in recommended dosage levels, combined with aggressive marketing materials and sales campaigns did, in fact, push Glaxo's Zantac past SmithKline & French's Tagamet to become the world's first $1.5 billion drug.

In addition, managers of businesses experiencing healthy market share growth feel that they have a great deal of freedom to act independently. In general, their businesses are more competitive and achievement-oriented.

Not surprisingly, these businesses are far more dynamic and entrepreneurial. Moreover, they are not as encumbered by a uniform management style and a single set of management practices.

These findings go a long way toward explaining the conditions that precede market share growth. All businesses face changes in their customer base, their competitors, and their product mixes. Companies that have successfully improved their market shares have been able to establish the responsive, market-oriented cultures needed to deal with these changes. Employees in these cultures believe they are part of dynamic organizations that value risk-taking, achievement, and success.

Lessons for Management

The decision to increase market share is one not to be made lightly. The improvement in profitability usually associated with a larger market share is clear. But the costs of increasing that market share may make greater profitability more difficult to achieve than management might initially expect. However, if a business decides it is worthwhile to make an investment in a market-share growth strategy, there is a great deal it can learn from the studies of companies that have already implemented successful strategies of that type. Those studies have attributed the firms' success to their ability to:

- Organize around markets;
- Keep their marketing and sales organizations as flat as possible;
- Ensure that the top of the organization has as much knowledge of marketing as it does about finance, production, and other areas;
- Introduce new people into the organization as needed; and
- Foster a culture that is responsive, flexible, and customer-oriented.

While market share may *improve* profitability, market share does not *cause* profitability. Rather, profitability is the result of sound implementation practices and programs in a number of key areas: strategy, structure, people, processes and culture. When an organization seeks to improve profitability through increased market share, it must plan for, and pay close attention to, all of these implementation areas.

CASE STUDY

To illustrate the points made in this chapter, the highlights of an actual (albeit disguised) client situation are discussed in this section.[12]

---

[12] The following is a discussion of a client situation in which the authors participated as consultants.

The Client Setting and Problem

The client was operating in an industry characterized as capital intensive, high technology, and cyclical, with relatively stable competitors. The client and its competitors were selling in world markets undergoing turmoil prompted by deregulation and increased competition. The company had its roots in defense-related products and, therefore, in government contracting sales and marketing. A complicating factor in the company culture and the corresponding management capabilities was the origin of the current company. It was a combination of six formerly independent and somewhat competitive companies.

Consultants were called in to the company after the appointment of a new CEO. He had developed a new strategic plan with top management that involved major changes in the emphasis and orientation of the management group—away from the manufacturing plant and technology strengths to a market-oriented operation. With this challenge, the consultants set about learning how the company had evolved, and why it had not generated a profit for the past ten years while consuming millions of dollars annually in newly injected capital. Figure 1-7 shows the company's actual and anticipated cash balances at year-end.

The company organization had recently changed from decentralized accountability for sales at each of its six manufacturing plants to a consolidated sales and marketing role at the company headquarters. This change

FIGURE 1-7

Case Study—Increasing Negative Cash Balances (experienced and planned)

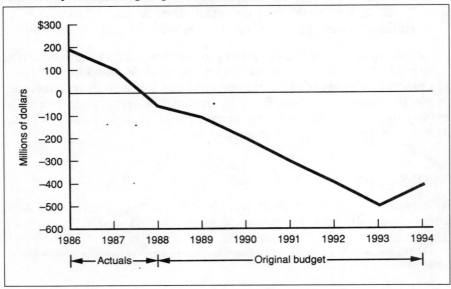

was strongly resented at each of the plants, which were individual fiefdoms. Furthermore, the CEO was not willing to confront the old cultural issue head-on by replacing the core management but was instead committed to keeping that group and still managing to change the culture. What he wanted from the consultants was help in determining the specifics of the change.

The company needed to simultaneously cut costs and improve its customer service—a tough balancing act for the best of managers. Customer service is a mix of marketing, sales, financing, product support, spare parts supply, and the training of customer on-line operating personnel and maintenance personnel. In planning, organizing, and delivering the right quality and quantity of customer service, the CEO had to lead top management to a common, simple, measurable objective: a positive cash balance.

Critical Success Factors

To get the management group to embrace the objective of a positive cash balance required several carefully thought-out implementation steps. The steps were derived from an agreed-upon list of critical success factors for the company. A critical success factor is an activity that a company must do well in order to fulfill its mission. The critical success factors, developed by the consultants from discussions held with the top managers and from their knowledge of the industry, were:

1. To meet customers' needs without exceeding competitive requirements,
2. To provide products that satisfy customer needs without "gold plating,"
3. To maintain technological strengths and competitive advantages in niche products, and
4. To segment markets and target marketing and sales to maximize product positioning and customer service capabilities.

Realizing these factors meant that the company had to cut its product costs and properly organize and manage its marketing, sales, technology, and customer service functions. Therefore, to apply the critical success factors in the implementation of the CEO's strategic plan required a complete reorganization.

Organizational Design Criteria

The next step in achieving the CEO's objective was to establish a set of organizational design criteria. These criteria had to be consistent with and supportive of the critical success factors. In other words, the company's structure, management processes, people, and culture had to be "in sync" with the goal of meeting the critical success factors.

The consultants developed a list of twelve organizational design criteria. Only a few of these criteria will be discussed here. One criterion dealt with organizing by the company's three markets. The three markets differed in their existing levels of business, profitability, growth prospects, technological strengths and weaknesses, competition, product acceptance, geographic concentration of customers, pricing sensitivity, and customer service requirements. This was a difficult criterion to implement: Management readily acknowledged that talent, technology, and sales and marketing resources were required to serve the company's three markets. Manufacturing, procurement, and after-sales servicing, however, were another issue, because reorganizing these functions impinged upon the manufacturing plant "fiefdoms."

Another criterion was to revamp the deal-making process. The product line was heavily weighted toward customers making large capital investments. In addition, the client's and the competitors' products were not directly comparable; that is, their operating and performance specifications and characteristics were different. Further, no one manager was accountable for deal-making besides the CEO. Deal-making requires the participation of many functions, not just marketing and sales. The key to success, once a company has suitable products to offer, is to efficiently and effectively conduct deal-making with prospective customers.

Constructing this process first required the implementation of the new organizational structure and appointing the top management positions. Second, the CEO decided that the head of marketing and sales would be accountable for directing the deal-making process. Third, all steps in the process were identified in sufficient detail to use in developing a series of recommended responsibilities for each function involved. Fourth, the sequence of the steps was analyzed to specify the positions within each function that would have accountabilities and when their participation would be needed. Fifth, delegations of authority were reviewed and revised, as necessary, to correspond to the new set of roles and accountabilities. Finally, the entire process was documented, reviewed by the appropriate management, and approved by the CEO. This may sound easy and straightforward, but it is not, when the organization is under pressure to survive, centers of power are breaking down, and new management relationships are evolving.

The deal-making process as it was implemented directly supported the critical success factors of meeting customer needs in the context of competitive conditions and targeting marketing and sales to maximize opportunities for success.

Strategy Implementation Results

The following four highlights show the company's performance improvement only one year after implementation of the strategic plan:

1. Sales up 19 percent.
2. Sales per employee up 96 percent.
3. A complete, convincing turnaround in profits—demonstrating the success of the company's efforts to cut costs and improve prices.
4. Positive cash balances at the end of the first year and projected throughout the next five-year planning horizon. (See Figure 1-8.)

It would be premature to conclude from the events and results to date that a new, more appropriate culture is firmly established within the company. It may reasonably take three to five years before such a change can be reliably substantiated. Nevertheless, things are clearly moving in the right direction. Company management's overall accomplishment during this arduous period was making strategy work for the company because of its considerable implementation planning efforts. These efforts far outweighed the strategic planning efforts.

CONCLUSION

Few executives still believe that highly detailed strategic planning processes are essential for superior performance. For instance, large corporate or business unit planning staffs are no longer the rule in corporations. The earlier belief in the power of strategic planning has given way to more realistic

FIGURE 1-8

Case Study—The Impact of Strategy Implementation on Cash Balances

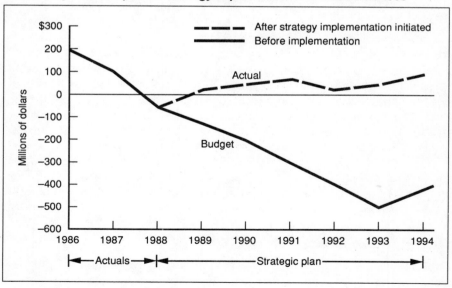

expectations about what planning can and cannot do. While planning can make a positive difference when it is oriented to the long term, serves as a management tool, and avoids time-consuming detail, executives today appreciate that superior plans do not automatically ensure superior performance. Success requires superior implementation as well as superior planning. In particular, a successful plan requires careful linkage with four key management areas: organizational structure, human resources, management processes, and business culture. Whatever a company's strategic goals or priorities, implementation planning must be a part of the strategic process from the beginning.

2

Avoiding SPOTS: Creating Strategic Unity

WAYNE BROCKBANK

DAVE ULRICH

School of Business, University of Michigan

INTRODUCTION

Strategic planning efforts often begin with great bravado and end with quiet humility. Too often, strategic plans become SPOTS (strategic plans on top shelf). SPOTS prominently sit on shelves as evidence of effort, but not of commitment to change. When SPOTS occur, a quick-fix alternative is to reject the overall strategic planning process. Not doing any planning avoids SPOTS, but does not help a company realize the benefits of effective planning. A major cause of SPOTS seems to be overemphasis on a traditional model of strategic planning that emphasizes formulation of plans without equal attention to or adequate theory on how to implement plans. This chapter reviews traditional strategic management practices and assumptions that generate SPOTS. Alternative assumptions and practices are offered that avoid SPOTS by focusing on creating strategic unity and that lead to more effective strategy management. The chapter concludes with a case study in which strategic planning was replaced with strategic unity.

TRADITIONAL STRATEGIC PLANNING PRACTICES

Traditional strategic planning follows four sequential steps:

1. Market research
2. Strategy formulation and planning
3. Strategy implementation
4. Control

At each step, a series of activities may occur that can lead to SPOTS.

Market Research

Market research to determine customer needs and identify future market trends is usually the initial step in strategic planning. In traditional market research, specialists or outside consultants design environmental scanning surveys that can be administered to select customers to identify market trends. Market information is then analyzed and summarized, highlighting key recommendations and action items.

Traditional market research may lead to SPOTS for a number of reasons:

1. Because market research specialists have primary responsibility for collecting and analyzing market data, they also have primary ownership of the results. A marketing department's influence often resides in the quality of the data collected and its control of access to that data. To maintain their power, marketing departments often subtly control access to data in order to maintain their centrality. In one company, for example, research data were intentionally complicated so no one except marketing could understand and apply the data.
2. With market research specialists designing environmental surveys, the survey may include specialized words that are not generally used by customers.
3. Customers may be reluctant to meet with and provide data to marketing specialists instead of their regular customer contact person-

nel. Thus, market research staff may have difficulty collecting accurate information about market dynamics.

4. Surveys may constrain customer responses. Customers may have concerns or interests beyond the survey itself. When customers do not know the individuals administering the surveys, they are less likely to offer additional information.

5. Customers may hesitate to discuss some problems without knowing exactly how the information will be used. For example, customers may not want to negatively evaluate a salesperson without knowing the influence that the information may have.

6. Managers are unlikely to use environmental scanning reports that have been prepared by staff specialists. Managers may assume that they already know the market information or that the information collected does not answer their specific questions.

For these reasons, many traditional marketing research efforts lead to SPOTS.

Strategy Formulation and Planning

Senior managers use market research to define company mission, goals, and strategic plans for one, three, and five years. Company mission statements become refined by specifying financial, market share, and product mix goals. Based on strategic goals, plans are prepared that allocate resources around advertising, product design, human resources, technology, customer relations, and pricing. Based on resource allocation decisions, staff specialists formalize strategic plans into a written document, series of memos, or meeting agendas. These formal plans embody the business strategy.

This traditional process of formulating plans may lead to SPOTS:

1. When senior managers discuss company strategies, they may not fully incorporate market research data. This may result from the data being too complex or abstract for easy interpretation and use. Frequently, senior managers rely on market data, which is based primarily on limited personal customer contact.

2. Although senior management may work on strategic plans, other members of the organization may be less aware of or committed to the plans. In one organization, the rumor was that the division general manager "wrote the strategic plan, then ate it." Many of the managers who were responsible for implementing the plan were not aware of its content. In another organization, the senior managers had spent two years working to agree on the mission, vision, strategic plan, values, operating objectives, goals, and control budgets. Their enthusiasm for this output was tempered when a random group of employees was asked their opinion and all but one of the

employees had not heard of the effort. The one employee's very positive response to the effort was also cynical—he said that it was a marvelous effort for the senior managers because it kept them in off-site workshops for two years and out of the way of those "really doing the work." When only senior personnel are involved in developing strategic plans, only they see the value; only they are committed to implementation. When managers further down in the organization fail to participate in the planning process, they see less value in the plans and can be cynical. Lack of lower level involvement may lead to SPOTS.

3. Because of limited awareness and use of plans, managers may begin to have disdain for the planning process, which they may view as an intrusion into their time and energy. In some organizations, a means/end inversion occurs. Strategic planning may begin as a means for managers to achieve useful ends, such as a greater understanding of the direction for the business. However, over time, staff personnel responsible for strategic planning become committed to adhering to a planning process. Thus, the planning process becomes the end, not the means. When such means/end inversion occurs, SPOTS are created.

Strategy Implementation

Implementation is the third sequential step in traditional strategic planning. Implementation generally occurs through official directives and control systems that flow through divisions, departments, sections, and, eventually, to individuals. Each individual eventually receives a set of objectives that, if achieved, allow the company to attain its mission and goals. In addition to issuing directives, efforts to implement strategy often rely on organization structure, management budgeting systems, and human resources systems.

Many well-intentioned efforts at strategy implementation fall short and give rise to SPOTS:

1. In some cases, individuals selectively implement strategic plan directives, depending on the individual's "zone of selective indifference."[1] When managers understand plans, they more willingly change behavior as recommended in the plan. However, if individuals do not understand the plan, their zone of selective indifference limits the changes they enact.

2. Managers often receive conflicting messages from strategic directives. In a company that prepared seven strategic planning documents, what emerged was "concept clutter": Each separate

---

[1] C. Barnard, *The Functions of the Executive* (Cambridge, MA: Harvard University Press, 1938).

document was interesting and useful, but each communicated a different set of potentially conflicting messages. When receiving conflicting messages, managers generally take personal initiative to resolve the dilemma. However, this kind of uncoordinated action sometimes results in SPOTS.

3. When managers find inconsistency between strategic actions and historical business values, they may slow implementation. In one company, the senior managers created a plan that centered on a feeder plant across divisions. Use of the feeder plant was intended to provide more efficient and economical production of materials for each division. However, this plan reduced the division manager's authority, so that the manager had less control over feeder plant operations. The five division managers understood the strategic plan and knew that it fairly represented senior management's vision of the company mission. However, it also reduced their individual autonomy. In response, the division managers engaged in a series of activities that were designed to subvert changes implied by the strategic plan. They failed to provide employees in the feeder plant with information that was required for the plant to operate effectively; they continued to contract long-term supply agreements to delay the need for the feeder plant; and they did not approve transfers of quality personnel necessary to operate the feeder plant. After about two years of attempting to implement the feeder plant, senior management decided that the cost of establishing such an operation was excessive. In essence, the strategic plan turned into SPOTS.

Control

The fourth sequential step in traditional strategic planning controls and monitors actions implied by the strategic plan. Control systems focus on individual outputs or behaviors in the organization. Controlling outputs emphasizes results, through management by objectives or key result area programs. Behavioral controls highlight employee actions, with less emphasis on direct results. To monitor strategy, most organizations adopt either output or behavior control systems. To control behavior, feedback and rewards may be designed to ensure that managerial actions coincide with the firm's strategic plans. Organizational rewards may focus on activities highlighted by the plan.

While control systems have merit in theory, what often emerges in practice has much less value. Employees who do not understand the philosophy, concepts, or values underlying the strategic plan may resist controls and monitoring mechanisms. When monitoring and control directives are created and imposed from the top down, employees feel distrusted and degraded. Their efforts turn to opposing the controls that accompany plan implementation. They establish lower-than-desired objectives; they identify exactly what activities are rewarded; and they perform well on those activities to the exclusion of other activities.[2] Because of these dynamics SPOTS accumulate.

Traditional Strategy Management Assumptions

While the four-step strategic planning process has various versions, it denotes a traditional view of strategic planning and rests on a number of assumptions:

- *Market research, strategy formulation, strategy implementation, and control are separate and sequential steps.* Generally, the staff function responsible for each of the four steps resides in a separate department. These departments often stem from different disciplines and are, to some extent, conflicting in their expectations. Marketing specialists, trained in marketing research, generally have very different skills from controllers, who emphasize the controlling and monitoring. Planners skilled in environmental scanning often have different competencies from experts in implementing organizational change. The differences between these functions may keep experts in each function from working together to ensure full plan implementation.

- *Commitment comes from reward expectation and/or involvement.* Under this assumption, individuals commit to the strategic plan not because they believe in the plan or because they are enthusiastic about it, but because they are rewarded for compliance. They are not committed to the plan; they are committed, rather, to the contingent rewards.

- *Strategy management is primarily the responsibility of senior management.* Most strategic planning processes view senior managers as the key players in strategic planning. Senior managers have responsibility for decisions that affect the overall company. They have access to information to prepare the company's strategic directions. They also tend to have the best view of the company as it relates to its global environment.

- *The focus of strategic planning is to allocate resources.* The overall process of strategic thinking should serve two purposes. First, it should help allocate scarce resources based on key success factors for a business. Making sure the proper investments are made in technology, products, people, and facilities helps meet customer needs. Traditional strategic planning models may adequately accomplish this purpose. Second, strategic thinking should build a commitment among employees to a common direction and focus. Often, this sec-

---

[2] S. Kerr, "Some characteristics and consequences of organizational rewards," unpublished working paper (University of Southern California, 1989).

ond purpose of a strategic plan is not accomplished through traditional strategic planning.

- *Control is cybernetic.* The flow of strategic planning up to the point of monitoring and feedback is sequential. The control process continues the sequential logic with goal communication, monitoring of performance, comparison of performance measures against outcome or behavioral goals, feedback, and reward. Compliance is achieved by stating or eliciting goals and then monitoring performance accomplishment.

These five assumptions underlie traditional strategy management. Because of these assumptions and practices, SPOTS have occurred. An alternative approach to strategic planning is creating strategic unity. This approach is based on different assumptions about strategy management and suggests alternative practices to strategy management.

CREATING STRATEGIC UNITY

Strategic Unity Assumptions

Strategic unity implies a common understanding of and commitment to business strategies. It can be measured as the extent to which both employees and external stakeholders recognize, accept, and aggressively execute strategic plans. By highlighting strategic unity, management can replace SPOTS with commitment, actions, and improved company performance. The creation of strategic unity is based on the following five assumptions:

1. Market research, strategy formulation, and strategy implementation are fully integrated processes.
2. Commitment comes from information exposure and enacted behaviors.
3. Strategic unity requires an organization-wide perspective.
4. The focus of strategic unity is not resource allocation, but commitment among all stakeholders.
5. Control is value-based.

Market Research, Strategy Formulation, and Strategy Implementation. Three components must be managed simultaneously to ensure strategic unity. The tenets of an integrated strategy are:

- *Research:* Market research is essential to learning the dynamics of the market and customer needs.
- *Planning:* Strategy formulation must be consistent with market research. Planning allows companies to integrate information, create new meanings, and make appropriate resource allocations.

- *Commitment:* Along with research and planning, the key to strategic unity is the commitment to act on the key activities identified in the strategic plan.

This approach assumes that commitment begins with market research, not after plans have been formulated as in traditional strategic planning. To achieve employee commitment to market research, strategic plans, and strategic implementation, a broad segment of employees must be involved in data gathering, market analysis, and/or planning. Finally, by conceptually integrating the three perspectives, initial data gathering is emphasized as the source of planning and commitment. As action items are implemented, continual research ensures that the actions are consistent with market dynamics. A key issue in implementing this assumption is increasing the level of interdepartmental respect and cooperation.

Information exposure and enacted behaviors. Too often, organizations rely solely on formal rewards to encourage compliance to strategic plans. As a result, employees become committed to obtaining the rewards and lose sight of the vision, mission, or direction embodied in the strategic plans. Strategic unity depends more on commitment than on direct rewards. While rewards serve an important motivational purpose, they can also lure employees away from the focus of the mission. Employee commitment comes from employee exposure to company information and from enacted behaviors. As employees receive more information about the company, they become more committed to company projects. In addition, enacted behaviors—behaviors that are voluntary, public, and irrevocable—cause individuals to become more committed to these behaviors and to the principles or values they reflect. At Hewlett-Packard, for example, staff engineers are often involved in recruiting new employees. During the recruiting process, the engineers make positive statements about the company, and as they do so, their own commitment to Hewlett-Packard is strengthened.

As more employees are involved in the three steps of integrative strategy management, more comprehensive commitment to strategy implementation occurs. For example, market research increases in importance as people involved in planning and implementation assist in gathering information. This diversity of experience exposes them directly to customers, who point out the importance of the company's products and services to their businesses. Constant exposure to such information also provides greater understanding of environmental demands to those who have primary responsibility for strategy planning and to those who must implement the plans. As people who implement plans are involved in market research and strategy planning, they have greater understanding and ownership of the entire process and its outcomes. Individuals see their jobs in the context of the entire company and its environment.

Organization-Wide Perspective. To maximize commitment to a company's goals and to understand the meaning behind the goals, people at every level should understand the company's strategic position. For example, as employees understand market dynamics and the company's response to such market pressures, they gain greater understanding, cohesion, and direction. This assumption also implies that planning occurs not only at the top, but throughout the company. When decisions are consistent with the strategic plan, individuals throughout the company understand the reasons for the decisions and implement them more quickly and accurately. Two challenges confront this assumption. First, management must ensure that the basic principles and values that guide the planning are clearly communicated and are based on credible assumptions and logic. Second, adequate effort must be made to ensure horizontal and vertical integration of plans into a unified whole that is consistent with the vision and direction of top management.

Commitment Among All Stakeholders. While traditional strategic planning focuses on resource allocation, strategic unity emphasizes commitment to the plan. By focusing on commitment, employees come to appreciate and accept customer values and requirements and recognize company practices must be aligned with internal company needs.

Value-Based Control. Building commitment through information sharing, enacted behaviors, and rewards results in a greater congruence between company goals and individual goals. Hence, there is less need for the explicit monitoring of plan implementation. When individuals share common values and assumptions, less explicit monitoring and control are required. Incentives and rewards can be allocated to those who share common values with the company. Such value-based controls elicit more commitment to the company and its strategies.

Practices to Build Strategic Unity

The assumptions of strategic unity imply practices that are different from traditional strategic planning, and a commitment by senior management to strategic unity is necessary. Senior management must begin by seeing the value of company-wide strategic practices. Senior management must also commit to spending time on understanding the alternative planning assumptions reviewed earlier, discussing the value to strategic unity, and spending considerable time and effort communicating with employees. Without these upfront commitments from senior management, the intended outcomes of strategic unity will not follow. Creating strategic unity requires more management time and attention than strategic planning. It requires that senior managers learn not only to write plans, but also to build commitment to accomplishing them. It takes time to involve people and to make sure that ideas translate into action. Given senior management support, a number of strategic practices can be undertaken in three phases: market research, strategy formulation, and strategy implementation.

Market research. Six steps are involved in using market research to build strategic unity. These steps are designed to collect accurate market data, to prepare plans that help the company adapt to the market dynamics, and to evoke company-wide commitment to customers. These steps provide a means for building strategic unity by getting employees close to customers. Strategic unity involves changing not only perceptions of employees within the company, but customer perceptions about the company. Establishing a unity among employees and between employees and customers requires substantially more effort than merely retaining marketing experts to do market analysis. The six-step process described here results in unity by integrating market research, planning, and commitment. By focusing on generating unity, SPOTS are replaced by commitment and action. The market research phase may take from two to four months, depending on the size of the company and the degree of involvement in the project.

1. *Preparational market research design.* To better communicate the importance of the research and to make sure that senior management feels a responsibility for the information, senior management should work with market research specialists to prepare a market research program. This action step works on the assumptions that (1) senior management has the ability to understand market research programs and (2) commitment comes from involvement and time allocation. The time senior management devotes to understanding and designing a market research program is well spent. Senior managers gain a vision of the potential payoffs that can inure to the firm from using a planning process that focuses on building strategic unity. They become more sensitized to the mechanisms by which system-wide commitment is established. By this means, they are also able to ensure consistency between their own leadership style and the principles for building a unified organization. Their involvement in market research also assists them in understanding the limitations and qualifications of the market research phase of the process.

2. *Survey design.* To build strategic unity, customer survey questions should be developed with a cross-section of customer-contact personnel, including key line managers, staff specialists, and sales personnel. Including representatives from throughout the company generates commitment to the research program and prepares people to be involved in using the infor-

mation that will be collected. Involving many people in generating questions for the survey allows specialists to refine questions and then submit the questions for review to those who were involved in question identification.

Each member of a task force then pilot-tests the survey with one to three customers. This pilot test provides a basis for fine-tuning the survey instrument, commits the task force to the research process, and prepares them to use the information that will come from the market research. Senior management should be involved in approving the final instrument. However, any changes recommended by senior management must be negotiated with the design task force.

Through this process of market research, a number of results occur:

- In all future meetings, a line representative will be present to defend and explain the process.
- The market research program gains company-wide legitimization by involving key individuals in the process.
- Line management accepts, understands, and owns the process.
- The question categories on the survey reflect actual customer concerns.
- Question wording is consistent with language used in the market.
- Senior managers have early notice of the information that will be collected and are then able to psychologically prepare themselves to use the type of information that will be collected.
- Success stories about the process are available as the process is implemented throughout the organization.

Skepticism exists when a cross-section of the company is first involved in designing the survey. People want to return to the traditional patterns of behavior and to delegate such activity to market specialists. However, after they are trained in generating question categories, participants become enthusiastic and committed. Enthusiasm and commitment increase as task force members become involved in pilot-testing the survey with customers. Word gets around that customers are willing to share information and that information can be used to help the company achieve strategic objectives. These success stories foster even more commitment to the process and prepare the company for making effective plans. The genesis of strategic unity is broad involvement in and an understanding of getting customer information into the firm.

3. *Sample selection.* Line managers and sales personnel involved in the market research program can help identify relevant customers to survey. Customers who might otherwise think that customer surveys are a waste of time might be more inclined to respond to salespeople with whom they have had previous contacts or to senior line managers.

FIGURE 2-1

Market Segmentation for Sample Selection

		Each customer's contribution to overall market	
		High	Low
Focal company's proportion of each customer's market	High	I PROTECT	III MAINTAIN
	Low	II ASSAULT	IV DEVELOP

When market research is performed solely by marketing department members, the number of customers to be contacted is severely limited. By involving task force members and other non-marketing personnel, the firm not only accrues the benefits of wider understanding and commitment, but also gains a larger sampling of customers, which allows for more rigorous analyses within more highly delineated market segments.

Customers to be interviewed may be selected from four possible market segments (see Figure 2-1). This market segmentation helps identify both current customers who are important to keep (quadrant I) and potential customers who are important to attract (quadrant II). It also helps to identify those customers who represent relatively low-value added sales volume. The four quadrants represent a cross-section of customers:

- *Quadrant I: Protect.* Customers in this quadrant are very active in the market. In addition, they give a high proportion of their business to the company. Customers in this quadrant are generally long-standing, big customers. To protect the company's market share, these customers must be given special attention.

- *Quadrant II: Assault.* Customers in this quadrant are each heavy contributors to the overall market, but the company has a low proportion of each customer's business. These are the most important customers to focus on, since they have a great deal of business, but the company is not receiving as much of the business as it could.

- *Quadrant III: Maintain.* Customers in this quadrant do not contribute much to the market, but the company has a high proportion of each customer's business. These customers merit less attention than customers in quadrants I and II, but they must be maintained to avoid market erosion.

- *Quadrant IV: Develop.* Customers in this quadrant are not contributing large amounts to the market, and the company has a low proportion of each customer's business. These customers deserve less attention than customers in quadrants I and II, but they should be included in the sample to ensure that future development activities include all customers.

This market segmentation process focuses not only on data gathering but on directing the company toward the appropriate market segments. By identifying customers in the four quadrants, some companies find that they are spending more time with customers in quadrants III and IV than with those in quadrants I and II. It is important to collect information from customers in each quadrant so that different strategies can be applied for each quadrant. Experience indicates that customer attitudes and expectations differ by quadrant. This is important, since a company wants to respond more directly to customers in quadrants I and II, where the greater portion of its business is. While other market segmentation frameworks exist, this approach is valuable because it emphasizes the relations between a focal company and alternative customer segments.

4. *Marketing and strategic planning training.* Once the survey instrument is designed and the sample is identified, a training meeting follows so that those involved in data gathering can learn about interviewing customers, strategic planning, and how the information they collect will assist them in making better strategic decisions. At this meeting, senior management also presents its commitment to the project and to the utilization of the information collected.

5. *Survey administration.* Using the task force-designed customer-contact survey instrument, personnel and key managers interview customers in the customers' offices. By meeting with and interviewing customers, the company not only receives complete and accurate information about what it needs to do to improve its performance, but also builds commitment from customers.

When completing surveys with company personnel, some customers (especially those in quadrant II) take the opportunity to request specific problem solving. As a result of being asked thoughtful and relevant questions and being exposed to a strong customer orientation, customers develop a more positive perception about the company. In a short period of time, market perceptions about the company will be positively altered.

In one case, an interviewer flew to a Middle Eastern country. The customer had been somewhat dissatisfied with the company's competitor, with whom he had been doing business, and was impressed with the strong customer orientation presented in the interview. Because the customer liked the content of the interview and because the interviewer was an actual employee (as opposed to a marketing consultant), the customer was able to place a substantial order at the time of the interview. The customer indicated that he would have continued with his current vendor if the interview had not made a strongly favorable impression on him. As a result of that single interview, the company grossed an additional $20 million over the following eighteen months.

A final benefit of having employees administer the survey is that those involved in data gathering become more committed to making changes that help the company respond to customers. Because these people have spent time learning about customer desires, they are more committed to making expected and required changes.

6. *Data analysis.* After all the data is collected, it is statistically summarized by research experts. No written report is generated. Too often written reports symbolize the end of the process rather than the beginning of action. If data are summarized into reports before management wrestles with their interpretations and conclusions, the result is usually SPOTS. The data summaries are reviewed with key management groups that interpret the meaning of the summaries and ask:

- What do the numbers mean?
- What are the customers saying?
- What can we conclude that we need to do to improve our performance?

After top management reviews data, the data are fed back to cross-sectional groups throughout the company. Each group is asked to perform the same data interpretation, highlighting what needs to be done in order for the company to better respond to its customers (see Figure 2-2).

As a result of such data feedback meetings, commitment increases to make necessary changes to respond to customer demands. This commitment comes, in part, because the individuals who are interpreting the data are likely to be members of the task force that designed and administered the survey. The individuals who are involved in these steps will also be heavily involved in implementing strategic changes that result from the data feedback meetings. From these meetings, no specific written reports are generated, but action items are established and implemented. The data feedback meetings also send a clear and consistent message through the company that strategy is a shared responsibility and that changes that come from the market research translate to immediate action.

Strategy formulation. Strategy formulation focuses on the development of a strategic identity. A company's strategic identity comes from the information collected through customer interviews. The strategic identity that flows from the market research should include both strategic imaging and a strategic reality. Strategic imaging refers to modifying customers' perceptions about the company's mission, goals, and activities. Strategic imaging assumes that a key factor in strategic unity is creating the image in the customer's mind that the company is working to satisfy the customer's

FIGURE 2-2
Iterative Feedback Meetings

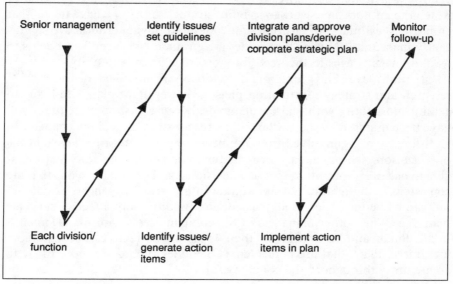

demands. Strategic imaging starts with effective market research. As employees collect information from customers about what the company can do to better meet their needs, customers revise their images of the company's mission and goals. Strategic images are further developed and solidified as company actions, consistent with the customer-driven image developed in market research, are taken.

Strategic reality refers to making specific changes in the company's products, practices, and policies to fulfill customer expectations. The plans that are developed to carry out the strategic reality involve individuals throughout the company. The survey design task force is involved to make sure that the data is interpreted consistently with its original intent; key staff are involved to ensure that specific action items are consistent with company values, mission, and direction policies and actions; and key line managers are involved to legitimate the plans that are derived.

One common difficulty in formulating strategic plans, which lead to strategic identity, is that some personnel assume a "business as usual" attitude. These individuals occasionally state that they already knew that the customers would respond as they did and that they have already made plans to meet those customer expectations. To avoid this tendency, once the final market survey is designed, personnel throughout the company should complete the survey, answering how they think customers will respond.

Statistical analysis generally shows that internal (company) responses and external (customer) responses differ significantly. In nearly every case in which the authors have worked to build strategic unity, we have found that employees' estimates of customer attitudes and buying criteria are significantly inaccurate. This data provides a legitimate "felt need" and helps to open managers' eyes to the need for greater accuracy and unity.

If multi-level and -function individuals are involved in the market research and strategy formulation phases, the resultant plans are likely to exhibit more unity with market demands, because customer attitudes will have been assessed by those who will be responsible for making changes. In addition, by being involved from the beginning with multiple levels in the organization, senior management better understands the information, is able to use the information to make decisions, and can create plans that are consistent with the information. Market information no longer is doubted, but can be better understood, trusted, and used in more effective strategic planning. When other managers in the company see senior management's involvement and commitment, their ideas and directives become more legitimate. Plans that are perceived as being legitimate are more likely to create unity throughout the company.

Strategy implementation. If the market research and formulation phases are successful, strategy implementation occurs quickly. This is because the employees who are central to making sure that strategies lead to action have been involved in the market research and strategy formulation phases. Through this involvement, they come to recognize the customer demands that compel the company to attempt new activities. Strategic reality matches strategic image for both employees and customers: That which is done inside the company meets the perceptions of the customers outside the company.

Strategy implementation translates into action when management ensures that people's time and behavior are focused on meeting strategic objectives. Human resources (HR) practices can be aligned with business strategies through the following techniques, which help to focus employee attention:

- Staffing practices that ensure that employees who are hired or promoted meet the requirements of the business;
- Development practices that help employees acquire competencies, which encourage competitiveness;
- Rewards that may be used to focus employee attention and build control systems;
- Performance appraisal, which may be linked to strategies to ensure appropriate standards and feedback processes.

In addition to these more formal HR tools, communication processes are critical to strategy implementation. When senior managers visit locations throughout the company and share aggregated company strategies, individuals are committed because they or their peers were involved in creating the strategies. When making presentations of company strategies, senior management must communicate clearly and consistently that the strategies are not solely a product of senior management, but are a part of a shared vision, based on the input of customers and individuals throughout the company. When communicating strategic plans, senior management can strengthen unity by sharing success stories. The example of the sales representative who visited the Middle Eastern country was widely shared in one company. This story encouraged others to become involved in the planning process and to be committed to responding to customers' needs.

Finally, as directives are issued from senior management, employees know more clearly the rationales for those directives and understand how those directives can improve individual performance. Throughout the company, a sense of clear direction is shared. With the clear direction, energy is focused and individuals are willing to behave in ways that are consistent with that strategic focus.

When company sales personnel revisit customers, on regular sales calls or to close deals, they can share the changes in the company's strategic reality with those customers. Such communication demonstrates the company's commitment to listen to customers and to respond with quick and accurate changes. Strategic imaging continues as customers begin to perceive the company in light of the actions that were taken in response to customer demands.

The Role of Management

The role of management in strategic unity must be clearly defined. Senior managers must be fully committed to the unity-building process. They must be willing to involve employees in planning activities that were traditionally performed by a few staff specialists and senior managers. They must be willing to listen and respond to employees' insights and customer information about how to better meet customer needs. They must be public champions of the process by constantly encouraging, reinforcing, and sustaining the effort. They must be willing to act on the information received from the market research phase. They must exhibit confidence as the process proceeds. They must be aggressive in their pursuit of customer commitment and of making the strategic reality consistent with the strategic image, as well as in building commitment among employees and between employees and customers. They must be patient to involve and empower employees. The management role for a strategic unity process includes the following steps:

1. Understand the overall process by laying out an eighteen-month strategic unity process in lieu of a strategic planning document. This step ensures that top managers understand and agree to the intent and processes of strategic unity.

2. Create a marketing research task force that includes customer-contact personnel throughout the organization. This task force ensures that employees from different functions and levels in the organization are involved in the process. It is a critical task force for managing the entire project.

3. Charge the task force with the responsibility to do marketing research and to make initial efforts at strategy formulation. Executives delegate enormous responsibility to the task force. The task force performs the market research activities, designs a survey, defines customers, and organizes a comprehensive customer-interviewing process. The task force also reviews the data and performs preliminary analysis of the implications of the research. Executives must ensure the integration of the activities of the task force with the existing management structure.

4. Work with the task force to clarify results and implement actions. Executives work with the task force in reviewing and refining action plans from the market research. As these actions are discussed and accepted, a company may begin immediately to implement its new strategic agenda. Executives must listen and lead by empowering others to act.

CASE STUDY

Creating strategic unity has been applied by companies in diverse industries. Focusing on strategic unity works best in industrial markets in which companies have a limited number of customers (i.e., fewer than 5,000). For example, in the health care industry, hospitals rely on a limited population of physicians (customers, in this sense) to supply patients to the hospital. In the electronics industry, semiconductor firms rely on a limited number of customers (computer manufacturers) to purchase their products. In the oil service industry, service firms rely on a limited market of oil drilling firms to purchase and service their products. In each of these industries, building strategic unity has been an effective alternative to traditional strategic planning. The most direct and measurable impact of this approach is market share increase.

An international producer and vendor of drilling supplies, which will be referred to here as "Oil Services Corporation," was one of four major international suppliers of its products. Over a five-year period, Oil Service's market share had dropped from 26 percent to 19 percent because of an increasing number of small, independent competitors and because of aggressive actions on the part of the other major producers.

The president of Oil Services was concerned about the precipitous drop in market share and the ensuing drop in morale within the company. To combat the decline, senior management worked with a number of strategic plans, but found that none of them helped. The president was impressed by the strategic unity concept and its strong customer-service orientation and ability to create internal commitment to action throughout the company.

Meetings were held with senior management to explain the project objectives and process. Senior management selected a market research task force of individuals across divisions and functions throughout the company to perform a customer analysis. This task force designed a survey and solicited a list of current and potential customers throughout the world in each quadrant of Figure 2-1. The final customer list totaled about 1,100 current and potential decision makers in customer firms. The task force pilot-tested its survey. A training session involved 50 selected company personnel (mostly in sales, but including individuals from other functions) who knew many of the 1,100 customers. These 50 personnel were trained and assigned to interview customers. All of the assignments to specific customers were based on historical customer contact records. For example, the Oil Service representative in Alaska was assigned to interview current and potential Alaskan customers.

After the interview assignments were completed, the collected information was statistically tabulated. A series of feedback meetings were conducted to acquaint management and employees throughout Oil Services with the data. The first feedback meeting with senior management identified key issues in the data and set general descriptive limitations of actions that could occur. Subsequent feedback meetings were held in each division to acquaint employees with the results and to generate specific action plans consistent with the data. A number of senior managers attended each division's feedback meeting. Each division's action plans were then shared with senior management, who integrated the plans and approved them as the foundation of the corporate strategy. Senior managers then finalized the strategic plan, issued directives consistent with it, and modified HR practices to ensure consistency with the plan.

As these activities unfolded, individuals in each division received affirmations of activities they had already begun. For example, in one division, customers placed a very high priority on service. To create a strategic image of service, the division initiated training programs and regular customer meetings. The division also began to record time between report and delivery of service. Even before senior management formalized customer service

FIGURE 2-3

Market Share Changes in Oil Services Company During Project

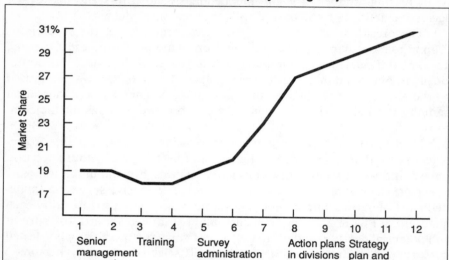

as a part of the strategic plan and approved these action items within this division, the division had already implemented the plans with great customer success. Senior management retained follow-up responsibility for the action plans of each division and ensured that actions occurred. The process of presenting data and generating action items at all levels of the company generated high enthusiasm within Oil Services. Senior managers were confident that their strategic reality reflected market demands, employees would act on the strategy, and the actions would influence key market customers by shaping a strategic image of Oil Service Corporation as a customer-driven, responsive company.

The desired results occurred. Figure 2-3 plots the twelve-month project and shows the market share change realized by Oil Service Company. The market share growth from 19 percent to 31 percent surpassed all expectations. Oil Service Company became known as the provider of choice and the provider that was most sensitive and responsive to its customers. Such quantifiable increases in market share alone validated the strategic unity approach to planning. In addition, there were qualitative changes within Oil Services: Employees who had been disgruntled by Oil Service's lack of responsiveness to customer needs were now encouraged by the company's aggressiveness in the market. Employees who had no previous input into company strategy felt ownership and responsibility for the results of the project. Qualitative measures of morale improved throughout the project.

CONCLUSION

Strategic unity differs significantly from traditional strategic planning. It emphasizes implementation of strategic plans at the initial stages of strategy formulation rather than as an afterthought. Senior management's awareness of and support for the strategic unity process is necessary. Senior managers signal to employees the value of strategic unity. Without such signals, employees respond much more slowly. These signals must be perceived as understandable, consistent, and legitimate by employees throughout the organization. Unless the company is willing and able to make changes, the strategic unity process will not work. In one case, a division increased sales significantly, but was unable to attain the required equipment to match increased customer demand because the equipment was not in the annual budget. As a result, customers were disillusioned with the company. This division would have been better off if it had not attempted strategic unity.

Follow-up is crucial after action plans are drafted; otherwise, there is a strong tendency to revert to old behavioral patterns. Also, unless departments are willing to share information and activities, and not be limited by traditional boundaries, the process will fail. Marketing and planning, must share responsibility for collecting data, and planning must be willing to involve marketing and sales in the design and implementation of plans.

Strategic unity rests on a number of assumptions that are different from those that underlie traditional strategic planning. It suggests a series of activities that evoke research, planning, and commitment in a mutually integrative and cohesive manner. It integrates marketing, planning, and implementation activities within a company. It rests on an implicit theory of organizations that suggests that individual commitment is necessary for fast, accurate, and complete strategy implementation and that individual commitment comes from involvement, ownership, and information exposure. Strategic unity succeeds. It avoids SPOTS. It induces company-wide enthusiasm to enacting changes that will help the company achieve its mission and objectives.

3

Management for Shareholder Value

WALTER MARDIS

The Hay Group

INTRODUCTION

What should shareholders reasonably expect from the companies in which they invest? Increasingly, corporate managers are recognizing that the answer is a return on investments that is at least equal to what could be obtained from equally risky alternatives, and most definitely greater than could be received from risk-free alternatives. This simple conclusion has led to the recent burgeoning interest in creating shareholder value and in finding ways both to achieve shareholder value growth and to effectively measure its accomplishment.

The impetus for this new attention by management to shareholders comes from two closely related sources. First, in the 1970s and early 1980s, a number of academicians, financial theorists, and consultants began to observe that many U.S. companies were failing in their basic mission to create real, measurable value for their owners. A number of companies were using misleading measures of performance that vastly overstated their levels of success in generating tangible, risk-adjusted returns. In fact, a large portion of U.S. companies were providing little, if any, real value to their shareholders, and in some cases, were actually losing value for their owners. Responding to these revelations was a broad group of Wall Street raiders and takeover artists who threatened to replace entrenched management in the corporations they acquired with managers who would focus on squeezing real economic value from the companies. For managers who survived the takeover frenzy, shareholder value became the "holy grail."

Today, few chief executive officers (CEOs) would deny that their primary mission is to provide shareholders with better total returns on their investments. Unfortunately, it still appears that only a minority of CEOs fully understands the total implications of a strategy to create shareholder value. More importantly, few seem to have instilled a comprehensive, company-wide commitment to this objective as reflected in the plans and actions of managers at all levels.

This chapter summarizes the existing approaches and techniques for achieving shareholder value that can be used by managers as a basis for defining and implementing successful programs for change. The discussion is organized around four main topics, and addresses the critical issues relevant to understanding and responding to the need to refocus corporate management to new principles of business management. The topic areas are:

- *The fallacies in the traditional accounting model.* Standard accounting techniques, when used as a basis for strategic financial analysis and planning, are severely flawed. They fail to accurately portray the true financial success of a business in creating shareholder value and provide a very poor basis for making financial decisions—particularly, capital investment decisions.

- *Basic concepts of shareholder value creation.* The real objective of any business is to generate free cash flow for investors, which means making investments that provide returns to shareholders commensurate with their risk.

- *Linking shareholder value concepts with total corporate strategic planning.* All strategic decision making should be based on a clear understanding of the difference between creating accounting returns for investors and creating true economic value.

- *Implementation techniques.* Adopting the concept that creating shareholder value is a company's basic mission requires changes in the way that business is managed. A variety of tools exist that can support the move toward a value-creation strategy, but they may require a substantial reorientation in the way managers think about the company.

WEAKNESSES IN TRADITIONAL TECHNIQUES FOR MEASURING PERFORMANCE

Most managers look to their net profit number as the key measure of performance in their business. Further, they rely on such ratios as return on equity (ROE) or return on assets (ROA) as indications of whether they are achieving an adequate return on the investments made in the business. They commonly assume that increases in net income (and, for example, in earnings per share), particularly if repeated year after year, will lead to improvements in share price or, in private companies, in the value of the business to its owners. Unfortunately, the relationship between traditional performance measures and the creation of real shareholder value is weak and often nonexistent.

The basic fallacy in employing standard net income measure as an indication of business performance is the accounting-based nature of these techniques. Although they offer certain benefits as a way to value accounting worth, they fail to properly measure true economic worth. Moreover, the lack of correlation between changes in earnings per share and changes in shareholder value results from the inability of traditional accounting-based measures to adequately account for risk, for the cost of capital, or for the time value of money.

Shortcomings in Accounting Measures

Alfred Rappaport was one of the first to point out that earnings per share (EPS) did not correlate with the creation of shareholder value. He showed that of the 232 companies in the Standard and Poors 400 industrial companies that had achieved at least 10 percent annual increase in EPS over the period 1974 to 1979, 55 percent had failed to provide to their shareholders total returns that exceeded the rate of inflation. In fact, 17 percent of the companies had actually generated negative returns to their owners. Even higher EPS increases seemed to have little effect. Of the 172 companies that achieved 15 percent increases in EPS during the same period, fewer than one half provided sufficient shareholder returns to even compensate for the inflation rate.[1] Nor is the duration of EPS increases a predictor of shareholder value. A 1983 follow-up analysis by Rappaport of major companies that had achieved

---

[1] Alfred Rappaport, "Selecting Strategies that Create Shareholder Value," *Harvard Business Review* (May/June 1981), p. 140.

continuous EPS growth over a ten-year period showed that many still witnessed reductions in actual shareholder wealth.[2] Moreover, the record of bookkeeping earnings as a predictor of shareholder value has not improved in recent years. In 1989, *Business Week* reported that 156 companies out of the 354 surveyed reported returns on equity of 15 percent or more. From 1986 to 1988, in terms of economic value creation, 46 of these companies actually lost shareholder value.[3]

As measured by traditional accounting techniques, earnings do not provide an indication of whether management is achieving its most basic performance objective: to provide shareholders with returns that are greater than they would obtain from risk-free investments, (e.g., government bonds). The reason for this failure lies in the intrinsic shortcomings in accounting assessments of value. Simply stated, standard accounting techniques rely on noncash and nontimely measures of performance and fail to consider the cost of capital in making evaluations of returns. Hence, returns that appear positive in an accounting sense may not be real and, moreover, may be inadequate in compensating investors for the risk associated with a business.

Rappaport offers six reasons why accounting measures fall short in tracking economic value creation.

1. Traditional accounting techniques can be manipulated to state higher or lower earnings, depending on nonmeaningful (in an economic sense) decisions on how to record revenues and expenses. For example, a switch from first in, first out (FIFO) to last in, first out (LIFO) in accounting for inventory makes no difference, economically, in a company's actual cash flow or in its real returns on investment; yet FIFO will, by standard accounting measures, produce better bottom-line profits. (In fact, because of tax advantages, LIFO actually leads to better true returns for a company—i.e., cash flow —even though it appears to reduce bookkeeping earnings.)

2. Earnings, as measured by standard accounting principals, do not reflect the varying costs of capital among the businesses within a company nor the differences in risk that alternative business strategies may entail. A more risky business or strategy, by definition, should offer greater returns to investors to justify their risk.

3. Earnings fail to account for working capital and fixed investment needs for any future growth of the company.

4. Changes in the environment, particularly in the current and anticipated rate of inflation, are not considered when a simple bottom-line accounting profit is used to evaluate performance.

---

[2] Alfred Rappaport, "Corporate Performance Standards in Shareholder Value," *Journal of Business Strategy* (Spring 1983), p. 29.

[3] *Business Week* (May 1, 1989), pp. 46–89.

5. What the company does with earnings (e.g., reinvestment in the business or payment of dividends) is not accounted for in traditional EPS measures. A company that reinvests earnings at a rate below what shareholders could achieve themselves from less risky investments is, in fact, detracting from shareholder value.

6. Earnings figures do not account for time preferences. A company that generates earnings that have not also covered the accumulated time cost of capital (i.e., from the point at which the investments in earnings generation were made) have, in fact, lost shareholder value.[4]

The Myth of Earnings per Share

Bennett Stewart offers a clear example of how reliance on EPS or earnings growth results in a misleading indication of real corporate performance. He describes two companies that have identical operating earnings and that are expected to grow earnings at the same rate. On this basis, traditional evaluation techniques (which suggest a correlation between EPS/earnings growth and shareholder value) would predict that the stock of the two companies would sell at the same price. However, if one of the companies requires more capital investment to achieve its earnings growth (or if it is viewed as a riskier business and therefore pays more for its capital), it would actually be providing poorer returns (or returns less able to compensate for increased business risk), and its shares would sell for less. The capital-hungry (or riskier) business will provide less free cash flow because it must pay for the cost of capital (or more for the risk-adjusted cost of the same capital). Since it is real cash, either reinvested in the business or distributed to shareholders, which ultimately determines a company's value, investors are simply less willing to assign a high value to such a company's shares.[5]

The Limits of Return on Investment and Return on Equity

Many executives, recognizing the fallacies in EPS calculations, have turned to return on investment (ROI) or ROE in an attempt to measure business performance more accurately. There are two basic flaws in this approach. First, the return, or earnings, number in the numerator is flawed. It does not reflect the actual cash available to a company to reinvest or to distribute to shareholders. Rappaport distinguishes between "accounting income" and "economic income" using the following calculations:

---

[4] Rappaport, "Selecting Strategies that Create Shareholder Value," p. 140 and *Creating Shareholder Value: The New Standard for Business Performance* (New York, Free Press, 1986) ch. 2.

[5] G. Bennett Stewart, *Stern Stewart Corporate Finance Handbook* (Stern Stewart Management Services, 1986), pp. 2-9, 2-10.

Accounting or book income
   = Cash flow
   − Depreciation and other noncash changes
   + Incremental investments in working capital and assets

Economic income
   = Discounted cash flow

$$= \frac{\text{Cash flow} + \begin{pmatrix} \text{Present value at end of year} - \\ \text{present value at beginning of year} \end{pmatrix}}{\text{Present value at beginning of year}}$$

$$= \frac{\text{Cash flow} + \text{Change in present value}}{\text{Present value at beginning of year}}$$

Book income is inadequate as a measure of return because it does not incorporate the current year's investment for working capital or fixed assets. Additionally, the treatment traditional accounting rules give to depreciation can present an inaccurate picture of time costs.

The second flaw is that the investment in the ROI ratio is meant to be an economic measure, but because it too has been derived using standard accounting techniques, it may be extremely misleading in showing the true value of the investment under management's control. ROI or similar measures have other shortcomings as well. In particular, Rappaport points out that ROI is a single period investment that is, it ignores events beyond the accounting period. (On the other hand, discounted cash flow returns in a given year clearly recognize estimates of cash flows over the entire forecast period.)

Rappaport cites work by Ezra Solomon demonstrating that ROI most often overestimates the actual economic performance of a company. Four key factors account for these discrepancies[6]:

1. *Length of project life.* The longer the project life, the greater the overstatement.

2. *Capitalization policy.* The smaller the fraction of total investment capitalized on the books, the greater the overstatement. At the limit, for investments that are expensed 100 percent, the book ROI will rise toward infinity. [Note: The accounting standard requiring that research and development (R&D) be expensed rather than capitalized (despite the fact that, in reality, R&D is like a capital asset in that it is a real addition to the long-term earning power of the company) can lead to extremely high ROIs in research-intensive industries such as pharmaceuticals, thus giving the appearance of superior performance.]

3. *The rate at which depreciation is taken on the books.* Rapid depreciation will result in higher ROIs. At the limit, the most rapid method

---

[6] Rappaport, *Creating Shareholder Value,* pp. 31–34.

of depreciation is, of course, tantamount to 100 percent expensing of outlays and, hence, leads to the same results.

4. *The lag between investment outlays and the recoupment of these outlays from cash inflows.* The greater the lag, the greater the degree of overstatement.

Recognizing Residual Value

A final shortcoming in traditional earnings measurements as an indication of shareholder value lies in their failure to account for the residual value of a business in assigning it an economic worth. As Bernard Reimann points out, typically less than one third of the economic (present) value of a firm, as reflected in its stock price, is attributable to expected cash flows for the next five to ten years. The greatest portion of the value comes from the discounted value of the business, as a going concern, beyond the end of the planning horizon.[7] The contribution of such future returns on shareprice was amply demonstrated in an article in *Fortune,* which also, parenthetically, demonstrated the inaccuracy of many CEOs' arguments that the stock market is irrational and only cares about the current quarter's earnings (see box).

The key point to understand in evaluating the accounting model of business performance is that it is not the approach used in the market to place a value on a company. In valuing a business, investors look to the real economic returns earned by a business (compared against the cost of capital), coupled with the level of confidence in management's capacity to continue to make economically sound business decisions on investments. Investors are not interested in accounting-derived earnings or growth or in non-risk adjusted returns. Instead, they seek continual generation of real cash that compensates them for risk taken, and they assign high values to those companies that demonstrate the ability to produce true economic gain.

THE ULTIMATE GOAL: CREATING SHAREHOLDER VALUE

Real shareholder/owner value can be defined as the present value of the anticipated future stream of cash flows from the business plus the terminal value of the company (if liquidated at some future point). Positive shareholder value is created when these cash flows are greater than the investor could have achieved from equally risky investments over the same time frame. Said differently, the worth of any business or business strategy equals the sum of its expected future cash flows discounted at a rate of return that reflects the systematic risk of those future cashflows. Ulti-

---

[7] Bernard Reimann, "Does Your Business Create Real Shareholder Value?" *Business Horizons* (Sept./Oct. 1986), p. 47.

Yes, You Can Manage Long-Term

Contrary to popular belief, the stock market is very conscious of the long-term capabilities of companies to produce results. Moreover, the market pays relatively little attention to short-term ups and downs in earnings and favorably responds to decisions by management to make investments today that promise economic returns in the future—even the very distant future. *Fortune* in an article in 1988 analyzed the stock prices of a number of large U.S. companies in an attempt to determine whether price levels were dependent more on short-term or long-term results. The conclusions, based on analysis done by the Alcon Group using Value Line forecasts were astounding. For large companies like Coca-Cola, IBM, General Electric, AT&T, Boeing, Proctor and Gamble, and many others, the greatest portion of the market value of their stock is explained by anticipated earnings beyond five years. In other words, the discounted value of the expected earnings for the companies over the next five years (which includes both funds reinvested in the business as well as dividends paid to owners) accounts for much less than one half of the stock value of the nation's twenty largest companies. Investors clearly look well beyond quarter-to-quarter earnings shifts and focus on how well they think the company can perform far into the future.

Parenthetically, they also tend to ignore short-term glitches in earnings or temporary missteps, despite what many CEOs appear to believe. Companies that report a down quarter seldom are punished in the stock market—unless investors perceive (usually correctly it turns out) that the short-term problem is an indication of long-term risks. Conversely, announcements of major investments such as in R&D or new plant investment are rewarded by the market—so long as investors believe that the company has demonstrated that the investments, over time, will provide superior returns. For example, when Citicorp announced that it would set aside a $3 billion reserve to cover Third World loans, resulting in a $2.5 billion quarterly loss, its stock actually rose. Investors had already taken the loan exposure into account in valuing the stock and were pleased to see Citicorp putting the problem behind it and gaining a tax advantage for having done so. Similarly, one researcher, Randall Woolridge of Penn State, concluded that on average, the day following announcements of major strategic investments, companies' stocks significantly outperformed the market.[8]

mately, the value created by a company for investors is reflected in the dividends paid plus increases in share price (capital gains).

Valuing the Business

An economic model for determining the value of an ongoing business moves away from traditional accounting measures and focuses entirely on

---

[8] Gary Hector, *Fortune* (Nov. 21, 1988), pp. 364–376.

the capability of the enterprise to produce cash for investors. To accomplish this, such a model must have several characteristics.

1. *Absence of noncash considerations.* Earnings must be free of book-keeping entries not affecting cash flow.

2. *Reflection of the time value of investments.* The timing of returns from investments must reflect their current value to the investor.

3. *Reflection of the riskiness of the business.* A cost of capital must be selected that reflects the level of uncertainty associated with a given company's performance.

4. *Calculation of real economic value added.* Both the efficiency of capital and the level of capital employed must be measured.

Several models exist for determining the actual economic value of a company to investors. The Stern Stewart component-based model, for example, defines value as a function of current operating efficiency, capital structure, tax policy, and forward business strategy.[9]

$$\text{Value} = \frac{\text{Value of current operations}}{\text{Cost of capital}}$$
$$+ \text{ Tax benefits of debt financing}$$
$$+ \text{ Economic value added by the strategic plan}$$

By adjusting the cost of capital to reflect the average weighted cost of both debt and equity, the tax benefits of debt financing are accounted for and the formula becomes:

$$\text{Value} = \frac{\text{Value of current operations}}{\text{Weighted average cost of capital}}$$
$$+ \text{ Economic value added by the strategic plan}$$

The components of this model and their significance in the equation are described in the following paragraphs.

The Concept of Value. Value is the sum of the returns on investments made by owners/shareholders in a business over the life of the business, discounted back to the present. For owners and stockholders, this value is primarily represented in free cash flow generated by the business and is evidenced in the form of dividends and stock price appreciation. Free cash flow is the cash the business can be expected to spin off over time. In the component-based model, free cash flow is

---

[9] Stewart, op. cit., pp. 4–8.

defined as revenues minus all costs of doing business (including taxes actually paid) and after all additions to working and fixed assets (e.g., plant investments).

Value of Current Operations. The value of current operations can be defined as the net operating profits after taxes (NOPAT) but before financing costs and bookkeeping entities not affecting cash flow or NOPAT. In the formula, NOPAT is typically based on current year results. It essentially reflects the economic earnings a company could be expected to return in perpetuity, assuming no changes in or additions to the investment base.

Cost of Capital. The cost of capital reflects the basic level of return expected by investors (e.g., typically the interest paid on risk-free government bonds) plus the premium they require in order to compensate for the degree of risk inherent in the particular business.

Tax Benefits of Debt Financing. Part of the inherent value of the company is the potential tax savings available from debt financing. Simply put, debt, within prudent limits, allows a company to shelter a portion of its profits, and those savings become corporate value. The tax benefits of debt financing are determined by multiplying the marginal corporate tax rate by the target level of debt used to finance business assets. In the adjusted formula shown previously, the tax benefits of debt financing are accounted for in the use of the average weighted cost of capital figure (C^*).

Economic Value Added by the Strategic Plan. The value of future businesses strategies is defined as:

$$\frac{\text{Amount of new capital invested annually (I)} \times \text{Rate of return on new investments (r)} - \text{Weighted cost of capital} \times \text{Time period for which superior returns will be provided (T)}}{\text{Weighted cost of capital} \times 1 - \text{Weighted cost of capital}}$$

or

$$\frac{I\,(r - C^*)\,T}{C^*\,(1 - C^*)}$$

The period noted previously for providing superior returns is a factor of the degree of cyclity of a business, the speed with which competitors can match a company's technological advances, ease of entry into the business, and macroeconomic factors.

An Alternative Model. Rappaport offers an alternative model that is also designed to value a company's worth to its investors.[10] He starts off with the basic concept that corporate value equals debt plus shareholder value. To solve for shareholder value, he rearranges this formula into the following equations:

Shareholder value = Corporate value − Debt

where corporate value is defined as a combination of:

- The present value of cash flow from operations during the forecast period
- Residual value representing the present value of the business attributable to the period beyond the forecast period
- Value of marketable securities

Therefore,

Corporate value
   = Present value of cash flow from operations during forecast period
   + Residual value + Marketable securities

Clearly, there are parallels between Stern Stewart's valuation technique and Rappaport's, though Rappaport uses a somewhat different approach to arriving at corporate valuations. Each of the key terms in his model are defined as follows:

1. *Cash flow from operations.* This term represents the differences between operating cash inflows and outflows. The present value of cash flows in the forecast period is equal to the sum of the discounted cash flows for the entering planning horizon where:
   a. The discount is the weighted average of the costs of debt and equity.
   b. Cash inflows minus cash outflows are defined as (sales in prior year) × (1 + sales growth rate) × (operating profit margin) × (1 − cash income tax rate) − (incremental fixed investment).

2. *Residual value.* This term represents the value of the company (i.e., cash flows) represented by operations beyond the planning period. It is derived from conclusions about the company's returns during the planning period combined with assumptions on how the environment for the business and its prospects will change in future years. For purposes of calculation, Rappaport assumes that after the planning period, the business on average will earn, in perpetuity, the cost of capital on new investments. He represents this with the following equation:

---

[10] Rappaport, *Creating Shareholder Value,* p. 52.

$$\text{Residual value} = \frac{\text{Perpetuity cash flow}}{\text{Cost of capital}}$$

A Hypothetical Valuing Situation. The following hypothetical situation illustrates the use of the Stern Stewart model in assigning an appropriate value to a company.

Company X

- NOPAT = $2 million
- Anticipated annual capital investments for the planning period (I) = $1.6 million
- After-tax rate of return (r) = 13%
- Growth rate = 12%
- Weighted average cost of capital (C*) = 11%
- Period for which management will have attractive investment opportunities (T) = 6 years

Using the valuation formula:

$$\text{Value} = \frac{\text{NOPAT}}{(C^*)} + \frac{I\,(r - C^*)\,T}{C^*\,(1 + C^*)}$$

$$\text{Value} = \frac{\$2,000}{11\%} + \frac{\$1,600\,(13\% - 11\%)\,6}{11\%\,(1 + 11\%)}$$

Value = $18,181 + $1,572

Value = $19,753 (not including short-term benefits from time value of
                  earnings during the operating year)

Determining the Cost of Capital

Both Stern Stewart's and Rappaport's models require that a cost of capital be derived in order to value a company's true worth. In fact, the basis for many of their criticisms of standard accounting-based measures of business performance reflect the failure of traditional methods to adequately account for the cost of capital.

In both models, the cost of capital is essentially the level of return a company must earn if it is to satisfy investor requirements for returns from investments. It is a combination of the risk-free return (e.g., as represented by government bonds) that investors can earn plus an appropriate risk premium.

According to Stern Stewart, there are several ways in which the cost of capital can be defined. For purposes of their model's valuation formulas, however, the average weighted cost of capital (C*) is the key form. In the Stern Stewart model, C^* equals the costs of equity plus the costs of debt, adjusted to reflect their relative weights in the capital structure of the company. A number of relatively complex processes may be employed to determine the requirements for return by equity investors. The Stern Stewart model uses a proprietary methodology based on extensive research that considers four main business characteristics:

1. Operating risk (volatility)
2. Strategic risk (particularly compared with peer companies)
3. Characteristics of assets (e.g., quality)
4. Company size and sources of income

Debt represents the average total costs of debt to the company minus the income tax benefits of debt. The cost of capital is calculated as follows:

$$C^* = \text{(After-tax cost of debt} \times \text{Target portion of debt)} + \text{(Cost of equity} \times \text{Target portion of equity)}$$

Both Stern Stewart and Rappaport continually emphasize that, in valuing a diversified corporation, it is essential that capital costs be calculated for each separate business unit of the corporation. If only a single rate is used, there will be a tendency to overrate the values of more risky ventures (and hence make inappropriately risky investments in them) and to underestimate the value of more stable businesses.

THE LINKAGE BETWEEN STRATEGIES AND VALUE CREATION

Once a clear understanding exists as to what contributes to the tangible value of a business, it becomes possible to define strategies and operating plans that will enhance that value. Conversely, managers can also better identify and reject investment opportunities that will ultimately lead to a decrease in shareholder value.

Proponents of the shareholder-value approach to corporate management believe that, traditionally, businesses have used the wrong yardstick to measure performance, and that, consequently, they have often adopted strategies designed not to achieve shareholder value creation but to satisfy performance criteria that have little relationship to real value enhancement. Once managers understand the correct measures of performance (i.e., real returns to stockholders and owners that are commensurate with risk and that recognize the time value of money), they can design and implement strategies that focus on value creation.

Measuring Economic Value Added

In designing or evaluating a given business strategy, managers need to focus on economic value added — i.e., the difference between the prestrategy and poststrategy value for the business. If the difference, discounted by the cost of capital, is positive, the strategy can be said to be generating value for its owners.

Rappaport provides a systematic model for valuing the contributions of business strategies.[11] He states that the value generated by a given business plan can be projected by calculating the capitalized value of the difference between operating margins and the minimum acceptable operating return on new sales. He designed the following equations to perform this analysis (Note: Book and cash income tax rates are assumed to be identical):

$$\blacktriangle E_t = \frac{(Pt' - Pt'_{min})(1 - T_t)\blacktriangle JS_t}{k(1 + k)^{t-1}}$$

Where:

$\blacktriangle E_t$ = Change in value of the equity in the company at time t

Pt' = Change in earnings before interest and taxes divided by the change in sales (i.e., incremental operating margin on incremental sales) at time t

Pt_{min} = Minimum acceptable return at time t defined as:

$$P'_{min} = \frac{(f + w)k}{(1 - T)(t + k)}$$

f   = Capital expenditure minus depreciation per dollar of sales

w   = Cash required for net working capital per dollar of sales increase

T_t = Income tax rate at time t

$\blacktriangle S_t$ = Change in sales at time t

k   = Weighted average cost of capital (see earlier discussion for determining the average weighted cost of capital)

To illustrate this model, Rappaport offers the following example:

Sales from most recent year   = $50

Projected sales growth rate   = 15%

Projected pretax earnings on incremental sales:
    First two years   = 13.5%
    Remaining three years   = 14.5%

Book and cash tax rate   = 46%

Working capital to sales ratio   = .20

Capital expenditures per dollar sales = .35

Cost of capital   = 14%

---

[11] Rappaport, "Selecting Strategies that Create Shareholder Value," *Harvard Business Review* (May/June 1981), p. 149.

TABLE 3-1

Estimated Impact on Shareholder Value, Using Rappaport's Model for Business Strategy Valuation (in millions of dollars)

Years	Sales	Sales increase	Projected return on incremental sales units minus minimum return	Shareholder present value increase
1	$57.50	$7.50	$0.01	$0.29
2	66.12	8.62	0.01	0.29
3	76.04	9.92	0.02	0.59
4	87.45	11.41	0.02	0.59
5	100.57	13.12	0.02	0.60
	$387.68	$50.07		$2.36

Table 3-1 shows the effect of strategy on shareholder value over a five-year period.

When evaluating alternative strategies available to a company, a key concern becomes assessing changes in the degree of risk associated with each option. Similarly, analysis of alternatives must account for changes in the timing of cash flows. Failures to reflect such differences will tend to overestimate or underestimate the value that each strategy alternative will ultimately provide to shareholders.

Assessing Strategic Performance

A company can determine the value created by its various units and assess the potential of existing business strategies to provide acceptable returns for investors by first determining the cost and timing of the original investments made in the business, starting with the discounted price of providing (or acquiring) the start-up assets of the business and adding discounted additions to the assets and working capital from subsequent investments. (The discount rate is a combination of the cost of debt applicable during the various time periods and equity costs, representing the level of risk associated with the businesses). The dividends and corporate charges paid by each business are then subtracted to give a present value of the net investment. Finally, a determination is made of the present value of the future cash flows the businesses can be expected to produce over time. The difference between the net present value of the investment in each business and the present value of expected returns equals the value created or destroyed.

In the second phase of such an analysis, the company determines the viability (i.e., ability to produce expected cash flows) of each of the business unit strategies. The key steps of the evaluation are (1) to apply appropriate hurdle rates—costs of capital that account for the true degree of risk associated with each business—and (2) to determine the likely timing of returns; returns provided later in the planning horizon are worth less than those available earlier in the period. The types of factors employed in determining the risk of each strategy typically include:

- Previous performance of the business and the perceived capabilities of management
- Current competitors' positions and existing or potential sources of competitive advantage
- Competitive and technological threats to the business
- Conditions in the marketplace

IMPLEMENTATION STRATEGIES TO ENHANCE SHAREHOLDER VALUE

The approaches and techniques available to managers to promote achievement of shareholder value objectives fall basically into four categories:

1. Changing the motivation of executive management
2. Taking advantage of the benefits provided by increased leverage (debt)
3. Evaluating acquisitions
4. Promoting a shareholder value culture

Motivating Management to Focus on Shareholder Value

In measuring and rewarding managers for performance, many companies tie bonuses, stock options, and other incentives to such measures as net profit, ROE, or EPS growth. However, as demonstrated earlier, there is little or no provable correlation between these accounting-based measures and the creation of real shareholder value. Managers can achieve high accounting returns or successfully grow EPS for years while the economic returns of the company decline and the value of the business is eroded. Many a corporate chieftain has grown rich while the stockholders have watched their investments deteriorate.

Many experts agree that the solution is to reorient managers toward performance measures that emphasize real economic value creation, and to make managers think like owners by linking their own compensation to the direct creation of wealth.

The list of misleading performance indicators that should be avoided reads like a list of the most common measures that businesses have traditionally used in evaluating and rewarding executive performance.

- *Revenue growth.* Revenues without commensurate earnings provide no value to a company.
- *Accounting profits.* The vagaries of the accounting system make accounting profits unreliable as a true measure of performance.

- *EPS growth.* EPS can always be increased, but at what price?
- *ROI/ROE.* The meaningfulness of both the return and the investment or equity can be distorted by accounting conventions.

More valid indicators of value creation, as discussed earlier, are those that take into account the real, free cash flow of the business, that incorporate risk and cost of money considerations, and that eliminate any irrelevant accounting discrepancies. Hence, when managers are rewarded on shareholder returns or economic value added, they are motivated to adopt strategies and to make financing and investment decisions that lead to wealth creation for shareholders. The Stern Stewart and Rappaport models on corporate valuation and strategy valuation lend themselves to incorporation in management performance ratings.

Ideally, an incentive plan that rewards executives for economic value added should have the following types of characteristics:

- Earnings opportunities of the plan should be tied as closely as possible to the same factors or conditions that affect the value of the company's shares in the marketplace. Hence, when the shareholder gains value, the executive also benefits. Conversely, if the company erodes shareholder value, management suffers financially as well.
- The plan should reward long-term performance, particularly by promoting continuing creation of shareholder value rather than single-year results.
- The plan should focus on the specific value drivers who demonstrably contribute to economic performance.
- The plan should provide for real ownership in the company by management, or at least encourage managers to adopt the same interests in the company as owners. (The very best incentive plans are designed to put management at real risk, for example, by expecting them to make upfront contributions of their own money to purchase stocks.)
- The plan should not limit or cap the payout opportunities of senior executives. The more economic value they create, the greater their reward.

In short, an incentive plan should be ruthless in driving executives to concentrate only on the interests of the shareholder and to avoid any strategic alternatives that fail to create economic value.

Making Use of Leverage

Despite the bad press given to overly leveraged companies, management should not lose sight of the fact that a prudent amount of debt can greatly contribute to increasing the inherent value of a business. Debt financing reduces the corporate tax burden. Therefore, the higher the ratio of debt to equity in a company's financial structure, the more real cash flow will be produced for the shareholders.

Joel Stern emphasizes that many companies should substantially increase their debt levels to take advantage of these tax benefits. He cites the following example of how debt can enhance value.[12]

1. The value of a company is defined as:

> Net operating profits after tax but before bookkeeping entries not affecting cash flow (NOPAT)
> Cost of capital + (Debt level × Tax rate) + Value of the business strategy

(For purposes of illustration, the third element of the equation is not relevant and will not be included in the remainder of the discussion.)

2. If a company's NOPAT equals $1,000, the cost of capital is 10%, and there is no debt, the company would be valued as follows:

$$\text{Value} = \frac{\$1,000}{0.10} + 0 = \$10,000 = \text{Equity}$$

3. If, however, the company takes on $5,000 worth of debt and the tax rate if 40%, all other things being equal, the valuation would be as follows:

$$\text{Value} = \frac{\$1,000}{0.10} + 0.40 \ (\$5,000) = \$12,000$$

Subtracting $5,000 in debt from the total value of $12,000 would reduce the equity to $7,000.

In taking on the debt and assuming sufficient cash flow to cover it (e.g., debt is at a prudent level), management substantially increase the value of the company to its shareholders. Essentially this is what leveraged buyout specialists do in taking over a company and why, despite common assumptions to the contrary, they have been able, in real terms, to increase the economic value of many companies. As Stern points out, high levels of debt also have the additional benefit of reducing discretionary cash flow. Thus, management is disciplined to focus on only those new investments that will generate superior returns and to avoid those that will not create shareholder value.

Evaluating Acquisitions

Michael Porter helped to demolish the myth that acquisitions can generally be expected to enhance the value of companies. As he demonstrates, the exact opposite is more often true; companies have typically overpaid for

---

[12] Stewart, op. cit., pp. 6-1 and 6-2.

their acquisitions or have bought businesses to which they could not add significant value.

There are only two ways a company can benefit from acquisitions. The acquiror either can increase the revenues of the acquisition (or increase its own revenues because of the acquisition) or it can decrease the acquisition's (or its own) costs. Absent one or the other, the combined companies will not generate additional cash flow above the level that would have been expected had the companies remained independent. (A third potential source of added value can be realized by improving the financial structure of the company; for example, by increasing debt levels, acquirers can also increase value.) Without additional cash flows (or economic value added), the premium that presumably was paid by the acquiring company for the acquisition will never be recouped and shareholder value will be lost.

In successful acquisitions or mergers, both the seller's and the buyer's stock or market value increase right away, which simply reflects the fact that, in combination, the companies will generate value beyond that which they could have provided independently. More specifically, the market determines that this value will exceed any premium paid by the acquirer.

Bennett Stewart suggests that potential acquisitions should be evaluated on the same economic value added basis that he recommends companies use in doing internal performance and valuation analyses.[13] Specifically, prospective acquirors should determine the net value added of an acquisition on the following basis, with value received reflecting any benefits provided by the combined organizations and value paid representing all cash, debt, or equity paid:

> Net value added
>> = Total (operating) value received
>> − Total (financial) value paid

Stewart emphasizes that value paid is not influenced by the accounting treatment of the purchasing process (except as it affects taxes paid). It makes no difference, for example, whether cash, debt, or stock is used; only the value of the payment is of concern.

Using the Stern Stewart formula, Stewart shows how benefits from acquisitions can be obtained and measured. Stern Stewart's model defines value as follows:

$$\text{Value} = \frac{\text{NOPAT}}{C} + tD = \frac{1\,(r - C)\,T}{C\,(1 + C)}$$

Stewart indicates that benefits to the acquirer come from three areas:

1. Operating benefits including improvement in efficiencies

---

[13] Ibid., pp. 7-1–7-8.

2. Financial benefits from unused debt capacity, tax loss carryforwards, or economies of scale in raising capital
3. Tax benefits

Promoting a Shareholder Value Culture

For many companies, adopting an aggressive value creation strategy means also making appropriate changes in the corporate culture (i.e., in its values, beliefs, and ways of doing business). There is a variety of ways to accomplish such a change, although a total cultural transition can take years to achieve and expected results are not realized immediately. One of the most effective methods for change is to refocus the compensatory system for executives by emphasizing economic value creation and making managers think like owners. Other steps that can be taken by management to reorient the culture of a company include the following:

- *Business mission.* Issuing a formal statement that the company intends to focus on enhancing shareholder value is, by no means, the total solution to creating a new culture. Nevertheless, it can be a first step. Companies such as Coca-Cola and Libby-Owens Ford, for example, followed up on their explicitly stated intention to build real economic value for investors by taking solid action that turned their objectives into realities.

- *Strategic planning/operational planning.* How a company develops plans and the objectives it sets in its strategic and operating plans send a strong message to managers and employees. When the CEO of a company begins to evaluate investments only on the basis of whether they will create real economic value, or when demonstrates that only programs or projects that enhance shareholder wealth will be accepted, managers will soon respond by eliminating uneconomic proposals from their plans and will reorient their efforts toward value-creating projects.

- *Training.* Not everyone in a company needs to fully understand the intricacies of the value-creation formula in order to be able to contribute to a value-enhancement strategy. Nevertheless, virtually all managers need to be taught the basics of what does or does not lead to economic value creation. Appropriate training programs for managers followed by continuous reinforcement can overcome misconceptions and point managers in the right direction.

- *Leverage.* Increasing the debt load within a company (at prudent levels) not only provides tax advantages but also forces managers to limit investments to only those opportunities that create shareholder value. The discipline of debt can be a powerful motivator and its ability to prevent uneconomic use of resources should not be overlooked.

CONCLUSION

Corporate management can no longer count on a passive marketplace to ignore failures to produce real value for shareholders. Managers who do not take advantage of all of the opportunities to maximize value creation will soon find themselves under attack by corporate raiders who know only too well how to enhance value. At a minimum, they will find that they can no longer find willing investors who will provide the financial resources they need to maintain and grow their businesses.

As management has become more attuned to the necessity of creating shareholder wealth, they have begun to think like owners and to guide their businesses toward creating real economic returns rather than meaningless accounting-based gains or unprofitable growth. Methods exist for accomplishing the transition to becoming a value creator; management's task is to take advantage of the available opportunities.

PART II

Tools for Strategic Planning

4

The Role of Science in Business Strategy

SIDNEY SCHOEFFLER

Founding Director, The Strategic Planning Institute

WHY EXAMINE THE ISSUE?

In most areas of human productive activity there is now, near the end of the twentieth century, absolutely no need to inquire what role science can and should play in that activity. The basic answer is obvious. Almost everyone understands that without science a modern doctor would be no better than a primitive medicine man, a modern engineer no more capable than a medieval artisan, and a modern farmer no more productive than a stone age hunter and gatherer. There are many issues on details and specifics (and always will be), and moral questions on use vs. abuse (and also always will be), but no disagreement on the basic notion that the laws of nature are capable of being discovered, important to know, and employable for the benefit of man. Moreover, the technology for making discoveries and applying them to human purposes is well developed, extensively tested, continually being further improved, and very extensively employed.

Curiously, this is not so in the area of business management, particularly strategic business management. The most popular concept here is still that business management is a craft. Strategic management is frequently seen as something that is learned by direct experience or from another craftsman, that consists of little more than the application of common sense plus native intelligence to a particular kind of problem, and that can be codified in relatively simple and unchanging procedures. In an increasing number of industries, one can see the remarkable spectacle of the product becoming better and better and the process of production becoming more and more efficient, while the business and its management remain qualitatively stagnant. The situation is very similar to military strategy, where the quality of the weapons keeps improving, but the quality of the generals remains the same.

How can science improve the situation? This is not the place for a treatise on scientific method; in any case, that would amount to pontification about the well known. Instead, the question is approached from the negative side: What business blunders are occurring because science is not used in business strategy, and how might these blunders be minimized? A summary of the key concepts helps to clarify the major points.

WHAT IS "SCIENCE"?

"Science," as used here, does not mean test tubes or telescopes, but refers to a method of thought. This method has proven exceedingly powerful in all areas of human endeavor to which it has been applied; it produces insights and capabilities that are cumulative, expanding, and improving without end and without upper limit. Progress is not, of course, always free of misstep or error (or even fraud), but part of the essential nature of science is that these errors are discovered and corrected.

Some of the key ingredients of this method of thought are discussed in the following sections.

Observation and Evidence

One learns about the world by observing the world. Likewise, one learns about business strategy by observing business strategy. Observation must be careful rather than sloppy: The observer measures, records, compares, and checks. All opinions and theories are provisional until they are verified by adequate evidence, and all evidence consists of careful observation of the real world. If the real world is kind enough to show the observer what he or she wants to see, then it is observed; otherwise the observer tries to coax the world to reveal its secrets by arranging suitable experiments.

Analytical Rigor

Evidence is interpreted through the use of logic. One does not jump to conclusions, but works toward them. When an inspiration or a flash of insight does occur, it is necessary to go back and check to see if the insight is logically consistent with the evidence and if the evidence is adequate. If the idea is inconsistent with the body of available evidence, it is rejected as erroneous; if it is consistent with the evidence but the evidence is inadequate, judgment is reserved until the evidence is adequate. The standards of adequacy are tight rather than loose.

Significance

When a pattern or relationship is observed, it must be tested for significance before it is accepted as a "fact" or "law." Thus the risk that the observed relationship is accidental and ephemeral rather than systematic and dependable is minimized. If an observed pattern is not significant, little credence is placed in it. If it is not known whether the pattern is significant (perhaps because its significance has not been tested), the pattern is not considered significant and little credence is placed in it.

Probability

Patterns and relationships are not expected to be black or white; they can be shades of gray. For example, cigarette smoking does not always cause lung cancer, and not smoking does not always prevent it, but the probabilities are different (and the differences are significant). The important thing is to measure the probabilities. Unknown probabilities are poor guides to action.

Hypothesis and Test

Knowledge accumulates by a cyclical and repetitive process of hypothesis and test. The hypothesis phase is the driving force; the test phase keeps it honest. Imagination, creativity, energy, hopes, and dreams come into play during the hypothesis phase; conscience, caution, and soundness come into play during the test phase. It is important that both phases be kept active all the time. (In this context, "theory" is an advanced form of hypothesis.)

Representative Cross Section

Conclusions with respect to a particular case are almost always derived from similar other cases. The criteria for similar other cases are subject to hypothesis and test. A sufficient number of similar other cases must be examined in order to test for significance. Therefore, when searching for reliable action guides in any particular situation, the trick is to find an adequate number of other cases that are similar to the present case. Failing that, there are no reliable action guides.

Respect for Others

Evidence is assembled and conclusions are reached in a way that can be communicated to others and verified by them. This minimizes the risk of wishful thinking, error, or fraud. It also minimizes the wastage that comes from reinventions of the wheel. The habit of communicating both evidence and logic is a manifestation of respect for others. The conclusions or recommendations of those who are unwilling or unable to support their views are rejected.

Cost/Benefit

The principles of scientific observation may be deviated from for clear cost/benefit reasons. Sometimes it is simply too much trouble to do things right;

for example, where the cost of error is small. When in doubt, however, all the principles should be applied in a conscientious and disciplined manner.

SCIENCE IN BUSINESS STRATEGY

The foregoing does not, of course, constitute a rigorous definition of science or a complete description of its methods. Emphasis has been placed on those precepts that, even though they are of great importance, are very frequently neglected in the formulation of business strategy and policy.

Strategic issues are, by definition, the critically important issues in a business—those that spell the major differences between success and failure. Therefore, they clearly deserve the best thinking and the most powerful methods and tools that can be brought to bear upon them.

Why, then, is the nonscientific approach to strategy-setting widely prevalent? Probably the most important fact is that the scientific base for business strategy is in a regrettably underdeveloped state and simply does not suffice as a guide to many of the decisions that must be made. It is not that the scientific approach is in principle unable to cope with business problems; it is that use of the approach has not been widely attempted. There is a vicious cycle at work here: The "supply" of the fruits of science is low, so the "demand" is low, so the "supply" is low, and so on.

The problem is how to break this vicious cycle and to turn it into the kind of benign cycle that works so effectively in medicine, engineering, and agriculture. Fortunately, some very good beginnings have already been made.

Chief among these, in the specific area of business strategy, is the Profit Impact of Market Strategy (PIMS) Program. This program, organized at the Harvard Business School in 1972 and operated by the nonprofit Strategic Planning Institute since 1975, is a larger-scale continuation of previous work done at the General Electric Company. It is, in effect, a cooperative venture, involving about 250 major companies in North America and Europe, designed to provide a set of observations, plus associated analytical procedures, for a more scientific approach to the planning efforts of the participating companies.

Each member company contributes information about its experiences in several different business areas to a combined data base. The PIMS staff analyzes this experience to discover the general laws that determine what business strategy in what kind of competitive environment produces what results. The findings are made available to member companies in a form useful to their business planning.

The program provides business managers and planners with tools and data to answer questions such as:

- What profit rate is normal for a given business, considering its partic- ular market, competitive position, technology, cost structure, and so on?
- If the business continues on its current track, what will its future operating results be?
- What strategic changes in the business have promise of improving these results?
- Given a specified contemplated future strategy for the business, how will short-term and long-term profitability or cash flow change?

In each case, the answers are derived from an analysis of the experiences of other businesses operating under similar conditions.

More specifically, four purposes of the program are:

1. To assemble a data base reflecting the business strategy experiences of a group of participating companies;
2. To conduct a research program on that data base in order to dis- cover the laws of the marketplace that govern (a) profit levels, (b) other outcomes of strategic actions, and (c) outcomes of changes in the business environment;
3. To conduct an applications program to make the findings of the research available to participating companies in a form and manner they can use effectively; and
4. To carry-out ancillary activities (publication, education, service to participants, study of planning methods, legislative recommenda- tions) that will enhance the value of the entire program to its mem- bers and to the economy at large.

The unit of observation in PIMS is a business. Each business is a divi- sion, product line, or other profit center within its parent company which sells a distinct set of products and/or services to an identifiable group of customers in competition with a well-defined set of competitors and for which revenues, operating costs, investments, and strategic plans can be separated in a meaningful way.

Currently the data base consists of information on the strategic experi- ences of more than 2,500 businesses, covering a three- to ten-year period. The information on each business consists of about 100 items descriptive of the characteristics of the market environment, the state of competition, the strategy pursued by the business, and the operating results obtained. Each data item has been pretested for significance and relevance to profit- ability.

The PIMS staff has devised a set of standardized forms to be filled out by the participant company for the contribution of its experience records to the data bank. The forms are designed to break the required data items into simple elements that can be assembled readily from financial or marketing records, or that can be estimated by someone familiar with the specific business.

One of the most encouraging aspects of the PIMS Program is the growing volume of academic research being performed on the PIMS data base. Numerous studies by academicians (faculty research and doctoral dissertations) have been completed. These studies, plus the increasing amount of other scientific work now being done at such institutions as Harvard, Columbia, Purdue, Michigan, Stanford, and New York Universities, are providing a demonstration to both the business community and business schools that substantial progress is indeed possible in this area.

The fruits of the effort will accumulate to the point where most decisions in the areas of business strategy and business policy may become as professional as corresponding decisions in, for instance, medicine. In the meantime, what is the practitioner to do? Life must go on, whether science is fully ready to assist or not.

The first thing to do is, of course, to take full advantage of the findings and the tools already available. They do not solve all problems, or even most, but they perform quite well as far as they go. Second, the effort to keep improving the data, the research, and the tools should receive support. Third, a sense of discrimination between the "good stuff" and the makeshifts is needed; in other words, the practitioner must become a more demanding consumer of business technology.

The field of health care, in addition to offering much instruction on how to become more scientific, also shows what can be done where the benefits of science have not yet reached. Where a disease can be cured, it is. Where enough is not yet known, (a) the patient is made as comfortable as possible; (b) his mind is occupied with good thoughts or distracting activities; (c) a miracle is hoped for; (d) if necessary, the process of dying is eased; and (e) work continues to do better the next time. A well-designed process of strategic planning does the same for the business executive.

CURRENT PERFORMANCE LEVELS IN THE BUSINESS COMMUNITY

The PIMS data base, in addition to providing observations for a scientific approach to business strategy, also affords a view of the damage done by the failure to use this approach.

The PIMS Program conducted a study to measure the shortfall from potential performance in a sample of 120 businesses. The approach took the following three steps:

1. For each business in the sample, measurements were made of the results of a "no-change" strategy (i.e., the operating results that the business will probably achieve if it simply maintains its current stra-

tegic posture and floats with the market). Operating results were measured in terms of the discounted present value of net cash flows plus capital gains (i.e., increase or decrease in the market value of the business) taken over a five-year period.

2. The potential operating results were then measured, using the same measure of performance. The potential was defined in terms of the results obtained by the good performers among "strategic look-alikes" (i.e., other businesses operating under strategically similar circumstances: having a similar position, in a similar market, facing similar competition, and employing a similar technology). The good performers were taken at approximately the eightieth percentile among the strategic look-alikes.

3. By direct comparison, a calculation was made for each business of its shortfall (if any) from potential.

The conclusions of this analysis certainly were not exact or indisputable, but they did produce a rough indication of the magnitude of the problem. The average business in the sample attained about half of its potential performance. This estimate of the current wastage of economic resources is in some respects too high (there is such a thing as simple bad luck, since the world operates on a probability basis, not a mechanical basis) and in other respects too low (the sample consisted of more outstanding companies than mediocre companies, and only of their surviving businesses). However, there is little doubt that the possibility of improvement is huge and that a scientific approach can make most of the difference.

COMMON BLUNDERS IN BUSINESS STRATEGY

Some of the specific mistakes that lead to the waste of resources can be identified. This discussion does not concern unlucky moves, but those that can clearly be expected, on the available evidence, to fail.

Making Moves Inappropriate to the Position

Many businesses make moves and take actions that have a high failure rate for the starting position of the business. Examine the following examples of inappropriate strategies:

- XYZ, Inc., a business with a low relative market share, simultaneously carries out an expensive and innovation-oriented research and development program and an expensive and leadership-oriented marketing program.
- Continental Flange, a business with a product of mediocre quality, attempts to compensate for lack of quality by an energetic marketing effort.

- R.P.H., Inc., a business with a low relative market share, becomes vertically integrated.

Building Productivity in the Wrong Way

Many businesses, in an effort to improve the productivity of their work force, mechanize or automate excessively, increasing their fixed costs considerably. As a result they stand to lose the fruits of their improved productivity by becoming embroiled in frequent and severe price wars or marketing wars.

Underdeveloping Strong Positions

Many well-positioned businesses (good product quality, well-segmented market, high productivity) tend to rest on their laurels and fail to take full advantage of the opportunities (e.g., for backward integration or for market-centered diversification) that their position provides.

Underdeveloping Weak Positions

Many businesses whose current positions have a few elements of weakness (e.g., slow market growth or low relative share) but other elements of strength give up prematurely and underinvest in the business by a considerable amount.

Going Down With the Flagship

Many companies depend heavily on a major "flagship" business. When confronted with maturity in that business or with a major new competitive challenge (e.g., from Japan), they fail either to restructure the business to cope with the new realities or to redeploy their strengths to other businesses or markets.

"Zigzagging"

Lacking the fortitude and clear-sightedness to see a strategy through to a successful conclusion, many businesses change position or strategy frequently, dissipating resources through wasteful "zigzagging."

Joining the Other Lemmings

Joining the rush into apparently promising new markets or technologies without adequate competitive strengths to succeed in these new areas, a business may well be unable to survive the inevitable shakeout.

Inappropriate Turnaround Efforts

When a business gets into profit trouble or cash trouble, it may predicate its strategy on moves that produce only a short-run appearance of improvement at the cost of an erosion of the fundamentals of the business. A common example is saving money by reducing product quality.

COMMON BLUNDERS IN LOGIC AND METHOD

The blunders in business strategy are attributable, in a general way, to shortcomings in logic and method. But under that broad heading, there are some specific errors that appear with particular frequency and cause an unusual amount of mischief.

Gullibility

Gullibility involves an uncritical acceptance of simplistic and/or unsupported principles of strategy and rules of business conduct. At least half of the most frequently cited principles of business strategy are not grounded in any visible evidence, or are inappropriate in major groups of businesses. It is easy to tell the sound principles from the unsound ones by examining the supporting evidence. If there is no evidence, or if the evidence is inadequate, the alleged principle is probably untrustworthy.

Failure to Test Consequences

Another common mistake is the adoption of a strategy for a particular business without a test of the consequences of that strategy. Many companies choose a strategy simply on the basis of where the business fits on a matrix, what their competitors are doing, what an expert recommends, or the prevailing consensus of the management team, without taking the trouble to test that strategy by a credible forecast of its consequences. It is not always easy to make this forecast, but it is always important to make the effort.

Poor Forecasting Logic

Inappropriate forecasting models are often used in strategy planning. The most frequent error is to employ time-series-based longitudinal models for strategic forecasting. This is almost always an error, because any change in the basic structure of the business or its environment will invalidate a longitudinal model, and strategic changes normally do involve the basic structure. The answer is to use models with cross-sectional bases, whose range of applicability spans both the old structure and the new structure.

Wrong Peer Group as Basis for Evaluations

A business may use an inappropriate group of observations to evaluate its strategic options. Many business people compare their own situation to that of other companies in their industry. This is usually misleading, because other companies do not always share the same strategic problems. For example, the passenger car business of General Motors has little to learn from the experiences of Ford, Chrysler, or Toyota with passenger cars, but a lot to learn from the IBM mainframe business or the General Electric lamp business, which also hold top rank in a maturing industry under severe competitive attack.

Tunnel Vision

This error consists of exploring too narrow a range of strategic options, thereby missing opportunities for substantial (rather than merely incremental) improvements in the business.

Erroneous Discounting

In evaluating future incomes or outgoes, businesses may use interest rates that are too high (thereby condemning the business to a harvest strategy) or too low (thereby ignoring an important element of opportunity cost). The villain is often inflation, which confuses many people as to which interest rate is really applicable. Most discount rates of less than 2 percent or more than 5 percent in real terms (i.e., relative to the rate of inflation) are suspect and probably wrong, unless the risk of the investment is very high. The use of a very short planning horizon (less than five years) is tantamount to a too-high discount rate.

Cost/Benefit Errors

Overinvesting or underinvesting in the planning effort, relative to the benefits achievable, is another common blunder in planning. There is a frequent inverse correlation between the cost and the benefit of a planning process. This happens because an inadequacy of logic or method is often compensated for by elaborate bureaucratic busywork or expensive consultant studies. Good planning is not very expensive, compared to bad planning, but it is not cheap either, because it must be done with considerable care and attention to possible missteps and errors.

CONVENTIONAL WISDOM VS. SCIENCE

Science often challenges conventional wisdom, with the outcome being improved potential for effective health care, space exploration, data processing, corporate performance, and so forth. The following examples illustrate the role of science in challenging conventional wisdom in business strategy.

Investing in Technology

The "Unprofitability" of Modern Technology. Of all the findings on business strategy yielded by the study of the more than 2,500 businesses in the PIMS data base, the following remains one of the most controversial: Businesses that are highly investment intensive, that is, those that use high levels of investment per dollar of sales revenue (airlines, bulk chemical-processing plants, or distributors of consumer goods requiring large inventories), are much less profitable than businesses with lower levels of investment per dollar of sales. Figure 4-1 illustrates this phenomenon in terms of return on investment (ROI).

This finding is controversial not because the phenomenon is rare, uncertain, or weak—it is common, quite clear, and extremely powerful—but because it is so unexpected. The conventional wisdom is that there is a strong positive relationship between investment intensity and modernity or progressiveness. Everyone knows that modern technology requires elaborate machinery, and thus heavy investments; that high labor productivity depends on extensive automation, and thus on heavy investments; and that

FIGURE 4-1

Investment Intensity and Return on Investment

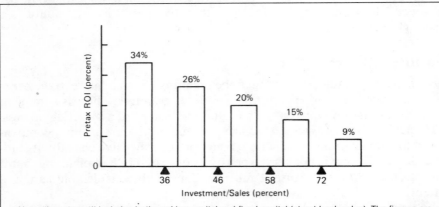

Note: "Investment" includes both working capital and fixed capital (at net book value). The figures are four-year averages. The cut points used have no significance in themselves, but are chosen to divide the businesses in the data base into equal groups. With a different definition of investment (e.g., predepreciation book value or current replacement value) or a different performance index (e.g., profit as a percentage of value added) or a different time period (e.g., three years or five years), the specific numbers are moderately different, but the strategic message is the same.

consumer goods must be readily available to customers to sell successfully, and thus require large inventory investments. Since modern technology, high labor productivity, and readily available consumer products are judged to be good things, they are expected to improve profitability rather than to hurt it. What in fact happens is that the commonly expected public benefits of investment-intensive technology (higher wages, lower prices, and improved product quality) do indeed occur most of the time; but, alas, the expected private benefits do not occur. Instead, the profits of companies that use an investment-intensive technology are usually rather poor.

Why does investment intensity hurt profits? Before answering this question, it is important to confirm that we are in fact dealing with an issue that is real and substantive, not just an optical illusion. For example, it might be argued that the negative pattern in Figure 4-1 is due entirely to arithmetic: that investment-intensive businesses have large denominators in their ROI ratios, and that their returns are low for that reason alone. That possibility can be excluded by using another measure of profitability. For example, Figure 4-2 relates investment intensity to the ratio of residual income to sales. The similarity of the pattern to that of Figure 4-1 confirms that investment-intensive businesses are actually less profitable.

Another possible argument is that the negative effect of investment intensity on profit is actually due to something quite different. Specifically, it is well known that businesses with high shares of their served markets are considerably more profitable than those with low shares. One of the reasons for that relationship is that high-share businesses tend to be more efficient

FIGURE 4-2

Investment Intensity and the Ratio of Residual Income to Sales

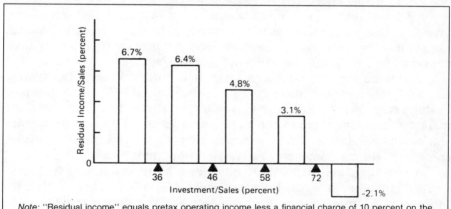

Note: "Residual income" equals pretax operating income less a financial charge of 10 percent on the investment used in the business. Other rates of financial charge produce different slopes but the same basic pattern. Even so unrealistic an assumption as a zero cost of money produces a slightly negative slope.

FIGURE 4-3

Effect on Return on Investment of Investment Intensity and Market Share

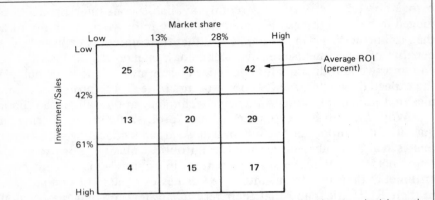

Note: The cut points between adjacent rows and columns were chosen to give approximately equal numbers of businesses in each row and each column. The ROI number in each box is the four-year average for the businesses falling into that box.

users of investment and are therefore less investment intensive, while low-share businesses are often inefficient users of investment and are therefore more investment intensive. The negative effect on profit of high investment intensity might therefore be no more than the reverse side of the coin of the favorable effect on profit of high market share. To exclude that possibility, it is necessary to establish that there is an effect on ROI from investment intensity in addition to that from market share. Figure 4-3 shows that there is indeed such an effect.

All the businesses in a given column have similar market shares, but investment intensity increases with each row. The fact that ROI decreases sharply moving down each column confirms that investment intensity has a negative effect on profit, regardless of market share.

Within each of the classes of investment intensity, one can examine not only ROI itself but also the degree to which the ROI of the group of businesses is lower or higher than would be expected from their levels of market share alone. Investment-intensive businesses are found to be even less profitable than would be expected from their market share, further confirming the phenomenon as a real and important one.

A third argument is that low ratios of sales to investment (i.e., high levels of investment intensity) are actually due to low levels of capacity utilization. A similar test of this hypothesis yields a similar result.

The major reason for this negative effect seems to be that the game of competition is played in a very different way in investment-intensive industries than in others. When each of the firms competing in a partic-

FIGURE 4-4

Increases in Selling Prices Related to Investment Intensity

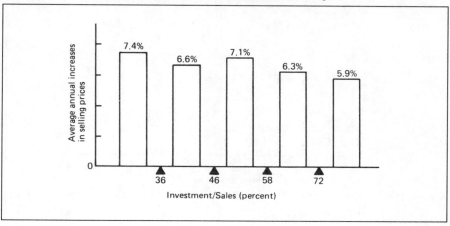

ular industry has committed heavy investments on which a reasonable return needs to be earned, each becomes rather eager to keep its capacity loaded. In an investment-intensive facility, volume is commonly believed to be the key to profitability. (Perhaps surprisingly, this belief is as common in industries where the investment consists largely of working capital as it is in those where the investment is largely fixed capital.) So the competitive process in investment-intensive industries readily degenerates into a volume-grubbing contest, punctuated with frequent price wars, marketing wars, and other over-intensive competitive measures that take most of the joy out of being modern, automated, or otherwise investment intensive. In particularly good years, when every company's capacity is almost fully loaded, this effect may not appear at all, but when good years are averaged with bad, as in the figures presented here, the negative effect on profit is quite clear.

Figure 4-4 illustrates this point by relating increases in selling prices to investment intensity. The contrasts are most obvious at the extremes.

The profit-depressing price squeeze also shows up clearly in examining the value added per employee in industries that differ in their investment intensity. "Value added" is the degree to which a business upgrades the market value of the raw materials or components it buys, i.e., the difference in market value between what the business buys and what it sells. Figure 4-5 shows that the value added per employee does not increase with added investment intensity over a surprisingly wide range.

Only on the extreme right of Figure 4-5 is there any significant favorable impact; in four fifths of all businesses, it appears that employees working with the support of large investments produce no more value than those

FIGURE 4-5
Value Added Related to Investment Intensity

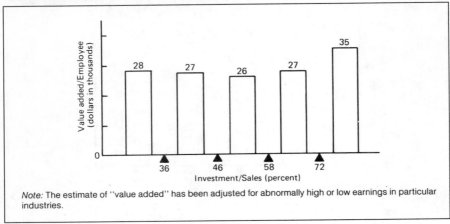

Note: The estimate of "value added" has been adjusted for abnormally high or low earnings in particular industries.

working with only small investments. How can this be? It is possible that the first group of employees is simply less productive as individuals, that they are less capable people. More likely, however, is that the more intensive price competition occurring in investment-intensive industries reduces the market value of the product of companies in those industries, and hence the value added by their activities. Even on the far right of Figure 4-5, the increase in value added per employee is usually insufficient to justify the higher investment and cash required, as verified by examining the profit and cash results of most of these businesses.

A closely related reason for the unprofitability of investment-intensive businesses lies in their apparent inability to manage their personnel levels in a suitable fashion: The number of employees per dollar of sales is just about as high as in less investment-intensive industries. The increased numbers of people in administrative, commercial, and other functions on average counterbalance the savings of people in manufacturing functions.

Before leaving this subject, it is worth noting that Figures 4-1 through 4-5 have undoubtedly slanted reality in favor of investment-intensive businesses, and therefore have understated the magnitude of the problem. This bias occurs because the statistics are drawn from accounting records that are kept in the conventional way. It is becoming widely recognized that conventional accounting procedures overstate ROI, particularly of investment-intensive businesses, both by overstating the numerator and by understating the denominator. The reason is the same in both cases: Fixed assets are valued at their historical cost, rather than at their current inflated worth, understating both depreciation costs (and thus increasing apparent earnings) and investment levels.

What to Do About Investment-Intensive Requirements. If the technology of a business clearly requires a high level of investment intensity, either of plant and equipment or of working capital (or of both), what actions should the business take?

First, the business should not automatically assume that more is better insofar as investment intensity is concerned. A highly automated plant is not necessarily a better plant than a less automated one. Of course, the recent series of cash crunches in the economy has already cured many businesspeople of this knee-jerk reaction, but old habits of thought die hard, particularly in industries, such as bulk chemicals, where increased capital intensification has long been a way of life. Most businesspeople still unquestioningly assume that good technology is synonymous with automated production or long and full pipelines in distribution. That assumption is valid just often enough in particular cases to save it from being ludicrous on its face. However, the proverbial "hard look" is clearly justified with regard to all investments that are larger than merely proportional to an increase in capacity.

Second, in evaluating a proposed investment that is clearly larger than merely proportional to an increase in capacity, the business should consider the strategic effect as carefully as it does the cost effect of the project. A negative strategic effect may more than offset a positive cost effect.

Suppose, for example, that a manufacturer is considering a capital-intensifying project (e.g., an increase in the degree of automation of plant) that on the basis of conventional cost calculations will have an annual operating cost, everything included, of $1 million, an annual saving of $3 million in reduced labor costs or reduced spoilage, and therefore a net benefit of $2 million per year. Suppose further that all of these estimates are absolutely accurate, and that the net saving of $2 million per year does in fact materialize as promised. Even then, the project may not be, and very frequently is not, profitable. While the business saves $2 million, it does not get to keep that $2 million. Instead, it gives the $2 million away, mostly to its customers, secondarily to its employees, and thirdly in the form of higher marketing costs.

A business is forced into such a move by the changed competitive climate. First, its competitors' and its own increased desperation for volume (to keep those expensive plants with their high fixed costs loaded) leads to price and other concessions to customers, particularly after the new technology has become widespread; second, increased fear of plant shutdowns leads to higher wage settlements and a greater reluctance to discharge unneeded people; and third, the business becomes caught in more and more intense marketing wars. So, frequently the net effect of the new technology is that its benefits accrue to the customer and to the labor union, while the business is left with the costs and the investments.

Now, the message of this scenario is not, of course, that any capital-intensifying investment should automatically be rejected, but rather that its strategic effect should be estimated as carefully, before the event, as its cost effect. The net result in many cases will clearly be against the contemplated project, no matter how glamorous it may be. However, while the project may have a negative net prospect as far as percentage ROI is concerned, it may quite often have a favorable prospect as far as dollar results are concerned, because the lower percentage is applied to a larger investment base. In such cases, a rather difficult management decision is required — difficult because it involves a tradeoff between an increase in sales and dollar profits on the one hand and a decrease in the rate of profitability on the other.

Third, the business should adopt a market strategy that minimizes the profit-damaging effect of capital-intensive technology. The PIMS data base suggests several ways of accomplishing this, many of them leading to increased dollar earnings, if not increased ROI levels or higher percentages on sales. Three of these moves are examined here.

The first is suggested by Figure 4-3. The bottom row, where the highly investment-intensive businesses are located, reveals a sharp increase in profitability moving from left to right, from 4 percent average ROI to 17 percent. Even at approximately equal levels of investment intensity, the high-share businesses do much better than the low-share businesses. This observation may seem rather obvious and unhelpful, until it is recalled that market share is measured relative to the served market, that is, relative to that segment of the total potential market in which the business is making a serious competitive attempt. So one way in which a business can obtain high market share is to concentrate its efforts on a segment of the total potential market — for example, a smaller geographic area or a more specialized class of customers. Since market segmentation efforts often can move a business toward the right on Figure 4-3, market segmentation or redefinition is clearly one strategic answer to the profit-depressing effects of capital intensity. The recent history of some segments of the specialty steel and pharmaceutical industries illustrates this principle.

A second approach is implied by Figure 4-6. Here businesses are divided according to their investment intensity and according to whether the breadth of their product line is narrower, about the same, or wider than what competitors are offering (to the same served market).

Focusing on the investment-intensive businesses in the bottom row shows that a product line that is broader than competitors' is clearly preferable to one that is not. This observation can be combined with the previous one: An investment-intensive business can be quite profitable if it focuses on a relatively narrow and conquerable market segment, and covers that segment really well, with a broad and diverse product line tuned to the preferences of that segment.

FIGURE 4-6

Breadth of Product Line Related to Investment Intensity

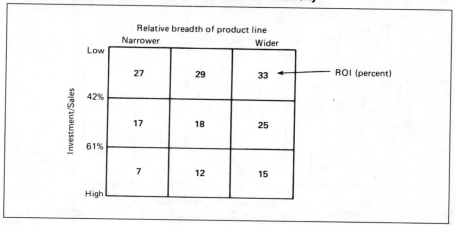

A third approach to profit protection in investment-intensive businesses is to be sure to obtain adequate productivity improvement for the increased investment. Productivity rises more rarely than one would expect, but where it does rise, it certainly helps. Figure 4-7 gives the key facts.

Pursuing Market Share

According to conventional wisdom, a business with a large share of its served market, especially if that served market is growing rapidly, not only

FIGURE 4-7

Adequate Productivity Improvement for Increased Investment

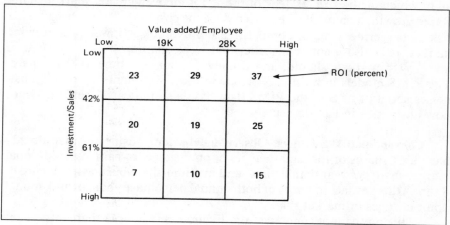

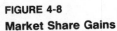

FIGURE 4-8
Market Share Gains

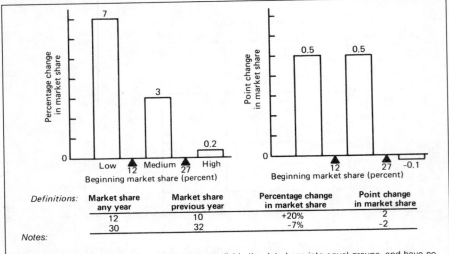

Definitions:	**Market share any year**	**Market share previous year**	**Percentage change in market share**	**Point change in market share**
	12	10	+20%	2
	30	32	-7%	-2

Notes:

(1) The market-share cut points were chosen to divide the data base into equal groups, and have no significance in themselves. Each group in the figure represents over 1,000 business experiences.

(2) The average market-share gain for the economy at large would seem to be zero, since whatever share one company gains another loses. The tables here do not average to zero because (a) more "good" than "poor" businesses are represented in the PIMS data base and (b) some businesses are implementing a segmentation strategy, in which almost everyone in the industry has a rising market share (though of a diminished served market).

finds it easy to gain additional market share, but also should pursue a share-gaining strategy. Many businesspeople believe that large-share firms possess advantages in resource availability, strategic position, and visibility—all of which facilitate a strategy of trying for an even greater market share. Rapid growth, meanwhile, helps to reduce the cost of the move, because the risk of triggering a major competitive donnybrook is lower in a growing market. It is also a common belief that weak-share businesses located in low-growth markets should, and usually do, harvest some of their share. The PIMS models in most cases confirm these judgments as to how businesses should act. But, the PIMS data base also indicates that this is not how businesses in fact do usually act.

Conventional Wisdom vs. Observed Behavior. Businesses that already have high shares of their markets tend, on average, to gain less additional market share per year than do low- and medium-share businesses. Figure 4-8 shows this key fact in terms of both annual percentage changes and annual point changes in market share.

While one cannot conclude from Figure 4-8 that large-share businesses

FIGURE 4-9

Effect of Real Market Growth on Share Gain

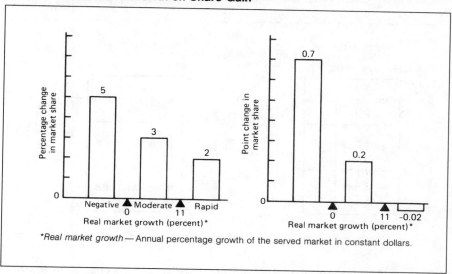

Real market growth—Annual percentage growth of the served market in constant dollars.

are or are not able to gain share more easily than small-share businesses, it is clear that large-share businesses have not gained the most share and have not protected their leading market positions. Weak-share businesses, in contrast, averaged a gain of more than a half point of share, an increase of over 7 percent from their initial position.[1]

Also contrary to popular belief is the fact that the highest market-share gains occur when the short-run rate of market growth is negative. The least amounts of share gain occur in rapid-growth markets. This relationship can be seen in Figure 4-9 (where, as before, each group represents well over 1,000 business experiences[2]).

To what extent are share gains in declining markets due to exit by some competitors? While some minor improvement in share performance does seem to be due to exits from the industry, the growth of market share of the survivors is greater than can be accounted for by this phenomenon alone.

Large-share businesses, on the average, lose share in rapid-growth environments, while weak-share firms gain share in such environments. Equally surprising, large-share businesses fare worse than weak-share businesses in negative market-growth situations. Figure 4-10 indicates the combined

[1] The result is the same if initial relative market share is substituted for the initial simple market share.

[2] The PIMS data base has five or more years of data for over 1,000 businesses. By taking every year-to-year move as a separate observation, over 4,000 year-to-year experiences are available for examination.

FIGURE 4-10

Effect of Initial Share Level and Market Growth Rate on Change in Market Share

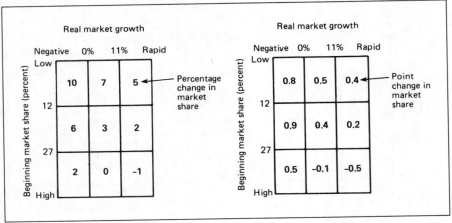

impact of initial share level and market growth rate on change in market share. It was the large-share businesses in rapid-growth markets that the conventional wisdom suggested would achieve the greatest share gains.

Why Do Businesses Act Counter to Their Beliefs? The focus here is on the large-share businesses, since they act in the most surprising manner. The observed results, counter to expectations, occur either because there really are natural market forces at work that lead such businesses to lose or give up share in rapid-growth markets, or because these businesses choose to follow that path. Among the reasons why large-share businesses may choose not to be aggressive could be the high costs of pursuing such a strategy.

Is it sensible, from a short-term performance perspective, for large-share firms to hold market position steady rather than to build it further? This question is examined in Figure 4-11 by comparing the cash flow, and in Figure 4-12 by comparing the ROI, of businesses that held market share steady and businesses that gained market share.

Figure 4-11 indicates the short-term cash costs incurred in gaining additional share. For example, among large-share businesses (bottom row), the market-share gainers earned a cash flow of 7 percentage points, compared to 10 points for the businesses holding their positions steady. Thus, the overall relative cash cost to the share gainers was 3 percentage points. Cash costs are moderately, but not significantly, lower for large-share businesses than for small-share businesses, both overall (−3 vs. −4) and per point of share gain (−1 vs. −2).

But, for short-term ROI cost, the story is quite different. Large-share

FIGURE 4-11

Cash Flows of Steady Market-Share Businesses vs. Gained Market Share Businesses

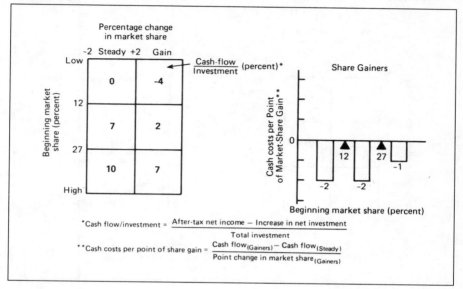

businesses must pay a short-run cost in terms of reduced ROI, while small- and medium-share businesses are able to increase short-term ROI and market share simultaneously. (Over a longer time horizon, however, large-share businesses will reap the ROI benefits of having a higher level of market share.)

Looking now at market-share change segregated by rate of market growth rather than by level of initial market position, conventional wisdom holds that it is least costly to gain market share in rapidly growing markets. The belief probably derives from the ability of all competitors to build their sales simultaneously in a growing market. Since no one's sales level needs to decrease, costly share-gain battles develop less frequently.

Cash and ROI performance, respectively, are illustrated in Figures 4-13 and 4-14.

Figure 4-13 indicates again that the process of building market share carries with it the cost of a lower short-term cash flow. Contrary to conventional wisdom, the cash costs of gaining share do not vary substantially between moderate- and rapid-growth markets. When cash costs are appropriately adjusted for average point change in market share in each environment, the cost of a point in share is only slightly lower in the more rapidly growing markets.

But, despite the modestly lower cash costs of building market share in

FIGURE 4-12

Returns on Investment of Steady Market-Share Businesses vs. Gained Market-Share Businesses

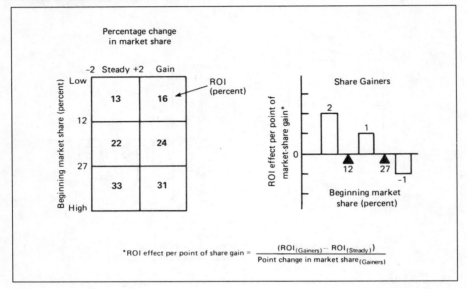

$$*\text{ROI effect per point of share gain} = \frac{(ROI_{(Gainers)} - ROI_{(Steady)})}{\text{Point change in market share}_{(Gainers)}}$$

rapid-growth environments and the general attractiveness of having a strong position in a growth market, little share growth is actually occurring, as shown in Figures 4-9 and 4-10. Managers in such environments are usually not under severe pressure to actually gain share, since as long as they

FIGURE 4-13

Cash Costs of Gaining Market Share

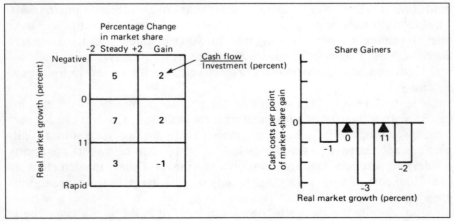

FIGURE 4-14

Effect on Return on Investment of Gaining Market Share

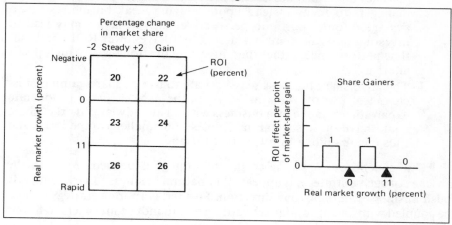

merely maintain share they will experience high profitability and significant sales growth.

Most surprising, perhaps, is the rapid share growth exhibited in moderate-growth markets—an environment where share growth is more costly and "harvesting" is frequently prescribed. Managers in this environment often turn to such tactics as creative product-line extensions to prolong the maturity phase of the product, and to build sales and market share simultaneously.

Businesses gaining market share do not pay a short-term ROI penalty regardless of the rate of market growth. The magnitude of the differences between those holding share steady and those building share, both with and without adjustment for the amount of share gain, does not allow a conclusion about whether building share costs more or less ROI in any particular market-growth environment.

While one can only speculate as to why so many people behave in a way counter to what they probably believe, the evidence suggests the following three explanations:

1. Managers have a short time horizon. Most managers are concerned with current results—profits this year and perhaps the next. They are encouraged to have this outlook by the fact that their own salaries, bonuses, and promotions may be tied to current performance. Thus, managers would be unwilling to suffer either cash costs or ROI costs now for higher share and higher ROI in the more distant future.

2. "Management by exception" is a management style that focuses upon things and events that are not behaving "normally" today.

This style, when applied to corporate strategy, may result in complacency about businesses that are very strong today, and encourage managers to focus instead upon bringing weak businesses up to average. From a portfolio perspective, such behavior may lead to investing in weak-share businesses that have lower ROI and cash-flow performance, rather than investing in strong-share, high-profit alternatives.

3. The large-share business may hesitate to use its share-gaining muscle out of fear of wreaking havoc in the market. Even a moderate expansionary move by a business with an already large market share could have quite substantial impacts on smaller competitors, and thus create quite a bit of market turmoil.

One conclusion: A strong corporate strategy is needed. Why? In the absence of such a strategy, it appears that natural business forces frequently push businesses in the wrong direction. Further, corporate strategy should be coupled with an appropriate reward system to induce managers to follow that strategy.

CONCLUSION

Good strategy planning consists of asking good questions, getting good answers, and effectively implementing those answers. The scientific approach is of major help in all three stages. It works because, on the positive, it increases the power of accomplishment and, on the negative, it minimizes the risk of costly blunders.

The scientific approach does have the drawback of a slow gestation period. But, while the accumulation of knowledge and method takes time, it is cumulative. The results get better and better, without any apparent upper limit. In any area of human activity in which the approach of science has ever been attempted, the step was always irreversible; it was never decided to go back to the old ways. There is every reason to expect that the field of business strategy and policy will travel the same course.

5

Using Computer-Based Simulations for Better Management Decisions

JOSEPH H. GEKOSKI,
President

LESLIE L. SPERO,
Chairman

STEVEN ZLOTOWSKI,
Director
Retail Practice Area Strategic Management Group, Inc.

INTRODUCTION

It has been called the corporate paradox: the all-too-common contradiction of having the finest professionals in every function, all notably adept at their respective responsibilities, yet with a limited view of the collective goal. Without a thorough understanding of each essential area of the business, managers often fail to see "the big picture"—the all-important strategic perspective. Without the opportunity to gain new insights, their view seldom broadens. The result is that the organization fails to develop a strategic thinking capability.

This situation is further complicated by the major challenges business organizations face in the 1990s: an increasingly complex business environment as volatile as it is competitive; heightened Wall Street expectations for profitability, growth, and cash flow; the call by *Fortune 500* chief executive officers for improved shareholder value; and the continuous presence of the forces of globalization.

This chapter discusses strategic thinking and the process of strategy development and implementation and shows how business simulations and the simulation seminar process can enhance the strategic thinking capability in large organizations by improving the strategic decision-making competency of operating managers.

WHY BUSINESS SIMULATIONS?

Computer-based business simulations are not new. For the past quarter century, students have used them as a framework to better understand the dynamics of various business issues. The first well-publicized business simulation was the University of Chicago's International Operations Simulation (INTOP) in 1963. Oriented toward international trade and the overseas operations of a multinational corporation, this fairly primitive simulation was programmed in Fortran and run on the IBM mainframe with input provided by keypunching eighty column cards.

Since that time, the state of the art in simulation design and application has advanced significantly. With the advent of personal computers and new software languages, completely portable and "user-friendly" programs have been developed, allowing a simulation developed in one country to be conducted anywhere in the world. Decision support systems and planning tools have also been created to aid the user in the decision-making process. Simulation seminars and training programs now focus not only on the dynamics within the simulation, as was the case with earlier business games, but also on the broader, more vital issues of strategic thinking and implementation.

Today's sophisticated business simulations are the best method of teaching managers strategic thinking. Experience suggests that operating managers often have difficulty grasping unfamiliar concepts. Particularly problematic for operating managers is visualizing a large number of interacting variables over multiple operating periods generally outside their daily operating experience. Simulation can place managers in such an environment to help them learn new concepts and gain experience applying those concepts to real-life situations.

Simulations designed specifically for the corporate environment are truly a learn-by-doing experience that allows managers to see the outcome of decisions they make in a given scenario. In this way they begin to understand the impact a selected set of variables can have on a function's performance results, on other parts of the firm, and on the bottom line.

Once a base case is established, the values of the variables can be changed so that a sensitivity analysis can be performed. This allows participants to evaluate the impact of strategic alternatives and to see the changes in the competitive and external environments.

In this process, executives and managers develop vision and implement their chosen strategy by means of a set of clearly defined tactical decisions. They develop an understanding of the key value drivers of a business strategy, which ultimately enhances strategic thinking capability.

ENHANCING STRATEGIC THINKING

All too often in business today, strategic planners and operating personnel find themselves on opposite sides of the same problem. Planners focus primarily on strategy formulation while operating managers focus on strategy implementation.

The mandate for operating managers to strategy application—what's supposed to be done with a strategy once it exists—is far removed from the process of strategy formulation itself. However, most management development efforts that call themselves strategy programs teach only strategy formulation. While some background in this is important, a management development program's emphasis should be on how to translate a strategy into a series of business decisions. The goal should be to communicate an awareness of how a strategy comes alive and guides corporate action. It is this understanding that leads to the development of a strategic thinking capability within the organization. Without it even the best business plans will go astray.

A well-thought-out and conceptually grounded management development program combined with a business simulation can significantly enhance the development of strategic thinking capability within an organization. (The Strategic Management Group (SMG) development program will be examined in greater detail later in this chapter.) The opening statement of such a program should convey to participants the usefulness of thinking of strategy as giving shape to a company much as a blueprint gives shape to a building. The purpose of a blueprint is not to teach the carpenters, plumbers, and electricians how to ply their trades, but to give them direction in applying their skills to create the form and function desired. Each person draws something different from the blueprint, yet the blueprint unifies all aspects of construction. In much the same way, the various levels and functions in an organization draw differently upon a strategy, but the strategy helps them all aim at a common, overall goal. Using this analogy as a central theme, such a program would focus on how one learns from a business's blueprint and how one then applies this knowledge in a dynamic environment.

THE STRATEGIC PROCESS

At the highest level of an organization, there must be a sense of what needs to be achieved. Upper or top management is then charged with the responsibility of devising a strategy that, if successfully carried out, will support these corporate objectives.

In order for top management to assess the organization's position and formulate a strategy, it must address the broad, critical inputs necessary for strategic thinking:

- What are our internal capabilities?
- What is our position in the marketplace?
- What environmental forces must be considered?
- What is the nature of our competition?
- What guiding principles and values must we uphold?

By exploring these dimensions, top management can begin to formulate a sound strategy.

Once formulated, the strategy needs to be communicated throughout the organization. A well-articulated strategy is the glue that holds an organization together by giving direction to all the individual parts. To get the entire company moving in the same direction, top management must convey to senior managers in the different functional areas an understanding of what is needed from them and why it is needed. Senior managers use the direction from top management to understand their functions' respective roles in the organization, whom they need to work with, and what outcomes are required from them. This is really strategy formulation at a different level. Top management shapes corporate strategy, and senior managers develop business unit or functional strategies (i.e., specific tactics) that will fulfill their responsibilities within the constraints and guidelines of the corporate strategy. The execution of these tactics is then entrusted to middle management.

At the corporate level, the emphasis is on evaluating what markets to compete in, integrating company-wide efforts, and developing a clear definition of sources of competitive advantage. This vision outlines the broad objectives of the firm. Strategy formulation at the senior management level has a narrower perspective. The objectives are, for the most part, already determined. The focus shifts from weighing possibilities to charting tactics. Senior managers assess internal capabilities, external forces, and competition on a tactical, action planning basis following the guidelines of the broad strategic objectives outlined by top management.

Senior managers play a vital role in communicating strategy throughout the organization. However, what they need to communicate to middle management is very different from what top management needed to communicate to them. Middle managers must see very concretely how they fit into the goals of their more immediate work environment (although some understanding of the "big picture" is also necessary). Compared to senior managers, middle managers are much more task oriented. However, middle managers, while taking direction from senior management, must also give direction to those below them.

The essence of the strategic fabric is this process of:

1. Establishing a strategy
2. Formulating tactics to achieve it
3. Communicating the importance and significance of each functional role
4. Managing the execution of those tactics
5. Incorporating feedback

Ideally, such a process rippling through the entire organization keeps everyone marching to the beat of the same drummer.

Armed with this understanding, managers can then translate strategy into what really matters: decision making. This can be understood at two levels. First, strategy should serve as a guideline to help managers make the best choice among alternative courses of action. At this level, managers rely on strategy to provide meaning in reactive situations. Second, strategy should serve as a proactive tool to help managers create sound courses of action in the future.

The three elements of formulation, communication, and implementation have been depicted here strictly as a "top-down" process. In truth, the process is extremely dynamic and requires a great deal of "bubble-up" if it's to be successful. People lower in the hierarchy of an organization are usually closest to the problems. It is the upward communication of problems, issues, and answers that underpins sound strategy formulation and tactical planning. In addition, a company's strategy cannot be a fixed vision. A strategy should provide direction while allowing for reassessment in the light of new developments.

In reality, there are many obstacles that can potentially turn this vision of the strategic process into science fiction:

1. Size of the organization
2. Lack of any explicit corporate strategy
3. Poor communication
4. Confusion among employees about their respective roles and contributions
5. Poor employee commitment
6. Weak analysis and decision-making skills of middle management
7. Deficient "hard" skills among employees

These obstacles can be overcome by having managers participate in a development process that broadens their view of the organization as a whole and of the need for cooperation among the separate functions and that enhances their strategic thinking capability and improves their strategic decision making.

Strategic Management Group, Inc. offers its corporate clients a development program that includes computer-based simulations as an integral part of its education methodology (see Figure 5-1).

Through the use of business simulations, participants are exposed to the issues and concerns in other functions and they begin to develop an appreciation and an understanding of how their actions are felt throughout the organization. Each phase of the process is described in more detail in the following sections.

Skills and Knowledge

The skills building and knowledge phase is primarily addressed through lecture, case studies, and group discussion. Initially, topics might include contemporary issues in strategic planning, evolution of strategic thinking, value-based strategic management, and an overview of the strategic planning process. As the program proceeds, additional subjects such as strategy formulation, strategic planning tools and techniques, competitive analysis, industry structure analysis, and creating shareholder value would also be included. These conceptual topics are divided so that they interface with appropriate periods of the simulation as identified in the agenda in Figure 2.

Appreciation and Understanding

As participants go through the business simulation exercise, they sharpen their own knowledge and skills, gain an appreciation for how these concepts

FIGURE 5-1
The SMG Development Program

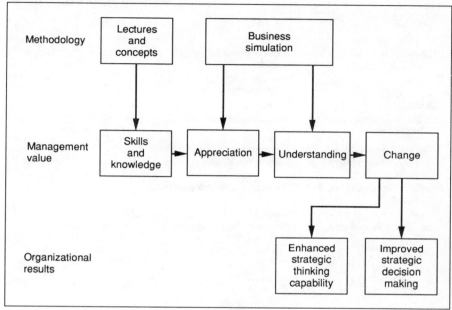

are applied, and receive a thorough understanding of how the concepts relate to their function specifically and to their organization as a whole.

This appreciation is then translated into a broader understanding of how the organization needs to interact and cooperate to realize its potential. Participants walk away with this message and subsequently apply this broader perspective to their own strategic thinking and decision making. Ultimately, they weave this generic understanding into a new outlook on their company's strategic vision.

Business Simulations

Characteristics and Features. Since numerous types of simulations exist, a definition of "simulation" as the concept is used in this chapter is useful, as is a description of the features a simulation must contain. A simulation has three basic characteristics.

First, it is dynamic, as it takes place over a number of periods. Its interactions usually change over those periods.

Second, it involves a number of variables, with at least a few of those variables interacting over time. These interactions are defined mathematically, but they should not be obvious to the person playing the simulation.

FIGURE 5-2
SMG Strategic Planning Agenda

DAY ONE	DAY TWO	DAY THREE
Morning Session		
Overview of Financial Management	Framework for Strategic Thinking	Simulation Workshop IV
	Strategy & Market Formulation	
Break	Break	Break
Strategic Financial Analysis Techniques	Simulation Workshop II	Implementing Differentiation
Afternoon Session		
Strategic Management Process	Competitive Analysis	Implementing Low Cost
Setting Missions Goals & Objectives	Developing the Strategic Plan	
Break	Break	Break
Simulation Workshop I	Simulation Workshop III	Strategic Assessment Presentation & Action Planning Workshop

Third, it is reactive to exogenous events. In some cases those events can change the way the variables interact. In such cases, the dynamics of the simulation will not hold constant from one period of use to the next.

Simulations of all types must contain a certain set of features in order to be effective. These are:

- Interactivity
- Feedback
- Accessibility
- Imitativeness
- Flexibility

Interactiveness is the ability of participants to see the likely results of their decisions before they actually commit to those decisions. This feature encourages the visualization of alternatives, which is the cornerstone of simulation.

Feedback is critical because the simulation is never as obvious to the participants as it is to the simulation designer. The process of feedback explains the environment to participants and provides a forum in which they can learn from previous decisions.

Accessibility refers to how easily a new participant understands the simulation environment and how readily a participant can use the computer program or paper-based simulation. Accessibility becomes more important as the complexity of the simulation increases, because accessibility eliminates the participants' concern over manipulating data and thus frees them to focus on understanding their alternatives.

FIGURE 5-3

Matrix of Types of Business Simulations

	Resource allocation–based	Event-based
Total enterprise		
Functional		

Imitativeness is the ability of the simulation to reasonably mimic the environment that it intends to simulate. For example, a good strategy simulation includes customers, suppliers, new entrants, and substitutes as part of its environment. This allows it to more closely mimic the environment it is intending to simulate. This imitativeness encourages "buy-in" by participants in any simulation.

Flexibility means that the simulation can be updated to reflect recent events—a necessity for all successful simulations. Flexibility is a natural outcome of the need for a simulation to be strongly imitative of the outside environment.

Types of Simulations. Within the broad definition of simulation, there are a number of types of simulations. Figure 5-3 shows these types in a simple matrix to illustrate the issues various business simulations are capable of addressing.

One dimension of simulation is whether it focuses on the total enterprise or on a particular business function. A total enterprise simulation looks at the entire business and involves the perspective of finance, marketing and operations. Its goal is to focus people on the necessary integration of these functions. It helps managers develop a respect for other functions by placing different departments in competition for scarce resources. Managers are able to see the impact each department has on the other departments and thus gain insight into the reasons for the behavior of various components of a company's value chain. Typical decisions in a total enterprise simulation include:

Marketing	Operations	Finance
Price	Capacity	Amount of money
Advertising	Scheduling	Debt/equity
Channel size	Cost control	Short term/long term
Channel motivators	Dividends	
Product		

A good total enterprise simulation restricts dollar availability and forces companies to choose a low-cost or a differentiation strategy. It creates conflict between Marketing's gung-ho sales goals and Operations' actual ability to provide for the market. It also creates competition for funding among various products and various stages of the life cycle, additional product features, and promotional campaigns. In a first-rate total enterprise simulation, the team feels the tug of too many demands on scarce resources and understands the need to set priorities among choices.

A second type of simulation, the functional simulation, is directed toward a particular business function. Its goal is to make people aware of the various balances that must be maintained inside the function and how that function must interact with the other functions it does business with. A functional simulation is similar to an enterprise simulation in that it focuses on integration within and outside the business area. But it is fundamentally different from enterprise simulation in that it is far more detailed about responsibilities inside the function. In this sense, the dynamics of the simulation become less important and the interaction of the variables becomes more important. For example, a good manufacturing functional simulation includes the following amount of detail regarding the basic decision of capacity: amount of capacity, when to add capacity, cost of capacity, location of capacity, the technological choices made regarding that capacity, and the flexibility of that capacity. This level of detail forces managers to be much more specific in developing a strategy and drives home the point that strategy is the accumulation of a set of tactical decisions: One or two inconsistent moves and the capacity is blown out of the water. Thus, functional simulations are in many ways the most strategic of all because they make obvious the need for a clear direction.

To date, total enterprise and functional simulations exist in the areas of industrial marketing, consumer marketing, sales management, financial management, manufacturing management, manufacturing scheduling, and human resource management. It is interesting to note that in all of these simulations, profit remains the ultimate goal. Simulation authors go to great lengths to maintain that goal, even though many of these departments are operated as cost centers in large corporations.

As shown in Figure 5-3, another dimension by which to differentiate simulations is whether they are resource allocation–based or event based. A resource allocation simulation focuses on where dollars are spent and forces participants to allocate a certain dollar budget among various investment choices. This type of simulation manages competition by comparing dollars spent to some sort of index. That index can be based on historical performance, preset targets, or competitors in the simulation itself. It assumes that all dollars have equal impact or, more simply put, that investments achieve results.

Event simulations are based on scenarios and the participants' reactions to the events of those scenarios. This type of simulation is best thought of as a play that unfolds over time, with opportunities for participants to interject their opinion of how that even should be dealt with. Such simulations are essentially long decision trees with each node being a separate event and having a number of branches. These simulations are useful for introducing managerial inefficiencies, external events of all types, and broader-based, qualitative decision making. Event-based simulations have been used for managerial assessment, management training, and scenario planning across the areas of management, leadership, sales management, and project management. Essentially, they can be used in any situation that takes place over a number of periods.

The Simulation Exercise

The SMG Simulation Exercise[1] begins with the participants being formed into senior management teams that take over a multi-million-dollar troubled company. Each management team inherits the same company and therefore starts the exercise from an identical position. However, as soon as they each take over, each becomes a separate entity competing against the others. Each team renames its company as its first decision, in symbolic recognition of its separateness from the other teams. Each team then faces a number of short-term problems, including: (1) a decline in profitability during the last few years; (2) a manufacturing facility operating on a costly overtime schedule; (3) a recent history of low cash flow; and (4) a warehouse loaded with inventory. Fortunately, a number of opportunities also exist, including: (1) market expansion; (2) new product introduction; and (3) a strong market for the company's core business. These are described in Figure 4.

In addition to the internal problems and opportunities just described, the teams must manage in an environment in which substantial forces surround the firm, as illustrated in Figure 5-4. The teams are encouraged to include an analysis of these forces as part of their decision-making exercise.

During the early workshop periods, the teams examine a number of strategic scenarios, ranging from low- to high-risk and focusing on growth or profitability or both. The teams begin to examine the market by evaluating both broad and narrow strategic targets and they decide how their organization should achieve sustainable competitive advantage: i.e., through differentiation or through cost leadership.

---

[1] This is a proprietary simulation offered by Strategic Management Group, Inc. as part of its executive development programs. For more information on this product, contact the authors at SMG, 3624 Market Street, Philadelphia, PA 19104; (215) 387-4000 or (800) 445-7089.

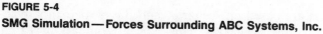

FIGURE 5-4
SMG Simulation—Forces Surrounding ABC Systems, Inc.

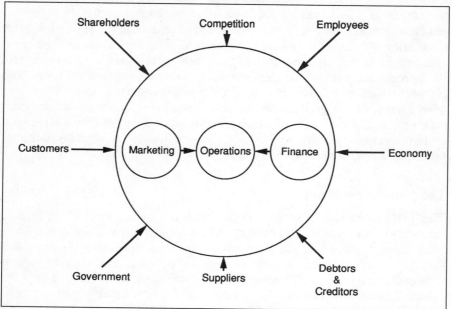

The First Workshop. During the first business simulation workshop period, the management teams, working in private breakout rooms, are asked to conduct a business assessment (situation analysis) of two areas:

- The external environment within which their company operates
- The internal environment, focusing on their company's strengths and weaknesses

Each team then prepares a mission statement that addresses its vision and long-term direction, and develops a set of objectives and quantifiable goals. Each group must also make its first set of annual decisions. (An example is shown in Figure 5-5.) During this workshop, a significant amount of time is spent on the business assessment and developing a vision and a long-term direction.

The teams make decisions by entering values into a computer planning model. Each breakout room is equipped with a personal computer loaded with a user-friendly software package that not only records decisions but acts as a planning tool that facilitates scenario analysis.

After each team has made a set of pro forma decisions and the simulation workshop is over, the decisions are read into a master computer

FIGURE 5-5

SMG Simulation—1989 Decision History for ABC Systems, Inc.

Marketing	Units	Decision for 1988	Decision for 1989	% Change 1988 to 1989
East				
1. Price of standard	Dollars	16.42	16.75	2
2. Price of premium	Dollars	23.23	24.95	7
3. Price of super	Dollars	.00	.00	0
4. Advertising of standard	1000s	400	450	13
5. Advertising of premium	1000s	300	400	33
6. Advertising of super	1000s	0	0	0
7. Sales force size	People	35	40	
8. Commission paid	Percent	2.0	2.0	
9. Sales on credit	Percent	45	50	
Operations				
Development				
1. Research & development	1000s	400	500	
2. R & D mix–standard	Percent	40	10	
3. R & D mix–premium	Percent	60	30	
4. R & D mix–super	Percent	0	60	
5. Process improvements	1000s	0	200	
Production				
6. Factory shifts worked	Number	2.00	2.15	
7. Production mix–standard	Percent	66	60	
8. Production mix–premium	Percent	34	40	
9. Production mix–super	Percent	0	0	
10. Factory expansion	1000s Units /8 hr. Shift	0	48	
Finance				
1. One-year loan	1000s	4000	4000	
2. Supplier payment period	Days	30	35	
3. Long-term debt sold (bought)	1000s	0	2000	
4. Common stock issued (bought)	1000s	0	0	
5. Common dividend per share	Dollars	.10	.20	

model that determines the industry environment and the actual team performance on the basis of a competitive evaluation of each team's decisions.

The Second Workshop. The teams begin their second workshop by evaluating results from their decisions for the first year; they conduct a detailed situation analysis and business assessment that includes an examination of the external environment and the competitive environment. They also prepare a variance analysis comparing actual results to their forecast pro forma financial projections from the prior workshop.

Upon completing the situation analysis, the groups concentrate on strategy formulation at both the business unit level and the functional level. They must ask: What is the competitive positioning of my business? Where do I have a sustainable competitive advantage? Michael Porter, in his book *Competitive Strategy*,[2] developed a simple matrix that allows managers to examine how their business is positioned on two dimensions: strategic advantage and strategic scope.

		Strategic advantage	
		Uniqueness	Low cost
Strategic scope	Broad target	Differentiation	Cost leadership
	Narrow segment	Focused differentiation	Focused cost leadership

Using this framework, managers can assess how their business is positioned strategically, whether they are attacking a broad target or a narrow segment, and whether they are attempting to compete by means of a differentiation strategy or a cost leadership strategy. This positioning framework in emphasized throughout the entire exercise.

The groups are also encouraged to consider other key issues, including sales forecasting, production planning, capacity planning, and cash management. They also examine the goals and objectives developed during the first workshop to see if they are on target in meeting them.

The Third Workshop. During the third workshop, the groups expand their competitive and industry analysis, using analytical tools such as the product life cycle, growth-share matrix, Porter's "five forces" model, product line margin analysis, value chain analysis, segmentation analysis, and strategic mapping. Each team focuses on critical issues that the business must address, and evaluates strategic alternatives by conducting "what-if" exercises. During the third and fourth workshops, each team examines whether its strategies are successful at creating shareholder value and develops a strategic plan for implementation.

In the fourth and final workshop, the teams continue to implement their strategic plan, attempting to create shareholder value, and examine several key financial issues, including balance sheet restructuring and dividend policy.

A concluding assignment in the exercise is the strategic assessment presentation. As an integral part of the exercise, each team prepares and presents a strategic assessment of its performance during the entire workshop

---

[2] M.E. Porter, *Competitive Strategy* (New York: The Free Press, 1980).

process. This ensures that the team has considered all aspects of the strategic planning process and helps it crystallize its position on each strategic issue. Each team's presentation includes discussion on its vision, mission, objectives and goals, latest situation analysis, competitive analysis, future vision, and biggest mistake.

CASE STUDY

No discussion of business simulations would be complete without a practical example. The strategies, tactics, and positions of five competing teams at the end of the second year based on their decisions in each functional area are described here.

- *Team A: Alert*
  - — Competitive strategy: Strongly differentiated in two major markets, attempting to create exceptional value.
  - — Tactics: Somewhat higher price but with industry average costs. Investing heavily in R&D to enhance quality and in advertising to achieve significant share of voice.
- *Team B: Beta*
  - — Competitive strategy: Driving to achieve the greatest market share across all markets and attempting to achieve the lowest cost position.
  - — Tactics: Price lower than competition in all segments. Spending on advertising at or above industry average. Producing acceptable quality products at lowest cost. Major plant expansion to support share strategy. No introduction of new product.
- *Team C: Crown Jewels*
  - — Competitive strategy: Attempting to improve profitability early on but not executing properly—neither a cost leader nor a differentiator.
  - — Tactics: Investing in R&D and advertising at industry average levels. Pricing set at industry average level.
- *Team D: Dynamic*
  - — Competitive strategy: A broad-based differentiator with penetration into all markets with all products. Dominated new product category in all markets.
  - — Tactics: Pricing above industry norm, reflecting value-added positioning. Advertising at a level just slightly behind industry leader. Heavy expenditures in R&D to enhance quality.
- *Team E: Excel*
  - — Competitive strategy: The smallest competitor in the industry, attempting a focus strategy but not clear on whether to be a differentiator or a cost-leader. A focus strategy is one in which the

FIGURE 5-6

SMG Simulation—Team Positions After Second Year

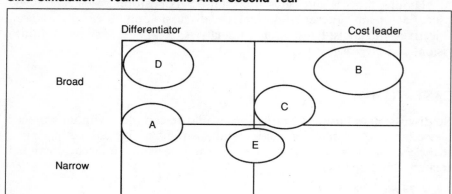

company directs its marketing efforts and business thrust at a narrow target group of customers rather than at a broad group. It is usually based on market, geographical, or product criteria.

— Tactics: Smaller investment in advertising than industry average. Lower price on mature product, higher prices on growth products. Very low quality due to low R&D expenditures. Highest production costs.

The positions of the companies at the end of the second year of play are as shown in Figure 5-6.

The team performance results at the end of the second year are shown here:

Team	Sales (millions)	Net income (millions)	ROS	Stock price
A	$35.7	$2,271	6.4%	41¼
B	46.9	612	1.3%	6⅝
C	35.9	1,286	3.6%	25¼
D	41.7	445	1.1%	10½
E	28.1	397	1.4%	11¼

These data show that in the short run, Team A is the best performer, followed by Team C, and Teams B and D are the worst performers. What is not apparent, however, is the longer-term positioning of Teams B and D. Their strategy in the short run is very costly, yielding low ROS earnings per share and cash flow. This, combined with higher risk, is reflected in their lower stock prices. The implications of their strategy,

FIGURE 5-7

SMG Simulation—Team Positions After Fourth Year

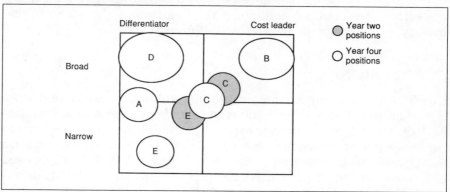

however, should be seen longer-term as they will be able to capitalize on their strategic positioning and the sustainable competitive advantage that they are developing.

Moving to the final year of play, Teams A, B, and D continued to consistently follow their original strategies. Team A focused on only two markets with a high value-added differentiation strategy. Team B continued with the broad-based cost-leadership strategy, and Team D continued to be the broad-based differentiator.

Team C was experiencing deteriorating quality and rising costs. Its prices remained in the middle of the industry range as did its advertising expenditures.

Team E introduced a harvest strategy on its mature product in an effort to enhance cash flow and began to use this to fund a quality enhancement program for its growth product. It showed signs of becoming a very focused differentiator. Profits grew during the last period as did stock price. The fourth-year positions are shown in Figure 5-7.

Team performance results at the end of the fourth year are shown here:

Team	Sales (millions)	Net income (millions)	ROS	Stock price	Total return to shareholder
A	$67.7	$6.4	9.4%	108½	62%
B	85.4	5.7	6.7	84⅛	52
C	62.1	4.0	6.5	57⅝	38
D	90.0	7.2	8.0	101	59
E	53.2	3.6	6.8	61⅝	41

Although all the teams achieved very acceptable levels of profitability during the final year, it is obvious from the stock price and return to shareholder data that Teams A, D, and B were the better performers. These teams achieved superior performance because they articulated their strategies early in the exercise, maintained an unwavering commitment to that strategy, and consistently implemented it from year to year.

CONCLUSION

Developing a strategic thinking capability within an organization is an important goal. Business simulations and simulation seminars are invaluable tools for improving strategic thinking and decision making. Experience has shown that simulation seminar participants are highly motivated, learn quickly, and retain a great deal from the experience. They become exposed to a senior manager's perspective on the business and see the major elements that affect the bottom line and shareholder value. They have an opportunity to deal with complex business issues and the interrelationship of the various functional areas of the firm. They see the trade-offs between short-term decision making and creating a long-term strategy, which ultimately enhances their strategic thinking capability and improves their strategic decision-making competency.

With this experience, participants become more effective change agents within their organization and the task of communicating and implementing strategy is made easier.

6

The Team Approach to Making Strategic Decisions

DAVID M. SCHWEIGER

WILLIAM R. SANDBERG

College of Business Administration
University of South Carolina

INTRODUCTION

Business managers are constantly faced with strategic choices, such as developing a new competitive approach to an existing market, evaluating a potential merger or acquisition, or divesting core products or businesses. While the circumstances surrounding the choices may be unique to a particular company, these decisions themselves are similar to those that regularly confront top management in every industry. Such choices often require substantial commitments of time and resources and may have broad, long-lasting effects. More-over, the problems or situations that spawn such decisions cannot be neatly compartmentalized. Each is connected to another strategic situation facing the firm and the solution of one problem may aggravate or even create another.

This chapter describes the process by which top management teams make decisions, highlighting the importance of valid and relevant assumptions, and emphasizing the need to exploit the diverse knowledge and capabilities of the top management team. The chapter also examines the pitfalls and errors that keep many organizations from increasing the effectiveness of their strategic decision making and describes the team approach that can overcome these difficulties.

CHALLENGES AND REQUIREMENTS OF STRATEGIC DECISIONS

Identifying Wicked Problems

Many of top management's crucial choices involve so-called wicked problems, in which the usual pressure of high-stakes decision making is compounded by several factors:[1]

- A dynamic, uncertain environment that forces management to accept unmeasurable risks and to respond to novel, unanticipatable events
- Top management acting on many interconnected fronts both within and outside the firm
- Incomplete information about the problem, including the cause-and-effect relationships among its elements
- Ambiguous interpretation of available information

Wicked problems would be troublesome even if top managers could see eye-to-eye on all major issues. Wicked problems, however, typically involve decision makers who represent conflicting interests, perspectives, or values: Managers may identify and assess problems from their own functional or organizational perspectives, or one management faction may push for a leading share of the market while another emphasizes a particular rate of return on capital at the expense of market share. These intrusions of personal power or career prospects can make decision making even more dangerous and enduring.

Factors in Decision Making

A top management team shapes the nature of a corporation through decisions concerning wicked problems that involve the company's mission,

---

[1] Richard O. Mason and Ian I. Mitroff, *Challenging Strategic Planning Assumptions* (New York: John Wiley & Sons, 1981), pp. 9–13.

objectives, competitive methods, and other elements of strategy. While such decisions may be explicit, perhaps following thorough analysis and discussion, they are also implicit. Managers may base both explicit and implicit decisions on assumptions—about the organization and its capabilities, how rival firms will react, how social trends will affect the company's principal markets, and so on—that escape examination or even identification.

Managers who face wicked problems make better decisions when their assumptions are valid and relevant.[2] They usually rely on assumptions about their company's key competitive strengths, the nature of competition within the industry, rivals' likely responses to their initiatives, economic and social trends, and the relationships among these factors. If valid, such assumptions are immensely helpful in making effective decisions; if invalid, their effect can be disastrous. Unfortunately once-valid assumptions can become dangerous if they are not periodically reexamined. Failure to reevaluate assumptions can lead management to overlook or dismiss important changes in the competitive market environment. For example, Sears, Roebuck & Company prospered for decades with an expansion and merchandising strategy built on assumptions about demographics, price sensitivity, credit availability, scale economies, and the impotence of rivals. These same assumptions, which were maintained tenaciously into the 1980s, delayed Sears's recognition of fundamental changes until Sears had suffered tremendous damage to its image and competitive position.

To be effective, a strategic decision must be appropriate to the organization and relevant to its situation. Specifically, a strategy should satisfy five criteria:

1. Internal consistency among all its parts and with the company's existing policies and goals;
2. Consistency with the current and future environment;
3. Appropriateness to the amounts and types of resources available to the company;
4. Acceptability of the degree of risk posed by the stakes and by the duration and irrevocability of the commitment; and
5. Timeliness of expected results.[3]

Where Top Management Goes Wrong

Many strategic decisions must be made under adverse circumstances, when external threats and competitive pressures allow no tolerance for poor

---

[2] David M. Schweiger, William R. Sandberg, and Paula L. Rechner, "Experiential Effects of Dialectical Inquiry, Devil's Advocacy, and Consensus Approaches to Strategic Decision Making," *Academy of Management Journal* vol. 32, no. 4 (Dec. 1989), pp. 745–772.

[3] Based on Seymour Tilles, "How to Evaluate Corporate Strategy," *Harvard Business Review* vol. 41, no. 4 (July–Aug. 1963), pp. 111–121.

choices or weak implementation. Yet many top management teams worsen the circumstances by drifting to a decision without identifying alternatives or consequences, failing to articulate their decision and its rationale, or failing to assign specific roles to subordinates whose support is vital, since they will implement the decision.

Communication of the decision and role assignments is necessary but does not ensure successful implementation. Even when top management communicates the gist of a decision to other managers, the implicit assumptions may go unrecognized. Thus, because key participants in implementation may not understand the full intent of the decision, they may unwittingly fail to comply with all of the nuances of their roles. Explicit assumptions, even if communicated and understood, will not always be shared by key participants, who may rely on their own, conflicting, assumptions in carrying out their parts of the decision. The organization's strategy loses coherence when conflicting assumptions govern the discretionary actions of middle and lower management.

Clarity and consensus about assumptions and decisions do not assure effectiveness. Explicit, shared assumptions may be invalid. In some organizations, such assumptions escape scrutiny because the company's culture does not tolerate even constructive dissent or because no one is able to challenge a powerful executive who holds the assumptions. For example, Kellogg Co. President Horst W. Schroeder allegedly rejected input from top managers and squelched dissent because he was confident that a popular Australian "he-man" cereal would succeed in the United States. When company researchers armed with market data disagreed, Schroeder is reported to have exploded in anger and ordered them to keep their conclusion quiet. The product failed miserably in the United States and the company demoted a product development manager.[4]

A MODEL OF TOP MANAGEMENT DECISION MAKING

Despite numerous differences in formal planning procedures from one company to another, there are similarities in how various top management teams make strategic decisions. In dealing with wicked problems, management faces a dynamic, uncertain environment that offers numerous potential points of leverage. This is complicated by the fact that frequently, available information is not only incomplete but also subject to ambiguous interpretation. Thus, it might be expected that wicked problems would prompt similar modes of decision making within otherwise dissimilar organizations.

---

[4] Richard Gibson, "Personal 'Chemistry' Abruptly Ended Rise of Kellogg President," *Wall Street Journal* (Nov. 28, 1989), p. 1.

A comprehensive study of 150 strategic decisions in 30 diverse British organizations[5] showed that while most organizations tend toward one type of decision process or another, they will adopt different processes for different types of decisions. That study identified several characteristics of the decision process common to organizations facing wicked problems:

- Decisions involve many parties or organizational interests.
- Disputes are common among decision makers or interested parties.
- Decision makers draw on numerous sources of information in which their confidence varies widely.
- Delays and impediments are prevalent.

Organizational researchers have offered several explanations of how top management teams make strategic decisions. The researchers' common aim is to trace the process from its origins in top management's perceptions about a situation through the various analyses and deliberations to a decision that leads to action and eventually to organizational performance.

Some researchers have focused on the top management team itself as the major determinant of strategic decisions, emphasizing the impact of individual managers' knowledge, beliefs, and assumptions on both perception and choice.[6] A second group of researchers has focused on consensus among top managers with respect to the organization's objectives and the means to attain them. They emphasize that understanding and commitment among the managers who make and execute decisions are vital to organizational performance.[7]

While these two perspectives on top management decision making are a useful starting point, they fail to address the key questions: How are individual managers' knowledge and assumptions incorporated in a team's decisions? In explaining organizational performance, how important is the quality of a decision in comparison to the degree of consensus surrounding it?

To capture these aspects of decision making, a third element has been added—the role of cognitive conflict in decisions. From this perspective researchers have focused on how decision-making teams arrive at consensus and how they use team members' diverse contributions. Emphasis is

---

[5] David J. Hickson, Richard J. Butler, David Cray, Geoffrey R. Mallory, and David C. Wilson, *Top Decisions: Strategic Decision-Making in Organizations* (San Francisco: Jossey-Bass Inc., 1986).

[6] See, for example, the model proposed by Donald C. Hambrick and Phyllis A. Mason, "Upper Echelons: The Organization as a Reflection of its Top Managers," *Academy of Management Review* vol. 9, no. 2 (Apr. 1984), pp. 193–206.

[7] See, e.g., the model proposed by Gregory G. Dess and Nancy K. Origer, "Environment, structure, and Consensus in Strategy Formulation: A Conceptual Integration," *Academy of Management Review* vol. 12, no. 2 (Apr. 1987), pp. 313–330.

placed on the impact of decision processes on both decision quality and the team members' ability to work together.

The result is an integrated model of decision making by top management teams (see Figure 6-1). This model represents the decision process in terms of inputs, transformation, and outputs. Data about the situation, the composition of the top management team, and the individual cognitive bases of team members are inputs that are transformed through the top management team's decision process. Outputs take two forms: (1) the choice itself, which can be assessed in terms of decision quality, and (2) individual managers' reactions to the decision and the process, which determine consensus among the team.

The Managers' Role

Managers have a limited field of vision. Their own interests and the responsibilities of their organizational roles influence their perceptions about a given situation. Furthermore, no organization can comprehensively monitor all aspects of its environment. The vastness and complexity of economic, technological, social, and political systems force even the largest organizations to target their intelligence activities to track only the more relevant events and trends. Information is restricted (and often distorted) as it flows through various organizational channels, where it is screened, abridged, and interpreted.

The System of Beliefs. Each top manager mutates the information by interpreting it "through a filter woven by one's cognitive base and values."[8] The existence and impact of such "filters" are documented in an intensive study by Donaldson and Lorsch of top management decisions at twelve successful industrial giants.[9] In each company they found "a distinctive system of beliefs"—a cognitive base—that served two functions: (1) It enabled managers to translate a complex, ambiguous reality into understandable, familiar terms, and (2) it provided continuity and stability whenever change threatened to undermine the lessons of experience to which managers referred for guidance.

A key element in the system of beliefs that shapes top management's perceptions about the company is management's vision of the company's distinctive competence—what the company should undertake and how to go about it. This vision greatly influences choices concerning products and markets, financial objectives, and exposure to risk. It also guides management in balancing the pressures and demands of constituencies within and

---

[8] Hambrick & Mason, op. cit., p. 195.

[9] Gordon Donaldson and Jay W. Lorsch, *Decision Making at the Top: The Shaping of Strategic Direction* (New York: Basic Books, 1983), p. 79.

FIGURE 6-1
Model of Top Management Decision Process

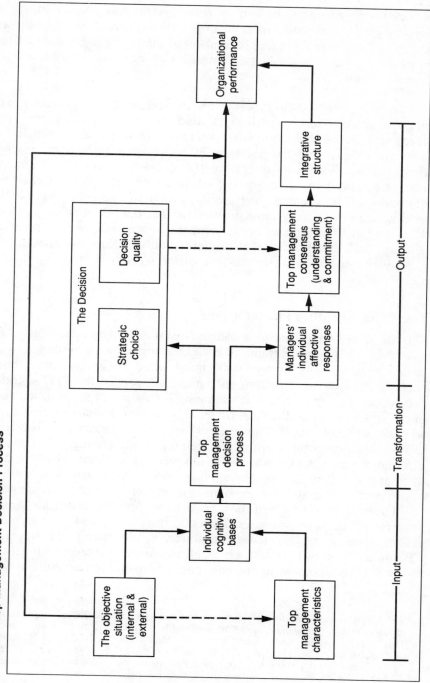

outside the organization. In fact, the belief system "becomes an important psychological commitment in its own right."[10] It is perpetuated by indoctrination and example from one generation of managers to the next. It provides the explicit and implicit assumptions for both formal and intuitive decision making.

The Decision-Making Process. Top management teams obtain and act on information to reach decisions. Beyond this obvious truth, there is considerable disagreement among observers as to the processes by which decisions are reached and the processes by which they ought to be reached. There are two rival camps of opinion.[11] One emphasizes rational, comprehensive decisions based on the logical, careful development of goals and alternatives. The other emphasizes an essentially political process that seeks adequate and acceptable decisions rather than the best ones. Under the second method, changes occur in organizationally digestible, incremental steps. Each camp claims that its method outperforms the other in complex, turbulent environments—in other words, in making wicked decisions.

The Chief Executive Officer's Role

The role of the chief executive officer (CEO) in strategic decisions is also controversial. At one extreme, the CEO is virtually an autocrat, setting goals and developing strategy with only limited assistance from subordinates. The moderate approach encourages support of the CEO's strategy and cooperation in its implementation by involving other senior managers in the strategic decisions. Sometimes, this concern about implementation will lead a CEO to involve lower-level managers in strategic decisions and to develop a corporate culture that reinforces the strategy. At the other extreme, there are CEOs who seek primarily to encourage other managers to emerge as champions of strategies, much as some organizations rely on champions to push the development and marketing of new products.

These divergent roles of the CEO are consistent with distinctly different strategic decision processes. They also impose on the CEO very different requirements of knowledge and power. At the autocratic extreme, the CEO must be knowledgeable about all elements of the environment—a formidable requirement in any case and a humanly impossible one when

---

10 Ibid., p. 108.

11 The rival views on decision processes and the appropriate roles of CEOs are nicely summarized by L.J. Bourgeois III and Kathleen M. Eisenhardt, "Strategic Decision Processes in High Velocity Environments: Four Cases in the Microcomputer Industry," *Management Science* vol. 34, no. 7 (July 1988), pp. 816–835. See also David R. Brodwin and L.J. Bourgeois III, "Five Steps to Strategic Action," *Strategy and Organization,* edited by Glenn Carroll and David Vogel (Boston: Pitman Publishing Inc., 1984), pp. 167–181.

wicked problems are involved. In addition, he must control all aspects of strategy implementation so as to induce compliance with the chosen strategy—an unlikely condition in a complex, multitiered organization.

The moderate approaches are less demanding of the CEO. Knowledge requirements are reduced through broader participation by top- and middle-level managers. The CEO serves as a coach, coordinator, or moderator as extensive discussions extract as much knowledge as possible from the decision-making group. Less power is required of the CEO because the managers who helped to develop the strategy, and are, therefore, committed to it, play major roles in its implementation.

At the other extreme, where strategy champions are encouraged, the CEO's knowledge and power requirements are greatly reduced. Although the CEO must be knowledgeable enough to establish the underlying premises of planning and to serve as a final judge of recommendations, he is relieved of the burden of conceiving and refining the strategy. To nurture good ideas and their champions, the CEO must have the power to fund and reward selectively, without submitting to elaborate organizational procedures. This type of power replaces the formal command over structure, staffing, planning, and control systems on which the CEO traditionally depends.

In sum, top management strategic decision processes breed contradictions. Their success depends on resolving several apparent paradoxes:

☐ *Decisions must be made quickly but after thorough investigations of alternatives and effects.* Yet rational, comprehensive processes are thought to be time-consuming and prone to delays.

☐ *Environmental changes require bold responses, but incremental adjustments are more easily implemented.* Can managers accept and support disruptive changes in strategy?

☐ *Diverse cognitive bases make for better decisions concerning wicked problems, but diversity within a group impedes consensus.* How can a top management team capture one without sacrificing the other?

Relationship Between Consensus and Implementation

A top management decision process can be evaluated on the quality of its decisions and on the consensus surrounding them. Unfortunately, quality and consensus do not always coexist peacefully.

Circumstances do not always permit all parties to come out ahead in strategic decisions. Hard choices may remain controversial because of honest differences or the political stakes involved, and the two may be difficult to disentangle. For example, Sears experienced a bitter struggle over strategy and organization between its Chicago-based buyers and its unharnessed, territorial sellers. Representing divergent cultures and views of retailing, the two factions shared little besides an allegiance to Sears.

Not only the choice but the manner of choosing may be problematic. For instance, *Fortune* attributes Jack Welch's "sterling" performance as chairman of General Electric to his methods of leadership. Welch and his executive council "enjoy intellectual roughhousing, and their debates make for fast, effective decision-making." But according to *Fortune,* "the arrogant brashness" of Welch's new culture has "alienated" managers in National Broadcasting Company and Kidder Peabody, subsidiaries that were acquired under Welch.[12]

Sometimes, the tradeoff required between decision quality and managers' acceptance of the decision can be treacherous. Research confirms that better decisions result from fully airing differences, identifying and evaluating assumptions, and debating alternatives. (In a classic study, Irving Janis demonstrated the effectiveness of these procedures by contrasting the decision process used by President Kennedy and his top aides during the disastrous Bay of Pigs invasion with that used a year later in managing the Cuban Missile Crisis.[13]) Yet many groups avoid such candor because it sparks personal conflict or because dissent is equated with disloyalty.

The desire for consensus is psychologically understandable. It is also justifiable, at least intuitively, for pragmatic reasons. Managers work more harmoniously when they agree about what is to be done. Yet researchers have not found a consistent relationship between management consensus and organizational performance, probably because the importance of consensus depends on the subject matter (does it concern environmental variables, goals, strategy, or tactics?) and the juncture in a company's decision process. For example, consensus about a solution soon after a problem has been identified may reflect premature agreement based on incomplete analysis or a hasty choice.

It is also helpful to think of consensus in terms of its two dimensions— *shared understanding* and *commitment.*[14] Managers may agree on what a decision means, yet work to subvert its implementation. Other managers may wholeheartedly want to implement a strategy, yet fail through misunderstanding. Either situation undermines organizational performance, regardless of the quality of a strategic decision. Despite the common diagnosis (lack of consensus) of these two conditions, top management must use very different approaches to deal with them.

---

12 Stratford P. Sherman, "Inside the Mind of Jack Welch," *Fortune* (Mar. 27, 1989), p. 50.

13 Irving L. Janis, *Victims of Groupthink* (Boston: Houghton-Mifflin, 1972).

14 Bill Wooldridge and Steven W. Floyd, "Strategic Process Effects on Consensus," *Strategic Management Journal* vol. 10, no. 3 (May–June 1989), pp. 295–302.

Resolving a lack of consensus is the task of an organization's integrating structure. If the difficulty stems from a lack of shared understanding, the solution usually requires a more effective dissemination of information. Informal contacts, routine reports, or the assignment of managers to coordinating roles are common options. Committees or task forces may handle broader information requirements. When facing a lack of commitment or opposition, the solution may involve finding alternate paths to the same end, refocusing attention on areas of agreement, modifying the rate of implementation, or direct action against the opponents (including removal from the organization). All of these latter steps were used by Edward Telling in his fight to bring a new strategy and organization to Sears.[15]

Finally, the quality of a strategic decision and the organization's ability and willingness to implement it also depend on environmental elements. Although some events cannot be anticipated or controlled, top management's decisions are a major factor in a company's performance and they are subject to influence. An effective decision process is vital to translating the organization's potential into reality.

THE TEAM APPROACH TO DECISION MAKING

The team approach to managing wicked decisions is based on six premises about top management decisions and organizational performance. The first premise is the key to the other five:

1. Timely, high-quality decisions that enjoy the understanding and acceptance of those who will implement them are the hallmark of effective top management. Organizational performance depends on maintaining such effectiveness over time.

The remaining premises explain how the elements of the first premise come into being and affect the others.

2. The individual capabilities of top management's members establish the potential for making and implementing effective decisions.
3. Utilization of members' capabilities determines the extent to which top management converts its potential into quality decisions.
4. Top management's decision-making approach determines how well it utilizes its members' capabilities.
5. Top management's decision-making approach determines how well its members understand, accept, and commit to decisions.
6. Certain organizational conditions influence the effectiveness of top management's decision-making approach.

---

[15] Donald R. Katz, *The Big Store: Inside the Crisis and Revolution at Sears* (New York: Viking Penguin, 1987).

An effective top management team is one that can arrive at decisions that enable the organization to survive and prosper in its environment (e.g., social, economic, industry). Because a top management team is not an ad hoc group, its members must be able to continue to work together effectively over time; that is, the decision-making process cannot lead to divisiveness that destroys cooperation among team members. Team members must understand, accept, and commit to decisions by supporting and implementing them. Also, the top management team must be able to make decisions within a reasonable period—many situations require immediate responses. Unless all of these criteria are met, it is unlikely that a top management team can effectively lead its organization into the future.

Selecting Top Management Team Members

The selection of participating managers is probably the most important consideration in designing the top management team. The composition of the team determines its maximum decision-making performance: the combined knowledge and capabilities of individual managers that can be utilized in making and implementing strategic decisions. When making these selections, a CEO should weigh three primary criteria: team diversity, constituent representation, and team size.

Ensuring Diversity. To ensure the rich mix of relevant knowledge and perspectives that is needed to make wicked decisions, the team of managers should be diverse in its capabilities. However, if not managed effectively, this diversity can lead to personal conflict among the managers, which, in turn, causes poor decisions and a lack of acceptance and commitment to them. Top managers may understand the need for diversity when constructing their teams but they often do not appreciate its effects when they are caught up in the heat of a decision. Thus, executives walk a thin line in deciding what types and degrees of diversity will be productive.

Although in its infancy, research on this topic has attempted to identify the characteristics of the ideal top management team. Hambrick has argued that the mix of managerial qualities desired in a top management team depends on the organization's strategic situation. Such qualities include each manager's values (fundamental beliefs or principles), aptitudes (such capacities as creativity, intellect, tolerance for ambiguity, and interpersonal awareness), knowledge (relevant to industry, markets, technologies, and so on), cognitive style (how he processes information and makes decisions), and demeanor (personal style or bearing).[16]

---

[16] Donald C. Hambrick, "The Top Management Team: Key to Strategic Success," *California Management Review* vol. 30, no. 1 (Fall 1987), pp. 88–108.

These qualities interact to form a gestalt that influences how a manager sees and understands the world, and how he approaches decisions. Moreover, the various gestalts of top managers interact to influence the team's decisions.

Research has not progressed to the point of identifying specific characteristics or gestalts that are most appropriate for managers in particular strategic situations. Even so, empirical evidence and experience suggest that successful decision making requires a top management team that possesses balanced knowledge about an organization's internal and external environments.[17] In many top management teams, there is a need for both those who think abstractly (sometimes called visionaries) and those who focus on details (who are needed to assess the vision's impact on the bottom line). Although most managers have diverse capabilities, they usually favor or are more interested in using particular ones.

Senior executives who design or refurbish their top management teams should examine their firms' situations and identify the capabilities that are required. Next, perhaps with the help of the human resources staff or consultants, the capabilities of current teams should be assessed. A large gap between the available and needed capabilities requires some tough measures: identifying and promoting successors, hiring replacements, or using consultants or other adjuncts to the team. Modest gaps and ample time to respond might permit less drastic measures: modified reward systems, executive development programs, coaching, or counseling.

A number of companies have instituted internal research programs to identify the qualities and capabilities that their top management teams will need in the coming decades. These programs, devised by human resources staffs and consultants, serve as the basis for future hiring and promotion decisions, compensation plans, succession plans, and executive development programs.

Representation on the Top Management Team. Managers whose direct roles or indirect support are crucial in implementing strategic decisions should be considered for participation in the top management team. This is simply an acknowledgement of the political realities in most organizations. Representation on the top management team of key organizational units or interests may be essential in gaining their acceptance and commitment to strategic decisions. Such involvement is not the only way to gain acceptance or commitment, but it certainly helps and may result in other benefits, too.

Team Size Consideration. In selecting a top management team, the CEO must consider his own style and ability to manage the team. Applying

---

[17] John P. Kotter, *The General Managers* (New York: The Free Press, 1982), pp. 34–120.

the criteria of diversity and representation, one might be tempted to include everyone. Nevertheless, a CEO must exercise restraint so that the team does not become unwieldy. In one organization, a division president included his direct reports plus the team's direct reports (a total of twenty-three managers) in his weekly staff meetings that were used to make strategic decisions (e.g., product introductions and acquisitions). The president believed that such a large group would ensure maximum diversity and garner the commitment of all the key managers in his division. Unfortunately, he discovered that the team process led to neither. As one vice-president put it: "Meetings are typically nothing more than a three-ring circus that frustrates all of us. Rarely do we make any useful decisions. Rarely do managers get an opportunity to speak. Frankly, the meetings are a waste of time."

Obviously, the president was incapable of operating effectively in a large group. Rather than encouraging interaction among team members (and taking advantage of the diversity), he typically squared off with individual managers in biting dialogues and even monologues. Not surprisingly, managers became reluctant to speak up, especially to indicate their disagreement. Confronted in private, the president admitted that he could not comfortably make decisions within such a large group, especially with subordinates of his direct reports. (Many of the president's direct reports also expressed concern about being reprimanded in front of their subordinates.)

The solution was to define a much smaller core team of eight members, including key functional and product area vice-presidents and two of the president's staff. The large staff meetings were retained, but their purpose was changed from decision making to information sharing. The new core team assembled to make strategic decisions. With some coaching and team development workshops, the president and his key managers dramatically changed their behaviors during team meetings. Managers were more inclined to speak up, to express the diversity of their views, and to be more actively involved in decision making. After a number of team meetings, there was less hostility and more open interaction among the managers.

The president took two steps to preserve the enthusiasm and commitment of those managers who were excluded from the top management team. First, the core team regularly requested their input as needed. Second, the president assigned them to newly established teams charged with developing implementation plans for the strategic decisions. Thus, although not directly involved in making the decisions, managers still had considerable influence in shaping them and even more in deciding how to implement them. The quality of decision making was improved without sacrificing the acceptance and commitment of the second tier of managers.

Decision Management and Cognitive Conflict

The composition of the top management team—its diverse managerial qualities and capabilities, its representation of organizational constituencies, and its size—determines its potential to make and implement high-quality strategic decisions. Whether this potential is realized, however, depends on the team's decision-making process. Many studies by social psychologists and management scholars, as well as practical experience, show that simply bringing diverse individuals together does not necessarily yield quality decisions. Research and experience with top management teams certainly confirm this lesson.

Diverse managerial qualities and capabilities increase the probability that a team will make good strategic decisions, but, if poorly managed, they can lead to destructive personal conflicts among team members. To combat this problem within the team approach and to utilize diversity while minimizing its potentially destructive effects, many companies deliberately structure, and thus endorse, conflict among team members. It is important to note that these companies encourage constructive, cognitive conflict as opposed to destructive, interpersonal conflict.

Cognitive conflict focuses on differences in ideas, whereas interpersonal conflict focuses on differences between individuals. Although the distinction is subtle, it is essential. When the focus is on individuals, the decision process tends to become personalized and political. Team members devote more time and effort to defending themselves and attacking others than to making good decisions. When the focus is on ideas, members turn their attention to exploring alternatives and the assumptions underlying them.

Programmed cognitive conflict procedure will not eliminate personal attacks and defensiveness, or prevent managers from pursuing personal interests, because to some extent, these behaviors are facts of organizational life. However, these behaviors are minimized when the decision process formally structures and endorses a constructive type of conflict (i.e., cognitive).

Using Programmed Cognitive Conflict

Formal debate is the principal mechanism to ensure cognitive conflict in the team approach. Debate may be structured in either of two ways: *devil's advocacy* or *dialectical inquiry*. Research and experience indicate that these two approaches are equally effective in producing high-quality decisions, and are more effective than non–programmed conflict approaches. A top management team can use either approach by following eight basic steps:

1. *Training.* Before attempting to use either approach, the top management team should be trained in the use of programmed conflict, its goals, and the conditions under which it is likely to succeed. This can be accomplished through training sessions involving formal instruction and experiential case exercises that use the procedure. The training sessions should help managers focus on how to explore decision alternatives, identify and analyze assumptions, and engage in cognitive, rather than personal, conflict. The training sessions also provide excellent opportunities for team leaders to state their expectations and to make clear their support for this approach to decision making and the types of behavior it requires.

2. *Forming subgroups.* After initial training, a programmed conflict procedure can be initiated in the top management team. Both the devil's advocacy and dialectical inquiry approaches require that the team be divided into two subgroups that will eventually engage in debate. To encourage substantial cognitive conflict, the CEO should assign team members to the subgroups in a way that ensures that there are ample differences between the two groups. For example, in one organization, "visionaries" were identified and assigned to one subgroup, and "detail-oriented" managers were assigned to the other. In another company, managers with extensive international experience were assigned to one subgroup and managers with no international experience were assigned to the other. Predictably, these diverse subgroups viewed the objective situation differently and proposed quite different decisions.

Differences between subgroups should be established on the basis of as many managerial qualities as possible. At a minimum, however, differences should be established in qualities that are deemed most relevant to the decision at hand. To avoid permanent coalitions and to promote team development, the CEO should vary the composition of subgroups from one decision to another. The human resources staff or consultants can help the CEO assess group and subgroup diversity in any of the managerial qualities discussed in this chapter.

3. *Developing recommendations.* Devil's advocacy and dialectical inquiry both require the subgroups to objectively analyze the situation. However, only one subgroup (designated by the team leader) is required to develop and recommend a decision, which should be supported by all the assumptions and analyses that led to it. If a decision involves several subdecisions, separate assumptions and analyses must be provided for each one. (The second subgroup is not required to document anything at this point.)

Such well-known group decision techniques as brainstorming are very useful in developing alternatives. In addition, group facilitators (e.g., human resources or organizational development staff members) can be very useful in managing interactions among the top management team, especially when the team is first learning to use programmed conflict procedures.

4. *Critique and negation.* After the first subgroup has prepared its recommendations, they are presented to the second subgroup for examination and response. The response formats will differ depending on whether the devil's advocacy or the dialectical inquiry approach is used. In devil's advocacy, the second subgroup is required to *critique* the first subgroup's assumptions, analyses, and decisions. In a dialectical inquiry, the second subgroup is required to *negate* or contradict the first group's assumptions, analyses, and decisions by presenting a diametrically opposed view. For example, diametrically opposed decisions include acquisition versus internal development of a new product, expanding internationally versus remaining domestic, and competing through low cost versus competing through product differentiation. Examples of diametrically opposed assumptions include growth versus decline of an industry and retaliation versus passivity on the part of rivals.

5. *Debate.* At this point, two positions have been established. With the devil's advocacy approach, there is an initial recommendation and a critique, whereas with a dialectical inquiry there is an initial recommendation and a counter-recommendation. The diversity of membership and the nature of the tasks involved for each subgroup set the stage for a debate that promotes cognitive conflict.

The debate procedure is iterative, with the two subgroups responding to each other's proposals, rebuttals, and revisions through written statements, oral presentations, or a combination of the two. The latter form of communication is preferable under most circumstances, although the written portions may be omitted when time is extremely limited.

After each assumption is debated, it is followed by a recommendation. To avoid premature acceptance of recommendations and promote cognitive conflict, the CEO (or preferably a facilitator) should encourage several rounds of revisions. The procedure continues until both subgroups agree that they cannot significantly improve the assumptions and decisions. If the subgroups are deadlocked, and time is short, the CEO may have to break the deadlock by making the decision. Although this is not normally a desirable approach, it may be the only way to meet the needs of the situation.

6. *Understanding and acceptance.* The CEO should make sure that all members of the team understand, accept, and commit to the decision. Any questions or concerns must be addressed immediately; otherwise implementation of the decision may be undermined. The CEO may meet with the full team to discuss this issue, have private sessions with each member, or have the human resources staff or consultants make independent assessments.

7. *Planning for implementation.* Once team members understand and accept the decision, implementation plans must be established. Each member of the team should be responsible for ensuring that specific elements of the decision are carried out. Responsibility charts are useful. This is also an excellent time to consider involving team members' subordinates in developing the implementation plans.

8. *Monitoring.* Because most wicked decisions are made in uncertain environments, they should be reviewed periodically and changed as necessary. It is important to remember that the strategic decision process is continuous. While the group may meet on a regular basis, it should be prepared to convene whenever necessary.

Effectiveness of Programmed Cognitive Conflict

Now that the steps in devil's advocacy and dialectical inquiry have been laid out, it is worthwhile to summarize the empirical evidence concerning their effectiveness. Several studies involving both executives and MBA students lead to the following conclusions:[18]

☐ Compared to teams using a group consensus procedure that did not incorporate programmed cognitive conflict, teams using devil's advocacy or dialectical inquiry produced better assumptions and decisions, made greater use of individual members' contributions, and reported more reevaluation of their own initial assumptions and recommendations. (Devil's advocacy and dialectical inquiry performed equally on these measures, and their effectiveness increased with experience in the procedures.)

☐ Teams using devil's advocacy or dialectical inquiry initially required more time to reach decisions, and reported less acceptance of their decisions, than teams using the group consensus approach. These differences disappeared as teams gained experience in the procedures. (Devil's advocacy and dialectical inquiry performed equally well on these measures.)

☐ There were no differences in satisfaction and willingness to continue working together between teams using programmed conflict procedures and

---

[18] David M. Schweiger, William R. Sandberg, and James W. Ragan, "Group Approaches for Improving Strategic Decision Making: A Comparative Analysis of Dialectical Inquiry, Devil's Advocacy, and Consensus," *Academy of Management Journal* vol. 29, no. 1 (Mar. 1986), pp. 51–71; David M. Schweiger and William R. Sandberg, "The Utilization of Individual Capabilities in Group Approaches to Strategic Decision-Making," *Strategic Management Journal* vol. 10, no. 1 (Jan.–Feb. 1989), pp. 31–43; David M. Schweiger, William R. Sandberg, and Paula L. Rechner, op. cit.; David M. Schweiger, William R. Sandberg, and Paula L. Rechner, "An Examination of the Subgroup Effects of Dialectical Inquiry and Devil's Advocacy," paper presented at the annual meeting of the Academy of Management, Washington, D.C., Aug. 1989.

those using the group consensus approach. Both measures improved with experience in the programmed conflict procedures.

In summary, the research findings suggest that programmed cognitive conflict, whether through devil's advocacy or dialectical inquiry, improves strategic decision making. Further, it does so without adverse reactions on the part of team members. Moreover, experience in using the procedures enhances both performance and team members' reactions.

Establishing a Proper Team Culture

Although dialectical inquiry and devil's advocacy formally structure and encourage cognitive conflict, they do not guarantee that members of the top management team will candidly disagree about assumptions and decisions and work toward a consensus. In many organizations, this will happen only if the CEO (team leader) takes an active role in establishing a supportive team culture regardless of whether the team already exists or is newly established. If the programmed cognitive conflict procedures are to work effectively, the top management team culture must discourage political behavior and promote candor, cooperation, and a clear sense of purpose. Although these attributes may seem obvious, they are often difficult to establish in practice.

Team leaders play the principal role in creating (or preventing) a supportive top management team culture—not only by articulating expectations, but also by their behavior and the behavior they encourage or tolerate. It is important to realize that cultures are created even when they are not planned. A CEO's actions do speak louder than words.

Because there are many cultural elements that influence the success of any top management decision process and the programmed cognitive conflict procedures, team leaders must reward (both in performance appraisals and through public recognition) cooperation and constructive disagreement and discourage (usually through private censure) undesirable behavior. Moreover, they must pay careful attention to their own behavior.

Using Facilitators

It can be difficult for team leaders to both moderate and take part in the decision process. In some cases, leaders who engage in both activities become so concerned about managing the process that they fail to participate in it. As a result, the potential benefits of their contributions are never realized, or they finish the process with little commitment to the decisions that were made. Neither outcome is desirable. In other cases, leaders who both moderate and participate inadvertently dominate the team's deliberations. Thus, the contributions and commitment of other key managers are never realized. Some team leaders use human resources staff members or consultants as moderators to permit their own active involvement without dominating the team's decision process. One top manager even used a facilitator for the sole purpose of managing himself during team meetings. He knew that otherwise the process would not work.

Facilitators are not always needed, as some team leaders can simultaneously perform both roles. But they may be a minority, and even they find it helpful to have someone else moderate when the team is learning to use the programmed cognitive conflict procedures.

CONCLUSION

Scholarly research and experience have shown that the best way to solve a company's wicked problems is through a cognitive conflict–based approach. Therefore, managers who are now using such an approach should be encouraged to continue to do so, while those who are not should be encouraged to consider it.

However, managers who are considering initiating the team approach must be aware that it is not a panacea for organizational problems, nor is it effective under all organizational conditions. The CEO or other team leader must diagnose the conditions under which the approach will be implemented. (This diagnosis may require professional help.) If conditions are right, he can decide whether to proceed with the team approach. If conditions are not right, the team approach should not be implemented unless there is careful intervention to change the top management team and its culture.

Financial Tools for Strategy Evaluation

RONALD G. QUINTERO

R.G. Quintero & Company

INTRODUCTION

Business strategy calls for an examination of many alternatives in such areas as potential products and markets, possible competitor actions, and financing arrangements. The major decisions a firm must make in selecting one strategy above all others requires a solid understanding of markets and products, competitors, and the firm's own capabilities. Among the tools available to help structure strategic thinking, financial statements, financial analysis ratios, and financial projections, in particular, are an essential part of the strategic manager's evaluative process.

This chapter examines these various financial tools and gives strategic managers insight into how identical figures can be presented and interpreted to offer widely divergent pictures of the company. This chapter also discusses valuation methods for acquisitions and the various methods of pricing venture capital, because these topics are closely related: The financial statements provide the raw data used to perform the ratio analysis, and the ratios, in turn, are used in the financial projections that are the basis for evaluating investment opportunities. An understanding of these financial tools and their significance can enhance the decision-making process and lead to better results.

USING FINANCIAL TOOLS

How do you support the selection of one alternative over another? How do you determine whether your company has the financial wherewithal to undertake a given project? How do you measure and evaluate performance? Financial tools provide objective means of analyzing these and other issues. Typical applications of financial tools include:

- Assessing the performance of a product, subsidiary, division, company, industry, or competitor
- Determining capital requirements
- Lease/purchase analysis
- Product pricing
- Acquisition and divestiture analysis
- Management evaluation
- Predicting business failure
- Deciding whether to make or buy a product
- Capital expenditure analysis
- Bond ratings

Financial tools transform financial statements from a myriad of data into useful information that can aid decision making. Any time a reader of financial statements uses them to draw certain conclusions, he or she is performing financial analysis. Financial tools aid the decision maker by providing an independent and objective means of supporting decision making. If properly used, financial tools can provide an unbiased assessment of past and future performance.

The Value Line Investment Survey, which for years has been recognized as an outstanding investment tool, is based entirely on financial and statistical algorithms, calculated on the computer. *Value Line* founder Arnold Bernhard claims that the times that he has deviated from the computer output, investment selections have frequently resulted in substandard performance. Consequently, his service tries to remain free of human bias by relying solely on the output provided by its investment tools, and to date it has been highly successful. Although this represents an extreme point of view, it reinforces the benefit of well selected and properly interpreted financial tools.

UNDERSTANDING FINANCIAL STATEMENTS

The concept of GIGO—garbage in, garbage out—is especially true in financial analysis. In order to use and interpret financial data properly, one must understand the data and how it was compiled. Essential issues that must be considered include data quality and integrity, reporting period, business unit, and accounting policies. The treatment of these issues and the assumptions and methodologies employed in compiling data can have a substantial impact on the resulting data.

The basic financial statements referred to in every auditor's opinion include the balance sheet, the income statement, the statement of changes in financial position, and the statement of stockholders' equity. The balance sheet is a "snapshot" of corporate financial position at a specific date, indicating assets, liabilities, and net worth. The income statement shows the revenues and expenses of the enterprise for a specified period. The statement of changes in financial position details the cash flow that is generated for a specified period. Annual changes in net worth are detailed in the statement of stockholders' equity. Examples of these statements are shown in Tables 7-1, 7-2, 7-3, and 7-4.

The Balance Sheet

Historically, the balance sheet has been the financial statement to which the greatest amount of attention is paid. It is the first financial statement mentioned in the standard auditor's report, and is often the only financial state-

TABLE 7-1
Sample Balance Sheet

XYZ CORPORATION
BALANCE SHEET
December 31, 1990 and 1989

Assets	1990	1989
Cash	$ 605,324	$ 944,871
Accounts receivable, net of $75,000 allowance for doubtful accounts	3,727,018	3,129,256
Inventory (LIFO)	4,018,627	3,254,508
Prepaid expenses and other current assets	316,253	402,619
Total current assets	$ 8,667,222	$ 7,731,254
Property, plant and equipment, net of accumulated depreciation	4,109,614	3,241,828
Investment in ABC Co.	699,951	—
Goodwill, net of amortization	475,000	500,000
Other assets	1,057,526	1,223,719
Total assets	$15,009,313	$12,696,801

Liabilities and stockholders' equity	1990	1989
Liabilities		
Notes payable	$ 460,000	$ 315,000
Current maturities of long-term debt	525,000	325,000
Accounts payable	2,519,938	2,325,423
Accrued expenses	1,099,282	1,080,877
Total current liabilities	$ 4,604,220	$ 4,046,300
Long-term debt, net of current installments	3,450,000	2,575,000
Deferred income taxes	304,025	257,968
Total liabilities	$ 8,358,245	$ 6,879,268
Stockholders' equity		
Common stock, no par	$ 724,500	$ 724,500
Retained earnings	5,926,568	5,093,033
Total stockholders' equity	6,651,068	5,817,533
Total liabilities and stockholders' equity	$15,009,313	$12,696,801

TABLE 7-2

Sample Income Statement

XYZ Corporation
INCOME STATEMENT
For the Years Ended December 31, 1990 and 1989

	1990	1989
Net sales	$22,579,488	$18,923,504
Cost of goods sold	16,121,754	13,189,682
Gross profit	$ 6,457,734	$ 5,733,822
General and administrative expenses	2,647,321	2,405,804
Selling expenses	1,845,997	1,499,318
Operating profit	$ 1,964,416	$ 1,828,700
Interest expense, net	496,924	351,284
Gain on sale of fixed assets	111,897	—
Equity in earnings of ABC Co.	72,438	—
Income before taxes	$ 1,651,827	$ 1,477,416
Income taxes	502,792	593,921
Net income	$ 1,149,035	$ 883,495

ment submitted to trade creditors. It is the "primal" financial statement, evidencing the most important corporate objective: survival. A company can have an outstanding product, idea, market share, sales force, or many other desirable traits; however, if it has insufficient assets to meet liabilities, its existence may be jeopardized. Conversely, a mediocre company may wallow in mediocrity for years if it has a strong balance sheet.

The balance sheet is of great importance to creditors because it is an indication of what assets are available to satisfy debts. To the extent that the balance sheet reflects a company's prospects for survival, it also is of interest to shareholders, employees, customers, suppliers, competitors, and the community or communities in which the company is located. Management uses of balance sheet data include:

- Monitoring assets available for current and long-term needs
- Identifying collections of accounts receivable or measuring the turnover of inventory
- Determining capital requirements
- Analyzing debt capacity
- Evaluating efficiency of assets employed
- Identifying leverageable or salable assets
- Analyzing insurance needs

Although generally accepted accounting principles (GAAP) prescribe permissible accounting methods, they allow sufficient flexibility such that a

TABLE 7-3

Sample Statement of Changes in Financial Position

XYZ CORPORATION
STATEMENT OF CHANGES IN FINANCIAL POSITION
For the Years Ended December 31, 1990 and 1989

	1990	1989
Working capital provided		
Net income	$1,149,035	$ 883,495
Items not affecting working capital		
Depreciation	465,291	309,421
Amortization	25,000	25,000
Deferred taxes	46,057	39,274
Gain on sale of equipment	(111,897)	—
Equity in earnings of ABC Co.	(72,438)	—
Working capital provided from operations	$1,501,048	$1,257,190
Long-term borrowings	1,400,000	225,000
Proceeds from sale of equipment	167,000	—
Proceeds from stock options exercised	—	75,000
Total working capital provided	$3,068,548	$1,557,190
Working capital used		
Repayment of long-term debt	$ 325,000	$ 316,000
Additions to property, plant, and equipment	1,422,487	364,852
Purchase of minority interest in ABC Co.	627,513	—
Payment of cash dividends	315,500	283,950
	$2,690,500	$ 964,802
Increase in working capital	$ 378,048	$ 592,388
Analysis of changes in working capital		
Increase (decrease) in current assets		
Cash	$ (339,547)	$ 227,153
Accounts receivable	597,762	284,528
Inventory	764,119	308,196
Prepaid expenses and other current assets	(86,366)	62,731
	$ 935,968	$ 882,608
Increase (decrease) in current liabilities		
Notes payable	$ 145,000	$ (27,000)
Current maturities of long-term debt	200,000	15,000
Accounts payable	194,515	133,219
Accrued expenses	18,405	169,001
	$ 557,920	$ 290,220
Increase in working capital	$ 378,048	$ 592,338

TABLE 7-4

Sample Statement of Stockholders' Equity

XYZ CORPORATION
STATEMENT OF STOCKHOLDERS' EQUITY
For the Years Ended December 31, 1990 and 1989

	Common stock (no par)		Retained earnings
	Shares	Amounts	
Balance, December 31, 1988	1,562,500	$649,500	$4,493,488
Stock options exercised	15,000	75,000	—
Cash dividends ($0.18)	—	—	(283,950)
Net income, 1989	—	—	883,495
Balance, December 31, 1989	1,577,500	$724,500	$5,093,033
Cash dividends ($0.20)	—	—	(315,500)
Net income, 1990	—	—	1,149,035
Balance, Decmeber 1990	1,577,500	$724,500	$5,926,568

misleading impression of financial condition may be derived from the balance sheet if the accounting method that was used is not taken into consideration. Asset and liability balances can vary widely depending on the accounting method employed. Also, the character of certain assets and liabilities can vary substantially among enterprises. Dollar balances alone can belie the true financial condition of a business concern. Examples of issues relating to balance sheets that should be analyzed are shown in Table 7-5.

The Income Statement

Once we know how much a company is worth, the question becomes how much money it made. The earnings of a company directly affect its new worth, since net worth is the cumulative product of historical earnings.

Companies commonly compile an annual income statement, with quarterly or monthly updates. The income statement represents an estimate of financial performance over a specific interval of time. In his landmark volume on auditing theory,[1] Dicksee reduced all accounting to the "single voyage" model. According to this paradigm, a ship is acquired, goods are bought, and a crew is hired in order to transport the goods to another port, at which time everything will be liquidated and the profits will be divided among the partners. The voyage could last months or even years. Revenues are realized only at the end of the voyage, when the goods are sold; meanwhile, most of the expenses are incurred before the voyage ever gets under way. Assuming that there must be a periodic accounting of

---

[1] Lawrence R. Dicksee, *Auditing: A Practical Manual for Auditors* (London: Gee & Co., 1892).

TABLE 7-5

Major Analytical Areas: Balance Sheet

Balance sheet item	Analytical area	Implications
General	• Independent verification	• Relative degrees of assurance, in descending order are audited financial statement, review, and write-up.
	• Auditor's opinion	• Financial statement integrity depends on whether opinion is unqualified, qualified, restricted, or adverse.
	• Accrual vs. cash basis	• Cash basis, often used for federal income taxes, may distort actual financial condition.
	• Seasonal variations	• May suggest different levels of assets and liabilities are required.
	• Operating vs. nonoperating	• Assets not integral to the business should be analyzed separately.
	• Payment schedule	• Useful in determining means by which they will be satisfied.
	• Valuation method	• Historical cost, current value, replacement cost, general price level accounting, or liquidation level can result in significant variations.
Assets	• Restrictions	• May be pledged, collateralized, or subject of pending sale; hence not freely available for future use.
Cash	• Dedicated uses	• Debt agreements, bank restrictions, and impending liabilities may limit alternative uses.
Marketable securities	• Cost or market value	• Net proceeds are market value, less costs of disposal and taxes.
	• Liquidity	• Large blocks of debt or equity securities frequently cannot be sold at prevailing market prices.

Accounts receivable Bad debt allowance	• Aging • Percentage or specific identification	• Older balances may present higher risk of noncollection. • May be inadequate.
Inventory	• Valuation method • Marketability	• LIFO, FIFO, or average cost can result in significant variations. • Historical cost may exceed market value.
Fixed assets	• Fair market value • Obsolescence • Depreciation	• Often varies substantially from historical cost. • Usable equipment may be technologically obsolete. • Accelerated methods such as sum-of-the-years'-digits and double declining balance result in more rapid write-offs, hence, lower balances and earnings than straight-line methods, as can estimated useful life.
Unconsolidated investments Intangible assets	• Ownership • Valuation method • Amortization	• Leased assets are capitalized, but not owned by the company. • Equity accounting value may differ substantially from fair market value. • Method and estimated useful life affect value.

Liabilities and stockholders' equity

Deferred taxes	• Rate of increase	• A growing company may never pay the net liability unless the "crossover point" is reached.
Long-term debt	• Interest rate	• Fair market value may differ from amortized cost, depending on relation between current and stated rate.
Convertible securities Treasury stock	• Conversion prospects • Costing method	• May signal a potential modification to capital structure. • May be accounted for at cost or par value.

voyage earnings, how do we estimate the portion of revenues and expenses attributable to each segment of the voyage?

This is the fundamental challenge of accounting: matching revenues and expenses. There is little dispute as to voyage earnings after the voyage has been completed and all accounts have been settled. Earnings are simply whatever is left over. The problem is that in most real-life situations, the voyage is still in progress.

There are two fundamental methods of accounting for earnings: cash basis and accrual basis. Cash-basis accounting is a simple tally of cash receipts and cash payments. It is commonly used in service businesses and by individuals and some corporations for filing income taxes. It is useful for depicting the financial reality of cash receipts and payments, which over the long run is the true measure of profitability. The problem with cash-basis accounting is that it fails to recognize that some revenues require several years to be realized, and some expenditures provide benefits that will last for several accounting periods. For this reason, GAAP requires in most instances that audited financial statements be presented on an accrual basis, which allocates revenues and expenses to the periods contributing to the income or benefiting from the expenses. Hence, a distinction is created between the realization and recognition of revenues and expenses.

Accrual accounting comes closer to approximating economic reality than accounting on a cash basis. Most financial data is prepared on an accrual basis. Major capital assets such as buildings or equipment clearly provide benefits that will last over several periods, and their expense should be charged accordingly. The problem lies in deciding what constitutes a reasonable basis for recognizing income and expenses. This problem is further complicated by the latitude that exists in income and expense recognition. The examples of income and expense recognition alternatives shown in Table 7-6 provide the potential for 165,888 different net earnings figures. Companies that are identical in every respect can report significantly differing results depending on how they recognize income and expenses. This does not mean that accounting data is simply a useless collection of numbers. Rather, it means that accounting data should be subjected to careful scrutiny before any conclusions are drawn. Accounting data is like a foreign language in that the substance of a message is the same irrespective of the language in which it is given. The economic reality of a company is largely unaffected by the accounting methods employed. The key challenge in using accounting data is correct interpretation.

The Statement of Changes in Financial Position

The income statement provides only a partial view of corporate performance over a given interval of time. It reflects revenues and expenses that have been recognized. However, as discussed above, there is often a

TABLE 7-6

Income/Expense Recognition Alternatives

Account	Method	Comments
Revenues	• Sales method	• Recognize at time of sale.
	• Installment sales method	• Recognize when payment is received.
	• Production method	• Recognize when product is completed (applicable to extractive industires).
	• Percentage-of-completion method	• Proportional recognition over performance of a contract.
Sales returns and allowances	• Specific identification	• Appropriate for low volume and/or high-ticket items.
	• Percentage of sales	• Assumes a discernible pattern.
Inventory cost	• First in, first out (FIFO)	• Assumes items sold in the order they are received.
	• Last in, first out (LIFO)	• Costing in reverse order to receipt.
	• Average cost	
	• Specific identification	• Most accurate method.
Inventory write-downs	• Minimize write-downs	• Maximizes reported earnings.
	• Realistic write-downs	
	• Maximize write-downs	• Minimizes taxable income.
Overhead	• Absorption costing	• Allocates to each unit of production.
	• Immediate recognition	• Assumes that overhead is an expense of the period.
Depreciation	• Straight line	• Assumes equal annual depreciation.
	• Double declining balance	• Assumes assets depreciate more rapidly in earlier years.
	• Sum-of-the-years'-digits	• Assumes assets depreciate more rapidly in earlier years.
	• Units of production	• Depreciation is related to output.
Depreciation/amortization period	• Minimize write-off	• Maximizes reported earnings.
	• Realistic write-off	
	• Maximize write-off	• Minimizes taxable income.
Warranty/product service expense	• Percentage-of-sales method	• Matches future expense with period revenues as generated.
	• Pay-as-you-go	• May contribute to earnings volatility.

(continued)

TABLE 7-6 *(cont'd)*

Account	Method	Comments
Patents, maintenance, construction interest costs	• Immediate recognition	• Based on cash payments.
Officer/shareholder compensation and fringe benefits	• Capitalization • Minimize • "Fair" • Maximize	• Assumes benefits in future years. • Done only where necessary or to increase selling price of company. • Minimizes taxable income; common in closely held businesses. • Assumes a discernible pattern.
Bad-debt expense	• Percentage of sales • Percentage of receivables • Specific identification	• Assumes a discernible pattern. • Appropriate for low volume/high account balance activity. • Immediate recognition.
Investment tax credit	• Flow-through method • Capitalization	• Tax benefit coincides with asset usage.

FIGURE 7-1

Flow of Funds

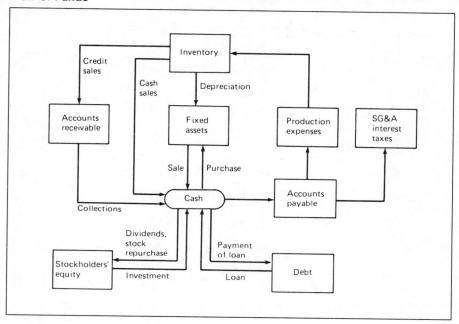

disparity between the point at which revenues and expenses occur and the point at which they are recognized. This disparity is reconciled through the statement of changes in financial position, which bridges the gap between the recognition of income and the flow of funds. Also referred to as the statement of sources and application of funds, sources and uses statement, statement of changes, and funds flow statement, it provides the details of funds (working capital and long-term capital) received and used by the business (see Figure 7-1). Viewed by many analysts as the most revealing financial statement, the statement of changes provides the best indication of "cash" income. It can readily be converted into a true cash-flow statement by using cash as the bottom line instead of using change in working capital.

Another important attribute of the statement of changes is that it shows how the company is spending its capital resources and where the money comes from. The liquidity of the company is more closely related to the working capital generating capacity shown in the statement of changes than it is to the amount of income shown in the income statement. Cash-flow projections and discounted cash-flow analysis are usually made using the format of the statement of changes.

FIGURE 7-2
Importance of Statement of Changes in Financial Position

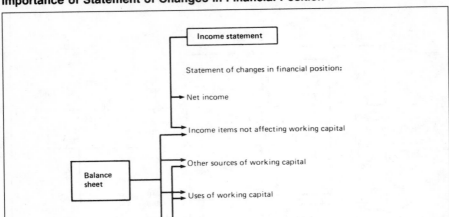

The importance of the statement of changes in relation to the other financial statements is best seen in Figure 7-2. To a greater extent than any other financial statement, the statement of changes is fed by and flows into each of the other basic financial statements. Using the prior year's balance sheet and the income statement, it is usually possible to create a current balance sheet and statement of stockholders' equity. The interrelationship of the financial statements demonstrates the primacy of the statement of changes and also reinforces the importance of viewing the financial statements as an interdependent unit rather than as individual perspectives of financial performance.

The Statement of Stockholders' Equity

The statement of stockholders' equity depicts the net worth of the corporation. Stockholders' equity is the residual of assets, less liabilities, at the values presented in the financial statements. It should not be confused with the value of the company, since the two figures can be quite different. There are often substantial disparities between the traded market value of publicly held companies and their stockholders' equity, or book value.

The significance of stockholders' equity varies according to the group looking at the figures:

- To creditors, stockholders' equity represents a safety cushion, since it shows the amount by which assets exceed liabilities.
- To shareholders, stockholders' equity represents the net investment in the company, and it reflects the original cost of their stock and retained earnings. The amount of stockholders' equity is often referred to as the capitalization of the company.
- To potential investors, stockholders' equity represents the net cost of entering into the business, at historical accounting costs. To the extent that the cost to potential investors of acquiring an interest in the company exceeds this amount or their pro rata share, stockholders' equity is often deemed to represent the downside risk of their investment.

The stockholder is more directly affected by transactions recorded in the statement of stockholders' equity than by those recorded in any other financial statement. Following are some examples of transactions recorded in the statement of stockholders' equity and their significance to stockholders:

- Changes in stockholders' equity normally result from earnings, losses, dividends, and changes in the number of shares outstanding.
- Earnings performance is perhaps the single most important factor affecting the value of stock.
- Prices are often referred to in terms of a multiple of earnings.
- Dividends and other distributions are the only cash flows that the stockholder receives from the company.
- Changes in the number of shares outstanding can signal changes in ownership control and dilution of ownership and/or earnings.

The statement of stockholders' equity reveals how the company is funding operations, exclusive of debt. It is important to note whether a company is building up its balance sheet (i.e., increasing net worth) as a result of profitable operations or through issuance of additional stock. The latter situation could indicate an inability of the company to fund operations internally, and the need to continue to issue additional stock in the future. Dividend payments may be evidence of superior earning capacity producing excess cash not required for reinvestment, or they may result from a policy necessitating periodic dividend distributions that essentially amount to non-tax-deductible expenses. Average after-tax corporate returns on equity have generally ranged between 15 percent and 18 percent in recent years. It would therefore seem more economical to reinvest earnings in productive projects than to provide taxable dividend distributions on which investors normally earn less on a pretax basis. Many profitable companies that have been superior performers in the stock market pay few or no dividends. Consider the example in Table 7-7.

TABLE 7-7

**Net Economic Benefit to Shareholders of
Alternative Dividend Policies**

	Dividend	No dividend
Pro rata income	$ 100	$ 100
Corporate income tax	50	50
Pro rata net income	50	50
Dividend	50	—
Individual income tax	25	—
Available for investment	$ 25 (a)	$ 50 (b)
Pretax return	8%	30%
Pretax income	$2.00	$15.00
Applicable tax	1.00	7.50
Economic benefit	$1.00	$ 7.50

(a) Available to individual
(b) Available to company

This example shows actual amounts experienced by corporations and investors. Obviously, the no-dividend policy provides the greatest benefit to shareholders.

Defining the Basis for Presentation

Financial statements can be prepared for any economic unit. This can include a single product, product line, department, division, subsidiary, geographical region, company, industry, or the entire national economy. The ease of preparing financial statements will depend on the availability and quality of underlying data. Often, the needed data is unavailable or requires so many assumptions as to be of dubious reliability. Competitor and industry profiles are frequently difficult to compile since most companies are privately owned and thus are not required to disclose financial information publicly. This is the case for small segments of some publicly held companies as well. Frequently, the financial data that is available fails to reveal the data needed. When preparing an analysis of how a company's labor costs compare to those of competing companies, for example, the preparer may find that even if the competitors publicly disclose financial data, their labor costs are buried in the costs of sales and general and administrative expenses. Efforts to obtain such data should not be discouraged, since some information is better than none. There are often industry trade groups or data services that compile industry data. However, intracompany data generally is easier to secure than data from other companies.

In compiling data for a portion of a corporate entity, the question of allocating common costs arises. Overhead costs may be allocated among businesses on the basis of relative sales, assets, units of production, net investment, square footage of occupancy, or number of employees, to name a few of the commonly used methods. Each form of allocation is likely to produce different financial results. The results may vary so widely that they make a difference between whether a product seems profitable or not profitable. Business decisions and management bonuses are often based on information generated, in part, using allocated costs. The cost allocation system can therefore have significant strategic and behavioral implications. There is no simple solution for the complicated issue of cost allocation. As a general rule, however, cost allocations should be designed to be both equitable and useful.

The use to which a financial statement will be put is an important factor in deciding on the amount of detail to be included in the statement. The format of financial data distributed externally is usually governed by GAAP and/or regulatory requirements. However, the format and the amount of detail in internal financial statements should be designed to facilitate decision making. The nature and content of financial information depends on the audience. The president of a diversified company may only require financial statements that provide an overview of the results of each business segment, while the executive in charge of the business segment may require much more detailed segmental financial data. Financial data should clarify rather than to obfuscate financial performance. It should be informative rather than exhaustive, and it should be user-oriented rather than accountant-oriented.

Another important issue in planning financial statements is distinguishing between variable costs (also referred to as incremental, marginal, or out-of-pocket costs), fixed costs, and total costs. Variable costs include only the costs of additional output, while fixed costs remain constant on a short-term basis, and are unaffected by output. Total costs reflect the combined total of fixed and variable costs. As long as the revenues derived from each incremental unit of production exceed the variable cost, it can be profitable to pursue production.

For example, suppose an opportunity exists to use excess capacity to produce for a variable cost of $1.75 per unit an item the company can sell for $2. If the cost allocation system would normally allocate $0.30 of fixed costs to each unit of production, the total cost per unit would be $2.05, seemingly making this an unprofitable item to produce. However, since fixed costs are unaffected by whether or not one elects to produce the item, it is evident that producing the $2 item will result in an incremental profit of $0.25 for each unit of production that the company would not otherwise realize. In this case, variable costing and total costing provide mixed signals that could lead to conflicting managerial decisions. For opportunities that arise to employ unused capacity, incremental analysis may lead to valuable business opportunities.

A final issue to consider in planning financial statements is the impact of changing prices and costs. For example, the fact that a company's sales have doubled in the last ten years is hardly praiseworthy if inflation has increased by 150 percent in the same period. If inflation is relatively modest, then historical financial data provides a useful benchmark for comparing annual results. However, in highly inflationary periods, annual comparisons can be almost meaningless.

Three methods of accounting have been developed to reflect the impact of changing prices: general price level accounting, current value accounting, and replacement cost accounting. General price level accounting is required as an additional disclosure of all large publicly held companies meeting certain financial criteria. Under this method, adjustments are made to certain assets, liabilities, and income statement items so that they may be presented on a common price level basis, as determined through the application of the Consumer Price Index for All Urban Consumers. Current value accounting and replacement cost accouting purport to do the same thing, except they use current values and replacement costs, respectively, as their measurement benchmark. Differences between earnings reported according to these methods and historical earnings constitute the gains and losses attributable to price level changes.

These methods are useful in that they provide a means of presenting financial data in a manner that will diffuse the impact of inflation. Nevertheless, they have been slow to receive general acceptance, due to the difficulty of identifying appropriate benchmarks that fairly and accurately reflect changing prices on a uniform basis. Historical-dollar financial statements have the advantages of being relatively straightforward and more easily verifiable. They adhere more closely to basic accounting theory, and their cash-flow patterns are based on realized transactions. Furthermore, the majority of assets and liabilities in most companies reflect fairly current costs, and are accordingly valued close to current price levels. As long as most managers have been trained in and are accustomed to using historical-dollar financial statements, and as long as there are tolerable levels of inflation, there will be a reluctance to embrace accouting methods that reflect inflation.

FINANCIAL RATIO ANALYSIS

Financial statements report the aggregate results of operations and financial conditions of a company at a specific point in time. Absolute numbers can signal important trends or can provide material for public relations releases (for example, "We are proud to announce that during the past year, total sales for our company exceeded one hundred million dollars"). However, by themselves, the numbers have limited significance. Raw financial data is of little value unless there is a frame of reference in which to view it. Financial ratio analysis provides that frame of reference.

We intuitively perform financial ratio analysis any time we read a financial statement. Relationships among accounts that are noticed or trends that are observed are forms of nonquantitative financial ratio analysis. The more formal procedure of financial ratio analysis provides a basis for enhancing or supplanting intuitive judgment.

Financial ratio analysis can be used to compare the current year's financial data to that of prior years or future years, competitors on an individual or aggregate basis, or businesses within an entire industry. Within a company, it can be used to evaluate the performance of divisions, subsidiaries, departments, product lines, or individual products. Since it is based on ratios rather than on absolute numbers, financial ratio analysis mitigates the problem of comparing business units of different sizes. The basic categories of financial ratios include composition ratios, liquidity ratios, leverage ratios, activity ratios, profitability ratios, and trend analysis. They are each described in the following sections, with sample computations shown in Tables 7-8 and 7-9 using financial data from XYZ Corporation in Tables 7-1 through 7-4.

Composition Ratios

The first step in performing any financial ratio analysis is to break down the balance sheet and income statement into their component parts. In breaking down the balance sheet, determine the percentage that each asset comprises of total assets, and the percentage of total liabilities and stockholders' equity represented by each item on the right side of the balance sheet. The income statement is broken down by calculating the percent of total sales that each expense and miscellaneous item constitutes.

Composition ratios are an excellent method for placing all firms on a similar scale. Irrespective of the sizes of the companies that are being compared, the sum of each category of accounts cannot exceed 100 percent.

Composition ratios highlight the relative magnitude of each asset account and indicate the proportional financing of total assets provided by each category of liabilities and of stockholders' equity. This type of analysis helps to isolate the reasons for shifts in profitability. There is no better tool for initiating the analysis of financial statements.

Composition ratios can also be used to develop common-size financial statements. Common-size financial statements make it easier to detect differences among units for which composition ratios have been calculated by placing them on the same scale. These statements can be developed by applying the composition ratios of another company to financial data of the company being analyzed, as shown in Table 7-10.

TABLE 7-8

Financial Ratio Analysis of XYZ Corporation

Ratio	Components	Amounts as of or for year ended December 31, 1990 (in dollars)	Financial ratio
Liquidity ratios			
Current	$\dfrac{\text{Current assets}}{\text{Current liabilities}}$	$\dfrac{8,667,222}{4,604,220}$	1.9
Quick	$\dfrac{\text{Current assets} - \text{Inventory}}{\text{Current liabilities}}$	$\dfrac{8,667,222 - 4,018,627}{4,604,220}$	1.0
Leverage ratios			
Debt	$\dfrac{\text{Total debt}}{\text{Total assets}}$	$\dfrac{8,358,245}{15,009,313}$	0.56
Debt/equity	$\dfrac{\text{Total debt}}{\text{Equity}}$	$\dfrac{8,358,245}{6,651,068}$	1.26
Long-term debt/equity	$\dfrac{\text{Long-term debt}}{\text{Equity}}$	$\dfrac{3,450,000}{6,651,068}$	0.52
Times interest earned	$\dfrac{\text{Earnings before interest and taxes}}{\text{Interest}}$	$\dfrac{1,651,827 + 496,924}{496,924}$	4.3
Activity ratios			
Accounts receivable turnover	$\dfrac{\text{Credit sales}}{\text{Average accounts receivable}}$	$\dfrac{22,579,488}{(3,727,018 + 3,129,256)/2}$	6.6
Average collection period	$\dfrac{\text{Average accounts receivable}}{\text{Credit sales}} \times 365$	$\dfrac{(3,727,018 + 3,129,256)/2}{22,579,488} \times 365$	55.4 days
Inventory turnover	$\dfrac{\text{Cost of goods sold}}{\text{Average inventory}}$	$\dfrac{16,121,754}{(4,018,627 + 3,254,508)/2}$	4.4
Days' sales in inventory	$\dfrac{\text{Inventory}}{\text{Cost of goods sold}} \times 365$	$\dfrac{(4,018,627 + 3,254,508)/2}{16,121,754}$	82.3 days

Working capital turnover

$$\frac{\text{Sales}}{\text{Average working capital}} \quad \frac{22,579,488}{(4,063,002 + 3,684,954)/2} \quad 5.8$$

Working capital per dollar's sales

$$\frac{\text{Average working capital}}{\text{Sales}} \quad \frac{(4,063,002 + 3,684,954)/2}{22,579,488} \quad 0.17$$

Fixed asset turnover

$$\frac{\text{Sales}}{\text{Average net fixed assets}} \quad \frac{22,579,488}{(4,019,614 + 3,241,828)/2} \quad 6.2$$

Fixed assets employed for each sales dollar

$$\frac{\text{Average net fixed assets}}{\text{Sales}} \quad \frac{(4,019,614 + 3,241,828)/2}{22,579,488} \quad \$0.16$$

Total asset turnover

$$\frac{\text{Sales}}{\text{Average total assets}} \quad \frac{22,579,488}{(15,009,313 + 12,696,801)/2} \quad 1.5$$

Total assets employed for each sales dollar

$$\frac{\text{Average total assets}}{\text{Sales}} \quad \frac{(15,009,313 + 12,696,801)/2}{22,579,488} \quad \$0.61$$

Profitability ratios

Profit margin

$$\frac{\text{Net income}}{\text{Sales}} \quad \frac{1,149,035}{22,579,488} \quad 5.1\%$$

Return on investment (ROI)

$$\frac{\text{Net income}}{\text{Average stockholders' equity}} \quad \frac{1,149,035}{(6,651,068 + 5,817,533)/2} \quad 18.4\%$$

Return on assets (ROA)

$$\frac{\text{Net income}}{\text{Average net assets}} \quad \frac{1,149,035}{(15,009,313 + 12,696,801)/2} \quad 8.3\%$$

Return on capital employed (ROCE)

$$\frac{\text{Net income}}{\text{Average long-term debt and stockholders' equity}} \quad \frac{1,149,035}{(10,101,068 + 8,392,533)/2} \quad 12.4\%$$

TABLE 7-9

Composition Ratios of XYZ Corporation

	1990	1989
Balance Sheet (percentage of total assets)		
Assets		
Cash	4.0%	7.4%
Accounts receivable (net)	24.8	24.6
Inventory	26.8	25.6
Other current assets	2.1	3.2
	57.7%	60.9%
Fixed assets, net	27.4	25.5
Investments	4.7	—
Goodwill	3.2	4.0
Other assets	7.0	9.6
	100.0%	100.0%
Liabilities and stockholders' equity		
Notes payable	3.1%	2.5%
Current maturities, long-term debt	3.5	2.6
Accounts payable	16.8	18.3
Accrued expenses	7.3	8.5
	30.7%	31.9%
Long-term debt	32.0	20.3
Other liabilities	2.0	2.0
	55.7%	54.2%
Stockholders' equity	44.3	45.8
	100.0%	100.0%
Income Statement (percentage of sales)		
Net sales	100.0%	100.0%
Cost of goods sold	(71.4)	(69.7)
Gross profit	28.6%	30.3%
General and administrative expenses	(11.7)	(12.7)
Selling expenses	(8.2)	(7.9)
Operating profit	8.7%	9.7%
Interest expense	(2.2)	(1.9)
Other income	0.8	—
Pretax income	7.3%	7.8%
Income taxes	(2.2)	(3.1)
Net income	5.1%	4.7%

TABLE 7-10

Using Composition Ratios to Develop a Common-Size Income Statement
(dollars in thousands)

Description	Composition ratios (%) XYZ Corporation	AB Corporation	Common size income statement AB Corporation
Net sales	$22,579	100.0	$22,579
Cost of goods sold	16,122	68.1	15,376
Gross profit	$ 6,457	31.9	$ 7,203
Selling, general and administrative expenses	4,493	22.6	5,103
Operating profit	$ 1,964	9.3	$ 2,100
Other expenses (net)	312	1.2	271
Pretax income	$ 1,652	8.1	$ 1,829
Income taxes	503	3.3	745
Net income	$ 1,149	4.8	$ 1,084

Liquidity Ratios

Survival is the most important objective of any company. Before the company can focus its attention on other plans and objectives, financial obligations must be met. Liquidity refers to the ability of a company to convert short-term assets to cash. Liquidity ratios measure the degree to which liquid assets are available to meet current obligations.

Current Ratio

Current assets
Current liabilities

The current ratio measures the relationship between current assets and current liabilities, which together are considered working capital. Current assets, which include cash, marketable securities, accounts receivable, and inventory, represent the most liquid assets of a firm. They are the assets from which cash most likely will be realized within a reasonably short period of time, and thus they are the most likely candidates to satisfy current liabilities. The higher the current ratio, the more liquid the company is said to be.

It would seem that a high current ratio is a desirable attribute. This is true only to a point. Although a high current ratio provides a measure of financial security, maintaining a needlessly high current ratio may reflect poor management of working capital. Most current assets earn little if any return, and they all have implicit, if not explicit, costs. It can be costly to tie too much into working capital.

A comparatively low current ratio should not automatically be construed as a negative attribute. There are many companies that thrive with barely enough current assets to satisfy current liabilities. They are able to do so if their current assets are highly liquid and can be converted into cash rapidly when current liabilities come due.

Quick Ratio or "Acid Test" Measurement

$$\frac{\text{Current assets} - \text{Inventory}}{\text{Current liabilities}}$$

The quick ratio or acid test is similar to the current ratio except that it excludes inventory. (Some applications will also exclude certain nonliquid receivables.) It is called the quick ratio because it includes only those current assets that can quickly be converted to cash. The reason for excluding inventory is that it is generally considered less liquid than other current assets. While cash is the most liquid type of asset and receivables normally represent legal obligations to pay cash, inventories depend on successful sales efforts and cannot always be disposed of above cost. Many financially troubled companies have excellent current ratios only because large amounts of unsalable inventory are on hand.

Leverage Ratios

Leverage ratios measure the relative amount of leverage, or debt, employed and the ability of the firm to meet its financial obligations. The two issues are interrelated, since the degree to which leverage is employed affects the fixed annual obligations.

Debt Ratio

$$\frac{\text{Total debt}}{\text{Total assets}}$$

This ratio is an overall measure of leverage employed. The left side of the balance sheet represents total assets, and the right side of the balance sheet shows how the left side is financed. The debt ratio calculates the proportion of the left side that is financed by debt.

It would seem to be desirable to have a low debt ratio. This is certainly true to the extent that it implies less risk. The more debt employed, the greater the fixed costs of interest and principal payments. However, this rationale overlooks the benefits that result from prudent use of equity. By "trading on the equity," it is possible to use leverage to help finance a company rather than to surrender control. This approach has been popular, and in several instances has been profitable, in the recent wave of leveraged buyouts, in which companies have been acquired almost exclusively through use of debt. Because debt is a tax-deductible expenditure, 14 percent debt costs 7 percent after taxes. This is often the least expensive form of financing.

Debt/Equity Ratio

$$\frac{\text{Total debt}}{\text{Total stockholders' equity}}$$

This ratio directly compares the two sources of business financing: debt and stockholders' equity, including preferred stock.

Long-Term Debt/Equity Ratio

$$\frac{\text{Long-term debt}}{\text{Total stockholders' equity}}$$

This approach measures the relationship among the two sources of capitalization for a business: long-term debt and equity. They comprise the "permanent" funding of a business. Short-term or seasonal needs funded by current liabilities are not deemed to be permanent funding.

The value of the business is often viewed as being the sum of the values of long-term debt and equity. To some extent these represent financing alternatives, because a business can normally be started or purchased using some combination of long-term debt and equity. Other common methods of assessing capitalization are to calculate long-term debt as a percentage of total capitalization or to calculate long-term equity as a percentage of total capitalization.

Times Interest Earned Ratio

$$\frac{\text{Earnings before interest and taxes (EBIT)}}{\text{Interest}}$$

Since periodic interest payments must be made when debt is assumed, interest expenses must be taken into account in the context of total pretax earnings. Income taxes normally are assessed only if net earnings exist after interest expenses. Interest expenses are therefore computed on a pretax basis, because the capability to pay interest is not affected by taxes. In the times interest earned ratio, a high multiple indicates that the company has demonstrated a considerble ability to pay interest, and there is substantial leeway in the amount that EBIT can decline before the company risks being unable to make required interest payments. It also is an important indication of a company's ability to secure bank financing.

Activity Ratios

Activity ratios, also known as turnover ratios or funds management ratios, measure the efficiency of working capital and fixed-asset use and management. Each activity ratio analyzes the relationship between an annual sales figure and an annual average of a balance sheet item or items. Annual averages are generally computed by calculating the average of beginning and year-end balances.

Accounts Receivable Turnover Ratio

$$\frac{\text{Credit sales}}{\text{Average accounts receivable}}$$

In what is gradually becoming a cashless society, the biggest source of cash for most businesses is accounts receivable. To some extent, sales and income, although recorded as accounts receivable on an accrual basis, are academic until receivables have been collected and cash has been received. Since accounts receivable are normally non-income-generating, and the financing of receivables may be expensive, it is important to collect receivables as promptly as possible. This is measured by the accounts receivable turnover ratio, which calculates the number of times that receivables "turn" annually.

It is generally more desirable to have a high receivable turnover figure than a low one. The exception to this statement is when a high turnover ratio is achieved because only the highest-quality credit risks were accepted, and several profitable opportunities of lesser quality were forgone. Also, analysis of an accounts receivable turnover ratio does not negate the need for analyzing accounts receivable in detail. It is possible that many of the accounts receivable currently outstanding were also uncollected as of the end of the previous fiscal year. An aging of accounts receivable, in which receivables are categorized according to length of time outstanding (e.g., less than 30 days; 30 to 60 days; 60 to 90 days; 90 to 180 days; and more than 180 days) is a good initial means of identifying problem accounts.

Average Collection Period Ratio

$$\frac{\text{Average accounts receivable}}{\text{Credit sales}} \times 365$$

This ratio converts the average collection period for accounts receivable into a figure expressed in terms of days. This figure is the multiplicative inverse of the accounts receivable turnover period times 365 days in a year. For example, if the accounts receivable turnover ratio were 6, then the average collection period would be approximately 60 days ($360 \div 6$).

Inventory Turnover Ratio

Cost of goods sold
Average inventory

Inventory, like accounts receivable, should be "moved" as quickly as possible. The costs of carrying inventory include financing, record keeping, storage, display, insurance, and losses due to damage, obsolescence, and theft.

Unlike the accounts receivable turnover ratio and other turnover ratios that use sales in the numerator, the inventory turnover ratio uses cost of goods sold in its numerator. This is because inventory is stated at cost; therefore, the volume figure that is used to express turnover—cost of sales —should also be stated at cost rather than at retail. The sales figure is often used in the numerator, which is incorrect, since it overstates turnover.

Normally, a high turnover figure is desirable. However, a few cautions are in order. Where companies that are being compared use different methods of valuing inventory (e.g., first in, first out vs. last in, first out), their turnover ratios may not be comparable. Seasonal fluctuations in inventory levels may make year-end balances nonrepresentative of balances that normally exist during the year. It may be more appropriate to use quarterly or monthly balances to calculate averages for purposes of estimating turnover ratios.

If a high turnover ratio is achieved because only high-volume items are in stock while profitable slower-moving items are not stocked, the high turnover figure may conceal the profitable opportunities that have been lost. Also, irrespective of turnover ratios, an analysis and aging of inventory should be done to ensure that the inventory is current and salable.

Days' Sales in Inventory Ratio

$$\frac{Inventory}{Cost\ of\ goods\ sold} \times 365$$

This ratio indicates the number of days' sales, based on annual sales volume, present in inventory at a specific time. It is not the same thing as the multiplicative inverse of the inventory turnover ratio multiplied by 365, since this measure is based on a year-end balance rather than on average annual balances. This ratio is a tool for management planning and for operations areas such as reordering inventory as well as being a measure of efficiency.

Since different lines of inventory are likely to move at different rates, this ratio should be calculated separately for each product line.

Working Capital Turnover Ratio

Sales
Average working capital

This measure is difficult to evaluate. A financially strong company with large cash balances may have a low working capital turnover ratio, whereas a financially distressed firm with a narrow margin of working capital may have an exceedingly high working capital turnover ratio. Notwithstanding the two extremes, it can generally be said that a high working capital turnover ratio is better than a low one.

Working Capital per Dollar's Sales Ratio

$$\frac{\text{Average working capital}}{\text{Sales}}$$

This ratio is the multiplicative inverse of the working capital turnover ratio, and is subject to the same limitations.

Fixed Asset Turnover Ratio

$$\frac{\text{Sales}}{\text{Average net fixed assets}}$$

The fixed asset turnover ratio is used primarily as an indicator of the productivity of net fixed assets employed. The various gradations can indicate whether a company or an entire industry is capital intensive. Its inherent limitation as an evaluation tool is that companies vary in depreciation policies, purchase/lease preferences, and average plant age, which can have a substantial impact on the cost shown for the plant.

Fixed Assets Employed for Each Sales Dollar Ratio

$$\frac{\text{Average net fixed assets}}{\text{Sales}}$$

This ratio is the reverse of the fixed asset turnover ratio.

Total Asset Turnover Ratio

$$\frac{\text{Sales}}{\text{Average total assets}}$$

The total asset turnover ratio measures how asset intensive a business is and the efficiency of total assets employed.

Total Assets Employed for Each Sales Dollar Ratio

$$\frac{\text{Average total assets}}{\text{Sales}}$$

This is the reverse of the total asset turnover ratio.

Profitability Ratios

Profits are the focus of most financial analysis. Each of the financial ratios discussed previously is intended to enhance decision making in order to improve profits. The financial ratios that follow are those that relate most explicitly to profits.

Profit Margin Ratio

$$\frac{\text{Net income}}{\text{Sales}}$$

The profit margin is a common bench mark often used to characterize the profitability of a business. It refers to the percentage of each sales dollar that filters to the bottom line. A high profit margin is more desirable than a low one, and is one attribute of a lucrative business. It allows the luxury of occasional mistakes, which are likely to be less damaging than in a low-margin business where errors can result in red ink. The downside risk is usually less in a high-profit business than in a low-profit business.

The profit margin cannot be regarded as an entirely independent measure of performance. Before making any conclusions based on profit margins, it is important to analyze the contributing factors. In reviewing the financial statements and analyzing the composition ratios described earlier, it may become evident that superior profit margins are the result of a single event that is unlikely to recur in future years. Another factor to consider is turnover. A company earning an 8 percent profit margin on inventory that only "turns" once a year will earn less than a company earning 4 percent on inventory that "turns" three times annually. It is desirable to have a high profit margin, but it should be understood, analyzed, and placed in a proper context before any conclusions are drawn.

Return on Investment Ratio

$$\frac{\text{Net income}}{\text{Average stockholders' equity}}$$

Also known as return on equity, this is the most significant profitability yardstick employed. Return on investment (ROI) is a valuable management tool because it provides a basis for dissecting profits and isolating factors that can lead to profit improvement. It is also a valuable tool for investors because it identifies the rate of return on their net investment and provides a good base for comparing alternative investments.

The benefits of ROI analysis become evident when it is broken down into its component parts, as follows:

Operating Factors

$$\frac{\text{Pretax income}}{\text{Sales}} \times \frac{\text{Sales}}{\text{Average total assets}} \times$$

Nonoperating Factors

$$\frac{\text{Average total assets}}{\text{Average stockholders' equity}} \times (1 - \text{Tax rate}) = \text{ROI}$$

The operating factors—the pretax profit margin and the total assets turnover ratio—are those that relate to annual business operations, which management can most readily effect changes upon. ROI can be increased by improving the pretax profit margin (for example, by increasing prices or reducing expenses) or by improving the efficiency of asset usage. The asset usage issue, or turnover, referred to in the discussion of profit margins can be more clearly seen in the ROI analysis. It shows why a grocery store, for example, with assets turning over every few weeks, can be much more profitable than an art gallery requiring a similar investment, in which assets may turn over only once or twice annually.

The nonoperating factors are less easily controlled by management, but they can have a substantial impact upon ROI. The ratio of total assets to stockholders' equity reflects the net investment in the business, exclusive of financing, and is less subject to annual fluctuations. All other things being equal, a highly leveraged business will have a higher ROI than one that is well capitalized.

The final nonoperating factor to come into play is the tax rate. This aspect of the equation results in the net income after taxes. Since this amount is greatly affected by tax rates, management should arrange good tax planning in order to minimize the tax bite taken from pretax income.

ROI may vary substantially from company to company depending upon the capital structures of the companies involved. As shown in Table 7-11, two companies that are otherwise identical can have vastly differing ROIs as a result of their respective capital structures.

The ROI of a rapidly growing company will often show a steady decline even though sales and earnings are growing at a record pace. This frequently occurs simply because in the early stages the company was undercapitalized; adding earnings to a low equity base causes the ROI seemingly to skyrocket. The more normal but depressed ROI figures that result from a better capitalized position should not be viewed negatively unless they lag behind industry averages.

Return on Assets Ratio

$$\frac{\text{Net income}}{\text{Average total assets (net)}}$$

An alternative to ROI is to ignore the capital structure of a business

TABLE 7-11

Return on Investment Based on Alternative Capital Structures

	Company A	Company B
Capital structure		
Debt	—	$ 50,000,000
Equity (1)	$100,000,000	50,000,000
Operating results		
Sales	$120,000,000	$120,000,000
Operating profit	30,000,000	30,000,000
Interest	—	6,000,000
Pretax income	$ 30,000,000	$ 24,000,000
Income tax	15,000,000	12,000,000
Net income (2)	$ 15,000,000	$ 12,000,000
Return on investment ((2) ÷ (1))	15%	24%

and simply to focus on the return on assets. The rationale for this approach is that the instrinsic profitability is unaffected by the method of financing. The financing method is simply a discretionary decision of management. The return on assets (ROA) ratio calculates a return on every asset employed in the business rather than only focusing on stockholders' equity. It is useful for identifying companies that have comparatively low returns on assets but appear attractive only because they are highly leveraged or undercapitalized, and as a result have a high ROI.

The problem with ROA is that the capital structure of a business should not be ignored, since it is an aspect of the business that cannot readily be modified. To focus strictly on ROA could lead to overlooking attractive investments in real estate, banking, or leveraged buyouts, which can have a low ROA but can be profitable in terms of ROI simply because of their susceptibility to leveraging. The best use of ROA is in conjunction with ROI and the other financial tools described in this chapter.

Return on Capital Employed Ratio

$$\frac{\text{Net income}}{\text{Average long-term debt and stockholders' equity}}$$

Return on capital employed (ROCE) is probably the best measure of the basic profitability of a business under the capital structure that is in place. It recognizes that the capital structure is often a discretionary decision of management; therefore, the return is calculated using all of the capital resources in place.

If the effect of financing alternatives is completely eliminated from our analysis, ROCE can be shown as:

$$\frac{\text{EBIT}}{\text{Average long-term debt and stockholders' equity}}$$

This format does not include interest expenses on long-term debt (it should include interest on short-term debt), or income taxes and the tax benefits resulting from the interest deduction. Considering, however, that these are bona fide expenses, the first format of ROCE is more commonly used.

ROCE gives a better perspective of the intrinsic profitability of the business. When viewing the business from a macroeconomic perspective, ROCE is the best measure. However, investors are most concerned with the return on their own investment; therefore, ROI prevails.

Trend Analysis

Trend analysis involves analyzing financial data over a multiple-year period in order to observe trends that seem to be in progress. The value of the financial ratios described previously is only partially realized if the reader fails to see how they have evolved over time. Financial ratios are best used within a comparative framework, and there is no better bench mark for comparison than the company's performance in prior years.

Trend analysis should include data from at least two years, but preferably three to five years. The subject of the trend analysis should include some if not all of the financial ratios discussed previously, as well as the growth rates of each significant balance sheet and income statement item.

Many observations may emerge as trends are analyzed. As with other forms of ratio analysis, trends should be compared to industry data and even to overall economic data in order to assess their significance. Growth rates should be analyzed, and the base upon which growth is measured should be considered. For example, if a high rate of earnings growth appears only because earnings in the base year were at a comparative low point, then this factor would have to be noted and other measures of performance in addition to earnings growth would have to be considered.

Using Financial Ratios

The objective of financial ratio analysis is not to calculate them but to use them. After the ratios have been calculated and analyzed, and appropriate comparisons have been made, a clear picture of corporate financial performance and corporate financial condition should begin to emerge.

Financial ratios are a good starting point for analyzing a company's financial condition, but they do not provide solutions. They can highlight potential problems, but they cannot solve them. They can identify potential strengths, but they cannot show how to develop these strengths. The purposes of financial ratios are to place financial data in a meaningful context and to highlight areas requiring further investigation. As with financial statements, the valuable skill is not in their compilation but in their interpretation and application to the decision-making process.

FINANCIAL PROJECTIONS

Financial projections should draw on the collective judgment and knowledge of executives from all significant activities within a business, including marketing, production, personnel, accounting, and finance. Incorporating information from these sources with data developed through the application of sophisticated analytical and quantitative techniques can lead to projections of which one can be certain of one thing: that they will probably be wrong. Given this probable outcome, why bother?

Financial projections are critical tools for business planning. To be without some sort of financial projection is like traveling through unfamiliar territory without a map. Financial projections provide a reference point around which business plans can be made.

Financial projections are frequently used for planning:

- Capital requirements
- Dividend policy
- Plant expansion
- Product development
- Wage increases
- Acquisitions and divestitures
- Debt amortization
- Income tax status

They are also commonly distributed to bankers and creditors.

Financial projections should include the four basic financial statements as well as a projection of net cash receipts. (The format for projecting cash receipts is shown in Table 7-12.) Omitting any one of these financial statements can lead to significant errors. For example, to project cash flow without projecting a balance sheet and an income statement can result in an erroneous projection of working capital requirements. In practice, however, many if not most projections fail to include at least one or more of the basic financial statements. Whether this failure is out of ignorance or out of expediency is not clear. However, the omission increases the potential for inaccurate projections. The advent of the microcomputer and the many financial spreadsheet

TABLE 7-12
Sample Projection of Net Cash Receipts

XYZ CORPORATION
PROJECTION OF NET CASH RECEIPTS
For the Year Ended December 31, 1989

	1989
Sales	$26,000,000
Cost of goods sold	18,800,000
Gross profit	$ 7,200,000
General and administrative expenses	2,850,000
Selling expenses	2,125,000
Operating profit	$ 2,225,000
Interest expense	480,000
Income before taxes	$ 1,745,000
Income taxes	700,000
Net income	$ 1,045,000
Add:	
Depreciation and amortization	500,000
Deferred taxes	50,000
	$ 1,595,000
Repayment of long-term debt	(525,000)
Additions to property, plant, and equipment	(400,000)
Payment of cash dividends	(347,050)
Increase in working capital	$ 322,950
Working capital to be funded:	
Increase in accounts receivable	(300,000)
Increase in inventory	(275,000)
Increase in other current assets	(50,000)
Funding provided by current liabilities:	
Decrease in notes payable	(15,000)
Increase in current maturities of long-term debt	25,000
Increase in accounts payable and accrued expenses	325,000
Net cash receipts	$ 32,950

software packages has taken much of the tedium out of developing financial projections. This should contribute to higher-quality and more timely and thorough projections.

Financial projections should include, at the very least, quarterly projections for the next four quarters and an annual projection of the next fiscal year. They should be updated continuously as new data becomes available or as each quarter passes. Many companies have monthly projections as well as annual projections going as far as five years into the future. Granted, projections of more distant periods are less likely to conform closely with actual results; they are important because capital expenditures, production and sales planning often depend upon the profile of the business several years out.

Financial projections rival the religions of the world in the number of methods that have been devised and in the sincerity of their proponents. Each company must develop an approach toward developing and evaluating financial projections that is appropriate for the company's unique circumstances and for the purposes for which projections have been devised.

Projection methodologies run the gamut from being strictly judgmental to being entirely a function of statistical formulas. The degree of verification with outside sources of key assumptions such as interest growth rates and other macroeconomic data varies substantially among companies, as does the number of executives from various disciplines that are involved in the process. The thoroughness of the process undertaken to develop projections should depend upon the use(s) to which the projections will be put, the amount of accuracy required, and the business implications, or downside, of inaccurate projections. Considerably less effort may be required if the implications of inaccurate projections are unlikely to be disastrous. At the same time, readers should never lose sight of the fact that irrespective of the thoroughness of the process employed to develop projections, there will almost always be deviations between projected and actual performance.

The essential features of the financial projection process include:

- Determining the purpose of financial projections
- Identifying the target audience
- Selecting the required input and analytical tools
- Obtaining source data
- Developing a financial model and supporting algorithms
- Integrating input with financial model to produce preliminary projections
- Ascertaining the reasonableness of projected output
- Analyzing, evaluating, and revising projections until they are suitable for distribution
- Integrating projections with business plans and other uses to which they should be put
- Revising projections, projection techniques, and financial model as subsequent experience dictates is appropriate

Some of the analytical tools that are employed in the projection process include:

- *Trend analysis:* This tool involves developing economic and financial trends using quantifiable historical data, which is projected on a linear basis according to observation, moving averages, or statistical trend line analysis.

- *Regression and correlation:* Trends that are linear or curvilinear may be projected based on relationships between dependent and independent variables developed through regression or multiple regression analysis. In practical terms, all one needs to know about this tool is that it measures the desired relationship according to a stated degree of confidence, and that it can be done entirely on the computer or electronic calculator.

- *Time series analysis:* This type of analysis is based on the premise that some factors change more as a result of time than as a result of the interrelationship among variables. Projections are made on the basis of historical performance and the trends, cycles, seasonal patterns, and volatility to which historical performance was subject.

- *Research:* External data is obtained from published reference sources, on-line data bases, microeconomic and macroeconomic forecasting services, and surveys. Data obtained by these means become input to some of the other analytical tools. They are also a means by which further results can be evaluated.

- *Financial ratio analysis:* Projected financial data can often be evaluated, explained, or developed through the application of financial ratio analysis. This can also be a tool for plugging "holes" in the projections. For example, if sales are projected to be $40 million, and an appropriate sales/working capital ratio is deemed to be 0.35, then projected working capital could be $14 million; this could be further broken down according to composition ratio analysis of the balance sheet.

- *Mathematical algorithms:* Once projections of certain items have been established, other items will result as the product or sum of the projected inputs. For example, if projections have been made of personnel and compensation, labor expense will be the product of the two. Financial projections normally consist of a myriad of algorithms that generate the required financial statements. Several useful computer software packages have been developed for the microcomputer and the mainframe computer that can facilitate this process, and generate the required data promptly, while affording convenient manipulation and modification of data.

- *Simulation:* Analyzing alternative outcomes is critical to testing the validity of the model, its input and output, and its sensitivity to changes in certain variables. The final projections are often presented in a format that contains alternative scenarios that depict the worst case, best case, and expected results.

- *Judgment:* This is the most valuable tool of all those described.

It would be fruitless to attempt to provide a laundry list of areas requiring analysis in developing projections. Any general list would be incomplete, due to the unique attributes of every company. Examples of some of the areas that should be explored are presented in Figure 7-3.

FIGURE 7-3
Areas Affecting Financial Projections

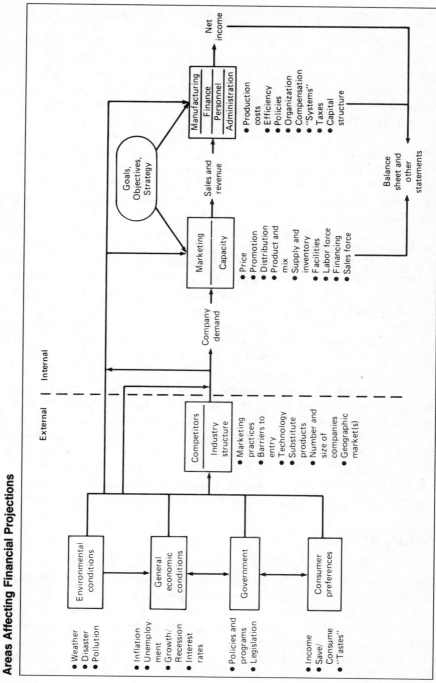
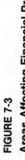

EVALUATING CAPITAL INVESTMENT OPPORTUNITIES

Four analytical tools are used to evaluate and prioritize capital investment opportunities: the payback method, average rate of return, net present value, and internal rate of return. These tools are discussed in detail in any corporate finance textbook. The purpose of this section is to highlight the essential features of each method and to demonstrate how the methods can be applied in financial analysis.

Each capital investment evaluation method is deterministic in the sense that it provides a single discrete number based entirely on financial projections and related assumptions. Given that financial projections are subject to a fair degree of uncertainty, problems can result from blind adherence to the output of the analytical method used. As with the results of any quantitative application, it is important that the results of cash-flow methods be analyzed and evaluated critically before they are used as a basis for decision making.

An essential premise of financial analysis is the existence of alternatives. Lacking alternatives, analysis is a moot exercise. For example, if the Environmental Protection Agency orders a factory to install a pollution control device and there is only one producer of the device, then there is no basis for making an analysis. If the device is not installed, the company goes out of business. As long as it is profitable to be in business, notwithstanding the cost of installing the equipment, then the company has no choice but to purchase the pollution control device.

To perform a worthwhile analysis, an investment alternative must have measurable results, and the results must be of sufficient magnitude to warrant the effort of conducting an analysis. Returns can be measured in terms of the incremental revenues generated, the costs saved, or a combination of the two. The factor that is evaluated is the net benefit of undertaking a project. In calculating the net benefit, the tax effects, disposal costs, and residual value of an investment all should be considered. An illustrative format for analyzing investment alternatives is shown in Table 7-13.

Payback Method

The payback method calculates how long it will take for an investment to generate enough cash to pay for itself. An investment should recoup its cost, and the sooner the better. If a $400,000 investment generates an annual cash flow of $100,000, then the payback period is four years. Using the example in Table 7-15, it is apparent that the payback occurs between the third and the fourth year (see Table 7-14). By interpolating to determine what portion of the fourth year's cash flows must be earned in order to attain the payback, it can be seen that by adding 0.42 of cash flows for the

TABLE 7-13

Format for Analyzing Investment Alternatives—Project Q

	1990	1991	1992	1993	1994
Investment cost					
Purchase price	$ 281,046				
Less: Investment tax credit	(18,746)				
Proceeds from sale of asset to be replaced	(15,000)				
Trade-in allowance on asset to be replaced	—				
Debt incurred to finance purchase (a)	—				
Add: Recapture of depreciation and ITC on asset to be replaced	3,085				
Installation costs	2,400				
	$ 252,785				
Investment benefits (b)					
Incremental revenues	$ 18,000	$ 21,000	$ 24,000	$ 27,000	$ 30,000
Net cost reductions	57,443	75,443	98,443	121,443	145,443
	$ 75,443	$ 96,443	$ 122,443	$ 148,443	$ 175,443
Less: Cost increases					
Depreciation	(50,557)	(50,557)	(50,557)	(50,557)	(50,557)
Interest (a)	—	—	—	—	—
Pretax benefit	$ 24,886	$ 45,886	$ 71,886	$ 97,886	$ 124,886
Income tax	(12,443)	(22,943)	(35,943)	(48,943)	(62,443)
Incremental income	$ 12,443	$ 22,943	$ 35,943	$ 48,943	$ 62,443
Add: Depreciation	50,557	50,557	50,557	50,557	50,557
Net proceeds from disposal/terminal value	—	—	—	—	12,000
Less: Debt repayment (a)	—	—	—	—	—
Net increase in working capital	3,000	3,500	4,000	4,500	5,000
Net investment benefit	$ 60,000	$ 70,000	$ 82,500	$ 95,000	$ 120,000

(a) Many practitioners analyze investments independently from financing costs.
(b) For new business ventures, the format shown in Table 7-12 is preferable, provided that a terminal value is included.

TABLE 7-14

Calculation of Payback Period—Project Q

	Net investment awaiting payback, beginning (a)	Net investment benefit (a)	Net investment awaiting payback, year-end	Contribution to payback period (years)
1990	$252,785	$ 60,000	$192,785	1.00
1991	192,785	70,000	122,785	1.00
1992	122,785	82,500	40,285	1.00
1993	40,285	95,000	—	0.42
1994	—	120,000	—	—

Payback period 3.42 years

(a) From Table 7-13

fourth year to the cumulative total from the preceding years, the investment is paid back.

The payback method provides an easy bench mark to evaluate an investment opportunity. It is simple and easy to apply and comprehend. Payback once enjoyed broad usage, and it is still part of the common parlance. Rules of thumb that are still applied include the adage that if the investment pays for itself within four to seven years, it is worth exploring.

The problem with the payback method is that is does not measure the effect of the timing or trends of cash flows. In the example shown in Table 7-15, two investment opportunities have a payback of exactly four years, and would therefore be judged as equal according to the payback method. The first alternative provides minimal cash flows in the first three years, a balloon payment in the fourth year, and begins to lose money shortly thereafter. The second alternative provides proportionally more cash flows in

TABLE 7-15

The Deficiency of the Payback Method

	Alternative 1		Alternative 2	
	Net cash flow	Cumulative cash flow	Net cash flow	Cumulative cash flow
Initial investment	$(100)	$(100)	$(100)	$(100)
Net cash flow:				
Year 1	5	(95)	20	(80)
Year 2	5	(90)	30	(50)
Year 3	5	(85)	25	(25)
Year 4	85	0	25	0
Year 5	0	0	40	40
Year 6	(10)	(10)	70	110
Year 7	$ (15)	(25)	95	205
Payback period	4 years		4 years	

TABLE 7-16

Calculation of Average Rate of Return—Project Q

	Incremental net income (a)	Net investment beginning of year (a)	Depreciation	Net investment year end	Average net investment
1990	$ 12,443	$252,785	$(50,557)	202,228	$227,507
1991	22,943	202,228	(50,557)	151,671	176,949
1992	35,943	151,671	(50,557)	101,114	126,393
1993	48,943	101,114	(50,557)	50,557	75,835
1994	62,443	50,557	(50,557)	—	25,279
Total	$182,715				$631,963
	÷5				÷5
Average	$ 36,543				$126,393

$$\text{Average rate of return} = \frac{\text{Average incremental net income}}{\text{Average net investment}} = \frac{\$36,543}{\$126,393} = 28.9\%$$

(a) From Table 7-13

the early years, which could be reinvested in other worthwhile activities, and provides rapidly appreciating cash flows during the years after the project has achieved the payback. Although this is an extreme example, and any competent executive would clearly select the second alternative despite the first's being equally rated by the payback method, it illustrates two basic flaws in the payback method: It fails to consider the timing of cash flows and their trends after the payback period. In less extreme examples it can be difficult to assess the impact of the timing of cash flows.

A second flaw that the payback method shares with all of the other cash-flow analyses tools is that it fails to distinguish between alternatives on the basis of the magnitude of the net benefit and to relate that net benefit to the original project cost. A $100 project that pays for itself in one year is deemed to be superior to a $1 million project that pays for itself in two years, even though the latter will clearly be of greater significance to the business.

The best use of the payback method is as an initial screening tool to ferret out investment opportunities that clearly cannot pay for themselves within any reasonable time period. That accomplished, other investment tools should be employed.

Average Rate of Return Method

The average rate of return, sometimes referred to as the accounting rate of return, is defined as follows:

$$\text{Average rate of return} = \frac{\text{Average net income}}{\text{Net investment}}$$

An example of this calculation is shown in Table 7-16. The average rate of return is often preferred by accountants because it is based on the net income presented on financial statements. It is consistent with the earnings figures reported to shareholders and quoted by the financial news media. Senior executives concerned with investor responses to reported earnings performance often prefer analyses that highlight reported earnings performance, since they satisfy investors by selecting investments that maximize reported earnings. Finally, the average rate of return shares with the payback method the advantage of simplicity—it is fairly easy to calculate and it provides a single percentage measure that can be compared against other investment opportunities.

The primary disadvantage of the average rate of return is that it fails to focus on factors affecting cash flow other than those reflected in net income. Other elements of cash flow, such as repaying the principal on loans or deferred taxes, are entirely ignored. The average rate of return also relies too much on the outmoded premise that investors rely on reported earnings to the exclusion of cash-flow information and other related data. Contemporary investment theory indicates that the stock market regards cash flow to be more significant than reported earnings in pricing securities.

Another fundamental weakness of the average rate of return, as with the payback method, is that it fails to attach any weight to the timing of income generated. Earnings generated several years in the future are treated no differently from earnings or losses presently generated. A project that requires several years to generate satisfactory performance levels may appear to be no worse than one that provides an adequate return within a more immediate time period.

Net Present Value Method

The net present value (NPV) represents the difference between the net cash flows of an investment and its cost, calculated on a present value basis to reflect the time value of money. The investment costs are deducted from the projected net cash flow, which is discounted at a rate that reflects the weighted average of capital to be employed. The result is the NPV. The higher the NPV of investment, the more desirable the investment becomes from a financial perspective.

NPV is regarded by many practitioners as the preferred method of investment analysis. Many businesspeople prefer to make decisions based on a single numerical value rather than a somewhat more nebulous rate of return or payback period. NPV is conceptually perfect in the sense that it provides a precise value for an investment opportunity. If the assumptions are correct, the NPV is the single "correct" net value of an investment. The problem is that assumptions regarding future events underlying the projected investment benefits are educated estimates at best, and assumptions

TABLE 7-17

Calculation of Weighted Average Cost of Capital — Project Q

	Pretax cost of capital	Income tax benefit (1—tax)	After-tax cost of capital	Weighting	Weighted average cost of capital
Long-term debt	15%	(1—0.4)	9%	0.30	2.7
Preferred stock	14	—	14	0.20	2.8
Common stock	19	—	19	0.50	9.5
					15.0

regarding the cost of capital are not entirely straightforward. The uncertainty of projections is a weakness shared by each of the four methods of investment analysis; however, the issue of cost of capital is unique to NPV.

There is little controversy surrounding the cost of debt and the cost of preferred equity. The cost of debt is simply the rate of interest, adjusted for the tax deduction resulting from paying interest (calculated as pretax interest rate times (1-T), where T is incremental tax rate) and the cost of preferred stock is its dividend rate. Both calculations are shown in Table 7-17. The cost of common equity is somewhat less obvious, as demonstrated by the various interpretations shown in Table 7-18.

Proponents of each method swear that theirs is correct and have some justification for their beliefs. Fortunately, each method normally results in a cost of equity capital that is reasonably similar. The differences are further mitigated by the weighting process, whereby the incremental cost of each component of capital is weighted according to its proportional use in the capital structure employed in the investment (see Table 7-17).

Practitioners often have difficulty identifying the sources of capital used in calculating the weighted average cost of capital. This issue is more problematic when the amount of capital is small, and has no immediate effect on the capital structure of the company. An example is a project funded by the use of surplus cash. In such situations, the incremental market rates on the existing capital structure are used to calculate the weighted average cost of capital. Where the financial markets have been tapped to finance a transaction, the identification process is more direct. Any capital not attributable to long-term debt or preferred stock is normally regarded as equity capital.

The weighted average cost of capital resulting from these calculations becomes the discount rate used to determine the present value of the future cash flows. The resulting amount, less the original cost, is the NPV.

Table 7-19 shows the NPV of an investment at alternative discount rates. As expected, the higher the discount rate, the lower the NPV. The variation in the resultant calculations of NPV is an indication of the impor-

TABLE 7-18

Alternative Methods for Calculating Cost of Common Equity Capital

Method	Basis for calculation	Advantages	Disadvantages
Target rate of return ("hurdle rate")	Decision of senior management	• Management sets investment objectives • Simple	• Lack of precision • Unsubstantiatable
Risk adjusted rate of return	Risk-free rate of interest (e.g., 5-year U.S. Treasury notes) + risk premium (beta × incremental return for equity investments)(a)	• Conceptually perfect	• May be unrealistic • Difficult to precisely determine the "correct" inputs
Return on equity (ROE)	Net income ÷ average equity, normally calculated over a 3- to 5-year period	• Over time, cost of equity capital will approximate ROE • Simple	• Variability among companies due to different accounting policies • Results in vicious circle of replicating prior performance
Analysts' proxy	Company's incremental borrowing rate on long-term debt + 4 percent	• Simple	• Lack of precision
Investor expectations	Expected annual appreciation in value of company's stock + expected dividend rate	• Correlates total returns on equity investments with expectations of sources of equity capital	• Nearly impossible to project

(a) Beta is a measure of variability in the value of the company's common stock in relation to stock market fluctuations. A beta of 1.00 signifies consonance with stock market fluctuations, whereas a beta below 1.00 signifies less volatility and above 1.00 signifies more. The equity risk premium is normally deemed to be at least 5 percent.

TABLE 7-19

Calculation of Net Present Value at Alternative Discount Rates— Projection Q

	Net investment benefits (a)	Present value of net investment benefits at		
		15%	18%	21%
1990	$ 60,000	$ 52,174	$ 50,847	$ 49,587
1991	70,000	52,930	50,273	47,811
1992	82,500	54,245	50,212	46,569
1993	95,000	54,317	49,000	44,318
1994	120,000	59,661	52,453	46,265
Total		$ 273,327	$ 252,785	$ 234,550
Net investment		(252,785)	(252,785)	(252,785)
Net present value		$ 20,542	—	$ (18,235)

(a) From Table 7-13

tance of carefully calculating the weighted average cost of capital and performing the calculation of alternative discount rates to provide a relevant range of value.

Internal Rate of Return Method

In order to calculate the NPV it is necessary to calculate the cost of capital to determine the discount rate to be applied to future cash flows. The NPV varies depending on the cost of capital employed. Several answers can result if alternative discount rates are used. The internal rate of return (IRR) provides a single convenient quantitative measure of investment performance that eliminates the need to calculate the cost of capital. Many managers prefer using a single percentage rate of return resulting from IRR analysis that can be compared to other measures, such as cost of capital, investment "hurdle" rates (minimum rates of return required for an investment to be acceptable), and financial market rates. The IRR places investments of all sizes on common ground by providing a single percentage measure that can be used to compare them, instead of the absolute dollar amount provided by NPV.

The IRR is calculated through a reiterative process that determines the discount rate at which the NPV equals zero. Conceptually, this is arrived at on a trail-and-error basis. In the example shown in Table 7-12, the NPV is greater than zero at a discount rate of 15 percent. If this calculation were to be performed manually, the next step would be to raise the discount rate in order to reduce the NPV. At 21 percent, the NPV is negative; therefore, the IRR must be between 15 percent and 21 percent. In this case, at 18 percent, the NPV is zero; therefore, the IRR is 18 percent.

TABLE 7-20

Example of Conflicting Results From Net Present Value and Internal Rate of Return Methods

	Initial investment	Annual cash flows				NPV at 10%	IRR
		Year 1	Year 2	Year 3	Year 4		
Investment A	$25,000	$10,000	$10,000	$10,000	$10,000	$6,699	21.86%
Investment B	25,000	—	5,000	10,000	30,000	7,136	18.20%

In practice, the IRR is seldom a percentage that can be directly obtained from the present value tables found in most financial texts. Instead of being an integer such as 16 percent or 17 percent, it is more often a fractional amount, such as 16.14 percent or 17.23 percent. These amounts can be approximated using the present value tables through interpolation; however, they are more often precisely calculated using electronic calculators with financial functions or computers.

In most cases, the IRR leads to the same decision as NPV in ranking alternative investments. Occasionally, however, they do differ. Table 7-20 illustrates an example in which an investment with a higher NPV has a lower IRR. The reason for the difference is that the NPV discounts cash flows at the stated discount rate, whereas the IRR discounts them at the computed IRR. In situations where the IRR exceeds the company's cost of capital, the IRR discounts at an inappropriately high rate. Investments that produce relatively lower cash flows in early years may have an inferior IRR even though the NPV exceeds that of a competing investment. In these circumstances the NPV is regarded as a superior measure of investment performance.

An additional shortcoming of IRR is that it does not differentiate among investments on the basis of their relative size. A $10,000 investment with a 19 percent IRR would appear to be superior to a $10 million investment with an 18.5 percent IRR, even though the latter clearly has the potential to be of greater significance to the investors. As with any financial tool, blind reliance on results cannot supersede prudent application and interpretation.

VALUING ACQUISITION CANDIDATES

Acquisitions of companies rank among the most significant capital expenditures made by businesses. The potential financial and business impact of acquisitions to the buyer can cause nearly any other type of capital expenditure to pale in comparison. For this reason, sound analysis of acquisition candidates is extremely important.

Well-publicized corporate bidding wars in which eager buyers increase purchase prices by tens if not hundreds of millions of dollars on short notice can make the valuation of acquisition candidates appear to be a superfluous issue that can be dealt with in a cavalier fashion. In fact, purchase price has the potential to be the determining factor of acquisition success, given that it is the bench mark against which subsequent results can be measured. An acquisition that is attractive at one price can be a money loser at a higher price. This is especially true in leveraged buyouts, in which purchases generate substantial principal and interest obligations that must be repaid.

Estimating the value of a company is not by any means a straightforward process. Well-trained experts can, at times, deviate substantially in their estimate of the value of an acquisition candidate. Unlike accounting, there are no generally accepted valuation standards that can be rigidly applied. Valuation is more an art than a science. Each situation must be uniquely analyzed, and often valued based, in part, on valuation methods peculiar to a specialized industry and/or the specific company.

Practitioners have developed several different valuation methods. Those that are most consistently applied are based on comparable companies, similar acquisitions, adjusted net worth, and discounted cash flow analysis.

Comparable Company Method

In contemporary portfolio theory, the stock market is presumed to be efficient in valuing publicly held securities. At any given point in time, the price of a company's stock reflects factors that affect the overall economy, the industry in which the company operates, the market for its products, and numerous factors specific to the company. They collectively determine the price at which a company's stock trades, a result of numerous independent transactions between value-maximizing investors.

Stock market data on publicly held companies are particularly relevant in estimating the value of a closely held concern. Especially useful are data on comparable companies that possess similar investment characteristics to the closely held business. In determining what constitutes similar investment characteristics, it is important not to take the term "comparability" too literally. A comparable company that resembles the closely held business in every way can never exist, and is unnecessary for valuation purposes. Investors buy and sell stock in order to achieve a financial return; hence, the group of comparable companies identified includes a body of companies that collectively displays investment characteristics that offer investors the prospects of achieving a rate of return comparable to the rate achievable through an interest in the closely held concern. Investment traits used to assess comparability may include lines of business, customer type or industry, geographical concentration, marketing methods, competition,

TABLE 7-21

Calculation of Weighted Average Earnings of Z, Inc.

	Earnings	Weighting	Weighted earnings
1990	$1,063,214	5	$ 5,316,070
1989	894,285	4	3,577,140
1988	952,193	3	2,856,579
1987	838,612	2	1,677,224
1986	725,484	1	725,484
Sum of weighted earnings			$14,152,497
Weighting			÷15
Weighted average earnings			$ 943,500

product complexity, sales and/or earnings trends, and overall financial condition. It is possible that none of the companies closely resembles the closely held company; collectively, however, they should display investment characteristics that would influence its value.

Value is translated from the comparable companies by applying their aggregate market capitalization multiples to the appropriate data of the privately held concern. The market capitalization multiples relate the stock prices of the comparable companies to certain per-share financial data, such as earnings, weighted average earnings (see Table 7-21), book value, and/or revenues. An application of these multiples to the related financial data of the privately held concern can result in several different values, as shown in Table 7-22. Each value constitutes a component of value that is not, by itself, fully indicative of value. The components of value are integrated into a single value by weighting them according to an informed judgment concerning the relative importance of each component in determining value, which may be supported by analysis such as that shown in Table 7-23. Other factors relevant to value may have to be considered that are not reflected in the stock prices of the comparable companies. Issues such as nonmarketability of stock, lack of management depth, appreciated assets, nonrecurring income or expense items, high cash balances, and others, may warrant adjustments to the value calculated through the application of capitalization multiples. Adjustments are normally made by applying premiums or discounts to the calculated value, and adjusting the earnings and book value of the acquisition candidate, where appropriate, so that the capitalized value is properly reflected.

The value developed by applying the aggregate market capitalization multiples of the comparable companies, with appropriate adjustments, is based on their stock prices, which are normally based on transactions for fractional interests in the underlying companies (e.g., 100- and 200-share

TABLE 7-22
Valuation of Z, Inc. Based on Comparable Public Companies

	Price/ earnings	Price/weighted average earnings	Price/book value	Price/ revenues	Calculation of value
Comparable public company					
P	9.1	10.2	1.24	0.33	
Q	14.0	12.9	1.36	0.49	
R	6.8	9.3	1.07	0.26	
W	15.0	16.8	2.28	0.81	
X	11.1	11.6	1.76	0.37	
Y	10.6	12.6	0.99	0.55	
Z	8.4	10.7	0.82	0.21	
Average of multiples	10.7	12.0	1.36	0.43	
	×	×	×	×	
Financial results of acquisition candidate	$ 1,063,214	$ 943,500	$6,343,518	$19,725,382	
Components of value	$11,376,390	$11,322,000	$8,627,184	$ 8,481,914	
Weighting (a)	× 30%	× 35%	× 20%	× 5%	
Weighted components of value	$ 3,412,917	$ 3,962,700	$1,725,437	$ 1,272,287	$10,373,341
Acquisition premium (b)					× 1.40
					$14,522,677

(a) Developed judgmentally or as shown in Table 7-23
(b) Based on general acquisition data of acquisitions with investment characteristics resembling Z, Inc.

TABLE 7-23

Method for Supporting the Weighting of Components of Value

	Price/ earnings	Price/weighted average earnings	Price/book value	Price/ revenues	Total
Average of comparable companies (a)	10.7	12.0	1.36	0.43	—
Standard deviation	3.0	2.5	0.51	0.21	—
Coefficient of variation (b)	0.28	0.21	0.38	0.49	—
Reciprocal of coefficient of variation	3.57	4.76	2.63	2.04	13.00
Reciprocal as percentage of total	28%	37%	20%	15%	100%
Weighting system to be applied	30%	35%	20%	15%	100%

(a) From Table 16-23
(b) Standard deviation ÷ average

lots); consequently, the value reflects a minority interest. The value of the entire company can be estimated by applying an acquisition premium to the previously computed value. The acquisition premium may be based on premiums paid over the existing market prices of selected publicly held companies to acquire control. The extent to which the price is bid up above the level that existed before the announcement of an acquisition is referred to as the acquisition premium. For example, if a stock price of $10 prevailed before an announcement of an acquisition that was ultimately consummated at $13 per share, the acquisition premium would be 30 percent ($3 divided by $10).

The comparable company method has the advantage of providing an independent basis for arriving at value that is relatively less subjective than other valuation methods. It shares all the advantages of the stock market as a pricing mechanism in the sense that it reflects a plethora of factors that collectively influence value. Like the stock market, the comparable company method displays some volatility in value over time if applied to value a single company because of changes in stock price levels and trends within the market. Companies within the stock market experience fluctuation in their prices. The main caveat to keep in mind regarding the comparable company valuation method is that it is only as good as the capability of the practitioner applying the method, and the care taken to select appropriate comparable companies, and reflect them properly in a valuation formula.

Similar Acquisitions Method

Recent acquisitions of companies with investment characteristics resembling those of the acquisition candidate provide useful valuation bench marks for many of the same reasons that comparable companies are significant. Similar acquisitions may even be viewed as more relevant in as much as they represent informed purchases of entire companies, rather than the partial interests that constitute the basis of the comparable company methods.

Both the similar acquisitions method and the comparable company method rely on the premise that fair market value is established by transactions between willing buyers and sellers that are reasonably informed of the relevant information. The capitalization multiples from similar acquisitions are used to develop value in much the same way as is comparable company market data (see Table 7-24). Where appropriate, adjustments are made to the resulting data or the underlying data of the acquisition candidate that is capitalized in order to account for any unique attributes requiring special consideration.

The major problem of the similar acquisition method is the difficulty of obtaining sufficient data on acquisitions to provide a meaningful indication of value. There are more than 12,000 publicly held companies from which comparable company data can be drawn, but only a few hundred acquisitions occur each year that disclose sufficient useful data. Also, acquisition prices may sometimes reflect factors that are specific to the transaction and not applicable to others. Those factors may include the relative negotiating skills of the parties to the transaction; the financial capacity of the acquirer; perceived synergies that would cause the merged value of the acquired company to exceed its freestanding value; and other aspects of the acquisition agreement that may not be reflected in the purchase price, such as employment contracts. Because of these and other shortcomings, the similar acquisitions method is often used as one of several valuation methods to develop a purchase price, rather than as the sole method.

Adjusted Book Value Method

Conventional wisdom dictates that there should be some relationship between the price paid to acquire a company and the value of its assets, less liabilities, which constitutes the adjusted book value. Many unsophisticated transactions are based exclusively on this amount. Although the value of a business ultimately derives from the earnings that it can generate rather than its adjusted book value, the latter measure is important since any transaction occurring at too substantial a premium over book value begs the strategic question of whether it would be more economical to build rather than to buy.

Adjusted book value is calculated by determining the fair market value of assets in place and reducing that amount by the market value of liabilities. Several interpretations are frequently provided for value that can confuse the issue, and are summarized in Table 7-25.

TABLE 7-24
Valuation of Z, Inc. Based on Similar Recent Acquisitions

	Price/ earnings	Price/weighted average earnings	Price/book value	Price/ revenues	Calculation of value
Acquisition					
A	11.0	13.8	1.42	0.62	
B	15.6	14.7	2.01	0.93	
C	14.8	17.2	1.61	0.72	
D	8.9	9.1	0.97	0.39	
E	12.1	13.9	1.39	0.52	
F	17.4	19.1	2.28	1.04	
Average	13.4	14.3	1.52	0.67	
	×	×	×	×	
Financial results of acquisition candidate	$ 1,063,214	$ 943,500	$ 6,343,518	$19,725,382	
Components of value	$14,140,746	$13,775,100	$10,213,064	$13,807,767	
Weighting (a)	× 30%	× 30%	× 25%	× 15%	
	$ 4,242,224	$ 4,132,530	$ 2,553,226	$ 2,071,165	$12,999,145

(a) Developed judgmentally or as shown in Table 7-23

TABLE 7-25

Asset Valuation Methods

Valuation method	Basis	Relative dollar value	Application
Book value	Net historical costs recorded on balance sheet according to generally accepted accounting principles	Variable	Accounting for a pooling of interests
Liquidation value	Net amount quickly realizable through a liquidation sale	Lowest	Liquidation; some asset-based loans
Current value	Net amount realizable through continued use in business or an orderly disposition	Middle	Purchase accounting; tax basis
Replacement value	Cost of replacing existing assets, without regard to enhanced functional performance of new fixed assets	Highest	"Make-or-buy" acquisition analysis

The result of adjusting the balance sheet to reflect the appropriate valuation is a calculation of adjusted book value. Table 7-26 provides an example of adjustments to the book value of Z, Inc. for purposes of acquisition analysis. The replacement value of assets is considered, as well as the cost of attempting to build a business of similar scope to the acquisition candidate. If the proposed purchase price were $14 million, the analysis in Table 7-26 indicates that there is an implicit premium of $554,439 associated with acquiring Z, Inc. instead of building it from the ground up. The advantage of starting a new business is greater control over determining many aspects of the organization that is ultimately established, while none of the bad aspects of the existing business is assumed. This must be weighed against the amount of time required to duplicate the business of the acquisition candidate, the risk that it may never be successfully duplicated, and the benefit of eliminating the acquisition candidate as a potential competitor.

Discounted Cash-Flow Analysis Method

The valuation methods described previously are essentially price-based valuation methods. Value is based on the prices of similar businesses or assets. The implicit assumption is that the market provides the best indication of value. Discounted cash-flow analysis (DCF) is a value-based concept, pred-

TABLE 7-26

Using the Adjusted Book Value of Z, Inc. for Acquisition Analysis

	Amount per balance sheet	Adjustment	Adjusted book value	Explanation
ADJUSTED BALANCE SHEET				
Assets				
Cash and short-term investments	$ 862,557	$ 14,316	$ 876,873	Accrued interest on investments
Accounts receivable, net	4,279,118	(104,286)	4,174,832	Doubtful accounts receivable
Inventory	2,744,322	718,669	3,462,991	LIFO adjustment
Other current assets	293,517	—	293,517	
	$ 8,179,514	$ 628,699	$ 8,808,213	
Net fixed assets	2,823,424	1,923,562	4,746,986	Appraised value of assets exceeds depreciated book value
Patents	145,322	54,678	200,000	Analysis of current value
Goodwill	108,617	(108,617)	—	No tangible value
	$11,256,877	$2,498,322	$13,755,199	
Liabilities				
Current liabilities	$ 3,045,918	—	$ 3,045,918	
Long-term debt	1,867,441	$ (203,721)	1,663,720	Long-term debt at below-market rates
Net book value	6,343,518	2,702,043	9,045,561	
	$11,256,877	$2,498,322	$13,755,199	

ACQUISITION ANALYSIS

Adjusted book value		$ 9,045,561
Other costs to duplicate Z, Inc.		
Start-up costs	1,000,000	Site location costs, employee recruitment expenses, professional fees, etc.
Replicative research and development	900,000	R&D costs to replicate product line similar to that of Z, Inc.
Differential of operating earnings of Z, Inc. during "catch-up" period	2,500,000	Estimated differential between operating earnings of Z, Inc. and start-up company during period of time required for start-up company to catch up to Z, Inc., not including start-up costs and losses reflected above
		$13,445,561
Premium for buying ongoing entity		554,439
Purchase price of Z, Inc.		$14,000,000

TABLE 7-27

Valuation of Z, Inc. Based on Discounted Cash-Flow Analysis

	Projected amounts	Present value of projected amounts (a)
Projected free cash flow:		
1990	$ 1,060,000	$ 929,825
1991	1,250,000	961,834
1992	1,463,000	987,483
1993	1,698,000	1,005,352
1994	1,952,000	1,013,808
1995	2,206,000	1,005,024
1996	2,493,000	996,296
Residual value ($2,493,000 ÷ 14)	17,807,143	7,116,399
	$29,929,143	$14,016,021

(a) Based on weighted average cost of capital of 14 percent

icated on the economic concept that the financial value of a business results from the cash flows that it enables the owner to realize.

The heart of DCF is the cash-flow projections upon which value is based. A format such as that presented in Table 7-12 is used to project cash flows over some foreseeable period—frequently five, seven, or ten years. The value of the acquisition candidate is deemed to be the present value of the cash flows that it can generate, discounted at the acquiror's cost of capital, adjusted for the risk of the acquisition candidate. The cash flows of the acquisition candidate have two components—the dividends or free cash flow that could be paid to the acquiror, and the residual value (also referred to as terminal value) that could be realized if the business were to be sold at the end of the projection period. The residual value is normally estimated by capitalizing the free cash flow at the cost of capital in the final year of the projection period (see Table 7-27), or by applying a conservative price/earnings ratio to the earnings in the final year, reduced to reflect the capital gains taxes that would result from the sale. The present value of these amounts is deemed to be the value of the acquisition candidate.

The process used in DCF is essentially the same as that employed in NPV calculations. Note the following similarities:

According to DCF:

Purchase price = Present value of cash flows + Residual value

By placing both components of DCF on the same side of the equation, it is evident that in applying DCF, the purchase price is always an amount where the NPV is zero. Applying another concept that has previously been discussed, with DCF, the purchase price is always an amount that will cause the internal rate of return to equal the cost of capital.

DCF shares the same major weakness as NPV: it is entirely dependent upon the reasonableness of the projections. A further weakness is the importance of residual value, which is often the most significant component of value. If it is difficult to estimate value at the time of purchase, it is even more difficult to estimate value several years hence. Some of this problem is partially mitigated since slight inaccuracies in the estimation of residual value are diminished by the discounting process. Also, sensitivity analyses are frequently performed under several alternative scenarios in order to arrive at purchase price parameters.

Despite these areas of concern, DCF remains an important valuation tool, often used in conjunction with the others to arrive at a consensus as to value or to establish price boundaries.

PRICING VENTURE CAPITAL

Pricing venture capital is one of the least well-defined areas of high finance. The process is a combination of horse trading, conartistry, and sophisticated analysis. The former skills are not readily imparted, nor germane to this chapter. The latter is important because it helps to clarify negotiating positions and establish a framework for arriving at an equitable arrangement. The use of analytical models can help remove part of the emotional element from what can be very difficult negotiations.

The central valuation issue is how large a portion of the company the venture capitalist will receive in exchange for the investment that is being made. Normally the companies receiving venture capital are not public, nor do they have a sufficient track record to be able to readily apply the valuation methods discussed in the previous section. Venture capital valuation methods are necessarily prospectively oriented, and tend to rely heavily on estimating future earnings and the timing and price at which the company will go public, since a public offering is normally the only means by which the venture capitalist can achieve the desired return on investment.

Traditional Pricing Method

The traditional pricing method focuses on the amount of the venture capitalist's investment, interim proceeds, and the value that it must have at the time of the initial public offering (target value) for the venture capitalist to achieve a target return on investment commensurate with the risk involved. The proportion of the total value of the company at the time of the initial public offering represented by the target value of the venture capitalist's investment is the amount of equity giveup required by the venture capitalist, according to the traditional pricing method.

The payoff on venture capital investments, if any, normally is realized when and if the venture capital recipient goes public or is sold. In the absence of an initial public offering (IPO) or a sale, it is unlikely that the venture capitalist will ever realize the 50 percent annual rate of return sought on successful investments. The apparently usurous rate of return on successful investments, giving rise to their nickname "vulture capitalists," is needed to compensate for the numerous failures that venture capitalists invariably invest in. Major venture capitalists generally prefer not to invest in companies that do not offer the prospects of an IPO within a three- to five-year timeframe. Although many venture capital investments are structured as debt (to give the venture capitalist a preferred interest in the assets of the corporation) with an "equity kicker," the venture capitalist is generally not content to receive a repayment of principal plus interest. The objective is to realize value through exercising the equity kicker.

The sample application of the traditional pricing method shown in Table 7-28 is based on a required annual rate of return of 50 percent, and what is deemed to be a conservative earnings figure and price/earnings multiple for the IPO four years in the future. By varying the earnings, IPO price/earnings ratio, target rate of return and/or timing of the IPO, different equity giveup percentages result. A matrix showing the equity giveup resulting from varying the aforementioned is useful for evaluating the giveup required. In practice, venture capitalists will make their decisions based on a conservative scenario, due to the risk and uncertainty of most venture capital investments. As a consequence, many successful venture capital investments yield considerably more than the required rate of return.

First Chicago Pricing Model Method

The traditional pricing method is simple and enjoys widespread use. By focusing solely on the returns required on successful investments, it addresses the major source of income for most venture capital firms. Unsuccessful investments yield nothing; mediocre investments yield comparatively little. A venture capitalist would not generally invest in a project that does not have the potential to achieve target rates of return achieved through an IPO or a sale of the company.

The flaw of the traditional pricing model is that is does not address the entire range of venture capital investments, the majority of which generally include companies that go under or fail to enable the venture capitalist to realize the benefit from his equity kicker. The broader portfolio issues of venture capital investments are reflected in the First Chicago Pricing Model (FCPM). This model quantifies the effect that alternative investment performance can have on required equity give-up.

TABLE 7-28

Traditional Pricing Method — Nu Corporation

	1990	1991	1992	1993
Venture capitalist's investment:				
Equity value of convertible debentures, January 1	$1,000,000	$1,420,000	$2,050,000	$2,995,000
Target total return at 50%	500,000	710,000	1,025,000	1,497,500
	$1,500,000	$2,130,000	$3,075,000	$4,492,500
Less: Annual interest on convertible debt	80,000	80,000	80,000	80,000
Target value, December 31	$1,420,000	$2,050,000	$2,995,000	$4,412,500
Venture capital recipient:				
Earnings (losses)	$ (350,000)	$ (50,000)	$ 350,000	$ 600,000
Assumed initial public offering price/earnings, December 31, 1993				× 15
				$9,000,000
Equity required by venture capitalist on January 1, 1990 to achieve target value			4,412,500 ÷ 9,000,000 =	49.0%

The essential premise of FCPM is that, in the most basic sense, there are three potential outcomes of a venture capital investment: success, as demonstrated through an IPO or buyout; survival, which enables the venture capitalist to recover principal and interest on convertible debt, without exercising the equity kicker; and failure, which results in a complete loss to the venture capitalist. Between these extremes there are several hybrids that may be readily incorporated into the FCPM, but that are omitted in the following example.

In developing the input for the FCPM, the task is to quantify the financial impact of each alternative outcome and judgmentally assign a probability to each alternative outcome based on past experience or an assessment of similar investments. The successful scenario shows a more optimistic earnings figure and price/earnings ratio than was used in the traditional pricing model because there is no attempt to dilute these figures or show a conservative presentation to accommodate for failures. The resulting value of the equity kicker at the time of the IPO is higher. Also, a lower discount rate is used to reflect the present value of future outcomes because risk is directly reflected in the projections of alternative outcomes rather than by increasing the discount rate. The survival scenario reflects only the repayment of principal and interest, which is discounted accordingly, and the failure scenario reflects a complete loss providing no cash flows. This model is prepared on a pretax basis, although appropriate adjustments could be made to incorporate tax effects in the calculations.

The present value of the financial impact of each scenario is assigned a probability and weighted, so that the resultant value reflects each of the

TABLE 7-29
First Chicago Pricing Model—Nu Corporation

	1990	1991	1992	1993	Present value of alternative scenario	Weighting or probability	Present value of probabilistic alternative scenario
Failure scenario							
Loss of investment and forfeiture of interest	0	0	0	0	0	30%	0
Survival scenario							
Interest	$80,000	$80,000	$80,000	$ 80,000			
Repayment of principal				1,000,000			
	$80,000	$80,000	$80,000	$1,080,000			
Present value at 40%	$57,143	$40,816	$29,155	$ 281,133	$408,247	40%	$163,299
Successful scenario							
Interest	$80,000	$80,000	$80,000	$ 80,000			
Present value at 40%	$57,143	$40,816	$29,155	$ 20,825	$147,939	30%	$ 44,382
Equity value of convertible debenture at December 31, 1993 initial public offering:							
Earnings of venture capital recipient				$ 900,000			
Price/earnings on initial public offering				× 25			
Total valuation				$22,500,000			

	1990	1991	1992	1993	Present value of alternative scenario	Weighting or probability	Present value of probabilistic alternative scenario
Equity value of convertible debenture			V% × 22,500,000				
Present value factor at 40%			× 0.2603				
				V% × $ 5,856,750	V% × $5,876,750	30%	V% × $1,763,025

Total $ 207,681

+ V% × $1,763,025

Investment = $1,000,000

Investment = Present value future investment proceeds

$1,000,000 = $207,681 + V% × $1,763,025

792,319 = V% × $1,763,025

$$792,319 = V\%$$
$$\overline{\$1,763,025}$$

V% = 44.9%

scenarios. The resulting equation is in the same form as a DCF equation: investment = present value of future investment proceeds. In this equation, the only unknown is the equity give-up (V). By solving the algebraic equation, the amount of equity giveup is computed.

The FCPM has the advantage of reflecting alternative scenarios more precisely than the traditional pricing model. As with other financial tools, the validity of the results of either of the venture capital pricing methods depends on the reasonableness of the underlying assumptions. At best, they provide an element of reason to a highly speculative area.

CONCLUSION

Strategic decision makers usually face a significant number of market, product, and competitor alternatives. Similarly, the number of financial tools available to strategic managers is also large. Planners and line managers alike need to understand how to use these financial tools to select one strategic alternative over another. This understanding requires that management know which tools to use and how to use them. Financial analysis requires that managers systematically lay out their assumptions and expectations. Effective financial analysis enables management to examine and compare these alternative assumptions and expectations. Ultimately, using the appropriate financial tools fosters the most rigorous strategic decision making possible.

8

A Step-By-Step Model for Strategic Planning

WALTER R. HOLMAN
Loyola College, Maryland

ALAN L. FARKAS
Farkas Berkowitz & Company, Washington, DC

INTRODUCTION

The strategic planning process in the private sector generally consists of the following four primary building blocks:

1. Assessment of the company's current position
2. Identification of the company's desired position
3. Evaluation of the strategic gap between the two and the critical issues to be resolved in order to close the gap
4. Formulation of strategies and action steps to resolve the critical issues

This chapter begins by presenting a generic model of the strategic planning process (see Figure 8-1). The model shows the specific steps involved in developing the four building blocks. The sections that follow discuss the building blocks and the steps in detail. The second part of this chapter presents an eight-step procedure for initiating a corporate strategic planning process quickly and successfully.

MAJOR STEPS IN THE STRATEGIC PLANNING PROCESS

Assessing the Company's Current Position

The assessment of the company's current position answers two fundamental questions:

1. What business is the company currently in?
2. How well is the company doing in this business?

Making this assessment involves a rigorous appraisal of the firm's operating and financial performance (evaluation of the internal environment) and a comprehensive analysis of the macroeconomic, regulatory, and marketplace trends (evaluation of the external environment) that shape the environment in which the company operates.

This performance appraisal permits the strategic planners to identify the key internal factors that contribute to the firm's success and to look at these factors in terms of the company's primary strengths and weaknesses. The evaluation of the external environment produces a clear picture of the current marketplace opportunities available to the firm and the significant risks and threats it faces in the marketplace. The mapping of company strengths and weaknesses against the current opportunities, threats, risks, and success determinants provides a concise assessment of the company's current position.

Evaluation of the Internal Environment. Evaluation of the internal environment involves making a comprehensive appraisal of the firm's operating and financial performance. The four primary resource bases that serve as the foundation for performance are:

FIGURE 8-1

Generic Model of the Corporate Strategic Planning Process

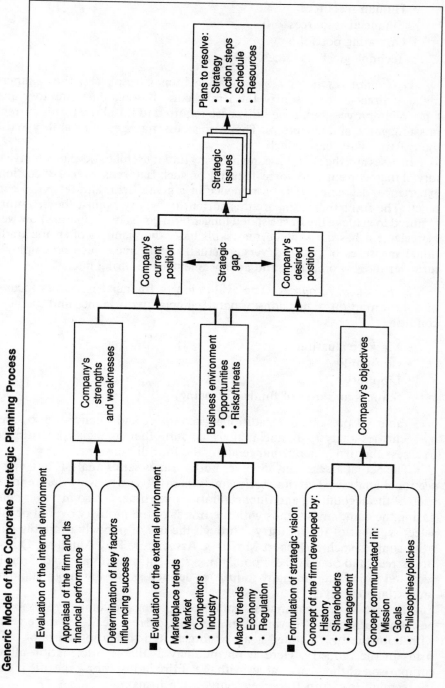

- Human resources
- Financial resources
- Operating portfolio
- Technological resources

1. *Human resources.* In evaluating human resources, the planners make a direct comparison of the firm's current skills base (number and types of employees) with the skills base required to fulfill the firm's current mission, goals, and objectives. They also assess management's ability to use the existing skills base effectively.

In assessing the skills base, many firms find it useful to develop an inventory of their current work force, focusing on such factors as level of education, experience, degree of skill, prominence in a given field, and technical currency. The firms then compare this current inventory against the inventory required to achieve the firm's stated longer term goals. In evaluating how well management has used the current skills base, the planners often use traditional measures of planned versus actual performance, such as employee turnover rates, promotions and advancements, and hiring rate.

2. *Financial resources.* The evaluation of financial resources focuses on four important dimensions of both financial performance and financial condition:

- Market valuation
- Profitability
- Liquidity
- Sources and uses of funds (financing)

Table 8-1 presents the traditional accounting and financial ratios used by securities analysts, financial analysts, and other financial practitioners to assess the firm's performance along the four dimensions.

The actual assessment involves both a times series analysis and cross-sectional analysis. The time series analysis involves assessing the trends in each of the accounting and financial ratios over time. It also involves comparing the company's trends with the trends of the industry overall or of a select segment of the industry. Through the use of publicly available data from sources such as Robert Morris & Associates, Troy Almanac, Dun & Bradstreet, and Standard & Poors, it is a straightforward task to obtain the required ratio data for many industries defined as the four digit standard industrial code level.

The cross-sectional analysis entails comparing the company's ratio values at a specific point in time (e.g., last year, current year, last three years) with both the firm's stated goals or targets and the ratio values of other firms in the industry. Here again, publicly available information allows comparison of the firm's values with the entire industry or a specific industry segment (e.g., top 10 percent, largest ten firms).

TABLE 8-1

Key Factors for Evaluating Corporate Financial Performance

Factor	Company values				Industry values (average)		
	1988	1989	1990	Target	1988	1989	1990
Market valuation							
P/E ratio							
Dividend yield							
Total annual rate of return							
Profitability							
ROE							
ROI							
Net profit margin							
Asset turnover							
Liquidity — short-term							
Current ratio							
Quick ratio							
Defensive assets as a percentage of current liabilities							
Liquidity — long-term							
Debt service coverage ratio							
Fixed charge coverage ratio							
Financing							
Debt-to-equity ratio							
Cash sources-to-cash uses ratio							
Cash from operations-to-cash uses ratio							

3. *Operating portfolio.* In assessing the firm's operating portfolio, the planners focus on the basic position of the firm within the industry and on the strategic position and profitability of the firm's major businesses or product lines. The planners begin their evaluation of basic position with an assessment of the overall attractiveness of the industry and of the critical factors that determine success in the industry. Industry attractiveness tends to be evaluated first and foremost on the basis of profitability and growth. The success factors evaluated in this step are primarily related to the firm's portfolio of products and services as a whole. The assessment provides answers to the following critical questions:

- How attractive is the industry overall?
- What product- and service-related factors determine the strength of the firm's basic market position in this industry?
- Does the firm's current product and service portfolio display these critical factors as strengths or as weaknesses?

The second step in assessing the firm's operating portfolio involves an analysis of the market position and profitability of each of the firm's business segments or major lines of business. This analysis provides answers to a second set of important questions:

- How attractive is a specific business segment?
- What is the firm's position in this market segment (e.g., market leader, minor player)?
- How profitable is this business segment for the firm?
- What are the critical determinants of success in this business segment?
- How well does the firm meet these critical determinants?

4. *Technological resources.* Technology assessment proceeds along the same lines as the assessment of the firm's skills base. The planners attempt to answer two fundamental questions: (1) What is the firm's current portfolio of technologies? and (2) What portfolio of technologies does the firm need to accomplish its stated mission, goals, and objectives?

Many firms develop a formalized "technology evaluation checklist" in which both the current and the required technologies are analyzed on the basis of factors such as:

- State of the art of the technology (emerging, developing, maturing, or declining)
- Personnel requirements to use the technology (education, knowledge, experience)
- Supporting facilities and equipment required
- Technological flexibility (range of products and processes that the technology can support)
- Source of the technology (domestic versus foreign manufacturers)
- Likelihood and time frame of technological obsolescence or replacement

Once the planners have completed the appraisal, they are able to review each of the firm's four primary resource bases in terms of historical performance, relative importance as a factor determining overall firm success, and current strengths and weaknesses.

Evaluation of the external environment. In many businesses, longer-run success is often more significantly influenced by the external factors that shape the environment in which the firm operates than by factors within the firm itself. The external environment produces both the opportunities and the threats and risks that management must contend with in order to fulfill the company's stated mission and goals. The evaluation of the external environment seeks answers to a number of very important questions:

- What are the external factors that shape the environment in which the firm operates?
- Historically, how have these factors affected the firm's operating and financial performance?

- What are the expected trends in these key factors over the longer term?
- What challenges (opportunities, threats, and risks) do these expected trends present to the firm?

1. *Identifying external factors.* Although each business and industry is different, the important factors that shape a firm's external environment usually fall into the following three categories:

- Market and industry trends
- Competitive environment
- Economic and regulatory trends

Within each of these categories, it is possible to identify a number of specific elements that are important to historical and to future company performance:

- Market and industry trends
  - Market size and growth rate
  - Number and type of customers
  - Industry profitability and financial condition
  - Product price elasticity and trends
  - Technological trends
  - Product development/basic R&D trends
  - Advertising and promotion trends
  - Merger and acquisition trends
- Competitive environment
  - Industry structure and concentration
  - Barriers to industry entry and exit
  - Industry entry and exit trends
  - Key competitors, competitor strategies, and competitor performance
- Economic and regulatory environment
  - Short-term and longer-term trends in interest rates and the availability of credit
  - Economic growth (regional, national) and inflation rates
  - Consumer, household, and business disposable income and spending
  - Federal, state, and local regulations affecting the firm, its customers and the industry

2. *Historical relationship of these external factors to firm performance.* With regard to analyzing the relationship between the key external factors and company operating and financial performance, the smaller, resource-constrained firms generally spend little time in-house conducting original research and rely primarily on the analysis of others. These firms emphasize inexpensive information sources such as reports of the federal government; industry and trade association studies; analyses published by Standard & Poors, Moody's, and Dun & Bradstreet; research findings provided by the research arms of financial services institutions; and market/industry intelligence found in business periodicals.

The larger, more resource-abundant firms conduct much of their own research in-house through marketing, sales, and corporate planning departments. The larger firms frequently purchase the more expensive and finely-tailored data and analyses available from a variety of market research organizations and combine them with the basic market research conducted by their own in-house staffs.

The end result of this ongoing analytical process is a concise picture of the key external factors and how they influence the operating and financial success of the firm.

3. *Trends in key external factors.* Since no one has a crystal ball that accurately forecasts the future, firms often develop a range of forecasts for each of the significant external factors. One of the most powerful and frequently used forecasting techniques is the scenario approach. Scenarios are comprehensive, internally consistent narratives describing a variety of plausible outcomes or forecasts for an individual external factor or set of external factors. As an example, a scenario approach can be used to establish the range of plausible long-term economic outlooks the company will face over the period of its current strategic planning horizon.

Figure 8-2 presents an example of the scenario approach. The economic outlook scenarios are based on five variables (gross national product (GNP) growth rate, inflation rate, unemployment rate, consumer disposable income growth rate, and level of consumer confidence) and the values each of these variables takes on under the three scenarios. A number of important points must be kept in mind when using the scenario approach:

1. The range of scenarios used for each external factor (e.g., economic outlook, competitive environment) must be realistic — it must establish the range or spectrum of feasible outcomes.
2. The scenarios constructed for a given factor (e.g., economic outlook) must be based on the variables most closely related to the company's operating and financial performance.
3. The values of the variables that make up the scenario must be internally consistent. For example, under the "highly favorable" economic outlook scenario in Figure 8-2, the values for each of the five variables must be likely to occur simultaneously.
4. The scenarios for all of the important external factors must be consistent. The optimistic scenario for economic outlook must be

FIGURE 8-2

Three Scenarios of the Future Economic Environment

Scenario	ECONOMIC FACTORS				
	GNP growth rate	Inflation rate	Unemployment rate	Disposable income growth rate	Consumer confidence
Highly favorable to firm	5.5%	3.0%	4.0%	6.5%	Highly optimistic
Slightly favorable to firm	3.0	5.0	5.5	4.0	Slightly optimistic
Highly unfavorable to firm	0.0	8.0	6.5	1.0	Pessimistic

linked with the corresponding scenarios for competitor environment, regulatory outlook, and so forth.

4. *Opportunities, risks, and threats presented by these trends.* The evaluation of the external environment reveals the primary opportunities available to the firm and the threats and risks it faces in the marketplace. These factors are ranked on the basis of the likelihood of their occurrence and the degree of their potential effect on the firm's future operating and financial performance.

Identifying the Company's Desired Position

As depicted in Figure 8-1, the planners develop the company's desired position by mapping the firm's strategic vision of itself against the opportunities, threats, and risks that shape its business environment over the planning horizon. The planners then translate the strategic vision into a specific set of longer-term objectives that, if realized, will successfully exploit the opportunities and sufficiently mitigate or manage the threats and risks.

A firm's strategic vision is shaped by its historical experience and by the active participation of its management, directors, and shareholders. A firm communicates its mission through its mission statement and its goals, philosophy, and policies. The company describes its desired position in terms of a set of objectives in the following areas:

- Industry/marketplace position
- Revenue size and growth rate
- Products and services produced
- Financial performance
- Technological objectives
- Organizational structure and culture

The planners state the objectives in measurable terms so that progress can be evaluated, and management can clearly determine when the objectives have been met.

Evaluating the Strategic Gap and Critical Issues

Figure 8-1 shows that the strategic gap is the difference between the firm's current position and its desired position. Operationally, the gap is a measure of the difference between the stated target values and the current values of the firm's primary objectives. Within the gap are the critical issues that must be resolved to move the firm from its current position to its desired position.

Table 8-2 presents a hypothetical example of measuring the strategic gap and identifying the critical issues. The company is a regional manufacturer and distributor of salted snack foods that aspires to be a leading national firm within seven to ten years. As a major step in this direction, the firm has committed to ongoing, comprehensive strategic planning. Table 8-2 represents the firm's assessment of its strategic gap over the next five years and its identification of the critical issues that it must resolve in order to close the gap. The critical issues for this company can be further described as the following:

1. *Growth.* Transition from a smaller regional firm to a much larger, national firm requires substantial internal and external growth.
   a. Internal requirements
      — Five-fold increase in retained earnings within five years
      — Doubling of employee base
      — Tripling of management cadre
      — Substantial increase in the firm's technological capacity (product development, R&D, quality control, manufacturing and packaging automation)
   b. External requirements
      — Four-fold geographical market expansion
      — Aggressive acquisition program conducted against a backdrop of limited experience.

2. *Taking the firm public.* Managing the complex public offering process and the transition from a family-held private company to a widely-held public firm.

3. *Internal culture and management.* Current management's ability to successfully embrace and manage the tremendous change in corporate culture that rapid growth will bring
   a. Sharing the reins of management with nonfamily members
   b. Developing mutual trust and confidence—elimination of a "we-they" culture

TABLE 8-2

Identifying the Strategic Gap and the Critical Issues

Strategic planning element	Plan	Actual	Critical issues
Mission	• Within 7–10 years become a leading national manufacturer and distributor of a high-quality full line of salted snack foods	• Among the top three leading regional (northeast) manufacturers and distributors of a limited line of mixed-quality salted snack foods	• Significant level of geographical, product line, and people growth required
Overall company strategy	• Become the lowest-cost salted snack food manufacturer • Grow geographically via acquisitions	• Medium-cost-range manufacturer of salted snack foods • Two minor acquisitions in past ten years	• Significant level of capital investment and technological know-how required • Limited acquisition experience
Marketplace position and reputation	• Become #3 national manufacturer/distributor of high-quality salted snack foods — Sales in all thirty-five major U.S. geographical markets — Rank at least #3 (in revenues) in twenty-eight of these markets	• Ranked third among manufacturers/distributors regionally (northeast) — Sales in twelve major U.S. geographical markets — Ranked #3 or better in four markets	• Firm virtually unknown outside northeast • Inconsistent rankings across northeast markets
Revenue objectives	• $150 million by year 5 • 20 percent annual growth over next 10 years	• $60 million in year 1 • 12 percent annual growth over last 5 years	• Desired growth rate well above projected industry level and recent company experience
Product objectives	• Develop 5 high-quality snack lines • Develop 2 new product extensions each year	• 2 high-quality and 2 mediocre quality snack lines • 4 new product extensions over last 10 years	• Ability needed to develop new snack products line and update quality of 2 existing lines • Historical inability to manage product innovation process
Technological objectives	• Completely automate manufacturing and packaging of 5 major product lines within 5 years	• One product line fully automated • Three product lines with moderate automation of manufacturing	• Capital investment and technological know-how required • Limited in-house engineering capability

(continued)

TABLE 8-2 (cont'd)

Strategic planning element	Plan	Actual	Critical issues

Financial objectives (profitability)	• 25% ROE
	• 12.5% ROI
	• 5.0% net profit margin
	• 2.5% sales/total assets
		• 15% ROE
		• 8% ROI
		• 3.8% net profit margin
		• 2.1% sales/total assets
			• Substandard profitability due to:
			  — Cost management problems
			  — Insufficient sales generation from asset base

Financing objectives	• $20 million external equity (over next 5 years) • Debt/equity ratio reduced to 1.0 within 3 years • $20 million additional retained earnings (over next 3 years) • No cash dividends over forseeable future	• Family-owned, privately-held common stock • Debt/equity ratio of 1.8 • No cash dividends paid	• Willingness/ability of family to take firm public • Comparable public firms pay out 40% of earnings as cash dividends
Organizational structure and culture objectives	• Expanded senior management team to include 3 non-family members • Decentralized operations management with geographical region (e.g. southeast) serving as profit center or strategic business unit • Expanded board of directors to include 4 outside, nonfamily members • Most management positions filled from within company • Caring, people-focused culture	• Senior management team consists of 3 family members (CEO, COO, CFO) • Highly centralized and top-heavy management structure • No outside or non-family board members • No pattern to management recruiting practices • High turnover, low morale	• Lack of trust concerning non-family managers • Historical inability to share company management with non-family managers • Short supply of qualified internal managers • Overcoming "we-they" management philosophy

    c. Decentralization of operations management
    d. Assimilation of acquisitions
    e. Developing a consistent track record of promoting from within the firm

Finally, the critical issues must be ordered on the basis of their overall importance and their timeframe for resolution.

Formulating the Strategies and Action Steps to Resolve the Critical Issues

This step in the strategic planning process requires the firm to develop the overall approach (strategy) to successfully manage each of the identified critical issues. It also requires the firm to formulate the specific actions that will be carried out to implement each strategy. Table 8-3 illustrates this strategic planning step for our hypothetical snack food company. Notice that the action steps are detailed with respect to the following:

- Specific content
- Time frame
- Individual responsible
- Resources required

Using this format, the firm can monitor the action steps and further refine them as it implements its strategic plan over time.

INITIATING THE STRATEGIC PLANNING PROCESS

This section presents several suggestions for initiating the strategic planning process quickly and successfully. The suggestions are presented in the form of an eight-step process:

1. Recognize the traditional planning problems
2. Understand the primary determinants of successful strategic planning
3. Take the firm's "planning pulse" to determine how effectively it currently plans
4. Effectively organize for strategic planning
5. Educate the key planners and managers
6. Develop a detailed work/plan for conducting the strategic planning process
7. Begin with the assessment of the current position
8. Plan up-front to institutionalize the strategic planning process

These steps are discussed in the following sections.

TABLE 8-3
Strategy and Action Steps to Resolve Critical Issues: Plan for Going Public

Strategy	Action steps	Individual responsible	Time frame	Resources required
Senior management team will commit 30 percent of available time over next 18 months to managing the process through the point of initial stock issuance	• Designated CFO as team leader (manager of offering process) • Work out 18-month schedules, activities for CEO, COO, CFO	• CFO (senior management team) • CFO	• Immediate • By month 2	• First seven months — CFO: 75% of time — CEO: 25% of time — COO: 25% of time
Firm will hire an outside financing adviser to assist in selection of an investment banking firm and to provide oversight guidance during entire offering process	• Select outside adviser • Adviser develops steps/schedule for selecting investment banking firm • Select investment banker • Adviser/investment banking firm develops steps/schedule for going public	• CFO • CFO/adviser • CFO • CFO/adviser	• By month 3 • By month 4 • By month 6 • By month 7	• Investment — $75,000 for adviser — $50,000 initially for investment banking firm — $30,000 other expenses

FIGURE 8-3

Checklist to Gauge the Firm's Level of Planning Sophistication

☐ *Do the firm's senior executives have a strategic orientation to the business?*
  — Knowledge of critical variables that determine the firm's success
  — Understanding of which variables can be controlled
  — Systematic approach to the management of the controllable variables

☐ *What kind of planning does the firm currently conduct?*
  — One-cycle planning (annual budgeting and forecasting only)
  — Two-cycle planning (functional planning, annual budgeting, and forecasting)
  — Three-cycle planning (strategic planning)

☐ *Is the firm's current planning characterized by any of the following problems?*
  — Planning becomes a mindless ritual rather than an opportunity for strategic thinking.
  — Various levels of the firm become locked into "we-they" battles.
  — Information required by planners becomes inaccessible or only grudgingly surrendered by "non-planners."
  — Future strategies often become unimaginative projections of current strategies.
  — Information presented in plans is managed to support parochial positions rather than to serve as a sound basis for comparing alternatives.
  — Attractive new strategies are often rejected in favor of more conventional and safer strategies.
  — Results of the planning process are ignored when actual long-range decisions are made.

Recognize the Traditional Planning Problems

The underlying causes of planning problems are seldom technical deficiencies in the planning process or the analytical approaches used. Instead, they are human and administrative in nature. Typically, planning is a resource allocation process carried out in a corporate reward-punishment system that emphasizes the short term. Managers tend to focus on short-term issues with near-term financial consequences rather than on the longer-term issues that should be addressed by strategic planning.

Corporate planners typically work at a hectic pace with constant interruptions; short, verbal encounters; and great varieties of subject matter primarily dealing with current, ad hoc issues. Many key corporate personnel are misinformed about planning, and the information necessary to make strategic planning work is often unevenly distributed throughout the firm.

Finally, the communications necessary for successful planning are made difficult by the large number of people who must interact and by the politics, informal alliances, and the friendships among key managers that often lead to less-than-optimal planning decisions for the firm as a whole and less than complete communication of these decisions.

By recognizing these traditional problems early on, the firm can take steps to dispel them where possible or to prevent them from undermining the strategic planning process.

Understand the Primary Determinants of Successful Strategic Planning

Many practitioners have discovered that the ease with which strategic planning can be implemented is a function of five important factors:

1. Performance problems: Firms with significant operating and financial performance problems tend to reach for strategic planning as a potential panacea
2. CEO role: Successful strategic planning requires commitment; the initial commitment and the staying power of the CEO are crucial
3. Resource imbalance level: The smaller the imbalance in existing resources among key managers (and thus the smaller the degree of reallocation required), the lower will be the resistance to strategic planning
4. Prior planning experience: Firms with prior planning experience are more likely to embrace strategic planning.
5. Previous management-by-objectives (MBO) experience: Managers who are familiar with MBO management systems more readily embrace strategic planning with its quantified goals and objectives.

Take the Company's "Planning Pulse"

In this step, the firm can use a checklist approach (see Figure 8-3) to gauge the current sophistication of its planning process and the extent to which its planning suffers from the traditional problems discussed earlier. Obviously, the companies that face the greatest challenges are those that (1) lack a strategic orientation to their business, (2) conduct only annual business planning, and (3) continue to be plagued by the traditional planning problems.

Effectively Organize for Strategic Planning

It is important to begin the strategic planning process with the company's existing planning committee or group. However, in the early phase of strategic planning, membership should be limited to the following key managers:

- Chief executive officer
- Chief operating officer
- Chief financial officer
- Senior planning executive
- Senior marketing/sales executive
- Senior managers from human resources, operations, and information systems

The planning committee should establish a regularly scheduled meeting time and place. If necessary, the meetings should be held away from the office. Frequent interruptions will quickly interfere with the process and send the message that the senior executives do not consider the strategic planning process a high priority.

The meetings should have well-articulated agendas that are well communicated before each meeting. The planning group should elect a chairperson and a recording secretary. The chairperson's role is to keep the process on track and on schedule. The chief executive officer or chief operating officer should not assume the role of chairperson, especially if he or she tends to dominate planning meetings. The strategic planning process must allow the participants to explore new ideas without political risk or fear of embarrassment.

Because of the large volumes of information typically generated during the course of a strategic planning effort, it is important to plan up front for information storage, retrieval, and dissemination. It is particularly important that each participant have an updated version of the evolving strategic planning document for each meeting. This important responsibility may be delegated to the chairperson or the recording secretary.

Educate Key Planners and Managers

The initial meeting of the strategic planning group focuses on both organizational details and orientation. In the orientation component, it is important to use the time to educate the participants about the important aspects of the process upon which they are about to embark. To this end, a formal "educational briefing" approach works very effectively. Here, participants are introduced to the following important topics:

- Concept of strategic planning and its importance
- Major steps in the strategic planning process
- Company's objectives for the process
- Typical strategic planning problems and ways to successfully address them
- Critical factors that determine the level of success in the process
- Role of the individual in the process

Develop a Detailed Work Plan for Conducting the Strategic Planning Process

Within the first two to three planning meetings, the planning group develops a detailed work plan to serve as a comprehensive blueprint for conducting the strategic planning effort. Based on the key steps in the strategic planning process (Figure 8-1), this work plan identifies the following:

- Each major strategic planning step
- Specific activities required for each step
- Information requirements
- Assignment of individual responsibilities
- Major milestones and schedule
- Resource requirements
- Design of strategic planning document and other supporting documentation

The group then uses this work plan to plan and monitor the activities and the progress of individual meetings and the overall strategic planning process.

Plan Up Front to Institutionalize the Strategic Planning Process

By spending the time up front to plan for the participation of other individuals in the strategic planning process (who, how, and when), the firm will not only enhance the likelihood of successful planning and subsequent implementation, but will also lay solid groundwork for a process that will continue long after the initial strategic plan has been developed.

The most effective way to institutionalize the process is to directly build institutionalization into the detailed work plan. Important elements include:

- Timing and type of participation by nonplanning group members
- Communication of planning process objectives, activities, and progress to nonplanning members
- Solicitation of comments and suggestions from those not directly involved in the strategic planning process

Begin With the Assessment of the Company's Current Position

By the third planning meeting, the administrative and orientation activities have been completed, and the group members are ready to begin work. By plunging directly into the assessment of the company's current position, the group members will quickly develop a sense of:

- The volume of work and the amount of time involved in the strategic planning process
- The significant differences of opinion among the group members concerning the firm's current mission, goals, strategy, and operating and financial performance
- The immense difficulties to be encountered in trying to develop consensus on where the company should go and how it should get there.

CONCLUSION

Strategic planning provides an explicit and shared understanding of the nature and purpose of the company. The strategic plan motivates and directs employees in meeting the threats and exploiting the opportunities available in the marketplace. It also stabilizes the firm in times of turbulence and uncertainty. In short, it is a blueprint for future success because it identifies what the firm is and can be.

9

Multinational Strategic Planning Systems

DAVID C. SHANKS

Arthur D. Little, Inc.

FIGURE 9-1
Multinationality as a Function of Markets and Products

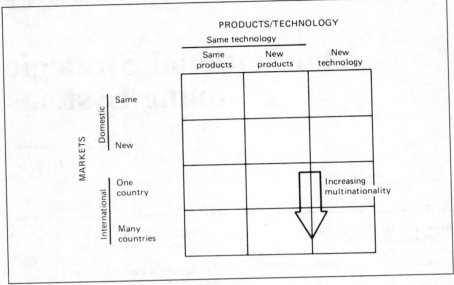

TRENDS AND DRIVING FORCES IN MULTINATIONAL ENTERPRISE

Multinational operations can be considered as an element of corporate strategy that involves the geographic scope of the enterprise. Multinationalism can be portrayed on a matrix model of corporate development activity, as shown in Figure 9-1.

A multinational corporation (MNC) is a corporate entity with a cluster of affiliated firms located in a number of countries. The more countries in which an MNC operates, the broader its scope and its acceptance into the "big league" of worldwide business enterprise. The affiliated firms of an MNC share several characteristics:

- They are linked by ties of common ownership.
- They draw on a common pool of resources, such as money and credit, information and systems, trade names and patents.
- They respond to the same strategy.

Since the 1960s, there have been significant shifts in the world economic and business environments that have affected MNC planning strategies. Some of these factors arose from reactions to changes in the world economy; others are actually the result of heightened MNC activity. Taken together, the following shifts have served as powerful driving forces that have shaped MNC strategy:

- Maturation of the economies of industrialized nations
- Emergence of new geographic market/business arenas (e.g., Soviet Union, Eastern Europe, Asia/Pacific countries)
- Growth of a new order of risk factors in conducting MNC operations
- A continuing increase in non-U.S. MNC ownership
- The appearance of state-owned enterprises in the roster of large MNCs
- Heightened scrutiny of MNC operations by U.S. (and other) governmental and regulatory agencies

Maturing Industrialized Economies

Since the mid-1970s, the economic growth rate of the United States, Canada, the United Kingdom, France, and Germany has slowed; it is not expected to perform at mid-century rates of 5 to 7 percent real growth. Performance on the order of 2 to 3 percent real growth is projected, and with more cyclicality than in earlier years. Among the reasons for this decreased growth rate are the final closing of geographic frontiers, slowing population growth, and aging infrastructures that are no longer maintained at the rate of physical depreciation. This is not to say that these markets are not extremely attractive for an MNC—the developed world is by definition both a producer and a consumer of most of our planet's goods and services. For established concerns, however, high product sales growth rates must be found by other means—through replacement markets, planned obsolescence, fashion, new or substitute products—or in other areas of the world where population and consumer demand is rising more rapidly.

Emergence of New Geographic Arenas

Significant geographic and political arenas have emerged recently as market and business opportunities for MNCs. During the 1970s and 1980s, the People's Republic of China was actively courted by MNCs following the normalization of diplomatic relations between China and the United States. The onset of the 1990s has brought immense change in the political structure and boundaries of Eastern Europe and the Soviet Union, requiring strategic response to rapidly changing diplomatic and political conditions. In this last decade of the twentieth century, Europe and the Soviet Union will be highly sought-after markets.

Other emerging nations, such as those with per capita incomes under $1,000 but with growth potential, also present future business opportunities. In fact, the U.S. Agency for International Development has designated several of these countries as opportunities for private sector investment by U.S. companies in joint ventures with locals. This is seen as a more effective way to promote economic growth than through direct government-to-government financial aid.

Increasing Risk Factors

Considering the history of commercial activity, trading risks have declined from the days when fire, shipwreck, piracy, and other business losses were commonplace events. Today's multinational strategist recognizes a new order of risks not present (or as prevalent) in earlier times: expropriation of assets, currency losses through exchange rate fluctuations and devaluations, unfavorable foreign court interpretations of contracts and agreements, social and/or political disturbances, import/export laws, tariffs, and suasions resulting in total or partial trade barriers.

Shift in Control

Over the past twenty years, there has been a gradual but definite shift in control of MNCs to corporations not based or owned in the United States. Almost 60 percent of the world's 180 largest corporations were controlled from outside of the United States in 1986, as opposed to less than 40 percent in 1963. The trend appears to be continuing.

The list of countries controlling major MNCs is growing larger, and is also concentrating in certain areas. Japan, the United Kingdom, Germany, France, Switzerland, and Canada have shown significant increases in the number of large MNCs. Also, emerging economics such as Korea, Brazil, the oil-rich nations in the Middle East, Venezuela, and Mexico have recently developed one or more large MNCs. These newer MNCs have different attitudes and incentives toward risk and return, fostered by different capital market structures (as in Japan), heavy government involvement (as with Mexico), or extensive international borrowings (as in Brazil).

State-Owned Enterprises

Multinational strategy must recognize that nationally owned enterprises are often managed in ways and for objectives that do not match free-market economic theories. State airlines are an example of single-product MNCs that compete with privately owned carriers worldwide. Such organizations are often viewed as instruments of national policy or visibility, and may offer services that are subsidized by the government and represent offerings with which a self-contained business operation cannot compete. Other examples of state-owned MNC activity include British Steel, Thomson, and Renault.

A cross-current trend in the 1990s is privatization, in which national enterprises are "unbundled" from government control and established as stand-alone competitors in the world marketplace. Under Margaret Thatcher, the United Kingdom has privatized a substantial number of national enterprises, including British Petroleum, British Airways, and Rolls-Royce—all major competitors in their respective global markets. Other examples include Alfa Romeo in Italy and Enasa in Spain. The driving force underlying all of these actions is making the enterprise more competitive with its global contenders.

Heightened Multinational Scrutiny

With the rise in U.S. multinational business activity during the 1960s came an increased awareness and scrutiny by governmental and regulatory bodies of the conduct of business in foreign countries. This intense examination was initiated, in part, by the realization that in some countries, foreign-owned MNCs represented effective control over a large sector of the country's economy. A case in point is U.S. oil interests in Middle Eastern nations, especially in Iran and Saudi Arabia, prior to the formation of the Organization of Petroleum Exporting Countries.

Adding to increased interest is another problem: overseas business practices conducted by U.S. and other MNCs that violate home country legal and ethical standards. Most notable are various payment schemes to foreign officials in return for contract awards. These "corrupt practices," as defined by the U.S. Foreign Corrupt Practices Act of 1977, are all the more problematic to foreigners whose home country laws and customs often permit such practices.

These two factors, economic control and corrupt practices, have led to a series of rules and regulations—voluntary and imposed—regarding MNC business operations, including disclosure or information, corrupt practices regulation, and codes of conduct.

DOMESTIC VS. MULTINATIONAL CORPORATION STRATEGIC PLANNING: A COMPARATIVE VIEW

Today's MNC must make strategic choices at several levels. These choices have the potential to change significantly the nature of the corporation's future business and performance. As shown in Figure 9-2, these choices exist at the corporate level, at the business unit or profit center level, and in the functions within each business unit, such as finance, manufacturing, marketing, sales, and research and development. This section concentrates on those planning concepts that are formulated,

FIGURE 9-2
Strategy Formulation Levels Within a Corporation

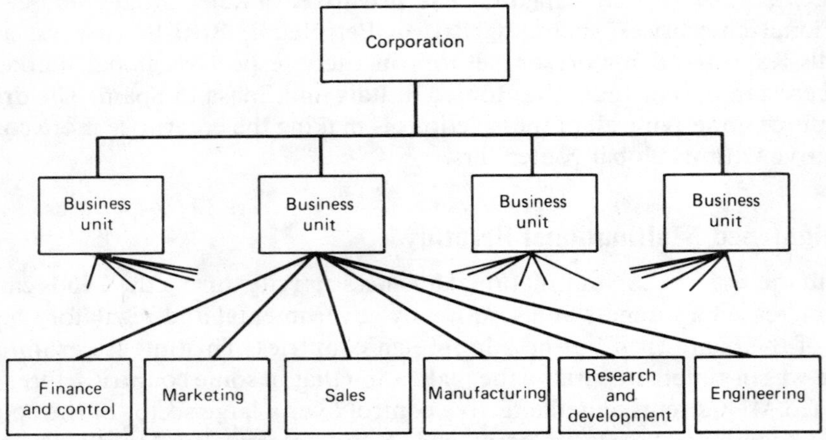

Note: Large corporations have introduced one or more levels between the business unit and the corporation, known variously as sectors, divisions, or groups.

approved, and executed at the business unit and corporate levels. Functional strategies, although important to the MNC, are beyond the scope of this treatment.

Domestic Strategy at the Business Unit Level

Among the most commonly adopted generic strategies at the business unit level of a domestic corporation are differentiation, overall cost leadership, and focus. Implementation of these strategies often involves adopting one of several strategic thrusts, as summarized in Figure 9-3.

FIGURE 9-3
Strategic Thrusts

• Start up	• Focus	• Catch up
• Grow with industry	• Renew	• Hang in
• Grow quickly	• Defend position	• Turn around
• Attain cost leadership	• Harvest	• Retrench
• Differentiate	• Develop niche	• Withdraw

For a domestic corporation, the strategic business unit (SBU) arena is limited principally to the selection of product line and associated technological breadth, depth, and diversity, and to the choice of markets and market segments within the home country's national boundaries.

In order for an accurate assessment to be made in most SBU strategic schemes, a microeconomic analysis of the industry is necessary. Success is greatest when there exists a more or less homogeneous set of factors, including a single market growth rate, competitor share concentration and structure, and level of demand saturation. Although such homogeneity may be found within the boundaries of the home country, it rarely is encountered in a multinational setting.

Multinational Strategy at the Business Unit Level

Because homogeneity rarely can be expected in a multinational setting, an SBU in a primarily domestic corporation must investigate and implement new and different planning strategies as it begins to expand into new markets beyond its national borders. One such strategy is to identify characteristics in each country of operation—individual industry, market, and relative competitive strength—and then combine these into a "portfolio" presentation, using the same analytical matrix for all countries.

The strategic options selected by a domestic SBU as it develops a multinational strategy often follow a common pattern of development, which can be outlined in a step-by-step procedure:

- Export
- Licensing
- Foreign sales representation
- Joint venture
- Establishment of foreign manufacturing
- Creation of a foreign SBU
- Creation of multiple foreign SBUs
- Rationalization of foreign SBU operations by specialization of function (global strategy)

As illustrated in Figure 9-4, an SBU's strategic degree of freedom increases (1) as its state of development in each country in which it wishes to operate advances and (2) as the number and diversity of countries of potential operation increases. When an MNC has operations and markets for one SBU distributed throughout several countries, and when these operations present opportunities for selective geographic leverage or focus for overall economic advantage, the range of strategic options broadens substantially.

FIGURE 9-4

Strategic Degrees of Freedom as a Function of Countries of Operation and Degree of Development

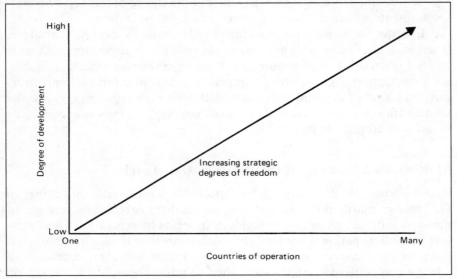

Recently, a clear distinction has been made between multidomestic and global industries. In the multidomestic case, business units follow separate strategies in individual foreign markets relatively unconnected with one another. In sharp contrast, global competition involves marshaling a worldwide business system against similar MNCs, or domestically oriented companies in each country. Individual country opportunities may be sacrificed, for example, to support a thrust in another geographic area. Companies involved in global competition are more likely to have a highly centralized planning operation. Some examples of global industries and principal competitors in the global arena are listed in Table 9-1.

Some important clues as to whether an MNC is dealing with a multidomestic or global industry lie in the abilities of purely domestic firms to combat foreign entrants in the market. For example, personal service companies such as law firms, accountancies, and insurance companies in every country have strong natural barriers to foreign competitors in detailed and complex local regulation, legislation, customs, and practice. Conversely, heavy subsidies by a home country government for a particular industry or technology may create a formidable economic advantage that can be exploited worldwide. The long U.S. dominance in commercial aircraft began with government-sponsored military airframe and engine technology. Until recently, no purely domestic competitor could match the world

TABLE 9-1

Global Industries and Competitors

Industry	Competitor
Watches	Timex
	Seiko
	Citizen
Nuclear reactors	Combustion Engineering
	Westinghouse
	General Electric
Construction equipment	Caterpillar
	Komatsu
Power generation equipment (turbines, generators)	General Electric
	Westinghouse
	Siemens
	Mitsubishi
Motorcycles	Honda
	Suzuki
	Kawasaki
Automobiles	Ford
	General Motors
	Toyota
	Volkswagen

market presence of Boeing and McDonnell Douglas in airframes, and General Electric and Pratt & Whitney in engines. Of concern to U.S.-based MNCs is the continuing lack of government industry cooperation in information technology and electronics, which signals erosion in long-term U.S. market position in those industries.

These clues, or criteria, can be divided into two areas: economic advantages and strategic strengths.

Economic advantages	Strategic strengths
• Capital costs	• Marketing
• Material and component costs	• Technology
• Economies of scale	• Information
• Government subsidies	• Quality control
	• Management systems
	• Market control
	• Human resources

Economic advantages are factors inherent in the countries of operation. Usually cost related, they result in lower labor, material, or critical overhead charges, such as transportation or taxes. Strategic strengths, under this definition, are the factors that facilitate the exploitation of economic advantages. Principally related to management and technology, they allow a global business system to be developed and efficiently operated.

FIGURE 9-5
Global Strategy Matrix

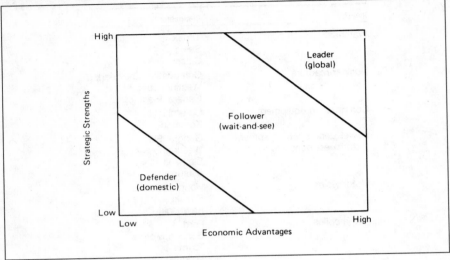

One possible analytical technique for assessing strategic and competitive advantages to determine an appropriate global competitive strategy is shown in Figure 9-5. Where a combination of economic advantages and strategic strengths appear low for global competition, as is the case with products such as Portland cement, beer, or glassware, a posture of defending individual domestic markets by stand-alone business units may be appropriate (the "defender" posture). Where both strategic strengths and economic advantages can be exploited through a worldwide network of business operations, as in consumer electronics, commercial aircraft, or motorcycles, the successful strategy may be an aggressive pursuit of a global strategy backed by sufficient corporate resources and exploitation of existing competitive position. This is represented in the "global leader" segment of the matrix. The remaining intermediate zone (the "follower" position) is an area in transition, where traditional domestic defense is giving way to global competition at an identifiable rate of change. It appears to present the most interesting strategic challenge: to identify correctly how fast the transition is occurring so investment and operations can be set in place to take maximum advantage of the change. Preemption is important, but being too early may result in unacceptable market returns and cash flow problems.

The color television industry, for example, moved through this transition in the ten years from the late 1960s to late 1970s. During that period, Japanese manufacturers, notably Matsushita, Sony, Toshiba, Sanyo, and

FIGURE 9-6

Possible Development Scenarios Toward Global Competition

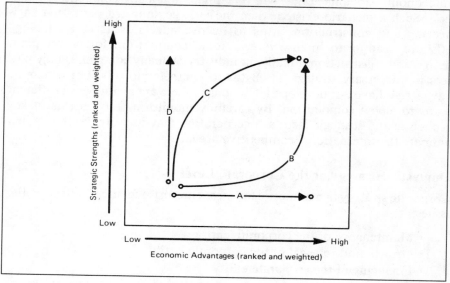

Hitachi, gained significant market-share advantages over U.S. and U.K. domestic producers, primarily due to their exploitation of the economic advantages of lower total costs and higher product quality, by means of exploiting strategic strengths in marketing and distribution.

This early identification of the transition from pure domestic to global competition is perhaps the most crucial element for both domestic and MNC-controlled SBUs. Obviously, the strategic strength and economic advantage factors illustrated in Figure 9-5 do not apply equally in all industries. These factors can be weighted and ranked according to relative importance, and the results plotted relative to time to assess the degree and speed of change toward global competitor status. Figure 9-6 illustrates the tracks of four different companies in their progression toward global competition.

The linear development of industry *A* indicates that although it may potentially benefit from substantial international economic advantages, global competition may never materialize because no company in that industry is able to exploit sufficient strategic strengths. In industry *B*, economic advantages develop over time and ultimately are coupled with significant increasing strategic strengths that will precipitate global competition. In the publishing industry, for example, the electronic communication of densely packed information is enabling publishers to compose printed material centrally and print locally by remote command.

Industry *C* has the advantage of significant strategic strengths. It is awaiting an economic advantage that will precipitate a globally competitive situation. Such a scenario existed when the U.S. government permitted engineering and construction firms to license nuclear reactor technology offshore, leading to intense international competition for power plant design and construction. Finally, in industry *D*, many companies may possess the necessary strategic strengths to compete globally, but economic advantages have not developed. Obviously, there are a number of different paths to global competition. By carefully monitoring movements of key economic and strategic factors, a corporation may identify the trends that animate the international competitive arena.

Domestic Strategy at the Corporate Level

Corporate strategy in a domestic business enterprise focuses on these major issues:

- Maintenance of the corporate entity
- Growth and renewal of the corporate entity
- Financing of the corporate entity
- Organization, measurement, and control of the corporate entity
- Management of external relationships

A domestic corporation contends with issues that are largely circumscribed within the boundaries of the home country. MNC corporate strategic planning must deal with these same issues; however, the complexity of the planning task increases with the introduction of new languages, cultures, currencies, and economic and political systems.

Multinational Strategy at the Corporate Level

An MNC must add several issues to the list of strategic priorities of a domestic corporation:

- International risk
- Logistics
- International finance
- Government relationships

International Risk. In recent years, international risk has been of significant importance in MNC corporate planning. The threat of economic and employee losses in operations increases when a corporation begins to move beyond its familiar frontiers. Expropriations in Cuba after the 1960 revolution and in Iran in 1979, executive kidnappings in Argentina, assassinations in Mexico, and contract repudiations in Nigeria are testimony to

TABLE 9-2

Examples of Risk Assessment Techniques

Technique originator	Technique	Characteristics
Arthur D. Little, Inc.	Custom forecasts	Business profiles that identify risk factors and offer alternative strategy development
Charles W. Hofer and Terry Haller	Globescan	Comprehensive analysis incorporating several decision and support models
Frederick T. Haner	Business Environmental Risk Index (BERI)	Expert weighting and ranking of 15 key economic and political variables
Political Risk Services (ICB-U.S.A., Inc.)	World Country Report Services	Scenario-based political risk forecasts
Probe International	Custom forecasts	In-depth narrative discussions of present/future conditions

the multiform and multicausal business problems that are compounded by the world's diverse economic, social, racial, and political forces.

A number of methods for assessing international risk have been developed during the past twenty years. Most rely on scanning a variety of social, political, and economic factors in a given country and rating and ranking these to arrive at an index of the likelihood of some business interruption. A sampling of these techniques is presented in Table 9-2.

Current international risk-assessment techniques consider political development, societal achievement, technical advancement, and resource abundance of the host country in assessing three types of risk:

- *Business risk*—fluctuations in operating income
- *Financial risk*—fluctuations in debt repayments
- *Catastrophic risk*—termination of operating income

Beyond assessing risk, an MNC requires a mechanism for dealing with the social and political forces that exist in its host country. Conflict management strategy is an important component of the overall MNC strategy for relationships with host countries.

Logistics. As operations expand throughout the world, logistics becomes an element of strategy with important dimensions. Attention to logistics must include data and information flow as well as physical product movement. Key issues in MNC information systems planning include:

- Transborder data-flow restrictions;
- Unionization of data processing departments outside the United States;
- Additional recordkeeping for compliance with the Foreign Corrupt Practices Act (and its equivalent in other governments);

- Increasing interdependence among operating units; and
- Rapid technological developments in information processing.

Facilities planning and location often determine the logistics of product movements. Capital-intensive manufacturing and distribution facilities often become a keystone in MNC strategic plans.

International Finance. All corporations must adopt financial strategies, including internal and external financing, debt and equity balancing, and other means of ensuring the growth and integrity of the enterprise. Multinationals, however, face significantly greater challenges in their financing operations than domestic corporations. Factors specific to multinational enterprises include:

- Currency exchange
- Currency translations
- Local inflation rates
- Local tax laws
- Regulations on repatriation of earnings

Beyond handling these factors, MNCs must deal strategically with pressure for local ownership and differing investment expectations. For example, Mexico has adopted a policy that requires local majority ownership of foreign multinational operations. In some instances, the local partner must be the government, as is the case with certain industries in France.

With local ownership often comes different expectations of appropriate business returns. Local owners, especially governments, may take a long-term view of profitability levels and the rates and timing of returns. For them, stable employment and the lack of more attractive alternative investment opportunities are the most important considerations. The foreign multinational may have better alternatives for investment, and typically desires a faster, higher return. Local borrowing has been one way to reduce foreign MNC direct investment and still enable the MNC to maintain control of the local venture.

Government Relationships. Some leading analysts of multinational enterprise maintain that relations with other countries are (or should be) the central strategic issue for an MNC. They believe that, depending on the circumstances, it is of strategic importance for a corporation to resist, comply with, or lead socioeconomic trends in a host country.

Most MNCs must pay special attention to their external relationships with host countries. It is not only in the Third World or less-developed countries that these relationships must be watched carefully. Especially in industries with high technological content, governments may require a range of considerations including, but not limited to, offsets, countertrade arrangements, local content requirements, and technology partnerships agreements; as well as requirements for local equity participation through a joint venture, alliance, or partnership agreement. In this context, successful MNCs such as IBM, Nestle, and Coca-Cola have adopted the strategy "think global, act local" as a way to become accepted into the variety of world communities in which they operate.

In his book, *The Competitive Advantage of Nations,* Michael Porter notes another important factor for consideration in the MNC strategy equation: the existence of related and supporting industries that speed production, assist in technology development, aid in distribution, or provide similar synergistic leverage to businesses. Examples include the "intelligence alley" group of software development firms in Cambridge, Massachusetts; the clusters of component and materials suppliers around the major Japanese automobile manufacturers; and the sustained focus on technological training and education coupled with a young, receptive labor force that is driving the information processing industry in Ireland.

MULTINATIONAL CORPORATION STRATEGIC PLANNING SYSTEMS

Given the range of planning factors and the variety of enterprises that must be considered, there are few hard and fast rules about MNC strategic planning systems. The factors needed to develop a sound plan vary, however, according to the level (SBU vs. corporate) and complexity (domestic vs. multinational) of the problem, making it possible to highlight those factors of key importance to a firm. The nature and scope of these factors in turn determine the type of planning system best suited to the strategic information and control requirements of that particular enterprise.

Strategic Planning Systems at the Multidomestic Stategic Business Unit Level

As illustrated in Table 9-3, a firm conducting a multidomestic SBU operation is faced with a geographic market portfolio planning problem. The individual markets have few, if any, points of commonality that call for centrally directed product or market strategies. Essential elements of a planning system for this type of MNC operation include:

- Wide latitude for individual countries to develop local (home country) plans and programs for dealing with unique products, markets, and sets of competitors

TABLE 9-3

A Comparison of SBU-Level Strategic Planning Factors

Factor	Single domestic	Multidomestic	Global
Industry			
Demand	Stems from a single set of factors	Different demands/factors by country/area	Unified by a common product or selling theme
Driving forces	Homogeneous set	Heterogeneous set	Multivariate, but may be used to balance/optimize a global system of competition
Trends	A single set	Vary; may offset/balance	
Market			
Growth	Homogeneous growth rate for overall industry	Several different growth rates; can vary widely	Several different growth rates; can vary widely
Key segments	A single set	Different sets may exist	Different sets may exist
Customer groups	A single set	Different sets by country	Different sets by country
Trends	A single set	May vary by country	May vary by country
Competitor			
Nature/ownership	Single set	May vary among countries	Trend toward concentration
Concentration/shares	Single set	May vary widely among countries	Trend toward concentration in a few globally active competitors
Bases of competition	Similar for all competitors across the industry or niche	—	—
Strategic thrust	—	—	Complementary roles assigned by country or region
Technology			
Products	Similar sets exist within the industry offerings	Different sets may exist; vary widely country by country	Common themes exist across international boundaries
Substitutes	If existent, present for all competitors	May exist only in some countries/areas	May exist only in some countries/areas
Raw materials	Tend to be equally accessible to all competitors	Individual countries/areas may have advantages	Individual countries/areas may have advantages
Financial			
Cost structure	A single range exists within the industry	Varies by country	Varies by country; used to fine-tune a global system
Investment intensity	—	—	Varies by function emphasized
Profitability	—	—	—

- Tight central control over flow of funds and resource allocations, based on operating and financial performance indicators from local operating units
- Central analysis, but with local input, of the overall SBU portfolio performance, including local political and economic risk, relative currency valuations, exchange rates, and operating and ownership policies and regulations

Kawasaki motorcycles, which entered the United States three decades ago, is a useful example of a multidomestic business. Kawasaki's planning system allowed a great deal of flexibility, enabling it to permit U.S. operations to develop creative product and market strategies without threatening the company's central control over basic financial factors, including the overall level of reinvestment in the U.S. business.

Kawasaki motorcycles have become a world-class competitive product through the efforts of Kawasaki Heavy Industries, the Japanese conglomerate. In the early 1960s, the Kawasaki motorcycle was produced in Japan principally for the Japanese market. Domestic sales were leveling off and management sought further opportunities for growth. At Kawasaki, motorcycles are produced by the Engine and Motorcycle Group, which is responsible for small internal combustion engines, motorcycles, and jet engines. Although part of a much larger entity, the strategy of the motorcycle business unit approximates that of a single-business company. The major strategic milestones in the evolution of Kawasaki motorcycles as a multinational operation include:

- Establishment of a U.S.-based marketing and sales office in 1965
- Introduction of export motorcycle sales to the United States, supported by heavy advertising and sales promotion expenditures in the late 1960s and early 1970s
- Development of an extensive independent domestic distribution and dealer network
- Establishment of a continuing stream of product innovations and models directed toward satisfying the recreational motorcycle buyer in the United States
- Ensurance of a prompt parts supply system through its distributors and a company warehouse system
- Establishment of the first Japanese motorcycle assembly facility in the United States, in Lincoln, Nebraska, in 1974

Kawasaki's successful penetration of the U.S. market required a considerable initial investment. The motorcycle division ran its U.S. operations at a loss for fourteen years, from 1964 to 1978. Kawasaki continues to assemble motorcycles at its Nebraska plant, and local U.S. content of the plant's motorcycle products has reached approximately 40 percent. In order to compensate for a slump in U.S. motorcycle demand during the late 1980s, Kawasaki also expanded its U.S. business to include production of automobile-related parts and components to maintain its Nebraska plant operating levels.

Kawasaki's overall U.S. entry strategy has proved remarkably successful in terms of gaining and holding a strong competitive position. The key elements of this strategy included (1) freedom for U.S. operations to develop distinctive products, distribution channels, advertising, and marketing, and (2) control over the flow of funds to ensure that the necessary investment was made to develop the market.

Global Competition

An MNC engaged in global competition, as shown in Table 9-3, tends to tailor its planning system along the following lines:

- Central (typically home country) control over the scope and contribution of individual countries' operations at the production, distribution, and marketing levels; based upon varying regional advantages in skills, raw materials, and other resources; energy costs; transportation; or rates of market growth.
- Central monitoring and control of resource allocation, performance goals, and risk indicators
- Central development, dissemination, and control of key factors in technological and product-related success, including product design, product quality, parts interchangeability, field service, and warranty provisions

Operating a planning system for a globally competitive product implies (1) a higher order of detailed communications with line and staff personnel in all countries of operation and (2) a method to motivate and reward individual country operations effectively and equitably for what may be perceived to be a suboptimization of that country's potential.

Timex Corporation, the Waterbury, Connecticut watch manufacturer, is a classic example of the development of multinational business operations with a single product line. Over a twenty-year period, from 1950 to 1970, Timex grew to dominate the worldwide wristwatch industry by radically changing the basis of competition. In doing so, Timex put into play a comprehensive mix of centrally controlled marketing, manufacturing, and distribution strategies.

The basic Timex product is an inexpensive pin-lever watch engineered for mass production and assembly. Most wristwatches in the early 1950s were of Swiss manufacture, built in a relatively labor-intensive process from individually fitted components. Unable to sell its watches through jewelry stores, the traditional distribution channel, Timex introduced its product through a wide variety of retail outlets, including drug stores, hardware stores, and large mass merchants. The product was backed by a generous one-year warranty, coupled with a lifetime low-cost service policy. Heavy advertising stressed high value in service, durability, and reliability. Timex built a worldwide network of over fifteen manufacturing and assembly plants to support its sales. These facilities were designed for the lowest-cost piece-part fabrication and incorporated the latest in automated small-parts assembly and testing equipment. Manufacturing, designed to produce interchangeable parts, took place under rigid quality control. The lightweight watch movements, cases, and straps were shipped by air freight for subassembly and final assembly at locations that took maximum advantage of import duty and tariff regulations.

Timex's integrated business strategy was formulated and directed from the top of the company by its founder, Joachim Lehmkuhl. It is interesting to note that the Timex strategic thrust remained essentially unchanged for more than two decades. Key strategic elements included:

- Low-cost manufacturing
- Broad, efficient mass distribution
- High product reliability
- Creative customer service

In the 1970s, however, Timex was battered by the popular introduction of the digital electronic watch. Late to enter this technology, which calls for radically different movement manufacturing techniques, Timex saw its worldwide market share erode. In an effort to catch up, Timex entered the consumer electronics field with a diversity of products ranging from digital electronic watches to cameras to home computers. Expanding into new products, each with their own highly competitive established markets, did not solve Timex's problems, but multiplied them instead.

In the mid-1980s, Timex management decided to return to the business Timex knew best—watches. Capitalizating on Timex's traditional strengths in watch manufacturing, distribution, and marketing, and adding to these outstanding product design and development talent, Timex has rebounded to capture 50 percent of the $10 to $50 watch market worldwide. Moreover, the company's foray into electronics has enabled it to become a successful computer parts and components supplier (i.e., printed circuit boards and disk drive heads).

Multinational Strategic Planning at the Corporate Level

As with the planning systems of domestic corporations, multinational strategic planning at the corporate level tends to address the business and environmental challenges and opportunities present in its planning horizon. However, these factors are usually more complex and varied than for a domestic enterprise. As outlined in Table 9-4, the multinational firm must usually pay close attention to these key factors:

TABLE 9-4
A Comparison of Corporate-Level Strategic Planning Factors

Factor	Domestic	Multinational
Internal environment		
Culture, values, heritage	Homogeneous	Homogeneous (parent nation); coupled with heterogeneous satellite country operations
Compensation and reward system	Simple; single-country customs, laws, regulations	Complex; multicountry customs, tax laws, regulations
Corporate strengths and weaknesses	Single set	Multiple set; satellite operations may either complement or offset parent company
Financial control system	Focused on single country operations control	Multivariate; requires understanding of each host country's regulations
Stakeholder interests/influences	Relatively homogeneous	Potentially heterogeneous; especially with widely distributed ownership situations
External environment		
Economic driving forces	Single set	Multiple sets
Social and political factors	Uniform set	Diverse and dissimilar; potentially clustered by stage of national economic development
Overall risk of operations	Usually well understood; managed by balancing investment in domestic business portfolio	Less predictable; managed by balancing investment in individual businesses and in overall multinational portfolio mix
Business portfolio		
Mix and diversity	Often more diverse than with multinationals; more industry sectors	Diversity often achieved through geographic scope rather than through product proliferation
Relatedness	Trend away from conglomeration; toward common themes	Varies; high degree of relatedness in globally competitive multinationals
Number and complexity of units	Varies	Varies
Ownership and control	Units tend to be wholly owned/controlled by parent corporation	High degree of parent corporation influence/control; tempered by local national regulation of foreign ownership

- A corporate culture more varied and diffused throughout several countries (especially if the MNC has grown through acquisition)
- A broader range of shareholders and shareholder interests (especially if the MNC operates in countries where significant minority or majority interests are part of a national policy)
- A need to understand and deal with a broad range of world economic, social, and political forces
- A need to communicate, control, organize, and reward employees worldwide, with sensitivity to local custom and practice, while supporting corporate goals and objectives

Given these requirements, research and experience with MNC corporate planning systems show the following general trends:

- Multinational corporate plans are developed at the parent company's headquarters.
- Business unit plans are developed:
  — Locally, if they are for domestic or multidomestic SBUs;
  — Centrally, with local input, if they are for globally competitive SBUs.
- Environmental factors are recognized as crucial to planning.
- Financial considerations dominate corporate plans.
- Contingency planning is receiving increased emphasis.

An interesting example of a corporation with a centralized, corporate-level plan development is Akzo, N.V., a chemicals and fibers MNC based in the Netherlands. It was formed in 1969 through a merger of Aku, a synthetic fiber manufacturer, and KZO, a chemicals manufacturer. In 1971, the Akzo board of management, dissatisfied with prior planning methods, called for a revised approach. The new system consisted of these major elements:

- Division of the corporation into units appropriate for strategic planning (about 100 within Akzo)
- Initial classification of each planning unit according to its strategic position and role for growth and funds
- Development of a strategic plan for each unit, with emphasis on:
  — Environmental analysis;
  — Portfolio positioning;
  — Strategic options; and
  — Proposed strategy and required resources
- Development of divisional and corporate objectives and strategies, including resource allocation guide lines
- Allocation of resources to the planning units

- Development of planning unit action programs, targets for financial performance (especially cash flow), and targets for capital expenditures

Akzo strategic plans for a five-year period were developed and revised each spring. Return-on-investment targets were established for each unit, based on that unit's strategic position, corporate expectations, and unit strategies. Unit plan reviews were conducted in three meetings between the Akzo Presidium and divisional boards of management. Although planning units were responsible for development of detailed strategies and programs, Akzo placed ultimate responsibility for portfolio strategy and resource allocation with the central authority. Akzo also has linked research and development planning with its corporate and planning unit strategies—an important step for a technology-based corporation.

As evinced by Akzo, centralized portfolio planning is an important tool at the corporate level of an MNC. Although individual SBU plans may be prepared by local or regional management (depending on the global nature of competition), a centralized approach is usually taken to monitor risk and exposure, adjust the overall mix of business activity, and achieve a coherent strategy for growth and renewal.

SOME IMPLICATIONS FOR FUTURE MULTINATIONAL CORPORATION PLANNING SYSTEMS

From the perspective of the United States, and probably of Japan and Europe as well, three developments—world environmental trends, advances in strategic planning methods and techniques, and MNC performance and the outcome of existing strategic directions—imply the following shifts in MNC planning systems:

- More use of strategic management techniques to enhance planning and analysis;
- An emphasis on technology as a major issue in strategy development;
- Recognition of specialization of function in country operations in global strategy formulation;
- A search for more relatedness in business unit portfolios; and
- An increase in risk-sharing through joint ventures, research and development partnerships, and other multicompany business operations.

Implications for Strategic Management

In contrast to strategic planning and analysis, strategic management encompasses the implementation of a corporation's plans and programs.

Domestic corporations are integrating "linkage" mechanisms—techniques to ensure plan accomplishment—into the corporate strategic planning process. These include tying the budgeting and control process to plans, adjusting the reward and compensation system to fit business unit mandates, and finding ways to ensure that business unit accomplishments are in line with the strategy selected. Highlights of this process include:

- Overall planning assumptions, goals, and objectives, and a statement of strategic guidelines are developed by corporate planning, and presented and discussed at a meeting of worldwide line and staff managers.
- Individual country business plans are developed and submitted to corporate management following overall planning guidelines.
- A corporate analysis of country plans is made and country business managers are notified of necessary adjustments.
- At an annual meeting, corporate and country business managers present and discuss plans:
  - A corporate operating plan covering the first year of each five-year plan, containing the necessary budget and program detail for financial and operational control.
  - The five-year corporate strategic plan, establishing overall business directions.

This process places high importance on the implementation aspects of the firm's strategy. As a result of focused discussions during planning meetings, strategic plans are prepared with specific program elements, key milestones, responsibility assignments, and associated expense and revenue targets, which are reported, monitored, and controlled.

Effects of Increasing Influence of Technology

With the proliferation of manufacturing locations, MNCs have created a diffusion of state-of-the-art process and product technology throughout the free world. Japanese and U.S. electronics companies have trained locals in Hong Kong, Singapore, Sri Lanka, and other developing Asian countries. These countries are now producing their own "me too" products, which often do not carry the overhead and research and development costs of the originators. The impact of technology diffusion will probably be to truncate lead times, and possibly shorten product life-cycles.

The natural reaction of technological leaders will be to protect lead time, which represents the recovery window for capital investment. Centralized research and development facilities in the home country and the careful division of manufacturing responsibility to avoid "complete systems" knowledge may be one way to achieve this objective. Another is to consider maintaining strict confidentiality on processes, formulas, and techniques, instead of placing them in the public domain through the patent system. Coca-Cola's secret soft drink formulation is a case in point. More recently, IBM has maintained a high degree of secrecy regarding its entry into the microcomputer industry with personal computers.

Specialization of Functions

The trend to maximize the efficiency of globally competitive businesses fosters the rational consideration of MNC functions. The search for low-cost labor in Latin America and Asia has been the most visible evidence of this trend. Other countries may offer different advantages, such as low-cost energy, inexpensive or readily available raw materials, low taxes (or high subsidies), favorable trade regulations, or available technical, scientific, or other critical skills. In a process similar to that used by domestic corporations that "rationalize" facilities by adding more efficient units and closing inefficient ones, MNCs will gradually focus each country's resources on areas of strength and away from areas of relative disadvantage.

A scan of recent national industrial development advertising sections in business periodicals demonstrates the emphasis that some countries have been placing on their relative advantages to the international business community:

- *Ireland*—productive assembly labor force, tax advantages, European Economic Community access
- *Germany*—skilled labor, technology
- *Brazil*—abundant natural resources, developing markets, attractive potential for foreign ownership
- *Japan*—skilled, productive work force; access via trading to world markets
- *Argentina*—natural resources

Search for Relatedness

Recent studies have shown that the earnings performance of pure conglomerates has not met that of single-business or closely related business companies. Current corporate portfolio analysis seeks relatedness among business units, as opposed to the pure financial "portfolio balance" models of the 1970s. Relatedness, or fit, can be achieved in many dimensions, including markets, customers, products, technology, management skills, and geography. Although many MNCs appear to have a single—or related—industry focus, future acquisition and divestiture programs may produce even more of a fit as MNCs, like domestic corporations, strive to perfect what they do best.

Increase in Risk Sharing

Entry into markets of significant size and growth requires heavy investments. Many high-growth areas of the world are also relatively unstable socially and politically. Furthermore, many countries require a local ownership share. For these reasons, joint ventures between two or more MNCs, a foreign MNC and a local partner, or between an MNC and a local government, will become increasingly common.

10

Surveys and Data Bases: Management Tools for Information-Based Organizations

MICHAEL R. COOPER

President and Chief Executive Officer, Opinion Research Corporation

BRIAN S. MORGAN

Vice President and Worldwide Practice Director, Opinion Research Corporation

INTRODUCTION

The trend for organizations in the 1990s to become increasingly driven by information represents a fundamental transformation of the corporation. It is not just a bolting-on of information systems and information technology to the existing structure. Drucker[1] characterizes this new organization as

---

[1] P. Drucker, "The Coming of the New Organization." *Harvard Business Review* (Jan.-Feb. 1988, pp. 45–53.

one in which work is done by cross-functional teams made up of specialists, each team with its own experience and knowledge base. These organizations place a premium on effective analysis and diagnosis. Therefore, the quality and the utility of information are paramount.

Surveys and data bases created from them are integral parts of this new fund of information. Primary information from surveys and data bases is becoming more and more integral to strategic decision-making. Managers at all levels in every department are relying on survey findings to guide their activities. Survey findings are indispensable for developing and maintaining competitive advantage. They replace speculation with quantitative information, providing management with vital perspectives on strategic, marketing, customer relations, and human resource issues.

To ensure that they have information, and not just data, managers must ask:

- Do I have the kind of information I need to guide and support my work? To track my progress toward meeting objectives?
- Am I getting high-quality information?
- Am I getting the most out of my information?
    — Is it analyzed, interpreted, and packaged to help me make decisions?
    — Are data bases being created? Can I monitor trends and develop benchmarks?

To be an effective management tool, information from surveys must meet all of the foregoing criteria and must complement other management information to enhance managers' capability to make effective decisions.

This chapter explores the effective use of surveys for management decision making, using case material from Opinion Research Corporation (ORC) survey programs. The issues covered include:

- Strategic uses of surveys and data bases in organizations
- Planning and conducting survey programs
- Building data bases of results and linking these data bases

STRATEGIC USES OF SURVEYS AND DATA BASES

Senior management can use information from surveys for strategy definition and company positioning. Then, once it sets a strategic direction, it can use surveys to track the effectiveness of organization components as each component strives for alignment with corporate strategy. The array of information that surveys can generate falls under the headings of strategy and positioning, product issues, and service issues.

A strategy and positioning survey might be conducted for a client consisting of the chief executive officer (CEO), the vice-president of planning, and other members of the senior management team. The issues addressed can include:

- *Image among shareholders and the investment community.* Information from these key publics provides an important perspective on the company, its management, its product and service quality, and its prospects as an investment. This information is useful for planning new strategic initiatives, evaluating reactions to recent financial results or other events involving the company, and evaluating and planning corporate communications efforts.

- *Image among customers.* Client and customer opinions of the company, the company's overall reputation, and its reputation for service and quality are important determinants of purchasing decisions. Management should be tracking these indexes on an ongoing basis as part of its effort to stay in close touch with the marketplace.

- *Image and valuation of possible acquisition candidates.* Corporate image is linked to value. An ORC study demonstrated that price/ earnings ratios are higher in companies in which management is viewed as innovative and forward-looking and quality is considered high (see Figure 10-1). For purposes of this study, companies in the ORC Corporate Reputation data base were divided among three categories representing low, medium, or high price-earnings ratios. Then, the reputations of companies in the three categories were compared. Reputation was defined as the ratings of the company given by a cross-section of executives in large U.S. companies on each of nine dimensions. The dimensions include:

  — Innovative and forward-looking management
  — Aggressive research and development programs
  — Good midterm personal investment
  — Responsive to customers' needs and problems
  — Reputation for offering high-quality products or services
  — Recognition of corporate social responsibilities
  — Effective corporate communications programs
  — Establishment and pursuit of high standards of ethical practice
  — Responsiveness to environmental concerns

As the results shown in Figure 10-1 indicate, the reputation of a company, and especially the characteristics of the company that make up its overall reputation, can provide important information to potential acquirers. Will the association between the acquiring and target companies enhance the reputation of either company? Of both? Of neither? Are there management issues in the target company that may produce obstacles to successful post-merger integration or that may signal potential hidden costs of integration?

FIGURE 10-1

ORC Corporate Reputation Value Index
Close Link Between Management, Quality, and Price/Earnings Ratio

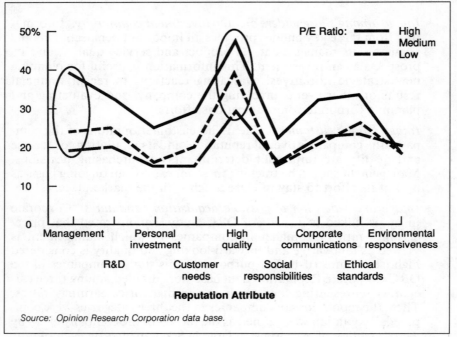

Source: *Opinion Research Corporation data base.*

- *Corporate brand equity.* Corporate brand equity, defined as the value of a company name in and of itself, can be measured by gauging customer reactions to the name and its competitors. In acquisitions, assumptions and judgments about the potential value of a company's name are often made on the basis of qualitative, sketchy information. A more quantitative approach can increase confidence in the accuracy of these important judgments, and can provide an assessment of the impact of the acquisition on corporate brand equity.

- *Emerging market trends.* Information on emerging customer needs and wants permits management to set product and service development priorities. In an era of extremely competitive markets, early alerts to changing market trends are essential for maintaining or building an advantage.

A product issues survey might be conducted for a client who is a vice-president of marketing, a brand manager, or a market research manager. Among the survey topics may be brand awareness, customer satisfaction, and pricing issues. Survey information on these issues has long been a mainstay of marketing management. What is new in this area are the growing reliance on instant information, using scanner technology, for rapid tracking of purchases and the use of large data bases to identify characteristics of purchasers.

A service issues survey might be conducted for a client who is a CEO, a vice-president of planning, a vice-president of quality, a vice-president of marketing, among others. Service quality is a major driver of customer attraction and retention. Service quality studies can cover such issues as responsiveness of sales and customer service staff, customer satisfaction, service to internal customers, and supplier relations. The uses of each type of survey for management decision making are explored below, and case examples of each drawn from ORC survey and consulting assignments are provided.

Strategy and Positioning

As noted earlier, management may require a strategy or positioning study for a number of reasons. Two cases encompassing a number of these reasons are described here.

- *A company is considering an acquisition.* A leading company in its industry is interested in acquiring a smaller company serving a similar client base. In addition to the hard financial data, management needs to know how investors, customers, and others view the target company, how these publics view the combined entity, and how the marketplace views the potential fit between a new brand and existing product or service lines. ORC assessed the reputation of the larger company, the target company, and other competitors among portfolio managers, individual investors, and customers. The results revealed that while customers viewed the target company as a preferred supplier, the investment community gave mixed readings of the target company's management, reputation, and track record. Investors also believed that the acquiring company's image was far superior to the target's image. Compared to the target, the acquiring company was far more likely to be seen as a good investment, a producer of quality products, a strong worldwide competitor, and a company with strong senior management. Few investors planned to acquire more shares of the target company, and current shareholders of the target company were far more likely to say that they planned to sell their shares than that they were going to buy more. The company decided not to pursue the acquisition at the present time, but to wait for an opportunity to buy the company at a lower price.

- *A company is reevaluating its position in the marketplace.* The management of a large service organization wants to plan new strategic investments, and needs to know how the organization is viewed in the markets it currently serves and in the markets it wants to serve.

ORC evaluated the visibility, overall reputation, and perceived strengths and weaknesses of the company and its key competitors. It interviewed the organization's clients and others in the industry to help define the attributes that drive decisions to purchase the type of services offered. Then, using a larger sample of the client base, it conducted structured telephone interviews, asking respondents to rate the importance of the attributes and to rate the client company and its competitors on these attributes.

Although the client company was widely recognized and highly regarded in many areas, it consistently came in second as a preferred supplier. It was recognized as having breadth, but was viewed as just outclassed in most of its major service areas. These results led the company to improve its services by putting staff with higher level expertise in day-to-day client contact roles and by custom-tailoring services to client requirements rather than relying on existing formulas. The company also conducted an image campaign to help redefine its position in the marketplace.

Product Issues

In the context of a well-conceived market strategy, it is appropriate to examine marketing issues related to particular products. A wide range of market research programs fall under the heading of "product issues," including studies on:

- Competitor and client brand strengths and weaknesses
- New product design
- Market sizing
- Segmentation of market needs
- Location of market gaps that offer new market opportunities
- Price and revenue optimization

Two examples of how companies have used these types of surveys are presented here:

- *A company wants to market a new product.* A major pharmaceutical company is interested in marketing a new prescription drug in an established market segment. The company asked ORC to study the market. ORC chose to use purchase decision modeling, a trade-off analysis technology, for this assignment. This technology allows the respondents, in this case allergy sufferers, to choose a product from an array looking much like a store shelf. The research task closely simulates the actual purchasing decision. By asking respondents to make a series of choices of the type just described, an attribute set can be created that contains information on various configurations of product features. The information gathered from this type of study can be used to identify important product attributes, to guide pricing decisions, and to estimate the size of the marketplace.

The results indicated that the nonsedating aspect of the drug was an important feature to the nation's sufferers of upper respiratory allergies, a market of over 42 million people. Moreover, the study identified a new market, "silent sufferers," who would not use then-available prescription drugs because of the drowsiness they induced.

Using the decision model to forecast the market, ORC developed a pricing strategy and recommended a price point two times higher than the one product management was considering. With this information, the company adopted a strategy that made the new drug the market leader within six weeks of introduction.

- *A company is considering producing a higher-quality product.* A manufacturer wants to produce higher clarity art-frame glass than any currently on the market. ORC conducted a study to determine:

  — Whether consumers were willing to pay for clearer glass
  — Whether the market could support a new, premium glass while the company maintained production of its current brands
  — Whether consumers would perceive the new brand's greater clarity and value

The study found that marketing a clearer glass would enhance the manufacturer's image as a technologically advanced company, but that projected revenue would not offset major increases in production costs.

As a result, the manufacturer made only minor production changes, which improved the clarity of the company's existing brands, and was able to redirect millions of development dollars.

Service Issues

In today's competitive market place, product quality alone is not sufficient to attract and retain customers. Service quality is also required. For example, in banking, service quality is far and away the number one factor driving customers to begin or terminate a relationship with a bank. In the auto industry, while product quality is the number one reason that customers choose a make, product and service quality are equally weighted as reasons that customers move on to another make. Expectations for service and perceived performance of the best and average firms varies substantially by industry. Gaps between expected and perceived performance are largest in the automobile and insurance industries, and lowest in the hotel industry.

In a service quality study, ORC assessed the methods used by a large telecommunications company for measuring customer expectations and satisfaction. ORC interviewed business purchasers and found that they place a high premium on product quality and service timeliness. Other interviews identified barriers at the company that hindered employees' ability to meet customer expectations. ORC recommended improvements in internal communications and interdepartmental cooperation and a new system for monitoring performance.

Guided by study recommendations, the company altered internal operational procedures and redesigned its internal service quality measurement methods to make them consistent with what customers viewed as high quality service.

PLANNING AND CONDUCTING SURVEY PROGRAMS

Regardless of the focus, an effective survey program typically contains the following phases:

1. Issues identification, in which issues to be studied are identified by means of meetings with management, exploratory interviews, and examination of any other data sources available, including company documents and reports, results of other surveys, and the like

2. Questionnaire design, in which questionnaires are constructed using custom items designed to address topics surfaced in the issue identification phase, data base items on which normative information is available, demographic items designed to segment respondents, and open-ended items used to provide respondents with an opportunity to make comments

3. Information gathering, in which data are gathered from respondents over the telephone, in personal interviews, and through the mail

4. Analysis and interpretation, in which computer analyses of data and interpretations of data are performed and presentations and reports are prepared

5. Implementation, in which the final presentation of results to management is made and the results are translated into actions. Action planning includes several steps:

   a. Ensuring management understanding of, and agreement with, the key issues that need to be addressed;

   b. For each concern, assigning responsibility for studying the issues, developing solutions, and planning for implementation;

   c. Reviewing progress against an established timetable; and

   d. Monitoring changes to ensure that desired goals are achieved.

Development of an action plan should begin early in the survey program. Without a well-thought-out strategy for translating results into action, a survey will produce lots of data but little valuable business information.

BUILDING AND LINKING DATA BASES

The final step in the effective use of information from surveys is to realize that the value of the information collected does not end at the conclusion of an individual study. Each survey produces information that can be used for additional purposes.

At the most basic level, a company can use information from a survey as a benchmark. When it later has other surveys done, it can chart progress, whether it is monitoring company image over time, tracking employee attitudes toward a performance appraisal plan, or keeping tabs on customer reactions to a new distribution program.

Beyond this, a company can link data bases with each other. For example:

- Corporate image data can be linked to valuation data such as stock prices and price/earnings ratios to assess the effects of reputation on market value
- Customer satisfaction data can be geocoded and linked to geographic profiles of the public. This marriage of data bases can provide an exceptionally rich picture of satisfied and dissatisfied customers in terms of income levels, life styles, housing preferences, product ownership, credit ratings, and many other variables.
- Information from a survey can be linked to comparative data bases. This can provide reference points such as norms for industry or geography or standards set by high-performing companies. For example, when a company is having a service quality or image study conducted, comparison data bases can provide benchmark numbers on high performing companies in the industry.

THE KEY TO MAKING EFFECTIVE USE OF SURVEY DATA AND DATA BASES

The key to making effective use of surveys and data bases is to actively manage the information as a resource. Principles include:

- Start with the strategy and follow with specific issue-oriented studies. Do not become diverted by evaluating products, service issues, and human resource issues that cannot be fit into an overall strategic picture.
- Design studies for decision making and action, avoiding information overload. A quality study does not mystify or overwhelm users by focusing on methodology or presenting them with reams of unnecessary detail. A quality study analyzes, interprets, and packages information to facilitate action and enhance decision making.

- Consider the link between studies and data bases. Conduct studies as part of an overall information strategy, and use data effectively as a resource for decision making beyond the context of the initial study.

CONCLUSION

As management builds information strategies to guide planning and decision making efforts in the years ahead, it will be faced with forging more active links between organizational units. To achieve this objective, management will have to merge the information resources of these previously disparate units. In the process, many organizations will find that their new integrated survey data and data bases are a key component of their new planning and decision making capability. They may even discover new questions or find answers to questions they never thought to ask.

11

Forecasts in Strategic Planning

DAVID A. KUDON
International Marketing Research, Abbott Laboratories

MARTIN R. FRANKEL
Bernard Baruch College, CUNY

INTRODUCTION

In 1974, U.S. electric utilities erroneously forecast a 7 percent growth in demand and built to meet this demand. However, actual demand grew at only 2 percent. This led to overcapacity, which led to higher rates and a diminution of the industry's profitability. Between 1980 and 1981, the petroleum industry forecast a 50 percent rise in oil prices and invested substantial amounts of money on this basis. In fact, demand fell, prices collapsed, and the industry experienced huge losses. In the early 1980's numerous brands of personal computers were introduced because of industry expectations of explosive growth. These growth forecasts were too high, and many manufacturers were forced out of business.[1]

In view of these disastrous consequences, it is obvious that accurate forecasts are essential to a corporation's ability to successfully plan its strategy and in some cases to ensure its survival in the marketplace. However, using forecasting in the planning process is not just a matter of selecting a forecasting model, buying some computer programs, and generating statistical models that predict product acceptance. That is forecasting "science," which, devoid of forecasting "art," generally yields unsatisfactory results. The statistical modeling (science) must be melded into a cohesive process with the planning (mostly art): There must be "form" along with "function." Thus, the forecasting process is broken down into two parts in this chapter: forecasting Process Maps for existing products and for new products (the "form" of the forecast) and qualitative and quantitative predictive models (the "function" of the forecast).

The product forecasting maps presented in this chapter are designed to provide the novice strategic planner with a template with which to initiate a forecasting process (or to understand an existing forecasting process). In addition, these maps will permit strategic planners with forecasting experience to compare and evaluate their corporations' forecasting procedures. The following discussion of forecasting is not a theoretical, mathematical, or statistical consideration of various forecasting models. It is a description of the components of the forecasting process designed to permit strategic planners to optimize the forecasting process in their corporations.

It should be noted that there are many forecasting maps. Only two are considered here.

Since a variety of well-documented models are available to produce the "functional" part of the forecast, the main thrust of this chapter is on the "form" of forecasting. For the convenience of the reader, some of the more common statistical techniques used in forecasting will be briefly described here. However, it should be noted that no attempt is made here to recom-

---

[1] F.W. Barnett, "Four Steps to Forecast Total Market Demand," *Harvard Business Review* (1988).

mend the use of one technique over another. This is a choice that must be made on one of three criteria:

1. Choose techniques that have been applied successfully in the past, or
2. Select techniques that are easy to use and that are accessible, or
3. Adapt a technique used for an analogous product to the product under consideration.

THE FORECASTING PROCESS

Many strategic planning departments use numerous idiosyncratic forecasting models in their planning process. The first thing that a strategic planning manager can do to increase the accuracy of the forecasting process is to centralize the forecasting process and use a unified model to produce forecasts. The benefits that accrue to the strategic planner who uses a unified forecasting process in place of multiple idiosyncratic forecasts are:

- Increased probability of producing reliable plans
- Increased probability of producing valid plans
- Increased likelihood of being able to track error variance and thus of being able to reduce error in the next year's plan

These benefits imply that even if the unified forecasting process that the planner selects is inaccurate, the forecast can be adjusted over time because each element of the process is specifiable.

Forecasting for a particular company and a particular product is often so situationally specific that it is difficult to select the right technique. However, as each year goes by, the forecaster must reevaluate the accuracy of the forecast by comparing it to reality. If the forecast is inaccurate, the forecaster must change assumptions, adapt the forecasting model initially selected, or choose a new forecasting model altogether. This reevaluation and adjustment process becomes almost instinctive with experienced forecasters. This reevaluation and adjustment process is why companies with rather stable products with long histories are able to produce extremely accurate forecasts. It is also why new product forecasting is often so inaccurate.

FORECASTING PROCESS MAP FOR AN EXISTING PRODUCT

The existing product forecasting process is shown in Figure 11-1.

There are five general input variables in this forecasting process: (1) baseline sales data (number of units sold), (2) growth in the number of customers, (3) growth in the amount of product (in units) used per cus-

FIGURE 11-1

Forecasting Process Map: Existing Product

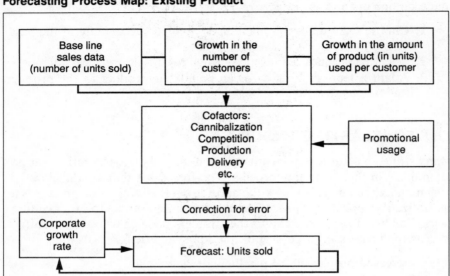

tomer, (4) cofactors (if any) and promotional usage, and (5) an error term. Basically, the number of units sold (TU) is a function of the number of customers (N_c) times the number of units used per customer (N_u) times any cofactors (C_i) that may exist plus a promotional factor (P_i) plus an error factor (e_t).

$$TU = N_c \times N_u \times C_i + P_i + e_t$$

Input Variables

Baseline Sales Data. This variable should be the easiest to deal with or estimate, yet it is usually the most difficult to obtain. A company's sales data are often "lost" in the management information systems (MIS) section of the organization. This means that the data, if obtainable, are often fragmentary, partially because the programs needed to compile the data or to segment the data are not available. This occurs because the managers responsible for collecting sales data are most likely collecting not for forecasting but for other reasons, such as billing or sales quotas. In addition, although sales data should be the most important data that a company can collect, usually they are gathered as an afterthought. Therefore, the data sometimes are not collected, are collected inaccurately, or are collected in a lagged fashion so that some of the data are current and some are old.

The planner must first gather what data are available and then ascertain whether they are complete and accurate. If the data are not accurate or are not obtainable directly, a market research effort is often called for, wherein the planner must survey various organizations (internal as well as external) to come up with a suitable estimate of company sales over time. Usually the information gathered in this way is fairly inaccurate, since it is based on people's recollections of past sales. The end result of either collecting what data exist internally, or surveying to get these data, is a series of sales figures extending forward from some earlier point in time.

Growth in the Number of Customers. Usually, the best data a company has are its sales data, since they are usually the most reliable or complete data the company has. Next best are the data on the number of customers. This information is often readily available from sales logs and other similar records. In addition, even though these data may be tedious to retrieve (since they are generally in paper form, not on electronic media), they are usually fairly accurate.

It is important to recognize that in many cases, the number of customers does not vary linearly with the number of units sold. In practice, growth in the number of customers usually levels off before growth in the number of units sold levels off. In other words the market becomes saturated, there are no new customers left, and growth can be garnered only through increasing the number of units sold per customer. This implies that knowledge of the number of potential customers to be sold a given product can be used to accurately predict the number of units that will be sold.

Growth in the Amount of Product Used per Customer. These data, if archived at all, are often stored in the same place that baseline sales data are stored; i.e., in the company's MIS department. Too frequently, these data are difficult to retrieve, and must be estimated by asking customers for current usage as well as past usage, as revealed by invoices and by memory, which means that these data are likely to be error-filled. It is tempting to estimate these data by simply dividing the number of units sold by the number of customers. However, this ignores the fact that there are cofactors that have an influence on the number of units sold. In addition, the change in the number of customers is probably not linear and a simple division may compound the distortion inherent in nonlinear functions.

Cofactors. Cofactors are the most difficult part of the forecast in terms of specificity, yet they are the easiest to produce. Cofactors refer to all the other possible nameable sources of influence that can affect demand, such as competition, sales incentives, production capacity, delivery capacity, damaged goods, destroyed product, sales budget, and growth rate from historical sales and estimated percent of users. It is here that management judgment often comes into its major use. Management judgment in this context is another name for a product manager's educated guess about the size of the market. This management judgment is applied in two areas:

1. Estimating what cofactors are influencing demand
2. Estimating what portion of variance each cofactor contributes to demand

Basically, the forecaster makes assumptions about market influences on a given product and then verifies these assumptions with the various product people. These individuals change or add to the list. Then the product people can usually be called on to provide the requisite estimators to factor into the demand forecast. However, these estimates are often inaccurate because they have a large component of subjectivity. The degree of inaccuracy in these estimates has been termed "management bias."

There are ways of reducing the amount of bias in management judgments, but they tend to be difficult for the average forecaster to apply and the methodologies are not generally available in commercial forecasting packages.

Promotional Usage. Often neglected in forecasts, promotional usage refers to the amount of product simply given away, used for testing, or used up in product demonstrations. Often, it can be a large component, although usually it exerts its main influence early in the life cycle of a product when demand is low and product giveaways are a rather large proportion of total sales. Since these data are usually not available in any data base, they must be estimated. However, growth in promotional usage is easily extracted simply by asking the marketing people how much of the product will be given away.

Errors in Forecasts and Forecasting Models. Even under the best of conditions, it is unrealistic to expect that a numerical forecast produced by a forecasting model will, in fact, be found to be correct with 100 percent accuracy. When this does actually occur, either a very rare and unlikely event has taken place, or one or more manipulations have been undertaken to ensure that a particular forecast occurs. Discounting these two possibilities, it is safe to say that all forecasting systems, even those which are viewed as highly accurate, will show some degree of error.

It is extremely important that the producers as well as the consumers of a particular forecasting effort fully understand the concept of forecasting error. From the producer's standpoint, the concept of forecasting error allows a quantification of the degree of certainty surrounding the single values produced by a forecasting model. The producer of the forecast is able to express a high confidence that the differences between the forecast and the actual results will be very small by assigning a very small error level to the forecast. On the other hand, the producer of a forecast may indicate a high degree of uncertainty associated with a forecasted value by assigning a high level of anticipated error to the forecast. In the latter case, the forecaster is saying that, given existing conditions, it is impossible to produce a forecast that has a high degree of anticipated accuracy.

From the perspective of the consumer or users of forecasts, the concept of forecasting error is even more important. By examining the anticipated error associated with the forecast, the individual who will make decisions on the basis of the forecast is able to recognize the risks and uncertainty that may be involved in taking certain actions. For example, if a particular forecast indicates a growth of 10 percent and the forecast is accompanied by a very small error, then the user of the forecast may be reasonably certain that this 10 percent growth will in fact occur. On the other hand, if the forecast of 10 percent growth is accompanied by a relatively large anticipated error, then the decision maker using this forecast must develop alternative strategies, since the growth may instead be 5 percent, or 15 percent, or even higher or lower.

Producing the Forecast

Now that the strategic planner has collected all the data, they must be used to produce a forecast. Let's examine a set of data for a fictitious company (see Table 11-1).

First, the forecaster must gather together all assumptions that must feed the forecast. This means listing the assumptions and then coopting agreement on them from all interested management personnel (especially senior management). This example uses the following five assumptions:

TABLE 11-1

National Widget Company Unit Sales Data (1984–1989)

Year	Number of customers	Units per customer	Cofactor	Recorded sales	Error	Actual sales
1984	3,610	10	—	36,100	0.2	36,300
1985	3,890	10	—	38,900	0.2	40,100
1986	4,180	10	—	41,800	0.5	42,300
1987	4,820	10	—	48,200	−0.3	47,900
1988	4,870	10	—	48,700	−0.1	48,600
1989	4,860	10	—	48,600	0.5	49,100

1. There are no significant promotional uses of widgets, since they are too expensive to give away.
2. The only operational cofactor is that there is an "old style" widget that National Widget still makes and sells that is cannibalizing sales of the new widget—to the tune of an estimated 5 percent a year through 1994.
3. Because of fixed government regulations, each customer can use only ten widgets. These government rules extend through 1994.
4. Since National Widget has a virtual monopoly on the widget market, the effects of competition are negligible.
5. Growth in products that National Widget sells has traditionally been logarithmic.

Table 11-1 shows that the actual sales for National Widget (i.e., the sales figures that the company maintains) have increased steadily from 1984 to 1989. However, in collecting the number of customers from internal files, and multiplying this out, a discrepancy is revealed. This error is probably due to error factors as specified previously. This error, which ranges from 0.2 percent to 1.2 percent (the difference between recorded sales and actual sales), is tolerable, and in this case cannot be specified exactly. However, this error must be accounted for when actually producing the forecast.

Table 11-2 was constructed using logarithmic trend analysis, which is part of several common graphing packages discussed later. In Figure 11-2, we can see that 1984 to 1989 data are first used to forecast number of customers using our product, and then multiplying out, unit sales are forecast. Then an adjustment is made for the 5 percent cannibalization estimated for the next five years, and the forecast is made.

However, the forecast does not take into account the error estimations. To include this error in the calculations, the figures are produced as ranges (0.2–1.2% error). Looking at Figure 11-3, we can see how the projected sales look for the next five years. The top line is the highest error, the bottom line is the lowest error.

TABLE 11-2
National Widget Company Five-Year Forecast (logarithmic trend analysis)

Year	Number of customers	Units per customer	Unit forecast sales	Forecast unit sales adjusted for cofactors
1990	5,920	10	59.2	56,200
1991	5,990	10	59.9	56,900
1992	6,120	10	61.2	58,100
1993	6,530	10	65.3	61,200
1994	6,680	10	66.8	63,500

FIGURE 11-2

Widget Sales Data: Five-Year Forecast of Potential Customers

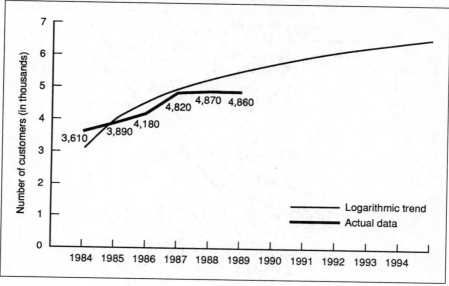

At this point, traditional marketing texts would consider the process more or less complete. There is, however, an element that many forecasters and strategic planners ignore. That is the corporation's "corporate goals," which are designed and implemented by senior management and too often based solely on management judgment. Many chief executive officers (CEOs) state the expected growth for a corporation in terms of a percentage each year; this process is often instituted independently of any forecast that is produced. Part or even all of a corporation's planning is then based on this figure. Sales goals and sales incentives often are implemented in line with this plan and are the determiners of how well a product or a whole line of products is sold. Production and capital outlay are even based on this percentage. To the extent that the corporation plans in this way, instead of planning to a forecast prepared by the strategic planning department, it makes the process of forecasting easier or harder. If the corporation plans totally to the CEO's "specified growth plan," the forecaster has only a few tasks. Since the forecast has no effect on the planning process, the forecaster merely has to mimic the specified growth, add a percentage point or two for error, and produce the "forecast." However, if the planning department has convinced the corporation that its forecasts have some applicability to the real world, then the forecaster must produce an

FIGURE 11-3

Widget Sales Data: Five-Year Forecast Error Estimation

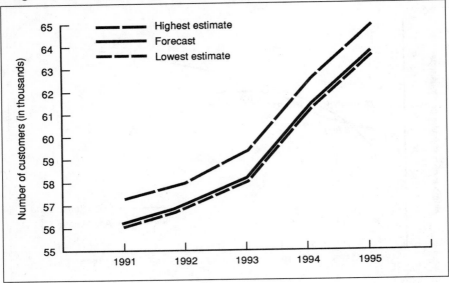

accurate forecast that specifies all the possible input variables either by modeling them mathematically, by culling them from historical files, or by guessing at them as accurately as possible. In most cases there is not such a polarity; however, the planner must include the effect of the corporation's desired growth rate in the forecast because it will have some effect on the sales of that corporation.

In the example, a check of the forecasted sales shows that they do fit the corporation's rather modest growth expectations. If they did not, the forecaster would have to adjust the figures or the assumptions used, or the forecaster would have to "reeducate" senior management so that the corporate goals and the forecasts were consistent. Thus, the method suggested here is to initiate the forecast process independently of the desired corporate growth rate, and then, through an iterative process, compare the forecast to the corporate goals. If the forecast is close to the corporate goals, then these goals have been validated. To the extent that the forecast deviates from the corporate goals, the planner must determine where this variance comes from. Assuming that the variance is not due to poor assumptions or error on part of the forecaster, the corporate goals should be adjusted to eliminate this discrepancy. Thus, if the entire planning process is based on the CEO's assumed growth rate, the forecast can serve as an error check on management judgment.

FIGURE 11-4

Forecasting Process Map: New Product

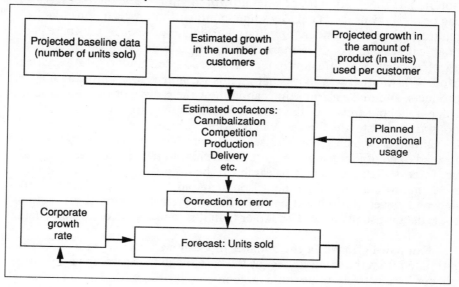

FORECASTING PROCESS MAP FOR A NEW PRODUCT

The new product forecasting process is shown in Figure 11-4. There are the same five general input variables in this forecasting process as in the forecasting process for an existing product: baseline data (number of units projected to be sold), (estimated) growth in the number of customers, (projected) growth in the amount of product (in units) used per customer, (estimated) cofactors (if any), as well as (planned) promotional usage, and an error term. The difference is that in the new products forecast there is no historical data from which to draw and most of the input variables must be estimated. It must be emphasized here that the forecasting process for the new products is the most difficult to perform accurately, and hence is the least reliable. Again, the equation for this process is as follows: the number of units sold (TU) is a function of the number of customers (N_c) times the number of units used per customer (N_u) times any cofactors (C_i) that may exist plus a promotional factor (P_i) plus a random error factor (e_t).

$$TU = N_c \times N_u \times C_i + P_i + e_t$$

Input Variables

Projected Baseline Sales Data. This variable can be projected using several techniques, yet is usually difficult to project accurately. Often market research is performed to have a suitable sample of the available population impart their estimates of what growth might be. This market research can be a survey or it can employ some semiquantitative technique like Delphi (discussed later, under "Qualitative Predictive Models"). If there is no practical way to conduct market research, a predictive model can be selected, such as a diffusion model (discussed later, under "Mathematical Models"). Another way of estimating this variable is to examine analogous products, and make assumptions about how the growth of the new product will parallel the growth of the older product. To the extent that the assumptions are accurate, the forecast will be accurate also. These assumptions can be validated by using market research to produce the same assumptions. Instead of conducting a survey or using Delphi to produce the actual product forecast figures, market research can be used to establish the assumptions that would allow for comparison of an older existing product with the new and as yet unproduced product. In any event the error of estimate in these data is usually quite a bit larger than it is in using historical sales data.

Estimated Growth in the Number of Customers. This variable can be estimated from the same sources as the baseline data. Again, the error component here is likely to be quite large in comparison with data on existing products.

Projected Growth in the Amount of Product Used per Customer. These data can be obtained in the same way that the baseline sales data are obtained, i.e., from market research, by comparing the new product to an existing product, or through modeling.

Estimated Cofactors. As with existing products, cofactors are the most difficult part of the forecast in terms of specificity, yet they are the easiest to produce. Cofactors refer to all the other possible nameable sources of influence that can affect demand, such as competition, sales incentives, production capacity, delivery capacity, damaged goods, and destroyed product. It is here that the major use of assumptions comes into play. In this context, assumptions are another name for a manager's educated guess about what the market will look like in the future.

The forecaster makes assumptions about influences in the market for the new product and then verifies these assumptions by comparison to existing products, by conducting market research (in this case, focus groups are a useful tool), or by checking with the various product people. However, as mentioned earlier, these estimates are often very inaccurate because of "management bias."

Planned Promotional Usage. The amount of product simply given away, used for testing, or used up in product demonstrations can be a large component and can usually be derived by examining corporate practices with earlier, analogous products, or by asking the marketing people for an estimate of promotional units.

Error. The error treatment for both new products and existing products is basically the same (discussed previously).

Producing the Forecast

Now that the strategic planner has collected all these data, they must be used to produce a forecast. To demonstrate, an example will be worked through, again using the National Widget Company. Table 11-4 presents projected sales data for 1991–1995. (For the sake of simplicity, this forecast deals only with the company involved and does not take into account the effects of competition. There, the numbers used are for the company's sales only, and the number of customers refers to only National Widget's customers, not all possible customers.)

This example focuses on National Widget's new product the "Framus Bracket," a very expensive item that replaces an older method of bracketing. National Widget has no product like this (so no analogies can be drawn) and there are no products like it on the market.

To actually begin producing the forecast, it is first necessary to list all the assumptions needed to produce the particular forecast. Then, as in any forecasting effort, all relevant personnel must be induced (coerced) into agreeing on their suitability. For this example, the following four assumptions were agreed on:

1. This is a revolutionary way of doing things, so there will be no competitors on the market for the next five years.
2. The old way of doing bracketing manually will be continued by 5 percent of the potential customer base (this is the cofactor).
3. The product management department estimates that seventy-five customers can be counted on to buy this new product in 1991.
4. The number of units will grow as specified in Table 11-4.

This forecast was produced by using the diffusion model described near the end of this chapter. There are three variables that had to be estimated: (1) the total number of customers who might buy the product, (2) the initial number of purchasers, and (3) a diffusion rate. The initial number of customers is given to the forecaster by the product managers; the total number of potential customers is obtained from secondary research; the diffusion rate was based on an educated guess by the forecaster.

Using these three elements, the number of customers from 1991 to 1995 was predicted from the model. The number of customers is then mul-

TABLE 11-4

National Widget Company Forecasted Sales Data for Framus Brackets

Year	Number of customers	Units per customer	Units of promotional use	Forecasted unit sales adjusted for the cofactor
1991	75	1.0	10	80
1992	135	1.4	10	189
1993	178	1.5	—	254
1994	206	1.6	—	314
1995	223	1.7	—	361

tiplied by the number of units estimated to be used by each customer factored down by the 5 percent of customers who will retain the old, manual bracketing method. This produces the forecast, shown in tabular form in Table 11-4 and graphically in Figure 11-5.

Again, the corporate goals must not be ignored. These goals must be compared to the forecasted sales and any necessary adjustments made. For this example, for simplicity's sake, it can be assumed that this new product does not produce enough revenue by itself to noticeably influence the 10 percent annual growth rate the CEO has set for National Widget Company. Therefore, in this example, we do not have to go through the adjustment problems described on those pages.

QUALITATIVE PREDICTIVE MODELS

In many forecasting applications, there is little or no quantitative data, and little or no chance of collecting any (a priori or post hoc). In these cases it is difficult to produce a forecast; however, senior managers of a company usually insist on a forecast regardless. The qualitative forecasts described in the following sections usually fill this need.

Delphi

The Delphi is an iterative process using a pool of recognized experts. These experts are given intensive questionnaires, along with controlled opinion feedback, many times to obtain consensus on a judgment. This judgment could be qualitative or quantitative. The traditional Delphi process is characterized by the following four features:

1. Selection of a group of experts to be surveyed
2. Anonymity of experts who respond
3. Repeated polling of these experts with feedback to each expert after each successive round
4. Statistical analysis of the degree of consensus achieved

FIGURE 11-5

Framus Bracket Forecasted Sales (1991–1994)

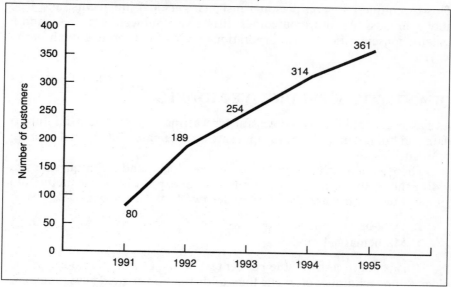

Experts are chosen generally on judgmental criteria: peer recognition, publication record, organizational affiliations, or any other information that establishes expertise in a given field. Anonymity of the experts is maintained by administering the questionnaire to the experts by mail or by phone. Thus, the experts never meet and their names are known only to those conducting the study. The reason for anonymity is to avoid both bias due to peer influence and other kinds of error that are inherent in group processes. The experts are then polled repeatedly until consensus is reached. The definition of consensus varies and the method of determining the degree of agreement sought needs to be selected with care. Historically, the measure of consensus has been the mean along with the score range. These statistical responses are used as feedback for successive rounds and as a basis for final analysis. In addition, these means and ranges of responses are given to the experts for reevaluation of their respective positions, in light of these new data. Another questionnaire is then administered and new estimates are gathered. A request for clarification of certain issues may also be included. Each participant responds to the new questionnaire and the iterative polling continues until statistical convergence (consensus) is reached or until practical concerns dictate an end to the study.

Prophetic Forecasts

This technique relies on personal insights, personal judgments, and facts about the possible future outcomes. It is a very subjective process, and is usually nonscientific. Many corporations forecast corporate growth in this way.

QUANTITATIVE PREDICTIVE MODELS

As has been noted, most successful forecasting systems use a mixture of data and human inputs. These inputs are amalgamated into a final quantity or quantities.

There are a number of different methodologies and techniques for providing these input quantities. For purposes of exposition, these methodologies and techniques are classified under two basic headings:

1. Data-based time series
2. Mathematical models

This is not necessarily the perfect taxonomy. Further, various methodologies and techniques cross the lines of distinction created here for exposition simplicity.

Data-Based Time Series

This section briefly covers some of the many methodologies and techniques that have been developed in order to extrapolate forward from a time-related series of data values. This is the common thread that links all of the data-based time series. All of these methods and techniques are designed to deal with the following scenario. A quantitative measure of performance is available at a discrete series of points in time in the past. For example, gross monthly receipts for a certain business unit may be available for the immediately proceeding forty-eight months. In this case, the forty-eight values (gross monthly receipts) and the corresponding information indicating the actual month with which the value is associated constitute the time series. The ultimate objective of any of the time series methods is to provide predictions of the values that will occur for this time series at some future time period. Time series methods are numerous and range from extremely simple to highly complex. The methods listed as follows are discussed briefly in later sections.

- Average absolute change and average percentage change
- Weighted average percentage change
- Moving averages
- Exponential smoothing

- Decomposition
- Regression
- Logarithmic trend analysis
- Autoregression
- Box-Jenkins

Average Absolute Change and Average Percentage Change. The average absolute change and average percentage change methods are probably the most frequently used techniques for producing a forecast. While these methods are sometimes criticized as being naive and oversimplistic, their simplicity gives them both understandability and intuitive appeal. With both methods, some time period is selected over which the averaging will be carried out. The choice of this period will have influence over the forecasted values.

In the method of average absolute change, the average year-to-year absolute change over the selected time period is determined and this average is used to extrapolate forward. For example, suppose that over the past five years, the yearly sales for a business unit have been (in thousands) 678, 698, 732, 760 and 800. The four year-to-year absolute changes are:

$$698 - 678 = 20$$
$$732 - 698 = 34$$
$$760 - 732 = 28$$
$$800 - 760 = 40$$

The average of these four values is 30.5. Thus, on the basis of the average absolute change over the past five years, the forecasted yearly sales for the sixth year are $800 + 30.5 = 830.5$.

The method of average percentage change determines the average year-to-year percentage change over the selected time period and uses this average to extrapolate forward. Using the same data, the four year-to-year percentage changes are

$$(698 - 678) \div 678 = +2.95\%$$
$$(732 - 698) \div 698 = +4.87\%$$
$$(760 - 732) \div 732 = +3.83\%$$
$$(800 - 760) \div 760 = +5.26\%$$

The average of these four percentage values is 4.2275 percent. Applying this percentage change to the last year sales of 800 produces a forecasted yearly sales for the sixth year of $800 + (4.2275\% \times 800) = 833.8$.

Weighted Average Percentage Change. The method of weighted average percentage change is similar to the method of average percent change, except more recent year-to-year changes are given more influence in the final forecast. For example, to base a forecast on a weighted average of the four most recent percentage changes (i.e., base data from the five most recent periods), instead of giving these four percentage changes equal weight, the most recent percentage change is given a weight of $\%_0 = 40\%$, the next most recent percentage change is given a weight of $\%_0 = 30\%$, and the remaining two least recent percentage changes are given weights of 20 percent and 10 percent, respectively.

Using the four percentage changes shown in the preceding method, this would produce a weighted average percentage change of $(0.4 \times 5.26 + 0.3 \times 3.83 + 0.2 \times 4.87 + 0.1 \times 2.95) = 4.522\%$. This would produce a forecast of $800 + (4.522\% \times 800) = 836.2$. The method of weighted average percentage change produces a slightly higher forecast than the method of average percentage change because more recent periods are given greater weight.

Moving Averages. Moving averages are a variation of simple averages. The difference between the simpler forms of averaging and the moving average methods involves the choice of a specific number of years to form the basis from which the average is derived. For example, a three-year moving average forecasting system always uses the three most recent years and ignores information from earlier periods.

A somewhat more sophisticated form of forecasting based on moving averages involves the use of double or triple smoothing[2] (typically referred to as double or triple moving average systems). For example, in the double three-year moving average approach, actual sales information would be obtained from the past five periods. These five periods of information would yield three three-year moving averages. These three three-year moving averages would then be averaged (a three-year average of averages) to yield an increment value to add to the most recent period. This moving average procedure may be extended to any number of averages, although three is a typical maximum upper limit. A triple moving average would involve forming a series consisting of n year moving averages. This new series would then be subject to an n year moving average in order to produce a second series. This second series would then be subject to an n year moving averaging procedure to produce a third series. The most recent value from this third series is used to update the prior year's value and produce the actual forecasted value.

---

[2] The terms "double" or "triple" refer to the number of times moving averages are taken. For example, in a double moving average system, the process of taking a moving average is repeated twice. In a triple moving average system, the process is repeated three times.

Exponential Smoothing. Exponential smoothing methods have been used in forecasting for more than 100 years. They are generally considered somewhat complex and archaic mathematical methods that have been eclipsed by more modern and sophisticated techniques. However, these techniques are used by some of the computer forecasting models that were developed for mainframe computers during the late 1950s and 1960s. In certain situations, exponential smoothing may provide adequate and robust forecasts that preserve some of the flavor of moving average methods while extending the level of sophistication and customization that is possible.

Forecasts based on exponential smoothing typically involve the use of single, double, or triple systems. Single exponential smoothing systems are appropriate when the underlying long-range trend is essentially flat, neither increasing nor declining. Single exponential smoothing makes use of all prior information in order to produce a forecast. The single exponentially smoothed value for period t (denoted S_t) is

$$S_t = ay_t + (1-a)S_{t-1}$$

where a is a constant between zero and one, y_t is the actual observed value at period t, and S_{t-1} is the smoothed value for period $t-1$. Thus, the exponentially smoothed value for period t is derived as a weighted combination of the actual value for the period and the exponentially smoothed value for the prior period. Since the exponentially smoothed value for the prior period is itself a combination of an actual value and a smoothed value from a prior period, the final exponentially smoothed value is influenced by all previous values. Mathematically, this may be seen in an alternative expression for S_t is given by

$$s_t = ay_t + a(1 - a) y_{t-1} + a(1 - a)^2 y_{t-2} + \ldots + a(1 - a)^{t-1} y_1 + (1 - a)^t S_0$$

where S_0 is an arbitrarily selected initial estimate and a is a constant between zero and one. It is, in fact, the form of this expression that is the reason the smoothing procedure is called exponential.

Forecasts based on single exponential smoothing essentially eliminate period-to-period variation, and assume that the long-range trend of the values is constant, neither increasing nor decreasing. For series with long-range linear (straight-line) trends that are either increasing or decreasing, exponential smoothing is often applied to the simple exponentially smoothed values in order to modify the resulting forecasts. The double exponentially smoothed estimate for period t is denoted by $S^{[2]}_t$. It is derived recursively (as is the case with single exponentially smoothed values) as

$$S^{[2]}_t = aS_t + (1 - a) S^{[2]}_{t-1}$$

where a is a predetermined constant between zero and one; and S_t is the single exponentially smoothed estimate for period t.

For series that exhibit long-term trend that is quadratic (a curve with single turning point), triple exponential smoothing is a more flexible alternative. Triple exponential smoothing makes use of the outputs of single and double smoothing. For time period t, the triple exponentially smoothed estimate is denoted as $S^{[3]}_t$. It is defined as

$$S^{[3]}_t = aS^{[2]}_t + (1 - a) S^{[3]}_{t-1}$$

It should be noted that forecasts based on any of the exponential smoothing methods are not unique. That is, for the same series, single (or double or triple) exponential smoothing forecasts will be different depending upon the choice of the constant a as well as the initial value S_0. Various systems have been suggested for choosing these values, but the choice is somewhat arbitrary and the final results may be highly dependent upon the system selected.

Decomposition. There are numerous methods of forecasting that are characterized as decomposition methods. Decomposition methods attempt to forecast future values by explicitly searching for and taking into account certain types of variation. Specifically, these methods attempt to built into the forecast factors that account for overall trend, seasonal variation, cyclical variation, and "irregular" variation.

In other words, y_t, the observed value for time t, is viewed as arising as the result of the multiplicative impact of four factors. Thus $y_t = TR_t \times SN_t \times CL_t \times IR_t$, where for period t: TR_t = trend, SN_t = seasonal factor, CL_t = cyclical factor, and IR_t = irregular factor.

Two widely used decomposition methods are "multiplicative" decomposition and Winters' method. Multiplicative decomposition uses various methods in order to estimate the four parameters in the four factors for y_t. Often these parameters are determined by least squares (regression) methods.

Winters' method uses a modification of double exponential smoothing in order to describe a series that is assumed to possess an overall linear trend coupled with seasonal variation.

Regression. Regression methods vary from the very simple (e.g., simple linear regression) to the highly complex (e.g., autoregression with linkages-transfers to associated series). Simple regression methods are discussed here. The more complex methods of autoregression and Box-Jenkins are covered in the next two sections.

The simplest regression method involves the use of least squares estimation to fit a straight line to all previous data. The forecast is derived by extrapolation of this straight line to future periods. The actual values observed in the time series from time 1 to time t are denoted $y_1 \ldots y_t$. It is assumed that y_i, the ith previously observed value, may be viewed as the additive combination of three components. These three components are (1) an initial value, B_0, (2) a linear trend factor that is equal to a constant times i, the number of periods (i.e., B_1 times i), and (3) a random noise component, e_i. This gives the simple linear regression model $y_i = B_0 + B_1x_i$. The values B_0 and B_1, typically called the regression coefficients, are usually estimated by the "least squares" procedure.[3] This procedure produces estimates of B_0 and B_1 that have two basic properties. First, the differences between the actual observed values of the series and the values predicted by the equation $y(predicted)_i$ will sum to zero. Second, the squared differences between the actual series values and the predicted series values are minimized over all possible choices of the estimates of B_0 and B_1. This means that if the differences $d_i = y_i - y(predicted)_i$ are formed, the sum of these differences is zero and the sum of the d^2_i are as small as possible. Once "least squares" estimated values of b_0 and b_1 are obtained, these values are used to produce a forecast for a future period (e.g., period $t+1$). If b_0 and b_1 denote these least squares estimates of B_0 and B_1, then the forecasted value for period $t+1$ is denoted as y_{t+1} and is obtained as $y_{t+1} = b_0 + b_1x_{(t+1)}$.

When a time series exhibits an overall trend that is not a simple straight line, but rather a line with one or more bends and curves, then simple linear regression will not adequately describe the series past behavior. Since it cannot adequately describe the series' past behavior, it would be unreasonable to expect that it would yield an accurate and reasonable estimate of future behavior.

An alternative available in the case of a nonlinear trend is the method of quadratic or polynomial regression. In an nth order polynomial regression (which can describe a trend with $n-1$ turning points), it is assumed that the ith value in the time series may be expressed as $y_i = B_0 + B_1xi + B_2 i^2 + \ldots B_n i^n$.

Typically, least squares methods are used to produce estimates of the coefficients B_0, B_1, B_2, $\ldots B_n$. Although conceptually appealing, polynomial regression methods are applied in only a limited number of forecasting situations.

Logarithmic Trend Analysis. This is a form of regression analysis that makes use of logarithms. The simplest form of logarithmic trend analysis replaces the time series values with the logarithms of these values. A linear

---

[3] There are several alternatives to least squared estimation that are occasionally employed under special circumstances. These methods include "maximum likelihood estimation" and the method of "minimum absolute difference."

regression equation is fit using these logarithms. The basic difference between simple linear regression based on original values and linear regression based on the logarithms is related to the basic model of period to period change. The logarithmic trend model assumes that the percentage changes rather than the original changes may be described as a linear function of time.

Autoregression. Autoregression has replaced linear and polynomial regression as the forecasting method of choice. Forecasting using the method of autoregression has both intuitive appeal and, with the increasing availability of personal computers, computational accessibility. Autoregressive methods explicitly recognize the empirical reality that a reasonably sound and robust predictor of what will happen today is what happened yesterday. A simple first order autoregression model assumes that the value of the series at time t is determined as an additive linear combination of a constant term B_0, a second constant term $B_1 \times y_{t-1}$ (the value of the series at time $t-1$) and a random error term e_t. Stated as an equation, the first order autoregressive model is:

$$Y_t = B_0 + B_1 \, y_{t-1} + e_t$$

Autoregressive models may use any number of prior periods in the prediction process. Thus the following model might be used:

$$Y_t = B_0 + B_1 \, Y_{t-1} + B_2 \, y_{t-2} + B_3 \, y_{t-3} + e_t$$

In this model, the value of the series at time t is assumed to be a weighted combination of the series at the three immediately preceding periods. This particular model may resemble the model that is used when the simple or weighted moving average technique is used. In autoregression models, however, the values y_{t-1}, y_{t-2}, etc. are previous values of the same series.

Box-Jenkins. The field of time series analysis has been greatly influenced by the work of George Box and Gwilym Jenkins. In their classic work *Time Series Analysis — Forecasting and Control*,[4] Box and Jenkins built on the technique of autoregression and developed a basic methodology and associated philosophy for the development of forecasts. The Box-Jenkins methodology involves three stages: identification, estimation, and diagnostic checking.

In the identification stage, the time series data and any other associated information and experience are used to determine whether the time

---

[4] G.E.P. Box and G.M. Jenkins, *Time Series Analysis — Forecasting and Control* (rev. ed.) (San Francisco: Holden-Day, 1976).

series may be represented with a moving average model, an autoregressive model, or a mixed autoregressive moving average model.

The estimation stage of the model involves determining the estimates of the model parameters. This stage typically involves computer intensive iterative techniques.

The final stage of the Box-Jenkins process involves diagnostic checking to determine the adequacy of the results produced by the model.

An important feature of the Box-Jenkins methodology is that it uses a technique called "differencing" or "backshifting." Differencing often allows time series that do not exhibit the property of stationarity[5] to be transformed into series that exhibit this property.

Models developed using the Box-Jenkins method are often termed ARIMA models with parameters *p, d, q*. These parameters refer to the moving average, differencing, and autoregressive aspects of the model.

Mathematical Models: Diffusion Model

With completely new products, or reintroduced products, data that would allow the use of traditional time series forecasting techniques do not exist. Under these circumstances various mathematical models are often examined in order to forecast the anticipated growth curve of the product. One of the most widely used techniques for forecasts of this type is the diffusion model.

Diffusion models may be fit to time series in which a large number of observations are available. However, diffusion models may also be used to produce forecasts when very limited or even no data are available. A simple form of the diffusion model will be discussed here, since it was used earlier in this chapter for the examples. On the basis of work done by Frank Bass (1974),[6] a three-parameter diffusion model has been constructed, wherein the initial input variables are number of initial purchasers, diffusion rate, and total potential purchasers. This is based on a contagion model, whose parameters are initial number of infected persons, contagion rate, and total potential infected population.

In the no-data or limited-data case, the users of the model must specify an initial number of purchasers/triers of the product and two constant parameters often described as coefficients of innovation and imitation. These three values will then generate a forecast of product sales over time.

---

[5] The term "stationarity" refers to the lack of a long-range trend upward or downward in the time series. Examples of nonstationary series include the average life expectancy of humans from 1700 to the present and the purchasing power of the dollar from 1945 to 1975. In some instances, the original time series may be nonstationary (showing upward or downward trend) but the series formed by taking period to period difference may not show this trend.

[6] F.M. Bass, "A New Product Growth for Model Consumer Durables," *Management Science,* Vol. 15, No. 5, 1969.

A distinguishing feature of the diffusion model is that unlike the time series techniques discussed earlier, the diffusion model actually attempts to reflect the process associated with the initial trial and adoption of a new product. In general, other time series methods are essentially empirical in that they do not attempt to reflect how the process operates, but rather how to best fit a series of data points.

CONCLUSION

Although there are many experienced planners, traditionally very few are trained in forecasting. Since forecasting is often critical to a corporation's ability to successfully meet the demands of an ever changing marketplace, many planners are forced to produce forecasts without any knowledge of how to do so.

This chapter has delineated the basic forecasting process in sufficient detail to allow a strategic planner to produce a rudimentary forecast. The process consists of two parts: forecasting process maps for existing products and for new products, representing the "form" of forecasting, and qualitative and quantitative predictive models, representing the "function" of forecasting.

In producing forecasts, the strategic planner must both select the right process and statistical technique and pay attention to the corporate growth goals, as these often influence the forecast both politically as well as in reality. Finally, any forecast should be validated over time, and adjusted for accuracy and credibility.

Corporate Development: Mergers and Acquisitions

12

Acquisitions and Divestitures

DAVID GAYLIN

JAMES W. DOWN

Temple, Barker & Sloane

INTRODUCTION

The buying and selling of businesses through acquisition, divestiture, and related forms of transfer are critical strategic activities for many corporations, large and small. While motives can vary widely, the decision to acquire or divest typically involves fundamental strategic issues of competitive product/market positioning, as well as financial issues of viability and shareholder value.

As the track record of public companies suggests, acquisitions and divestitures are not easy to accomplish and can often yield outcomes below expectations. However, by understanding the reasons companies acquire or divest, how this decision fits in with overall corporate strategy, and the nature of the acquisition and divestiture processes, the chances of success can be increased. In general, research in both areas shows that successful outcomes involve the creative evaluation of all options and disciplined, careful planning.

While acquisitions and divestitures are often flip sides of the same transaction, the motives, processes, and guidelines for each can be different. This chapter therefore treats each perspective separately, with numerous case examples provided for illustration.

ACQUISITION AS A STRATEGY

The word "acquisition" is used in this chapter to describe the addition of a business enterprise to a parent company through merger, consolidation, or takeover. Although "acquisition" can technically refer to any purchase of ownership control, this section focuses on acquisition as a business strategy with operating intent, as opposed to a financially driven strategy in which the

TABLE 12-1

**Net Merger and Acquisition
Announcements 1969–1989**

Year	Number	Year-to-year percentage change
1969	6,107	+37%
1970	5,152	−16
1971	4,608	−11
1972	4,801	+4
1973	4,040	−16
1974	2,861	−29
1975	2,297	−20
1976	2,276	−1
1977	2,224	−2
1978	2,106	−5
1979	2,128	+1
1980	1,889	−11
1981	2,395	+27
1982	2,346	−2
1983	2,533	+8
1984	2,543	—
1985	3,001	+18
1986	3,336	+11
1987	2,032	−39
1988	2,258	+11
1989	2,366	+5

Source: W.T. Grimm & Co., Mergerstat Review (1989).

buyer expects to restructure and then divest the purchased business. There is thus somewhat less emphasis on certain types of leveraged buyouts and "raider" takeovers that were common in the mid- and late 1980s, and that were made possible largely by the availability of "junk bond" financing.

Since the mid-1960s, acquisition activity has fluctuated widely. It peaked in 1969 with over 6,000 mergers, decreased during the early 1970s, and leveled off in the late 1970s and 1980s at between 2,000 and 3,000 mergers per year (see Table 12-1). The reduction in the number of mergers, however, has been more than offset by the significant increase in the size of mergers, many of which fall into a new category called "megadeals." Table 12-2 shows the increase in the number of mergers in excess of $100 million from 1979 to 1989. The significant jump from $44.3 billion of "large" deals in 1980 to over $200 billion at the end of the decade reflects the development of the megadeal, mergers in excess of $1 billion, the largest being the $24.7 billion acquisition of RJR Nabisco by Kohlberg Kravis Roberts (KKR).

Some of the most notable companies in U.S. industry were acquired

TABLE 12-2

Increase in the Value of Acquisitions

Year	Acquisitions in excess of $100 million	Total dollar value paid (billions)
1979	83	$ 43.5
1980	94	44.3
1981	113	82.6
1982	116	53.8
1983	138	73.1
1984	200	122.2
1985	270	179.8
1986	346	173.1
1987	301	163.7
1988	369	246.9
1989	328	221.0

Source: W.T. Grimm & Co., Mergerstat Review (1989).

during the 1980s merger wave, including Conoco, Marathon Oil, Bendix, Gulf, General Foods, RCA, Kraft, Federated Department Stores, and RJR Nabisco.

There are differing opinions on the long-term effects of the merger wave of the 1980s. Some analysts believe that the mergers are, for the most part, a different type from those that took place during the conglomerate wave of the 1960s. In the 1960s, many companies pursued a corporate strategy, attempting to increase earnings per share and spread risk through investment in diverse enterprises. Although this strategy worked for a time, the longer-term performance of the resulting conglomerates led the stock markets to accord them below-average price/earnings (P/E) ratios. By contrast, the merger movement of the late 1970s and 1980s centered more on the attempt to produce synergy between the companies, e.g., to create global scale and market position, and thereby increase shareholder value.

Critics of the recent merger movement, however, cite concerns over the high premiums paid and the significant debt incurred to finance the deals, and they question whether the claimed synergies will materialize. Although the average premium paid over market has leveled off at around 40 percent, many deals go far higher and place a crippling burden of debt on the merged company (e.g., Robert Campeau's $6.5 billion purchase of Federated Department Stores Inc.).

MAKING THE ACQUISITION DECISION

The overall objective of any acquisition is to maintain or increase profits. The pursuit of this broadly stated policy, however, is one of the major reasons that many acquisitions fail. To guard against failure, an acquisition program should be soundly based on specific objectives.

Acquisition Objectives

Acquisitions can be made for a variety of specific reasons. Some of the more common reasons are discussed in the following sections.

To Strengthen or Protect the Base Business. The desire to acquire elements such as key personnel, assets, and purchasing power is often the driving force behind an acquisition. Grand Metropolitan's $1.2 billion purchase of Heublein from RJR Nabisco in 1987 greatly strengthened its base business of wine and spirits. News Corporation's 1986 purchase of six independent television stations from Metromedia Inc. is another example of a tactical purchase of assets. Without the clout of Metromedia's presence in New York, Los Angeles, and Chicago, News Corporation's chairman, Rupert Murdoch, would have a slim chance of achieving his strategic goal of a fourth major network in the United States.

Many acquisitions are made to adapt to competitive or environmental changes. As the airline industry became more and more competitive following deregulation in 1987, the larger carriers developed "hub-and-spoke" systems, channeling most of their flights through a few major relay points. This structural change in the industry, which put a premium on scale, led to a wave of consolidation as smaller players became less viable. In 1986, Delta acquired Western Airlines, and NWA, parent company of Northwest, acquired Republic Airlines, for $900 million and $884 million, respectively. In 1987, USAir Group acquired Piedmont Aviation for $1.56 billion to strengthen its position in the southeast, and the following year acquired Pacific Southwest Airlines to establish a west coast presence. In 1988, AMR, parent company of American Airlines, continued the buying spree, purchasing three connecting regional or commuter carriers for a total of $145 million.

Competitive changes can often lead to a chain reaction of merger activity within an industry. Nabisco's acquisition of Standard Brands in 1981 started things off in the food industry. In 1984, Nestlé acquired Carnation, and RJR soon thereafter acquired Nabisco. The following year, Philip Morris bought General Foods, and in 1988 it also acquired Kraft. More recently, Grand Metropolitan acquired Pillsbury for $5.8 billion. Other circumstances (e.g., deregulation) can also lead to a chain reaction, as in the airline, banking, and insurance industries.

To Diversify. Acquisition can be a way of gaining entry into new markets or businesses. Several major railroads have bought trucking, barge, and ocean carriers to hedge their bets and offer "one-stop shipping" (e.g., Norfolk Southern's acquisition of North American Van Lines in 1985, Union Pacific's acquisition of Sea-Land Service in 1987). Sears, Roebuck & Company used acquisition to diversify even further from its base business. Facing slow growth and depressed profits in retailing, Sears made two major strategic acquisitions in 1981. Sears added the stock brokerage firm, Dean Witter Reynolds, and the largest real estate broker in the United States, Coldwell Banker & Company, to its existing Allstate insurance business as part of its major effort to diversify into financial services.

Acquisitions of large, multibusiness companies can serve several strategic objectives at once. The acquisition of RCA by General Electric (GE) is an example of both strengthening the base business (industrial and consumer electronics) and diversification (RCA's broadcasting business). GE then sold some radio stations and other assets for $2.5 billion. Then GE decided consumer electronics was not strong enough and continued its diversification strategy by trading its combined GE-RCA consumer electronics business (keeping the industrial electronics base business) to Thomson of France for Thomson's medical imagery business where GE saw greater promise.

To Avoid a Takeover. Acquisition can be used to defend against an unfriendly takeover attempt. In the highly publicized 1989 battle between Time Inc. and Paramount Communications, Time switched its merger plan with Warner Communications to an outright acquisition of Warner to fend off the unwanted takeover bid by Martin Davis, chief of Paramount Communications. The courts upheld Time's acquisition under the argument that it was in the company's strategic best interests, giving added ammunition to corporate managers in dealing with raiders. Additionally, although it is not always the case, a recent large acquisition makes a corporation's financial balance sheet more debt-laden and hence, less desirable for a takeover attempt.

To Improve Financial Returns. A company often makes an acquisition to improve its return on excess capital or to take advantage of tax benefits. Gulf + Western, under chairman Charles Bluhdorn, employed a policy of acquiring companies whose assets it believed were undervalued. This strategy was particularly successful with the acquisitions of Paramount Pictures, Marquette Cement, and Kayser-Roth, but failed with Brown Company (divested in 1980) and New Jersey Zinc (divested in 1981). Since Bluhdorn's death, however, Gulf + Western management has reversed course, selling off most of its non-entertainment businesses and ultimately changing its name to Paramount Communications in 1989.

Other companies have improved financial returns by redeploying capital from a maturing or threatened business to a faster-growing, higher-return business (e.g., Eastman Kodak's acquisition of Sterling Drug). Similarly, Seagram's purchased Tropicana because of the low growth of the liquor industry.

Corporate Evaluation

Before a corporation can determine the goals of an acquisition program, it must evaluate both its present and its future positions. It should evaluate the external environment, analyze the company's internal strengths and weaknesses to compete in this environment, and assess its corporate objectives and the company's ability to fulfill them. The external environment includes the economic, competitive, political, legal, social, and institutional pressures that bear upon any company. The internal environment includes corporate strengths and weaknesses, shareholder goals, management style, and corporate culture. Some of the key strategic questions to ask during the evaluation are:

- What are the corporation's long-term financial and nonfinancial corporate objectives?
- How mature are the corporation's current businesses, and what growth potential remains?
- What technological trends are taking place, and what threats or opportunities do they pose?
- What legal or regulatory changes are taking place, and how will they affect the corporation?
- What is the corporation's competitive position? How is it changing?
- Should the corporation deepen its penetration in existing businesses or expand into new business areas?

The result of this evaluation is typically a set of long-term corporate objectives and an evaluation of the capability of the company's present business to satisfy these objectives. The evaluation should include the identification of any expansion or diversification needs.

Acquisition Alternatives

Before embarking on an acquisition program, a company should evaluate alternatives to acquisition as a means of achieving its long-term corporate objectives. It should consider joint ventures as an acquisition alternative, even though joint ventures can be difficult to manage. Over time, the goals of the joint venture partners may diverge, resulting in disputes, attempts by one partner to buy out the other, or, in some cases, protracted legal battles. For example, when, because of the poor economy, Conoco decided not to provide $12 million in funding for testing a new industrial boiler, it left its partner, Stone & Webster, with the prospect of funding part or all of the testing cost.

The company should also evaluate the internal start-up of new ventures as an acquisition alternative. This strategy is probably most appropriate where a company has skills and resources it can apply to new areas and has significant time to develop the new venture. Such new ventures typically suffer substantial losses and negative cash flows in their early years of operation and, on average, require eight years before they achieve profitability and ten to twelve years before their return on investment equals that of mature businesses.

PLANNING ACQUISITION STRATEGY

Once a corporation has determined that an acquisition program is the best means of achieving long-term goals, it must develop an acquisition strategy to guide the program. This strategy addresses issues such as the strategic direction of the corporation, the size and type of the firm to be acquired, and the type of acquisition desired.

Strategic Direction

The corporation must decide whether to seek horizontal expansion (e.g., May Department Stores–Associated Dry Goods; Bristol-Myers-Squibb; Tyson Foods–Holly Farms), vertical integration (e.g., Conagra–Banquet Foods; General Motors–Electronic Data Systems), or diversification. If the corporation selects diversification, it must decide whether the new firm should be related to existing businesses (e.g., Time-Warner; American Express–Shearson Loeb) or unrelated (e.g., ITT-Sheraton).

Although there are no hard and fast rules on these issues, the financial performance of diversifying companies is closely correlated with the way in which firms relate new business ventures to their old businesses, rather than to the magnitude or the pace of diversification. Even more important, companies that exhibit the best financial performance (i.e., highest returns to capital and least variability in earnings relative to growth in earnings) are those that have tightly controlled and consistently focused their diversification efforts by building on a single core of existing skills, knowledge, or experience. In contrast, companies that have either disregarded their existing core of skills and knowledge or tried to build in various different directions, each new direction drawing on a different skill, knowledge, or experience, have not performed well.

This point is supported by the authors of the best-selling *In Search of Excellence,* who point out that all the companies they identified as having particularly effective management have grown by building on their strengths.[1] Not one of the companies they designated as excellent is an unrelated conglomerate. Further, a January 1990 study[2] found that the most successful

---

[1] Thomas J. Peters and Robert H. Waterman, Jr., *In Search of Excellence* (New York: Harper & Row, 1982).

[2] "The Best and Worst Deals of the '80s," *Business Week* (January 15, 1990).

deals of the 1980s were those in which the acquired company was in a business directly related to the existing business. The highest success rate came among acquisitions involving companies in the same industry.

Related diversification can be divided into two types.

1. *Related-supplementary diversification* is accomplished by diversifying into new markets requiring functional skills identical to those the company already possesses. The purest form of this strategy is horizontal integration, with minimal departure from key functional activities.

2. *Related-complementary diversification* is accomplished by adding key functional activities in order to participate in the same market but in a broader fashion. The purest form of this strategy is vertical integration, in which the company adds new skills but makes minimal change in market orientation.[3]

The two major criteria for choosing between related-supplementary diversification and related-complementary diversification are the attractiveness of the market (e.g., rate of growth) and the company's competitive position within the market (e.g., market share). The research concluded that (1) companies with strong positions in low-growth markets should pursue related-supplementary diversification, and (2) companies with limited positions in attractive industries should pursue related-complementary diversification.

Type of Company

The corporation must decide whether to seek a private company, a public company, or a company division that is being divested. This decision is greatly influenced by the availability of the various types of companies. Despite the fanfare surrounding many acquisitions of public corporations, the data presented in Table 12-3 demonstrate that in the 1980s, the predominant activity in mergers and acquisitions was acquiring divestitures and private companies.

Size of Company

Is the corporation looking for a $50 million company or a billion-dollar company? This usually depends on the corporation's objectives and resources. Alco-Standard follows a strategy of acquiring small companies that can be operated on a decentralized basis but that can still benefit from being associated with a multi-billion-dollar corporation. Sears, on the other

---

[3] Malcolm W. Salter and Wolf A. Weinhold, *Diversification Through Acquisition* (New York: The Free Press, 1979).

TABLE 12-3

Composition of Acquisition Announcements

Year	Acquisitions of divestitures	Acquisitions of public companies	Acquisitions of private companies	Total
1980	666	173	988	1,827
1981	830	168	1,330	2,328
1982	875	180	1,222	2,277
1983	932	190	1,316	2,438
1984	900	211	1,351	2,462
1985	1,218	336	1,358	2,912
1986	1,259	386	1,598	3,243
1987	807	286	855	1,948
1988	894	462	836	2,192
1989	1,055	328	867	2,250

Source: W.T. Grimm & Co., Mergerstat Review (1989).

hand, had to acquire very large corporations (Dean Witter and Coldwell Banker) in order to succeed in diversifying from its $20 billion retailing business.

Type of Approach. Is the corporation looking for a "friendly" deal (e.g., Burroughs and Sperry merging to form Unisys)? Is it willing to be an "unfriendly" acquiror (e.g., Tyson Foods and Holly Farms; Brown-Foreman and Lenox)? Does it want to play the role of the "white knight" (e.g., Allied opportunistically coming to the rescue of Bendix)?

Pursuing a friendly acquisition usually increases the chances of retaining the acquiree's management, but it limits the opportunities available, since the managements of many companies are not interested in being part of a merger. Pursuing unfriendly acquisitions, however, has some serious risks, as evidenced by the notorious four-cornered battle among Bendix, Martin Marietta, United Technologies, and Allied Corporation.

In 1982, Bendix attempted to acquire Martin Marietta. In a series of moves that resembled a game of checkers more than chess, Martin Marietta turned from prey to hunter by teaming with United Technologies and tendering an offer for Bendix at the same time that Bendix was tendering its offer for Martin Marietta. Bendix finally was forced to turn to Allied Corporation in a merger that kept it out of the hands of Martin Marietta, but it cost the initiator of this battle, Bendix Chairman William Agee, his job. Similarly, in a futile attempt to take over Conoco, Seagrams ended up owning 20 percent of Du Pont-Conoco, and shortly thereafter it incurred a $650 million paper loss as the price of Du Pont's stock tumbled.

The role of the white knight is not always clear. For example, shortly after Allegheny International came in as a white knight to rescue Sunbeam

Corporation from IC Industries, it terminated several hundred Sunbeam managers ranging from high-level executives to middle managers. Similarly, Wheelabrator-Frye "rescued" Pullman, Inc., from McDermott, Inc., only to terminate more than 1,500 Pullman employees beginning the day after the merger was completed. There can also be significant risks for the white knights. They often enter as the battle is in progress, and they have little time to negotiate or do research. Chairman Robert Buckley of Allegheny commented that he discovered hidden problems in Sunbeam that were greater than they seemed. Eventually these problems contributed to Buckley's ouster in 1986. Occidental Petroleum reached an agreement in only nine days to acquire Cities Service for $4 billion.

ACQUISITION PROCESS AND IMPLEMENTATION

Once a corporation decides to make an acquisition, it should develop an implementation plan. The level of formality of the plan depends upon the time available and the management style of the corporation. Formal plans tend to be inflexible and stifling, whereas informal ones are usually inefficient and risky. The best plans incorporate both formal and informal elements, allow for speed and innovating, but take an organized approach that promotes efficiency and minimizes risk.

The basic elements of an acquisition program are discussed below.

Development of Criteria

Acquisition criteria serve three purposes:

1. They ensure coherence with corporate strategy and objectives;
2. They guide personnel in evaluating and screening industries to enter and companies to acquire; and
3. They assist board members, management, bankers, attorneys, and brokers, who play a role in identifying and evaluating acquisition candidates.

Criteria should not be formulated so tightly that nothing passes through, nor so loosely that too much passes; they should be flexible and be allowed to change over time to reflect changing experience and priorities.

There are many types of acquisition criteria; the criteria discussed here are typically included in an implementation plan, either formally or informally.

Industry Focus. Is the corporation looking for a company involved in any manufacturing industry, or is it seeking a company involved in a specific area (e.g., the manufacture of specialized heavy truck equipment?)

Synergy With Acquiror. What type of synergy with its present operations is the corporation seeking? Old-style conglomerates such as Textron or Gulf + Western, which did not necessarily require acquisitions to have any synergy with existing operations, are few and far between. Most companies today are in the acquisition market to strengthen existing operations. Examples of areas of synergy between acquirer and acquiree include the following:

- *Functional* synergy, such as a strong marketing company acquiring a company with a solid product line but limited marketing expertise (e.g., Quaker acquiring Stokely-Van Camp's Gatorade)

- *Distribution* synergy, such as a company with an existing distribution chain acquiring a company that is seeking to expand the distribution of its products (e.g., Sears acquiring Dean Witter; Chesebrough-Pond acquiring Bass Shoe and in turn being acquired by Unilever)

- *Financial* synergy, such as a cash-rich company acquiring a company whose growth is limited primarily by a shortage of capital (e.g., Bayer AG acquiring Matrix Corporate Development, a computer imaging firm; United Technologies acquiring Mostek).

Financial and Economic Criteria. Financial and economic criteria typically include the following:

- *Growth.* Is the corporation looking for a high-growth company or an average growth company? Or is growth unimportant?

- *Return on equity/return on total capital.* How should the returns compare to those of our existing operation, to those of U.S. industry on average, or to those of the acquisition candidate's competitors?

- *Financial leverage.* Is the corporation seeking a company with high or low leverage? How does the leverage compare with that of the corporation's existing operation, or with that of the candidate's competitors?

- *Operating leverage.* What should the acquisition candidate's relative level of fixed and variable costs be? What level of capital and labor intensity does the corporation want?

Competitive Posture. Is the corporation looking for a company that is a leader in its primary market and that could, therefore, command a premium price? Or is it seeking a troubled company that has the potential for turnaround and, therefore, the potential for a substantial increase in value? How important is potential competition, obsolescence, or substitution? The Pritzker family, owners of Hyatt Corporation, have successfully employed a strategy of acquiring troubled companies, usually at a price substantially below book value, and turning them around.

Management. Should the company have experienced, stable managers who will continue to run the operation, or will the corporation provide its own managers? Should the firm's management have the same style and culture as the corporation's (e.g., the polished investment bankers of Salomon Brothers merging with the commodity traders at Phibro)?

Geography. Does the corporation want a company with primarily domestic revenues, or one with international revenues? Does it matter where the company is headquartered? Will it consolidate physically with the corporation?

Acquisition Search Process

Approaches. There are several approaches to the acquisition search process. The choice depends on a corporation's objectives, time horizon, prior planning and analysis, resources available, and corporate culture. There are three major types of approaches: opportunistic (starting from what is already for sale), research (starting from acquisition criteria), and combination (a blend of the two approaches).[4]

- *Opportunistic approach.* This method first identifies companies available for sale and then determines which are attractive. It permits immediate movement into the flow of deals and consideration of a wide range of candidates, while not wasting time on companies that may not be for sale. Some disadvantages of this approach are that it requires a heavy reliance on third-party brokers, it can result in significant time and effort devoted to inappropriate candidates, and it may not support an overall strategic direction. The opportunistic approach is usually most appropriate for companies that have extensive acquisition experience and are bargain-hunting or pursuing a conglomerate strategy.

- *Research approach.* This entails performing detailed screening and research to determine which industries and companies fit the acquiror's strategy and criteria, selecting the companies that fit, and then determining what companies may be for sale. The advantages of this approach are that it is highly focused and is likely to yield candidates that "fit" with the acquiror. The major disadvantage is that it involves a significant commitment of research time and effort. It is particularly effective for companies that do not have much acquisition experience or that are unsure of the industries they wish to enter.

- *Combination approach.* This approach blends elements of both the opportunistic and the research approaches. It is a flexible

---

[4] Jerold L. Freier, "Acquisition Search Programs," *Journal of Corporate Venture* (Summer 1981).

method that involves researching and identifying industries and companies that should be pursued while still being open to attractive deals that may become available. This method is not as structured as the research approach or as loose as the opportunistic approach. It appeals to companies that have a good sense of where their acquisition program is headed but that could benefit from the additional research.

The first step in the research approach or the combination approach is to screen potential industries by identifying all those that meet the company's criteria. The company could begin the process with a broad criterion of seeking a consumer products company, for example. The next step is identifying all standard industrial codes (SICs) that fall into this category. After this initial screening, the company conducts financial and secondary research (using on-line data bases, such as Disclosure and Compustat, and trade journals) to provide a preliminary evaluation of each industry. It then ranks the industries in terms of potential, and chooses several of the highest ranked for in-depth analysis. It should perform this analysis using (1) interviews with individuals and groups such as industry participants and trade associations; (2) secondary research (e.g., published industry reports, consultants, investment reports); and (3) a complete literature review aided by the on-line data bases. The output of this process should be a comprehensive report on each industry containing the following information:

- Industry size
- Industry growth and projections
- Industry structure and dynamics
  - Number and market shares of participants
  - Profitability
  - Historical and projected changes
- Competitive profile of significant participants
  - Financial analysis
  - Products
  - Organization
  - Management
  - Performance
- Criteria for long-term success
- Determination of interest in entering each of the industries analyzed and list of target companies for further analysis

Acquisition prospects can be generated from many sources, including industry analyses directors, consultants, investment and commercial bankers, attorneys, accountants, and other brokers.

Initial Contact With Candidates. Once a corporation identifies a prospect, it must decide whether to attempt a friendly or unfriendly takeover. If a corporation undertakes an unfriendly takeover, it proceeds directly to the in-depth corporate analysis. If a corporation attempts a friendly takeover, it initiates contact with the candidate in addition to undertaking in-depth research. There are several ways to initiate this contact, including direct contact by letter or telephone and indirect contact through mutual friends or professional intermediaries. The initial contact with the candidate serves many purposes, including:

- Assessing potential management and cultural fit
- Assessing potential business fit and value added
- Determining the candidate's interest in merging
- Creating interest in merging

Detailed Company Investigation and Appraisal. If the corporation is still interested after the initial contact, or if it bypassed the contact stage, its next phase is an intensive analysis and appraisal of the candidate. The following activities should be included:

- Conducting preliminary operations, legal, and financial audits (e.g., for possible major lawsuits pending, the candidate's balance-sheet strengths, accounting policies that have been used to govern reported earnings)
- Performing an appraisal of the assets
- Commissioning special studies needed in areas such as pension funds or antitrust
- Developing detailed marketing, technical, management, manufacturing, and financial/economic information
- Consulting with experts on accounting, financing, legal, and regulatory issues (e.g., pooling versus purchase, tax-free options, antitrust)
- Determining the impact of the merger on both parties under various scenarios
  — Purchase price
  — Merged business forecast
  — Financial plans (e.g., pricing, volume, cost)
  — Industry and other microeconomic outlooks

Negotiations. The form of negotiations varies with every transaction. Negotiations usually begin informally at the initial meeting, and they become more formal in subsequent discussions as the price, terms, and conditions are refined. However, it is important that the acquiror develop a negotiating strategy prior to serious discussions. This strategy should include a plan covering the following:

- *Price.* How much does the corporation want to pay? What is the maximum that it will pay?
- *Type and terms of financing.* Will cash, notes, stock, or another form of payment be used?
- *Employment contracts.* Will specific contracts or other incentives be provided? If so, what will the general clauses be?
- *Organization.* How will the candidate report to the acquiror? What flexibility and what constraints are envisioned? What cultural issues can be anticipated?
- *Employee benefits.* Will the candidate retain its present policies, or adopt those of the acquiror? Will the candidate's employees retain the perquisites to which they are accustomed (e.g., company cars, offices, travel arrangements, bonuses, vacations, sick days)?

Documentation, Confirmation, and Closing. Acquisition negotiations can often take a long time, and many changes can take place within the candidate company during this period. Prior to closing, the corporation should carefully review and update all studies and analyses. This includes final legal and accounting audits, final forecast and scenario analyses, and analysis of any major changes that have occurred in the personnel, financial, marketing, or operational areas. In addition, the closing itself usually involves significant legal review for both parties to the transaction.

Implementation of Transition Plan

The closing of the deal does not end the acquisition process; instead, it begins the transition phase. The chances of a successful relationship are increased greatly if a detailed transition plan has been developed prior to the closing. The turnover of top management in an acquired company is extremely high in the first few years following acquisition. This turnover can often be attributed to the changing work environment. Managers often cite the new parent's information reporting requirements or a real or perceived loss of status as reasons for the high turnover. The transition plan should address the following:

- Integration with parent's systems (e.g., accounting, personnel)
- Level of autonomy
- Reporting relationships
- Reporting requirements (e.g., budgets, plans)
- Compensation and benefits
- Perquisites (e.g., company cars, travel arrangements, bonuses)
- Other policies and procedures

TABLE 12-4

Participation in the Acquisition Process

Acquisition stage	Participants						
	Top management	Corporate development	Finance/ accounting	Legal	Other functional groups	Consultants	Investment bankers
Criteria	XX	XX	X			X	
Industry analysis and candidate identification	X	XX				X	X
Preliminary candidate analysis	X	XX	X			X	X
Candidate contact	XX	X				X	X
Detailed evaluation	X	XX	X	X	X	X	X
Negotiations	XX	X	X	X			X
Documentation, confirmation, and closing	X	X	XX	XX	X		
Transition	XX		X		X		

XX = Major participant
 X = Participant

Source: Temple, Barker & Sloane.

PARTICIPANTS AND RESOURCES IN THE ACQUISITION PROCESS

As shown in Table 12-4, the acquisition process usually involves multiple participants, both internal and external, in almost every stage. Some participants, such as top management, are usually involved in every stage, whereas others, such as consultants or internal functional groups, are usually involved in very specific areas, such as evaluating one facet of the candidate's business.

The resources required to support an acquisition program depend on the type of search process used and the number and size of acquisitions planned. For example, a research-based search process requires a more significant in-house staff than an opportunistic process that relies primarily on intermediaries to identify prospects. Similarly, the staffing required to consummate one acquisition will be less than that required to support multiple acquisitions. There is, however, some basic internal support that is required in almost all cases.

Internal Resources

There should be one person who is the recognized leader in planning and implementing acquisitions. This could be the chief executive officer, the chief financial officer, the corporate planner, or the head of the merger and acquisitions group. Large, active acquirors usually have a staff dedicated to identifying and analyzing prospective deals. Smaller or less active acquirors often rely on a multidisciplinary internal task force to analyze opportunities as they are identified. Even companies with merger and acquisition staffs usually use task forces, drawing, as needed, on internal resources in areas such as finance, taxation, labor, and operations.

In addition to the efforts of internal personnel, the acquisition program should have access to some of the many on-line informational data bases that are available for screening and analysis (e.g., Disclosure, Compustat, Mergex) and access to financial valuation models (either internal or external).

External Resources

Almost all acquisitions involve external parties. The degree of their involvement depends on the availability of internal resources and the complexity of the acquisition. The following is a brief description of the types of external support usually employed and the circumstances under which they are most effective. Note that although there are potential pitfalls in using any external resource, the well-respected firms that provide merger and acquisition support have succeeded over the years by developing strong relationships with their clients based on competent guidance and trust.

Investment Banks. Supporters swear by the assistance they receive from investment bankers; detractors often refer to them as "salesmen in pinstripe suits." Bankers can assist both the buyer and the seller in a variety of areas, including the following:

- Industry and company identification
- Initial contacts with prospects
- Financial valuation
- Negotiating the terms of the deal
- Financing arrangements
- Takeover defenses

In large acquisitions, it is common for the buyer and the seller each to be represented by one or more investment banks (see Table 12-5). It is clear that numerous investment banks came out winners in the $25 billion leveraged buyout between RJR Holdings (a group led by KKR) and RJR Nabisco. KKR's fee was an unprecedented $75 million, while Drexel Burnham Lambert, Merrill Lynch, Morgan Stanley, and Wasserstein Perella each received $25 million for assisting KKR; and Dillon Read and Lazard Frères, representing RJR Nabisco, each received $14 million.

TABLE 12-5

Participation of Financial Intermediaries in the Largest Acquisitions of 1989

Rank	Value of deal (billions)	Companies	Financial intermediaries	Fee (millions)
1	$25.1	RJR Holdings (Group led by Kohlberg Kravis Roberts)	Kohlberg Kravis Roberts	$75
			Drexel Burnham Lambert	25
			Merrill Lynch	25
			Morgan Stanley	25
			Wasserstein Perella	25
		RJR Nabisco	Dillon Read	14
			Lazard Frères	14
2	$12.7	Bristol-Myers	Goldman Sachs	25
			Shearson Lehman Hutton	4
		Squibb	Morgan Stanley	24
3	$ 8.3	Beecham Group	Kleinwort Benson	N/A
			Wasserstein Perella	N/A
		SmithKline Beckman	Goldman Sachs	15
			J.P. Morgan	15
4	$ 7	Time	Merrill Lynch	2
			Shearson Lehman Hutton	16
			Wasserstein Perella	16
		Warner Communications	Alpine Capital Group	6
			Goldman Sachs	1
			Lazard Frères	20
			Merrill Lynch	1
5	$ 5.8	Grand Metropolitan	Morgan Stanley	14
			S.G. Warburg	7
		Pillsbury	Drexel Burnham Lambert	10
			First Boston	10
			Kleinwort Benson	1
			Shearson Lehman Hutton	10
			Wasserstein Perella	10
6	$ 4.1	Imperial Oil	First Boston	0.1
			Gordon Capital	7
		Texaco	Morgan Stanley	N/A
			Scotia McLeod	N/A
			Wasserstein Perella	N/A
7	$ 3.9	Tennessee Valley Authority (federal corporation) sells bonds	First Boston[b]	24
			Goldman Sachs	
			Merrill Lynch	
			Morgan Stanley	
			Salomon Brothers	
8	$ 3.9	HCA-Hospital Corp. of America	Morgan Guaranty Trust	50
		Hospital Corp. of America[a]	Morgan Stanley	8

(continued)

TABLE 12-5 (cont'd)

Rank	Value of deal (billions)	Companies	Financial intermediaries	Fee (millions)
9	$ 3.9	Tennessee Valley Authority (federal corporation) sells bonds	Morgan Stanley[b] First Boston Goldman Sachs Merrill Lynch Salomon Brothers Shearson Lehman Hutton	24
10	$ 3.8	Dow Chemical	Morgan Stanley	16
		Marion Laboratories	Shearson Lehman Hutton	17

(N/A) = Not available
(a) = Group formed by Hospital Corp. of American management, Morgan Capital, and other investors.
(b) = Lead manager

Source: "Deals of the Year," Fortune (Jan. 29, 1990), pp. 137–139.

To make effective use of investment banks, it is important to determine what functions they can perform that cannot be handled by internal resources. For example, investment banks will gladly perform industry and company analyses for a fee, but they usually bring no more expertise to this undertaking than exists within many companies' planning staffs. On the other hand, in terms of entering the flow of deals or providing guidance on financing issues, investment banks often can be of significant value.

Similarly, it is important to understand how the terms of payment might affect the actions of the investment bank. For example, investment banks are usually paid a percentage of the purchase price. For smaller deals, this often still involves the old Lehman formula of 5 percent of the first million dollars, 4 percent of the second million, 3 percent of the third million, 2 percent of the fourth million, and 1 percent of all monies over $4 million. However, large deals are usually a straight negotiated percentage of the purchase price. This provides incentive to the seller's investment bank to find a buyer and receive the highest price possible; however, it may cause a conflict of interest for the buyer's investment bank. It also can result in the investment banks on both sides being more interested in finalizing the transaction than in determining whether strategically it is the right transaction for either party.

Consultants. Consultants are often used for many of the same functions that investment bankers perform, such as assisting in industry and company identification, making initial contacts, and assisting in valuation. Their primary role, however, is usually in the area of performing special studies, which can range from technical engineering studies to market research surveys to comprehensive industry or strategy studies.

Compensation for consultants is most likely to be on a per diem or a project basis and is not tied to the acquisition itself. Fees vary significantly, depending on the size of the project and the quality of the firm retained.

Attorneys. Attorneys, either internal or external, are involved in all acquisitions. Their primary functions are to perform a legal audit; evaluate legal issues, such as antitrust and taxation issues; assist in the negotiations; and draw up the detailed legal paperwork that accompanies most acquisitions. The legal audit is an extremely important step in the acquisition process, because it identifies potential liabilities (e.g., lawsuits pending, product liabilities) that the acquiror may inherit.

Accountants. Outside accounting firms are usually brought in to perform an accounting audit; to assist in evaluating such issues as valuation, taxation, and financing; and to provide financial advice during the negotiations. The accounting firm may be the acquiror's auditor if there is no conflict of interest (that is, the accounting firm may also be the acquiree's auditor). An accounting firm should be selected for its expertise within an industry or area.

Appraisers. Outside appraisers are usually retained to appraise specific assets, such as inventories, real estate, or the physical plant and equipment. It should be noted, however, that appraising can be an extremely subjective process. For example, an appraiser might value a piece of real estate at $1 million, but there is no guarantee that that price could be obtained in the open market within a reasonable period of time. The valuation of assets with fairly limited markets, such as industrial plants and equipment, becomes even more subjective.

ACQUISITION VALUATION AND PAYMENT ISSUES

Valuation

Almost every company is for sale if the price is high enough; therefore, one key to the success of any acquisition is the price that is paid. An acquisition that seems very desirable at $75 million may seem less attractive at $100 million.

There are no scientific rules that determine how a company should be valued. If the candidate is a public company, the market has already valued it; however, corporations usually must pay significant premiums over market value in order to obtain a controlling interest in the acquisition. For the years 1984 to 1989, the average premiums paid over market[5] were:

1984	1985	1986	1987	1988	1989
37.9%	37.1%	38.2%	38.3%	41.9%	40.0%

One way to value a candidate is to analyze recent acquisitions of similar companies. The acquiror should analyze the P/E ratio of the tender offer, the premium over market price before the offer, and the market-to-book-value ratio of as wide a sample of comparable companies as possible.

It should be noted that analyzing similar companies is not a straightforward task, because the definition of "similar" companies is often subjective, particularly for companies that participate in multiple businesses. For example, if one were trying to value Tiger International, would it be compared to trucking companies, air freight companies, or leasing firms? It should also be noted that comparative analysis by itself is not a valid basis on which to value a company; however, it can provide useful valuation information.

Probably the most widely used method of valuing acquisitions is to discount their expected cash flows over a specified period of time. Although this process is relatively straightforward from a technical standpoint, projecting future earnings and cash requirements usually requires great familiarity with the company and its environment, and even then will involve subjective judgment.

Table 12-6 illustrates a simple model valuing an acquisition under two different growth rates. This example demonstrates how critical the assumptions are to the valuation (for example, increasing the expected growth rate from 10 percent to 20 percent doubles the value of the acquisition, and therefore doubles the P/E ratio that could be justified). Since the development of the assumptions does involve subjectivity and risk, it is usually advisable to value the company under a variety of scenarios (e.g., optimistic, most likely, pessimistic) or to consider the impact of specific strategic jeopardies. Each of the major assumptions that drives this type of model is discussed below:

- *Time span:* The cash flows should be projected for a period that the forecaster feels comfortable analyzing.

- *Cash flow:* Cash flow is defined in this model as net income plus noncash items (e.g., depreciation), minus planned capital expenditures minus any changes in working capital. The example in Table 12-6 assumes that capital expenditures equal depreciation plus 10 percent of earnings but the actual projections of both earnings and capi-

---

[5] W.T. Grimm & Co., *Mergerstat Review* (1989).

TABLE 12-6

Conceptual Relationship Between Acquisition Earnings Growth Rate and Maximum Multiple Payable

Proposed Acquisition
Revenue: $200 million
Net income: $10 million
Reinvestment = Depreciation + 10 percent of earnings
Ending value multiple: 8
Desired ROI: 14 percent

Year	10 percent growth			20 percent growth		
	Earnings	Cash throwoff	Discounted value	Earnings	Cash throwoff	Discounted value
1	$ 11.0	$ 9.9	$ 8.7	$ 12.0	$10.8	$ 9.5
2	12.1	10.9	8.4	14.4	13.0	10.0
3	13.3	12.0	8.1	17.3	15.6	10.5
4	14.6	13.2	7.8	20.7	18.7	11.1
5	16.1	14.5	7.5	24.9	22.4	11.6
6	17.7	15.9	7.2	29.9	26.9	12.3
7	19.5	17.5	7.0	35.8	32.2	12.9
8	21.4	19.3	6.8	43.0	38.7	13.6
9	23.6	21.2	6.5	51.6	46.4	14.3
10	25.9	23.3	6.3	61.9	55.7	15.0
Residual value	$185.0		$ 49.9	$442.1		$119.3
Total discounted value			$124.2			$240.1
Maximum multiple payable			12.4			24.0

Source: Temple, Barker & Sloane.

tal expenditures should be based on analysis of the company's historical performance and announced plans (e.g., capital expenditure commitments).

• *Residual value:* The residual or terminal value of the acquisition often plays a major role in the valuation. This is the market value that the acquisition is assumed to have at the end of the forecast period. The example in Table 12-6 illustrates one method commonly used: setting the terminal value by using an anticipated P/E ratio. Another common method is to discount the value of the perpetual cash flows beyond the forecast period.

• *Discount rate:* The discount rate allows for comparison of the acquisition to other available investment opportunities. The most widely used method is to use a discount rate equal to the corporation's weighted average cost of capital. However, as Alfred Rappaport points out, "The acquiring company's use of its own cost of capital to discount the target's projected cash flows is appropriate only when it can be safely assumed that the acquisition will not affect the riskiness of the acquiror. The specific riskiness of each prospective candidate should be taken into account in setting the discount rate, with higher rates used for more risky investments.[6]

Payment

The form of payment is also usually a critical factor in negotiations. Companies can use cash, common stock, preferred stock, debt, or a combination of stock and cash. According to W.T. Grimm, in 1988, cash was used in 56 percent of the acquisitions, stock in 21 percent, stock and cash combinations in 22 percent of all transactions.[7] The advantages and disadvantages of payment with cash versus stock relate to the tax implications, the risk involved with stock, and the effect on earnings per share.

Although a buyer probably has more flexibility with cash, if it uses stock for at least 51 percent of the payment, it can usually structure the transaction so that it can defer any federal taxes until the eventual sale of the stock. (Table 12-7 illustrates the various types of mergers that can take place and the resulting tax implications.)

The potential tax liability on capital gains is typically of concern to the seller, who may have a cost basis far below the selling price. By offering terms that minimize the seller's tax liability, the buyer may be able to strike a better deal. Capital gains may also come into play on the buyer's side if the buyer intends to restructure and sell off pieces of the acquisition. Although strategic and business criteria should generally control the acquisition decision, tax and legal effects can have an important impact on structuring the deal.

Federal tax legislation in the 1980s eliminated many opportunities to avoid or defer tax liabilities. The incentive for two-stage stock swaps, in which the buyer purchases shares of the seller and then swaps them for the desired assets, was eliminated by the Tax Act of 1982. This technique had enabled Conoco to save $400 million in taxes on its sale of Hudson's Bay Oil and Gas to Dome Petroleum in 1980.[8] The Act also eliminated the loophole for partial liquidation, a technique used in U.S. Steel's 1981 acquisition of Marathon Oil. Normally, the purchasing company tries to revalue the assets of the acquisition to generate higher depreciation and tax credits. This can be done by buying the assets of the company and technically liquidating the acquiree. However, as an offset to tax benefits, the government requires tax payment on the recapture of past depreciation deductions and investment tax credits taken on the acquiree's assets prior to the buyout. To avoid these payments, U.S. Steel only partially liquidated Marathon, saving an estimated $500 million in taxes. The

---

[6] Alfred Rappaport, "Strategic Analysis for More Profitable Acquisitions," *Handbook of Mergers, Acquisitions, and Buyouts* (Englewood Cliffs, NJ: Prentice-Hall, 1981).

[7] W.T. Grimm & Co., *Mergerstat Review* (1989).

[8] "Tax Law's Effects on Mergers," *The New York Times* (Sept. 7, 1982), p. D-8.

TABLE 12-7

Types of Mergers and Business Combinations

Characteristics/ requirements implications	I Statutory merger	II Exchange of stock for stock	III Purchase of assets for stock	IV Purchase of stock for cash or non-voting securities	V Purchase of assets for cash or non-voting securities
Nontaxable to shareholders of acquiree if specific requirements met	Yes, except for "boot"	Yes, except for "boot"	Yes	No	No
Transaction medium and steps	Generally 50 percent or more of purchase price must be in stock to meet continuity of interest rule	Voting stock only; voting preferred stock may be possible but not for pooling treatment	1. Voting stock with possibililty of up to 20 percent nonstock 2. Corporate shell of acquiree remains and may be liquidated	No restriction as to purchase medium	1. No restrictions as to purchase medium 2. Corporate shell of acquiree remains and may be subsequently liquidated to avoid double taxation
Type of accounting treatment	Purchase or pooling of interests	Purchase or pooling of interests	Purchase or pooling of interests	Purchase only	Purchase only

Source: James W. Bradley and Donald H. Korn, Acquisition and Corporate Development (D.C. Heath & Co., 1981).

Tax Act of 1986 repealed the *General Utilities* doctrine, named after a 1935 Supreme Court case, which had provided another escape clause from capital gains taxes. A new loophole, popular with raiders, was then discovered, in which sellers could set up subsidiaries that "mirrored" a newly acquired business and then sell their stock instead of the assets. The Tax Act of 1987, however, quickly eliminated this loophole too. Now if a buyer sells off assets, it has to pay the regular 34 percent corporate tax rate on any gains.

Several tax-saving techniques are still currently available, however. Using an installment sale and borrowing against the notes, for example, Robert Campeau deferred capital gains worth about $200 million when he spun off several of his newly acquired department store chains in 1988. (Campeau's heavy use of debt eventually drove him into chapter 11 bankruptcy, tax savings notwithstanding.)

In 1988 May Department Stores, a successful retailer that purchased stores from Campeau, found a tax-saving swapping ploy when it decided to retire some of its stock with cash. May raised the cash by selling a half-interest in its shopping center development subsidiary to PruSimon, a venture involving Prudential Insurance, with a three-step, tax-free transaction: (1) May and PruSimon formed a 50/50 partnership, with PruSimon putting in $550 million in cash and May contributing its real estate subsidiary, worth $550 million; (2) May tendered for about $550 million worth of its publicly held stock; (3) May sold the stock to the partnership for about $550 million. Since May effectively owned half of this stock position, it thus cut its ownership in the subsidiary by $275 million and retired $275 million of stock.

A potential disadvantage of stock deals is that the acquiree, by taking the acquiror's stock, has pinned the value of the acquisition to the future performance of the acquiror's stock, especially if the acquiree's shares are encumbered by agreement in some fashion. For example, the Conoco stockholders who received Du Pont stock watched its value plummet from $54 a share in 1981 to the low $40s in early 1984. Eventually, however, Du Pont's stock climbed to $125 a share in 1989.

The effect on earnings per share of using stock versus cash also has to be considered. Depending on the expected earnings per share issued (i.e., the acquiree's earnings divided by the shares issued to buy it), the use of stock could potentially dilute earnings per share, with consequent repercussions in the investment community.

As shown in Table 12-7, straight cash deals require the use of purchase accounting. Table 12-8 compares the implications of purchase versus pooling accounting. The following are some of the circumstances under which purchase accounting or pooling accounting are preferred:

- Purchase accounting may be preferred when:
  - The fair market value of the net assets exceeds the cost of acquiring the stock of the company. The resulting "negative goodwill" will have a positive impact on future earnings.
  - The seller has had recent losses or poor earnings. A pooling would require restating all prior period earnings to include the seller's poor earnings performance, while a purchase would not.
- Pooling accounting may be preferred when:
  - The purchase price significantly exceeds the fair value of net assets, and a material amount of goodwill would otherwise be recorded.
  - The restated historic earning trends are improved by the pooling.

GUIDELINES FOR SUCCESS AND REASONS FOR FAILURE

Despite the continuing popularity of acquisitions as a method to create shareholder value and the time and attention devoted to acquisitions in

TABLE 12-8

Purchase vs. Pooling Accounting

Characteristics	Purchase method	Pooling method
1. Theory	Acquisition of assets or stock	Uniting of ownership interests; "pooling of risks" concept is important.
2. Consideration	Buyer can use cash, notes preferred or common stock; warrants or convertible securities. Contingent payment is allowed	Must be an exchange of voting common stock for voting common stock; no shares to be issued can be contingent on future events.
3. Percent sought	May purchase all or any part of assets or stock; may increase prior minority interest in stock	Ninety percent or more of combining company's stock must be exchanged for issuing company's stock (10 percent or less can be cash or notes, including any stock acquired prior to the pooling).
4. Recorded amounts	Seller's assets and liabilities are adjusted to their fair value. Previously unrecorded assets and liabilities are also recorded.	Combining company's assets and liabilities retain same basis as before.
5. Goodwill	Amortized over not more than 40 years; amortization is not tax deductible. If cost is less than net assets acquired, noncurrent assets are reduced; if they are reduced to zero, then "negative goodwill" is recorded and amortized over not more than 40 years.	No goodwill recorded.
6. Reported earnings	Earning of seller included in operations from date of acquisition. Footnote disclosure or pro forma current and prior year earnings required. Subsequent periods' depreci-ation and other expenses are computed using adjusted asset and liability values.	All prior years' earnings must be restated to include pooled company and effect of additional shares issued. No adjustments to methods of computed earning.

Source: I. Robert Levine and Richard P. Miller, "Accounting for Business Combinations," Handbook of Mergers, Acquisition, and Buyouts (Englewood Cliffs, New Jersey: Prentice-Hall, 1981).

many companies, research indicates that the odds of success are no better than 50/50. In a study of over 2,000 acquisitions by 33 leading U.S. companies from 1950 to 1986, Michael Porter found that about 55 percent were later divested; among acquisitions in unrelated industries, the subsequent divestiture rate was 74 percent.[9] Porter's research confirmed an earlier

[9] Michael E. Porter, "From Competitive Advantage to Corporate Strategy," *Harvard Business Review* (May–June 1987).

study by James B. Young, who, looking at a broader sample, found an acquisition failure rate of about 50 percent going back to the 1940s.[10]

Although very little quantitative research has been conducted on the reasons acquisitions fail, much of the qualitative research indicates that a general lack of acquisition planning and too little emphasis on the human aspect of absorbing a new organization play major roles in acquisition failures.

What can be done to ensure a successful acquisition? There is no single answer; each acquisition is unique; and success is never guaranteed. However, following the straightforward guidelines offered here should significantly increase an acquisition's chances of success:

1. Develop a comprehensive diversification plan as part of an overall development strategy. It is important for the firm to have a clear definition of what business it is in and what business it wishes to be in. Should General Motors be in the automobile industry, the transportation industry, or the durable goods industry?

2. Buy a firm that meets sound strategic and economic criteria; do not buy simply whatever is available. Many firms become impatient or "lovestruck," and abandon their screening criteria.

3. Understand opportunity and have the resources to develop it and the commitment to exploit it. Companies should seek a good fit with their own operations; expecting perfection is not realistic. The buyer should take the time to understand its own strengths and weaknesses as well as those of the acquired company.

4. Evaluate the management of the acquired company for intelligence, style, energy, and motivation. Will the managers fit in as part of the corporate family? The value of sound management is difficult to overstate, but fit with the buyer's corporate culture is equally important. For years, pharmaceutical companies have attempted to merge with cosmetic companies, but often the managers of a "serious" business such as drugs are not comfortable with a business such as cosmetics.

5. Make the right advances; acquisition requires courtship. Gains for owners of both firms should be specified, and people should be absorbed into an organization with great care and sensitivity to needs for status and autonomy. Anticipate problems and discuss them openly with the management of the prospective acquisition. It is important that the top management of the acquiring company be involved in all aspects of acquisition planning and implementation.

6. Determine the price beyond which the deal ceases to be attractive. Keep in mind that, for the right price, almost any company can be

---

[10] James B. Young, "A Conclusive Investigation into the Causative Elements of Failure in Acquisitions and Mergers," *Handbook of Mergers, Acquisitions, and Buyouts* (Englewood Cliffs, NJ: Prentice-Hall, Inc., 1981).

bought. The key is to make the purchase at a price that allows for an attractive return.

7. Avoid making a big mistake. Small mistakes can be solved or will dissipate over time. If a company frivolously bets on a acquisition and makes a mistake, there may be few options left.

Analysis of several acquisition failures uncovers the violations of these guidelines by some of the largest, most successful companies in U.S. industry. Exxon's $1.2 billion purchase of Reliance Electric in 1979, described by *Fortune* as "perhaps one of the worst mergers ever made,"[11] is an example of oilmen using a wildcatter's betting mentality to venture into manufacturing. Exxon bought Reliance mainly to mass-produce and market a new, energy-saving electric motor that Exxon was developing. Within a year, however, it became apparent that the new product was neither technically nor economically viable. Exxon's problems were compounded by the payment of a much higher purchase price than originally intended (to outbid an unfriendly offer for Reliance) and by the belated discovery that a Reliance subsidiary had been cheating on the safety-testing of its equipment. Exxon eventually sold Reliance to a management group for $1.35 billion in 1986, but the initial mistakes were very costly.

Another example of poor acquisition planning and analysis is Honeywell's $1 billion purchase of Sperry Aerospace from Unisys in 1986. Intended to complement Honeywell's existing defense business, Sperry turned out to have serious problems, including large cost overruns on several fixed-priced military contracts. These problems contributed to Honeywell's substantial loss in 1988 and a fall in its stock price. Honeywell subsequently sued Unisys, its investment banking firm, and four former Unisys executives, seeking over $350 million in damages for alleged misstatements of financial information regarding the acquisition.

Poor integration planning can be another cause of failure. In 1985, James Dutt, then chairman of Beatrice Companies, acquired Esmark Inc. for $2.7 billion. Dutt launched the bid during a major restructuring of Beatrice's own operations. The ultimate confusion caused the Esmark management to flee, resulting in depressed earnings for Beatrice. In 1986, KKR broke up Beatrice after a $6.3 billion leveraged buyout, and Dutt lost his job.

DIVESTITURE AS A STRATEGY

Divestiture is the selling of a company, subsidiary, division, or a product line as a going business. Selling a business is just as important an investment decision as acquiring a business. The seller in effect believes it can

---

11 "Exxon's $600-Million Mistake," *Fortune* (Oct. 19, 1981).

earn a greater return on the funds used by that business by selling it (at market value) and using the funds elsewhere. Whether the proceeds of a divestiture are in the form of cash, equity, debt securities, or some combination, the seller's implicit assumption is that those proceeds have better investment applications than in the divested property. The buyer, of course, is making a similar economic comparison, but in reverse. The fact that two opposite points of view can coexist, often to mutual benefit, simply reflects the different objectives, expectations, capabilities, or strategies of buyer and seller.

Although the widespread restructuring and asset deployment strategies of recent years have led to significant divestiture activity, the initiative is still with the buyer in the majority of cases. The business press typically covers a divestiture transaction from the buyer's side, i.e., as an acquisition. Much attention is paid to buying techniques, little to selling. In part, this reflects the business community's preoccupation with size and growth. To divest a business may be seen as a sign of failure; yet a well-planned, well-executed divestiture can create significant value for the seller's stockholders. The seller's remaining business or businesses may benefit from increased management attention and the infusion of new liquid assets. Managers, employees, and customers of the divested unit may also benefit, as, for example, when the divested unit receives needed additional capital from its new owner.

A successful corporate divestiture requires specific, action-oriented skills. The corporation must first determine its objectives and priorities. It must analyze the internal operations and external environment of the divestiture candidate in light of those objectives. Then, it can develop a divestiture sales plan, contact prospects, conduct negotiations, and manage a smooth transition. In the business environment of the 1980s, the skills to implement these activities became increasingly important. The 1960s and late 1970s were boom times for mergers and acquisitions and represented —in many, if not most, instances—a seller's market. The 1980s, with high interest rates, stiff global competition, and corporate belt-tightening and restructuring, were more a buyer's market, with a heavier burden placed on the seller to plan for and consummate a satisfactory deal. For most industries, this environment is likely to continue in the 1990s.

This discussion takes the perspective of the corporate, multibusiness seller, i.e., one with several different subsidiaries, divisions, or lines of business. The issues that sellers of single businesses face (e.g., following the retirement or death of the principal owner-operator) may be largely similar, but the decision to sell the entire enterprise may revolve less on economic considerations than on the seller's personal objectives and judgments of the competence of potential management successors. This discussion also assumes that the selling organization will continue to be in business after the divestiture (perhaps in a significantly different form), although total liquidation is briefly considered as an option. Excluded from discussion, therefore, are financially driven leveraged buyouts and "raider" takeover activities in which businesses are acquired with the express intent of restructuring and divesting them. For purposes of nomenclature, the divestiture candidate is referred to here as "the division," although it may range from a freestanding, incorporated subsidiary to a single product line.

MAKING THE DIVESTITURE DECISION

In too many cases, the divestiture decision is a reactive one, often arising from despair over a division's poor financial performance or an unsolicited purchase offer that seems too good to refuse. Proactive sellers, i.e., sellers who see the divestiture option as an opportunity, usually have better results than reactive sellers. In either case, however, it is usually harder to make a divestiture decision than it is to make an acquisition decision, because divestiture requires a company to let go of something familiar. The division may still generate cash or have some potential. It may once have been the core of the company, and it may still have strong emotional appeal and well-placed defenders. Divestiture usually generates some difficult "people problems." Although this discussion focuses primarily on the logical, analytical aspects of the divestiture decision, a sensitivity to the emotional aspects is also important.

Determining Objectives

A company considering divestiture must know why it is doing so. Prospective buyers will be interested in the seller's reasons for divesting, and the seller's rationale should still leave them with convincing reasons to buy. Understanding the objectives that it hopes to achieve through divestiture will also help the seller or its negotiators in structuring the proper deal. A classic reason for divestiture is to unload a disappointing acquisition. In such a case, it is critical for the seller to know why the division is falling short of expectations. Is it poor financial results? Lack of fit with overall corporate strategy? Other reasons? It is also important for the seller to know what use it will make of the funds it gains from disposing of the division.

The reasons for and objectives of divestiture discussed in the following sections apply to most business situations, but they are not exhaustive. Objectives may overlap, since the sale of a division may serve several corporate purposes simultaneously.

Financial Reasons for Divestiture. Poor financial performance is probably the most commonly cited reason for divestiture, and a prospective buyer is likely to suspect this reason even when it is not the case. Intractable loss operations, which are unattractive to most potential buyers, are sometimes purchased by private investors, management groups, or employee stock ownership plans (ESOPs), particularly if the business is relatively small. Selling the division to such buyers may be seen as a better alternative, for economic or noneconomic reasons, than liquidating it. A small, "dog" (poorly performing) division in a large, high-overhead corporation, for example, may be turned around by entrepreneurs who can give it more attention.

In 1980 Colgate-Palmolive sold its Helena Rubinstein division, which had lost $50 million in 1979, to a private firm. Colgate received $1.5 million in cash and $18.5 million in notes payable over fifteen years, but it agreed, in turn, to guarantee $43 million of the division's bank debt. Philip Morris was unable to turn its marginally profitable American Safety Razor subsidiary (makers of Personna and other blades) into a major industry contender. Philip Morris tried unsuccessfully for three years to sell the subsidiary, and it had almost liquidated it, when a management group agreed to purchase it in 1976 for $16 million. Squibb's sale of its Beech-Nut baby food division (1973), Sperry's sale of its Remington electric razor division (1979), Beatrice's sales of its International Playtex division (1986), and Kraft's sale of its Celestial Seasonings division (1988) are other examples of well-known but marginal businesses sold by large parents to small investor groups. Some well-known ESOPs, where employees gained full or partial control of the business to strengthen it, include Rath Packing Co. (Waterloo, Iowa) and Okonite Co. (Ramsey, New Jersey), as well as Chrysler and Pan Am.

A division may be profitable yet still be a candidate for divestiture for financial reasons. Some examples are as follows:

- *Not meeting corporate objectives.* In 1981, Beatrice Foods sold Dannon, the yogurt company, for $84 million, or twenty-three times Dannon's earnings. Although it was profitable, Dannon failed to pass rigorous, new corporate standards—5 percent real sales growth per year or 18 percent return on equity—and its positive cash flow was threatened by the recent entry of two well-financed competitors, Kellogg and General Mills. The buyer, however, French dairy producer BSN-Gervais Danone, saw Dannon as a good vehicle for its own entry into the U.S. market. A similar logic led Westinghouse to sell its electrical transmission and distribution to ABB of Switzerland in 1989 and led General Electric to sell its consumer electronics business to Thomson of France in 1988.

- *Pressing need for capital.* A company may sell a profitable but nonessential division to cover losses and its core businesses. In 1982, LTV sold Lykes Brothers Steamship Company and its fleet of forty-six ships to a new company for $150 million, posting a $30 million pre-tax profit. LTV had relatively little background in marine transportation, and it needed cash to strengthen its two large steel operations, which were suffering from a severe industry recession. In 1989, Zenith sold its promising personal computer division to Groupe Bull to raise capital for its hard-pressed television business.

- *High debt burden.* Acquisitions financed by "junk bonds" almost inevitably lead to selective divestitures, but these can occur in more conventional deals as well. Du Pont sold some of Conoco's oil and gas properties to Petro-Lewis for $716 million in order to reduce the large amount of high-cost debt it incurred in financing its 1981 acquisition of Conoco. (It should be noted that this transaction was more a sale of assets than a sale of a going concern.) Divestiture may also be a matter of survival. In 1982, Chrysler sold its profitable combat tank manufacturing subsidiary to General Dynamics in order to satisfy creditors and other parties to its bailout agreement. Seven years later, in 1989, an again-faltering Chrysler chose to sell its Gulfstream aerospace subsidiary.

Divestiture as Part of a Larger Strategy. A divestiture may be part of a broader corporate strategy of asset redeployment. The division may no longer fit with the rest of the seller's business. It may be in a slow-growth market, or in an industry that is changing because of new technologies, mergers by large competitors, or other reasons. The division may be in an attractive, high-growth industry, but the seller may lack the capital required to maintain market share, or it may prefer to channel its capital elsewhere. The seller may also want to remain in the industry but simply want to correct imbalances in size, product line, or geography.

In October 1988, United Telecommunications sold United TeleSpectrum, a subsidiary providing cellular telephone and paging services, to National Guardian Corporation for about $775 million. While the fast-growing cellular industry was very attractive, United Telecommunications's core strategy was to strengthen its position in long-distance telecommunications. United and GTE had merged their long-distance telephone businesses into an equally owned company called US Sprint in 1986. The huge investments required for US Sprint's ambitious national fiber-optic system cost United more than $1.5 billion. In order to boost cash and pay down debt, United was later able to increase its stake in US Sprint from 50 percent to 80 percent. In April 1990, United acquired GTE's remaining 20 percent stake in US Sprint for $500 million.

External Reasons for Divestiture. Some divestitures may be motivated less by operating strategy than by considerations external to the business. Some examples follow.

- *To improve the market value of common stock.* This has become a major reason for divestiture in recent years. Given the unpopularity of conglomerates, a diversified firm may spin off peripheral divisions in order to simplify itself for stock market analysis or to improve its image in the financial community. Holiday Inns sold its Delta Steamship subsidiary for $96 million in 1982, in part because the stock market had typically accorded a higher price/earnings ratio to firms in the lodging industry than to those in the maritime industry. Burlington Northern spun off its energy businesses into a separate entity in 1988 because, as its chairman said, "the market doesn't like conglomerates." Similarly, Dekalb Corporation believed that the sum of its parts was worth more than the stock price of the whole company. Having spun off several peripheral units, in August 1988 it split the remaining core into three parts—Dekalb Energy Co., Dekalb Genetics, and Pride Petroleum Services Inc. In September 1989, total stock prices of the split-up companies had risen 130 percent since the time of the initial break-up announcement in October 1987.

- *To avoid a takeover.* Divestiture of an attractive division may be used to thwart a potential takeover of the entire company. In 1986, Westinghouse Electric sold its promising cable television business (which it had acquired in 1981) for $1.7 billion in cash, yielding a capital gain of $650 million. The company considered its stock price undervalued and was seriously concerned about a potential takeover by raiders. By divesting Group W Cable, Westinghouse was able to repurchase about 20 percent of its common stock and set up a reserve for restructuring its remaining businesses, making it less vulnerable to a raid.

- *Domestic regulatory pressures.* While antitrust activity was relatively light during the Reagan administration, government regulations or court decisions can sometimes require a firm to make a divestiture; other regulations may indirectly force a divestiture by increasing the cost of doing business. Schering-Plough, the drug company, acquired Dr. Scholl foot products in 1979, but was quickly forced by the Federal Trade Commission to sell Dr. Scholl's athlete's foot powder product line because it competed with Schering's Tinactin remedy. On a larger scale, AT&T's 1982 modified consent agreement with the Department of Justice required it to divest its local telephone operating companies; this was the largest divestiture in history. As part of the agreement, however, AT&T was accorded greater freedom to compete in unregulated markets.

- *Foreign pressures.* For companies with international operations, foreign government policy or political risk may encourage a divestiture or force a company to share ownership with local interests. Responding to anti-apartheid pressures from stockholders, employees, and various government entities, many U.S. corporations sold their South African operations. In 1988, Bausch & Lomb, Unisys, and Sterling Drug all sold their holdings in South Africa. In 1989 Mobil completed the sale of its twelve South African businesses for about

$150 million in response to legislation that withdrew tax credits and sent profits declining.

Other Reasons for Divestiture. Problems with management succession are a common reason for selling smaller or family-owned businesses, and this problem may also occur in a corporate division. The parent may believe that the division's junior managers are not qualified to replace senior managers who are about to retire. Divestiture may solve personality conflicts; for example, the division may be managed by a former owner who is unhappy in a large organization.

Divestiture may simply be an opportunistic response to an unexpected but attractive offer. Earnings may be at a peak and the timing may be right from the perspective of stockholder interests. However, the company must weigh attractive offers against longer-term objectives. Even if a company decides a division is not for sale, someone else's interest may provide new insight on a division's strategic opportunities.

Evaluating the Division

In addition to determining what corporate objectives might be served by a divestiture, the corporation should analyze the division's strengths, weaknesses, and future potential. Management needs this analysis so that it can make a sound decision regarding the unit; this analysis will also provide data that the corporation can present to prospective buyers. The evaluation should cover (1) internal strengths and weaknesses, (2) environmental conditions that will affect future performance, (3) competitive position, and (4) the division's relation to the rest of a corporation.

Information for the analysis includes financial statements (at least five years, if possible), budgets and long-term business plans, market research data, competitive intelligence, and industry forecasts. Any unusual accounting practices or economic conditions that affect the division's reported performance should be identified. The capabilities of upper and middle management should also be considered.

The evaluation process prior to divestiture is similar to that conducted during acquisition planning. Questions about strategic direction, business fit, and competitive position must be addressed. In principle, the corporate parent has an advantage over outsiders in obtaining information about the division, particularly in assessing the quality of earnings, confidential plans, and the caliber of division management. In fact, however, division plans may be overoptimistic. Smaller or more autonomous divisions may not be accustomed to providing detailed information to the corporate level, and attempts to gather accurate information may disclose the company's intentions prematurely. It may be helpful to use outside assistance, such as consultants, investment bankers, or industry analysts, in gathering information.

It may be necessary at this early stage for the corporation to decide how involved the division's management should be in divestiture planning. It is generally best to let at least a few key managers know about the division's evaluation; they will find out soon enough and the corporation will need their cooperation. General or specific assurances to these managers on the safety of their positions following divestiture may encourage the desired cooperation. During the divestiture process, it is also advisable to restrain the division from making long-term commitments that might hinder its sale. However, if the divestiture decision is relatively uncertain, such restraint must be imposed subtly and indirectly. Strict confidentiality is vital during the decision-making stage to avoid rumors and morale problems, which will only aggravate any existing problems and reduce the division's market value.

An analysis of a divestiture candidate must also include its relation to the rest of the corporation. Selling an ailing acquisition, for example, may only undo the diversification or synergy that the acquisition was designed to accomplish in the first place. Are the division's earnings countercyclical to those of other divisions? Does the division possess functional expertise, technology, distribution, or other assets that are of value to the rest of the company? Are its products needed for filling out certain product lines or for an internal, vertical source of raw materials or components? Can the indirect overhead associated with the division be eliminated upon divestiture, or will it merely be spread over the remaining businesses? What will the impact of separation be on the rest of the business, and how will employees, customers, suppliers, and the financial community perceive the separation?

Divestiture is a long-term decision that is generally irreversible. The corporation's evaluation of the division should therefore focus on its longer-term prospects. The macroeconomic, industry, and regulatory outlooks also have to be considered. The definition of "long-term" depends on the type of business, the level of risk, and the company's ability to make forecasts. However, five years should be considered a minimum. It may be useful to construct several environmental scenarios (e.g., optimistic, pessimistic, most likely) and attempt to assess probabilities for the division's future performance under each scenario. The evaluation of the division provides the basis for projecting its expected earnings, cash flow, and capital requirements, as well as making a qualitative determination of its role in the corporation's overall strategy.

Identifying and Evaluating Alternatives to Divestiture

Alternatives to divestiture depend on the company's reasons for considering a divestiture, e.g., poor earnings, slow growth, capital requirements, or a lack of fit with its other businesses. Each alternative will probably involve tradeoffs, whose financial implications the company should measure and compare. The tax implications of the alternatives may vary substantially, so the company should give some attention to after-tax effects. The specifics will depend on the structure of the final settlement. Tax effects are often critical, since tax basis and book basis frequently differ. In some cases, an ostensibly profitable transaction may turn sour when taxes are considered; in others, an unacceptable deal may become more attractive through proper tax structuring. Unless the company has already identified a likely buyer, the results of a decision to divest are highly uncertain, and it may be helpful to make an assessment of the probable outcomes. The following alternatives are oriented toward the most common type of divestiture: a problem division.

Retain the Division. Retention should be regarded as a positive action rather than a matter of default. Several options are as follows:

- *Improve operations with a view toward keeping the division for the long term.* In several cases of problem divisions, an evaluation of disposal alternatives led instead to a turnaround plan. The cost and commitment required, however, must be well understood.

- *Improve operations in order to make the division more salable at a later date.* The time frame must be defined, and the incremental return on any additional investment must be carefully estimated.

- *Phase down operations.* This option may be undertaken for several reasons: (1) to squeeze cash out of the division, e.g., by raising prices, tightening credit terms, cutting inventory, selling nonessential assets; (2) to shrink the division's size and thereby make it easier for a smaller buyer to acquire it; and (3) to prune problem operations and retrench in strong areas. Implementation of a phasedown must be done carefully to avoid detrimental rumors.

- *Do not act.* No action is always an option, although it is often unrecognized as such. However, the company should use this alternative only if it needs more time to make an informed decision. The problems that originally motivated the analysis of the division are unlikely to solve themselves.

Enter a Joint Venture. Through a joint venture, the division's problems can be shared with another company whose strengths, operating or financial, may help turn the division around. An example is Fiat-Allis, created in 1972. Allis Chalmers' Construction Machinery Group had low market share, marginal profitability, and difficulty in competing with Caterpillar, Komatsu, and others on a full-line, worldwide basis. Allis considered several alternatives, including more outside sourcing of finished product, becoming a short-line producer, and taking more component production in-house to increase value added. Allis preferred outright divestment to all these; however, it could not find a buyer and expected liquidation to bring less than book value. Fiat, which desperately wanted a foothold in the U.S. market, was willing to enter into a joint venture. Allis traded control of the division for cash up front and a deliberate, phased withdrawal from the venture.

Liquidate or Dissolve. The company may prefer this option where sale of the division's individual assets would yield a better return than continuing to operate those assets or divesting the division as a going concern. Goodwill and patients can be liquidated as well as tangible assets. In instances where inflation in fixed-asset replacement costs has been very high, liquidation may realize more than book value. Any losses, on the other hand, will be partly offset by tax savings. If the division has a high profile in its community, the company should pay attention to public relations; special efforts may be needed to minimize economic dislocation to the area.

Liquidation of the entire corporation may create substantial value to public stockholders if the market has persistently undervalued the company. In most such liquidations, elements of the business continue to operate under successor (often private) structures (e.g., Metromedia in 1986 and MGM/UA Entertainment in 1987). Sometimes, however, a public company may completely dissolve itself and cease to exist. In early 1979, UV Industries was selling for about $20 per share, versus a book value of about $25. Stockholders approved management's liquidation plan, as follows: (1) UV's Federal Pacific Electric Company subsidiary was sold to Reliance Electric for $345 million in cash in March, and stockholders received a liquidating dividend of $18 per share in April; (2) UV's oil and gas properties were sold to Tenneco for $135 million; (3) UV's remaining assets, principally gold mines, coal mines, and other natural resource properties, were sold to Sharon Steel Corporation, which controlled 23 percent of UV, for $518 million in cash and subordinated sinking fund debentures. A final per-share distribution of $7 in cash and $27 in debentures was made in September 1980. Shareholders thus realized a total of $52 per share (including the debentures at face value), versus a stock market value of $20 before the liquidation began. In addition, the liquidation plan complied with the nonrecognition of gain provisions of Section 337 of the Internal Revenue Code, which resulted in a tax savings to UV of about $42 million.

Shut Down. Under this option, the company terminates the division's operations, but it retains and "mothballs" the division's assets. A shutdown might be done while management waits for economic conditions to improve, looks for a buyer, or refurbishes facilities in order to transfer them to another division. Temporary shutdown will involve ongoing expenses such as maintenance, security, insurance, and property taxes.

Abandon. If the situation is desperate, a company may simply walk away from a business, taking whatever write-offs are necessary. United States business interests in Iran were abandoned during that country's revolution and the ensuing hostage crisis, although suits were later filed to recover compensation. In 1983, Time Inc. closed its TV-Cable Week magazine after five months of publication. Faced with the prospect of continued heavy losses, Time decided that abandonment at a $50 million loss was its best option.

Spin Off to Investors or Take Public. A spin-off is a form of restructuring in which stockholders continue to own the same assets but in a different legal form. For example, the seller can create a subsidiary to own the divestiture candidate and then distribute shares of the subsidiary to the company's stockholders, severing or reducing the division's ties to the parent. The subsidiary must be large enough to be viable as a separate entity. Spin-off is sometimes done under court order, as in the landmark 1911 antitrust decision against Standard Oil of New Jersey, which forced the company to spin off its Indiana, Ohio, and California companies. Under a 1982 consent agreement, AT&T spun off its Bell operating companies in 1984; each share of AT&T common stock was exchanged for one share of the reorganized parent and prorated shares of the seven newly organized regional operating companies. The Esmark and Brunswick/Sherwood spin-offs cited earlier were, on the other hand, purely voluntary.

One argument for voluntary spin-off is greater shareholder value. Consider a company with two unrelated divisions: Division A, in a high-growth industry, contributed $1.50 in earnings per share; Division B, in a static industry, contributed $0.50. If the company's total earnings per share was $2.00 and its stock market price was $24, it would have a P/E of 12. As two separate companies, the stock market might accord Division A a P/E of 15, for example, and Division B a P/E of 9. Shareholders would then hold shares worth $22.50 and $4.50, respectively—an increase of $3 per share as a result of the spin-off.

Spin Off to Employees. Since the late 1970s, ESOPs have been used increasingly to keep financially troubled businesses afloat. ESOPs provide substantial tax advantages, and they are a means of giving employees a stake in the business and raising equity without going public. Under an ESOP, a trust is created that buys stock in the company or division on behalf of the employees. The stock purchases are typically financed by bank debt. The company then contributes up to 25 percent of its payroll expense per year to the trust, which uses these contributions to retire the trust's debt. The company gains a tax deduction for the total amount of its contributions while also raising needed equity capital.

Choosing Among Alternatives

In choosing among divestiture alternatives, it is again important to remember that disposing of a business is an investment decision. A useful economic concept for evaluating this decision is return on recoverable assets (RORA). Consider, for example, a division earning $5 million on assets with a net book value of $100 million—5 percent return on assets. The division's assets *recoverable* upon disposal, however, may be valued at $50 million, which could be invested in some other activity. The division's current RORA is then, in fact, 10 percent ($5 million ÷ $50 million), and this is the rate of return that should be used in comparing alternative investments of the recoverable funds.

Deciding to divest a division, particularly an older one, may be a difficult and even emotional process. For companies that are not accustomed to selling divisions, time may be required at top management levels to raise awareness, change values, and generate a consensus before presenting a divestiture plan to the board of directors for approval. This incremental approach was seen in General Mills' divestiture of its once-dominant flour milling business, which was preceded by many staff reports, management meetings, the development of new data reporting systems, and the divestiture of many smaller, less-central businesses. On a broader scale, it took Westinghouse over a decade to exit many of its core electric businesses, such as lighting, motors, and transmission gear, which had been founded by George Westinghouse almost a century earlier. How long a company's divestiture decision takes will depend on the decision-making procedures, the corporate culture, and the particular situation of the division. Once a decision has been made, however, it is important to begin the divestiture program as rapidly as possible. Otherwise the division remains in a harmful state of limbo. A specific strategy for selling the division must be developed and implemented.

PLANNING DIVESTITURE STRATEGY

As with any complex transaction, there are no firm guidelines on the time required to complete a divestiture. The condition of the general economy, the stock market, and the industry will exert influences beyond the seller's control. Buyers who express interest but then back out will add to the time requirements.

Some practitioners suggest a target of six months from making the decision to closing, although this is generally a minimum. A rough schedule might be as follows: several months for gathering information and planning strategy; several months for contacting prospective buyers and making presentations; several weeks for conducting negotiations; and about two months for the detailed preparations prior to closing.

Key Functions in the Divestiture Program

One of the first questions to address is who should be involved in the divestiture program. Before staffing for divestiture, however, it is useful to consider the key tasks and functions that will be required. An overview of these is presented in the following sections.

Major Policy Decisions. This function is typically the domain of the chief executive officer (CEO) and the board of directors. Final approval of the divestiture decision, program management, schedule, price, terms, and buyer will be required.

Overall Program Management. A senior manager must be selected to oversee the selection and contacting of prospective buyers; "packaging" of the division for presentation to prospects; selection and relations with outside consultants and intermediaries, if any; negotiations; and closing. The program manager should have direct access to the CEO. Since the CEO is likely to have other responsibilities, the day-to-day management of specific aspects of the program may be delegated to key subordinates. It is important, however, to keep the program on schedule; any delays should be the fault of the buyer, not of the seller.

Data Gathering. This function will primarily involve assembling financial and operating information needed for presentations and negotiating. Although the data collected during the divestiture decision-making stage provide a beginning, buyers are likely to require considerably greater detail concerning factors such as the quality of receivables and order backlog, the actual and book depreciation of major fixed-assets, management agreements, labor contracts, and pension liabilities. The seller must exercise good judgment in determining the amount and format of information provided to prospects, in deciding whether this information is given voluntarily or on request, and in planning the timing of the release of information. The seller must also identify tax and other legal considerations that may affect the structure of the final agreement, such as prior agreements with customers, lenders, creditors, lessors, licensors, and government agencies. The data-gathering function may also assist in identifying prospective buyers.

Selection, Contact, and Presentation to Prospects. Active efforts are required to bring a suitable buyer to the negotiating table. As discussed below, a company can notify prospects that the division is for sale in many ways, from making a public announcement to making a casual comment over lunch. A company may also use intermediaries. Skill is required to arouse serious interest in a prospect without distorting or omitting facts or weakening the seller's position. To avoid confusion, a company should designate a single point of contact for communications with each prospective buyer.

Negotiations. Serious discussion of price and terms may be friendly or combative. It may involve a time-consuming chain of decisions, such as the signing of a letter of intent, a preliminary agreement, or supplementary agreements. A single, chief negotiator should be clearly designated, so that the buyer cannot take advantage of any conflicts within the seller's organization. The chief negotiator should have stature, credibility, experience, and thorough preparation. The seller should give the chief negotiator firm guidelines on its primary objectives regarding price and terms, but the negotiator should have latitude to bargain over secondary issues. The negotiator should have the judgment to distinguish major and minor issues, but will need direct access to the program manager or CEO when additional guidance is necessary.

Preparation for Closing. Considerable legal and accounting work will be required to document exactly what is and what is not included in the transaction, and to translate the two parties' understanding of their agreement into mutually satisfactory legal language. The legal documentation may be voluminous, but it is needed to avoid subsequent misunderstandings and possible litigation. The divestiture program is not completed until the final settlement has been signed, so the seller's management must be ready to see the program through to a successful closing. The seller should also be prepared to give some assistance to the buyer during a transition period after the closing. This transition period, in fact, is likely to begin before the final agreement, as the buyer gears up to take control of the division, and the seller should try to make this transition as smooth as possible.

Staffing the Divestiture Team

The specific assignment of functional responsibilities in the divestiture program will depend on the relevant skills and experience of the seller's personnel, the pressure of their other responsibilities, and the size and complexity of the transaction. Some functions may be combined; for example, the program manager might also take responsibility as the key contact point and chief negotiator with serious prospects. Because of the range of functions required, however, it is likely that the divestiture program will be managed as a special project that cuts across existing organizational boundaries within the seller's corporation.

The initiative to consider divestment may have begun among corporate staff in the parent, for example, or at some management level between parent and division, such as group or region. Some of these same people may also assist in carrying out the decision. Except in large conglomerates, it is unlikely that there is a designated staff function for handling divestitures, but personnel in an acquisitions, strategic planning, or financial planning department may have relevant experience or skills. It is generally best to take a team approach, with a senior manager and one or two other managers involved from start to finish. This ensures unity of purpose, continuity, and timeliness. The corporation's chief financial officer and its top in-house attorney should also be involved. Tax and legal implications should be considered as early as possible.

Use of Intermediaries. It will probably be necessary to engage outside experts and intermediaries at different stages of the program, such as lawyers, accountants, management consultants, investment bankers, and business brokers. Ultimate responsibility for the success of the program, however, must remain in the seller's organization.

Outsiders may assist in negotiating and closing, as well as in identifying prospects and developing presentation materials. They should be selected on the basis of demonstrated experience and ability, but the program manager's judgment will be necessary. Most companies have established relationships with law and public accounting firms. These firms may have expertise in divestiture; if not, they can probably supply references of firms that do have such experience. It may also be useful to request references from previous clients of these firms. Any potential conflicts of interest should be identified. If outsiders are to play a major role in the divestiture program, it is also important that they get along personally with key people in the seller's organization.

Compensation for outside consultants and others may be a per-diem rate, a percentage of the divestiture proceeds, a contingency payment, or some other arrangement. Attorneys and management consultants often charge a per-diem rate, while investment bankers typically charge a percentage fee. Fees can range widely, depending on the size of the deal, and they usually are negotiable. For large, *Fortune 500* transactions, total fees to outsiders can run in the tens of millions of dollars, although this may represent less than one percent of the proceeds. The value added by good consultants and other intermediaries is likely to be many times whatever fees they charge.

Involvement of Division Personnel. Division personnel must play some role in the divestiture program. During the presentation stage, the prospective buyer will visit the division's facilities, and it will probably want to meet the division's key managers in order to solicit their views of the division's prospects. The division's employees, moreover, are assets. A prospective buyer may be looking for certain management skills to augment those in the buyer's existing business. The buyer may even consider key division managers essential to the transaction. Even if the buyer is likely to make personnel changes or reductions after taking control, most of the division's employees will probably be retained, at least during a transition period. What division employees say and do during the divestiture program may have a major influence on a prospect's interest and subsequent negotiating position.

The division's managers are in an awkward position during a divestiture program, and their response to it may be hard to predict. If financial performance is a problem, they may feel unfairly blamed for failure and fear for their jobs. They may be bitter and feel that the fault lies with the parent. Or they may see divestiture as an opportunity to strengthen the division and enhance their careers. In any case, division personnel can jeopardize the sale or at least damage the seller's negotiating position. This remains so even as divestiture becomes more likely, since the division's managers may begin to transfer their loyalties from seller to buyer and curry favor with the buyer.

The seller's divestiture team must therefore take careful account of division personnel in its planning. A policy of openness and fairness is usually best. The seller should try to convince key division managers and other employees that their welfare is being considered, in the form of employment security, severance pay, and other benefits. The interests of division personnel, in fact, may provide useful guidance in planning the divestiture and identifying prospective buyers. Although confidentiality should generally be maintained during the decision-making process, once divestiture has been chosen, it must be dealt with openly. Disgruntled employees will hinder the sale; enthusiastic employees will help it.

Assessing the Division's Marketability

In order to set pricing limits and identify and sell likely prospects, it is first necessary to conduct an inventory of the division's marketability. This enables the seller to tailor the sales plan and presentations to particular buyers. The process begins with a determination of exactly which items are for sale, which are excluded, and which are negotiable. Comparable asset values, P/E ratios, acquisition transactions, and other measures provide useful guidelines for valuation. The seller can then estimate the financial value of the division as an outsider might perceive it. This analysis should include an evaluation of internal strengths and weaknesses that an outsider would be less likely to know about, such as functional skills, technology, and other nonfinancial assets, that could have a significant impact on the division's attractiveness and value.

What Is for Sale? Unless the division is a fully freestanding entity, defining the business to be sold can be difficult. Facilities and equipment may be shared with other divisions. Certain functions such as legal, personnel, cash management, collection, and data processing may be performed by parent staff, and even general management personnel may be primarily affiliated with the corporation. Which employees go and which stay? Although neither buyer nor seller can decide for employees, attractive compensation packages can be designed to help persuade them. If the division is not a complete business entity, it may be restructured as such, if that will make it more saleable. On the other hand, it may not be desirable to sell the entire division as a single entity. The seller might want to break the division into pieces or reduce its assets to make purchase more feasible for smaller buyers. Profitable product lines might be segregated and sold on the basis of earnings power; assets associated with unprofitable lines could be sold for book value or whatever the market would bear. Other considerations include the following:

- *Fixed assets* that are essential to the business must generally be included. Unused or underutilized assets, however, such as real estate, buildings, or equipment, might be retained or sold separately.

- *Current assets* are more subject to negotiation. Receivables are likely to be discounted by the buyer, and if the seller has a strong collection function, it may be best to exclude them altogether. Marketable excess inventory might be sold separately, particularly if some of it has already been written off. Cash is a highly variable item, and it is usually allocated at closing on the basis of a previous negotiation.

- *Expense items,* such as fuel and office supplies, may have value not represented on the balance sheet. Insurance, a prepaid expense, must be carefully examined; disposition may depend on the type of policy or whether the seller self-insures.

- *Liabilities* may often be excluded in order to facilitate a sale, or the seller may be willing to guarantee certain debts incurred by the division. Reserves and accruals must be examined for adequacy and relevance. Product or service warranties to customers must be identified and evaluated.

- *Patents and trademarks* may be included, or the seller could license them to the buyer. On the other hand, the division may hold certain licenses or distribution rights that are not transferable to a different owner.

- *Off-balance-sheet items,* such as order backlogs, long-term leases, and research and development, may have substantial value or liability, and should not be overlooked. The backlog, in particular, may be a better indicator of the division's future potential than recent operating statements.

Attractiveness to Buyers. Once the seller knows what it wants to keep and what it is willing to divest, it can assess the division's attractiveness to prospective buyers. The detailed analysis of financial and nonfinancial assets and liabilities discussed in the preceding section will provide a basis for this assessment, but industry, market, and competitive information must also be considered. Even if the division has been a poor performer, the company must remember that the division's future, not its past, is being sold. Historical earnings are important, and they should be restated to account for any unusual or nonrecurring charges or corporate overhead allocations, but a wise buyer is likely to look at qualitative factors as well.

The seller must therefore give attention to the division's functional skills in such areas as marketing, production, and research and development; current and projected funding needs, and whether those funds are needed for growth or defense; and the feasibility of division management's objectives. Prospective buyers may even be concerned with intangible factors such as the division's organizational culture.

The seller should also identify potential problems such as the following:

- *Antitrust considerations* may restrict the types of buyers that can be approached. Foreign governments may also impose restrictions, or may make it difficult to repatriate the divestiture proceeds.

- *Pension and benefit plans* may involve large obligations and may be unfunded or inadequately funded. Restructuring the plans, with Internal Revenue Service approval, may be necessary to attract a buyer. Employees will also be concerned about any changes. All plans and changes should be carefully reviewed by experts.

- *Labor unions* will certainly be interested in the divestiture program, although in most cases union approval is not necessary. Depending on the situation, union leaders may be advised of the seller's intent, although such disclosure is often left to the buyer. Most buyers will not want to walk into an unpleasant labor situation. If a union contract is about to expire, the seller should probably defer any disclosures about the divestiture program until a new contract has been negotiated; otherwise, the union may try to extract special concessions.

Determining Price and Structure

The company cannot address decisions about price and structure without a general determination as to the type of firm likely to buy the division. In many cases, some potential buyers will have been identified in earlier phases of the planning process; e.g., firms in the same industry or firms known to be making similar acquisitions. Moreover, there are no scientific rules to calculate one correct price and structure, because value is a highly subjective matter that will also be influenced by the changing market forces of supply and demand. Regardless of any other arguments, the price must permit the buyer a reasonable return on its investment. Too high a price could prevent the sale and could conceivably result in the buyer's bankruptcy and the seller's repossession of the business. Guidelines about desired payment and structure should therefore be flexible enough to permit negotiation and accommodate the needs and financial constraints of the buyer.

There are two main aspects of the structure of a divestiture transaction, each of which may have significant tax effects: (1) the form in which ownership of the division is conveyed to the buyer and (2) the form in which the seller is compensated. The buyer typically receives control of the division in the form of stock, if the division is a subsidiary with its own ownership structure, or in the form of title to all or selected assets and liabilities associated with the division. The forms of compensation to the seller are virtually limitless. Although most divestitures are for cash and notes, the seller may receive equity in the buyer's company, equity in the division, shares of the sellers' stock previously obtained by the buyer, mortgages, merchandise credits, contingency payments, or a combination of payment methods. The timing of these transactions can vary from the closing date to a longer schedule.

Expert tax counsel should be sought in order to determine an optimal structure, bearing in mind, where possible, the relative tax circumstances of buyer and seller. Prior to the Tax Act of 1986, for example, it was advantageous for a seller to structure the divestiture as a sale of stock rather than assets to obtain preferential capital gains treatment on the difference between the net proceeds and the cost basis. While current tax laws no longer distinguish capital gains from ordinary income, a stock sale may still be advantageous in avoiding recapture of accelerated depreciation as taxable income and in thoroughly removing the seller from the business and any contingent liabilities. A buyer would generally prefer to receive assets rather than stock in order to maximize the value of depreciable assets for cash flow purposes. Even if the division's legal structure permits a stock sale, the seller should be willing to consider the sale of specified assets as the more practical alternative for many buyers. The degree of flexibility required will depend on how the seller perceives its bargaining position.

Pricing Techniques. It may be useful first to establish minimum and asking prices on the basis of cash up front, if only for internal purposes, to serve as a reference for evaluating pricing alternatives. Book value, as stated for financial reporting purposes, is a useful starting point. The corporation may have to adjust the division's balance sheet to represent its true book investment in the division, since certain asset and liability items may not be carried on the division's books or may be commingled with those of other divisions. It should also restate book value in light of the potential tax treatment of the transaction, since the division's tax basis is likely to differ from its financial reporting basis (e.g., accelerated versus straight-line depreciation of fixed assets).

Even though an adjusted book value may bear little resemblance to the division's current liquidation value or future earnings potential, it nonetheless represents the seller's breakeven point for financial reporting purposes. A prospective buyer, meanwhile, may look at book value as a benchmark for negotiating, believing that the seller has set book value as a minimum objective. Many buyers and sellers do in fact use book value as a standard, but too great and adherence to it can be unrealistic, since the business could be worth considerably more or less.

Various other techniques are available to assist the seller in determining a fair market price. Current liquidation value of the division's individual assets and estimates of the division's future earnings both provide useful guidelines. Comparison with similar companies may be helpful; the current market value of publicly listed companies can be readily obtained, and recent merger and acquisition activity should also be looked at.

P/E ratios for comparable firms in comparable industries may be used as a reference. However, use of P/E ratios in negotiations may lead to disagreements, for example, over what constitutes a fair P/E ratio and which year's earnings should be used in the calculation. Discounted cash flow or net present value analysis is also a useful tool, but, again, disagreements may develop over estimated future earnings and the appropriate time horizon and discount rate. It has been suggested that a buyer in its second year of ownership should be able to earn a return on its total investment equal to between one and one-half and three times the rate of high-grade corporate bonds or other low-risk investments. Although this formula may be somewhat simplistic, it highlights the fact that the buyer will be comparing the potential return on its investment in the division with the potential return on alternative investments. A buyer may consider total investment particularly important, since it may expect to invest capital in the division beyond the price it pays the seller.

Negotiating Posture. During the presentation stage, before serious negotiations begin, the seller should be willing to quote a fixed or minimum asking price so that a consistent position is communicated to different buyers. The seller may also discuss broad objectives concerning divestiture structure, but it should avoid getting mired in details too early in the discussions. Successful negotiations typically proceed from the general to the specific, starting with agreement on the overall structure of the sale (e.g., stock or assets) and then moving to price. The terms of the sale permit the greatest flexibility and are usually dealt with last.

Regardless of the pricing techniques employed, the seller must be able to give convincing arguments to justify its price, and it must support these arguments with a logical analysis of the division's prospects. The asking price should be realistic, but at the same time sellers should not be afraid to be bold if the supporting analysis is well-founded.

DIVESTITURE IMPLEMENTATION

Selling the Division

After determining the general attractiveness of the division and price objectives, an aggressive seller will actively seek prospective buyers, either directly or through intermediaries. An active approach is likely to speed the divestiture process and also give the seller more control over its outcome.

Finding Prospects. Compiling a list of prospects is analogous to the screening process in an acquisition search. The seller should screen prospects on the basis of business fit, ability to pay, antitrust considerations, corporate objectives, and other factors. Suggestions can come from a variety of sources, including the seller's personal contacts, the board of directors, and the division's own managers, suppliers, and customers. The seller should not hesitate to use outside assistance when necessary. Consultants, bankers, lawyers, and accountants may suggest suitable public or private buyers or investor groups whose potential interest in the division might be totally unknown to the seller. Data base services may be used in screening large numbers of prospects, e.g., companies of a certain size range in certain SIC-code industries. Many corporations, moreover, have publicly announced acquisition programs. Publications such as *Who's Who of Corporate Acquisitions, Mergerstat Review,* and *Mergers and Acquisitions* may provide names of active acquires and their acquisition criteria.

Making Announcements. An alternative approach to prospecting is to announce publicly that the division is for sale and wait for interest to develop. This approach has been used successfully by many companies. If the division is relatively unattractive, a list of likely prospects may be difficult to compile. If the division is highly attractive, the seller may hope to conduct an auction among many bidders. Public announcement, however, often puts the seller in a reactive position and may give the division a bad name if much time elapses while buyers shop around. On the other hand, even a seller who actively seeks prospects on a confidential basis may eventually have to make a public announcement once rumors have begun to circulate.

Negotiating. Once a serious prospect has been identified, the two negotiating teams meet. The size of the teams is itself negotiable, but an expert lawyer (internal or external) should be included. Tax, accounting, and other analysts or consultants should also be available. Detailed analysis of counteroffers is generally best done away from the heat of the bargaining table, however. The chief negotiator should try to find general areas of agreement before discussing technicalities. Many minor details can be worked out in the period prior to closing, but the negotiators should reach agreement on all key points to prevent a deal from unraveling because of some later misunderstanding. It is common to allow the final price to fluctuate after negotiations to reflect the specific conditions at the time of closing.

Closing. Following the negotiations, the seller must provide updated, audited statements and documents for the division. A certified public accountant should certify that the statements were prepared according to generally accepted accounting principles, but responsibility for their accuracy lies with the seller. Prior to settlement, the buyer is likely to try to uncover the division's worst problems, since afterward those problems belong to the buyer. The seller's divestiture team should cooperate with the buyer and avoid petty disputes to ensure that the divestiture program reaches a successful final settlement.

GUIDELINES FOR SUCCESS

In divestitures (as in acquisitions), the theme is simple: Careful analysis and planning—or executive homework—increase the chances of success. Moreover, experience suggests that following some guidelines should significantly increase the divestiture's chances of success.

1. First and foremost, do the strategic homework—for both the parent and the division. Make sure that all attractive options have been fully considered. The benefits of the divestiture to the parent should

clearly and substantially exceed both the direct and indirect costs of divestment.

2. Once the decision to divest is made, act quickly. The problems that originally motivated the decision will not solve themselves. Rumors can sap morale and harm the seller's negotiating position.

3. Approach the decision positively. In many cases, divestiture may be genuinely positive not only from the parent's perspective but also from the perspective of the division. Where this is so, make every appropriate use of division management in carrying out the process.

4. Plan the divestment process carefully. Avoid a fire sale and try to reduce to the unavoidable minimum any personal trauma. The biggest risk in divestiture is the destruction of the division's economic value caused by the departure of key employees and other disruptions to the division's business. Therefore, it is essential to have a clear strategy for approaching prospective buyers and for determining when and how to bring division management on board.

5. Clearly delineate and assign responsibilities in the divestiture process. It is useful to have a dedicated, accountable team involved from start to finish.

6. Finally, anticipate the people problems. Where possible, take steps to mitigate them and compensate key people for the personal disruption they will experience. Even where substantial costs are involved, they may be a lot less than the indirect costs of perceived or real insensitivity.

CONCLUSION

Overall, winning in the acquisitions and divestitures area requires a disciplined approach that, in effect, enables a company to create its own opportunities rather than react under pressure to the short-term exigencies and apparent opportunities of the moment. For both buyer and seller, creating value requires a clear articulation of the objectives to be served by the proposed transaction; a careful and creative analysis of all strategic alternatives; a disciplined search for potential partners in the transaction; a valuation and deal structure that take into account economic realities and the other party's point of view; and a solid, well-paced plan for implementation.

13

Creating Merger Value: Acquisition Motives and Their Implications

SAYAN CHATTERJEE

The Weatherhead School of Management,
Case Western Reserve University

INTRODUCTION

Once among the most prominent activities on the U.S. economic scene, mergers and acquisitions have now come under fire from those who question their economic validity. Proponents of mergers and acquisitions claim that mergers create value, pointing to the fact that mergers almost always make the target firm's stockholders richer because of the premium they are paid. In contrast, some opponents—frequently led by industrial organization economists—believe that mergers are usually bad for the bidding firm, pointing to the poor postmerger performance of the newly combined firms. Other opponents echo the same theme when they argue that acquired firms are often divested soon after the acquisition.

All mergers do not create value for the bidding firm. In fact, on average, bidding firms do not create value for their shareholders; instead, most of the value accrues to the shareholders of the target firm. In specific instances, bidding management can increase its chances of success by (1) concentrating its acquisition activity on certain kinds of strategically related firms, and (2) paying particular attention, from the very beginning, to the issues that are necessary for a successful transition and integration.

Just as importantly, management frequently overlooks the value implications for rivals of the target and bidding firms. To the extent that managers neglect these implications to rivals, they diminish the chances for value gains in their own companies.

MERGERS AND ECONOMIC VALUE

Stock price reactions at the time of merger announcements are an important measure of economic value, since they start with a baseline of the market's evaluation of how the acquiring firm would have fared without the acquisition. Typically, the stock price change is computed after the movement of the broader market, such as the Standard and Poors 500 (S & P 500), is taken into account. This ensures that the change in the stock's price is specific to the merger announcement and not due to changes in the broader market. For this reason, the change in the stock's price at the time of the merger announcement, on average, provides a good forecast of the benefits or damage that will accrue to the new firm. It is difficult to sort out the effect of a merger, or any strategic change, after the fact, because other complicating factors that may have nothing to do with the decision to merger, may affect the performance of the new firm.

Creating Economic Value

Economic value is created when an existing resource is used to take advantage of an opportunity. The resource can be in the form of excess physical capacity or funds, marketing or innovative ability, new technology, the ability of a firm to control the total output in a market, or general managerial capabilities. The magnitude of the economic value will depend on the scarcity of the resource and the degree to which it can be utilized. For example, a pharmaceutical company that has a patented drug can make money only to the extent that an appropriate malady exists in the population. To assess the economic value of a proposed merger, management must first understand how, and to what degree, value accrues to the bidding and target firms.

A merger's economic value to the bidding and target firms depends on two factors:

1. *The magnitude of the total value created or destroyed.* Specifically for mergers, economic value is the result of one or more factors. A merger can increase the target company's operating efficiency. A merger can also increase the market power of the new, combined firm. A merger may provide a target firm with cash so that it can pursue opportunities that it would otherwise not be able to afford. These respective factors, or merger motives, may be called operating efficiency, market power, and financial efficiency. The magnitude of the gain in a particular merger will depend on how much each of these factors improves the combined firm's overall performance.

2. *The proportion of economic value accruing to the bidder and the target.* Typically, targets are purchased at a premium, so that in most mergers the target firms receive at least some part of the expected gains, as represented by the premium. The situation is less clear for the bidding firm. The proportion of the gains realized by the bidding company's shareholders is a function of the difference between the present value of the gains anticipated from the merger and the merger premium. Because the capital market often deems merger premiums too high, in many instances mergers actually decrease the bidding firm's value. A case in point is Phillip Morris's recent acquisition of Kraft. In spite of the obvious synergies between the General Foods division of Phillip Morris and Kraft, the market penalized Phillip Morris by nearly $5 per share when it announced the proposed acquisition. Clearly, large apparent gains by themselves do not automatically benefit shareholders of the bidding firm—too high a premium in the eyes of the capital market can wipe out the expected gains.

In any transaction, the amount of the actual merger premium will depend on the relative bargaining powers of the bidder and of the target firms involved in the negotiations. Typically, the goal of a merger is to have the use of the resources of both the bidding and target firms jointly to create more value than these resources could generate individually. However, if other firms believe that they can combine their resources with the target to create similar value, they, too, will bid for the opportunity to create the additional value for themselves through a merger with the target company. Through this process, gains from the merger will accrue to the shareholders of the target firm, since it is the target firm that has the negotiating leverage. In other words, the portion of the economic value that will go to the shareholders of the bidding firm will be lower when the market for acquisitions is more competitive.[1]

---

[1] J.B. Barney, "Returns to Bidding Firms in Mergers and Acquisitions: Reconsidering the Related Hypothesis." *Strategic Management Journal* vol. 9 (1988), pp. 71–78. S. Chatterjee and M. Lubatkin, "Corporate Mergers, Stockholder Diversification and Changes in Systematic Risk." *Strategic Management Journal,* forthcoming.

Strategic Relatedness and Economic Value in Bidding and Target Firms

To understand how economic value accrues to the bidding and target firms, two dimensions must be considered: the motivations behind the merger and the nature of the strategic relatedness between the merging firms. Strategic relatedness exists to the degree that the merging firms share common business activities, such as marketing channels or production processes. The greater the commonality in markets, technologies, processes, or products, the greater the strategic relatedness.

For these purposes, it is useful to categorize mergers as being of three types: horizontal, related, and unrelated. In horizontal mergers, both the bidding and the target firms come from the same industry. Related mergers are those in which the bidding and target firms have some functional activity in common, such as the market or the end customer. All other types of mergers can be considered unrelated.

Strategic Relatedness and the Magnitude of Gains

Students of strategic management argue that the more strategically related the bidding and target firms, the greater the potential for creating value through a merger. Related mergers offer opportunities for improving the specialization and/or market power of the merging firms' resources. Firms can reduce costs and/or enhance differentiation through the exploitation of scale and scope economies in such tangible areas as manufacturing, research, distribution, and brand extension. Study after study has demonstrated that these opportunities are more likely for related mergers.[2]

By definition, unrelated mergers involve the combining of noncompeting products that incorporate different markets and product technologies. Therefore, while unrelated mergers may provide financial economies, they are less able than related mergers to provide operating efficiencies or market power.

The potential for greater market power is most available through horizontal mergers. By becoming larger, the combined firm may be more capable of influencing the price of its outputs or the cost of its inputs.

Finally, the financial efficiencies that are available in unrelated mergers should also be available in related and horizontal mergers, while the nonfinancial benefits that are potentially available in more related mergers

---

[2] M. Lubatkin, "Merger Strategies and Stockholder Value." *Strategic Management Journal* vol. 8 (1987), pp. 25–37. M.S. Salter and W.S. Weinhold, *Diversification Through Acquisition.* (New York: The Free Press, 1979); H. Singh and C. Montgomery, "Corporate Acquisition Strategies and Economic Performance." *Strategic Management Journal* vol. 8 (1987), pp. 377–386.

are not normally present in unrelated mergers. Thus, the absolute magnitude of gains is likely to be higher for related and horizontal mergers.

Strategic Relatedness and the Sharing of Gains

The proportion of gains accruing to the bidding firm's shareholders will depend on the difference between the present value of such gains and the merger premium. To retain some of these gains, the market for mergers must be less than perfectly competitive. This is possible if the merger has some unique features.

In mergers that are motivated by efficiency or market power considerations, a related bidder that shares the most valuable functional activities with the target firm is in a distinctly better position to outbid less related suitors. The more related the bidder, the greater the proportion of new economic value it can retain. This is especially true for horizontal mergers in which (1) there is a small number of potential bidding firms to start with and (2) there may not be any incentive for the other firms to bid for the target if the merger is undertaken primarily to increase market power. Typically, mergers resulting in increased market power are likely to benefit all the firms in an industry. Unrelated bidding firms, on the other hand, can primarily hope to seek financial efficiencies. Because an unrelated firm cannot bring to a merger the unique contribution that a more related bidding firm can, other cash-rich firms can come into the bidding process, raise the premium, and actually reduce the gains to the successful unrelated bidding firm. Table 13-1 summarizes these various relationships. Related mergers create more value, and in these types of mergers, the bidding firm keeps a larger portion of the economic value. Horizontal mergers create the most value. The value creation relationships can be summarized as follows:

Merger Economic Value Creation
Horizontal Mergers → Related Mergers → Unrelated Mergers

TABLE 13-1

Sources of Gains and Value Created for Bidding Firms

Type of merger	Sources of gains			Degree of competition for same target firm	Value created for bidding firm
	Market power	Operating efficiency	Financial efficiency		
Horizontal	Possible	Possible	Possible	Low	High
Related	Unlikely	Possible	Possible	Low	Medium
Unrelated	Unlikely	Unlikely	Unlikely	Highly	Low

Economic Value to Rival Firms

Management that is involved in acquisition and divestiture activity is usually acutely aware that such activity can have a pronounced effect on the price of its stock, even if management does not agree with the capital market's assessment of a given purchase or sale. Like all strategic moves, a merger can affect rival firms in the merging firms' industries.

The impact that a merger will have on rivals depends on how the merger changes the dynamics of the competition in the industry. It is usually more difficult to identify the impact that the merger will have on the acquiring firm's competitors, since the acquiring company is generally larger than the target and tends to operate in more industries. In contrast, because target firms are usually smaller and more focused, and are identified with a particular industry, the merger impact on their rivals is likely to be greater than it is for rivals of the bidding firm.

Managers can assess the impact of a merger on rivals by considering two offsetting factors—price effect and information effect, which frequently influence the future earning possibilities of rival firms.

Price Effect. If a merger produces a more efficient target firm, the increased efficiency will allow the postmerger firm to reduce prices, which will have an adverse impact on the profitability of the entire industry. Because of price reductions by the newly merged firm, other industry participants will probably have to lower prices to remain competitive. The price effect can easily have a negative impact on the profitability of rival firms.

Information Effect. If a merger (or any other event) allows an industry as a whole to raise prices or cut costs, value is created for all participants in that industry. For example, when hurricane Hugo struck North Carolina, the stock price of insurance companies with exposure in the region went up. At first blush, this would seem perverse, since the hurricane would cause a cash drain on the insurance companies as they met the claims of those insured against the hurricane's effects. However, the stock market looked past the immediate claims (which were not going to affect the reserves of insurance companies in any case) to the future. The market expected that the payment of claims would stop a price competition that had developed among regional insurance companies with fat reserves. Thus, the hurricane led to an upward revision of premiums, creating value for all the firms. In this instance, the hurricane provided information to the market that led it to upwardly revise the future probability of earnings. In a merger, similar information effects usually have a positive impact on rival firms. The net change in the market value of the rival firms can, therefore, be represented by the following relationship:

Change in Value of Rivals = Information Effect (Gain) − Price Effect (Loss)

Accordingly, the value change of rival firms depends on the combination of the information and price effects.

Strategic Relatedness and Economic Value in Rival Firms

Rivals in Horizontal Mergers. In horizontal mergers, the impact on rival firms comes from the underlying motive of the merger. If the motive is to increase market power, the merger gives a signal (information) to the capital market that all the firms in the industry can benefit. For example, the recent consolidation of airlines enabled the industry, as a whole, to raise prices. It is not surprising that in recent years that transportation average has far outperformed broader market indices, such as the S&P 500.

However, if a large sample of horizontal mergers is considered, there is no guarantee that all the mergers will be undertaken to increase market power. (In fact, depending on the antitrust environment at any given time, some horizontal mergers will not be permitted by the Federal Trade Commission or the Justice Department, which are extremely sensitive to potential increases in market power that may result from horizontal mergers.) But many horizontal mergers are undertaken to increase the operating efficiencies of the target firms, usually by taking advantage of scale economies in areas such as manufacturing, distribution, research and development, and marketing or sales.

Increased operating efficiencies, which are brought about through merger activity, are frequently countered by others in the industry. Mergers involving major players often prompt further merger activity by the remaining players in the industry, which in turn reduces the impact of the price effect on rival firms. This is one of the main reasons that there are frequently a number of mergers in the same industry within a short period.

Operating efficiencies that were sought by the initial bidder and target are often imitated by industry rivals. For rivals, the change in value of horizontal mergers will depend on the relative importance of information and price effects. Because the price effect is usually the smaller of the two, most rival firms should improve their economic value.

Rivals in Related Mergers. In horizontal mergers, the price effect is usually relatively less than the information effect. On the other hand, with related mergers, the likelihood is that price effect will be the more significant of the two. A related merger will result in a more competitive target firm, which has the potential to reduce rivals' profits. Rival firms frequently lack recourse to a similar combination; that is, they cannot find targets that will provide them with the same advantages that the original bidder found. (The original related merger is typically undertaken to exploit a particularly advantageous combination that may be difficult for others to duplicate.) Hence, the price effect is much more difficult to offset than is the case for rivals in horizontal mergers. A case in point is Pillsbury and Kraft, rivals in the food industry. Kraft purchased General Foods. Kraft's products complement General Foods' products in ways that cannot be duplicated by Pillsbury.

Related mergers can, in some instances, also have information effects. For example, a related merger may be undertaken to utilize a technology that was developed in a different field. If such a technology transfer proves successful in the initial related merger, other related mergers are likely to follow to take advantage of the technology, which, while not new to the original industry, is new for the acquiring industry. Anticipation of future mergers can actually increase the value of the rival firms. The information effect is usually minimal, however, and the value of the rival firms can be expected to decrease in related mergers.

Rivals in Unrelated Mergers. In unrelated mergers, there is a possibility of a price effect if the postmerger target firm is perceived as a stronger competitive entity. However, if, as expected, an unrelated bidding firm can do little to increase the competitiveness of the target (short of a cash infusion), the gains to the target firm will be much smaller than the operating efficiencies generated from a related merger. In other words, there should not be much in the way of a price effect. Consequently, rivals should not lose much value, if any at all. There is also some likelihood of an information effect in the form of technology transfers. Typically, however, technology transfers between unrelated markets are even less likely than between related markets. These arguments are summarized in Table 13-2. Putting the preceding arguments together, the expected change in value for rival firms will generally be:

Horizontal Rivals → Unrelated Rivals → Related Rivals

TABLE 13-2

Types of Mergers and Value Impact on Target Firm Rivals

| Type of merger | Probability | | Change in stock price of rivals |
	Price effect (negative)	Information effect (negative/positive)	
Horizontal rivals	Low	Medium	Positive
Related rivals	High	Low	Negative
Unrelated rivals	Low	Low	Unchanged

TABLE 13-3

Empirical Findings of Value Impact on Bidding Target and Rival Firms

Type of merger	Bidding firms	Target firms	Rival firms
Horizontal	Positive gain	Positive gain	Positive gain
Related	No gain	Positive gain	Positive gain
Unrelated	No gain	Positive gain	Positive gain

EMPIRICAL FINDINGS AND IMPLICATIONS

A number of studies have established the relative changes in value for bidding, target, and rival firms (see Table 13-3). In horizontal mergers, bidding, target, and rival firms all gain in value. However, gains to both related and unrelated bidding firms are usually nonexistent, though the respective target firms do increase in value. Contrary to widely held expectations, strategically related mergers do not always create value for their shareholders. In fact, detailed studies have shown that gains of the related target firms are smaller than or equal to those of unrelated target firms.[3] This means that the magnitude of the total gains in a related merger can be smaller than that of an unrelated merger. Apart from the extreme form of relatedness (the horizontal merger), strategic relatedness in itself does not seem to confer any advantages to the bidding firm.

The researchers have also discovered that rivals of the target firms almost always gain at the time of the merger announcement. While this result was expected for rivals in a horizontal merger, it was not anticipated in the cases of related or unrelated mergers. For management, a number of important implications arise from these findings.

There are basically two reasons that related bidding firms do not create more value than unrelated bidding firms. First, the magnitude of operating efficiencies in related mergers is often overestimated by management—frequently as a result of major cultural clashes between the merging units. Expectations that motivated management to acquire a target firm simply are not met to the degree planned. Second, for both related and unrelated mergers, the competition for target firms is equally high and, consequently, all gains accrue to the target firms.

---

[3] S. Chatterjee, "Types of Synergy and Economic Value: The Impact of Acquisitions on Merging and Rival Firms." 7 (2) *Strategic Management Journal* vol. 7, no. 2 (1982), pp. 119–139. M. Lubatkin, "Merger Strategies and Stockholder Value." *Strategic Management Journal* vol. 8 (1987), pp. 25–37.

Gains and Culture Clash in Related Mergers

Efficiency gains in related mergers are likely to be influenced by cultural fit and the process of actually managing the consolidation process. Mergers are neither financially successful nor unsuccessful simply because two businesses share related features, whether these features are products, markets, or technologies. Rather, the success of a merger depends, among other things, on how cooperative and committed the managements of the merging firms are.[4] Moreover, the level of cooperation and commitment can be greatly influenced by differences in culture.

The likelihood of a culture clash will not be the same for all types of mergers. The strategy behind a merger determines the extent to which the cultures of the two firms will come into contact. In unrelated mergers, in which the products and markets of the combining firms are dissimilar, the buyer may impose changes in the acquired firm's financial system, but, otherwise, it will allow the acquired firm's operations to remain fairly autonomous. This is less likely to occur in related mergers, where the motivation to merge generally stems from the buyer's belief that operating efficiencies can be achieved between the two firms. Accordingly, in related mergers, there is likely to be a greater need for the managers of the acquired firm to conform to the goals, control systems, and beliefs of the buyer's top management team.

One study suggests that the degree of cultural differences can affect the related firm's gains.[5] While related bidding firms usually do not benefit from a merger, there are circumstances in which they can gain. In related acquisitions, bidding firms that are most culturally compatible with the target firms' culture are the most likely to create values for their shareholders. Those that are the least compatible actually destroy value. Firms that plan to undertake related mergers for the sake of greater operating efficiencies must pay serious attention to the problems involved in implementing these changes after the acquisition. The recent problems of Unisys serve as an example. Efficiencies that were expected to be reaped from the merger of Burroughs and Sperry failed to materialize. Former managers and other observers have commented that cultural differences frequently prevented the new company from achieving the integration that was necessary for many of the desired efficiencies.

Unrelated mergers, on the other hand, present less severe cultural problems. The more related the merger, the greater the expected efficien-

---

[4] M.E. Porter, *Competitive Advantage: Creating and Sustaining Superior Performance* (New York: The Free Press, 1985). P. Shrivastava, "Post Merger Integration." *Journal of Business Strategy* vol. 7 (1986), pp. 65–76.

[5] S. Chatterjee, M. Lubatkin, D. Schweiger, and Y. Weber, "Cultural Differences and Shareholder Value: Explaining the Variability in Performance of Related Managers." Paper presented at the Academy of Management National Meetings, Washington, D.C., 1989.

cies, but greater also are the potential barriers represented by cultural differences between the acquiring and acquired managements.

Competition in the Market for Targets

There is a second reason for the poor value gains of related bidding firms: Increased competition in the market for acquisitions bids away the merger gains in the form of the higher premiums that must be paid to make the acquisition. In this situation, neither the related nor the unrelated bidding firm is likely to keep any of the gains for its shareholders.

If the competition for acquisitions is higher than expected, a basic premise upon which the superiority of related mergers rests becomes suspect. The underlying premise of related mergers is that they somehow lead to a unique combination of resources that is not easily duplicated by other firms. Often, mergers release information about how the gains are to be obtained. More often than not, this information can lead to other mergers in the target firm's industry that can just as easily take advantage of the efficiencies hoped for by the firms in the initial merger. This is especially true if the gains come from some form of technology transfer or inside information about the target company.

For example, shortly after EMI announced the invention of the CT scanner, a number of other firms introduced their own CT scanners, despite the slowing effect of patents. This rapid information dissemination may have acted as a disincentive to exploit an innovation through mergers, since the information could be used by the target firm to negotiate a higher premium. Even if the merger with one potential acquirer fails, the target company has the option of realizing gains through market transactions with other companies. Public knowledge about the technology's advantages only increases the attractiveness of the target firm to other companies.

A second type of information transfer involves inside information. In the buyout of RJR, management's original bid price was quickly challenged by other bidders who read the bid price as being indicative of a higher inside value that the management wanted to keep. As a result, other bidders were willing to pay a greater premium.

This suggests that the information effect may be much stronger in mergers than previously thought. This conclusion is supported by empirical studies that show that rivals of related and unrelated target firms benefit from the original acquisition. The findings for rival firms indicate that gains resulting from an announced merger can be duplicated by other firms.

Because the uniqueness of the merger gains cannot be sustained, competition for the targets implies that no gains will accrue to the bidding firms. Also, because rival firms can duplicate these gains, the price effect is reduced, and this, in turn, reduces the competitive advantage of the original merger. These findings make a strong case for utilizing unique resources through internal development, where the information effect can be much more tightly controlled.

CONCLUSION

Management must appreciate that strategically related mergers do not necessarily lead to gains in value for their shareholders. In fact, rival firms may prosper. Frequently, incompatibility between management teams will reduce the operating expectations that originally served as the basis for the acquisition. Management must appreciate the difficulties involved in all types of mergers, whether they are horizontal, related, or unrelated. Management and shareholders are well served only when strategically important mergers are well managed. Merger activity will result in gains only when the merger reflects and complements good management.

14

Making Mergers Work: A Strategic and Cultural Challenge

MICHAEL H. LUBATKIN

School of Business Administration, University of Connecticut

INTRODUCTION

Since 1983, over 12,000 companies and corporate divisions—representing about one fifth of the market value of all traded stocks—have changed hands. Investment bankers and corporate lawyers have prospered, and the business lexicon has gained such new terms as "raiders," "greenmail," "white knights," and "golden parachutes." But has anyone or anything else been enriched by all of this activity?

The popular business press clearly does not think so. It continues to publish articles that recount, in painstaking detail, problem-plagued acquisitions such as Exxon's $1.2 million blunder with Reliance Electric, Kennecott's mismanagement of Carborundum, and Coca-Cola's surprising setback with Taylor Wines.[1]

Legislators in Washington have also cast "no" votes on mergers through the introduction of more than two dozen bills designed to restrict merger activity. Proponents of these bills claim that mergers have a nega-

---

[1] *Fortune* (Apr. 30, 1984), pp. 262–270 and (May 27, 1985), pp. 20–24.

tive net impact on the U.S. economy by squandering resources in the pursuit of illusory gains in efficiency.

In addition, there are the verdicts of such respected financial economists such as Professors Michael Jensen of Harvard and Richard Ruback of MIT whose opinions are more tempered, but still lead to less-than-ringing endorsements. They conclude that shareholders of selling firms benefit from mergers, but those of buying firms do not. At best, the economists say bidding-firm shareholders do not lose. They also find mergers to be ineffective in reducing shareholder and business risks.[2]

All of these observations combine to present a rather unflattering assessment of the acumen of today's corporate decision makers. But if the majority of mergers do not create value for the acquiring firms, why do business leaders continue to initiate them? Are they oblivious to the legacy of those who have failed before them? Or are they acting solely in their own interests, because their rewards are more closely tied to corporate growth than to corporate value?

This chapter presents a different view—one shaped from a growing body of literature that takes a closer look at the strategies behind mergers and cultural compatibility of merging firms as well as the widely held beliefs about the negative value of mergers.

The chapter begins by reviewing the theory of corporate diversification as it pertains to mergers. The potential benefits and practical impediments of both related and unrelated mergers are discussed. Whether a firm can create value for its shareholders through a merger is examined from the perspective of two conditions that are of great importance to shareholders. The first condition is when stock returns (appreciation plus dividend) increase as a result of a merger, and the increase exceeds the merging firm's cost of equity and general stock market movements—in other words, when a merger creates abnormal returns. The second is when the cultures of the selling and buying firms are compatible.

Finally, practical suggestions are offered for improving the effectiveness of mergers—suggestions that are particularly timely in light of the increased attention now focused on shareholder value and the revelation that many executives are unsure about exactly how their firms' actions affect stock prices.

DOWNPLAYING THE CASH-FLOW TEST

A strategic approach to mergers holds that they cannot be judged as a one-time event, or as ends in and of themselves. Instead, mergers are viewed as

---

[2] M. Jensen and R. Ruback, "The Market of Corporate Control: The Scientific Evidence," *Journal of Financial Economics* (1983) 11, pp. 5–50; A. Michael and I. Shaked, "Evaluating Merger Performance," *California Management Review* (Spring 1985), pp. 109–118.

means for executing a long-term strategy. In this light, conventional discounted cash-flow hurdle rates are less useful for determining the worth of a merger than they are for other capital investments. When a merger is intended to change the competitive position of a business, the merger may be expected to have a detrimental short-term effect on a business's cash-flow pattern. This strategy was evident in United Technologies' (UT) mergers with Otis Elevator in 1976, Carrier in 1979, and Mostek in 1980. When viewed as a stand-alone investment, each combination made little sense from a discounted cash-flow perspective; but after all three mergers were completed, the soundness of the strategy could be seen. Mostek's microprocessor technology provided Otis and Carrier with a competitive edge in the market for designing "intelligent" buildings. Linked within UT's Building Systems Division, the combined companies were able to make advancements that they could not have attained separately.[3]

This same thinking was behind IBM's 1984 purchase of Rolm. IBM was willing to pay a substantial premium for Rolm because Rolm represented IBM's best avenue for quickly establishing itself as a competitive force in the fast-growing telecommunications market. As will be discussed later, the downfall of this merger was not an ill-conceived strategy, but rather a poor cultural fit between the two merged entities.

Both of these examples suggest that the true worth of a merger is determined by how it contributes to a firm's competitive advantage or strengthens the defense of a chosen market position against outside market and economic forces. If a merger successfully enhances competitive advantage, a firm can maximize upside opportunity while minimizing downside risk.

LESSONS IN COMPETITIVE ADVANTAGE

IBM is a firm with unquestioned competitive advantage in many of its markets. As long as it retains that edge, the returns to its shareholders will be greater than those of its less competitive counterparts, regardless of economic conditions. This gives IBM unique opportunities for sustaining or generating growth. Its options range from expanding its product lines to increasing promotions to introducing new technological breakthroughs. Growth, via the merger route, can also fit comfortably within this range.

Anheuser-Busch was recently profiled in the business media, which noted, "Per capita [beer] consumption has been declining for years, yet Busch sells twice as much beer as it sold a decade ago—more beer than its two largest rivals combined, more beer than anyone else in the world."[4] Anheuser-Busch has apparently pushed the burden of market decline onto its less competitive counterparts through a strategy that calls for segment-

---

[3] "Mergers that Worked," *Fortune* (Apr. 30, 1984), p. 270.

[4] See "How Busch Wins in a Doggy Market," *Fortune* (June 22, 1987), pp. 99–111.

ing the market "with a vengeance," demanding loyalty from distribution channels, and monopolizing prime promotional outlets. In other words, Anheuser-Busch has also been able to lower its overall market risk through shrewd use of its competitive advantage.

RELATED OPPORTUNITIES

How can mergers be employed as part of a strategy to enhance competitive advantage? The most logical applications seem to be in "related mergers." These combine distinct business units that are linked by certain core technologies. Related mergers provide several opportunities for making business strategies more competitive. They can reduce costs and/or enhance differentiation by exploiting economies of scale and scope in areas that are both tangible (manufacturing, research, and distribution) and intangible (administrative "know-how," brand extensions). Procter & Gamble's acquisitions of Charmin Paper, Duncan Hines, and Folger's are excellent examples of related mergers that were motivated by economies of scale in distribution and marketing "know-how."

Related mergers provide the potential for power gains if the merged firm, by becoming larger, can influence the price of its output or the cost of its input. For example, a recent *Fortune* article described the muscle tactics that Anheuser-Busch used on greedy wholesalers.[5] The article relates the experience of one distributor of Budweiser beer who decided to sell a rival brewer's brand. Without overtly demanding that the distributor stop selling the rival brand, Anheuser-Busch representatives visited the distributor and heavily criticized his methods of operation in general. Another distributor who also tried to sell a rival's brand said that twenty-two Anheuser-Busch field managers descended on his operation. The distributor was then called to St. Louis to talk with top management about his lack of loyalty. The threat of power gain was also the primary reason that the proposed Coca-Cola/Dr. Pepper and Pepsi/7-Up mergers were disallowed.

In contrast, unrelated mergers offer far fewer advantages. By definition, unrelated mergers involve the combination of noncompeting products that utilize different product and market technologies. While they may still provide allocation efficiencies, it is far more difficult, if not impossible, for unrelated mergers to produce tangible and intangible efficiencies, or power gains.

A note of caution: Even though related mergers may have greater potential than unrelated mergers for creating additional shareholder value, they should not automatically be deemed superior in all cases. Many merg-

---

[5] Ibid.

ers are sold to shareholders on the premise that the two companies have a natural fit, when, in reality, the fit is illusory.

MEASURING THE VALUE OF A MERGER

Related or unrelated, a merger's success is ultimately determined by its ability to create or improve shareholder value. High valuation allows a firm to satisfy the financial claims of its constituencies: employees, customers, suppliers, and stockholders. It also inhibits proxy battles for corporate control and enhances the firm's future effectiveness by providing less-costly access to additional debt and equity capital

Shareholder value is defined by the market price of a firm's common shares. The price reflects the market's expectations about future performance—the discounted present value of all cash flows expected from prospective as well as past corporate investments. Shareholder value is "created" only when expectations about future performance increase.

When evaluating the ability of a merger to create value for the buying firm's shareholders, it is critical to recognize that the price of an acquisition is set in a highly competitive market. In a seller's market, it is not surprising that the selling price is usually substantially higher than the going rate was before merger negotiations began.

From the perspective of the selling firm's shareholders, mergers clearly create value. From the perspective of the buying firm's shareholders, there are two important questions: Are mergers, in general, a good investment? Do certain types of mergers represent better investments than others?

Strategic management investigations (see Table 14-1) suggest that the answer to the first question is yes: On average, mergers appear to be in the best interests of the buying firm's shareholders. The investigations also dispel the commonly held belief that the market is so competitive that it prevents the buying firm from gaining along with the selling firm.

Which mergers produce the largest gains? As might be expected, some studies, such as the one by Shelton, show that returns to buying firms are highest when the merger combines distinct but related business units. However, as Table 14-1 shows, the superiority of related mergers over unrelated mergers is not clear in all cases. Frequently, the mergers that offer the greatest potential advantages in theory prove to be the most difficult to achieve in practice. Those difficulties can usually be traced to cultural incompatibility between the merging firms.

A CLASH OF VALUES

To realize the economies of scale and scope that a merger is designed to produce, considerable consolidation of product lines may be required in

TABLE 14-1

Shareholder Returns: Buying Firms[6]

Investigator (date)	Finding
S. Chatterjee (1986)	On average, buying firms appreciate in value during a five-day period surrounding the merger announcement. However, unrelated buyers gain an average of $24 million, while related buyers gain only half as much.
M. Lubatkin (1987)	Regardless of "relatedness," buyers gain 11 percent in their stock value during the two-year period preceding the merger transaction month.
L. Shelton (1988)	On average, buying firms lose 1.4 percent of their equity value during the three days surrounding the merger announcement. However, related buyers gain in value and perform noticeably better than unrelated buyers.
S. Chatterjee and M. Lubatkin (1990)	Buying firms involved in related mergers are able to reduce the rate of return required by shareholders (i.e., their cost of equity) by about 17 percent. This gain to shareholders is less evident for unrelated buyers, whose cost of equity declines by only half as much.

areas such as distribution channels, control systems, and research and development. These efforts are often resisted by the people who must carry them out. Professors Philippe Haspeslagh and David Jemison explain:

> Ironically, acquisitions often destroy noneconomic value for those who are asked to create economic value after the transaction is made. Creating economic value requires the cooperation and commitment of operating-level managers of both firms, in order to combine the skills, resources, or knowledge of the two firms. Yet it is precisely this group and their subordinates for whom the acquisition destroys noneconomic value through the loss of job security, status, or career opportunities.[7]

Researchers in organizational theory believe that the culture of an organization is a powerful determinant of organizational effectiveness. Broadly speaking, organizational culture affects practically all aspects of the way in which people interact with each other—leadership styles, administrative procedures, rules of conduct, and perceptions about the environment.

Every social group has a culture, and each culture is somewhat unique,

---

[6] The studies cited in Table 14-1 were all published in the *Strategic Management Journal.* They include S. Chatterjee, "Types of Synergy and Economic Value" (Mar.–Apr. 1986); M. Lubatkin, "Merger Strategies and Shareholder Value" (Feb. 1987); L. Shelton, "Strategic Business Fits and Corporate Acquisition: Empirical Evidence" (May–June 1988); S. Chatterjee and M. Lubatkin, "Corporate Mergers, Stockholder Diversification, and Changes in Systematic Risk" (May–June 1990).

[7] P. Haspaslagh and D. Jemison, "Acquisition—Myths and Reality," *Solan Management Review* (Winter 1987), pp. 53–58.

shaped by the group's particular history and shared experiences. Culture is the "normative glue" that holds an organization together, and unlike implementation tactics such as reward systems, it holds fast and cannot be easily modified. To the extent that practicing managers are concerned about shareholder gains, therefore, they should pay at least as much attention to cultural fit as they do to strategic fit during the premerger search process.

The full potency of organizational culture can be seen when two autonomous cultures are brought into close contact with each other, as typically happens when two related firms merge. In related mergers, the motivation to merge generally stems from the buyer's belief that it can utilize the acquired firm's physical and human capital more efficiently than is currently the case. This often leads to considerable pressure on the acquired firm to conform to the buyer's goals, control systems, and values (culture). For example, in conglomerate mergers in which the products and markets of the combining firms are dissimilar, the buyer may impose changes in the acquired unit's financial system but otherwise allow the acquired firm to operate autonomously as a separate subsidiary.

The pressure to accept the culture of the buyer may be resisted, depending on how dissimilar the employees of the acquired firm perceive the two cultures to be. Conflicting corporate cultures can produce feelings of hostility and significant discomfort. Conflict between cultures can also lower commitment and cooperation, especially on the part of the acquired top management team. Key employees of the acquired firm who are unwilling to adapt to the new culture may either resign or actively resist any of the buyer's consolidation tactics.

It is not surprising that conflicting corporate cultures have been the undoing of many related mergers that appeared to make good strategic sense—e.g, IBM and Rolm. From the perspective of the acquiring firm's shareholders, differences in corporate cultures may be an important determinant of the relative success of a related merger.

A recent study[8] found strong evidence to support this point. After surveying the perceptions of managements of recently acquired firms and relating their perceptions to investor expectations, the study found that when significant cultural differences were perceived to exist, the buying firm's equity value was much more likely to deteriorate during the sixteen-trading day period surrounding the merger announcement. When low cultural differences were involved, the opposite pattern emerged: Investors tended to view the mergers favorably and bid up the buying firm's stock price.

---

[8] S. Chatterjee, M. Lubatkin, D. Schweiger, and Y. Weber, "Culture Differences and Shareholder Value." Presented at the 1989 meetings of the Academy of Management, Washington, DC.

CONCLUSION

Recent evidence challenges many of the widely held beliefs concerning the effectiveness of mergers. In general, mergers are valuable to the shareholders of both the selling and buying firms. Firms that pursue related mergers can achieve increases in shareholder value that are not available to individual investors or to firms that pursue unrelated merger strategies. However, related mergers are not always superior. While they offer the greatest potential, in theory, they can also be the most difficult to achieve in practice.

Steps to Improve Effectiveness

The studies suggest four practical steps that should be taken to improve the effectiveness of a merger of any kind:

1. Estimate the cash inflow to be gained through improved competitive advantage. From an investor's point of view, a merger that develops strong competitive advantage will generate large returns that are fairly immune to general economic and competitive pressures. However, sources of competitive advantage may be subtle and difficult to identify. Therefore, practicing managers should begin planning for a merger by identifying all meaningful tangible and intangible interrelationships; determining whether any advantages from these relationships will improve the competitive positions of the merging businesses; and estimating the effect that those advantages will have on the size and timing of the company's cash inflow patterns.

2. Estimate the cost of shared strategic capabilities. Managers cannot assume that merger benefits will automatically be low. Effective planning will identify the steps that are necessary to facilitate cross-business cooperation. This must be done before the deal is consummated—to ensure a more realistic assessment of theoretical advantages and practical costs—and reviewed again after the transaction has been completed. Skill transfer takes time and requires continual fine tuning. Rigid adherence to preconceived integration actions can destroy the culture of the selling firm, wipe out its skill base, raise investor uncertainty, and, in the process, amplify business risk and lower shareholder return.

3. Estimate the total added value produced by the merger. After systematically assembling estimates of benefits and costs, managers can use the standard net-present-value procedure to determine the current value of future earnings. Estimates from this procedure should provide a good approximation of the merger price and the contribution that the merger will make to the value of the firm.

4. Share these estimates with investors. Managers cannot lose sight of the stock market's informational needs. Companies constantly provide the market with information by means of published reports, actions, or the absence of action. The market continually gathers and evaluates this and other information and impounds its view of the company's future prospects in its market price. Thus, the manner in which a company manages its information flows will determine its market reputation. Information management is particularly critical in a merger situation. The market prefers to be convinced about the merits of a merger, rather than have one sold to it by shallow promises. A substantive estimation of the added value that will be generated by the merger can provide the structure that management needs to sharpen its judgments and provide it with the numerical "vocabulary" that it will need to communicate with investors in a language they understand.

15

Managers Under Siege: Corporate Control Contests and Management Turnover

JAMES P. WALSH

Amos Tuck School of Business Administration, Dartmouth College

INTRODUCTION

Management changes often are made either in anticipation of a corporate control contest (a merger, acquisition, or leveraged buyout) or as a consequence of it. While these changes may represent a needed cleansing of entrenched and inefficient management, a corporate control contest can also be a stimulus for pruning deadwood from the corporate ranks.

The author wishes to thank Anant Sundaram for his helpful comments on an earlier version of this chapter.

The high turnover that generally occurs in acquired companies is not necessarily the result of management discipline, as many would assert. The consequences of management turnover can be immense for the acquiring company. The underlying key to success in any acquisition is sound management. It is therefore crucial for the acquiring management to take a number of immediate steps to ensure that the new business has stable management in place.

Acquiring management should first systematically identify the key management contributors throughout the organization. Management gaps should be filled from within the acquired company whenever possible. Keeping the identified key contributors, however, is just as important as filling management gaps. Long-term incentive compensation programs are often instrumental in retaining these key contributors. At the same time, the acquiring management must work with the remaining management to instill a sense of shared strategic direction. Strategic changes and new implementation programs should reflect the views of both the new and existing management.

It is not automatically true of an acquisition that the new management is superior or that existing management must be disciplined. Early on, the universally accepted rhetoric was that the acquiring management was better than existing management, and any opinion to the contrary was seen as defensive and self-serving. With the benefit of both hindsight and systematic research, however, it is apparent that much of that dissent has been borne out. High post-takeover management turnover sometimes is a result of a need to replace inadequate management, but an acquiring management team must have a clear understanding of when it is necessary to maintain continuity and when it is not. Acquiring companies should generally work to reduce management turnover by making management changes only in cases where performance or strategic redirection is merited.

This chapter examines the impact that corporate control contests (specifically, mergers, acquisitions, and corporate raider ownership) have on the careers of top managers. Top management turnover patterns in a variety of corporate control contests are reviewed. In addition to the consequences of this activity on managers' careers, this chapter will consider the impact that these career changes may have on a firm's management. (Carl Icahn's acquisition of TransWorld Airlines (TWA) articulates many of the lessons that were supposed to have been learned from the control contests of the past decade.)

CASE STUDY OF A CONTROL CONTEST

In 1985, Carl Icahn's bitter struggle with Texas Air, Resorts International, and a group of employees' unions for control of TWA captivated the nation.

TWA's management asked Congress for protection from the buyers; only the Reagan Administration's lack of support for such protective legislation doomed the effort. The Missouri State Senate, however, unanimously endorsed a bill that obstructed Icahn's efforts. Only after a federal court overturned the measure was Icahn able to acquire the company.

In the heat of the takeover battle, it was difficult to evaluate the claims and counterclaims about the merits of the acquisition. Icahn's stated goal of improving the inept management of TWA was often ignored or dismissed as a ready smokescreen to mask what others saw as his more nefarious motives (e.g., the pursuit of a large greenmail payment). Retrospectively, the veracity of his intentions can now be evaluated.

A little more than a year after he assumed control of TWA, readers of *Newsweek* discovered that indeed, Icahn had been making management changes. In an interview about the acquisition, he said:

> At TWA—to make it simple, we basically replaced all the top management. That's one of the steps we took in the first few months. We really replaced the whole 42nd floor. There's nobody there on the 42nd floor at 605 Third Avenue who was there before. Possibly there's one, but I think he's leaving. And it had to be done.[1]

With the passage of time, this management turnover can be assessed in light of TWA's performance before and after the management changes. Figure 15-1 captures the relationship between the performance of TWA's stock and a variety of corporate control milestones. Performance was assessed in two steps. First, the performance of TWA's stock was compared against the average performance of twenty-four of its competitors in the airline industry. Then TWA's performance was contrasted against an equally weighted market index for the entire New York Stock Exchange. The two approaches revealed similar results. The excess returns were summed from February 24, 1983 (when TWA was first publicly traded) to August 26, 1985 (when Icahn assumed control), and again from August 26, 1985 to October 25, 1988 (when Icahn took the company private). The horizontal line at the zero point on the vertical axis represents average performance in either the airline industry or the stock market as a whole. Any points under the line represent performance below the industry or market average. Similarly, any points above the line represent times when TWA was outperforming either benchmark. The results show clearly that, with the exception of the typical increase in firm value around the control contest, TWA underperformed the industry and the entire New York Stock Exchange before Icahn took control and for two and one-half years afterward. The figure also illustrates that TWA enjoyed a steady improvement in market performance, beginning eight

---

[1] "Confessions of a Raider: An Interview With Carl Icahn." *Newsweek,* October 20, 1986: pp. 51–55.

FIGURE 15-1

TWA's Cumulative Excess Returns and Corporate Control Milestones

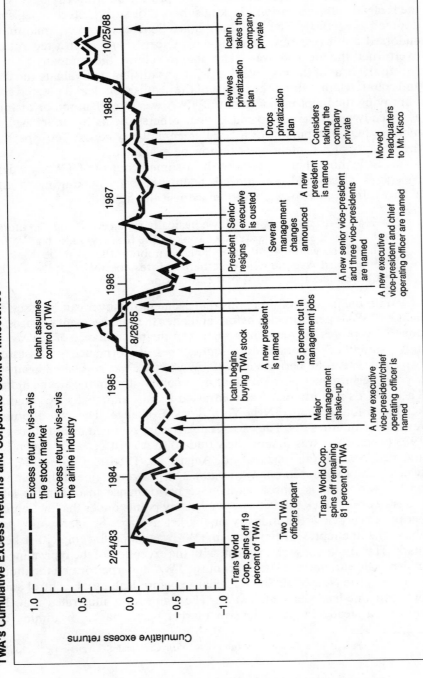
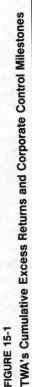

months after Icahn took control and ending in 1988. At the time TWA was delisted, it was outperforming both the industry and the stock market.

A review of the corporate control milestones reveals that TWA was a company that struggled to succeed after it was spun off from the Trans-World Corporation (a diversified holding company). After a few apparently futile attempts to discipline its top managers, TWA attracted the attention of Icahn and a number of other potential owners. In retrospect, it is now clear that TWA was recognized as an undervalued and perhaps misman-aged company. Figure 15-1 illustrates that the management discipline imposed by Icahn probably saved TWA from bankruptcy. It is beyond the scope of this chapter to assess in any detail the actions of the managers running TWA before and after Icahn. Although Icahn and his managers were criticized for paying for the acquisition with the wage concessions they exacted from labor, the fact remains that TWA's performance improved after a profound management shakeup.

What lessons can be learned from TWA? First, it appears that internal and external corporate control systems can work in a complementary fash-ion to overcome each other's inefficiencies. In this case, the external corpo-rate control market (represented by Icahn) worked to correct TWA's performance problems that were associated with an ineffective internal control system. As a result, the owners of the firm were spared catastrophic losses.

In the best of circumstances, a board of directors has a difficult time monitoring, appraising, and motivating managers so as to ensure that they behave in the best interests of the firm's shareholders and, indeed, a myriad of shareholder groups. Boards are burdened with incomplete information, time pressures, and the imperfect control options of either adjusting com-pensation contracts or dismissing management. Just the same, research suggests, perhaps surprisingly, that boards (especially those with a prepon-derance of outside directors) do discipline (i.e., dismiss) their managers for poor performance.[2] However, research also suggests that managers can, if they so desire, easily entrench themselves by neutralizing the monitoring and control efforts of a board of directors.[3] In such instances, the new man-agement team associated with a takeover may represent the only hope for abused shareholders and stakeholders.

Of course, there is no guarantee that a new management team will be able to turn the situation around completely. A firm may have to undergo a num-ber of control contests in order to survive and prosper. Indeed, TWA's success in 1987 and 1988 was not matched in 1989, and, in early 1990, *The New York*

---

[2] J.B. Warner, R.L. Watts, and K.H. Wruck, "Stock Prices and Top Management Changes." *Journal of Financial Economics* 20 (1988): pp. 461–492; M.S. Weisbach, "Outside Directors and CEO Turnover." *Journal of Financial Economics,* 20 (1988): pp. 431–460.

[3] M.L. Mace, *Directors: Myth and Reality.* (Boston: Harvard University Press, 1971).

Times labeled it "a troubled airline."[4] It may be that TWA will be restructured or taken over in the future. The company could also go bankrupt. Even though Icahn turned around TWA for a two-year period, there are no guarantees that he can sustain this record of success, and, in fact, he may fail.

D.L. Birch tracked the history of 12 million U.S. business establishments between 1969 and 1986 and, in part, examined their mortality rates.[5] He found that "for every group of companies that opened their doors, approximately half will last five years, 38 percent will be around after 10 years, and 31 percent will survive 15 years." While few firms are destined to last forever, control contests can be instrumental in promoting organizational longevity. Carl Icahn is no doubt aware of these odds. He also seems quite aware of the benefits associated with control contests. Perhaps as a consequence of his TWA experience, he has embraced the academic viewpoint and become a critic of entrenched and inefficient management.

Despite Icahn's reform rhetoric and the suggestive case study evidence, the extent of this problem — and the wisdom of the TWA lesson — are still not known. To avoid prematurely celebrating the takeover artist and crucifying contemporary management, it is important to discover if all, or most, corporate control contests serve to discipline entrenched management.

Approximately 75,000 mergers and acquisitions have been announced during the past twenty-five years. The TWA lesson might suggest that they were all motivated by a desire to discipline incompetent top managers. However, tender offers (such as Icahn's) represent only 3.3 percent of all merger and acquisition activity since 1980. Moreover, there are many other motives that might produce merger and acquisition activity — for example, synergies of various types, tax savings, wealth transfers from other constituencies, and even hubris on the part of the acquiring company's management team. It is dangerous to judge the frequency of an event by the ease with which an example of it comes to mind. The ready availability of Icahn's success story of management discipline at TWA might result in an overestimation of the frequency with which such success stories have occurred in the past.

TOP MANAGEMENT TURNOVER FOLLOWING CORPORATE CONTROL CONTESTS

The first step in understanding the nature of reform associated with corporate control contests is to document the extent of top management turnover following them. When the top management team turnover rates for 102 of

---

[4] A. Salpukas, "Icahn on TWA Woe: 'We're at a Crossroads.' " *The New York Times,* February 10, 1990: Sec. B1, p. 35.

[5] D.L. Birch, *Job Creation in America* (New York: The Free Press, 1987).

the 444 largest mergers and acquisitions (during the 1975–1979 period) were profiled and compared to the turnover rates in 77 of the acquiring companies and a matched control group of 75 companies (over the same period),[6] the target companies' top management team turnover rates were higher than those in both the control group and the acquiring firms for every year following a merger or acquisition (see Figure 15-2). However, while these rates are abnormally high, they are not of the magnitude one might expect after examining the TWA case. Still, the abnormally high turnover in the target companies' officer groups is consistent with the view that mergers and acquisitions serve to discipline entrenched and inefficient top managers.

Obviously, postacquisition top management turnover is an important and sometimes controversial topic of study. If the dismissed executives, in fact, are entrenched and inefficient managerial deadwood, then few would mourn their passing. The problem is that it is often difficult to know if managers are culpable for their firm's poor performance. The managers may be wrongly accused. It may be that the chastised managers should be

FIGURE 15-2

Cumulative Top Management Turnover Following Mergers and Acquisitions

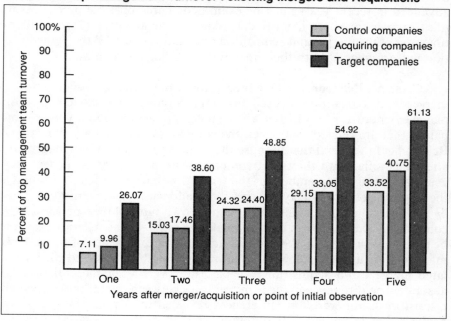

---

[6] J.P. Walsh and J.W. Ellwood, *Mergers , Acquisitions and the Pruning of Managerial Deadwood: An Examination of the Market for Corporate Control* (Unpublished manuscript, Amos Tuck School of Business Administration, Dartmouth College, 1990).

celebrated for keeping a bad situation from getting worse. It may also be that target company managers lost their jobs because of a mishandled integration process. Acquiring company managers are often warned against the "prima donna urge," which causes some acquiring company managers, who consider themselves in some sense to be victors in a corporate struggle, to treat their new managers with disrespect and condenscension.

The consequences of discharging top managers can be profound for the managers themselves and for the newly combined firm. Moreover, the consequences for the firm can be great if the lost leadership was central to running the new business. Ironically, top managers may depart from a mishandled integration situation when the motivation behind the acquisition, in fact, was to buy this very management talent. With this in mind, it is important to understand the origins of postacquisition turnover.

The Origins of Top Management Turnover

In light of the fact that many managers leave their firms after takeovers, it is important to understand if the origins of these changes were rational and productive. That is, both the theory and rhetoric of reform that have been advanced in recent years must be examined. Three possible precursors to this turnover have been identified: (1) company relatedness; (2) the contentiousness of the merger and acquisition negotiations; and (3) the preacquisition performance of both the target and acquiring companies.

Company Relatedness. One theory about the turnover associated with mergers and acquisitions focused on company relatedness: the idea that top management turnover is higher when a merger or acquisition involves companies that are related than when the companies involved are unrelated.[7] Researchers theorized that because the acquiring company's managers are already familiar with the target company's business, they might feel they could afford to lose members of the target's management team. Similarly, the acquiring company may feel that it can add value to the target company by replacing the target's managers with its own more skilled personnel. In contrast, an acquiring firm that completes an unrelated acquisition may not be able to afford to lose the product and market experience of the target's managers. As a result, a low turnover rate should be associated with unrelated mergers and acquisitions. In fact, however, researchers discovered absolutely no difference in the turnover rates between related and unrelated acquisitions, nor were any differences revealed in a more finely grained analysis that examined four different types of relatedness along with the unrelatedness measure.

---

[7] J.P. Walsh, "Top Management Turnover Following Mergers and Acquisitions." *Strategic Management Journal* 9 (1988): pp. 173–183.

Merger and Acquisition Negotiations. In recent years, merger and acqui-sition negotiations have become something of a spectator sport. The business press delights in reporting on who swallowed a poison pill or who applied a shark repellent in the hopes of warding off a possible suitor. Pac-Man defenses, white knights, scorched-earth policies, and greenmail payments are common to many mergers and acquisitions. Negotiation research shows that a contentious negotiation can alter, if not shatter, the prospects of any pro-ductive post-acquisition relationship between the parties.

An examination of 102 mergers and acquisitions and the data dealing with such variables as the length of time required to negotiate a deal, the number of counteroffers made, hostility, the method of payment, and public assurance of management retention, reveal that only the hostility of the nego-tiations explained any of the sizable first-year turnover.[8] Perhaps one of the most surprising results to emerge from this research was the absence of a statistically significant relationship between an acquiring company's public assurance that the target company managers would retain their jobs and the empirical evidence reflecting the fulfillment of those assurances. The finding may give some managers pause. The turnover rate among those whose jobs were guaranteed in the premerger period was, on average, 5.74 percent higher than their colleagues who received no such assurances. Such counterintuitive results explain why observers find these negotiations so intriguing.

Preacquisition Performance. The TWA example cited previously revealed a relationship between the company's preacquisition performance and the subsequent top management turnover. It was only after the presum-ably inefficient managers departed that Icahn was able to turn the company around. In an effort to test if this is a valid generalization, researchers exam-ined the relationship between preacquisition performance and subsequent turnover.[9] When examining the performance/turnover relationships in a set of control companies, or companies that were not involved in merger and acquisition activity in this period, researchers found a modest asso-ciation. Absent a control contest, boards of directors appear to be able to discipline their top managers for poor company performance. An even stronger relationship between these two variables exists in the acquiring companies, which claim, with justification, that they are very capable of disciplining inefficient managers. However, in contrast to the TWA example, management theory, and the reform rhetoric heard in the press, there was no association between the preacquisition performance

---

[8] J.P. Walsh, "Doing a Deal: Merger and Acquisition Negotiations and Their Impact Upon Target Company Top Management Turnover." *Strategic Management Journal* 10 (1989): pp. 307–322.

[9] Walsh and Ellwood, op. cit.

of the target firm and the high postacquisition top management turnover.

Researchers also tested whether target companies' managers are entrenched as well as inefficient, examining the turnover patterns in the target companies and control companies in the five years that preceded the takeovers. If the target companys' managers were entrenched, there should be very low historical turnover rates. In fact, there was little difference between the two sets of companies. The only difference observed was in the year immediately preceding the acquisition. At this point, the target company turnover rate was higher than the normal rate established among control companies—a result directly opposite from the one predicted by the entrenchment theory.

Researchers explored the relationship between an acquiring company's poor performance history and the target company's turnover rate because they assumed that target company managers were departing involuntarily. Subsequently, they considered the possibility of voluntary turnover among acquired managers who did not want to be associated with a new, poorly performing parent company. Two distinct patterns of turnover evolved. The first-year turnover rate was associated with a history of poor parent company performance, while the second-year turnover rate was associated with a history of good parent company performance. In the case of poorly performing parent companies, it may be that the talented managers who do not wish to be a part of a poorly performing company (and have employment opportunities elsewhere) will depart. Ironically, the managers that remain after such an acquisition may be the "managerial deadwood" who could not find a job elsewhere. Little first-year turnover was associated with parent companies that demonstrated a strong performance history. It seems that such companies wait a year to form their own judgments about the talents of their acquired managers. The observed relationship with second-year turnover may represent a pruning, but because this turnover is unrelated to the managers' past performance, the basis of these departures may represent an assessment of the fit between the managers and the future goals and objectives of the new company, rather than a judgment about their past performances.

The results of this study should temper the enthusiasm of critics of contemporary management practice, especially those who see external control contests as an effective antidote to managerial incompetence. While there is also the possibility that managers are the victims, rather than the culprits, in these control contests, the TWA experience remains as evidence of the pruning deadwood hypothesis.

Corporate Raider Discipline

The management-discipline motive does not drive every acquisition, but it may drive some. The challenge is to find when it operates.

Researchers examined the nature of managerial discipline associated with the hostile tender offers made by a group of noted corporate raiders, identifying sixty publicly traded companies in which these raiders had acquired at least 5 percent of each company during the 1979–1983 period.[10] The researchers also created a matched set of control companies. Their goal was to examine the relationship between performance and top management turnover in the target and control companies. In addition, the researchers investigated the historical performance/turnover relationships in the ten years prior to raider ownership, as well as the theoretical relationships between preraider performance and postraider turnover. Consistent with the managerial-discipline motive, they expected that the postraider turnover would be higher than the firm's historical turnover rate and the turnover rate in the firm's control company. They also expected to see little in the way of a historical performance/turnover relationship, but did expect to see the postraider turnover to be strongly associated with the firm's preraider performance.

The investigation showed that postraider management turnover was indeed higher than normal. However, the effect was not immediate. Abnormally high turnover was not in evidence until three, four, and five years after a raider purchased a stake in a company. As such, this turnover pattern was consistent with the managerial discipline motive. However, a historical relationship between performance and turnover in the control companies was nonexistent, in direct contrast to the studies that found that boards typically do discipline their managers for poor performance. It may be that corporate raiders acquire firms in poorly disciplined industries, but the firms they buy do show a modest historical relationship between performance and turnover. Perhaps raiders acquire the best firms in poorly disciplined industries. Indeed, one investigation found that poorly performing industries seem to attract hostile tender offers. Corporate raiders may lead this activity by first identifying such industries and then acquiring those firms that have the best performance prognosis.[11]

Surprisingly, no relationship was found between performance in the five years preceding raider ownership and the abnormally high turnover found in the five years following raider ownership in these sixty companies. Once again, high management turnover was uncorrelated with past performance. Perhaps the most interesting result to emerge from this research was the effect of corporate raider ownership on the target firms' nearest competitors (the control companies). Previously, they demonstrated no historical

[10] J.P. Walsh and R.D. Kosnik, *Corporate Raiders and Their Disciplinary Role in Corporate Control Contests* (Unpublished manuscript, Amos Tuck School of Business Administration, Dartmouth College, 1990).

[11] R. Morck, A. Shleifer, and R.W. Vishny, "Alternative Mechanisms for Corporate Control." *American Economic Review,* 79 (1989): pp. 842–852.

performance/turnover relationship. All this changed, however, after the raiders acquired a part of their competitors. Suddenly, the control companies demonstrated a very strong relationship between their preraider performance and the turnover after the raiders bought their competitors. So, while the effects that corporate raiders have on the management of their own companies is unclear, the effects that they have on competitors is clear and dramatic. Accordingly, raiders play a disciplinary role at the industry level of analysis. Suddenly, after the announcement of their ownership positions, their targets' competitors revealed performance-contingent, top management turnover. The raiders seem to have taught them a lesson. Ironically, this vicarious lesson appears to have been an illusory one.

Research Summary

Taken together, these research results illuminate and clarify many of the claims about the disciplinary role of corporate control contests. Although researchers were able to document that many top managers do lose their jobs after corporate control contests, they learned to be cautious about attributing most of this job loss to a managerial discipline motive. In contrast to the popular rhetoric, not all managers are punished for suboptimal performance—although, clearly, some are. The TWA evidence is incontrovertible. Moreover, corporate raiders seem to provoke the competitors of their acquired companies to better control their own managers. Researchers failed in their attempts to document the origins of much of the acquired firms' management turnover. The high turnover rates could not be explained by company relatedness, the contentiousness of the negotiations, nor preacquisition performance. Indeed, most corporate raiders did not discipline their acquired managers for poor performance histories. The prior performance of the acquiring firms explained any of the high postacquisition turnover rates. One can only conclude that many of the displaced managers were the casualties, rather than the culprits, in these control contests.

The evidence prompts more careful thought about managerial discipline in light of the many motives that can drive acquisition activity. Indeed, an acquisition may say more about the incompetence of the acquiring firm's managers than it does about the acquired managers. An incompetent management team may embark on a string of acquisitions for no other reason than to build a corporate empire that will provide them with many of the perquisites associated with such power and influence. Who can blame a talented acquired manager for not wanting to be a part of this self-aggrandizing empire?

The point is that these research findings must be built upon a more refined understanding of the role of acquired and acquiring firms' managers in corporate control contests. Until then, acquired firms' managers should not be indicted by business observers for their supposed incompetence. These easy assumptions are not helpful, especially if they compromise the abilities of managers to manage in turbulent times. For better or worse, control contests have profoundly altered the contours of contemporary management practice. In particular, control contests are giving form to a number of trends that promise to severely strain the capabilities of all managers in the years ahead.

CORPORATE CONTROL CONTESTS AND FIRM MANAGEMENT

To this point, the discussion about the consequences of corporate control activity has focused largely on top managers who have lost their jobs as a result of this activity. Equally important is a look at how these corporate control contests affect the managements of the firms involved and the impact of this activity on those who remain to manage.

The first point to be recognized is that there are fewer managers running today's corporations than there were ten years ago. In light of what has been said here, it should come as no surprise that many companies have trimmed their management ranks. Almost 1.3 million managers and professionals lost their jobs between 1979 and 1986:[12] Nearly 10 percent of all nongovernment managers left their professions each year during this period.[13] As the management ranks thin, the problems facing the remaining managers burgeon, and profound changes in the natures of both managerial discretion and control promise to test their abilities.

A Challenge to Managerial Discretion

One of the fundamental tenets of management theory and practice is that slack resources should be marshalled to enable a firm to innovate in good times and weather crises and jolts in bad times. Some have argued that organizational survival is critically dependent on the presence of slack resources. In this era of corporate control contests, it has become increasingly difficult to maintain slack resources. Companies with excess slack become takeover targets. Indeed, financial economists argue that excess cash properly belongs to the shareholders, not to the managers. As a consequence, the discretion of the contemporary manager has been curtailed and the margin for management error has been cut.

---

[12] S.R. Sanderson and L. Schein, "Sizing Up the Down-Sizing Era." *Across the Board* 23 (1986), pp. 15–23.

[13] D.L. Birch, *Job Creation in America* (New York: The Free Press, 1987).

A Challenge to Managerial Control

An accompanying problem is that the coordination and control of today's company is becoming increasingly difficult and costly. In the late 1970s and early 1980s, the trend was toward the development of strong organizational cultures. Employees preferred to work in firms that built a strong commitment to a corporate vision. Day-to-day activities became more exciting and meaningful as they contributed to some greater goal. As company loyalty and commitment increased, it became less necessary to provide the kind of direct supervision that was required under the more antagonistic relationships established by earlier management practices. Companies with strong corporate cultures needed fewer managers. The problem with corporate control contests, however, was that with their attendant restructurings, it became very difficult for managers to create strong cultures that simultaneously bound an individual to an organization and decreased the managerial costs of coordination and control.

It has become commonplace to read in the business press about the demise of corporate loyalty or the disappearance of the "company man." Employees and managers alike now worry about job security as firms attempt to anticipate or deal with the reality of corporate control contests. In one provocative paper, researchers argued that it is becoming increasingly common for firms to break implicit contracts with employees.[14] They provided the example of an older worker who was fired in a cost-cutting move because the company could no longer justify his salary. (The tragedy was that such a worker accepted lower wages when he was young, in return for the promise of a steady job when he was old.)

Corporate loyalty and commitment are nearly impossible to maintain when the implicit contracts upon which they are based have been severed. Only an organizational alchemist can transform employee self-interest and job insecurity into company loyalty and commitment. Unfortunately, absent any such legerdemain, the basis for coordination and control that so well served a lean administrative hierarchy has been compromised.

CONCLUSION

No one questions that the pace of domestic and international competition has increased in recent years. Perhaps as a consequence, companies have been bought out, merged, and acquired at a rate unequalled in history. In some cases, this corporate control activity represents a valuable and timely purging of entrenched and inefficient managers. For example, with the ben-

---

[14] A. Shleifer and L.H. Summers, "Breach of Trust in Hostile Takeovers." In A.J. Auerbach (Ed.), *Corporate Takeovers: Causes and Consequences,* (Chicago: University of Chicago Press, 1988), pp. 33–56.

efit of hindsight, no one can doubt that TWA was a better company for being acquired by Carl Icahn. In other cases, notwithstanding the commonplace rhetoric of reform, research shows that often, the purging of presumably incompetent management does not represent a sound acquisition motive. Just the same, this research also indicates that many managers' jobs are at risk. Setting aside the personal toll of executive job loss, consideration of the surviving managers' situations revealed enormous challenges as they must face these competitive pressures with less financial discretion and greater coordination and control problems. Although no cure for these difficulties is on the horizon, at least one palliative prescription may be offered to relieve many of the attendant symptoms of this distress.

Most fundamentally, the seductive logic that places incompetent managers at the root of corporate control activity must be checked and challenged. While compelling, the TWA lesson proved to be limited in its application. Such logic, more often than not, serves as a smokescreen to obscure the motives of an incompetent acquiring management team bent on empire-building or looting another firm's assets. This reform logic may provide the rationale to "blame the victim" for another's crime. From a less devious perspective, this reform logic may subtly contribute to the acquiring company's arrogance that frequently complicates and confounds the postmerger integration of otherwise well-conceived organizational combinations. (Even the often-used term "parent company" signals that the acquiring company must possess an unusual degree of managerial acumen.) Such attitudes do little to promote harmony in the new organization and may, in fact, help to explain much of the so-far inexplicable management turnover. Ultimately, this rhetoric of reform unfairly indicts and no doubt demoralizes many competent managers who have been caught up in the finger pointing frenzy of the past decade. If corporations hope to meet the management challenges posed by corporate control activity, they must be clear about its origins. Management scapegoating serves no one.

Formulating Business Unit and Corporate Strategy

16

Market Research and Business Strategy

GORDON WYNER

Senior Vice-President, M/A/R/C Inc.

INTRODUCTION

Today, business strategists and marketing researchers operate in worlds that are far apart. Strategists tend to take a top-down view of business, whereas market researchers take a bottom-up view. Strategists look at the resources and strengths of their corporations and ask questions like "What kind of a company do we want to be?" Researchers gather data from current and potential customers to find out what they need and want in terms of specific products. Strategists have a much freer hand to pursue alternative business scenarios. Researchers are constrained to deal with the consumer as a given. Strategy develops new scenarios. Research is most often utilized to evaluate the likely market response to a given scenario.

Although it does not happen easily, nothing prevents practitioners of the two approaches from communicating. The research function can be actively managed to ensure that research and strategy are synchronized to support the strategic objectives of the firm. For example, in some situations there is inherent strategic content to the research, and thus the design of the research can directly reflect strategic concerns. In most market research projects, the details of the actual research are worked on by the researchers themselves, but their work can be guided by input from the strategists as to the overall goals.

While there is little direct acknowledgment of the role of market research in the strategic perspective, much of the same vocabulary is used by both groups. Words like "competition," "market segments," "product differentiation," "positioning," "brand image," "brand switching," and "customer" appear frequently in both camps. Furthermore, the development of business strategy is based on a large body of knowledge about products and markets that ultimately comes from some type of research. Each of the shared terms just listed is measurable in some way by market research. For example, business strategy often analyzes various ways to deal with different kinds of competitors. Market research can identify, from the consumer's perspective, who the competitors are, how loyal consumers are to them, how frequently consumers actually switch brands, on what criteria brands are differentiated in the consumer's mind, and so on.

Additionally, some of the advanced research techniques contribute much more than static measures. These techniques make it possible to understand the dynamics of consumer behavior. Future behavior can be predicted to allow the strategist to anticipate the likely outcomes of strategies before they are implemented.

Given the apparent relationship between the two disciplines, and the great need for market information by strategists, it is worthwhile to establish the links between business strategy and marketing research. Better information, from well-designed research, can lead to better business strategies and performance against those strategies.[1]

In this chapter, the relationship of business strategy to research design is described to show how the research is actually conducted. There is also discussion of how the market research function is organized within a company, and how that organization can be altered for greater achievement of the company's business strategy objectives. The chapter concludes with a look at how organizational issues relate to the financial arena. If research is

---

[1] This chapter does not represent a comprehensive summary of all the types of marketing research that might bear, in some way, on business strategy. For an exhaustive survey of the field, see Paul E. Green and Donald S. Tull, *Research for Marketing Decisions (4th ed.)* (Englewood Cliffs, New Jersey: Prentice Hall, 1978); or David A. Aaker and George S. Day, *Marketing Research* (Toronto, Canada: John Wiley & Sons, 1989).

to support the strategic goals of the firm, then it should be managed financially in ways that actively pursue those goals.

BUSINESS STRATEGY AND RESEARCH DESIGN

Product Testing and the Product Portfolio

One of the most basic forms of market research is product testing. This research is designed to obtain consumers' evaluations of products in order to guide management decisions as to what products to offer and how to modify them to achieve improvements that result in increased sales. Product testing is also used to monitor the performance of products in the market in order to track quality and value, relative to the competition. Of all the types of market research done in the United States, product testing constitutes the single largest category. This kind of research is especially prevalent in certain product categories, such as foods, personal care, and household products. It plays a smaller role, although it is still important, in services and durable goods.

Product testing takes place within a strategic context, whether or not this context is ever acknowledged. The products or new product ideas being investigated all fit somewhere within the company's portfolio of products. For example, in many instances, a company has different expectations for each product in its portfolio, depending on the growth rate of the industry and relative market share currently enjoyed by the product. These expectations for the product usually influence the research objectives, the questions asked of research respondents, the sample selected, and the experimental design.

The well-known Boston Consulting Group (BCG) growth-share matrix defines products as "stars," "cash cows," "question marks," and "dogs" in terms of high or low positions on these two dimensions of growth and share. The high share/high growth star products use a lot of cash to finance continued, rapid growth and to maintain their high shares. Cash cows generate large amounts of cash that support other business units. Their markets have matured, and one goal is to "milk" profits through cost efficiencies. Question marks need cash infusions to increase shares in high-growth categories, while dogs have performed poorly in low-potential markets.

What then are the strategic implications of location in the portfolio for product testing research design? First, why might research be conducted? What kinds of questions would be asked regarding each type of product? What customer groups should be targeted for market research?

There is no rigid set of rules for setting up the research design, and the requirements of the research will vary in real applications. However, concepts familiar to business strategists can play an important role in setting research objectives and actually implementing the research. The four BCG

TABLE 16-1
Research Implications for Products

BCG Product type	Sampling	Measurement
	Brand users	Increased usage
Stars	Nonusers of brand	Brand switching, attributes
	Nonusers of category	Trial
Cash cows	Brand users	Increased usage, discrimination
Question marks	Nonusers of brand	Brand switching, attributes
	Nonusers of category	Trial
Dogs	Target segment	Specialized usage occasion

product types help to define research objectives and identify the sampling and measurement design issues for a product (see Table 16-1).

Stars. By definition stars need to continue high growth. Therefore, the question for a star product might be whether it is capable of sustaining the high growth that it has achieved historically. Product testing should be designed to help determine whether consumers will continue to purchase the product. If the product's star status is based on product superiority, then testing should substantiate this assumption. If superiority is not evident in the product, then other factors (e.g., distribution, promotion, advertising) must be responsible, and the testing strategy should take this into account.

Market research for star products should include a sample of current users of the product because it is important to maintain those consumers who have contributed to past successes. The questions asked of these consumers in the study should determine whether increased usage is possible. For example, is there reason to believe that consumers might consume more per usage (e.g., larger soft drink sizes or larger candy bars) or engage in more purchase and usage occasions (going to a pizzeria for lunch, or having soup as a meal in itself)?

Another sample should be drawn from the consumers who currently do not use the brand, but use a competitive one. Growth can come from these types of consumers, but only if they can be induced to switch from the competition. The questions in the study should therefore allow consumers to indicate whether they would switch or perhaps have switched in the past. To make this determination, comparative questions can be used that cover each of the important attributes that distinguish the product from competitors' products. For example, a study of competitive frozen pizzas that differ on crust, sauce, cheese, and toppings should include questions that ask consumers to compare each of these characteristics for each of the products being considered.

The design of the study might take into account the comparative nature of the problem. For this type of situation, a *paired test*, in which a consumer is asked to directly evaluate the two competitive products, may be in order. For food products this can mean tasting two different products and using them for some period of time. If consumers have the opportunity in the real market to make these comparisons, it makes sense to reflect this in the research design. The tasks performed by the respondent in the research should parallel, as closely as possible, their actual, in-market behavior. It has become widely accepted that paired tests are more sensitive in picking up differences between products, since each person is directly asked about both.

By contrast, the *monadic* study design, in which only one product is tested by each consumer, is generally thought to be less sensitive, since the comparisons between products are made from different samples of people. However, in some situations there is no relevant comparison for the consumer, so a paired design would not be appropriate. For example, if a telephone company is testing a new network-based service, such as call waiting or call forwarding, there may be no direct competition. The monadic design would then parallel the consumer's real-world decision to try or not to try the new service. Monadic designs have the advantage that a consumer's reaction to a product is not biased or influenced by his exposure to another product. This can be a problem, however, when multiple tastings of food products are done.

A third sampling consideration for the star product is consumers who do not yet use any products in the product category. They should be included to determine whether they represent a potential growth segment. Again, by definition, it is assumed that there are growth opportunities to be had. It is up to the research to find and quantify them. In this instance, potential consumers would be asked questions relating to trial of a "new" product. Since they have not yet tried it, they have no basis for comparison with competitive products. Neither the extended usage questions nor the attribute comparison questions are appropriate for them. The design almost has to be monadic rather than paired, but questions can be included relating to the benefits of entering the category versus using alternative products. For example, consumers who do not buy frozen dinners can be asked about the potential benefits of convenience relative to home-cooked meals.

Cash Cows. For cash cows, the key market research question is likely to be whether the product can sustain its position among its current users. If the market is mature, then new users are not likely to emerge. If the product has been correctly classified as a cash cow, then there is little reason to include nonusers of the brand or category in the study. Either these nonusers literally do not exist (e.g., everybody uses toothpaste) or there are some barriers to new users entering the market (e.g., decaffeinated coffee users may be outside the category for regular coffee because they do not want to use caffeine).

Since expanding the market for products of this type is impossible, often the business strategy is to reduce their costs to further increase profits. From a research standpoint, this leads to a concern with the impact on consumers of product modifications. Typically, a lower-cost ingredient (such as a less expensive oil or spice in snack chips) is tried in the hope that consumers will not notice the difference. If there is no evidence of consumer dissatisfaction during the study, then the change is made. Specialized designs are available to estimate the true discriminating capabilities of consumers as distinct from errors of judgment and guessing. (Two examples of these designs are the triangle and repeat pairs designs.) However, in many instances, a simple paired preference test is used to make the decision.

Question Marks. Question marks have a fairly urgent need to expand their user base. Their location in the product portfolio says that there is growth potential in the category. The potential users are both current nonusers of the brand and nonusers of the product category. The research implications follow those for the stars, except for the fact that current brand users are not as important. While it may be prudent to include some users for comparative purposes (e.g., to find out why they like the brand so that these criteria can be used to attract nonusers to the product), the real growth has to come from outside the existing group of consumers. Additionally, if the brand currently has a small share of the market, it will probably be difficult and costly to find users to include in the research sample.

Dogs. One of the few recommended strategies for dogs is to identify a niche and determine whether this kind of business is sustainable at levels that meet corporate financial objectives. The implications for product testing are to sample people who qualify for the various niches and to measure preferences and other product evaluations for the specific occasions of use that are relevant to the niche. For example, premium priced candy might be a niche product in a diversified snack food company's portfolio. To investigate product acceptance, the researcher first has to locate users who have an interest in these types of candies. This may be a subsegment of the users of snacks with greater mass appeal, or perhaps a different group altogether. Second, the product may be appropriate only for certain occasions and purposes, such as gift giving. The context for the respondents in product testing research interviews should reflect this "occasion" framework, and the questions asked should elicit answers that reflect preferences of the respondent in what he buys for others rather than what he buys for himself.

Conjoint Analysis and Generic Business Strategies

Three generic strategies are at the core of many real-world business strategy applications. They are:

- Cost leadership
- Product differentiation
- Focus

To what extent can market research contribute to a firm's analyses of these strategic options? It can add significantly to the information base that supports decisions through the application of the methodology of conjoint analysis. This method for measuring is an example of a situation in which marketing research can go beyond static measures of the current market and contribute to scenario building and testing.

Overview. Conjoint analysis is a method for measuring the preferences of individuals with regard to various products, services, and other types of alternatives. It provides an understanding of consumer preferences for specific product features or attributes. It answers the question, "Why do consumers buy the products they do?" Conjoint analysis approaches the answer to this question in terms of the attributes that have an impact on consumer choices among alternative products. Of course, there are variables other than product attributes that affect choices, but the researcher must first understand how consumers evaluate the attributes. Then, external factors, such as distribution, advertising, and promotion can be taken into account.

The attributes of a personal computer, for example, include the internal memory, the hard disk memory, the screen size, the price, the manufacturer, and potentially many more features. The specific options ("levels") of the attributes might include one, two, three, or four megabytes of internal memory, a screen of 8, 10, or 12 inches, and a price tag of $3,000, $5,000, or $7,000. Categorical attributes, such as manufacturer, can be identified in a conjoint analysis as well—for example, IBM, Compaq, or Apple. In any given analysis the specific attributes that are chosen and defined represent what is most important to the buyer and include any new features or options being contemplated by the manufacturer.

Conjoint analysis utilizes product descriptions that contain one level for each attribute. For example, in a study of personal computers, one description for an IBM computer might be:

Internal memory: 1 megabyte

Hard disk memory: 20 megabytes

Screen size: 10 inches

Price: $5,000

A respondent might be asked to evaluate as many as fifteen or twenty different descriptions for one study. Because each description reflects a different set of levels for the attributes, it is possible to produce the entire range of possible attribute combinations. The benefit of this approach is that respondents evaluate and express their preferences for whole products rather than for individual attributes, and the findings are therefore more realistic.

Each level of an attribute is assigned numerical values, called utility values, that are based on individual responses to the product descriptions. The utility values derived for each respondent reflect the worth to that respondent of any possible product that might be offered in the marketplace. This is a very powerful feature of conjoint analysis because it can be used to evaluate the hundreds of attribute combinations that are possible for a single product, without the need to go back to the field and conduct additional consumer surveys.

The key assumption of conjoint analysis is that consumers follow a fairly simple decision-making model. This is the linear, additive model, which says that the consumer has an overall utility, or value, for a product that is simply the sum of the utility values for the component parts. In the example used here, the overall value for a computer would be found by adding the utility values associated with internal memory, hard disk, screen, price, manufacturer, and so on.

Benefits. Conjoint analysis can provide some rich data for the marketer interested in the demand side of the market. The technique yields consumer preferences for various products and component attributes. Typically, the results are used for product development (what features should be offered to make it attractive enough?) and for competitive pricing (how much can be charged before market share erosion occurs?). The information can also be useful at the strategic level in the context of differentiation strategies. Specific product or service features that are highly valued by consumers can be identified and measured. Quantitative evaluation of product features makes it possible for strategic planners to assess the real impact of differentiation.

This technique reveals the trade-offs that consumers are willing to make in deciding among alternatives. Suppose, for example, that a particular computer buyer attributes a higher value to IBM than to Compaq. Being a rational buyer, this individual would prefer to pay as little as possible for a computer. If a particular IBM computer costs more than a particular Compaq, there is a choice to be made. Would the consumer pay $5,000 for an IBM versus $3,000 for Compaq? The utility values indicate the point at which a manufacturer preference is equated with a price reduction, i.e., the trade-off point. It reveals what kind of premium a consumer is willing to pay to obtain a product from the preferred manufacturer. Conversely, it reveals how much of a "discount" the other manufacturer needs to offer to induce the consumer to buy a product.

Once utility values are estimated from survey data, they can be used to simulate the market response to alternative competitive scenarios. A data base created from the survey data is used for "what if" questions in which hypothetical and real products are placed in competition with each other and the computer calculates the shares of choices that would go to each.

Overall utility scores are derived from the sums of the utility values for each attribute level. In the simplest application of the conjoint analysis model, the overall utility scores are compared for the products being simulated. The product with the highest score is the one that would be chosen by the consumer. The manufacturer can run the model with different attributes to estimate what would happen if a price is lowered or features are added to a product and the product competes against existing products in the market. The segments of the market that would switch as a result of these changes can be isolated for further analysis.

Application to Differentiation Strategy. Conjoint measurement research can be an important source of input on several sides of a differentiation issue. Not only can it provide support for an established strategy, but it can also support untried strategies. As long as the product differentiation can be incorporated into the conjoint design, the results can be used to simulate what would happen if the new features were offered.

The competitor that is the object of a differentiation strategy may also use this kind of analysis to counterattack. By examining the consumer's evaluation of differentiating features, the competitor can see whether it would benefit from offering some version of those same features. The end result might be to blur the distinctions created by the original manufacturer, thus reducing the effectiveness of its strategy.

For example, Apple Computer has obviously done much to position itself as a leader in easy-to-use computers through its Macintosh product. Ease of use can be translated into several different product features, such as pull-down menus, pictorial representations of data to be manipulated (icons), and a mouse to manipulate data by pointing to the screen. These kinds of features may have constituted a unique differentiating characteristic of the company's strategy at one point in time. Other personal computers on the market required the user to learn how to use coded function keys on the keyboard to accomplish the same operations.

Conjoint measurement could have been used to quantify the appeal of these features to Macintosh users, and to IBM users, to see the extent to which they affect overall preferences for computers. How popular would Apple computers be if they did not have the ease-of-use features? Comparison of preferences for computers with and without specific features reveals the value to the manufacturer of having them.

In recent years, many ease-of-use features that are similar to those offered by Macintosh have been introduced for IBM computers. For instance, the Windows and Presentation Manager software accomplish many of the same things that the Macintosh does. Conjoint measurement could be used for an assessment of the impact of this product differentiation. For example, how much do buyers value these features at this point in time? Are the benefits strong enough to persuade loyal Macintosh users to switch to IBM?

Application to Low-Cost Strategies. All the actions taken internally to maintain a cost advantage ultimately have an impact on the consumer in terms of the price paid for the product and the quality of the product. A conjoint analysis enables the manufacturer to measure the price sensitivities of individual buyers in the market, and the utility values for specific features show the degree to which consumers respond to changes in all the aspects of a product that ultimately make up its quality.

Segments of more and less price-sensitive buyers can be isolated. Simulation of the market response to changes in price can show what would happen if the price advantage were extended further, i.e. if price is lowered. How many new consumers would choose the product at the lower price? Is the total profit generated at the lower margin adequate to justify the strategy? Ideally, the strategist would like to know, in advance, what kind of demand for the product can be anticipated if costs are reduced significantly and some of the savings are passed on to customers in the form of price reductions.

Alternatively, the analysis can be used to see what would happen if the cost advantage were to disappear. This could come about as the result of a conscious strategy of raising prices. It could also come about as the result of losing production efficiencies—for example, having to replace plant and equipment at more expensive current prices. If prices are raised, do the additional revenue and profit from remaining customers more than offset the lost customers?

One new element is being added here to the discussion of conjoint analysis. Now the cost of production has entered into what has been, to this point, solely a demand analysis. For example, a manufacturer might need to know what costs could be eliminated if some product features could be eliminated. In this situation, conjoint analysis reveals how the consumer values quality in the product in terms of specific product performance characteristics. How much does the car buyer value reliability? How much is he or she willing to pay to obtain a long-term warranty? The manufacturer can use this information to determine just how much quality must be built in to attract customers, while considering what it will cost to deliver that level of quality.

The simulation capability of conjoint analysis can be used to anticipate the consequences of a low-cost strategy before the company attempts to implement it. Based on company or industry experience curves, what efficiencies can be expected at higher volumes of production? If efficiencies are possible, the analysis can project what kind of volume would be expected with the modified product. This information can, in turn, be used to assess whether the financial scenario makes a product modification worthwhile.

Application to Focus Strategies. The basic techniques applied to differentiation and low-cost strategies can be applied in the context of a focus strategy. The analysis concentrates on identifying target segments in the market and then applying the principles of a differentiation (or possibly a cost) strategy to those groups. Data from a conjoint analysis study can be used to great advantage to identify segments, since the utility values represent consumers' desired benefits for specific product features. This is an unusually precise way to isolate groups that share a common profile of desired benefits. It has the potential to be much more precise than other techniques, such as attitudinal, demographic, or usage segmentation schemes. Unlike the subjective interpretations of attitude profiles or the descriptive, but not actionable, demographic summaries, conjoint analyses of concrete product benefits characterize and describe the segments.

ORGANIZATIONAL ISSUES

The market research function is organized in numerous ways in U.S. companies. It ranges from centralized (all research directed by one group) to decentralized (separate research groups for individual business units). Its reporting relationship varies from direct accountability to marketing, or to marketing services, or to information services, or to a corporate authority.

All the various research activities that are conducted by a corporation can and do contribute importantly to business strategy. However, the fragmented nature of some of the activities often obscures the whole research enterprise. Within a large research department, individual analysts often design and conduct studies independently of others doing similar work. Within large corporations, departments often independently sponsor research that is similar and related to research sponsored by other departments. The potential impact and value of market research companywide can only be appreciated if all the research activities are viewed as part of a whole.

This whole is the company's commitment to expending resources to learn about its customers, products, and markets through information gathering. Of course, there are many ways to organize individual departments to realize the benefits of research, but what is important is the potential that resides in most companies to get more leverage out of their research by thinking about it as a system for corporate learning. The advances and efficiencies of new information technology make this possible because information can easily be shared across departmental boundaries.

A Systems Approach

In concrete terms, what are the components of a system for corporate learning? The first consideration is that a company has limited resources to spend on information acquisition. Research competes for money with all the other investments and expenditures, such as capital equipment, marketing and sales, and product development. Although it is difficult to quantify the return on investment for research dollars, these dollars must at least provide a return that subjectively satisfies management. One way to enhance the return is to pool the resources of the different departments that spend money on research and, perhaps even more importantly, pool the information they obtain. If resources are pooled, then potential efficiencies of scale can be identified and exploited. If information is shared, then entirely new kinds of learning about the business become possible. When the information is left compartmentalized, the overall learning potential is limited.

Corporate Level Analysis. In many companies the earliest research conducted on new products is done internally under the auspices of the research and development (R&D) group. Food companies may conduct sensory research with panels of employees who taste products and give their feedback. Typically, their input is limited to describing what they tasted rather than how much they liked it. (Evaluative judgments are obtained in other studies with randomly selected consumers, as opposed to company employees.) Durable goods companies may conduct product research done by engineers. They might acquire competitive products and tear them down to isolate certain performance features and then build prototypes for new products. They also might test them with internal staff. They would focus on how the user handles the product, ease of use, and long-term performance.

In the market research department, studies are conducted on products to determine consumer reactions to the product itself (e.g., features and packaging) and the marketing communication about the product (e.g., advertising and imagery).

In another part of the company, research is being done to track product performance after it is in the market. In food and consumer durables companies, this research can take the form of competitive product testing, quality audits of products on the shelf, and tracking of complaints registered by consumers who experience problems with the products. The department that oversees this research may be related to manufacturing, and is often titled "quality control" or "quality assurance." In service companies, the operations function might oversee this kind of research and call it "customer satisfaction measurement."

Whether officially defined as a research system or not, these three kinds of research are related parts of a whole system. The same products are being investigated, but at different points in their "life." In the early stages, research helps to determine which product attributes to manipulate to achieve a physical product that meets corporate goals. In the middle stages, a focus on marketing variables is added to the product focus. Research helps decide how to spend marketing dollars to achieve sales success. In the latter stage, the research monitors performance to isolate problem areas that need attention. Once again, the research identifies specific product variables that can be modified.

There is considerable learning potential in linking the research from all stages. Ideally there would be a vehicle for all researchers to find out what product formulations have been tested before in the company's history, how many and what kinds of products went into marketing testing, how many and what kind went into the market, and how successful they have proven to be over time. Each contributor to the product (in its development, marketing, or long-term management) can do a better job with access to information at all phases.

The whole range of products tested represents a sample, albeit a nonrandom one, of all products that might have been tested or actually produced. This particular sample is the result of the experience of an organization—what it has elected to test for various historical reasons. It is probably made up of many successes, but includes some failures. Thus, the successes and failures can be compared to determine if there are common themes that distinguish one from another. This is a corporate level analysis. Examples of questions asked in a corporate level analysis are the following:

- Does the company always seem to do well when it has a superior product, at premium prices, but not as well when it attempts to provide a commodity product at the lowest price?
- Does the company tend to do well when it targets a particular market segment, but do poorly when it tries to serve the entire market?
- Does the company tend to have long-term staying power with its products when the marketing function is decentralized (e.g., to regional levels) as compared to when it is nationally controlled?

TABLE 16-2

Profile of Company Experience, for Corporate Level Analysis

Product stage	Successful	Unsuccessful
Development	Superior product overall Parity on product attributes	Parity product overall Superiority on some, inferior on other product attributes
Marketing	Targeted to key segments Heavy advertising support Premium priced	Mass marketing Heavy promotion support Low priced
Long-term management	Regional marketing control Consistent product quality	Centralized marketing control Varying product quality

Table 16-2 is a hypothetical illustration of corporate level analysis across products for a company.

Corporate level analysis requires research at each stage of the product's cycle. If the various kinds of research are never integrated into this type of analysis, the learning potential is lost, even though the resources have been expended. When research is integrated in this fashion, a new level of knowledge is achieved at the company level. Each product and each department is an important component of the overall picture, but the view is incomplete to any single participant in the process. Only at the corporate level can the full view and the full value of the research information be realized.

Master Research Plan

Despite the considerable benefits of this kind of a corporate level analysis, there are substantial limitations. Precisely because the products represent the experience of the company, they do not represent all the possibilities that the company did not pursue. Even if many alternative formulations of products are tested at the earlier stages, the selection of products to test further or modify is constrained. Success at earlier stages is a prerequisite for follow-up. This is most obviously the case when it comes to actually going into the market. Companies enter the market with what they believe to be the best products. Product ideas that were rejected at the earlier stages never get tested in the later stages.

The limitations of a corporate level analysis suggest that there is a need for more than the capability to synthesize the history of research within a company. How can a company use research to expand its understanding of the strategic options that could be attempted? A general answer to this question is to consider a master research plan for the company that cuts across the divisional and departmental boundaries. If management articulates a research design philosophy, the research function can be more actively managed to achieve strategic goals. With the larger, corporate view in mind, research can be designed to investigate new product possibilities that make sense corporately but would not be investigated by a single department. For example, in the area of product testing, the standard research approaches can be linked with the corporation's strategic objectives. The conjoint analysis approach represents a further extension of the notion of a design philosophy. It relies heavily on experimentation as opposed to measuring responses in the current market.

Experimentation is a relatively inexpensive way to expand the options under consideration. The cost of research to simulate the marketing environment is usually a very small fraction of the cost of the actual marketing action. For example, the technique of pretest market forecasting of the success of new grocery products has become an extremely accurate tool. At a fraction of the cost of a live test market, a survey-based study can predict in-market performance to within 10 to 20 percent most of the time.[2]

Implementation

Inventory. The first step toward a corporate research plan is to inventory what kind of research is currently done. Research can be found in the market research department, marketing itself, R&D, manufacturing, quality assurance, corporate affairs, communications, strategic planning, and perhaps other departments. The following questions are helpful in creating the inventory:

- What kinds of studies are done by each of these groups?
- What research designs are employed?
- Are measures of product acceptance consistent from one study to another so that they can be compared?
- Are some questions, such as "intent to purchase," asked in an identical (or at least compatible) way across products and categories?
- What type of respondents are studied?
- Is there a consistent definition of what a customer is? For example, if brand loyalty is a concept that relates to many products in the line, does it always mean the same thing?
- Are the study respondents drawn from all business segments?
- Do they include important non-customer groups that are potential customers?
- What kinds of time frames are used in the research? For example, do all survey studies about advertising measure the same periods, such as the week or month?

[2] Glen L. Urban and Gerald M. Katz, "Pre-Test-Market Models: Validation and Managerial Implications," *Journal of Marketing Research* vol. XX (Aug. 1983), p. 221–234.

- Do tracking studies conducted over time have compatible reporting periods so that across-product and across-category analyses can easily be accomplished?

Once an inventory is completed, then decisions can be made to consolidate research where appropriate. For example, some firms conduct multiple tracking studies that separately measure responses to advertising, intent to purchase, and inventory of current products. It might be possible to integrate these into a smaller number of data collection efforts that allow these measures to be taken from the same individuals. The analysis would be considerably more powerful if based on individuals rather than limited to only aggregate analysis of changes over time.

In addition to analytical advantages, there could be cost efficiencies if studies can be combined. In general, it is desirable to group studies according to the similarity of their objectives and designs. If there are substantial similarities, then perhaps with minor modification studies can be standardized to facilitate across-study comparisons.

There are always unique studies that do not fit within an established pattern of research. A pioneering study may have a completely different research design from those in other studies. It may eventually lead to a new standard in the corporation for conducting research, even though it does not compare to anything else in use at the time it is conducted. Obviously, this kind of creativity should be allowed and encouraged in the area of market research.

Communication. An important implementation step is to create a vehicle to communicate about research across organizational boundaries. One way to do this is to assign a chief information officer to the task. This individual does not control all the research functions in the company but does have knowledge of all the research activities, and is a major participant in—or the manager of—corporate level research, such as the corporate level analysis and the master research plan.

Other ways to coordinate research information are to be found in technology. Whether or not a corporation assigns coordination of research information to a chief information officer, this information can be made accessible to all data bases and local area networks. Computer systems are available that can automate the entire research process so that all documents are entered into a single data base and the process is controlled according to preestablished routines. In addition to the efficiencies of automation, this kind of system makes the across-product, across-time learning an essential component, rather than a post hoc project. It builds in the communication among research that is critical to creating a truly integrated research systems environment.

FINANCIAL ISSUES

The systems approach makes it possible for a corporation to get the maximum leverage out of research expenditures through consolidation of resources. It facilitates decisions about conducting research, i.e., which studies to do. It also can be applied to decisions about purchasing research from other companies that provide research products and services.

Deploying Research Resources

The value—current or potential—of a business provides a useful guide to research expenditures. In general, the larger the business or potential business, the greater the permissible expenditure on research. Of course, actual expenditure may not follow this pattern closely in some situations—for example, if there are greater or fewer researchable issues in some areas of business.

Research dollars can also be spent according to the timing of other business expenditures. An example of this approach is in advertising. It makes sense to expend the most to track the effectiveness of advertising during time periods when advertising is at its heaviest. In this way the level of precision required of the research (and hence the extensiveness and cost of the research project) can be adjusted to relate directly to the need for precision. If, for instance, advertising is relatively light during the summer months, then the research probably does not need to be quite as precise. If advertising picks up dramatically in the fall, then the precision of the measurement of advertising effectiveness should follow suit. Put more generally, research expenditures should relate to the risks of the business decisions being made. The greater the financial exposure of the company, the greater the research precision required.

Buying Research From Research Companies

If research activities are to be actively managed to support business strategy, then this intention affects the purchase of research itself. In order to gain more leverage for research dollars, many companies utilize the same principles they use with suppliers of other products and services. Specifically, they have consolidated their lists of research companies with which they will do business. In many cases the result has been substantial reductions in the number of "approved" suppliers. A small number—perhaps fewer than five—can be actively managed centrally by the research director. A large number—close to 100 in some companies—cannot be managed in this way. If standard research procedures are to be adhered to, the smaller number is essential. It is feasible to communicate on a regular basis with the smaller number and to reinforce the requirements of the corporation. It is not feasible to communicate with a large number on a frequent basis.

A reduced list of suppliers implies that each one will be asked to do a significant amount of work for the client. Participating research companies can look forward to a steadier stream and larger volume of business. This situation is intended by the buyer of the research to increase leverage over the suppliers. When a significant volume of business is at stake, it follows that the supplier will be more responsive to the client than when small, unpredictable amounts of business are involved. Thus, the corporation can anticipate greater compliance by suppliers with corporate research goals and procedures than could ever be accomplished with a large, unmanaged supplier group.

The corporation can also expect to gain valuable consulting advice from the reduced list of research companies. In this environment, the supplier typically has access to more information about what the corporation is trying to accomplish than in the unmanaged situation. The supplier is doing more business with the corporation, understands better what needs to be done, and can even benefit from conducting its own R&D efforts to create improved products and services.

CONCLUSION

The success of business strategy depends on an accurate understanding of the market, and companies would therefore benefit from bridging the communication gap between business strategists and market researchers. There are some significant opportunities for these two groups to work closely together. All that is required is a mutual understanding of the relationship between the two perspectives so that they can be synchronized to achieve business goals and enhance company performance.

17

Market Segmentation

SUSAN SCHWARTZ MCDONALD

Booz Allen & Hamilton, Inc.

INTRODUCTION

Today buying a telephone requires sorting through a remarkable array of models and features, and a glance out the window reminds us that some of the great automotive successes of more recent years have emerged on the basis of well-defined market segmentation strategies. Most products today are designed and positioned to satisfy some segments of the market very well while deliberately overlooking others.

If properly conceived and executed, this approach can yield an increase in profitability, despite a reduction in unit sales. Consider watches. The Rolex is obviously targeted at mature buyers who can afford an expensive timepiece and are willing to pay for the privilege of owning one. Meanwhile, in another segment of the market, Swatch has captured the youth segment with a fun, faddish, quasi-disposable strategy that defines its benefits and its audience in a way that traditional watch companies never have before.

One of the most important missions of marketing research is to help businesses develop and target their products by identifying relevant market segments and discovering their distinctive needs. The word "relevant" is key because there are a number of different ways in which customers—both people and businesses—can be segmented, and there are no clear guidelines for how best to do it. Since every individual plays many roles and has many sources of affiliation, there is no one ideal way to classify any purchaser of a product. The appropriateness of a segmentation scheme depends on the product category, the history and life cycle of the product, and the marketing objectives, among other considerations. To appreciate these subtleties, it is necessary to review the various segmentation approaches available and the kinds of options and constraints they imply.

WAYS TO SEGMENT A MARKET

Demographic Segmentation

Socioeconomic variables, or demographics, are a cornerstone of market segmentation because pricing strategy, distribution, and media access are all closely tied to such variables as income, employment, age, and gender. Demographic classifications also have the clear advantage of being relatively easy to construct and apply. In fact, some "products," such as retirement communities, are literally defined in demographic terms.

Historically, the primary segmentation scheme in marketing was men and women, and it remains a basic principle for organizing the marketplace, even in this era of greater equality and role redefinition. However, demographic classifications are equally relevant in business-to-business marketing. Any industry that targets businesses instead of people will naturally need to distinguish small businesses from large ones, for example, because size tends to have very direct implications for the sorts of product or service requirements and resources a business will have. So, too, do organizational structure and operations requirements. In the health care industry, for example, different types of hospitals and provider organizations will have differing levels of price sensitivity or receptivity to technical innovation, depending on factors like size, for-profit status, patient census, and the like.

A notable advantage of demographic segmentation is that there is usually a great deal of syndicated data available in most markets to help organizations discern key relationships between category usage and demographics. Geodemographic segmentation enables marketers to reach relatively homogeneous zip code segments whose residents appear to share much in common demographically and behaviorally. The underlying assumption—that "birds of a feather" live in similar communities—can help a marketer target promotional mailings to receptive segments. The availability of ready-made demographic segmentation schemes does not mean that more sophisticated, custom-tailored data bases are not also required for effective marketing. It does mean, however, that a market research department can easily purchase data off the shelf and then build a more sophisticated data base on that platform.

The chief drawback of demographic segmentation is that not everyone in a given demographic segment will behave in precisely the same way. For example, two thirty-five-year-old mothers of three with the same general socioeconomic characteristics may use different detergents, drive different cars, and so on. Similarly, AT&T can expect to encounter a number of small businesses that share the same general characteristics but that, owing to different management styles, for example, have markedly different telecommunications requirements. A sophisticated marketer must therefore be knowledgeable about other ways to approach market segmentation.

It has become increasingly clear that changing socioeconomic factors are requiring more sophisticated principles of market organization. Some of the demographic variables marketers emphasized in the past are now less important than they used to be, while others are emerging as more prominent. For example, the market for certain health foods, such as high-fiber cereals, was originally primarily people with specialized medical needs. Today the market has broadened to include a much larger prevention-oriented group defined by such factors as education, age, and a health-conscious attitude as well as by medical requirements. Similarly, the very term "yuppie" brings to mind a target group defined simultaneously in terms of income, education, family structure, and social values. When manufacturers of baby products envision a target audience of new mothers, they no longer only think of women in their twenties who spend all their days caring for infants. Instead, they are concerned with a segment that spans at least two decades in age and represents a variety of lifestyles and family structures that defy the old stereotypes of motherhood and baby care. The proliferation of products and the challenges and rewards of addressing this enormously complex market reflect that new variety.

Behavior Segmentation

Another common way to segment markets is to classify customers on the basis of how they behave—for example, how actively they participate in a particular category, how much of a brand they use, where they shop, and so on. Like demographic segments, behavior segments are relatively easy to define and track. Purchase data are available through numerous syndicated services and have the potential to become even more accurate in the future if consumers allow their purchase data to be accessed directly by means of scanning technologies.

To maintain market intelligence, marketers must understand the behavior of different user groups—who they are, what they like, how they shop, and why they buy what they do. It is also appropriate sometimes to define target markets on the basis of volume. For example, Frequent Flyer perks were created explicitly for the airlines' heavy users; many services provided by credit card companies were designed specifically for individuals who already hold these cards.

On the other hand, defining a market strategy in terms of current user behaviors has significant limitations. So that they can serve the market more proactively, marketers need to know how particular user groups might behave if a different constellation of products were available. For that reason, marketers should be prepared to segment current or potential users on the basis of feelings, attitudes, and motivations in order to take into account unmet needs and create new transactions.

Attitude Segmentation

In its broadest sense, attitude segmentation refers to a variety of segmentation approaches that reflect psychographic (lifestyle) or product-specific consumer needs and preferences. Attitude segmentation attempts to organize the marketplace according to complex attitude structures that transcend demographics or behavior. Because it tends to be multidimensional—i.e., to reflect a variety of feelings and needs simultaneously—attitude segmentation is typically derived through multivariate statistics, which makes it more controversial and challenging than other methods of segmentation, but no less important as a marketing device.

The tools available for attitude segmentation allow for considerable flexibility in how consumer needs are conceptualized. For example, markets can be segmented according to the negative as well as the positive attributes associated with a particular product category and its purchase or use. A case in point is the fast food industry, which was launched when restaurant chains began structuring their kitchens, menus, and promotions to address the problems and limitations associated with many traditional restaurant formats (e.g., high cost of menu items, long waits for meals).

The theory behind attitude segmentation is that different consumers have different product requirements and motivations, and that it is possible to group individuals on the basis of those needs in order to engage their attention and loyalty. There is a variety of ways to approach the process, however, and all of them have potential value.

Psychographic Segmentation.
One of the earliest and best-known approaches to market segmentation, psychographic segmentation assumes that the personalities and views of consumers yield important clues to their behavior and preferences in a variety of product categories. There are, in fact, several syndicated segmentation schemes, virtually all of which classify consumers on the basis of such characteristics as personal goals and values.

Psychographic segmentation schemes tend to be especially useful for products positioned around broad social and demographic parameters. However, the approach has only a limited capacity to explain category-specific behavior or to guide product development on the basis of category needs and experiences. For example, while the term "yuppie" evokes general images of self-indulgence and connoisseurship, and implies an interest in expensive, sophisticated products, members of this group do not represent a homogeneous segment whose consumption behavior in any given product category is easily predicted. They may purchase vans or sedans, eat Cheerios or Chex, use Polaroids or Nikons, subscribe to *Money* or *Sports Illustrated*. A marketer of any of these products needs to know more about this group—e.g., family size and leisure-activity preferences—before tailoring a marketing program to address their needs.

Benefit Segmentation. Benefit segmentation is an approach that segments consumers on the basis of their product requirements. Amateur photographers, for example, are inspired by a variety of needs and motivations, including the practical need to archive events, the psychological need to arrest time, or the more creative need to achieve artistic self-expression. Cameras are designed and marketed around these different needs, just as cars are designed and positioned to satisfy an interest in, say, luxury and style versus economy and safety. Often what is needed to reflect this variability is an approach to segmentation defined with respect to the motivations and requirements associated with each particular product category. For example, the photography buff with high-tech, high-status camera equipment may have a no-frills requirement when it comes to automobiles and may drive a reliable economy car. A marketer of cars would want to know this individual's needs and feelings about the automotive category, not about status products or sophisticated technology in general.

Under some circumstances, it may be desirable to segment usage occasions rather than users' overall product requirements in a particular category—that is, to group purchase or consumption events on the basis of the immediate needs that triggered them. This approach first surfaced in the beverage category, where it was noted early on that the same consumer could be expected to have different requirements at different times: thirst, boredom, and so on. Applications have broadened to a variety of other categories in which needs and product choices are situational and do not reflect consistent or stable patterns of individual behavior. Florida citrus growers attempted to convince the public some years ago that orange juice was not just for breakfast anymore. In depicting the telephone call between life-long friends, AT&T reminds its customers of the pleasure of calling someone just for the emotional gratification it brings, not necessarily only to relay news.

IMPLEMENTING SEGMENTATION FOR EFFECTIVE MARKETING STRATEGY

The proliferation of segmentation options and the challenge of implementing them successfully places a heavy onus on both marketers and market researchers. The more abstract segmentation schemes in particular have attracted criticism. Charges leveled at attitude segmentation, for example, center on theoretical concerns about the accuracy of the methods, practical difficulties in applying the information, and the relative cost of conducting this type of study. Even advocates of multivariate segmentation techniques generally concede these difficulties, but they also advance the counterargument that attitude segmentation brings a company closer to understanding its marketplace and makes it better equipped to define a positioning and targeting strategy than it could without access to such tools.

Since most, if not all, contemporary product marketing strategies are based on market segmentation of some type, and no single market segmentation scheme is appropriate or desirable for all product categories or scenarios, a marketer must be willing to consider a variety of approaches in order to acquire a solid understanding of market structure and market opportunities. However, there is no simple set of principles that relate different marketing problems to corresponding segmentations. An attempt to grow share in the crowded soft drink category might require an occasion segmentation; a program to increase the appeal of low-fat beef might make use of a food attitude segmentation or a segmentation based on barriers to beef consumption. Each market must be approached on a case-by-case basis, with the guidance of experienced market research professionals to review options and maximize the returns on the segmentation scheme ultimately chosen.

The importance of market research in segmentation goes almost without saying, even though many successful product strategies have evolved from an intuitive segmentation of the market. No matter how intuitively obvious a market segmentation strategy may seem, it is important that it be based on research to help conceptualize market structure, identify targets, and develop product and message strategies. Of course, the more complex the segmentation scheme, the more complex—and costly—the research.

The marketer uses segmentation research to determine:

- Kinds and number of segments in the marketplace
- Approximate size of each segment
- Kinds of consumers in the identified segments and how they can be reached most effectively
- Product requirements of the consumers
- Kinds of marketing messages or themes that are most likely to get a response

Identifying Market Segments

Identifying market segments poses stiff challenges, particularly if segmentation has been conceptualized in fairly abstract terms. An important misconception about segmentation outside the research community is the presumption that market segments are real and simply waiting to be discovered. This view puts a premium on accuracy, when, in fact, market segments are an intellectual convenience—a way of structuring reality to help reduce the complexity of the marketplace. The fact is, there is no truly objective or absolute segmentation scheme waiting for discovery, and this is as true of many demographic and behavior segments as it is of more creative psychological ones. No one is absolutely young or old, rich or poor; even basic demographic concepts like upper-class and middle-class are arbitrary categories created to help marketers cope with a complex social structure.

Selecting Targets

Once the marketer has identified segments in the marketplace, the next requirement is to select targets. There is a variety of criteria that can be used to select targets, including one or more of the following:

- The size of the segments (number of consumers and the volume they represent)
- The brand allegiance (or "availability") of the segment
- The match between the product attributes or technological capabilities and the needs of the segment
- The regard in which the brand or product is held
- The age or life cycle stage of the segment, and the prospects for a continuing revenue stream once brand allegiance is cultivated
- Mean income of the segment (and any other demographic characteristic that might have an impact on purchase behavior)
- Media accessibility of the segment
- Compatibility of your distribution access with the segment's consumer purchasing patterns and channels

A common misconception about segmentation is that it requires a narrow focus on one group to the exclusion of all others. Actually, effective market segmentation draws as broadly as it can—often on more than a single segment—so long as the segments targeted all require compatible product features and messages. Low salt/low fat products, for example, were originally targeted at people whose diets were medically restricted, but these products are now directed at companion segments defined by weight-consciousness and general concern about nutrition.

In targeting multiple segments, however, it is important that they be truly compatible constituencies that can safely coexist and can "overhear" one another's messages. For example, it is possible to market a sporty family sedan—often seen as a contradiction in terms—but only so long as segmentation analysis suggests that there are consumers seeking the best of those two automotive worlds. By contrast, Days Inn motel chain could not simultaneously talk about luxury extras to the upscale traveler while speaking of clean, spare comfort to the thrifty one. Such an attempt to span both market positionings with an all-things-to-all-segments strategy would risk confusing and alienating both of these segments with a logically inconsistent product premise.

Accessing Segments

Accessing attitude segments that have been defined and identified poses a challenge to the marketer attempting to implement strategy. Suppose, for example, that marketing research suggests that a manufacturer of jeans aim for the "rugged sophisticate"—an underserved segment, average age 30, 60 percent male, that values durability and casual elegance. It is entirely reasonable for the manufacturer to ask the marketer: "How do I find these people? How will I know them when I see them? How will they recognize that I have their brand? And how do I track success with them?"

Consumer segments that are defined in abstract terms—like "rugged sophisticate"—are admittedly more difficult to identify and access than Republicans or women who are thirty-something, but the task is by no means impossible. The marketer can determine the media usage of target segments and can selectively appeal to that audience by structuring the product and defining its benefits in a way that research suggests meets the needs of this group. It is also possible to monitor marketing success within the target segment through tracking research, although this task requires more sophistication and finesse when attitude segments are targeted rather than behavior or demographic segments.

CONCLUSION

It is crucial for the marketer to understand how the needs and perceptions of a market segment may be changing and how well the product is meeting those needs. For example, Cadillac's failure to recognize that contemporary car owners were redefining luxury in terms of automotive performance, not merely price, left America's original luxury car vulnerable to a new generation of German—and now Japanese—competitors who have put engineering teeth in the luxury positioning.

Although a sound segmentation strategy should have at least several years of durability, rapidly changing trends and technologies can cause realignments in the marketplace. The current Baby Boomlet, for example, has done more to promote attention to automotive safety than years of zealous crusades by Ralph Nader, and car manufacturers are now capitalizing on parental sensitivities with appropriate features and positionings.

It is also important to make certain that the audience is, in fact, hearing the marketing message as it is intended to be heard. Market performance is usually a good indicator, but periodic reconfirmation is desirable to check for signs of "drift" or miscommunication. Skilled market research is an indispensible tool for this sort of market surveillance.

Effective marketing requires a customer weighting process that sometimes forgoes breadth of opportunity for market fit. Developing a segmentation strategy demands a candid assessment of the product and the available technical capabilities as well as a shrewd appraisal of the customers. Intensifying competition and, in many industries, dwindling margins place a premium on sound segmentation strategy. This environment requires marketers to aim for new levels of creativity and selectivity in their market assessments in order to garner strategic advantage in progressively narrower and more crowded domains.

18

Strategies for the Knowledge-Based Business

ANDREW GELLER

GEORGE MANDERLINK

LEE HAWLEY

ANDY BEAULIEU

The Hay Group, Inc.

INTRODUCTION

The technological revolution has significantly increased the amount of information available to businesses. This increase in data, together with the development of advanced technology for collecting information, has lead to the emergence of the knowledge-based business. In this type of organization, information is used to gain competitive advantage. This information may cover a wide range of areas, including customers and competitors. The resulting internal organizational structure is characterized by a flexibility and innovation that enable it to react more quickly and effectively than the competition to new ideas and rapidly changing market conditions. Knowledge-based organizations are structured so that accountability and autonomy exist at all levels rather than within a formal hierarchy. There are fewer levels of management, decentralized decision-making, and interdisciplinary teams of specialists working together at all levels of the organization.

The success of knowledge-based businesses stems in part from the ability of their employees to rapidly process large quantities of information into knowledge that can be used to competitive advantage. The speed with which information is processed has become a critical success factor in the information age. As market life cycles shorten, rapid, efficient integration of information across stages of development (e.g., market opportunity identification, design, production, delivery) has become increasingly important. In the auto industry, for example, U.S. manufacturers are scrambling to halve their product development cycles, which traditionally have run about five years from conception and design to production model.

In their search for information, businesses are also becoming increasingly integrated with other institutions. Specific information needs are spawning strategic alliances with customers and suppliers. To be sure, alliances have existed in the past, but the ability and willingness to share information among allies is new. For example, suppliers are expected in many cases to allow their buyers to look directly at production data, and at times, suppliers may tap directly into product performance data maintained by their buyers.

Business are even expanding their ties to academic institutions as sources of innovative information and potential employees. This type of integration differs from the full-scale vertical integration of the past, where every stage of production, from the extraction of natural resources to the final product, was controlled by the firm. In knowledge-based businesses, integration occurs among separate firms or groups, such as customers and employees. Integration in knowledge-based businesses accommodates the swift action demanded by the information age and fosters mutual benefit without compromising individual identity.

Despite the promise of greater autonomy and authority, knowledge-based businesses are not without challenges. Foremost among them are:

- *The need for more highly skilled employees.* Knowledge-based businesses require employees who can learn new skills, adapt to new situations, and make decisions under uncertain conditions. This demand for higher skills comes at a time when skilled labor is scarce.

- *Increased employee stress.* The quickening pace of technological change, the competitive pressures for continuous improvements in productivity, and ongoing organizational restructuring are making the information age increasingly stressful for employees.

• *Employee segmentation.* The upward mobility of employees engaged in "routine" work will diminish as "knowledge" work becomes more specialized and complex. Tomorrow's highly valued knowledge workers will require new ways of managing.

Strategy development and implementation require that management be aware of the new knowledge-based environment in which they and their organizations work. Planners and managers must adapt to a new strategic environment. This chapter discusses the implications and action alternatives of such an environment, and offers prescriptive measures that managers can take to overcome knowledge-related strategic challenges and thrive in the information age.

KNOWLEDGE-BASED ORGANIZATIONS AND EMPLOYEE CAPACITY

The knowledge-based organization is characterized by the need for workers with highly specialized skills and capabilities. Because knowledge-based businesses are geared to gathering and processing information by state-of-the-art methods, they require employees with the advanced education, training, and skills to work with sophisticated process technologies. These technologies have eliminated many low-skill positions, requiring workers in the remaining less-skills-intensive jobs to possess more analytical and diagnostic capabilities. For example, remaining workers on a welding line where robots have replaced some positions must maintain the robots and interpret production and quality data being compiled.

Employees at all levels of the knowledge-based organization are finding their jobs increasingly demanding. Employees need to demonstrate an ability to learn new skills, adapt to new situations, and to make decisions under conditions of uncertainty. The competitive success of the knowledge-based organization depends on the ability of its employees to create knowledge from information and apply that knowledge to add value to the company.

Opposing Demographic and Educational Trends

While the skill demands of knowledge-based businesses are increasing, the "baby bust"—the decline in U.S. birth rates that occurred after the post–World War II "baby boom"—has resulted in fewer college graduates and, consequently, a smaller entry-level work force. This decline will significantly affect companies heavily involved in new technologies (e.g., telecommunications, computers, robotics) that require a work force with skills learned mainly in the past few years.

Not only is the number of college graduates decreasing, but the percentage of science and engineering graduates is also on the decline. This trend will make it increasingly difficult for knowledge-based businesses to fill positions requiring highly specialized skills in the latest technologies.

The decline in the efficiency of the U.S. educational system to produce well-educated graduates is also affecting knowledge-based businesses. In addition to lacking the technological skills required by these organizations, recent graduates often are not proficient in basic language, math, and reading skills. In knowledge-based businesses, these skills are becoming increasingly important as flexible processes replace routine ones and as decision-making authority is given to employees at lower levels within the company.

Recruiting and Retaining Skilled Workers

The rising skill requirements of knowledge-based organizations and the dynamics involved in the supply of such employees have several implications for the business planner. First, human resource planning is becoming more uncertain and complex. For example, ongoing technological advances constantly require new skills, and trends in the labor market, such as increased competition, make recruiting more difficult and costly.

For hired employees, learning itself becomes a critical job skill; as the "half-life" of job skills shortens, learning new skills becomes a requirement to holding one's job. This requires ongoing training in order to maintain the competitiveness of the organization's knowledge resources. As knowledge-based businesses increase their internal training, they need to look externally and determine their role in the broader educational process. In addition, to attract and retain employees, these businesses must consider alternative actions that address nonwork issues and that use nontraditional strategies.

Addressing Nonwork Issues. To maximize its attractiveness to the available labor pool, the knowledge-based business can provide services to meet some of the nonwork needs of employees. For example, arrangements can be made to provide day care for children and elderly family members. In some cases, it may be possible to provide these services at an on-site location.

If such services cannot be provided, knowledge-based businesses can offer employees other options. For example, alternative work schedules can be instituted, including flex-time, where the start and finish time can vary by as much as two to three hours; job sharing; time-off banks, where time is given as a reward and used at the employee's discretion; and the work-at-home plan, which has the added benefit of reducing or eliminating commuting time.

Job discontinuities created by reduced-time schedules or leaves of absence can be "back-filled" by trainees who are phased in and out as part of a rotational assignment. Additionally, an internal temp pool can be created, possibly using retirees. Career discontinuities can be minimized by planning the reduced-time period or time off in the context of a longer-term career. For example, while the employee is on a reduced-time schedule or leave of absence, career discontinuities can be minimized through an active informal network with members of the organization. Special work projects can be created for the duration of the reduced time period (e.g., development work, proposal writing, special study).

Alternative, nonlinear career tracks (e.g., "mommy tracks") must be supported by strong top management and the appropriate organization culture. Such support is more forthcoming in knowledge-based organizations because emphasis is focused on results rather than methods, and the retention and use of all knowledge resources are more highly valued than in more traditional organizations.

Companies can benefit from a clear definition of their position on family issues. A position that demonstrates an awareness of family needs can be used to market the company to prospective employees. As family issues continue to receive a great deal of legislative attention, the company can help guide lobbying efforts either on its own or in partnership with other businesses.

Using Nontraditional Strategies. A number of action alternatives that employ nontraditional strategies can be used to increase the supply of skilled workers. For example, strategies can be developed to recruit and train women who have never been in the labor market. One such target group is the relatively large population of women over age 35 attending college (especially community colleges). In addition, special programs can be developed to alleviate potential fears and low self-confidence of women who have never worked outside the home.

Other strategies focus on identifying and recruiting skilled workers from outside the United States. These strategies might involve recruiting on overseas campuses and offering high-school graduates from other countries a company-sponsored college tuition reimbursement plan. Skilled workers can also be found by establishing employment networks in immigrant communities within the United States.

Another nontraditional strategy for increasing the supply of workers is to tap two frequently overlooked groups: the disabled and the elderly. Companies can profit from the pool of physically and mentally handicapped workers merely by paying attention to issues of ease of access and job appropriateness. For example, jobs made quite routine by automation are often ideally suited to some mentally handicapped employees who are able to maintain much higher levels of concentration and motivation for these repetitive tasks than nonhandicapped employees. In the case of the elderly, older workers could be recruited by offering alternative, flexible work arrangements. In addition, retirees could be recruited and retrained for special projects.

The more conventional strategy of moving work to where the workers are may have some novel applications, such as moving work into the home. A less traditional strategy of increasing the supply of workers would be to move workers to where the work is. This strategy might involve company-sponsored long-distance transportation or subsidized housing.

Company-Level Action Alternatives. Another broad category of action alternatives concerns company support of programs at the national, local, and corporate level to ensure a supply of skilled workers. Involved in this effort would be determining how the knowledge-based organization could support national education reform. Several other types of programs that could be established at the company level include:

- Multiservice adopt-a-school programs
- Company-run programs for teacher development
- Placement of company employees or retirees as teachers
- Transfer of advanced human resource management practices to schools
- Offering special business courses

A range of other programs could be developed within knowledge-based organizations that may perform such functions as:

- Training employees to be better managers of their children's education
- Providing resources to help parents assist in their child's education
- Involving employees as education volunteers

Other Action Alternatives. Knowledge-based organizations can add to their skilled work force by increasing employee skill level through special training. The most effective training approaches integrate organizational needs, adult-learning principles, and technological developments. The objectives of training programs developed out of such an integration are to:

- Support individual needs and learning styles
- Allow for continuous learning
- Incorporate employee evaluation and measurement
- Create universal delivery
- Provide training "on demand"
- Increase the portability of training

Technology itself can be used to increase the supply of workers. For example, particular tasks or activities may be simplified through technologies such as artificial intelligence or computer-based automation, thereby freeing workers to perform other tasks. However, using technology can create additional problems: Other tasks may be made more complex as a consequence; employee control may be reduced, which may increase stress and decrease motivation; opportunities for on-the-job skill development may be limited; and work simplification may help perpetuate a two-tier work force.

The level of technological sophistication of human resources professionals at knowledge-based businesses also has an impact on how effectively skilled workers are recruited and trained. The greater their understanding of the technological side of their organization, the more accurate human resources professionals will be in evaluating company needs vis-à-vis employee capabilities.

One way human resources professionals can acquire technological sophistication is by studying the impact of new technologies in specific areas of the company. Human resources professionals can also add value to their human resources programs by incorporating technologies such as computerized taxonomics of skills and tasks and computer-driven, multimedia educational delivery systems.

THE INFORMATION AGE AND STRESS

In hierarchically based organizations, authority ultimately rests at the highest management levels, and information is concentrated in the hands of a few. Knowledge-based organizations, however, distribute information to all concerned employees. Thus, the ability to make decisions—and the stress associated with that responsibility—is also distributed.

The Information Explosion

Knowledge-based organizations are more stressful than hierarchical ones in a number of ways. Not only are workers faced with the decentralization of information, but they must process great quantities of data. Fax machines, computers, mobile phones, and electronic mail all are increasing the amounts of information available to workers. In addition, the pace of work seems to be quickening. Communication is more rapid, creating pressure to think, decide, and act faster.

Escalating Skill Requirements

The same technological advances responsible for increased information are forcing workers to constantly update their skills. Clerical workers, who in the past could depend on the skills they acquired in high school to serve

FIGURE 18-1

Percent of Frequent Health Problems Related to Computerized Monitoring of Work Performance

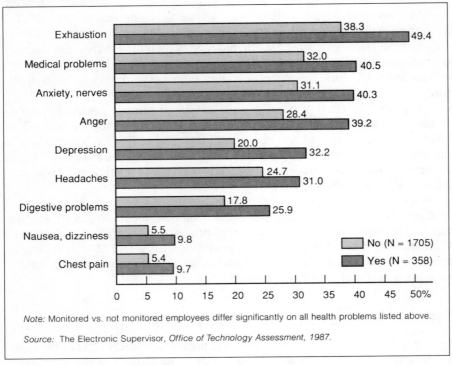

Note: Monitored vs. not monitored employees differ significantly on all health problems listed above.

Source: The Electronic Supervisor, *Office of Technology Assessment, 1987.*

them throughout their careers, must now be retrained to use computers. They must also be trained again whenever a new software or hardware program comes on line. The stress these workers experience from having to constantly update their skills is exacerbated by the fact that, as a result of new technology, close employee monitoring is now more widely used. Such monitoring is itself a source of stress and frequently leads to health-related problems, as shown in Figure 18-1.

Organizational Causes of Stress

Particularly in knowledge-based businesses, workers are having to "run faster just to stay in place." Changes in the external competitive business environment are continuing to raise expectations and demands for improved productivity. Increased competition is lowering tolerance for poor (and even average) performance; as a result, compensation and job security are becoming more contingent on performance. Figure 18-2 shows

FIGURE 18-2

Percentage of Employees Reporting "Poor Performance Not Tolerated"

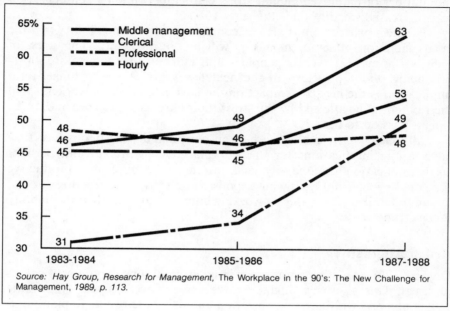

Source: Hay Group, Research for Management, The Workplace in the 90's: The New Challenge for Management, 1989, p. 113.

an increasing trend by employees at all levels to report that their company does not tolerate poor performance.

Even when individual performance is good, there can be increased stress. Organizations are increasingly passing on to their employees the risks of the overall business performance. Base salaries may be cut, and incentives, dependent on performance, substituted. Jobs themselves are more at risk, contingent on annual or even quarterly company performance.

Continued, frequent, and rapid organizational transformations are also sources of stress. Turbulence from changes in organizational ownership as well as more rapid entry into new markets also contribute to stress.

Organizational Implications

Business planners must take into account several significant organizational implications arising from the stressfulness of the information age. Most apparent are the significant economic and human resources costs and liabilities that are likely to result from these increased stress levels. Heightened stress levels can increase employee medical costs—as well as time lost on the job—at a time when U.S. health care expenses have risen sharply and are expected to continue to escalate through the year 2000. In addition, the number of employee mental stress claims for worker's compensation have increased steadily since the early 1980s.

Business planners must also be concerned with the possibility that the next generation of senior managers will be "burned out." The stress of today's jobs may leave fewer people willing and able to assume more stress-producing senior positions in the next few years. An even longer-term implication is the negative impact on the next generation of workers. Will their potential be affected by the stress their parents experience and, to an extent, pass on to them?

Although family matters are often considered nonwork issues, they have strong implications for the workplace. A significant and perhaps costly implication is that family needs interfere with employees' productive time on the job. Employees whose spouses also work often feel pressured to attend to family matters during working hours, or to limit their availability for overtime work.

Action Alternatives

Organizations can adopt strategies aimed at modifying certain root causes of stress. This approach might involve surveying employees on specific causes of stress within the organization and using the results to plan intervention programs. For example, well-planned communications distributed before and during periods of company reorganization can minimize the negative impact of such transitions by enabling employees to understand, predict, and perhaps control the impact of the change.

Other preventive strategies include analyzing how new technologies will affect employee stress before they are introduced into the company. Additionally, existing jobs can be analyzed and redesigned in terms of key stress-related dimensions (e.g., job demands and work control). The organization's culture can also be examined to determine how effectively it buffers stress (for instance, the extent to which the organization values employee effort, loyalty, and diversity). Supervisors and managers can be trained to identify signs of stress and to create methods of management that will minimize stress. Other programs that can alleviate stress include time off in addition to normal vacation, planned sabbaticals, and realistic job previews and socialization experiences.

Treatment programs for employees experiencing stress can be explored. Employees can be encouraged to have periodic stress evaluations by licensed health professionals and can be educated about stress-reducing treatments. The corporation's employee assistance programs can also be expanded to deal with such stress-related problems as alcoholism and drug abuse.

SEGMENTATION OF THE KNOWLEDGE-BASED ORGANIZATION

In knowledge-based organizations, the tradition that workers can move from bottom to top through native ability and hard work is becoming obsolete. Instead, the key segmentation is between "routine workers" and "knowledge workers." Routine workers are those with relatively simple, scripted tasks; knowledge workers engage in more analytic, specialized work. Frequently, though not always, the two groups differ in educational background, with the knowledge worker generally having a college or advanced degree. Because of the skill demands of knowledge work, it is increasingly difficult to move from routine work to knowledge-level work without returning to school.

Routine Work

The availability and viability of routine work is diminishing. Technology is a major contributor to this trend, having replaced so much unskilled labor. Notice, for example, the recent change in the telephone operator's job. After the operator performs the telephone number look-up (aided by a computer data base), a voice-generator announces the number to the caller. This new system reduces errors, but it also reduces the number of telephone operators needed.

Many routine jobs are now filled on a just-in-time basis; that is, workers are hired only for those hours or periods of the year when their services are required. While this saves the company money, it also makes these jobs less desirable.

The trend is clear. Workers with few technical or analytic skills are becoming less able to earn a decent living, and are becoming less able to bridge the gap and move into higher-paying positions. As we continue to move into the information age, a growing portion of the population is in jeopardy of being left behind.

Knowledge Work

While there will continue to be some routine work within the organization, knowledge-level work is expanding as a result of the sophistication of the technology used by the organization and it implements that technology. In addition, certain production work has now become "knowledge" work because of the more advanced technical and problem-solving requirements of the job. For example, robotics have replaced some routine jobs with fewer but more highly skilled operator and maintenance positions.

Organizational Implications

Knowledge-based organizations must understand the special needs of knowledge workers in order to attract and retain them. These needs include learning, autonomy, opportunities to make socially recognized contributions, and special, or star, status.

Management systems must undergo changes in order to motivate, develop, and provide a suitable environment for knowledge workers. Within this new system, emphasis must be placed on developing the ability to self-manage; manage the boom-bust cycles of performance; move from job definitions to role definitions; design compensation packages without a comprehensive understanding of the scope of the job; and maintain direction in the absence of clear career paths.

The challenges of managing key contributors and teams are continuing to increase. The management of knowledge workers within knowledge-based organizations requires adjustments to the concepts of performance management, job evaluation, compensation, and authority and control.

Action Alternatives

To address the challenges of a more highly divided work force, it is necessary to develop an understanding of the typology of workers within the organization. This includes distinguishing routine work from work that is becoming more knowledge-based, and identifying the needs, values, and attitudes of workers in these two categories. The resulting profiles should influence the appropriate management processes and human resources practices. Uniform and standardized policies and practices are likely to be untenable.

A tendency will be to "spotlight" key contributor knowledge workers. Before such a "star system" is implemented, however, the negative attitudes associated with it need to be understood. Spotlighting can be demotivating for those not recognized, especially when they have contributed to the success of the "stars." Human resources management techniques should be developed to "diffuse the spotlight" in order to maintain a stability of purpose and culture within the organization. For instance, career paths can be structured around the stars of the organization. Culture seems to be an especially important variable in providing the bond between the knowledge worker and the organization.

Given the increasing emphasis on productivity and performance, and the tendency for some young knowledge workers to become tense and inflexible under pressure, knowledge-based organizations need to develop means for managing failure so that innovation and appropriate risk-taking are supported. The object is to increase the resilience of knowledge workers —especially those subject to unusual amounts of stress.

Knowledge-based organizations can help control conflict between routine and knowledge workers through public-private partnerships for economic and community development. Businesses can also counsel social-service agencies in management practices and offer outreach programs to underprivileged youths to assist them in obtaining the skills necessary to obtain jobs in their organizations. In addition, company policies and perquisites can be made more egalitarian, and the interaction of different employee groups can, if managed well, improve mutual understanding.

CONCLUSION

Business strategy formulation requires close attention to the components of the company's competitive advantages and the requirements for sustaining that advantage. These components include proprietary technology, capital, and customer relationships. In the 1990s, however, competitive advantage will come increasingly from the company's employees and its use of information.

In an increasingly tight market for skilled workers, the organization that can attract and retain the best of them will have an advantage. The ones that organize in ways that allow expression of special skills will be able to exploit that advantage. Only by doing so will a company be able to fully utilize the new technologies of the information age.

Business planners must therefore pay close attention to human resources trends both within and outside their organizations. They must carefully chart the complex interactions between these trends and the changing requirements of the organization's information technology.

If all of these elements can be incorporated into the organization's strategic business planning, and those plans are successfully implemented, the organization will have created a significant and sustainable competitive edge.

19

Turnaround Strategies

DONALD C. HAMBRICK
Columbia University

INTRODUCTION

A turnaround is a special management situation, typified by limited resources, poor morale, skeptical allies, and urgency. Heated global competition, the high cost of capital, and maturing markets have made situations requiring turnarounds more common than ever.

This chapter discusses the main issues and options confronting a turn-around manager, with some practical considerations for implementation. It draws on actual studies of troubled firms and turnaround efforts to portray key issues. While discussions of some points, such as the four recurring causes of downturn and the five main types of turnaround strategies, may seem oversimplified, this approach is necessary, since it is hardly useful to lay out a long stream of anecdotes along with the shallow wisdom that no two turnaround situations are the same. The goals of this chapter are to broaden the turnaround manager's vision of the kinds of analyses and actions that may be undertaken and to help the manager narrow the choices to those most pertinent in his own situation.

OVERVIEW OF THE TURNAROUND SITUATION

Most firms would like to be performing better than they are, but only a fraction can be said to be in need of a "turnaround" as the word is meant here. A precise definition of a turnaround situation is not important, but it is useful to put rough boundaries on the terrain. As a starting point, a turn-around situation is defined as one in which business performance is persist-ently below some minimally acceptable level. A business whose mission is generating profits would be in a turnaround situation if it earned less than the firm's cost of capital. Excluded from the definition are businesses that are moderate performers and those whose poor performance is due to short-term industry cycles (such as cement and fertilizer companies.)

Distinguishing Features

Turnarounds call for a different way of thinking and different types of actions than do other strategic situations. Four factors serve to set apart turnaround situations from other strategic settings: limited resources, poor internal morale, skeptical stakeholders, and urgency.

- *Limited resources.* Almost by definition, a troubled firm has limited resources for improving its situation. Depending on how long the firm has been performing poorly, a turnaround manager can encoun-ter a situation of high debt levels, overextended payables, and aged plant. Banks and the parent firm are usually reluctant to infuse more funds. A classic example is Scripto. Herbert Sams took over the presi-dency of ailing Scripto in 1971, following three years of losses. Retained earnings were at a ten-year low, debt (most of it current) was at an all-time high, fixed assets were dated, and the bloated inventories were generally unsalable. This situation is not unusual for the turnaround manager. The challenge for such a manager is to work with what is available, find ways to stretch resources, and find terrain that somehow tolerates the firm's sharply restricted resources. Some of the strategies open to managers in other settings—aggressive pricing, heavy advertising, product development, and plant modernization—are effectively ruled out because of limited resources, at least in the short run.

- *Poor internal morale.* The turnaround manager usually confronts a dismal personnel situation. If the firm has been a longtime poor performer, there are probably few talented or aggressive people left. A general malaise will have set in, such that even if there are capable people who remain, they will feel sapped. Even in situations where a downturn has been recent, it is not unusual to find poor morale, bickering among units, and lack of confidence among employees at all levels. A common wag among turnaround specialists is "All the stars are circulating their résumés, while the deadwood is circulating the water cooler." It is not enough that the turnaround manager has limited financial resources. The people needed to apply those resources creatively are usually in short supply or in disarray.

- *Skeptical stakeholders.* An organization exists in a broader environment and is dependent on certain stakeholders in that environment. Examples of stakeholders are suppliers, creditors, distributors, franchisees, and unions. For the troubled firm, there is a natural tendency for these parties to withdraw support, especially if they feel that they have viable alternatives. For example, angry creditors, bondholders, and shareholders forced a federal court to remove effective control of Eastern Airlines from its parent corporation. Management was turned over to a court-appointed trustee, who daily faced the prospect of Eastern's liquidation. Not only is the turnaround manager in a position of having to work with limited resources; there is also the threat that even those resources will be taken away.

- *Urgency.* Taken together, the above factors clearly suggest the fourth distinguishing characteristic of turnaround situations: Time is of the essence. Unlike the manager of a more stable status quo operation, the turnaround manager must act promptly, since allies are getting restless, key employees are preparing to leave, and competitors typically are making rapid inroads. Poor corporate performance, gone unchecked, becomes a rapidly deteriorating spiral. This urgency has implications for the ways in which decisions must be made, for the substance of those decisions, and for the sequence of actions.

What is clear is that the turnaround manager basically only gets one round of moves. Everything attempted must work; there is no slack; there is no organizational resilience; patience is frayed. Therefore, the selection of moves must be sound, and the orchestration must be smooth.

The turnaround situation is one of awesome responsibility, where many jobs, careers, and financial and physical resources lie in the balance of a few key decisions. Analysis must be quick, but not cavalier. Turnaround managers have an important job, but they do not operate from on high. They must know the limitations of their data and their limitations in acting on the data.

Stages of the Turnaround

Most turnarounds can be thought of as having three stages: crisis, stabilization, and rebuilding. In practice, these stages are blurred together and cannot possibly be conducted in strict sequence. But, knowing about them gives the turnaround manager some sense of the ground that needs to be covered.

It is tempting to treat evaluation as the first discrete stage in a turnaround. After all, the manager needs a period—even a brief one—in which to gather data and deliberate on alternative courses of action. But, it is preferable to view evaluation as something that is done throughout a turnaround, not only at its start. The front-end planning needs to be done, but it cannot be exhaustive. All of the contingencies cannot be foreseen at the outset. Throughout the entire turnaround effort, the manager is re-evaluating and adjusting course. There is an incremental element to turnarounds, just as there is to any other strategic situation—possibly even more.[1]

The features of the three stages are as follows:

- *Crisis.* Depending on the severity of the situation, the manager's first task is to ensure the survival of the business. This primarily means arresting cash outflow, or what many turnaround specialists call "stopping the bleeding." This can involve small steps such as putting clamps on accounts payable or instituting restrictive travel and expense account policies. It can also mean major steps such as disposing of inventories, closing down or selling plants, and firing people.

- *Stabilization.* After the trauma of the crisis stage, the task is to stabilize the remaining operations. The company is no longer shrinking, but it is not growing, nor is it capable of growth. Attention is directed at improving margins, fine-tuning the product mix, targeting new high-return market segments, and seeking new efficiencies. New control and information systems are often put in place. At this point, these systems are not elaborate; they are only the minimum necessary to support the firm's quest for stability and breathing room.

- *Rebuilding.* Only after successfully dealing with the crisis and stabilizing the firm can the turnaround manager attempt once again to expand the business. In the rebuilding stage, several activities of an entrepreneurial quality can be started or accelerated: product development, aggressive marketing campaigns, and asset renewal/expansion. In addition, more ambitious programs can be started in the

---

[1] James B. Quinn, *Strategies for Change: Logical Incrementalism* (Homewood, Ill.: Richard D. Irwin, 1980).

areas of human resource development, control, and information systems. In many respects, the rebuilding stage is like any other strategic situation, since many of the extraordinary features of the turnaround will have passed. If the firm is lucky, the lessons learned will remain.

There are no convenient rules of thumb to predict how long each of these stages will last or how long the whole process takes. Obviously, the time periods vary depending on the severity of the situation, the nature of the industry, the size of the firm, and other factors. However, available research generally supports the time frame elaborated by one author.[2]

The length of time necessary to perform each stage can vary dramatically. It takes anywhere from two weeks to six months to make value judgements about a business. A small company takes two weeks; a billion dollar company takes six months. If you are going to liquidate parts of the business, it takes ninety days from the time you decide to liquidate until you actually clean out the warehouse. If you are selling off segments of the business, it's a six-month process from the time you decide to sell. The period of stabilization takes six months to a year. The return-to-growth phase takes at least another year. Altogether, we are talking about anywhere from one to three years, with a $20 million company taking one year, and a [billion-dollar company] taking three years.

SITUATION ASSESSMENT

The turnaround manager's first task is to gather and analyze facts about the firm's situation. Since resources and time are limited, this assessment of the situation must often be less thorough than would otherwise be ideal. The manager must be creative and astute in deciding what types of analyses are most important and where the underlying data will come from.

Diagnosis of Severity

Just how bad is the company's situation? This is the starting point for the turnaround manager. A host of factors will eventually be of interest: morale, product quality, equipment reliability, and so on. But, at the broad level, the interest is financial: How far is the firm from making money, and how much longer can the bills be paid? The classic techniques for answering these questions are break-even analysis and cash-flow analysis.

- *Break-even analysis.* The technique of break-even analysis is discussed in most managerial accounting books, but its relevance usu-

---

[2] Donald B. Bibeault, *Corporate Turnaround: How Managers Turn Losers Into Winners* (New York: McGraw Hill Book Co., Inc., 1982).

ally eludes executives in healthy businesses. For turnaround managers, however, break-even analysis is of central importance. So, a brief review here seems appropriate.

A firm's break-even point, as seen in Figure 19–1, is that level of volume at which revenues equal total costs. Total costs consists of two components: fixed costs and variable costs. Fixed costs, as the name suggests, do not vary with output levels. Examples of fixed costs are depreciation, supervisory salaries, interest, and advertising. In reality, of course, these costs are fixed over some range of output, but they can be adjusted if volume rises or falls sharply. Thus, a more accurate portrayal of fixed costs would be as a series of steps—level over a small range and then increasing abruptly. The schematic is much easier to follow, however, if the portrayal is perfectly flat, since this implies that these costs will occur regardless of volume.

Variable costs are those that vary directly with volume. Direct labor, direct material, power, and sales commissions are examples of variable costs. Thus, when volume is zero, variable costs are at zero. For schematic simplicity, variable costs are portrayed here as rising in a linear relationship with volume, even though nonlinear relationships (through quantity discounts, critical mass efficiencies, and so on) are possible.

Strategic turnaround options are discussed in a later section. However, it is apparent at this point that the situations facing turnaround managers in Firms A, B, and C in Figure 1 are very different. Firm A is actually operating slightly above the break-even point. The firm has some leeway and may not have to pass through the crisis stage. To some extent, the managerial task in Firm A could be seen as fine-tuning a generally viable enterprise. Firm B, operating slightly below the break-even point, is in a more serious situation, and will have to undertake more severe actions than Firm A. And, finally, Firm C, is far below the break-even point and faces the most radical reshaping of its volume/cost/capacity relationships. Firm C has to acknowledge that it is not going to be as large as its decision makers once thought that it would be.

• *Cash-flow analysis.* If break-even analysis gives an indication of the magnitude of the firm's problems, cash-flow analysis sheds light on the degree of urgency. There is nothing elaborate about preparing a cash forecast, and, in fact, it is more straightforward than preparing an earnings forecast. Usually, a cash forecast is broken out on a monthly basis. The starting point is today's cash on hand. To that is added the expected cash receipts for each month (accounts receivable stemming from earlier sales, less bad debts) and any special infusions of cash (e.g., from inventory liquidations and sale of assets). Then subtracted out are all expected cash outlays (such as wages, payables due, taxes due, and equipment purchases). The remaining figure is the expected cash balance at the end of the month.

FIGURE 19-1

Example of a Break-Even Chart

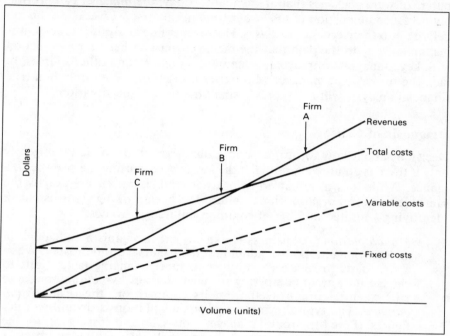

It is not unusual for a healthy firm to develop projections in which cash flow for some months is negative. For the troubled business, there is the prospect of an unending procession of such months, and the turnaround manager needs to know how long it will be—under current conditions—until cash will be completely gone. Businesses that have a seasonal element—which most businesses do—need to do a particularly careful cash-flow analysis. Of course, businesses that are part of larger firms often have their parents' coffers to tide them through a severe period. But, even in such a case, a cash-flow analysis is important.

The use of break-even and cash-flow analysis provides opportunities for the turnaround manager to ask a variety of "What if" questions. For example, what would be the effect on cash flow if payables could be stretched out by another 30 days or obsolete inventories are disposed of? What would be the effect on the break-even point if a five-cent-an-hour concession is won from the union or if an underused facility is closed down? Asking these sorts of questions is a valuable way for the turnaround manager to grasp the dimensions of the situation. With the help of a qualified financial analyst who knows how to use any of the spreadsheet microcomputer software packages that are available today, the manager can profitably invest some portion of his or her time in the first six weeks on the job delving into these types of analyses. However, while analysis is crucial, it is just an adjunct to the data that the manager must gather from interaction with key managers, employees, customers, suppliers, and other sources. In fact, the turnaround manager who buries himself or herself only in sterile financial analysis will grasp only a small fraction of the situation.

Diagnosis of Cause

Decisions about how to turn around a business can be made intelligently only if there is an understanding of the key factors causing the poor performance. While it is true that no two turnaround situations are exactly the same, research on organizational failure has been strikingly consistent in identifying a limited number of common failure syndromes.[3]

- *Maladaptation.* A business is like any other organism embedded in an environment: It must adapt in order to survive and prosper. When a firm fails to revise its product to meet changing tastes, fails to change its way of competing to meet changes by competitors, and fails to differentiate itself from its competition, the firm is *maladapted.* The typical symptom of maladaptation is dwindling sales figures. If the turnaround manager plots sales and cost figures for the past few years and observes a drop-off in sales (either in absolute dollars or in market share), but no major changes in costs, the conclusion must be that the firm is maladapted (Figure 19-2a). Maladaptation means either that volume is down or prices are down, both of which indicate that the firm is not in attractive terrain or is not well-positioned within its terrain.

- *Poor controls.* Some firms are troubled primarily by poor internal controls. Their sales are relatively healthy, but they are lacking in their ability to monitor and manage their various cost and current asset categories. Poor controls are often especially a problem in firms that are growing rapidly and/or are growing by acquisition. A look at the recent sales and cost figures for a firm plagued by poor controls will reveal steady or even growing sales, rapidly increasing fixed costs (inventory carrying costs, general and administrative expenses), and ballooning variable costs (e.g., poor labor controls, inefficient purchasing, shipping and distribution, and bad-debt write-offs) (Figure is not only 19-2b).

- *Excessive risk-taking.* If the essence of management is risk-taking, then the essence of good management is prudent risk-taking. Many firms end up in trouble because of excessive risk-taking—expanding at a rate in excess of the resources that the business will have avail-

---

[3] John Argenti, *Corporate Collapse: The Causes and Symptoms* (New York: John Wiley and Sons, 1976), p. 40.

FIGURE 19-2
Some Common Failure Patterns

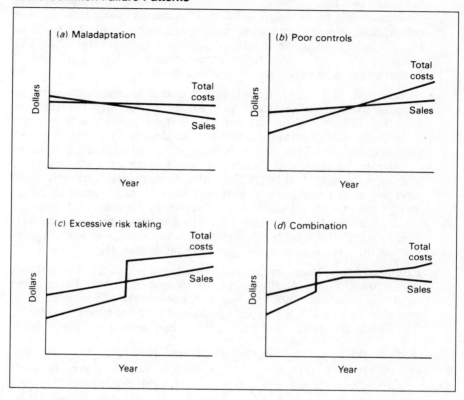

able in the near future. The most typical form of this is "the big project"—especially new plant and equipment installed in advance of sales at hand. The recent sales and cost figures for such a firm are portrayed in Figure 19-2c. Usually, there is a healthy sales trend which encourages the firm to make a major expansion, resulting in a sharp increase in fixed costs. Unfortunately, sales do not increase as steeply as the fixed costs. It could be said that this is a problem of maladaptation; but, frequently in this situation, sales are occurring at a respectable rate, and overoptimism is the real culprit. Variable costs per unit may actually diminish, since the new plant may result in somewhat greater efficiencies. The net effect, however, is usually substantial overcapacity, depleted cash, and a heavy debt burden. Other forms of excessive risk-taking are acquisitions, launching a new product, bulk purchase of materials, or any obligation that is large in relation to the resources of the firm.

For the turnaround manager, there is a great irony in the excessive risk situation. Often, the situation is more severe than one brought on by maladaptation or poor controls. That is, the gulf between costs and sales can be very great. However, the source of the problem tends to be more isolated. It is not as likely that there is widespread malaise, chaos, or ineptitude throughout the firm, as there would tend to be in other turnaround situations. Thus, the manager may have more reliable resources in the form of people, organization, and processes with which to work.

- *"Uncontrollables."* This term is put in quotes because managers are prone to attribute their problems to forces outside their control. It is true that factors such as foreign competition, government actions, technological discontinuities, and natural disasters can play a major part in crippling a firm. But, only some subset of such circumstances —probably a small one—is totally unforeseen or unmanageable. Management needs to be vigilant about such possibilities; it must navigate so as to avoid their potential impact, and it must find creative ways to respond when they do occur. The turnaround manager must decide whether the problem really has emanated from the outside or whether the problem is systemic, and resides in some fundamental internal weakness that needs to be dealt with.

- *Combinations.* Many turnaround situations, of course, stem from some combination of the problems described above. Often, one weakness brings on another: The firm encounters one form of trouble, and then acts in a way that brings on another type of problem. The financial symptoms of such a firm are portrayed in Figure 19-2d.

What should be clear from this discussion is that even though the details of turnaround situations occur in endless variety, there are some major commonly recurring classes of turnaround situations. Strategic responses can also be grouped in ways to help managers find the most logical matches between sources of problems and avenues for recovery.

Internal Assessment

The turnaround manager should delve beyond financial indicators in order to determine the firm's strengths and weaknesses. He or she must conduct an internal analysis quickly and with generally sketchy information. Thus, the manager must target the inquiry. One way to proceed is to identify the dimensions of key importance in the industry. This will normally be a list of at least five factors, but it should not contain more than twenty factors. Then, the manager must try to learn how the firm rates on each dimension. The manager should be able to conclude whether the firm, when rated against key competitors, is in the bottom third, the middle third, or the top third on each dimension. Those dimensions where the firm scores low are those that either (1) the firm should steer clear of in crafting a turnaround strategy, or (2) the firm must correct if the dimension is a key survival factor in the industry. Those dimensions on which the firm is strong should form the basis for locating a way of competing.

Precision in this assessment is not as important as objectivity, since firms routinely fool themselves as to their strengths and weaknesses. Hard data should be used whenever available. If only subjective impressions are available, it is important to obtain such impressions from multiple sources, including some outside "objective" parties, with the aim of striving for convergence in identifying the firm's real strengths and weaknesses.

Environmental Assessment

A turnaround attempt must, of course, take into account what is occurring in the environment. Strategy books and articles can provide excellent frameworks for conducting an environmental analysis, which should address technology, markets, competitors, suppliers, the economy, political scene, and cultural/demographic factors. As with an internal analysis, the environmental assessment must be done more hastily than might be the case in other strategic situations. So, here again, targeting is important. Four examples of questions about environmental factors that seem most germane in turnaround situations are the following:

1. How rigid are market shares? Can the firm realistically expect to increase its volume? As a product life cycle matures, customer loyalties become entrenched and competitors become more tenacious, such that certain turnaround avenues are effectively cut off.

2. What are the current pockets of market opportunity? For example, what segments are "hot" right now? In order to pull through the crisis era of turnaround, the firm may have to be opportunistic. Attention to long-term, secular trends can be postponed until the firm is ready for its rebuilding phase.

3. What are the firm's competitors doing? For example, are they leaving any vacuums that the firm can fill? Are they preempting some segments? Are there some inexpensive "me too" tactics that can be pursued?

4. What are the economics of this business? For instance, can some subassemblies be economically contracted out? Can goods be shipped from just one plant instead of three regional plants?

Sources of Information

A major frustration for the turnaround manager is that the information needed to do a situation assessment is often not at hand. After all, the company probably got into trouble because its management was not scanning the right information. Subordinates in the marketing and control functions, for example, may be completely in the dark about some important facts.

The turnaround manager must be creative and aggressive in pulling together the important facts. The first source is internal. It may be that the functional heads *do* have good data that the previous general manager had not asked for or had ignored. The turnaround manager must open up all information passageways, even if it means bypassing a functional head to tap into a subordinate's information base.

The firm has stakeholders who can be sources of good information. Suppliers and customers can be experts on the economics and competitive trends in the industry. Certainly, it is important to tap these sources regarding the firm's posture relative to competitors. Also, if the business is part of a larger corporation, it is likely that some line or staff units elsewhere in the firm are knowledgeable about key events and trends in the industry. Their expertise should be tapped, even though there is often a natural hesitance to go to the parent for advice or help.

In addition, there is an abundance of publicly available data on most industries. Trade journals, government statistics, industry yearbooks, and newsletters are good examples of data sources for the turnaround manager —especially one who is new to the industry. All of these sources, along with sparing use of consultants to help mold the data into a meaningful whole, can give the turnaround manager a reasonable picture of the firm's internal and external situation in as short a time as six weeks.

STRATEGIC COMPONENT OF TURNAROUND

At the heart of the decisions facing the general manager are those dealing with strategy: choices of where to compete (in terms of products and markets) and how to compete (e.g., asset structure, functional emphasis). Strategy is the topic of this section

Generic Turnaround Strategies

Turnaround strategies, like the failure syndromes discussed previously, can be concisely grouped: (1) revenue push, (2) cost cutting, (3) selective product/marketing pruning, (4) major retrenchment, and (5) combination strategies.[4] These options are listed roughly in ascending order of their degree of short-term unpleasantness, with revenue push being least traumatic and major retrenchment typically being the most traumatic for an organization. Each strategy consists of sub-moves that must "hang together" to allow it to succeed, although the timing of turnaround strategies varies.

---

[4] Charles H. Hofer, "Turnaround Strategies," *Journal of Business Strategy* (Spring 1980), pp. 19–31; Donald C. Hambrick and Steven M. Schecter, "Turnaround Strategies for Motive Industrial-Product Business Units," *Academy of Management Journal* (Fall 1983), p. 50.

Revenue Push. In some turnaround situations, it is possible and appropriate to put the primary effort into increasing sales. Such a strategy can be successful only if market shares are not rigid and/or if niches exist where the firm can use some special advantage. A revenue push strategy, of course, requires that the firm have some underused competence in product development, sales, or marketing. If these functions are generally deficient, then a revenue push strategy will not succeed, at least not without first replacing or revitalizing the sales/marketing or product development staffs. At least one study has found that revenue push strategies are not often successful in mature industries.[5]

Since time and money are limited in a turnaround situation, a revenue push strategy must somehow be crafted so that large upfront outlays are not required. This usually rules out totally new products, where tooling, customer education, and sales force education are required. Instead, selective reintroductions of products earlier dropped, expansion to new geographic markets or to different types of users, and taking on subcontracting work to help fill capacity are among the relatively inexpensive and quick avenues open for expanding the revenue base.

Some mention should be made about the tactic of price cutting to build sales. In general, this is a flawed move in a turnaround situation. Usually, the turnaround firm does not have the financial resources to wage any sort of price war. And, as often as not, the turnaround firm—as part of its broader symptoms—does not have the efficiency edge that will allow it to have the lowest unit costs in the industry. Price cuts will only provoke retaliatory moves by stronger competitors who can generally afford even lower prices and who can sustain those prices for a longer period of time than the troubled firm. A wise revenue push strategy will involve differentiating and niche-seeking behavior and will avoid price cutting. The key seems to be in locating new markets based on competitors' weak spots.

Cost Cutting. Some turnaround situations are best dealt with by various forms of belt tightening, or cost cutting. Sometimes, such moves require careful negotiations, as when wage or work rule concessions are sought from a union. Other such moves can be made more unilaterally. Examples are decisions to cut advertising, research and development, travel/entertainment, or managerial pay, or to centralize purchasing. Also part of a cost-cutting strategy—although not involving costs per se—are attempts to drive down inventory levels and to seek quicker collection of accounts receivable in order to free cash.

A cost-cutting strategy has the advantage of achieving its results quicker than the other strategies. But, the magnitude of those results is usually lim-

---

[5] Hambrick and Schecter, op. cit., p. 51.

ited. That is, in many circumstances, cost cutting alone is insufficient to turn the firm around. It is also important to note that cost cutting sometimes so enfeebles the firm that it is sent into an even deeper slide, thus further delaying (or even ruling out) the eventual stabilization process.

Selective Product/Market Pruning. This strategy is aimed at having the firm focus on those arenas that are most lucrative or in which the firm's position is most defensible. Sometimes, whole product lines are dropped, but often, there is careful pruning of each product line's breadth and depth to get rid of marginally profitable items that proliferated during earlier good times. Sometimes, pruning will be done around market considerations—scrapping lines where demand is dwindling or where competition is fierce. And, sometimes, pruning will be done around competence considerations—scrapping lines where the firm is at a competitive disadvantage or is just a "me too" player whipsawed by stronger competitors.

A look at the profile of a firm after it has executed a pruning strategy will reveal some or all of the following changes:

- Decrease in sales by 10–20 percent
- Decrease in capacity utilization—letting least-efficient plants sit idle (or, ideally, disposing of the assets)
- Increase in gross margin percentages—the firm is now in lines where prices are stronger and where it has relative efficiency
- Decrease in marketing expenses and inventories as a percent of sales— the firm has a more homogenous set of customers and products, allowing for improved efficiencies in these areas
- Reduced receivables as a percent of sales—the firm drops marginal customers or those who exert a great deal of power over credit terms.[6]

Major Retrenchment. The most traumatic turnaround strategy is one that involves a major retrenchment. This strategy differs from the pruning strategy in terms of the magnitude of the cutbacks. Here, major plant closings and consolidations are required, and the primary aim is to reduce fixed costs and the asset base. Selection of this strategy amounts to an awareness that the firm simply cannot be as large as earlier decision makers thought it could be.

With this strategy, as with pruning, selectivity should be exercised. But the selectivity here is not nearly as fine, since more of the business must be closed down. Generally, only assets that are certain to be used in the near term should be kept. The sale of assets should be done aggressively but with great deliberation, since the sale price of most fixed assets can vary within a wide range, depending on timing and careful identification of interested buyers. Unfortunately for the firm, newer facilities are those that bring the high-

---

[6] Ibid.

TABLE 19-1

Matches Between Turnaround Situations and Strategies

Source of problem	Severity of situation	
	Mild	Grave
Maladaptation	Revenue push	Product/market pruning or major retrenchment
Poor controls	Cost cutting	Cost cutting or product/market pruning
Excessive risk taking	Revenue push	Major retrenchment
Combination	Combination, with emphasis on revenue push and cost cutting	Combination, with emphasis on major retrenchment and cost cutting

est price, so there is an obvious trade-off between how much cash the business will get and the quality of the remaining assets.

Combination Strategies. In practice, the four turnaround strategies discussed here are often used in various combinations. Sometimes, if time allows, they are employed in series, for example, first pruning and then cost-cutting. Other times, the strategies are used simultaneously in a balanced effort. Such an approach is very complex, and usually requires a nucleus of talented managers in addition to the general manager. Still, this approach can be necessary if the firm's situation is severe and stems from multiple weaknesses.

Matching the Strategy With the Situation

Different situations call for different turnaround strategies. In order to discuss this "matching" process, the earlier classification of problem sources must be considered: maladaptation, poor controls, excessive risk taking, and "uncontrollables." A classification of the severity of the firm's troubles must be added to the list. Severity means the amount of negative gap between sales and costs. A firm making modest profits or operating just below the break-even point would be in a situation of mild severity. A firm operating well below the break-even point would be in a position of grave severity. The two classification schemes yield the framework for Table 19-l.

If maladaptation is the source of the problem and the situation is of mild severity, a revenue push strategy is logical. The firm has some financial resources with which to engage in new product/market initiatives. Its costs and assets are not necessarily out of line; rather, it primarily needs to update its offerings and to be more aggressive in the marketplace. Often, key marketing, sales, or product development personnel will need to be replaced to execute this strategy. If a maladapted firm's situation is of great severity, it will not have the resources to embark on any immediate entrepreneurial initiatives. Instead, selective product/market pruning or major retrenchment will probably have to be undertaken in order to refocus the business around a viable core. After stabilization has been achieved, product/market initiatives can be undertaken.

For a firm suffering from poor controls and facing a situation that is not severe, a cost-cutting strategy is generally appropriate. The primary emphasis must be on getting costs under control. Since the situation is not severe, the generally limited impact of a cost-cutting strategy may be sufficient to move the firm to much better health. On the other hand, if the situation is severe, a firm plagued by poor controls must often go beyond cost cutting and also engage in some form of scaling down—usually pruning. This is needed to allow the firm to become more manageable and to free up resources to see the firm through the turnaround.

If a firm is suffering the aftermath of excessive risk taking, but the situation is of mild severity, a revenue push strategy is often called for. The task is to achieve enough volume to fill the unused capacity. Since the situation is of mild severity, resources will often be available to engage in product/market development activities. If an excessive risk situation is severe—that is, if assets are far underutilized—then the realistic strategy is major retrenchment. It would be quixotic to attempt to achieve enough revenues to close such a huge gap, and cost cutting would barely make a dent and would not address the problem at all.

If "uncontrollables" are the primary cause of the firm's troubles, the strategy must be selected to respond to the particular circumstances. So many types of "uncontrollables" can occur that it is not possible to narrow down to one or two likely strategies here. (Uncontrollables are not included in Table 19-1 for this reason.) For example, a strike would suggest very different actions than would import dumping. Turnaround managers should ask themselves candidly whether the underlying problem really has been "uncontrollable" or whether there might not be some notable deficiency in the organization that will impede an effective turnaround.

If a combination of problems plagues the firm, then, logically, some combination of strategic moves is probably necessary. In situations of mild severity, an emphasis on revenue push and cost-cutting measures will often be sufficient to stabilize the firm. In situations of greater severity, the more stringent strategies of pruning and retrenchment must likely play major roles in a turnaround.

In sum, there are three key patterns evident in Table 19-1:

1. The turnaround strategy must somehow respond to the real source of the problem, not the imagined source.
2. Situations of mild severity can often be dealt with by use of the less traumatic strategies such as revenue push and cost cutting, whereas situations of grave severity require pruning or major retrenchment.

3. Situations of mild severity can often be dealt with by use of a single strategic theme; situations of grave severity usually call for multiple themes.

Common Patterns in Unsuccessful Turnarounds

Far from all turnarounds are successful. Some turnaround failures are generally hopeless situations in which no one could possibly succeed. Other failures can be traced to managerial mistakes in the turnaround attempt. There are three broad classes of such errors: overkill, underkill, and inconsistency.

Overkill is the managerial error of excess. An obvious example is when the turnaround manager cuts costs to the bone, only to drive out all talented employees, strangle the marketing effort, and slash product quality. A more subtle example occurs when the manager retrenches far more than is necessary. For example, as a result of the turnaround effort at A&P, the supermarket chain is just one-third the size it was in the early 1970s. Was that much cutback necessary? Some would say "yes," although the company did rebound sharply in the 1980s. But the turnaround manager can reach the point where he or she only relies on more and more surgery to achieve his or her aims. This is unimaginative management, and the resulting tiny firm— even if it is healthy—is not a turnaround; it is a new firm consisting of reassembled leftovers. A turnaround can easily be a "success" if the finished product is only one-third the size of the original.

Underkill is the more common error of not doing enough. Often, turnaround managers will make relatively minor adjustments in the hope that they will be adequate for a turnaround. The most common is to cut costs in only one or two areas, for example, research and development or advertising. By and large, such cuts are trivial, even though they may be painful and momentous in the eyes of the management. (As noted previously, sometimes, minor cuts are all that is needed.) Another form of underkill occurs when a strategy is poorly balanced. A relatively common example is the firm that attempts to expand its revenue base while allowing its efficiency and controls to deteriorate further. Clearly, the turnaround manager can avoid the polar pitfalls of overkill and underkill only by conducting an early and accurate situation assessment.

A final type of turnaround failure arises because of inconsistencies. In such an instance, the various components of the strategy are not mutually reinforcing and may even be flatly incompatible. An example found with striking frequency in one study is the firm that introduces a wave of new products at the same time that it cuts marketing expenses across the board.[7]

---

[7] Ibid.

Not only must the strategy fit the situation, but the individual pieces of the strategy must fit one with the other.

POLITICAL COMPONENT OF TURNAROUND

All businesses rely on striking favorable relationships with outside parties: suppliers, distributors, unions, and so on. For troubled businesses, attention to these links is especially crucial. This is because, as noted earlier, some stakeholders become skeptical and want to reduce their support for the troubled firm, just at the same time the firm needs more generous support. The successful turnaround manager must be able to conceive and execute an effective political component to the turnaround.

The starting place in a political analysis is to determine the amount and nature of the vested interest each major party holds in the turnaround firm. To the extent that a party is (1) very dependent on the firm and (2) has few alternatives, there is the basis for political maneuvering or negotiation. At one extreme is a party who is barely dependent on the firm and who has many alternatives. For example, if a supplier provides a firm with only a small portion of its output, and/or if there are ample alternative buyers for that output, then there is not much of a basis for negotiation. And, in fact, this will be the type of external party who will most promptly sever ties with a troubled firm. At the other extreme is the case of the supplier who sells 50 percent of its output to a firm; and all of the firm's major competitors are vertically integrated backward and so have no interest in the supplier's output. Such a situation is fertile ground for political maneuvering by the turnaround firm.

The turnaround manager needs to look beyond simply financial considerations in determining how dependent an ally is on the firm and the nature of that dependence. The key factor to bear in mind is that decisions by allies—like decisions by all organizations—are made by people, not by a black-box profit maximizer. These people have values, career aims, and political battles peculiar to their own organizations. Examples of these varied types of vested interests follow. At this point, it is important to understand that the turnaround manager will often find it worthwhile to learn something about the inner workings of a stakeholder organization and the values and perceptions of its key decision makers.[8]

The turnaround manager should be imaginative and comprehensive in identifying potential allies. Suppliers, distributors, franchisees, unions, trade associations, government agencies, and even competitors are among the numerous groups who might have an important stake in the survival of

---

[8] Ian C. Macmillan, *Strategy Formulation: Political Concepts* (St. Paul, Minn.: West Publishing Co., 1978).

the firm. Discussed below are political maneuvers involving these types of allies. That is followed by a discussion of political moves with a much more obvious constituency: creditors.

Arousing Support of Stakeholders

There are basically two ways to arouse support from stakeholders. The first is to alter the substance of the situation so that the stakeholder is even more dependent on the firm and its survival. This usually takes time, resources, and a naive stakeholder—all of which are usually in short supply for a turnaround firm. The second approach is to alter the stakeholder's perception of the situation. This usually amounts to extending graphic reminders of how dependent the ally is on the firm and providing some clear picture of the consequences—short-term and long-term—if the ally does not make concessions. Since this basically involves making threats, which often evoke personal antagonism and hence stubbornness, it is sometimes necessary to communicate with an ally through a third party—e.g., a board member, trade association executive, or even the press.

Some examples of extracting concessions from allies are in order:

- A troubled manufacturing firm convinced a local union leader to support its bid to revise the labor contract by presenting a detailed analysis of the cost makeup of the product and of the most direct Asian competitor's product. The company went on to stress that it would be prepared to provide the press with these figures. The national union had recently been the object of negative publicity regarding its intransigence in the face of inexpensive, high-quality imports and was eager to appear more flexible in negotiations. Since the local leader aspired to office in the national union, his cooperation was secured, and the contract negotiation was successful.
- Harley Davidson, the only maker of motorcycles in the United States, was able to obtain strict quotas on competing imports. Because it was a small company, its appeal could not possibly be on the grounds of overall economic impact. Instead, it sought out key parties in Washington and built a subtle, emotional appeal about the uniquely American "Harley," and how this instance of David and Goliath was a precursor of future such problems.
- Troubled Hudepohl Brewing Company, which serves primarily its hometown of Cincinnati, is able to get preferential shelf space and retailer support because it constantly reminds the dealer—sometimes explicitly, sometimes subtly—of the uncomfortable squeeze they will feel if Hudepohl (with about 25 percent of the Cincinnati market) were gone and only giants Miller and Anheuser Busch were left.
- Crown Cork and Seal, when severely troubled in the late 1960s, was able to get the major steel producers to undertake major product and

process research on its behalf, since the big can makers, American and Continental, had switched to aluminum. Tinplate had been a major revenue producer for the steel companies, and so they had a vested interest in keeping Crown Cork—a major tinplate user—afloat.

- Burger King, in the midst of a turnaround attempt, faced the threat of mass defections and even lawsuits from its disgruntled franchisees. The company had nothing substantive it could offer, but its top managers worked to communicate the details of the turnaround plan, including its content and timetable to the franchisees. The threatened defections were partially forestalled by the candor and aggressiveness of this communications campaign.

These examples are far from exhaustive, but they illustrate the types of concessions a turnaround firm might seek, the array of parties from which it might attempt to gain concessions, and the basis on which the negotiations might occur.

Negotiating With Creditors

Usually, the most nagging problem for a turnaround manager is a shortage of cash with which to fund strategic moves or even to pay off existing obligations. Negotiating with creditors is, in concept, no different from negotiating with any other ally. However, since favorable negotiations with creditors are so crucial to a turnaround, some special considerations are worth noting.

Banks are most responsive to a request for leniency or for more funds if the troubled firm can present a realistic but creative plan for the turnaround, along with some indication that the turnaround is already underway. For example, a bank might be more comfortable about a troubled firm's prospects if a new general manager is in place, the firm's labor contract has been renegotiated, and key suppliers have extended the firm's payable dates. For this reason, it is important to carefully plot the sequence in which negotiations with stakeholders are conducted. In the same vein, banks can sometimes be influenced by contacts from the firm's key suppliers or customers, especially if they too are key clients of the bank.

Banks also like to see benchmark dates by which the firm will make certain progress. A firm may ask to pay off a loan in 18 months, but the bank will be far more comfortable if the firm can point to interim dates by which key steps will be achieved—sale of some equipment by a certain date, a new product launched by a certain date, and so on. This is basically what Pan American Airlines did several times in the 1980s. The airline formulated detailed survival plans which, although not upbeat, were realistic and comprehensible. The banks, led by Citibank, concluded that they could keep a close pulse on progress, and so they agreed to provide the bridge financing for the survival plan.

A common mistake by turnaround firms and their banks is that they set their sights on the crisis stage of the turnaround and fail to lay the groundwork for financing the stabilization and rebuilding stages. Some would-be turnarounds are stopped short because of overanxious creditors. The task for the turnaround firm is to have some idea of how much money will be needed, and when it will be needed, to complete the entire turnaround. The firm should either portray the full picture to the bankers up front or have in mind a way of unveiling and negotiating the increments as the turnaround progresses.

HUMAN AND ORGANIZATIONAL COMPONENTS OF TURNAROUND

A turnaround manager, like any other general manager, is dependent on the firm's people and organization to achieve his or her aims. Before turning to potential actions in these areas that turnaround managers may wish to consider, it is important to review some common human and organization pathologies found in troubled firms.

Research has consistently concluded that firms often get into severe trouble because of an ineffective top manager. The most common form of this problem is the long-term autocrat: the top manager who requires all information to flow to him or her and who, in turn, makes basically all decisions. Such a "strong" chief executive can be the factor behind a firm's success as long as his or her biases and values are in line with what is required by the environment. But, as soon as there is a mismatch, severe trouble develops.

A turnaround manager who steps into the aftermath of this common situation generally finds that the upper-level and mid-level managerial talent is sparse, or at least atrophied. Talent could be sparse for two reasons: (1) The autocrat did not search for or select truly strong managers into the organization, and (2) over time, any capable and aggressive managers will have left the autocratic firm if they had alternatives. Generally, the longer the autocrat has been in place, the fewer creative and aggressive managers there are to assist in the turnaround. A more generous, yet sometimes quite accurate, view is that substantial managerial talent may reside in the firm, but it is simply atrophied from lack of use. Obviously, an important early task for the turnaround manager is to evaluate key people—a subject to which we will turn in a moment.

Studies of organizations under crisis have identified some other common symptoms that a turnaround manager must address. First, people in troubled organizations tend to act erratically; they make genuinely bad decisions in the face of crisis.[9] They misperceive data, integrate data poorly, and engage in precipitous and harmful interpersonal and interunit bickering. There are two broad implications from this for the general manager. The first is that tasks, structures, and processes must be put together in a way that responds to these problems. The emphasis must be on simplicity, explicitness, and pinpointing of responsibilities. The second implication is that the turnaround manager needs to sort out whether seemingly weak performers are inherently weak or are basically capable people just revealing various stress behaviors. If the latter, they still might have to be released, or they might somehow be harbored or reassigned so that their real talents can be tapped.

Another major symptom in troubled organizations is that behavior tends to be very rigid.[10] People seem to restrict information flows by limiting their scanning, relying only on formal information channels, and communicating in abbreviated form (for example, yes/no, stop/go, buy/sell). People also try to tighten control during a crisis by restricting information flows, attempting to concentrate power, and introducing complex systems of approvals for every action. To some extent, such control is called for in some turnaround situations, but its negative consequences should also be clear.

Evaluating Key Mangers

Since the general manager probably cannot intelligently make all decisions alone (even though he might be tempted to try) and certainly cannot execute and monitor all those decisions, he or she must compose a suitable managerial team as quickly as possible. Thus, the evaluation of key managers is one of the first and most important tasks to be conducted by the turnaround manager. As noted previously, there is a distinct likelihood that some managers will have to be fired or reassigned.

In evaluating key subordinates, the turnaround manager should be interested in three qualities: knowledge, aptitude, and attitude. In this context, knowledge means the degree to which the manager "knows" his or her job and/or possesses information that is crucial to the organization. Sometimes, a manager is absolutely crucial to the turnaround effort because of some important knowledge he or she possesses. Examples would be the sales manager who possesses detailed but undocumented knowledge of key customers' buying patterns and processes, or the operations manager who

---

[9] Carolyn Smart and Ian Vertinsky, "Designs for Crisis Decision Units," *Administrative Science Quarterly* (Summer 1977), pp. 640–657.

[10] Barry M. Staw, Lance E. Sandelands, and Jane E. Dutton, "Threat-Rigidity Effects in Organizational Behavior: A Multilevel Analysis," *Administrative Science Quarterly* (Autumn 1981), pp. 501–524.

has mastery over otherwise unruly and uncooperative equipment. However, sometimes subordinate managers have highly specialized knowledge but not any broader knowledge, such as key trends in the industry, competitors' moves, or new technologies. In such a case, the choice is between the safe continuity available from the manager with specialized internal knowledge and the possibility of new insights/directions from a manager brought in from the outside with broader knowledge.

Aptitude refers to the abilities of the manager to do things—to analyze, to lead, to control, and so on. Sometimes, a manager can have tremendous knowledge but not the wherewithal to do much with it. For example, a manager may not be capable of complex reasoning, may not be decisive, or may not bring out the best in subordinates. Depending on the type of turnaround envisioned and the mix of talents within a management team, key people could have to be replaced because of limited aptitude.

Attitude is a third quality to look for in a subordinate in a turnaround situation. The turnaround manager needs people who do not feel defeated by the situation, who are capable of psychologically reinforcing each other, and who are supportive of the top person and the direction in which he or she wants to head. Subordinates who are not supportive are not only lackluster performers; they also tend to poison the atmosphere so that others' attitudes are affected as well.

The turnaround manager, of course, relies heavily on informal observation and his or her sense of people to conduct evaluations of subordinates. But, the astute manager, recognizing that time is of the essence, will devise tests to determine the capabilities of people in the three broad areas discussed here. The most common test is to request the subordinate to conduct an analysis of some limited part of his or her area within a fairly short deadline, such as two days. An example would be to ask the marketing manager to identify the three largest orders won and the three largest orders lost over the last year, and to analyze the factors underlying the outcomes. In doing this task, the marketing manager will have to demonstrate his knowledge (Can he even identify the orders? The competitors to whom the firm lost?), his aptitude (Does he demonstrate sound logic? Does he extract any reasonable common threads from his analyses?), and his attitude (How eager to please does he appear? Did he take the request seriously?).

For such tests to be genuinely useful, some caveats must be borne in mind. First, these tests should not be labeled as such. Savvy subordinates in a turnaround situation know they are always under careful scrutiny, and will only resent a single contrived exercise to put them on the spot. This raises the second caveat: No test like the one described should be used in isolation to evaluate a manager. Rather, several such tests over the first few weeks of a turnaround, in concert with informal observation and other data, provide the information to make a reasoned decision about the person. The third caveat is that these tests should never involve detours for the managers. That is, they should only involve asking the manager to do something that genuinely is needed to conduct the turnaround. Time and resources are too tight to be asking key subordinates to engage in academic side trips.

The turnaround manager should extend his or her evaluation of key people to at least two levels below, since there may be some very capable managers who are obscured by their bosses. Knowing what talents exist at multiple levels will be important in making all other moves—firings, reassignments, even choice of strategy. Another reason for opening communications with mid-level people is that they are often valuable repositories of information about markets, technologies, and their bosses' capabilities. The textbook nicety of always strictly observing the chain of command when communicating in the organization is probably poor procedure in most firms, and it is especially ill-suited for a turnaround firm.

At this point, it is useful to say a few words about firings—the logical aftermath of the managerial evaluation process in many turnaround firms. Actually, firings are not inevitable, and they should not be seen as such. However, if a major strategic retrenchment is needed, there is usually no choice.

Firings are always agonizing, but their harmful effects on individuals and on the organization are minimized if clear criteria exist. In contrast to across-the-board cuts, the usual starting criterion is to cut by product or function. Cuts are made in those areas that are losing the most money or that are grossly overstaffed. The most talented people in these areas should be considered for reassignment to continuing operations, since it makes little sense to get rid of strong people or to keep mediocre people just because of their departmental affiliations. In general, merit should be the guiding principle in firings (except, of course, in laying off unionized employees, where seniority usually must be observed).

Since managers at each level will be responsible for ranking their subordinates, a difficult dilemma arises: Should firings proceed from the top to bottom or from bottom to top? If done from the bottom to the top, it is possible that a subordinate will be rated (and either kept or fired) by an inept supervisor who in a few weeks will be fired himself or herself. If firings are done from the top to the bottom, there is the possibility that subordinates will be rated by a new supervisor who cannot accurately assess their performances. An additional consideration is that firings from the top down can carry great symbolic and negotiating power. There is no easy answer to this dilemma, but recognizing it may allow the manager to think through the factors involved.

Probably the most crippling thing a turnaround manager can do is to have waves of firings. If after one round people know that more firings are imminent, their productivity will be disastrous. It is far better for the manager to do all the firings at once and to pledge that there will be no further firings. Since an airtight pledge of this sort can be difficult to honor, a compromise position might be to stress that there will be no more firings, as long as certain turnaround goals are met. Such an approach supplants the employee's negative preoccupation with a very positive, constructive goal.

Rewards and Motivation

The turnaround manager is usually short on resources with which to bestow rewards to key people. This means that motivation must center on intangibles and on the promise of later rewards, in addition to the obvious fear of being fired.

Fortunately, turnaround managers often encounter situations where intangible rewards are powerful motivators. Many troubled firms get into that condition because of an autocratic, dictatorial general manager. The turnaround manager who selects a team of managers with some raw talents, and then pushes them to start initiating improvements and to exercise discretion, will, after some initial skepticism on their part, often find those managers utterly exhilarated by the challenges of managing. They will be motivated by being part of an organization with renewed momentum and a sense of direction.

Now, this phenomenon only occurs if there is substantial progress. Achievement brings about motivation, just as much as motivation brings about achievement. This means that subordinates should be given challenging tasks that can be broken into discrete parts, so that they will have a series of short-term goals and can enjoy a steady stream of small but motivating victories. Managers, like other people, respond to reinforcement. Particularly in a turnaround, they need to be put in situations where progress is called—loudly called—"a win."

Intangible motivators alone will not keep good people for long. Even though financial straits sometimes prevent it, every effort should be made to keep salaries at competitive levels. Turnaround managers sometimes cut salaries instead of cutting people, but this is generally a way to send the best people looking for jobs elsewhere. As the firm approaches stabilization, the turnaround manager should also consider announcing the point at which incentive compensation will again start, and maybe give some indication of how the incentive compensation plan will be structured so as to bring the bright horizon into sharper focus for the managers.

Organizational Structure

The turnaround manager often will find a situation in which the organization's structure needs to be changed, due to confused roles and relationships and poor suitability of the structure to the turnaround strategy. There are two specific things that an organization's structure must accomplish in a turnaround situation: pinpoint accountability and eliminate information blockage.

The assignment of responsibilities must be absolutely clear in a turnaround situation. This often means revising tasks so that each person has an identifiable domain and goals (with interim benchmarks). In general, structure must be simple in order to achieve this aim. Complex matrices and standing cross-functional teams usually run counter to the aim of pinpointing accountability. Effective turnaround managers will often set up talented subordinates as "champions" of discrete tasks or projects, even though the tasks could legitimately be woven together across departments to achieve so-called synergies or economies of scale. The key seems to be in assigning or instilling "problem ownership."

In a turnaround situation, organizational structure can be a key to eliminating information blockages. A typical move is to reduce the number of layers in the organization, so that information does not have to travel as far, either upward or downward. The greater the number of levels, the longer it takes for the information to flow, the less information gets through, and the more distorted the information becomes. Another way to open up information flows—this time laterally—is to convene two-person or three-person ad hoc task forces to deliberate on key policy issues. Often, these will consist of functional heads who have not been communicating with each other at all up until now. Such task forces must be temporary (with a rigid deadline—sometimes no more than two weeks), high-level (with the authority to implement), and focused on some issue with cross-functional implications (such as the marketing and production heads developing policy and tactics regarding product quality). The task forces should not have any lingering operating responsibilities, since operating accountability must reside with individuals.

Information and Decision Processes

The turnaround manager needs to make decisions about what information is needed, where it is needed, how it should flow, and, in general, how decisions should be made. Here again, the emphasis should be on simplicity and fluidity. The manager, possibly with the help of a consultant or inside aide, should draft some very simple forms for reports to track information about the key areas of the business. Ideally, each report will require only a handful of figures and will pertain to a crucial dimension of the business. The manager must resist asking for information on every possible facet of the business.

It is crucial to engage key subordinates in the process of refining these reports, since they will be providing the eventual data and since they often have important insight into what type of data is most necessary. In fact, it is useful to first establish a set of simple, highly focused reports that will flow from the functional heads to the general manager and then charge the functional heads with doing the same within their respective areas. The quality of the first set of reports will dramatically shape the quality of those developed at middle and lower levels of the organization.

It is important that turnaround managers not rely only, or even primarily, on formal written information flows. In fact, many turnaround managers replace chief executives who had essentially cut off personal contact with subordinates. The effective turnaround manager will engage in face-to-face exchanges with subordinates, rather than relying on more detached and sterile media. Such meetings—especially when one-on-one (as opposed to larger groups)—promote fluid and subtle information flows. In a situation where rigidity, confusion, and lack of trust probably abound, achievement of these aims is essential.

SYMBOLIC COMPONENT OF TURNAROUND

A symbol can be defined as anything that has meaning beyond its inherent substance. A manager's formal language, informal language, decisions, use of time, and general demeanor convey far more than their substance might indicate. In fact, symbols are the very stuff of top management. And, they take on particular importance in turnaround situations, since, as noted above, substantive resources for accomplishing goals are in short supply. When people's nerves are frayed, they are particularly sensitive to signals.

Managers do not really have a choice about using symbols. They emit them all the time. In fact, every substantive action—a statement, a meeting location, a walk through the plant—can be thought to have symbolic fallout. Managers mismanage their use of symbols in two ways.

The first is failing to understand that the symbolic fallout exists. A common example is the turnaround manager who holes up in his or her office, often with the door shut, at the same time he or she is asking people to step forward with ideas. The inconsistency is far from obvious to the general manager, but it is profound in its impact on subordinates.

The second way of mismanaging symbols is failing to use them to their fullest. Through careful staging, the potential symbolic fallout from an action can be greatly expanded. For example, a new turnaround manager came into a situation where the executive offices were located in a modern, fairly expensive office building a few blocks from the company's main plant. By happy coincidence, the office lease lapsed two months after his arrival. And, he knew that the prudent thing—both substantively and symbolically—was to move the executive offices back to the plant where there was older, unused office space. He decided to heighten the impact of the move by having the moving trucks start the unloading on a workday, just at the time employees were going to lunch down a long corridor where the moving was taking place. Everybody was made aware of the move, and they had the remainder of their lunch hour to talk about it and the general manager's personal commitment to cut costs.

Some will argue that such behavior is manipulative and slick, and is not going to "fool" anyone. But, truly great leaders through history have been separated from the merely good leaders by their astute and persistent use of symbols. And, if these examples seem trivial, it is worth noting that the exceptional manager seeks every way imaginable to convey a point to the people whose acts and attitudes he is trying to influence. Sometimes, this will be through grand settings, but, more often, it will be through fairly mundane contexts.

When symbols are used consistently, and with appropriate frequency, they form a theme. Turnaround managers need such themes to provide clear direction and motivate people who are, in various degrees, confused, frightened, and skeptical.

To a great extent, symbols represent the manner in which the turnaround manager uses all the other levers available—strategy, political initiative, structure, rewards, and people. Symbols, then, overlay the entire turnaround task.

CORPORATE-LEVEL TURNAROUND ISSUES

This chapter has focused primarily on the manager who has been charged with the turnaround of a business unit. But, there are also important issues that must be addressed at the corporate level of a diversified firm, often before the turnaround of one of its businesses can get under way. Chief among these issues are: whether to attempt the turnaround or to sell off the business, what kind of manager should head up the turnaround, and how much time should be allowed for the turnaround.

Turn Around or Sell?

A turnaround should be attempted only if there is a high probability that the going-concern value of the business is substantially greater than its liquidation value. To reach that determination, someone at the corporate level must do an analysis of the prospects for the industry and for the business within its industry. Often, this analysis must be done even more quickly and with less data than the eventual analysis conducted by the turnaround manager.

The corporate analysis must not rely only on the financial statements of the business, no matter how unequivocal they may seem. Rather, the analysis must extend to the overall health of the industry, and data—even if impressionistic—must be gathered from a variety of sources, including the business' suppliers, customers, key managers, and employees. If the prospects for the industry appear dismal or if the problems of the business are particularly deep-rooted or pervasive, selling the business or its assets may be more sensible than attempting the turnaround. Of course, sometimes firms are prevented from exiting, due to such factors as union severance agreements, long-term contracts with customers, and crucial synergies between the troubled business and other healthier businesses within the corporation.[11]

In weighing the sale of a business (or of its assets), two key factors should be borne in mind. The first is that the business may well be worth much more to someone else than it is to its current management. That is, the business may fit particularly well with the strategy or competence of another firm, such that they would pay a reasonable price—perhaps even a premium—to acquire it. Second, the business will yield a much higher price if sold in an orderly, deliberate fashion than if it is sold under duress or crisis. Among other things, this means that assets are usually worth more before a turnaround attempt than after an *unsuccessful* turnaround attempt, when the firm is desperate and has only confirmed the poor health of the business in the eyes of potential buyers.

The corporate analysis of the liquidation value of the business must be communicated to the turnaround manager. Such a figure provides the turnaround manager a reference point against which all actions and timetables can be measured. It is especially important for the turnaround manager to know that he or she has a "walkaway" position in negotiating with stubborn stakeholders.

There are substantial costs and risks in attempting a turnaround rather than getting rid of the business. Some of these costs are obvious, but there are also hidden tolls in the amount of time, creativity, and emotional energy the troubled business diverts from other more promising operations within the firm's portfolio. Probably, far more turnarounds are undertaken than should be.

Selecting a Turnaround Manager

Once the company has decided a turnaround attempt is warranted, there is the decision as to who should lead the effort. Here, two questions are rele-

---

[11] Kathryn R. Harrigan, "Exit Decisions in Mature Industries," *Academy of Management Journal* (Fall 1982), pp. 707–731; Michael E. Porter, "Please Note Location of Nearest Exit: Exit Barriers and Strategic and Organizational Planning," *California Management Review* (1976), pp. 21–33.

vant: Should the present general manager be replaced? If so, by what kind of person?

Some authors feel strongly that replacement of the present top manager is crucial in a turnaround situation.[12] The rationale for such a view is that the present manager has already demonstrated ineptness by allowing the business to deteriorate; he or she is psychologically wedded to the present way of doing things, and so would be unable to generate and accurately weigh alternatives; and, because of his or her close ties to subordinates, customers, and other parties, he or she could not make the hard decisions that must be made in a turnaround situation. There is no systematic data as to whether or when this view is correct. However, it seems to be widely subscribed to, as judged by one finding that three quarters of the executives heading up eighty-one turnaround attempts were new to the job.[13]

Not all such new managers are from outside the firm, and, in fact, the idea of picking a turnaround manager from among the present management team is an appropriate compromise in some situations. Such a person has the advantage over an outsider of knowing the business and its key players, and may have a relatively open mind about changes that need to be made. In larger companies, a subordinate is more likely to have held truly responsible general management experience yet still be psychologically detached from the incumbent executive's view of the firm. For example, at NCR, William Anderson was the extremely successful chairman of the firm's Japanese subsidiary. He was known for experimentation and deviation from the established NCR approach. He had the combined advantage of knowing NCR but not fully accepting it, and so he was an obvious (and eventually successful) choice by the board to head up the firm's turnaround. NCR pruned operations, streamlined its work force, and focused its business lines around several key organizational concepts. Under Anderson, NCR's financial performance markedly improved.

Any further discussion of selecting a turnaround manager inevitably becomes a litany of "it all depends." It depends on what type of turnaround is most likely, for example, revenue building versus cost cutting. It depends on whether the person is being selected only to bring the business through the crisis or whether he or she will also engineer the rejuvenation. It depends on the mix of talents and attitudes of the key subordinates in the business. Additional contingent factors could be listed. In short, there are no clear guidelines. It is clear, however, that corporate decision makers need to become knowledgeable enough about the troubled business so that they can identify intelligently the most appropriate type of turnaround manager.

---

[12] Hofer, op. cit., p. 25.

[13] Bibeault, op. cit., p. 95.

How Much Time to Allow

A fitting—in fact, crucial—question for corporate managers to ask is, "How long will this turnaround take?" Here again, there are no rigid guidelines. Chrysler tried to turn around for fifteen years. Other firms accomplish it in a year or two. Turnaround researchers have found fairly consistently that the *average* elapsed time from start of a turnaround to satisfactory profits is about three years. But the range is immense, as one could easily expect. The key determining factors are the health of the industry, the severity of the firm's condition, the strategic position of the firm (often indicated by market share), its capital intensity, and its middle management quality.[14]

Instead of trying to delineate exactly how long a turnaround might take, corporate-level executives should set benchmarks and a timetable for the business during the turnaround. A tentative timetable can be established based on the early analysis that is done to determine whether a turnaround is viable. Then, the timetable should be renegotiated after the turnaround manager has had a chance to develop his or her own estimates. Interim benchmarks should be set so that the parent firm is not in a "wait and see" situation. Progress must be continually visible, and there should be logical points in the timetable when bailing-out can be reconsidered.

A CLASSIC TURNAROUND—THE CASE OF ARTHUR KELLER

This chapter has stressed that there are a vast array of components, or levers, that the turnaround manager can draw upon, and that the levers chosen must fit the situation. But orchestration of these levers—appropriate balance, sequence, and pace—is also crucial to a successful turnaround. The best way to illustrate orchestration of a turnaround, and at the same time summarize how the various levers can be used, is through discussion of an actual turnaround. The example is from a case study that continues to be widely used in university and corporate executive programs.[15]

The Situation

Arthur Keller became the general manager of a major Swedish dressmaker when it was acquired by the large Austrian yarn producer for which he worked. Keller knew before starting the job that the dressmaker, Hedblom, was in trouble, since he had been involved in the (often bitter) acquisition

---

[14] Ibid., p. 98; Dan Schendel, G.R. Patton, and James Riggs, "Corporate Turnaround Strategies: A Study of Decline and Recovery," *Journal of General Management* (Fall 1976), pp. 3–11.

[15] L'Institute pour l'Etude des Methodes de Direction de l'Enterprise (IEMDE), "Hedblom (A)" and "Hedblom (B)," distributed by Harvard Case Services, 1968.

negotiations. But he scarcely could have known the real magnitude of the problems.

Sales had dropped by 50 percent over two years, due to delivery delays, poor merchandising, and increased competition. New machines were on order, despite the fact that the company was operating at 25 percent of capacity. With its present cost structure, the firm would have to double its sales just to break even.

Keller found that at the core of the company's problems was the owner-founder, Mr. Hedblom. It seemed he had exercised a very centralized, authoritarian management style. He personally processed all the company's mail, required all managers to punch a time-clock, and, needless to say, made all the key decisions for the firm. Unfortunately, he was slow and risk-averse in his decision making, which, in this seasonal industry, led to very peaked and costly production cycles, late deliveries, and poor channel relations.

The human resource situation that Keller encountered was in keeping with the rest of the picture. The six key managers were cold and skeptical. The marketing manager said he would probably leave. The controller still had obvious loyalties to the old Mr. Hedblom, and the production manager was demoralized because Mr. Hedblom had him reporting to a consulting engineer who was retained to install a production control system. The work force complained openly about lack of work, while at the same time a substantial amount of work was subcontracted outside.

Controls and budgets were nonexistent. In fact, the only two reports generated were a daily report of the firm's bank balance and a daily report of sales orders (but only for those orders received by mail). Since Mr. Hedblom had been the funnel for all information, there was essentially no communication among the functional heads.

The Turnaround

The situation facing Arthur Keller sounds unappealing, but it is not unlike the turnaround conditions described throughout this chapter: urgency, skeptical stakeholders, poor morale, and a vacuum left by an autocratic chief executive. As will be seen, Keller measured up to the task. This discussion of Keller's various moves will be tied to the array of turnaround levers.

It is difficult to improve on Keller's own words for describing how he entered the organization and conducted his situation assessment:

My main task at the beginning was to gather information and to get cooperation. I knew nothing about the dress business and little about Hedblom. I therefore conducted a detailed and systematic investigation of all aspects of company operations. Every time [I am in the plant] I walk around the building, meet the people, talk to them as best

I can in my broken Swedish, and particularly ask questions, questions, questions. You simply take nothing for granted. By having people explain and justify what they have been doing for years as a matter of unquestioned routine you often discover what needs to be investigated and appraised. Also, in this way you learn a lot about your people.[16]

In terms of strategy, Keller faced the option of either a major retrenchment or pushing sales up past the break-even point. His assessment of the industry and his diagnosis of Hedblom's problems led him to conclude that a sales-push strategy was feasible. So, Keller sought ways to expand volume. These included the introduction of four off-season dress collections (in addition to the customary two peak-season collections), a line of separately branded dresses to be sold through chain stores, sale of fabrics to other dressmakers, and expanded sales in other Scandinavian countries. The off-season dress collections were an especially important move, since they were directly responsive to the growing uneasiness of retailers to make big semi-annual inventory commitments, and they helped to even out Hedblom's own production cycles. This was a major innovation in the industry, and it was made possible by Keller's fresh view and persistent questioning.

Keller also introduced some important cost-cutting measures. By advancing the start of each season's production cycle, inefficient peaks and valleys were nearly eliminated. Changes in plant layout were made to facilitate product flow and reduce costs, and new fabric cutting processes were introduced to reduce waste. Keller's search for quick, creative ways to cut costs is perhaps best illustrated in his decision (recommended by someone in production) to use transparent thread in sewing, which permitted the use of just two threads (one light and one dark), thereby facilitating sewing operations and minimizing thread inventories. This decision and other cost-cutting moves reinforced the primary strategy of expanding revenues.

Only sketchy data is available on how Keller used political moves to aid in his turnaround attempt, but there is some indication that he was imaginative on this front as well. Using his parent company as a fulcrum, he was able to obtain a sizeable cooperative advertising budget from one of the parent's biggest fiber suppliers. Similarly, he was able to get credit on good terms by working through the parent company's lead bank.

Keller conducted his turnaround effort without replacing any of his managers. As badly as the firm had been performing, he concluded that the remaining managers were not to blame. Of course, they were not dynamos, but he sensed that they were generally competent and, in addition, they carried a great deal of information which, even if unwanted or unused by his predecessor, would be invaluable in the turnaround effort.

---

[16] Ibid., p. 10.

Naturally, the company could not afford financial incentives for the managers. Instead, Keller had to rely on—and accentuate—the degree to which the managers could be motivated by a sense of teamwork, vitality, and expanded discretion. On the heels of his predecessor, these were powerful motivators.

He modified the structure only slightly, by putting one manager in overall charge of the new dress line. And, after releasing the consulting engineer, he put the production manager in overall charge of the production function. Both of these changes were prompted by Keller's desire to give key managers clear and bounded areas of responsibility.

Keller's attempts to introduce new controls and information flows centered on the themes of simplicity and timeliness. He concluded that a budgeting system could only be put together on an incremental basis, by starting with the information on hand and adding to its detail and quality in each successive month's budget. He set up three quality-control posts through the production process, so that problems could be caught before the whole production cycle was completed. He designed a set of four one-page weekly reports on crucial aspects of the business and encouraged his subordinates to develop similarly simple and straightforward reports in their own areas. Overall, Keller delegated many decisions, but he exercised control by maintaining close personal contact with each manager and persistently asking questions.

Finally, Keller was a master in the use of symbols. He engaged in numerous substantive actions which, when enhanced by appropriate staging and timing, greatly helped to reinforce the themes he was striking in the turnaround effort. Here are several of those actions and the themes he tried to accentuate with each:

- *Action:* He gave early, visible attention to the next year's line.

  Theme: "We're going to start making decisions and taking risks."

- *Action:* He moved the executive offices from across town to the unused top floor of the plant.

  Theme: "We're going to start talking with each other."

- *Action:* He eliminated almost all outside subcontracting.

  Theme: "We have a lot of talent and resources right here."

- *Action:* He fired the consulting engineer.

  Theme: "I want *you people* to start making the key decisions."

- *Action:* He held open houses for employees' families, press, and community.

  Theme: "We've got plenty to show off."

- *Action:* He made many personal tours of the plant.

  Theme: "I'm involved and interested."

- *Action:* He sent personal letters to customers, guaranteeing on-time delivery.

  Theme: "Things are changing here. I am personally involved in the changes."

In contrast to his predecessor, Keller used powerful themes, and he drove them home by the careful and persistent use of symbols.

Keller's turnaround of Hedblom was exceptionally successful. Within nine months, the business was breaking even; and, within fifteen months, it was earning roughly 10 percent on sales.

Keller's turnaround effort is a snapshot of the key points of this chapter. He conducted an early, quick, but in-depth analysis of his situation and players. He charted a course that was responsive to the nature and magnitude of the firm's problems. He creatively engaged all the components of an effective turnaround: strategic, political, human, organizational, and symbolic. And, he engaged them in a balanced fashion, so they were mutually reinforcing.

CONCLUSION

Turnaround managers must be ready to make moves as soon as they enter the turnaround picture. Because turnarounds are unique situations, there is tremendous pressure on the manager to do a quick, early analysis and to move on to key actions. The luxury of an exhaustive period of evaluation is generally not available. However, the turnaround manager must carefully orchestrate the use of strategic, political, human, organizational, and symbolic measures, because generally he is allowed only one round of moves.

Turnaround managers must match the various strategy options to the unique circumstances of their companies while continually updating their evaluations concerning the effectiveness of these strategies. Also, clear lines of responsibility and accountability must be drawn for middle and low level managers. In choosing these subordinates, turnaround managers should assess each candidate's knowledge, aptitude, and attitude.

Depending on the industry and the company's own situation the time frame for completing the turnaround can be anywhere from a few months to several years, although three years is usually concerned average. Managers faced with a turnaround should set a tentative timetable that includes not only benchmarks for determining the effectiveness of their strategies, but logical points at which the feasibility of selling out can be considered.

20

Business Strategy for the Political Environment

JANET A. WEISS

University of Michigan

MANAGING THE POLITICAL ENVIRONMENT

Business strategy in the 1990s will be preoccupied with capitalizing on some of the remarkable and interrelated changes that came about during the last decade: the globalization of the marketplace, the explosion in information technology, and the pervasive interdependence of the public and private sectors. As a consequence of this interdependence, policies and practices in the public sector are crucial to business success.

Regulating business activities is a major governmental concern, and business cannot afford to ignore the political environment that shapes public policy. Companies in every industry must learn to act within constraints and to capitalize on the opportunities created by the actions of federal, state, and local governments. Companies that compete internationally must also be sensitive to the changing political situations abroad.

This chapter focuses on how to evaluate the political atmosphere in the U.S. context, how to anticipate changes in the political environment, and how to develop a political strategy that is compatible with the company's business strategy.

In a society in which corporate executives decide which technologies to develop and which to abandon, where industry and jobs will be located, what quality of goods and services to produce, how to compensate different kinds of people for different kinds of work, and which people will work together, the relative well-being of the entire society is in the hands of business. Society cannot be indifferent to how business makes these choices. A major function of government in a capitalist system is to encourage business enterprises to perform effectively in various roles. The standard of living and the relative distribution of wealth for everyone depend on the outcome. As a result, many groups throughout society seek to influence these basic decisions.

Business Consequences of Political Action

The business consequences of these influences are twofold. Many of the influences constrain managerial discretion. Such policies as the regulation of prices and services, legal liability, restrictions on how firms treat their employees, environmental and safety standards, standards of product quality, prohibitions against deceptive advertising, disclosure requirements, minimum wages, and mandated benefits all limit the ways in which business may be conducted. Other social and political influences provide opportunities for business to grow and flourish. Policies such as the bailouts of troubled companies and savings and loan institutions, job training and expanded public education, loan guarantees, infrastructure improvements (e.g., transportation facilities, water projects, roads, rail spurs), international trade policies, research and development (R&D), tax advantages for investment or research, and the promotion of U.S. exports all enhance the opportunities for businesses to profit and expand.

Competitive Consequences of Political Action

Business managers need to understand the Iron Law of Public Policy: "Every act of government, no matter what its broader merits or demerits for society at large, creates winners and losers within the business world."[1]

---

[1] Robert A. Leone, *Who Profits: Winners, Losers and Government Regulation* (New York: Basic Books, 1986), p. 3.

For example, the 1988 decision of the National Highway Traffic Safety Administration to modify the Corporate Average Fuel Economy standards from 27.5 miles per gallon to 26.5 miles per gallon resulted in significant financial gains for Ford and General Motors (which would have paid multi-million dollar fines if the standard had remained at 27.5) but losses for Chrysler (which could have met the higher standard, reducing its costs relative to its domestic competitors).

Managers often fail to realize that policies that burden or benefit an entire industry do not have identical effects on all firms within the industry. Some firms are inevitably hurt or helped more than others, thus altering the competitive balance.

Many kinds of public action shape the competitive environment. By imposing new costs of doing business, environmental regulation creates advantages for those firms that find it least costly to come into compliance, and disadvantages for those firms in the same industry with older plants, dirtier fuels, or limited technical expertise in pollution control. When faced with policies that are designed to reduce the cost of doing business, producers that can quickly take advantage of the changes in policy will benefit at the expense of those who have invested more heavily in the status quo. For example, proposals by the Environmental Protection Agency (EPA) in 1981 to relax the standards on lead content in gasoline offered relatively small price reductions (about one tenth of a cent per gallon) to large refiners, a larger savings (about nine tenths of a cent per gallon) to small refiners, and the largest saving (nearly five cents per gallon) to blenders who purchase fuel from other refiners and sell it to retailers. Although it might seem surprising that key players in the refining industry should resist policies designed to reduce their costs, after looking at the competitive implications of the EPA's policy, the lack of enthusiasm from the major companies becomes much easier to understand.

Sophisticated managers also realize that the form of government intervention has competitive implications. When the Consumer Products Safety Commission set out to design safety standards for chain saws, its intent was to prevent injuries caused by saw kickback. However, the three major chain saw manufacturers advocated two different regulatory solutions. Two advocated nose guards or antikickback chains—relatively cheap solutions that did not require redesign of the entire machine. The third advocated chain brakes, a more expensive and effective solution that did require redesign. The third manufacturer had already installed chain brakes on its saws, and competed on the basis of quality and safety. Obviously, it would prefer a requirement that would force its lower-cost competitors to increase their prices and redesign their saws. Each side sought to have its preferred standard accepted as official government policy.

Regulation is not the only kind of government action that has competitive consequences. Changes in government funding for scientific and medical research may give an advantage to firms whose R&D portfolios complement those of publicly funded laboratories, and create a disadvantage for those whose work becomes redundant with that being done in the public domain. Improvements in employees' access to quality public education may be an advantage to firms that require well-trained workers, but a disadvantage to firms that do not take advantage of their employees' skills. Legal protections for women, older workers, people of color, and the physically disabled may have little effect on the employment practices of many firms, but a large impact on competitors who have lowered their costs by underpaying these employees.

The constraints and opportunities posed by the political environment are constantly changing in response to internal and external pressures on both business and government. Although major issues such as environmental regulation and tax or trade policy remain on the agenda year after year, the public sector frequently changes directions and tactics for reasons that seem bewildering to the managers whose work is affected. Without training or experience in the world of politics and policy, managers often respond to these changes in ways that are blind or even counterproductive to the interests of their firms.

COMPONENTS OF A PROACTIVE ORIENTATION

Five strategic skills can improve a firm's ability to realize competitive advantage in the political environment:

1. Keep alert to trends, events, and processes in the nonmarket sphere that may affect the business. Do not wait for regulation or litigation to land on your desk—anticipate it.
2. Cultivate the skill of diagnosing the causes and consequences of political and social trends, events, and processes. Learn what is systematic and predictable in the social and political environment.
3. Think through how changes outside the industry and the firm might affect the firm's competitive position. For example, do not jump to the conclusion that all cost increases or regulatory constraints are bad; some may actually enhance the firm's competitive position.
4. Develop strategic responses to the political environment that enhance the firm's competitive position in the long run. These build on knowledge about the firm and of the other entities (public and private) that have stakes in the same resources, markets, locations, and people.
5. Create organizational mechanisms to integrate the firm's strategy for dealing with the social and political environment with its strategy for financial, product, or human resource purposes.

Unlike specialized staff skills, strategic orientation to the political environment is a general management skill. Given the smaller size and authority of corporate staff in many companies, top management must place increasing responsibility on general managers to cope with the social and political forces that bear on the success of their product, operations, or unit. Their contributions are essential to an effective business approach to managing the threats and opportunities presented in the political environment.

Keep Alert

How do firms build the capacity to anticipate an issue before it creates serious threats? Many large corporations have taught their staffs to identify issues in the environment beyond the marketplace so that they can detect changes and trends that may have business implications. Midsize and smaller corporations tend to rely on trade and professional associations or external advisers for this function.

Scenario Construction. Scenario construction and issues identification are designed to develop the capacity for foresight. Managers and staff are invited to consider the full range of forces that may influence the success of the business. These may involve social attitudes, values, technological changes, demographics, scarcity of human or natural resources, trends in political preferences and activism, regulation, litigation and so on, depending on the industry and the business. Early identification of such issues allows time for management to understand the issues and the entities involved, and to assume a positive rather than a negative orientation. It also affords managers the opportunity to seek out and meet experts and activists, to learn their concerns, and to share the business's information and perspectives so that others might have a more realistic understanding of feasible business responses.

Scenarios help managers imagine plausible alternative futures in the social and political arena. By focusing on a handful of key factors and forces outside the marketplace, scenarios suggest how these forces might influence one another to create different trajectories. For example, current U.S. policy toward international trade is delicately balanced between forces favoring protectionism and those promoting unencumbered international flows of trade. It is not difficult to come up with scenarios in which widespread public xenophobia, political pressure from firms losing business to international competitors, and a successful populist candidate for president combine to tilt U.S. trade policy toward a more protectionist stance, with major financial implications for firms with significant overseas investments. Laying out such maps of the future keeps managers alert to the possible environments in which they must compete.

Scanning and Monitoring. Scanning and monitoring are similar to scenarios, except that these techniques are applied to the present. By systematically collecting intelligence about the external world, scanning permits managers to see trends in early stages and to detect events as they unfold. Businesses may designate individuals to act as scanners of print media, industry data bases, political events, trade association activities, and research outlets. The scanners collect information to keep managers or management committees aware of environmental changes of potential relevance.

Trends and events that managers deem of special importance are monitored. Monitoring alerts managers to medium-term pressures and opportunities. For example, pending legislation or patterns of government procurement might be monitored by firms that will be directly affected. Community attitudes toward development and the environment may be monitored by firms seeking to construct new manufacturing facilities. Educational and research trends may be monitored by firms that expect to recruit large numbers of scientific personnel.

Together, scenario construction, scanning, and monitoring of the social and political environment allow managers to avoid surprises. Although social expectations and constraints on the firm may increase, managers who anticipate the constraints are better positioned to accommodate them in their business planning. For example, DuPont, the largest manufacturer of chlorofluorocarbons (CFCs), closely monitored growing scientific evidence that CFCs cause significant harm to the ozone layer. Not much imagination was required to recognize that such environmental damage might lead to political pressure to cease CFC production. Because of this early recognition, DuPont was able to begin the long, arduous process of developing alternative products in the event of a possible ban on CFCs. Its scientists had ample time to produce alternative products that seemed commercially feasible. Knowing that the environmental damage might be catastrophic and that their substitute products could compete successfully, DuPont began to support the imposition of a worldwide ban on CFCs. Monitoring gave them the advantage of a long lead time in developing a strategy that enabled them to do well while also doing good.

Cultivate Understanding

If managers treat social and political events as inexplicable, irrational, or corrupt (or all three), their willingness or capacity to shape those events will be impaired. Although many dynamics in the social and political environment are discontinuous and unpredictable, others are both predictable and systematic. The public sector operates differently than the private sector, but no less understandably.

For both pragmatic and ideological reasons, many managers fail to make systematic diagnoses of what is happening in the political sphere. The pragmatic reason is that few of them learn how the public sector works. The ideological reason is that most managers have personal political views that lead them to regard public officials as irritants. Groups representing the interests of consumers, communities, the environment, or labor often seek to influence the operation of the firm through public action, articulating concepts of the public good that are unrelated to the ideology of free enterprise. These concepts have often gotten short shrift from business managers, who dismiss the concerns of external constituencies as illegitimate interference with the appropriate functions of the firm.

Such ideological distaste for government or for activist groups has led many managers to leave the "dirty" business of politics to paid consultants, lobbyists, or trade associations. Rather than learning about the concerns and issues raised by government officials, they seek quick fixes for political problems. This lack of attention to developments in the political sphere frequently means that managers learn about political problems only after they have become serious and difficult to resolve. For example, why bother to learn much about the status of prolonged, complex, and controversial battles over product liability legislation? Only after managers are staggered by the extent of their firm's liability, through direct experience, are they likely to realize the business implications of the issue.

Through better training and opportunities for regular involvement in public affairs, managers can learn more about why governments behave as they do, and why other stakeholders seek help through the public sector in their dealings with the firm. This enhanced sensitivity enables managers to differentiate between trivial and serious threats to the well-being of the firm. It enables managers to respond to the reasonable concerns of external groups before they become demands or requirements. It also enables them to present, as effectively as possible, the company's point of view in deliberations about policy.

Business managers become more effective in their dealings with external groups when they understand the differences in perspective and incentives between people who work in the private and public sectors. At the risk of caricaturing these differences, there are four dimensions that sophisticated managers learn to appreciate in their dealings with the public sector at local, state, and federal levels.

1. *Decision procedure vs. outcome.* In governments, decisions are often made by specifying the procedures for making decisions, and permitting the procedure to produce what outcome it will. For example, Americans select a president not by careful, reasoned consideration of the best person for the job, but by specifying a nomination and election process that narrows the field to a final candidate. Similarly, Congress did not seek to design optimal tax legislation in 1986; instead, it sought to design a package of tax changes that could attract enough votes to become law. Most local governments are not legally permitted to make purchasing decisions on the basis of contractor or vendor reliability, quality, or reputation; the procedure specifies that contracts shall be awarded on the basis of price. The consequence of this preoccupation with procedure is that agencies at all levels of government are much more procedurally constrained than corporations. Civil service, purchasing and contracting, freedom of information, budgeting procedures and hearings, and required administrative procedures all reduce the discretion of public managers in their work. How they do their jobs becomes at least as important as how well the agency performs. Although many businesses are also concerned with how decisions are made and how managers conduct themselves, they nearly always accord managers more flexibility to pursue desired outcomes.

   2. *Equity vs. efficiency.* Public decisions are often guided by concerns about who benefits and who loses if public action is taken. Decisions that benefit nearly everyone but place heavy burdens on some regions or groups of people are very difficult to make. An obvious example is the great difficulty that states experience in locating sites for the disposal of toxic or nuclear wastes. Safe disposal sites for such materials are a universal need, but vociferous opposition from the neighbors of proposed sites nearly always outweighs the public's needs in the political calculus. Of course, business decisions also take into account the distributional effects of gains and losses. More often than in the public sector, however, they are guided by concern for whether the company's overall gains will exceed overall losses. Less successful divisions or product lines are closed or sold in order to bolster the health of the enterprise as a whole. This kind of thinking makes it difficult for managers to appreciate the intense concern of politicians for the differential impacts of proposed legislation or regulation.

   3. *Bottom-up vs. top-down initiative.* Most businesses are hierarchical in nature. Major decisions are made by the people at the top of the hierarchy. Planning and forecasting occur at the top. When major new initiatives are considered, the top of the organization is best positioned to consider the value of the initiative for the organization as a whole. Typically, the senior managers have spent their careers in the corporation and know it well. By contrast, most initiatives and decisions in government agencies are made at much lower levels. The staff and middle managers have far more power than corporate officials expect. Legislation and regulations are written in the middle of the organization. Waivers and grants are made at the initiative of staff. Staff are the gatekeepers for the legality and feasibility of proposals made by senior officials. Part of the reason for this bottom-up strategy is that the most senior people in government are there for short stints—two years or so—and never get to know their organizations very well. These senior managers serve at the pleasure of the elected officials, the president, governor, or mayor. They leave office because of the arrival of new elected officials, a change in policy direction, or the need to get back to their previous careers. Because of differences in both structure and career paths, people at the tops of corporations must learn not to go straight to the top of the government organization they seek to influence. Instead, managers must learn who has the power to make the decisions, and work with them, whoever they may be, regardless of title.

4. *Short-term vs. long-term commitments.* No government decision is forever. New elected officials reverse course. New political dynamics change the balance of power. Coalitions form and then unravel. Legislation expires, and must be reconsidered. Budgets are reconstructed yearly. New resources become available, or disappear. Although a firm or an industry may lose one round, there are always more rounds to come. Even huge capital investments, such as federal procurement of major weapons systems or the construction of a proposed interstate highway, are perpetually open to reconsideration, acceleration, or cancellation.

Because so many constituencies may be involved in public decisions, and because there is no clear hierarchy of control, policy decisions are more like truces among competing interests than crisp, enforceable decisions from the top. Such decisions by government officials should not be treated as though they are permanent commitments of the agency's resources or authority. Win or lose, when significant decisions are at stake, managers should stay involved in the policy process to protect the corporation's interests, to defend gains, or to notice opportunities to reverse losses.

Compared to most businesses, governments tend to operate in ways that are slow-moving, consensus-seeking, and remarkably open to comment and participation from interested outsiders. The differences in operating style may obscure the predictability in the political system. Uncontrollable or irrational forces do not dominate government decision making. The system is quite understandable on its own terms. Managers who make the investment in learning those terms often find it possible to make compelling cases for their companies' interests.

Consider Competitive Implications

If a firm has developed a process for tracking developments in the political environment, and understanding what they mean and how they might unfold, the next step is to consider the competitive implications of those developments. This is a very focused version of the "so what?" question. Having built up the capacity to scan, monitor, interpret, and predict the political and social world outside the firm, managers must now develop the capacity to translate that understanding into competitive terms. Government action may open new markets (e.g., pollution control equipment, waste recycling facilities, military applications), or it may reduce costs associated with existing products and services (e.g., improving airport or highway facilities to ease access to remote areas, generating electricity, or subsidizing job training in certain industries). It also may close existing markets (e.g., asbestos products, aerosol packaging), or increase the costs associated with existing products or services (e.g., tobacco or alcohol, banking or insurance services).

As discussed earlier, the Iron Law holds that government actions will always have competitive implications, not only for the industry but among firms in the industry. All kinds of actions by all levels of government (federal, state, county, local) have implications for the relative success of private firms as compared to their competitors. Depending on the initial costs, resources, strategies, and the flexibility of each firm, the same government action that poses huge burdens for one firm will create exciting opportunities for another. Some of these competitive implications are tangible and immediate. For example, when Congress passed 1986 legislation imposing a ban on all new investment and bank loans to South Africa, some banks suffered immediate losses; other banks that had pulled out of South Africa earlier or that had never invested there did not suffer.

Some competitive implications are more long-term. Deregulation of the airlines at first seemed to hurt the established carriers, but, with time, the large, well-capitalized, and sophisticated carriers, like American, found ways to derive competitive advantage from flexibility in route structures and pricing. After years of resisting governmental control over health care, some business leaders have found that their health care costs are much higher than those of their international competitors—so much higher that they are now ready to consider some variety of national health insurance to help bring these costs under control.

The competitive implications of government action are not always immediately obvious. Frequently, management's first reaction is to resist public policy that may increase costs or restrict decision-making power, without considering the competitive consequences. Managers are concerned or outraged at the prospect of intervention, which strikes them as an illegitimate claim on corporate resources. However, as with DuPont and the CFCs, public pressure may actually create competitive advantage, and the corporation needs mechanisms that enable it to recognize this. Some sophisticated companies, such as Cummins Engine, Pacific Gas and Electric, and 3M, have created systems to reap business advantages from what might be seen as policy constraints. For example, 3M has created a program called "Pollution Prevention Pays" to identify and support initiatives that save money while reducing air and water pollution. Since 1975, the program has chalked up $1 billion in savings.

Competitive position is also affected by the public's perception of a company's response to public policy issues. Many activist groups monitor and publicize corporate performance that affects the environment, worker safety, affirmative action, and other issues of widespread public concern. In extreme cases, boycotts are organized against companies whose actions, while legal, violate public norms of responsible behavior. In many cases, companies suffer a loss of reputation. Exxon's response to the Valdez oil spill, for example, seems to have caused long-lasting harm to the firm's image of competence among consumers and public officials. Companies are quite sensitive to such reputational concerns. In 1990, two tobacco companies rolled back new product introductions after the Secretary of Health and Human Services charged that their products exploited blacks and teenagers. Sustained pressure on fast-food companies to minimize their waste streams has prompted McDonald's to seek competitive advantage (and fend off the attacks of environmentalists) by instituting a much-publicized waste reduction and recycling program.

Finally, companies must consider the competitive consequences of public actions that weaken or strengthen their entire industry. Although a given railroad may profit from a safety requirement that weakens its competitors, it must pay attention to policies that make it more attractive for customers to ship by truck. Savings and loan institutions that profited while their competitors have been plagued by recent troubles are nevertheless tarnished by the massive losses suffered by the industry. Like classic competitive analysis based on business considerations, competitive analysis of the political environment must examine both the immediate market environment and the larger economic system in which the firm operates.

Develop Strategic Responses

The fourth step in coping with the political environment is to develop enlightened company policies based on what has been learned. If sensitivity to the political environment never translates into specific corporate or managerial action, it cannot justify a claim on company resources. If the competitive analysis has been done well, it will be clearer to management whether strategic changes in products, locations, processes, employee relations, public communication, or lobbying are in the interests of the firm. The appropriate parties to develop and execute these responses will also be easier to identify.

Reach Out to External Entities. One strategy for taking advantage of changes in the political environment is to become a more active participant in the political process. Many companies choose not to participate, leaving this task to trade or professional associations, business lobbying groups, or the largest firms in the industry. The Iron Law shows that all firms in an industry will not be equally affected by any given policy intervention. Accordingly, each firm may want to bring its particular circumstances to the attention of legislators, regulatory officials, or other political actors. Only through individual action can the company have its interests represented aggressively and fairly.

An active individual response might involve many formal and informal activities. To develop closer relationships with elected officials in the communities and states where the company is located or does business, managers may want to learn more about the political forces at work in their districts and states. When the Arkansas Business Council became concerned about the quality of the state's higher education, it financed a study not only of education, but of the state's spending and tax policies. Business participation in electoral politics can be channelled through campaign contributions by political action committees or grass-roots efforts to get out the vote. There are other kinds of grass-roots programs: educating shareholders, employees, retirees, and other corporate constituents about issues important to the firm through programs of guest speakers; objective (i.e., two-sided) analyses of issues in company newsletters; alerts about pending legislation; and surveys. When elected officials learn that not only the business itself, but individuals as well, are concerned about a policy issue, they are more likely to take notice.

Managers should also contact administrative officials who often control decisions crucial to the success of the firm. These civil servants and political appointees usually have more technical expertise than elected officials, and may work on a much narrower band of issues. Often, they can be persuaded with sound technical arguments that are backed up by systematic information and analysis. In controversial cases, many interested parties may try to introduce information into the policy debate. Companies that can provide reliable, credible data about the potential impact of government policy options are more likely to succeed in influencing the choice among the various options.

These dynamics also apply in the international arena. As U.S. firms operate on a global scale, their operations are affected by foreign governments as much as by the domestic political environment. International developments such as the integration of the European Economic Community, the change of regimes in Eastern Europe, or the departure of Britain from Hong Kong pose great risks to business success. Sophisticated firms have learned how to enlist the support of the U.S. government in their efforts to do business abroad. Through official channels, such as bilateral or multilateral trade negotiations, or through less formal channels, U.S. government offices can assist U.S. firms in negotiating with host countries.

These trade and consular officials, like domestic regulatory officials, are career employees who have considerable expertise in their fields. A well-documented analysis of the company's arguments, coupled with an understanding of the government's legal options and political interests, can be very persuasive. However, a lack of sensitivity to the larger diplomatic and economic context of trade negotiations can lead to asking these officials to do the impossible—which is likely to defeat the purpose.

Finally, companies are often advised to keep in touch with activist groups that have continuing interests in their business. Environmental groups, civil rights groups, and community organizations, for example, may raise issues that signal the onset of major risks or liabilities for a company. Early awareness of such issues and attempting to understand them at a preliminary stage prepare firms for responding promptly and responsibly. To illustrate, McDonald's successfully countered pickets in Vermont who wanted to ban polystyrene packaging for hot food. The company's aggressive local education campaign persuaded activists of the advantages of recycling polystyrene products. Often, these types of activities help managers appreciate the political legitimacy of perspectives other than their own. Understanding the reasoning of those who seek to constrain them helps managers develop persuasive arguments that acknowledge the reasonable claims of other perspectives and limit the costs to their individual firms.

Making Internal Adjustments. A complementary strategy is to respond to the political environment by changing some aspect of the company's internal operations. As firms see the writing on the political wall, they can move to take advantage of coming public policy. For example, many companies believe that environmental laws will become more stringent during the 1990s. Meeting high standards in pollution control when designing and constructing facilities is far cheaper than retrofitting after new standards have been adopted and enforced. The business opportunities for pollution control equipment and waste management are likely to expand. Similarly, the movement toward integrating handicapped workers into mainstream employment poses challenges and opportunities to businesses that seek to hire more individuals with physical disabilities as well as to those who provide products and services that enable other businesses to hire people with disabilities. Employment practices, product development, service innovations, manufacturing, marketing, sales—nearly all aspects of business may require reexamination in light of changing political conditions.

Organize for Ongoing Sensitivity to the Political Environment

Businesses have employed many mechanisms for developing strategies to respond to political challenges and opportunities. Strategy development and execution may be handled by:

- A specialized staff that is devoted to public or regulatory affairs
- A committee of the board of directors
- The office of the chief executive officer (CEO)
- Staff task forces that draw on both staff and line personnel
- Delegation to line management
- External consultants

Each of these mechanisms has some distinctive strengths and weaknesses, and typically several are used at once.

Specialized Staff. During the 1970s, many firms instituted Issues Management or Public Affairs programs that built up separate staffs of specialists with expertise in monitoring and interacting with the political environment. Because of the downsizing and restructuring of corporations during the last five years, many of these programs have been eliminated or reduced and their functions absorbed into the managerial ranks. Nevertheless, a number of companies continue to maintain specialized staffs that are responsible for monitoring and responding to the political environment. These staffs may be located at corporate headquarters, in Washington, DC, or at several major corporate facilities.

The strengths of these specialized staffs are their technical expertise in the public sphere, their network of contacts outside the corporation, and their ability to interpret the political world to top managers. Only a fraction of the work of these staffs is substantive; most involves communication within the business and with external constituents, marketing, education, coalition building, and outreach.

The risk of this approach is that such a staff has the potential to become peripheral to the major strategic thrusts of the company, and thus isolated from line managers. If this happens, the staff will not be able to effectively communicate either the company's needs and problems to the outside world or problems of the outside world to the company. When a specialized staff is effective, it serves as a powerful bridge between the business and its external constituencies. When it is not effective, it buffers the company, without helping either the company or the external constituencies to learn from one another or to function more effectively.

As a variation on the specialized public affairs staff approach, some firms make their legal staffs responsible for monitoring issues that arise in the political environment. Because many dealings with governments have legal components, bringing in lawyers at an early stage can help the business to position itself so as to limit legal liability. However, filtering all such issues through lawyers makes it difficult for line managers to notice the competitive opportunities and challenges posed by government action. Thus, this mechanism for handling strategy for the political environment tends to produce a more reactive stance.

A second variant is to integrate planning for the political environment with planning for the business environment by assigning responsibility to strategic planners. Because both kinds of planning are done by the same group, this approach guards against the risks of marginality of a specialized public affairs staff. It keeps people with public affairs responsibilities focused on business implications for the firm. Compared to a public affairs staff, a combined staff does not offer similar incentives for the development of specialized expertise in public affairs and the nurturing of relationships between the business and its external constituents.

The two kinds of planning can be quite different. Strategic planning for the political environment tends to be less quantitative, less reliant on available data, more reliant on relationships and coalitions with other entities, and more laden with political, moral, and ethical values. Although both kinds of planning need to be interpreted and sold to line managers, planning for the political environment triggers some kinds of resistance that strategic planners typically do not face—i.e., challenges on political or ethical grounds to company positions or alliances. For example, Pacific Bell's active support of employees with AIDS created puzzlement and some hostility among many supervisory employees.[2] Why, they wondered, would their company adopt policies and sponsor events that allied it with homosexual activist groups? It is a rare strategic planning group that can also manage hot political issues in a constructive way both within and without the business.

Committees of Boards of Directors. Some corporate boards of directors have formed committees to deal with public policy issues facing their firms. These committees are typically chaired by outside directors. The strengths of this approach to the political environment are that it provides a vehicle for attracting top management attention to public policy issues while providing the firm with the perspectives of the outside directors on the political challenges that face the firm. As boards face increasingly active institutional shareholders, a formal mechanism to consider social and public issues provides an orderly way to deal with the concerns and demands of these groups.

The disadvantages are that the board does not have the time, knowledge, or resources to translate many of these issues into operational strategies for the firm to pursue. This mechanism can work well for a handful of pressing issues that face the company, but not for the full range of day-to-day constraints and opportunities, or for the anticipation of gradual, long-run change.

---

[2] David Kirp, "Uncommon Decency: Pacific Bell Responds to AIDS," *Harvard Business Review* (May/June 1989).

Chief Executives. Some CEOs have taken considerable personal responsibility for navigating their companies through the political environment. Often, this is triggered by a major crisis that threatens the business with significant losses. For example, Robert Malott of FMC undertook a personal crusade for tort reform after his company was forced to pay several huge legal judgments for manufacturing equipment that had been involved in industrial accidents.[3] Lee Iacocca of Chrysler personally led the fight for federal loan guarantees when his company was on the verge of bankruptcy. Several CEOs have spearheaded efforts to improve the education of the labor force by working with the public schools.

The advantages of CEO involvement are significant. A CEO has a company-wide perspective that frames political issues in the context of the company's business interests. At this level, priorities for public affairs are not separated from business strategy, because the CEO is necessarily responsible for both internal and external constituents. CEOs also have a great deal of credibility when they are knowledgeable about the political process and proactive in pursuing the interests of their firms. Politicians are more interested in the views of the CEO than in those of the staff representative of the CEO, provided, of course, that the CEO is not naive about what the political process can and cannot do. Involvement of the CEO also legitimizes interest in the political environment throughout the firm. Other managers come to see the importance of public policy for the success of their products or services.

These advantages are accompanied by some disadvantages. The CEO, even in a small, single-product company, never has enough time to handle all the ways in which the company is affected by the political environment. If all initiative for dealing with the political environment originates with the CEO, many things will not get the attention they deserve. In a firm of any size, the CEO's efforts must be complemented by the significant involvement of other managers. Mechanisms for encouraging that involvement are also necessary. A related disadvantage is that the CEO is also responsible for the performance of the company; short-term pressures on performance tend to divert sustained attention to problems in the political environment, even though they are eventually linked to performance.

Line Management. Some firms leave political issues in the hands of their managers. The capacity to see threats and opportunities in the environment is a fundamental skill of general management, and good managers notice pertinent threats and opportunities, regardless of their origins. One great advantage of this approach is the easy translation from awareness to

---

[3] Martha Wagner Weinberg, "The Political Education of Bob Malott," *Harvard Business Review* (May/June 1988).

strategy development and execution when the same person is responsible for all stages. Another great advantage is that by decentralizing the responsibility for monitoring and developing strategy, the firm has many opportunities to take advantage of the complex political environments that surround its various activities. Line managers have an immediate grasp of the business's capacity to respond to challenges from external constituents. They are also well positioned to balance the needs of customers and employees against the demands of other constituencies. This is a strong argument for locating much of the responsibility for the political environment at the level of strategic business units.

The risk of leaving strategy for the political environment in the hands of line managers is that many managers are too preoccupied with pressing matters of performance and competition to devote much attention to external, nonmarket constituencies. In addition, many managers do not have the training or the inclination to understand the dynamics of the political environment. As mentioned earlier, many believe not only that politics is outside the realm of their interests and competence, but also that politics should not interfere with legitimate business activities. Such naive beliefs interfere with managers' effectiveness in dealing with legitimate actions of government that, like it or not, affect their competitive success.

Companies that want to rely on their line managers to develop strategies for dealing with the political environment can educate managers to operate more effectively in this sphere. Training can teach managers how to understand the political environment. Staff support can bring issues to the attention of line managers (compensating in part for the problem of scarce time), reminding them of the importance of strategy in the political environment. Regular surveys of managers and other employees about pressing issues facing the firm in the future can also remind managers to pay attention to the long-run implications of changes in the social and political world. Firms can also offer incentives to reward managers for reaching out to nonmarket constituencies. If people understand that their responsibilities include liaison with community groups, elected officials, or local and state governments, and that their performance in managing these responsibilities will be evaluated regularly, line managers can be expected to take on significant responsibility for this sort of strategy. Bear in mind that some central direction or focus is necessary to encourage people to discharge these responsibilities effectively on an ongoing basis.

More line manager involvement in political relationships does not necessarily rule out the need for specialized staff, but it does change the role of that staff. Rather than buffering the rest of the organization from the hurly-burly of politics, the staff now must work to involve people in external relationships and activities. They coordinate and direct attention to issues that they deem important. They move information around the organization. As senior management recognizes the importance of political factors, specialized expertise becomes more important in a strategic sense, but this requires different organizational arrangements to be used effectively.

Task Forces. Task forces combine some of the advantages of the mechanisms already discussed. Many firms create task forces on an ad hoc basis to meet immediate challenges or to prepare for long-term changes. These task forces may draw on people throughout the organization, from both staff and line functions, to marshall the expertise of the business to cope with new demands or opportunities. Sometimes task forces are headed by a designated "issue manager," whose job is to monitor developments or to coordinate the implementation of the task force's plan.

The advantages of this approach are that task forces bring together people with diverse expertise and experience. They facilitate implementation by allowing the task force members to disseminate the results of their work to their groups and divisions. Task forces enhance the legitimacy of corporate decisions by offering many kinds of people, with many kinds of views, the opportunity to participate in controversial decisions. Because task forces are temporary tools, the firm that uses them acquires some flexibility in the use of resources, compared to firms that commit resources to permanent staff. For a business that develops a strategy to cope with child care and parental leave one year, recycling hazardous wastes the next, and the implications of the integration of the European Economic Community for sales in Europe after that, task forces provide a flexible way to mobilize the organization's talent pool to address these diverse challenges.

The disadvantages of using task forces include the lack of continuity in relationships between the business and external constituencies, the lack of in-house expertise for all issues in the political environment, the variable quality of task force products, and the lack of follow-through in implementing task force recommendations.

Third-Party Assistance. Many small- and medium-size firms leave their political strategy in the hands of those outside the firm. Trade associations, law firms, and lobbying firms do the work of scanning the environment, considering the implications, and developing and executing responses. Firms rely on these consultants for their expertise, knowledge of the political process, and capacity to mount coordinated efforts to achieve desired results. The advantages of specialization are obvious. Economies of scale are available when many firms are similarly situated with respect to legislation, regulation, or other government action. Expertise that the firm does not require on a full-time basis can be sensibly contracted out for efficiency's sake.

The disadvantages are also significant. Information from a trade association is equally available to all of its members, which means that competitors also have access to the same information. A second, more significant disadvantage goes back to the Iron Law. Although a trade association or lobbying group may help some firms in the industry, not all firms will have the same goals or benefit equally from government action. Thus, most firms will discover at some point that the policies advocated by their trade association will actually harm their particular competitive position within the industry.

External consultants, law firms, and lobbyists suffer from a milder version of the problem posed by the Iron Law. Although they may be familiar with the industry, they seldom know enough about the competitive situations of individual firms to fully appreciate the implications that various government actions will have on those firms. Because they are not full-time employees, they cannot know as well as managers at what point compromise or negotiation begins to threaten the firm's interests. Leaving political relationships in the hands of third parties may also mean that no one in top management really understands the options and uncertainties involved. As a result, no one is well situated to pursue the firm's interests effectively.

No single approach offers a business a sure-fire way to manage the development and execution of strategy for the political environment. Reliance on any single mechanism leaves the firm vulnerable to the considerable risks of mismanaging its opportunities. Combinations of mechanisms are necessary to compensate for the advantages and disadvantages of each approach. In particular, some combination of staff and line involvement offers the possibility for specialization and continuity in external relationships plus the integration of political concerns with ongoing business operations.

GUIDELINES FOR STRATEGY IN THE POLITICAL ENVIRONMENT

Because industries and firms differ so widely in their exposures to political and social influences, only general recommendations that apply across a wide range of cases are offered here.

Do Not Wait for Issues to Gather Momentum

Calvin Coolidge is reputed to have said that he never bothered to take action when he saw a problem coming down the road; nine out of ten would run off the road before they got to him anyway. This strategy has been a recipe for disaster for many U.S. companies. By waiting until issues have gathered enough momentum to reach their desks, managers find themselves face to face with roaring locomotives. It is a lot easier to divert or at least influence political action at early stages. Political issues develop over long periods of time, offering many opportunities to participate early in the process. By the time city, state, or federal governments come to the brink of adopting legislation, or a regulatory agency implements standards, much of the game is already over. Managements that react to government action after it occurs confront not only nonbusiness interests but also entrenched interests in their own industry who are among the beneficiaries of the policy that has been adopted. Managements that participate in the development of policy and regulation have the opportunity to shape policy to achieve goals while minimizing the costs to themselves and maximizing the costs to their competitors. Thinking in terms of prevention, not cure, means that a company must always have some antennae out, to anticipate, scan, and monitor the world beyond the marketplace.

Companies should focus on those issues that are likely to affect them over a three- to five-year time horizon. Short-term crises tend to get management's attention regardless of the firm's political sophistication. It is difficult to justify spending scarce resources on issues that develop over longer time horizons. Three to five years permits intelligent anticipation, providing the firm with enough warning to take sensible action.

Integrate Strategy for the Political Environment With Other Business Strategy

Political strategy is competitive strategy. A firm's political positions and activities affect its competitive position, and vice versa. Although companies may undertake activities for philanthropic reasons, with no expectation of business payoff, most companies need to be sensitive to the interrelationship of their political and business agendas. This does not mean that a firm should remain single-mindedly focused on profitability or other business outcomes. Quite the contrary: Devoting company resources to community relations, environmental goals, public education, and other public purposes can be a highly desirable way for a company to satisfy many objectives at once, at the same time allowing it to contribute to the larger well-being in such a way that the firm strengthens its own reputation, influence, and long-term success. Being a good corporate citizen helps the corporation attract the social legitimacy and approval that are required to permit sustained economic success. Business strategy and political strategy are both facets of enlightened self-interest.

Maintain Multiple Links to the Political World

The political environment is complex with both opponents and allies coming from many directions. Elected officials must respond to multiple constituencies, and any single business is only one constituent. No single relationship with government officials, trade associations, or political parties can cover all of the political and social issues that a company faces. A range of people from different functional and geographical units of the company can help to build the links necessary to attract a web of external support.

Be Adaptive but Persistent

Business interests nearly always face organized and vocal opponents who advocate policies that impose considerable costs on their companies. Seldom are businesses able to get precisely the policies that they want. Compromise is inevitable. Although companies must be prepared to compromise, they must also be prepared to persist in demands that they consider to be reasonable and legitimate. Decisions are never final. Losing one round is not the end of the process. Companies that persist in a reasoned and informed way are more likely to see their proposals endorsed, at least in part, in the political environment.

Search for Common Ground With External Groups

Whether external groups place demands on a firm or a firm asks for help from government, having allies is better than going it alone. Allies may be found among other private domestic firms in the same industry, or in the community. However, they can also be found where least expected. For example, consumer, environmental, civil rights, labor, and religious groups may be business adversaries on many issues, but they can turn into allies on others.

The search for allies is the search for common ground between the firm's interests and other interests in the community and society at large. A strategy that is based on alliances tends to pull a firm away from the narrow pursuit of self-interest at the expense of others and into a search for common goals. Companies that have sought nontraditional allies have strengthened their own claims to legitimacy and influence on issues such as trade policy, public education, deregulation, and community development. This tends to produce more satisfactory political results in the short term, but also has some constructive long-term payoffs. Working with external groups as potential allies, at least some of the time, builds understanding and acceptance on both sides. This improved understanding can be helpful to a company even when its one-time allies are back on the other side of the picket line. When businesses focus their energies on those business objectives that also benefit other groups in society (e.g., creating jobs, designing better products, or improving employees' skills), they strengthen public acceptance of the whole enterprise.

CONCLUSION

Many sectors of society are interested in business activities and will make and use channels to influence those activities. Government, the most important such channel, is here to stay. So are concerned citizens and institutions that have ideas about how businesses should be run. Sophisticated businesses have learned to work with activists, the media, politicians, and bureaucrats instead of against them. At a time when American business needs a favorable public, legal, and political environment to support its international competitiveness, success may depend on whether more managers can master a comparable strategic orientation to the political environment.

21

Strategy of Market Entry: To Pioneer or Follow?

MARVIN B. LIEBERMAN
John E. Anderson School of Management, UCLA

DAVID B. MONTGOMERY
Graduate School of Business, Stanford University

INTRODUCTION

This chapter presents a framework for understanding how profitability is tied to the order in which companies enter a market. Does it always pay to be first? In first-mover situations, the pioneering firm has a period of head start before followers enter. During this initial period, the firm may have an opportunity to make strategic investments in numerous areas, including facilities, distribution, product positioning, patentable technology, natural resources, and human and organizational know-how. If imitation is costly or occurs with a long lag, then preemptive investments during this early period can be leveraged into significant long-run benefits to the pioneering firm. Further, lack of competition during this initial period prior to entry by others may reduce the cost of acquiring resources, relative to the resource costs that will prevail later in the evolution of the market. But if imitation is easy, later entrants may be able to "free ride" on the innovator's investments and thereby gain most benefits without incurring the innovator's cost. In such circumstances, it may be better for the first-mover to invest relatively little and simply skim the market cream during the early period of little or no competition, or perhaps not to invest at all.

Potential first-mover advantages arise in three areas: (1) new products, (2) new processes, and (3) new markets. For a given firm, a specific first-mover opportunity may arise as the result of unique product or process development by the firm, because the firm has the vision to see a new market opportunity not yet perceived by others, or because the firm chooses to be the first to act on an opportunity perceived by many. While the availability of first-mover opportunities is partly under the control of the firm, there is often a significant element of luck. One example is 3M's development of "Post-Its" from a failed glue; 3M's innovative culture was prepared to respond when fortune smiled.

Some of the major competitive issues confronting managers in relation to first-mover opportunities are:

- How to identify first-mover opportunities
- How to exploit these opportunities and defend the resulting first-mover advantages
- How to avoid first-mover disadvantages
- How firms that enter late can successfully attack an established first-mover.

This chapter provides a reference point for managers who are faced with such issues. It aims to help managers exploit opportunities and avoid pitfalls in both first-mover and follower positions.[1]

---

[1] For a more theoretical treatment of these issues, see M. Lieberman and D. Montgomery, "First-Mover Advantages," *Strategic Management Journal* vol. 9 (Special Issue, 1988), pp. 41–58.

The first section of this chapter deals with the phenomenon of first-mover advantages. Do they exist? Over what time frame? What is their magnitude? The second section considers specific sources of first-mover advantage. An understanding of these sources provides a backdrop for specific management action. The third section explores the converse of first-mover advantage: drawbacks of early entry, and the relative advantages that can accrue to follower firms. The final section suggests managerial implications and offers prescriptions for both first-movers and followers.

FIRST-MOVER ADVANTAGE: FACT OR FICTION?

What Is a First-Mover?

Defining a first-mover is not as clear-cut as it may at first seem to be. First-movership may entail being the first to produce a new product, the first to use a new process, or the first to enter a new market. A given firm may be the first in one or more of these senses and a follower in others. Consider, for example, the disposable diaper industry. Expensive, two-piece disposable diapers had been introduced in Europe and in the United States by the time Procter & Gamble (P&G) began test-marketing Pampers in the early 1960s. The expense of the early disposable diapers virtually guaranteed that the product would be used by most families only for travel. P&G believed that disposable diapers could substantially compete against the traditional cloth diapers if the cost per diaper could be held to five cents or less. When P&G achieved this goal, the disposable diaper revolution began in the United States. Later, P&G was the first to introduce disposable diapers to the Japanese market and achieved a ninety percent market share. Unfortunately for P&G, Japan's Unicharm and Kao both launched a superabsorbant diaper that offered significant advantages. P&G's market share in Japan was driven as low as 7 percent (it has subsequently risen to over 30 percent), causing the company to reassess its diaper design. A chastened but more savvy P&G learned its lesson in the Japanese market and was first to introduce the superabsorbant product to the United States. P&G's first move in the U.S. market preempted Kao and Unicharm from building a strong U.S. beachhead with a superabsorbant diaper.

The question is, Was P&G first? It certainly was in introducing disposable diapers to Japan. It was the first to introduce the superabsorbant product to the United States. It was the first to lower the cost per diaper, fueling the U.S. disposable diaper revolution. It has gained and maintained substantial global market share advantage from these moves. Yet P&G was not the first to introduce disposable diapers to the global or U.S. markets. Others had gone before. It was not the global first-mover when it came to the new, improved superabsorbant diaper, but it was the first to introduce the new product to the U.S. market.

Do First-Mover Advantages Exist?

Many first-movers enjoy lengthy periods of market prosperity, often becoming household words. Coca-Cola has maintained a leading position for a hundred years. Sony commands a substantial position in the "no-hands" portable cassette player market, which it pioneered with its Walkman. Perrier built a prestige image in the United States with its original healthful appeal as an alternative to alcohol, rather than as an alternative to tap water, which had been the position taken by previous bottled water companies. Additional examples abound of long-term success being sustained by the first-moving, pioneering firm.

Being a first-mover, however, does not guarantee long-term success. For example, in 1947 Cott was the first to introduce sugar-free soft drinks, and in 1962 Royal Crown was the first to introduce a sugar-free cola. Both were overtaken and dominated by Coca-Cola and Pepsi, later entrants into this market. Sperry Univac missed the ultimate potential of mainframe computers and yielded its early first-mover lead to IBM. Rheingold's Gablinger's low-calorie beer was a regional first-mover in the 1960s, yet it has been displaced by Miller Lite, Bud Lite, and others. The Osborne portable computer was a first-mover and an early winner before strategic error and bankruptcy took it out of contention. In 1974, Docutel had 100 percent of the emerging automatic teller machine market. Four years later, its share had slipped to 8 percent, because of the introduction of systems selling by IBM, Burroughs, and Honeywell as automatic teller machines became a mere component of electronic funds transfer systems.

While not absolute and immutable, as illustrated by these examples, pioneering advantages do appear to exist empirically. Using the Profit Impact of Market Strategy (PIMS) data, Robinson and Fornell have shown that on average, market share advantages accrue to pioneers and early followers in both industrial and consumer products.[2] As shown in Table 21-1, pioneering market share advantage is substantial for both industry groups. Nevertheless, the advantage appears to be greater for consumer goods, measured either in terms of differences in share between pioneers and late followers, or in terms of the statistical contribution of entry order to the explanation of market share differences.

A further empirical analysis of pioneering advantage in consumer packaged goods was conducted by Glen Urban and his associates.[3] For a

---

[2] W.T. Robinson, "Sources of Market Pioneer Advantages: The Case of Industrial Goods Industries," *Journal of Marketing Research* vol. 25 (Feb. 1988), pp. 87–94; and W.T. Robinson and C. Fornell, "The Sources of Market Pioneer Advantages in Consumer Goods Industries," *Journal of Marketing Research* vol. 22 (Aug. 1985), pp. 297–304.

[3] G.L. Urban, R. Carter, S. Gaskin and Z. Mucha, "Market Share Rewards to Pioneering Brands: An Empirical Analysis and Strategic Implications," *Management Science* vol. 32, no. 6 (June 1986), pp. 645–659.

TABLE 21-1

Average Market Share per Entrant Position

	Consumer goods	Industrial goods
Pioneers	29%	29%
Early followers	17%	21%
Late followers	12%	15%
Number of businesses	371	1,482
Percent of variation in market share due to order of entry	18%	8%

sample of 129 products, they found that 77 percent of the variation in the relative market share of each brand to enter, compared with the market share of the pioneer, could be explained by (1) order of entry, (2) ratio of preference for a brand relative to the pioneer, (3) advertising of the brand relative to the pioneer, and (4) the elapsed time since the previous entry. As expected, earlier entrants benefited from a larger market share. That is, the second entrant had some advantage over the third entrant, etc.; but the first-mover enjoyed an advantage over all.

The market share disadvantage of later entrants can be estimated from these results. Assuming that there were no differences in consumer preferences and advertising between the pioneer and later entrants, the shares of successive entrants relative to the share of the pioneer would be 71 percent, 58 percent, 51 percent, 45 percent, 41 percent, etc., respectively. Thus, the second entrant would tend to achieve about 71 percent of the pioneer's market share if it merely matched the pioneer in customer preference and advertising, while the sixth entrant could expect to realize only 41 percent of the pioneer's share under these circumstances.

Thus far, the evidence of first-mover advantage has concerned market share effects. What about profits? The systematic evidence here is very sparse. To be sure, one can easily conjure up examples such as Coca-Cola to suggest that first-movers may be very profitable over a substantial period of time. However, an analysis of several hundred consumer businesses from the PIMS data base found that for the average firm, pioneering was marginally unprofitable.[4]

Another aspect for which little evidence is available is the question of risk. If pioneering is riskier than following, it should yield higher expected returns in order to compensate for the added risk. However, as will be seen later in this chapter, there are risks, albeit different ones, to be faced in both the pioneer and follower strategies.

---

[4] W. Boulding and M. Moore, "Pioneering and Profitability: Structural Estimates From a Nonlinear Simultaneous Equations Model With Endogenous Pioneering," Research Paper, Fuqua School of Business, Duke University (May 1987).

Duration of Advantage

While nothing lasts forever, market share advantages to pioneers exhibit some tendency to persist over substantial periods of time. Davidson notes that in eighteen United Kingdom grocery product categories, largely developed since 1945, fully twelve of the pioneer brands remained the market leader as of the mid-1970's.[5] By the same token, the advantage is not guaranteed, as six of the eighteen pioneers were overtaken by rivals (for example, Gillette overtook Wilkinson in stainless razor blades). Further evidence of the market position persistence of lead brands is cited by Ries and Trout.[6] They note that for twenty-five leading brands in 1923, twenty were still first some sixty years later. Four had slipped to second, while one of the lead brands had plummeted to fifth. While this study was largely, but not exclusively, of pioneering brands, it illustrates the potential for long-run advantage that a pioneer might capture.

Brown and Lattin, for example, have examined the duration of both order of entry and headstart effects on first-mover advantage in regional markets of a new segments of the pet-food market.[7] "Headstart" refers to the lead time the pioneer has in the market prior to the entry of the second brand. They found that although the market share advantage due to order of entry persisted even three to five years after the entry of the second brand, the headstart effect dissipated over time. That is, the longer the time the pioneer had been in the market prior to the competitor entering, the greater its headstart advantage, but the longer the second brand had been in the market with the pioneer, the more the initial headstart advantage was diminished.

Given evidence of the advantage conferred by order of entry, what might a later entrant do to overcome this handicap and shorten the duration of the pioneer's advantage? Urban et al.[8] provide a market-based calibration showing later entrants can overcome the pioneer's advantage by better positioning their product relative to consumer wants and by spending more heavily on advertising. Product positioning, they found, was approximately three times as important as order of entry in explaining relative market share, while advertising expenditures were just over twice as important as entry order. Thus, a later entrant can overcome a pioneer's natural advantage by developing a better product (perhaps as a result of observing the limitations of the pioneer's product), by advertising more than the pioneer, or both. However, a pioneer can avert loss of

[5] J.H. Davidson, "Why Most New Consumer Brands Fail," *Harvard Business Review* vol. 54 (Mar.-Apr. 1976), pp. 117–122.

[6] A. Ries and J. Trout, *Marketing Warfare* (New York: McGraw-Hill, 1986).

[7] P. Brown and J. Lattin, "The Headstart Effect as a Source of Pioneering Advantage," Research Paper, Graduate School of Business, Stanford University (Jan. 1990).

[8] Urban et al., op. cit.

market position by being at least as good as later entrants in satisfying customer needs and providing advertising support. Consequently, the only way that later entrants can successfully erode the pioneer's first-mover advantages is if the pioneer provides the opportunity by failing to at least match the later entrants in meeting customer needs and in spending on advertising.

The evidence suggests that first-mover or pioneering advantages do indeed exist, that they may persist over very substantial periods of time, and they may be derived from product, technology, and market pioneering. But the anticipated rewards to pioneering are not a natural "birthright" to which every pioneer is entitled. They are an opportunity that will be realized only if the firm earns them in competition with other firms.

SOURCES OF FIRST-MOVER ADVANTAGE

First-mover advantages arise from three basic sources: (1) proprietary technology, (2) preemption of resources, and (3) the ability to lock-in customers through switching costs.

Proprietary Technology: Research and Development and Innovation

A firm with a new product or process technology can often gain a competitive advantage. However, this advantage can be sustained only if the technology can be kept proprietary for a reasonable period of time. Technology can be kept proprietary through patents, copyrights, or secrecy.

Patents. In a few industries, such as pharmaceuticals and chemicals, where innovative product characteristics can be clearly defined, patents have been an important mechanism enabling first-movers to capitalize the value of their innovations. For instance, the high average profitability of prescription drug companies largely reflects first-mover advantages protected from imitation by patents. In another example, Xerox maintained a highly profitable monopoly in plain paper copiers for over a decade based on its original patents. To extend this period further, Xerox patented a thicket of alternative technologies that shielded the firm from entry until challengers used antitrust actions to force compulsory licensing. General Electric's long-term dominance of the electric lamp industry was initially derived from control of the basic Edison patent, and later maintained through the accumulation of hundreds of minor patents on the lamp and associated equipment. Similarly, Polaroid continues to maintain its monopoly in instant photography, bolstered by its victory in patent infringement suits against Kodak.

Copyrights. Copyrights sometimes serve as an effective substitute for patents. In computers, for example, Apple protected its Macintosh from direct imitation by copyrighting the operating system software and aggressively challenging infringers in court. Similarly, Intel is protected by copyrights on the design of key integrated circuits used in all IBM-compatible personal computers.

Secrecy. Secrecy is often utilized to sustain advantage over competitors. In industries where process advantages are competitively important, companies may bring key sources of such advantages "in house" in an effort to keep them proprietary. Thus, many companies themselves produce or modify their process equipment. For example, S. C. Johnson uses internally developed injection moulding machines to produce many of the caps used on its products. This capability enabled the design of a unique "scrubber" cap for Shout laundry stain remover. Other proprietary filling equipment is used to fill the patented can, which permits dispensing of Edge shaving gel, an innovative product of S. C. Johnson emulsion technology. Similarly, P&G spends several hundred thousands of dollars tailoring each new disposable diaper processing machine, in part to maintain proprietary process advantage. In some cases it is better not to patent a process, since competitor monitoring of patent applications is readily and commonly done. This is especially true when it seems likely that a competitor could use the patent knowledge to readily invent around the firm's patent.

Managerial and Organizational Innovation. Research and development and innovation need not be limited to physical hardware; firms also make improvements in managerial systems and may invent new organizational forms. Organizational innovations can be difficult for competitors to understand. This makes them slow to diffuse, so that they often convey more durable first-mover advantages than product or process innovations. Toyota, for example, has honed its vaunted production system since the 1950s, maintaining a continuing productivity advantage over U.S. auto producers as well as most of its domestic competitors. While the basic features of the Toyota system are now generally understood, the subtlety of the system and existence of many interdependent elements relating to work force, equipment, quality control, and supplier relations makes implementation by competitors difficult. Indeed, General Motors has made little progress in adopting the system in its own plants, despite the opportunity for first-hand observation provided by its joint venture with Toyota in Fremont, California.

Learning Curve. The well-known learning curve effect can also reinforce first-mover advantages. An early entrant with great accumulated production experience may be able to maintain a cost advantage over later rivals. However, this is true only to the extent that the relevant process technology can be kept secret. Process information flows to competitors through numerous channels, including "reverse engineering," employee mobility, plant tours, research publication, and informal communication by employees, vendors, and consultants. Typically, only a small fraction of process-based learning remains proprietary for more than a short period. Learning-based advantages can be sustained only if initial learning is augmented by continued improvements, or protected by an unusual degree of secrecy.

Firms that have successfully reaped large first-mover cost advantages based on proprietary learning-based improvements include Dow in magnesium, DuPont in titanium dioxide pigments, Lincoln Electric in welding equipment, and Toyota in "just-in-time" automobile manufacturing. In the latter two examples, learning-based advantages have been maintained by the firms' ability to sustain continued learning. Lincoln Electric's early market entry with superior patented products, coupled with a managerial system promoting continued cost reduction in an evolutionary technological environment, has enabled the company to maintain high profitability for decades.

Frequently, managers overestimate the degree of advantage that can be maintained on the process side. For example, although there is a tendency for process technology to leak to competitors more slowly than product technology, competitors typically gain access to detailed information on both products and processes within a year of development. Even if the pioneering firm can keep its own process advances secret, rivals are bound to narrow the gap as their own production experience increases. If rivals are more proficient than the pioneer in their engineering capabilities, they may well surpass the pioneering firm despite lower cumulative volume.

Preemption of Scarce Resources

The first-mover in a market is frequently able to preempt later rivals by acquiring the most desirable resources at relatively low cost. These resources include natural resource deposits, geographical locations, marketing channels, product positioning, and, to some extent, skilled personnel. Latecomers may be forced to use inferior resources, or to incur higher costs to attain parity with the pioneering firm.

If the first-mover firm has superior information, it may be able to purchase assets at prices below those that will prevail later in the evolution of the market. Natural resource deposits are the most obvious case. For example, the concentration of high-grade nickel deposits in a single geographic area in Canada enabled Inco, the first company in the area, to secure rights to virtually the entire supply and thus dominate world production for decades.

The pioneering firm may also be able to preempt the best technical or marketing personnel. However, this seldom confers a sustainable advantage, since unlike natural resources, human beings are highly mobile. Late entrants can easily offer a compensation premium for skilled personnel, which must be matched by the pioneering firm to prevent loss of employees. For the first-mover to gain a true advantage on the personnel side, the firm must be able to retain skilled workers without paying the full premium offered by competitors. The premium may be avoided, for instance, if followers are perceived to have risky prospects for survival.

First-movers may also be able to deter entry through strategies of spatial preemption. In many markets there is room for only a limited number of profitable firms; the first-mover can often select the most attractive niches and take strategic actions that limit the amount of space available for subsequent entrants. Preemptable space can be interpreted broadly to include not only geographic space, but also shelf space and product characteristics space (i.e., niches for product differentiation).

Locations in Geographic Space. First-movers have greatest choice of retailing locations and may be able to preempt the best sites without paying a premium. In some instances, large-scale spatial preemption has proven feasible, leading to huge financial returns for the first-movers. A prime example is Wal-Mart in discount retailing. Wal-Mart sought out regions of the southwestern U.S. with towns too small to support more than one discount retailer. (Initially, other retailers thought these towns were too small to support any discount retailer). Wal-Mart then blanketed these regions with retail outlets and efficient distribution facilities. By coupling spatial preemption at the retail level with an extremely efficient distribution network, the firm has been able to defend its position and earn sustained high profits. The Price Club has pursued a variation on this strategy in the California market, with warehouse stores packed just closely enough in the most lucrative suburban locations to block openings for competitors.

Airlines have pursued similar strategies with their hub-and-spoke systems. Airlines that dominate a particular urban hub or city-pair market have often been able to charge a premium. Eastern gained dominance in the New York to Washington market with its pioneering shuttle service, whose profits helped support the remainder of the Eastern system for decades. Similarly, USAir, which dominates a large proportion of its geographic markets, earned one of the highest profit rates in the industry in the 1980s. Once it has become firmly entrenched at a given hub, an airline becomes extremely costly for competitors to dislodge.

Marketing and Distribution Channels. Similarly, a first-mover may be able to preempt the best marketing and distribution channels. For example, shelf space is a critically scarce resource in most retail outlets, and late entrants may be unable to gain access to retailers' shelves or may be able to do so only with exceptionally differentiated products, exorbitant promotional expenditures, or deep retailer discounts. Preemptive distribution advantage is especially available to first-movers with products that are physically bulky or that come in a wide assortment of flavors or sizes. For example, Gerber's baby food and P&G's disposable diapers are stocked by virtually all supermarkets. Since shelf space limitations restrict the number of competing brands to at most two or three, these two pioneers face limited competition. In disposable diapers, P&G was also able to tie up with the premier distributor of hospital maternity kits, Gift Pax, thereby blocking access to this channel by later entrants.

Preemption of Consumer's Perceptual Space. The pioneering firm may also be able to acquire space or positioning in the perception of consumers more readily or cheaply than later entrants. If they are able to generate sufficient consumer awareness and product trial, pioneers often play a critical role in defining the attributes that consumers perceive as important within a product category. For example, Coca-Cola, as the pioneer, defined for consumers around the world what distinctive attributes, such as taste, a cola should possess. The first-mover's messages stand alone and are noticeable, while those of later entrants tend to crowd each other out. A late entrant must have a truly superior product, or else advertise more frequently (or more creatively) than the incumbent in order to be noticed by the consumer. In such cases large pioneer market shares tend to persist because perceptions and preferences, once formed, are difficult to alter.

Pioneers such as Coca-Cola and Kleenex have become prototypical, occupying a unique position in the consumer's mind. The same phenomenon exists in business and industrial markets. Xerox made its name so virtually synonymous with plain-paper copying that its name has become a verb. Many people have xeroxed on their Canon copiers, but who has "canoned" on their Xerox? Similarly, the name Cray has become almost synonymous with supercomputers.

Another factor in the persistence of large pioneer market shares is that new consumers continually enter the market and form their own preferences. Since these new consumers are more likely to be exposed to the high-share pioneering product than to the lower-share follower product, they may form a preference for the pioneering product, as did consumers who tried the product immediately on introduction. As Carpenter noted, for example, growing up in a home that uses only Vaseline petroleum jelly may have the same impact on a consumer's petroleum jelly preferences as no competition.[9] Thus, successful pioneering entry results may be sustained based in part on customer preference formation mechanisms.

Filling Product Line Gaps. Pioneers may be able to reinforce their early lead by filling product differentiation niches. Kellogg has sustained its extraordinary profit rates, in part, by proliferating an array of new cereal products. McDonald's, which has long dominated the hamburger fast-food market, reinforced its advantage by moving into breakfast foods and fried chicken. The breakfast move provided extended hours of utilization of McDonald's fixed assets, while chicken enhanced McDonald's attractiveness by offering consumers variety. Indeed, many successful consumer product pioneers that initially held product quality superiority over imitators subsequently developed advantages in the form of a broader product line even as their quality superiority was eroded by competition. Broad product lines convey advantage by enhancing the supplier's bargaining power, providing the opportunity to gain economies in operations, and by attracting customers through variety. For example, P&G's broad product line enables it to achieve distribution advantages by means of discounts for full car shipments. Full product lines reduce the number of supplier relationships for business customers; for retail consumers they provide opportunities for convenient one-stop shopping.

Preemptive Investment in Plant and Equipment. Another way that an established first-mover can deter entry is through preemptive investment in plant and equipment. When markets are regional because of high transport costs or tariffs, it may be important to establish an early local presence. In disposable diapers, for example, P&G rushed to build a network of plants across the United States, and then in Europe and Japan. Such capacity can block opportunities for new entry. If pioneers fail to build plant capacity quickly enough, they may leave an easy beachhead for competitors.

When the incumbent holds adequate capacity, an added deterrent to competitive entry is the threat of a price war if overcapacity develops. In titanium dioxide pigments, for example, DuPont pioneered a new process and quickly moved to build a plant of twice the conventional scale. The resulting excess capacity and threat of price erosion deterred rivals from building the new facilities required to imitate DuPont's process. Similarly, Dow Chemical maintained a near monopoly position in magnesium for several decades, based partly on preemptive investments (threatened or actual) in plant capacity.

---

[9] G.S. Carpenter, "Market Pioneering and Competitive Positioning Strategy," *Annales de Telecommunications* vol. 42, no. 11-12 (Nov.-Dec. 1987).

Buyer Switching Costs

First-mover advantages also arise from buyer switching costs. A customer who invests time and energy adapting to the supplier's product will lose these investments if he switches to another supplier. Late entrants must therefore invest extra resources to attract customers away from the first-mover firm. If the benefits of switching to a new supplier are uncertain, risk aversion may lock in the buyer even more strongly.

Initial Transactions Costs in Adapting to Supplier. Several types of switching costs can arise. First, switching costs can stem from initial investments that the buyer makes in adapting to the seller's product. These include the time and resources spent in qualifying a new supplier, the cost of ancillary products such as software for a new computer, and the time, disruption, and financial burdens of training employees.

Industrial buyers make vendor-specific investments in the design of their products and processes, in computer software, and in organizational systems. These investments must be made anew if the firm changes vendors. For example, travel agents using the pioneering Sabre and Apollo reservations systems made significant system-specific investments in training and office procedures.

Individual consumers face switching costs for similar reasons. With personal computer software, for example, the considerable investment the consumer makes in learning a particular package is largely lost if he switches to new software. The continued popularity of Lotus 1-2-3 is derived, in part, from the training costs that must be incurred anew if existing users switch to another package. For inexpensive package goods, once the consumer has found a satisfactory brand, the potential benefits of experimenting with a new brand are often too small to warrant much additional attention. This can give rise to substantial brand loyalty.

Switching costs may be different between leading firms and also-rans. McKesson, the giant drug wholesaler, has developed numerous services for its independent retail drug customers. These services include computer-based order entry and inventory control, shelf design and layout procedures, credit card systems, third-party claims processing, and terminal systems for pharmacy records. Independent retail drug stores come to depend on the efficiency of these systems for their very survival. Consequently, drug wholesalers that do not provide these services have little chance of capturing significant demand. However, the switching costs between McKesson and Bergen-Brunswick, which also provides such systems, is surprisingly low. McKesson can convert a Bergen-Brunswick customer to its "Economost" system in a day or two and visa versa. For example, McKesson's system can convert Bergen-Brunswick stock numbers into McKesson stock numbers automatically. Hence, technology may enhance switching costs for some competitors while lowering them for others.

Supplier-Specific Learning Over Time. A second category of switching costs arises from supplier-specific learning by the buyer that occurs in addition to the initial investment of time required to gain basic proficiency. Over time, the buyer adapts to characteristics of the product and its supplier and thus finds it costly to change over to another company's product. For example, nurses become accustomed to the intravenous solution delivery systems of a given supplier and are reluctant to switch. The skills acquired over time by users of Lotus 1-2-3 become partly obsolete if they switch to another package. In a related fashion, Cray benefits from the large cumulative development of specialized software by its existing users, which is costly to adapt for competing machines.

A creative approach to raising switching costs by means of supplier-specific learning was taken by the semiconductor firm Intel. Intel's customers faced serious competition for available electrical engineering graduates. Intel turned this shortage to its own advantage by providing resources to university engineering laboratories so that a given school's graduates would be trained on Intel microprocessors. Given this training, a graduate of a school with an Intel lab could immediately go to work for an Intel customer without having to learn the idiosyncrasies of microprocessors made by Intel's chief rival, Motorola. This made Intel customers more attractive to these graduates, thus giving Intel customers an edge in recruiting. Further, these graduates were cost effective in that they required less additional training.

Contractual Switching Cost. A third type of switching cost is contractual switching cost that can be intentionally created by the seller. Airline frequent-flyer programs fit in this category. Similarly, many travel agents have signed long-term lease contracts for use of the SABRE reservations system; these contracts raise the costs of switching to a competing system. Travel agents must pay a penalty to terminate contracts early, in addition to other costs of disruption and retraining. Moreover, the contract periods on different components of the system are often staggered to prevent switching costs from falling to zero on a single expiration date.

Risk and Uncertainty. Another type of switching cost stems from the uncertainty of buyers regarding product quality. In such a context, buyers may rationally stick with the first brand they encounter that performs the job satisfactorily. Buyer risk aversion may push the market strongly in favor of the first-mover product, assuming that its performance is of adequate quality. For example, Federal Express and Tandem Computers are first-movers that have achieved enormous success based on their early reputation for reliability.

Brand loyalty of this sort can be particularly strong for low-cost package goods where the benefits of finding a superior brand are seldom great enough to justify the additional search costs that must be incurred. In such an environment, first-mover firms may be able to establish a reputation for quality that can be transferred to additional products through umbrella branding and other tactics.

These uncertainty effects tend to influence individual consumers more than corporate buyers, since the latter's larger purchase volume justifies greater research on alternative suppliers. Switching costs in industrial markets often dissipate over time as buyers become more knowledgeable about competing products. For example, as overnight delivery volumes have increased, corporate purchasing departments have evaluated the reliability of alternative vendors that are less expensive than Federal Express. By establishing contracts with these vendors, purchasing departments have been able to wean individual employees away from using the higher-cost service.

Compatibility Advantages. When new buyers of a class of product find it desirable to be compatible with existing users, an additional set of first-mover advantages can arise. Once Lotus 1-2-3 became established as the dominant spreadsheet package, new buyers were willing to pay a premium to be compatible with the existing base of users. Compatibility enables easy transfer of data and routines, and it reduces duplication in training costs. Similarly, once Microsoft's DOS became the dominant operating system for IBM-compatible personal computers, users were forced to purchase the Microsoft product to gain access to the existing base of software programs.

A related point is that the pioneering firm can often benefit through the establishment of industry product standards. De facto industry standards are more likely to be set by first-movers than by later entrants, who may have little choice but to conform to the standard already set. Early entrants who have established such standards, which can be defended through patent or copyright protection, have often been enormously successful. One example is Intel, which convinced IBM to adopt the Intel microprocessor as the centerpiece of the IBM personal computer. This made it essential that other makers of IBM-compatible machines purchase chips from Intel or a licensee. However, many firms have been less successful in their efforts to establish such favorable industry standards. In video cassette recorders, Sony made substantial early investments to establish its Beta standard, but was overshadowed by Matsushita and JVC, whose VHS format had some technical advantages (longer recording/playback time) but also disadvantages (picture quality). (In part, Matsushita and other followers chose a competing format to keep their longtime rival Sony from setting the industry standard and thereby gaining a first-mover advantage.) Even when a firm is successful in establishing its product as the industry standard, the results are not always beneficial. For example, industry standardization around the initial IBM personal computer proved to be more curse than blessing for IBM, since it has reduced entry barriers into the IBM-compatible market.

FOLLOWER ADVANTAGES

As has been seen, pioneering firms have often carved out large advantages through early investments in proprietary technology, superior physical or marketing resources, or customer switching costs. But business history is replete with first-movers who failed miserably, or who succeeded initially but were quickly overtaken by competitors. Prime examples include Bomar in calculators, Sperry in computers, and Sony in video cassette recorders.

Just as some factors favor first-movers, others favor firms that enter later. In many instances, late-movers can "free-ride" on the pioneering firm's investments in technology and market development, thereby avoiding some of the costs of early entry. Late movers also benefit from the resolution of technology and market uncertainty as they learn from the experience of first-mover firms. Technological discontinuities can provide gateways for late entry. Finally, various types of incumbent inertia can make it difficult for the incumbent to adapt to environmental change. All of these phenomena can reduce, or even completely negate, the net advantage of the first-mover derived from mechanisms considered previously.

"Free-Riding" by Later Entrants

Late-mover firms may be able to "free-ride" on the first-mover's investments in a variety of areas: product and process research and development, buyer education, employee training, regulatory approval, and infrastructural development, including the development of necessary inputs and complementary products.

Technology. Research and development and learning-based advances diffuse to competitors through various channels, including employees, suppliers, contractors and consultants. As a result, imitation is less costly than innovation in most industries. Unless the pioneer can protect its innovations through patents, copyrights, or secrecy, followers will ultimately be able to duplicate these innovations at lower cost. (Note, however, that pioneers enjoy an initial period of limited competition that is not available to imitator firms. If high prices can be sustained during this period, the pioneer may be able to recoup its initial investment, even if first-mover advantages are ultimately dissipated.)

Buyer Education. Follower firms may benefit from the pioneer's investment in education of buyers. Bomar, for instance, engaged in extensive television advertising, which enhanced consumers' awareness of the new electronic calculator technology. This stimulated greater sales by Texas Instruments and other challengers following Bomar's demise. Similarly, in the U.S. robotics industry, heavy investments in buyer education by the pioneering firm Unimation during the 1960s and 1970s largely served to benefit other competitors.

Employee Training. Followers can often hire employees from the pioneering firm, thus avoiding many training costs. Moreover, followers sometime spring from the pioneer's own employment ranks. Waves of talented personnel left Fairchild, the most important pioneer in the fledgling semiconductor industry of the late 1950s and 1960s, to form their own spin-off companies. Many of these spin-offs, such as Intel and AMD, grew rapidly to dwarf the parent firm in both size and profitability.

Infrastructure Development. Often, much of the pioneer's investment in infrastructure development and regulatory approval goes to benefit follower firms. For example, when color television was under development in the United States, RCA as the pioneer produced both the color television sets and broadcast the largest number of hours of compatible color through its ownership of the National Broadcasting Network. Other color television set manufacturers let the RCA/NBC team build the market but were prepared to jump in when demand began to surge. Similarly, in the U.S. market for video cassette recorders, Sony found it necessary to pursue a costly lawsuit to establish the right of consumers to record television programs off the air for their own use. This benefited later followers as well as Sony, which paid the cost of its pioneering in money, time, and management attention. Casio delayed becoming the first company to market digital audio tape in the United States for fear of lawsuits such as those faced by Sony in video cassette recorders.

First-Mover Errors in Technology and Marketing Strategy Decisions

Technology and Customer Needs Are Uncertain During Early Stages. The ultimate value of the first-mover's investments depends on the firm's accuracy in predicting the evolution of technological developments and customer needs. Initial uncertainty surrounding technology and market demands raises the risk that the first-mover will be off the mark. Under these conditions, there are obvious advantages to waiting, particularly when large upfront investments are required.

A would-be pioneer can stumble in the research and development stage, or it can introduce a commercial product or process that is eventually perceived as inferior. The British Air Corporation introduces the first commercial jet, the DeHaviland Comet, which was initially a success but soon proved to have fatal flaws in design. Boeing came up with a superior design in the form of the 707 and thus came to dominate the global aircraft industry.

Uncertainty is often resolved through the emergence of a "dominant design." The Model T Ford, DC-3, and Boeing 707 are examples of dominant designs in the automotive and aircraft industries. After emergence of such a design, competition often shifts to price, thereby conveying greater advantage on firms possessing skills in low-cost manufacturing.

A related point is that a late-mover may be able to learn from the first-mover's mistake. For example, when Toyota was first planning to enter the U.S. market, it interviewed owners of Volkswagens, the leading small car at that time. Information on what owners like and disliked about the Volkswagen was incorporated in the design process for the new Toyota, which ultimately displaced Volkswagen as the leading small car in the U.S. market.

Technology and Customer Needs Are Subject to "Discontinuities" Over Time. In addition to uncertainty regarding the gradual evolution of a new technology or market, discontinuities often arise. New technologies may become economically feasible, and consumer tastes can shift dramatically. Later entrants can exploit these changes to displace existing incumbents. In some industries, discontinuities can be anticipated (e.g., multigeneration products), but even so, pioneering incumbents are often caught off guard. VisiCorp, the firm that introduced the first spreadsheet program, failed to recognize that the next product generation would require integration with graphics. The firm was thus upstaged by Lotus.

Since the replacement technology often appears while the old technology is still in place, it may be difficult for an incumbent to perceive the threat and take adequate preventive steps. Examples include American Viscose's failure to recognize the potential of polyester as a replacement for rayon, and Transitron's inattention to silicon as a substitute for germanium in semiconductor fabrication. This perceptual failure is closely related to "incumbent inertia."

Customer needs are also dynamic, creating opportunities for later entrants unless the first-mover is alert and able to respond. Docutel, as the pioneer, supplied virtually all of the automated teller machine market up to late 1974. Over the next four years, its market share plunged to less than 10 percent under the onslaught of competitors who offered computer systems to meet the emerging need for electronic funds transfer.

Incumbent Inertia

If the firm pursues a first-mover opportunity and is initially successful, the problem then arises of how to maintain this advantage. A common trap is "incumbent inertia"—the firm becomes locked in to its initial technological or marketing approach and is unable to adapt to changing opportunities and defend itself against competitive threats. Over time, successful incumbents often become inflexible and slow to recognize and respond to their changing environment. Eventually, such incumbents can become quite vulnerable, enabling late entrants to achieve sizable gains at the incumbent's expense. A prime example of this phenomenon is Xerox's feeble response during the 1970s to major competitive challenges posed by Japanese rivals on the low end and U.S. rivals on the high end of the plain-paper copier market.

Why do incumbents so frequently exhibit this lagged or frozen response to competitive threat? The reasons are several: (1) Organizational routines hinder perception and response to environmental changes, (2) sunk costs slow response, and (3) incumbents are often overly concerned with cannibalization of their current products.

Organizational Routines. One reason for inertia is the tendency toward organizational "hardening of the arteries." Standard routines and procedures increasingly block the firm's ability to perceive environmental change. The firm's established view of technology and customer needs may be internally reinforced. Factors that limit adaptive response by incumbents include the development of organizational routines and standards, internal political dynamics, and the development of stable exchange relations with other organizations.

Numerous dysfunctional examples of such inertia can be cited. Henry Ford persisted in production of the Model T long after changes in the competitive environment had made it clear that new products were required. When the automobile was initially replacing the horse in rural America, low cost was the vital element in success. However, Alfred Sloan at General Motors recognized changing needs in the marketplace as America urbanized and the automobile became, in many cases, a statement of the persona of the consumer. Ultimately, Ford had to close its factories for twelve months between mid-1926 and 1927 in order to retool. Ford's continuation of its low-cost strategy long after the need for differentiation became apparent is a classic case of incumbent inertia.

Established distribution relationships contributed to the decline of the Swiss watch industry. Timex introduced the disposable watch in drug stores and other mass channels, but the Swiss were unable to follow for fear of offending the jewelry stores that were their prime mode of distribution.

Organizational blinders also promoted the decline of the major potato chip producer in Great Britain. Historically, the vast majority of chips were consumed by men in pubs. It took the incumbent five years to realize that the challenger had invented a whole new market segment: supermarket sales to women and children. By that time, the incumbent had lost half of its original market share. Indeed, even when an incumbent recognizes the threat and makes a commitment to change, organizational factors often sabotage the effort.

Sunk Costs. A second reason for inertia is that the firm becomes locked into a specific set of productive assets. In this case, an inertial response may be rational, at least initially, since the benefits of product or process change may not be large enough to justify the new investments required. The danger for the incumbent is that it persists too long in this behavior. Ford's decision to remain dedicated to the Model T during most of the 1920s, despite competitive pressure from General Motors, was initially a rational response given Ford's enormous investment in product, process, and established reputation. Like many successful late-movers, General Motors perceived where Ford was most vulnerable. Ford's error was in sticking with the Model T for too long, so that the ultimate conversion of product and facilities proved unduly traumatic and costly. Similarly, P&G lagged in upgrading its pioneering Pampers disposable diapers because of the tremendous cost in plant and equipment. After Pampers lost substantial share to Kimberly-Clark's Huggies, the investment ($500 million) was belatedly made.

A firm with heavy sunk costs in fixed plant or marketing channels that ultimately prove suboptimal may find it rational to "harvest" these investments and ultimately exit the market, rather than attempt to transform itself radically. The appropriate choice between adaptation and harvesting depends on how costly it is to convert the firm's existing assets to alternative uses. Moreover, organizational inertia has often led firms to continue investing in their existing asset base well beyond the point where such investments are justified.

Reluctance to Cannibalize Existing Lines. A third reason for incumbent inertia is reluctance to cannibalize the firm's existing product lines. Often, an established firm has less incentive than a new entrant to introduce new or improved products. A late entrant that aims its new product offerings correctly can exploit the incumbent's reluctance to cannibalize, using it, in effect, as a lever to defuse incumbent retaliation. Xerox exhibited such cannibalization-avoidance following the expiration of its patent-enforced monopoly. Xerox lagged in introducing innovations that would have made its existing technology less attractive, and it was sluggish to cut prices on account of its large fleet of rental machines in the field. This provided a gateway for entry by Canon, Ricoh, Savin, and others. Similarly,

U.S. automakers were reluctant to enter the small-car segment in the 1970s for fear of cannibalizing their larger, more profitable models. This enabled Toyota, Nissan, Honda, and other Japanese companies to expand their U.S. market shares.

PRESCRIPTIONS FOR MANAGERS

The First-Mover vs. Follower Decision

It is clear that pioneering carries both advantages and disadvantages. The ultimate net impact of pioneering generally depends on the firm's skills and position, competitors, and changes in the environment. Thus, pioneering may prove advantageous to some firms in some circumstances, but it is not necessarily a superior strategy for all entrants.

Although the issue is often couched as an either/or proposition, in fact most companies are both first-movers and followers. This can occur even in a single product category, as in the case of P&G in disposable diapers.

As a matter of corporate policy, some firms emphasize pioneering while others prefer to follow. Sony, for example, aggressively pursues first-mover advantages from new product innovation. Sony's major rival, Matsushita (whose nickname in Japanese, *maneshita denki*, translates as "electronics that have been copied") generally lets Sony and others innovate. It then enters later, leveraging its manufacturing and marketing capabilities to wrest share in the growing market from the pioneers. Matsushita invests in research and development to be ready to enter the market when it begins rapid growth, but the firm generally will not launch new products until others have proven the market.

Sony and Matsushita are polar cases; most firms lie somewhere in between. The degree of emphasis that should be placed on pioneering depends on the firm's specific characteristics and skills. Firms whose entrepreneurial vision and new-product research and development are excellent tend to find first-movership attractive, whereas firms having relative skill bases in manufacturing and marketing may not. Then, too, firms having a strategy of first-movership may often be forced to follow in related product areas in order to provide a more complete product line.

The first-mover versus follower decision process is presented schematically in Figure 21-1. In order for a firm to become a first-mover, there must be a feasible opportunity. The occurrence of such an opportunity depends on the firm's own foresight, skills, resources, and good fortune—and that of its competitors.

First-mover opportunities are often created by changes in technology, customer needs, distribution channels, competition, and governmental actions. For example, a first-mover opportunity was created by the miniaturization of electronics, which facilitated the development of

FIGURE 21-1

First-Mover vs. Follower Decision

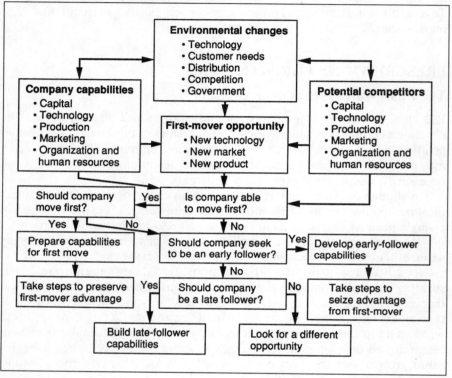

portable computers, radios, and televisions, as well as nearly invisible hearing aids that fit inside the wearer's ear. Increased customer demand for better quality microwaveable prepared food has provided food companies like Stouffer's with a first-mover opportunity in this market. As distribution by means of telephone sales and other forms of direct marketing have grown, new opportunities have arisen for innovative firms to develop first-mover advantages. The entry of Japanese automobile manufacturers in the U.S. marketplace has weakened U.S. firms' first-mover advantage in their home market. The executive, legislative, and judicial branches of the U.S. government, through regulation, deregulation, and policy decisions, have created first-mover opportunities for some firms and substantial difficulties for others. For example, export restrictions, especially on high-tech products, have hindered the ability of some companies to secure a first-mover position in an increasingly global marketplace.

While the ability to be a first-mover is not under the control of the firm alone, the firm contributes proactively to its own pioneering opportunities. It must decide whether and how much to invest in search of such opportunities.

The first question a company must ask when such an opportunity arises is whether the firm has the capabilities to become the first-mover and build a sustainable advantage. If the answer is yes, the firm must decide whether to exploit the opportunity and how best to do so. Once a firm has chosen a pioneering strategy, it must invest resources to make its move and also begin to take steps to preserve its first-mover advantages.

If a company decides not to be a first-mover, or if a rival has preempted this position, then the company must decide whether and how to follow, and whether to do so early or late. If the pioneer is small, lacks resources, or has not yet achieved much market penetration or recognition, it may be vulnerable to attack by an early follower. Entry as a late follower may be attractive if incumbents have become complacent, if environmental changes have caught them off guard, or if the late-entering firm has strategic reasons to enter. The latter may reflect a need to broaden a product line to maintain satisfaction among customers and distribution channels, or it may reflect a need to be present in certain markets in order to deny resources to rivals or to keep more intimate track of a competitor's capabilities.

Rx for First-Movers

A company that regularly pursues first-mover opportunities must be able to perceive these opportunities before they are apparent to competitors. The firm must be capable of initiating and nurturing innovative projects that give rise to first-mover positions. It must also take into consideration the length of time that it can reasonably expect to maintain any advantages associated with first-movership. Even when pioneering advantages are likely to be ephemeral, entry can be profitable if sufficient profit margins can be sustained during the early phase of the market. Indeed, many pioneers exploit their initial advantages, then exit or sell out to others.

A pioneer that aims to maintain its position over the longer term must exploit the sources of first-mover advantage while avoiding (to the extent possible) the disadvantages of first-movership. After creating the market, the pioneer needs to keep followers from eliminating its first-mover advantages. Depending on the industry context, a range of tactics are potentially available for this purpose.

Preempt Potential Opportunities for Entry. A pioneer can protect its first-mover advantages by blocking entry opportunities through patents or copyrights. If patents are effective in the industry, the firm can attempt to patent as many technological approaches as possible. As mentioned previously, Xerox created a patent "thicket" in the 1950s and 1960s that successfully defended the firm from late entrants until it was forced by the courts to license outside parties. Polaroid pursued a similar patent-based strategy with considerable success. Currently, firms in the biotech industry are attempting to create such patent defenses for specific products. In the computer field, where patents tend to be less effective, Apple has used copyrights to protect its Macintosh operating system from imitation.

On the marketing side, the firm may be able to preempt entry opportunities by filling positioning gaps. If the product is one where consumer switching costs would be high, it may be essential for the pioneer to induce trial purchases by the majority of potential customers before rivals have an opportunity to do so. Similar tactics can be important even in markets where switching costs are more moderate. For example, while building the market for disposable diapers in the United States, P&G advertised heavily, distributed samples to new mothers, and constructed manufacturing plants in all regions of the country, thereby blocking opportunities for geographic entry. Later, P&G introduced a higher-quality product, Luvs, in addition to its Pampers line in order to block opportunities for followers to enter as a premium brand. P&G also preempted its Japanese competitors, Kao and Unicharm, by being first to introduce superabsorbant diapers in the United States.

Minimize Technological Leakage. A firm's own employees are often a major source of technological leakage. Leakage can be reduced by offering incentives for key employees to remain with the firm—e.g., stock options, premium pay, and favorable working conditions. The firm can also take legal action against former employees who divulge key information to competitors. Such lawsuits have proven difficult to win but can have strong demonstration and deterrence value. A less costly but sometimes most effective, method of controlling leakage is for the firm to emphasize to its employees the importance of maintaining a close-lipped mentality when dealing with outsiders.

Technological leakage can also be reduced by limiting access. The firm can restrict the number of contractors and consultants it deals with, and require them to sign enforceable nondisclosure agreements. The firm can cut off access by discontinuing plant tours, as Kellogg has recently done in response to the discovery that European producers were taking the tours to learn Kellogg's production secrets. The firm can also tie up key suppliers through purchase contracts and other arrangements. Finally, products can sometimes be designed in ways that make "reverse engineering" more difficult.

The incumbent can also reduce leakage while furthering its lead by developing organizational capabilities. Organizationally embodied skills are hardest for competitors to duplicate. One reason is that competitors are unable to observe exactly what the incumbent is doing—i.e., precisely what constitutes the key to the incumbent's success. A second reason is that organizationally embodied skills are distributed throughout the firm and thus cannot be carried off by a single employee or group of employees. For example, the Toyota production system is embodied in thousands of employees and pieces of equipment widely dispersed throughout the company. Japanese rivals have thus been able only to approach, but not to surpass, Toyota's productivity after several years of effort to emulate the system.

It may also be important for the pioneer to invest in capabilities that are likely to become critical as the market evolves. For example, the biotechnology company Amgen has invested heavily in drug manufacturing and distribution, rather than contract these functions out to potential competitors.

Avoid Excessive Inertia. A certain amount of incumbent inertia is desirable. It makes economic sense for a pioneer to exploit its existing investment base. However, the danger is that the pioneer will become too myopic and inflexible. There are several ways to guard against this.

First, the firm should track the continued evolution of customer needs. Customers become more sophisticated over time, and new market segments develop. Xerox's failure to perceive customer needs at the low end of the market enabled Japanese competitors to enter and carve out a successful niche. Strength in low-end copiers gave these firms a strong base to challenge Xerox in other areas.

Shifts in consumer preferences can sometimes result from the firm's own inattentive actions. In the late 1970s, for example, Kleenex tissues, which had established the industry standard, lost significant market share. Subsequent research indicated that consumers' preferences had shifted to competing brands that were softer. This preference shift was the result of Kleenex's production economy choices that had gradually increased the level of recycled wood pulp in the tissues. Once Kleenex restored and enhanced the level of softness, it regained and even surpassed its previous market share.

Continual product innovation is another key to retaining competitive advantage. Caterpillar, by neglecting to re-engineer their low-end models in the early 1970s, gave John Deere an opportunity to enter the over-100 horsepower bulldozer market using an innovative transmission as a differentiating feature.

The firm should also be willing to make investments that may cannibalize existing products and processes—i.e., "better to eat your own lunch." Successful first-movers must sacrifice some short-term revenue to maintain long-term leadership. In many competitive struggles, the firm with the longest time horizon ultimately wins. Steel and semiconductors are two of many industries in which U.S. producers have lost leadership positions to their less myopic Japanese rivals.

Many pioneers have needlessly or inadvertently painted themselves into a corner by making inflexible investments in manufacturing and marketing systems. Henry Ford's initial success with the Model T was followed by financial disaster once Alfred Sloan perceived changes in buyer tastes and mounted an aggressive assault based on new product features. With its innovative but inflexible transfer lines, Ford had emphasized efficiency at the expense of flexibility. Similarly, P&G's production equipment for Pampers disposable diapers, installed in the 1970s, was highly efficient but made it difficult for P&G to modify and add product features. This enabled Kimberly-Clark and other later rivals to upstage P&G's product without invoking major retaliation. When P&G ultimately replaced its Pampers lines—at a cost of over half a billion dollars—it installed more flexible equipment that allows for easy alterations in product features. In general, the advent of computer-aided manufacture and flexible automation technologies now makes it possible to adopt increased amounts of manufacturing flexibility at reasonable cost.

Flexibility is also essential in other areas, such as research and development and marketing. Faced with uncertainty about the best architecture for future supercomputers, Cray split itself into two separate companies in order to track technological alternatives without generating excessive conflicts within the organization. The Swiss watch industry was decimated following Timex's entry, largely because it was unable to develop a low-cost product line and set up new distribution channels. To maintain long-term dominance, pioneers must use flexibility and monitoring as antidotes for the potentially destructive impact of changing technology and customer needs.

Finally, a firm must learn from history and competitors. Cummins, for example, took steps to preserve its position versus the Japanese after observing the historical behavior of its Japanese competitors. Cummins noticed that the Japanese had a tendency to advance from a low-end beachhead to challenge incumbents in the high end in such industries as motorcycles, automobiles, and plain-paper copiers. In order to avoid repetition of the Japanese triumph in their industry, Cummins embarked on a drastic program of cost and price cutting. Although this required substantial restructuring of the company, Cummins has thus far been able to avoid losing market share to the Japanese. Xerox and Ford have used competitor benchmarking to understand and improve upon competitor's activities and products. This has enabled Xerox to rebound in its plain-paper copier market share and has led to Ford achieving over half of the U.S. auto industry profits in recent years.

Rx for Later Movers

Firms with a follower strategy—whether by design or inevitability—face two major questions:

1. How long is it prudent to wait before entering?
2. Should the pioneer be attacked directly, or should the entrant seek a less confrontational, differentiated position?

The appropriate answer to these questions depends on the strength of the pioneer's position and the challenger's own specialized capabilities.

Confronting the Pioneer Directly. If the pioneer is small, lacks resources, or has not yet achieved much market penetration or recognition, it may be vulnerable to aggressive attack by a follower. If the pioneer is capital-constrained, it may be unable to take full advantage of its first-mover opportunities, thereby leaving the door open for larger, better-financed firms. The onslaught of the well-heeled Coca-Cola and Pepsi on Diet Rite's pioneering move in low-calorie colas is a case in point. In situations where large followers lack some necessary skills, these can often be obtained by means of purchase or acquisition of early-mover firms, often without paying an exorbitant premium.

If the pioneer is extremely weak, direct imitation of the pioneer's product can be a reasonable strategy. Urban et al.[10] found that for consumer packaged goods, a follower could overcome a pioneer's market-share advantage by outspending him on advertising. However, "me-too" strategies have proven to be generally unsuccessful. For example, doctors ignored a "me-too" ethical pharmaceutical introduced by one of the premier drug manufacturers. It was seven years before the gross dollar sales of this "me-too" product equaled the introductory promotional expenditures on this drug. For consumer packaged goods, Montgomery (1975) found that "me-too" products suffer extreme disadvantages in obtaining supermarket shelf space, a prerequisite for successful consumer sales.[11]

In general, "me-too" strategies seem to be effective only when the innovator has not done its marketing properly or intensely enough. "Me-too" brands tend to fail when positioned close to the pioneer, but they are often successful when positioned close to differentiated later entrants. A brand that mimics an entrenched pioneer usually finds it difficult to generate trial purchases, due to the dominant perceptual position of the pioneer. However, a brand positioned near a differentiated later entrant can make it

[10] Urban et al., op. cit.

[11] D.B. Montgomery, "New Product Distribution: An Analysis of Supermarket Buyer Decisions," *Journal of Marketing Research* vol. 12 (Aug. 1975), pp. 255–264.

easier for both to generate trial purchases at the expense of the pioneer. Thus, some "me-too" positions are superior to others.[12]

If a relatively young pioneer has locked into the wrong technology or customer features, a differentiation strategy is obviously warranted for followers. Again, the study by Urban et al. on consumer packaged goods found that a follower could readily overcome a pioneer advantage by developing a product that was better positioned to meet consumer needs.[13] To support such a strategy, a follower needs to be keeping up with research and development and market research. A mature pioneer can be successfully confronted with a differentiated product if the pioneer has missed a major shift in technology or customer needs or suffers from a serious inertia problem.

Followers may also have advantages if they possess assets or resources that the pioneering firm lacks. Followers may bring reputations for quality or reliability, as in IBM's entry into the personal computer market. Successful followers often possess strong technical skills or control key marketing channels. For example, EMI developed the first computerized tomography scanner but lost to GE in the marketplace because EMI lacked a technology infrastructure and marketing base in the medical field. In calculators, Bomar lost to Texas Instruments because it lacked the semiconductor manufacturing capability needed for low-cost production as competition drive prices down. Many Japanese firms have been successful late entrants, based largely on their manufacturing skills.

Entering Through a Market Niche. Followers may find it preferable to avoid direct confrontation with a strong pioneer, at least initially. Early entry through a market niche may be attractive if the pioneer has achieved a strong position but the follower has advantages in some particular segment. Hewlett-Packard (HP), for instance, was an early entrant in the electronic calculator market, where it carved out a position at the high end with calculators specialized for scientific and financial applications. HP established an early reputation for quality in this segment (derived in part from the firm's more general quality reputation), which protected its calculators from much of the price erosion that occurred in the mass market.

One common strategy of Japanese companies has been to enter via the low end of the market, as exemplified by Toyota and Canon. In the zipper industry, YKK noticed that the dominant incumbent, Talon, had an average pricing policy. YKK entered by discounting the most popular colors and styles, which it could service efficiently from its focused factories in Japan. After gaining a strong beachhead, YKK broadened its line and introduced a series of innovative products. Today, it is the dominant global competitor.

---

[12] See G.S. Carpenter and K. Nakamoto, "Market Pioneers, Consumer Learning and Product Perceptions: A Theory of Persistent Competitive Advantage," Research Paper, Columbia University (Nov. 1986).

[13] Urban et al., op. cit.

One major advantage of a niche strategy is that incumbents will often not notice or react. The niche follower, once it is secure, may choose to roll up-market. For example, the Japanese entry in the U.S. auto market culminated in their entry into the luxury car segment with Honda's Acura, Toyota's Lexus, and Nissan's Infiniti. In motorcycles the Japanese followed the same course. The largest of the early Honda motorcycles in the United States was one third the engine size of the then smallest Harley Davidson. Harley-Davidson viewed them as toys; but once Honda and other Japanese companies had entered at the low end, they gained aspirations of moving up-market. Ultimately, they very nearly put Harley Davidson out of business.

The strategy of not attacking a strong incumbent, at least until having developed strength is termed a *sukima* strategy in Japan. (A *sukima* is a small crack where a Japanese sliding paper door doesn't quite fit its frame.) In the United States, Japanese companies entered in such fashion through the low end of markets for motorcycles, autos and plain-paper copiers. In Europe, the Japanese executed a niche strategy geographically in the automotive market. The Japanese first entered the European auto market in Finland and Switzerland, where there was no indigenous auto industry to be protected. This afforded the Japanese an opportunity to learn how to operate and market in a European context. Their next entries were into the remainder of Scandinavia, the Benelux countries, and Great Britain. The opportunity here was relatively weak or nonexistent competition from local firms. Only after the Japanese had mastered operations and marketing in the rest of Europe did they attack France and Germany, which had local industries to protect and strong competitors.

CONCLUSION

This chapter has surveyed the sources of first-mover advantage as well as the disadvantages of pioneering that can make follower positions relatively more attractive. Managers must decide whether a strong emphasis on pioneering is appropriate, given their firm's resource base. In situations where skill and good fortune have generated a first-mover opportunity, managers must decide whether the firm should pursue it, and if so, how best to enhance its value. Managers of follower firms must determine whether and how the first-mover advantages of the pioneer can be subverted. Many pioneering firms, following a period of initial success, fall into a trap of arrogance and complacency and thereby become vulnerable. However, pioneers that build adequate capacity, innovate to meet changing technologies and customer requirements, fill up available market niches, and adapt to evolving patterns of distribution are formidable opponents and exceedingly difficult to overcome.

22

Logistics and Operations for Global Strategy

DAVID G. DEROULET

JAMES C. SPIRA

Cleveland Consulting Associates, Cleveland, Ohio

INTRODUCTION

No business strategy for the 1990s can overlook the critical strategic role of business logistics in the total supply chain. This chapter explores the principles that must guide overall strategic thinking if a business is to achieve a sustainable competitive advantage for the coming decade. Specifically, it suggests the value of increasing the business's flexibility to deal with—rather than its attempts to anticipate—future events. In line with that proper basis for strategy, the process of "reengineering" operations to build in more flexibility and responsiveness is discussed. An inherent part of this process is an integrated approach to logistics and the linkages it establishes both within the organization and among the company, its vendors, and its customers. Because these logistical linkages are the key to retaining flexibility while maintaining structure, they represent important leverage points for strategic improvement.

Separate subsections of the chapter address how reengineering translates to various areas of logistics, including supply chain and network planning, distribution operations, materials management, and transportation. It concludes with brief case studies of companies who have successfully reengineered their logistics operations for increased flexibility and competitive advantage.

THE PROPER BASIS FOR STRATEGY

Business strategists have two basic desires: to foresee the future and to know how to act on that vision. Although it is impossible to predict the future precisely, the coming decade will be marked by the following features:

- New markets will continue to spring up worldwide, as will global competitors.
- Information technology will continue to advance rapidly.
- The pace of change in both global affairs and technology will accelerate.
- Worldwide competition will become much more intense.

Recognizing the fact that exact business forecasts are impossible to make does not render strategic business planning impossible or inappropriate. It simply shifts the emphasis of the strategy from one of targeted response to one of flexibility. Instead of straining to see further into the future, it makes better sense to build organizations that are more capable of responding quickly to changing conditions. The aim of strategic business planning must be to build greater flexibility into the organization to deal with the unknown. The strategy must also accommodate short-term factors that can be anticipated, but these factors should act as partial tests of the validity of the strategy, not drivers of its creation.

"FLEXING" THE CORPORATION

A program for building flexibility into a business is dependent on four directives:

1. Gaining a thorough understanding of the state of the art
2. Developing a global perspective
3. Reengineering the business internally for greater integrations
4. Reengineering external relationships to create seamless integration

The idea of building flexibility into the company is not new and has been implemented in various ways. Generally, and correctly, it is tied to the theme of increased integration between functions like engineering and marketing internally, and between the company and its vendors and customers externally. Some strategists have even called for a "boundary-less" organization, in which no internal barriers exist between people, as the way to allow the company to move faster, communicate more clearly, and involve everyone in a focused effort to serve ever more demanding customers.

Unfortunately, that idea is both inadvisable and infeasible. Not everyone in the company has the independent initiative, global perspective, or commitment of the chief executive officer. People need organizational structure to give them focus, direction, and even a sense of allegiance. Instead, the focus must be on making boundaries more rational, redrawing them to reflect real affinities and dependencies, and establishing or reinforcing the links between all areas of the organization. What must be done, in effect, is to reengineer the company to make it more effective and efficient. Externally too the company's relationships with vendors and customers must be redesigned to achieve a seamless pattern of service. To do this, it is necessary to identify and forge authentic partnerships that yield real benefit for all parties involved

Before any reengineering can take place, however, the strategist must gain a thorough understanding of the state of the art and develop a truly global perception.

Gaining a Thorough Understanding of the State of the Art

Throughout business history, obtaining thorough information and insight into the current state of affairs has offered a significant competitive advantage; today it is a requirement to remain competitive. Unfortunately, now more than ever, sorting through the glut of accessible information for relevant facts is a daunting task. Whether through observation or in consultation with others, a strategist must gain a thorough understanding of the company's performance, competitors, and customers. Beyond that, it is necessary to become familiar with other industries that are using technology in innovative, relevant ways. It is also helpful to know what technological capabilities now exist to help the business, and what new tools are on the immediate horizon.

This level of insight is what business strategists have traditionally sought in order to get the jump on competitors. Gaining a knowledge of what is happening now and what is imminent is the necessary first step toward any type of strategic thinking, because it sets the baseline for specific future actions. However, in order to create a strategy that effectively deals with the continuing rapid advancements, it is also necessary to develop a global perspective.

Developing a Global Perspective

One of the most significant challenges facing American business leaders is the consolidation of the developed world into a single marketplace. Knowing how to capitalize on emerging demand for products in Eastern Europe and the Soviet Union, for example, is a question of first educating oneself in the business history, culture, and tastes of the people there, and then becoming familiar with the real limitations of the existing infrastructure. With regard to Europe, where the "1992" directives are gathering momentum, American managers must keep abreast of the opportunities being made available with each month's rulings, as well as potential changes that will establish new product standards, import regulations, and, possibly, foreign-entry barriers. The prospect of a unified European market of 300 million consumers makes this part of the world a critical focal point for American business. At the same time, it would be a mistake to focus on a single region and ignore the rest of the globe. Latin America, the Far East, or Africa could be the next "hot" area, and American business leaders must be poised to act on a boom in these regions.

Of course, a global perspective should consider global competitors as well as customers. The chief result of the contracting world market is much greater intensity in global competition, which is causing enterprises worldwide to have to perform much better than they ever did before. Knowledge of how these competitors have successfully approached their own regions, and how those approaches will translate to new areas, will allow U.S. managers to hold their own ground while making forays into new territories.

Reengineering the Business for Greater Integration

The major hurdle that companies must overcome now is the inadequacy of their current business practices to respond to new developments in technology and markets. To gain the kind of flexibility required to stay on top, today's business leaders must do more to link individuals, functions, departments, organization levels, suppliers, and customers.

The problem, in simplest terms, is a "business as usual" approach that supports existing operational processes designed to recognize and accommodate barriers to flexibility. Progressive companies are realizing that today's technology offers the power not simply to automate those processes, but also to alter them. This means rethinking the traditional ways in which business is run and changing, or eliminating, some age-old steps. In sum, it means reengineering the supply chain away from its usual operation to capitalize on the information inherent in its components. This requires a three-stage process of redesigning, retooling, and reorchestrating.

Redesigning. The heart of successful business reengineering is the careful consideration of how the basic processes of the business—in terms of buying, manufacturing, and selling—can be made more responsive to the demands of the future. The emphasis must be on flexibility rather than rigidity, and there must be an awareness that the future is uncertain, despite the fact that a few of its features can be anticipated. Thus the overarching goals of the redesigned operations must be to:

- Facilitate rapid communication of new information
- Enable the focus of activity to be shifted into new areas
- Allow additional resources to be mobilized as appropriate

To create this kind of flexibility, it is necessary to first identify the many components of each functional area for individual consideration, and then regroup them into more rational sets, based on information affinities and dependencies. Note that functional areas will still be distinguished by organizational lines—this is no boundaryless company—but they will be redrawn according to a more relevant pattern. Once tasks have been reorganized into functional areas, the linkages between those functional areas must be optimized so that information and cooperation flow freely among them. When the new design is complete, it should be evaluated in light of how it will accommodate developments on the foreseeable horizon and theoretical scenarios in the longer term. While such an evaluation is not a total test, a negative indication surely calls for another redesign.

Finally, it is necessary to identify the key leverage points within and between functions and attempt to make immediate improvements there. A leverage point is a point where a small incremental improvement in management will yield a large financial impact. An example would be the process used by a steel processor to decide how to cut up an ingot once it has been rolled out. Because this is a fundamental operating decision, the company would benefit greatly by using technology to improve the management of that task. In the early 1980s, factors such as transportation deregulation, the oil crisis, and high inflation rates made managing transportation costs a leverage point for many companies. In general, these points provide sufficient yield on investment to justify their short-term orientation.

Retooling. Once the operational processes have been redesigned, the next step is to retool the work practices and information systems required to support them. Managers must have computer systems that deliver critical operation information, enabling them to redirect, accelerate, and sharpen their planning, decision making, and control. A new technology infrastructure—of computers, communications equipment, software, and data—must be constructed, and people need to gain new skills to match the demands of the redesigned business.

Reorchestrating. Reorchestration refers to the leadership that top management must provide to embark on and successfully achieve a large-scale redesign in business processes. It is the easiest element to accept in concept, and the most difficult one to plan and implement. The task falls squarely on the turf of senior line management, who must change the beliefs, understandings, culture, structure, and behaviors of the organization to succeed in the transition from current business practices to those of the future.

The Potential of Reengineering. As a departure from the ordinary way of doing business, reengineering can be a somewhat unnerving concept. Undertaking such an effort means acting on a presupposition that a better way can be found before formulating a clear idea of what the new configuration will look like or achieve. Yet the wholesale alterations brought about by some recent technological advances—advances that were intended only to automate—indicate that this is not an unfair presupposition. A case in point is scanning technology, which was justified and installed to improve check-out clerk productivity in supermarkets. As it turns out, the information being provided by these systems has given retailers increased insight into and control over nearly every aspect of their business. This example is evidence of the power of reengineering even when it happens haphazardly. The potential for gain when it is planned is enormous.

REENGINEERING EXTERNAL RELATIONSHIPS TO CREATE SEAMLESS INTEGRATION

The process of reengineering internal operations has its parallel for external relationships as well. Again, the initial question is where to draw the boundary lines: To achieve optimum flexibility, where should the company's total operations begin and end? Again, once those lines are established, the effort must be undertaken to ensure that no line represents an informational blockade. With information tools such as electronic data interchange (EDI), there is no excuse for a company not to be linked with its vendors, carriers, and customers.

Management has been talking for years about forming information-based partnerships that benefit every participant in the supply chain, from vendors of raw materials to carriers, manufacturers, retailers, and customers. The problem is that in practice, instead of searching for real symbiosis, companies have simply tried to leverage knowledge about the strengths and weaknesses of customers and vendors for their own benefit. What managers must do now is look for opportunities for authentic partnerships.

An authentic partnership is one that recognizes the needs of each party in a business transaction so that the transaction proves beneficial to both.

For example, a tire manufacturer can establish a true partnership by providing just-in-time delivery of mounted tires to an automaker's plant in return for annual sales commitments. Sustaining this relationship requires both parties to merge physical and information assets—e.g., inventory, schedules, and forecasts—to create a national supply system and to share cost savings. This working relationship differs substantially from the arm's-length transactions that often result in duplicate inventories and expensive emergency shipments.

The same type of authentic partnerships may be on the rise in the grocery retailing business, where the emphasis on everyday low price is causing retailers to rethink their relationship with grocery manufacturers. Instead of buying periodically on promotion, retailers are beginning to express an interest in forecasting their requirements and tying that forecast into the production schedule of the grocery manufacturer.

As a measure of their interest, a recent survey of 40 major retailers,[1] each with annual sales in excess of $250 million, found that 90 percent considered partnerships desirable, and 75 percent also believed that partnerships will increase in the future. In addition, while merchandising remains the most popular linkage area, partnerships that address operational components of the retailer/supplier relationship are regarded as increasingly attractive opportunities. For example, 60 percent of those retailers surveyed strongly agreed that operational partnerships are effective for inbound transportation; 45 percent strongly agreed that operational partnerships benefit inventory management; and 30 percent also felt strongly that such partnerships benefit store operations.

It is important to note that in these operational partnerships, the critical bridge-building is performed by the two company's logistics functions. Because logistics management focuses on the linkages along the supply chain, it is best able to identify the partnership and leverage point opportunities that build flexibility into a business. The following sections discuss at greater length the strategic role of logistics, as well as issues of particular strategic concern in the areas of supply chain and network planning, distribution operations, materials management, and transportation.

THE ROLE OF LOGISTICS IN THE CORPORATE STRATEGY

Clearly, good logistics management is required to reengineer a business to achieve greater integration, both among internal functions and in external operational partnerships. Logistics integration responds to competitive

---

[1] Survey conducted by Cleveland Consulting Associates in the fall of 1989; included 20 food chains, 5 grocery wholesalers, 10 mass merchants and 5 specialty retailers.

intensity by meshing the economics of the vendor and the customer, thus providing customers with better service and getting product from vendors at lower cost. Just as importantly, it establishes a strong web of connections that remains flexible to respond to constantly changing business demands.

In short, the role of logistics is to reengineer, from an operational point of view, relationships that are established within an organization and among vendors and customers globally. The following sections detail some of the key issues surrounding the reengineering process in each area of logistics.

Supply Chain Strategy Issues

Supply chain strategy directs the application of operational assets toward meeting customer needs at minimum cost and investment. A well-conceived and -executed strategy improves performance in manufacturing, marketing, and sales, as well as providing delivery cost savings and inventory reductions. To achieve these improvements, the strategy must take into consideration:

- Customer needs and required services
- Competitive delivery capabilities
- Gaps between current performance, requirements, and competitive offerings
- Financial performance objectives across operations
- Trade-offs among transportation, inventory, storage, and production costs
- The role of information in reducing assets and improving performance
- Logistics organization
- Logistics planning, control, and measurement approaches

A key aspect of supply-chain strategy is distribution channel selection, in which the sales and physical distribution practices used to get products to consumers are specified. Traditionally, channel selection has been important to marketers because it affected market penetration and retail price point. Once consumers were sold the benefits of a product through advertising, then broad availability and low price points were all that was needed to build market share.

Now, however, channel selection and management have become more important because channel partners are exerting greater influence on consumption. Many manufacturers are increasing the incentives offered to customers to gain "trade franchise," i.e., influence over their marketing and selling activities. Trade franchise is as important as brand franchise in sustaining consumer preference for many products, especially those in mature categories.

As logistics managers work closely with their marketing peers to build market share, many find it advantageous to delegate the traditional physical distribution functions to third parties. This trend reflects the ability of third-party providers to vend a broad range of transportation, distribution, and inventory control services. In fact, vendors are even bidding to replace internal production planning and purchasing functions as part of the full-service concept.

In evaluating opportunities available from third parties, logistics managers must remember that their value is based on three principles: scale, functional specialization, and investment avoidance. Scale brings greater efficiency than what could be achieved internally. Functional specialization ideally improves quality. Investment avoidance works just like contract manufacturing, where products with lower volume, unique production technology, or a speculative future are sent to "copackers." With today's concentration on asset management, outside production and distribution are an attractive alternative to adding to the balance sheet. Finally, to determine whether new services have value for the company, the logistics manager must also evaluate them in terms of strategic fit, potential loss of business control, cost and investment, reliability, and adaptability.

Network Planning Issues

The location of a company's manufacturing and distribution facilities is the biggest factor in the ability to provide superior customer service at competitive costs. Yet few companies have facility networks that are rational, efficient, or synergistic. Instead, these networks typically reflect the company's history of intermittent internal growth and mergers and acquisitions. The result is a patchwork network that is superfluous in some regions and threadbare in others. Why do such networks persist? Because the analysis required to optimize them is complex, and implementing the revisions can be expensive and cumbersome. Network planning decisions must take into account the following concerns:

- *Capacity.* Do current facilities provide insufficient capacity? Excess capacity? Facilities must be evaluated with an eye to future demand projections.

- *Customer service.* Facility location is key to responsiveness. Planners need to be able to quantify the service impact of opening or closing a plant or warehouse or of changing sourcing or stocking policies.

- *Transportation costs.* Savings in this often overlooked area translate directly to the bottom line. An optimal network minimizes these costs.

- *Global sourcing.* Network planning cannot stop short at the U.S. borderline. As trade barriers throughout the world continue to fall, foreign product sourcing will make sense for many businesses.

- *U.S./Canada trade.* The recently ratified Free Trade Agreement between the United States and Canada significantly broadens cross-border market opportunities and has important ramifications for network planning.

- *New product sourcing.* Launching a new product is always chancy enough. The right network will help to ensure that the company can provide the service and competitive pricing it needs to succeed.

- *Postmerger synergy.* Consolidations yield real economies of scale for manufacturing and distribution. With the right network, they can be realized.

Although the task of network planning can seem daunting, it is greatly simplified by the availability of computer modeling tools with the capability to model entire facility networks and support "what if" analyses. Management can use such tools to evaluate with precision the relative merits of numerous scenarios before proceeding with a change.

Strategic Issues in Distribution Operations

Distribution operations encompass all the necessary components of achieving excellence in functional performance within and among distribution facilities. This involves consideration of facility design, materials handling systems, labor productivity, order servicing, and unitization and packaging. The goals of management in this area must be to increase the rate of return on facilities investment by improving task execution, schedule methods, control procedures, and coordination with the transportation and production functions.

Investments in distribution systems and materials handling equipment are usually designed to fit the distribution characteristics of a business. Yet distribution characteristics do not remain fixed. Competitors, consumer channels, marketing efforts, and profit performance requirements continually alter a company's order profile, service expectations, and supply chain partners. Strategic logistics planners need to respond to these changes by reengineering operations so that the company is able to provide a range of distribution capabilities. They link these capabilities with marketing to create the mix of service and cost characteristics that maximizes profitability. Reengineered operations may include highly focused facilities, multicapable facilities, and flexible, reliable partners for short-term needs. Most importantly, the system will be able to provide the service requirements and cost structure that is correct for each customer, product, or special program.

Essential to this capability will be the management of distribution information. Recent technology, such as bar codes, portable transaction computers, and radio frequency transmission, provide little more than basic data about the status of orders, inventory, and shipments. Yet successful companies will use this data to create information on how customers order — not just what they order — and the distribution characteristics of individual customers and products. Distribution and marketing can then use this information to create programs whereby distribution characteristics are managed to create profits and not only to manage costs.

Strategic Materials Management Issues

The concept of materials management, and the terms associated with it, have been around for thirty years, but only in the past decade have great strides been made in this area. The focus of materials management is to minimize total investments in all inventory and to achieve close coordination between production and delivery. This requires detailed knowledge of capacity planning, production scheduling, inbound transportation planning, and order management activities that are linked to inventory requirements. However, advances in personal computer technology — with off-the-shelf integrated systems solutions now available — have made it possible for even the smallest company to quantify the complicated supply chain trade-offs involved in these issues.

Successful materials management programs balance trade-offs between supply (inventory and production capacity) and demand (orders and forecasts). These trade-offs are resolved in a way that provides competitive levels of customer service at minimum investment. Investments in raw materials, work-in-process inventory, finished goods inventory, and production capacity are all considered. Nevertheless, good materials management is not an end in itself; rather, it is a critical ingredient in linking purchasing, manufacturing, distribution, and sales. If materials management fails to span all of these areas, attempts to improve other areas often founder. For example, a company may implement aggressive DRP and inventory reduction procedures only to find that the plant is unable to maintain the required reliability of these programs. On the other hand, just-in-time improvements designed to reduce lead times and minimize work in process are often lost in the inefficiency of finished goods distribution and inventory planning. When materials management is applied to reengineering the links among these supply-chain functions, improvement efforts are leveraged for maximum effectiveness.

Transportation Strategies

In the 1980s, it was not difficult to cut major costs from the transportation function. With the convergence of the oil crisis, deregulation of the transportation industry, and high inflation rates, there was a major competitive crunch for carriers to reduce transportation costs, and they responded accordingly. As we enter the 1990s, however, many carriers are being driven out of the market as the costs of capital and fuel continue to increase. Although the pressure is still on logistics planners to keep their transportation costs low as a percentage of sales, it is likely that many of them will overrun their budgets substantially.

Nevertheless, in terms of strategy, logistics organizations have been placing increasing emphasis on the transportation piece of their management portfolios. This is happening for two reasons. First, the implementation of just-in-time production techniques by customers has created ordering patterns and service requirements that complicate shipment planning and delivery. Second, there is greater awareness that transportation can often be substituted for expensive inventory and facilities to obtain the responsive service levels needed to compete.

An important component of this renewed emphasis on transportation strategy is dedicated capacity in the form of either a private fleet or a contract operation. These alternatives to common carriers can provide advantages in service and cost predictability, but they also require careful planning and attention to operational detail. Contemporary fleet management systems can enable logistics managers to meet planning and operating challenges by scheduling and dispatching dedicated capacity over a user-specified time horizon. Properly applied, they can help companies of all sizes achieve consistent savings and increased return on assets. On a strategic level, they help management address questions of fleet sizing, location of driver domiciles, equipment selection and mix, alternative operating practices (e.g., one-shift vs. two-shift operation, use of double teams and/or trailer pools), and location of maintenance and refueling facilities.

Of course, for most companies, common carriage will remain the most manageable alternative. To optimize the use of these resources, the best strategy for these businesses will be to form strategic partnerships with a few select carriers. In this postderegulation era, and in the midst of a transportation industry shake-out, it is important to remember that unprofitable carriers make weak business partners. Thus, the carrier selection process must go beyond seeking the least-cost carrier for each traffic lane. Instead, shippers should choose carriers according to such quality-based criteria as experience, operating authority and geographic coverage, on-time performance, operating efficiencies, equipment availability, and information accuracy.

Because the shipper-carrier partnership can only be maintained by sharing information about shipment volumes and costs, service performance, operating procedures, and strategy, information accuracy is a critical consideration in the carrier selection process. On-board satellite communications, Local Area Networks, artificial intelligence, expert systems, outsourcing of operations, EDI, and strategic systems are all concepts or technologies that carriers are evaluating or using today. To take full advantage of these attributes, a shipper needs the capability to establish strong informational linkages with its carriers.

CONCLUSION

All of the issues outlined in this chapter point the way to innovative reengineering of operations to achieve greater flexibility for the 1990s and beyond. In every case, this flexibility has to do with the kind of integration achievable through excellent logistics management. Several industry examples depict successful results of reengineering that were achieved either by cutting links out of the supply chain or by reorganizing aspects of internal operations to become more efficient and effective.

Perhaps the most striking example to date is the grocery industry. Today, nearly half the total output of major dry grocery manufacturers is being picked up at the point of manufacture by the customer, who transports product directly to his plant or warehouse. Out of eight million grocery loads a year, four million are being tendered without the use of outside carriers or manufacturers' warehouses. Customers take direct and immediate responsibility for damage and delivery performance to leverage fixed assets, such as their fleets and distribution centers.

The grocery antithesis is an equally notable increase in direct store delivery (DSD). Manufacturers are assuming more responsibility for getting product directly to the store by bypassing the warehouse or the wholesaler. The trend has even gone beyond the traditional DSD areas of perishable, breakable, or returnable products. Items like paper goods and other bulky items are also going direct to stores, because, as stores get bigger, they can handle greater volumes while avoiding some warehouse throughput costs and store labor expense.

In the retailing arena, Wal-Mart, for example, has opened a new experimental store, where manufacturers are given an agreed-upon quantity of space to merchandise their products. For their part, Wal-Mart provides store space, check-out counters, and receiving docks. In this case, with the exception of providing a receiving dock, Wal-Mart is not involved in distribution.

A more significant example is the "Sears revolution." After eighty years of building a warehousing empire and maintaining heavy control of its distribution, Sears is reengineering its entire store supply system. The majority of its central and regional warehouses has been or will be closed, and primary responsibility for transportation will be shifted to suppliers. In essence, the distribution system that Sears grew up with became outmoded.

Lead times were too long, inventory levels were too high, and distribution and transportation costs had ballooned to almost double that of many of Sears' streamlined competitors. Now, with fewer warehouses and off-loaded responsibility for distribution, Sears has paved the way for

- Dramatic speed up of product movement to stores
- Huge reductions in inventories
- Extensive amounts of warehousing space freed up to be sold
- Reduced responsibility for damage

Another example of achieving more with less through reengineering is the use of third parties. Companies are frequently engaging intermediaries to provide services that suit the needs of a particular manufacturer or retailer. For example, LTL consolidators are used to ship products to approximately 2200 KMart stores. Various manufacturers' products are mixed by the consolidator and reshipped economically to KMart stores around the United States.

Certainly there are numerous companies and products for whom cutting links from the supply chain does not result in savings, and can actually cost market share. Every organization needs a distribution approach that is optimized for the business and competitive environments in which its customers or end users operate. However, as the preceding examples demonstrate, a willingness to be bold in undertaking changes to build greater flexibility into operations can position companies for further growth and profitability.

PART V

Strategy Implementation

23

Organizational Structure and Management Process

PETER LORANGE

Handelshøyskolen BI
Norwegian School of Management
The Wharton School, University of Pennsylvania

INTRODUCTION

There has been strong interest over the past few years in the role an organization's structure and management processes play in effective strategic management. Important progress has been made regarding these issues within the research community, and practitioners have added important insights based on their experience. In this chapter, a firm's structure and its related management processes are presented as highly interrelated phenomena, and an integrated point of view is offered for considering management structures and processes as complementary vehicles for implementing strategies effectively. Treatment of only selected aspects of a firm's structure or management processes is likely to have significantly less effect on implementation; it is the consistent consideration of both structure and process that will prove to be effective.

A key to assessing the appropriateness of a particular structure and its accompanying management processes is an understanding of the strategic pressures that a firm faces from its environment, both for pursuing new opportunities and for coordinating internal activities to compete efficiently in already existing businesses. Thus, this chapter begins with a brief discussion of how environmental pressures affect the structure and processes a firm adopts. It then moves on to discuss major, broad patterns in the evolution of organizational structures and their accompanying processes, with particular emphasis on seeing them as vehicles for an organization to achieve a better alignment between its environment and its internal capabilities.

The discussion in this chapter of alternative structures and processes focuses on five different archetypes: the functional form, accompanied by a business planning and control process; the divisionalized structure, with its multilevel planning process and decentralized control support; the geographic/multinational organization, with its associated process backups; and two full-blown multidimensional structure/process alternatives, one that emphasizes the structural approach, and another that emphasizes process considerations (the so-called strategic/operating structure approach).

To a large extent, each structural process builds on the former, and significant parts of one archetype can also be found in the next. That there are common elements among the archetypes underscores that, in real life, a continuity of hybrid options will evolve rather than the dichotomized archetypes presented. Typically, management will anticipate emerging environmental pressures, and it will respond by modifying the firm's management structure and processes. Structural modifications usually affect only certain parts of the organization at one time, not the entire corporation. Different aspects of the management processes also tend to be strengthened on an ongoing basis. More "clean sweep" realignments of structure and process at one discrete point in time are typically much more difficult; hence the emergence of hybrid structural/process patterns.

Since a company normally consists of a multitude of businesses, each facing different strategic realities and challenges, the effect of different structures and processes on particular business elements within the firm also needs to be addressed. For this reason, structures and processes must be designed to fit different strategic business settings within the firm, just as the firm's overall structure and processes must be tailored to its general environment.

Throughout this chapter, an attempt has been made to emphasize up-to-date information that will be useful to the practitioner. This current information, however, builds on the long and rich traditions of research on the interrelationships between strategy and structure.

STRATEGY AS A DETERMINANT OF STRUCTURE AND PROCESS

This section focuses on the interrelationship between the strategic challenges, the resulting pressures an organization faces, and the organization's need to develop a formal structure and an associated management process to respond to these pressures.

A basic, overriding task of strategic management is to increase the value of the organization through the following steps:

- Attempt to identify a set of attractive business opportunities, judged in terms of the market.
- Attempt to develop organizational strengths that meet the requirements for success in the attractive business segments.
- Set aside resources today in order to be able to build the strengths required to carry out future strategies. This strategy-implementing activity takes place in tandem with the organization's ongoing efforts to keep the present pattern of business activities going.

Thus, there is a complex challenge for management that requires an understanding of a diversity of issues. For example: What makes some environments more attractive than others? What are the critical requirements for succeeding in each setting? How can a firm assess the appropriateness of the match between its position in the environment and its internal capabilities? As a firm strengthens this match by building new strategic capabilities, what resources is it applying?

A precondition for addressing questions relating to structure and process is an analysis of the environmental setting or settings at hand. Then the firm can establish a view of the critical strategic pressures that it may be facing. In a competitive business setting, one way to succeed is by having a product that is sufficiently unique to allow a firm to charge a higher price than its competitors, and to enjoy thereby a higher margin of profit. Alternatively, the profit margin can be created by bringing the product to the market place at a lower cost than the competition. An organization's choice of business strategies, therefore, when it comes to decisions about products and costs, depends on two major considerations of the environment: (1) What opportunities does a particular business environment provide for the adaptation of a firm's product to the environment so as to emphasize the product's distinguishing features (e.g., novel design, unique quality, better service, a reliable source of availability), and to what extent can this environment create a basis for more or less continually modifying a product to keep ahead of a competitor's products? (2) What opportunities does a particular business environment provide for the integration of organizational activities so as to achieve comparative cost advantages, for example, through attempting to standardize in order to achieve so-called experience-curve effects in manufacturing, distribution, or marketing.

An organization must face up to a combination of pressures to adapt to its environment and to integrate its activities; the importance of each of these tasks will be dictated by the environmental setting at hand, will tend to differ from business to business and from company to company, and will probably change over time.

Of course, the complexity of the firm's environmental strategic exposure depends on several underlying factors, three of which are particularly important. First, the diversity of the firm is critical; e.g., how many businesses it is in, how these businesses are related, and whether the firm can be managed so as to benefit from a common core of know-how. Second, the stability of each of the firm's particular businesses is likely to differ, for example, in terms of sales growth rates, evolution of the business, and the effect of environmental factors such as consumer shifts, technological change, or initiatives from government and other stakeholder interests. Third, the fierceness of the competitive climate that each business faces varies depending on the type of competition, the structure of the particular industry, and the competitive strengths enjoyed by the competing firm in a particular business.

The complexity of the firm's strategic response is, of course, derived to a large extent from environmental factors. The environment determines what it takes to compete successfully. Environmental pressures might lead to a variety of responses, depending on what level of the organizational hierarchy is affected: the business element level, the business family level, or the corporate/portfolio level.

At the business element strategy level, a firm's response to environmental pressures may be manifested in its decisions about whether to remain within the present product/market configuration or to extend into the new product or market applications. Conceivably, a business element strategy may also be simplified further by concentrating on an even narrower set of products or markets. At the business family level, the environment might lead a firm to emphasize coordination among business elements in the external competitive arenas, as well as to attempt to achieve competitive advantages from clearer internal coordination of research and development (R&D), manufacturing, sales, and so forth. At the corporate, or portfolio, strategy level, environmental pressures might affect the degree to which management chooses to pursue corporate-wide transfer of strategic resources (e.g., funds, key management talent, or technological know-how). Or, alternatively, management may rely on having the business families consider redeploying strategic resources among subsets of business elements within themselves. The latter method implies that a smaller fraction of resources might be reallocated with a corporate-wide focus in mind. The corporate portfolio strategy might be said to be more complex if the environmental circumstances call for a corporate-wide strategic resource allocation.

It should be noted in passing, however, that how effective an organization wants its strategy to be greatly affects its willingness to face up to environmental complexity. With a highly ambitious vision and performance challenges for itself, the organization can tolerate less evasion of environmental reality. Pressures to modify the organizational structure and processes thus might be expected to be felt earlier and stronger in such instances.

By choosing an appropriate organizational structure and management processes, an organization can develop a relevant strength posture for meeting environmental challenges. However, an organizational structure (i.e., the delineation of the patterns of formal tasks and authorities assigned to the members of an organization) cannot, of course, be changed too frequently. The costs associated with reorganizing should not be ignored. To reorganize represents a fairly drastic way of bringing the organization's capabilities in line with its environmental requirements; such discrete adjustments from one organizational setup to another can uproot working relationships and otherwise affect motivation. Reorganization may be disruptive, and it may be some time before the organization is back to working at full speed. These considerations should be kept in mind when considering the properties of the five major organizational forms that are discussed later in this chapter. A firm cannot easily switch back and forth between the archetypes.

The development of management processes can be seen as complementing choices about a firm's structure, in that they further delineate specific patterns of executive interaction and behavior within the basic organizational framework chosen. Tailor-made management processes represent an overlay on the formal structure; that is, they are a more incremen-

FIGURE 23-1

Functional Organizational Structure

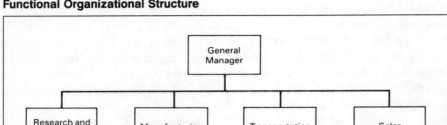

tal, flexible mode of adjusting a firm's ability to integrate its activities and otherwise adapt to its environment. As long as the organization's structure is designed to meet the strategic pressures it faces in the first place, the management processes can help extend the firm's ability to adapt to those pressures. Management processes can thus be seen as complementary, more dynamic fine-tuning on top of structure. It should be stressed that even though an organization may have matched its adaptive and integrative capabilities to the strategic challenges at hand, such a fit does not tend to be a stable one. Environments tend to change more or less continuously, revealing new opportunities as well as emerging threats, and putting pressure on management to develop and modify continually the firm's ability to respond to such environmental challenges.

An important implication is that an organization must continually channel resources into building future positions of strategic strength, at the expense of its immediate performance. An accurate assessment of the environment is thus essential for determining the trade-off between building for the future and attempting to achieve immediate short-term results. An appropriate structure and process for a given setting is critical for making such decisions. It is a major challenge to management, functioning through a particular structure and its associated management processes, to allow for a realistic commitment of resources to strategic change, by channeling appropriate resources into building new strengths, i.e., by protecting them from all being used to meet today's short-term performance pressures.

THE FUNCTIONALLY ORGANIZED FIRM

Figure 23-1 provides an example of a functional organizational structure. This type of structure is used when the various tasks engaged in by the business have been specialized as much as possible. Each major function is assigned to a particular department in order to take advantage of employee experience and the benefits of scale that result from the specialized activities that might be carried out within each of these departments. Duplication of effort is kept to a minimum.

This form of organization has major benefits as well as limitations, all of which are well known. It is used primarily by corporations with uncomplicated strategic settings, primarily ones that focus on one business or on a few highly interrelated ones. The general manager in such a firm must be closely associated with the business, because he or she must provide the generalist's "glue" to pull the specialist functions together into a cohesive business. The major strength of this form, above all, is that it offers strong integrative capabilities; it provides a basis for carrying out each function in a cost-efficient manner, for building a specialized organization that can benefit from the accumulation of focused efforts, and for investing in specialized equipment. Its major limitation is that it provides a relatively poor vehicle for adapting quickly to new opportunities and threats from the environment. Because each functional unit in the organization has a specialized and narrow purpose, a relatively inflexible pattern is created. Thus, for this setup to be an appropriate structural choice for a firm, there must be some degree of stability in the business's environment. Rapidly changing external circumstances would easily defeat the very purpose of this form, which is to provide a stable, efficient organization by pursuing the benefits of integration.

The functional structure is suited to a firm that finds itself in a relatively narrow span of business. Such a business may frequently be well established and relatively mature, in which case its environment is likely to be relatively secure. The strategic success of such a firm typically hinges on its ability to achieve lower costs than its competition. The functional organization lends itself to such a requirement, because it represents a structural vehicle that is well suited to pursuing integrative, efficiency-oriented strategies. The functional structure may also be well suited to the smaller, rapidly growing firm in which the lack of size justifies choosing this relatively "inexpensive" structure and in which the pressure to maintain profit margins sufficient for the firm to survive calls for integrative discipline.

The strategic management process in this type of organization needs to strengthen further the integrative focus of the business. This can be achieved by continuing to improve the coordination of internal activities as well as by developing related products or markets. A formal planning process might be established to facilitate this. The process would help management reassess the strategic direction of the business, delineate strategic programs for implementing the business strategy, and reserve room in the budget for the tasks required to carry out the strategic programs.

The process of setting objectives consists of reassessing the basic strategic direction of the business by considering changes in the environment and by articulating the internal requirements for pursuing new business opportunities vigorously. The delineation of underlying assumptions or factors that are critical to the success of a particular objective is a particularly important aspect of this planning step. Subsequent changes in these assumptions may lead to a revision of the objective.

The next step focuses on articulating how the objectives are to be carried out through appropriate strategic programs. Many strategic programs normally call for a cross-functional team effort. For example the development of a new product might require close cooperation between research and development, manufacturing, and marketing. Similarly, a strategic program for improving the efficiency of the production process might require the combined involvement of research and development and manufacturing. Thus, although each functional department is engaged in specialized cost-efficient operating activities, each will need to carry out additional roles if the firm is to implement the overall strategic program successfully.

The link between the strategic programming step and the budgeting step of the planning process thus becomes critical. Each functional department's role in carrying out the overall strategic program should be clear, and each department should receive sufficient resources earmarked for realistically carrying out its share of these tasks.

Figure 23-2 provides a formalized picture of how strategic programs link up with the budgeting process. For each strategic program, the tasks that must be performed by each functional department and the required resources are described. The overall resource requirements for each strategic program are provided in the right-hand column of the figure. The total set of derived strategic implementation roles that each functional department is requested to carry out, and the associated resources that each function would need for this, can be seen in the bottom line of Figure 23-2. The budget for each functional department should have specific lines that articulate these resource needs.

The setting of strategic direction within a business can be aided by making use of a business planning process in a functionally organized company. Such a process should delineate business objectives and identify strategic programs that enable the firm to remain competitive. Process improvement, renewal of products or markets, or a move into new businesses less directly related to the core business might be the result. Also, each functional department's part in the team effort to carry out a strategic program, as well as the resources needed to carry out the required activities, must be spelled out carefully. Finally, functional departments should be given the resources necessary to carry out their derived strategic roles (as illustrated in the bottom line of Figure 23-2).

There must be a trade-off if a firm is to meet both strategic and operating pressures; sufficient resources must be provided for strategic purposes,

FIGURE 23-2

Delineation of Strategic Program Tasks to Be Carried Out by Functional Department, and the Implied Resource Requirements

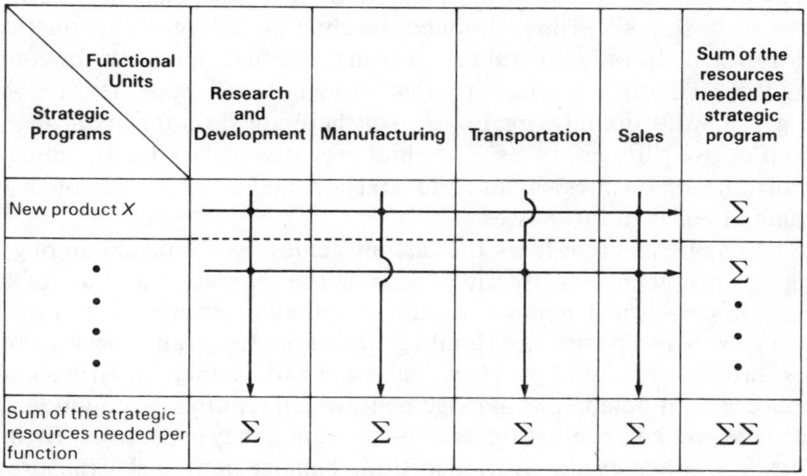

Functional Units / Strategic Programs	Research and Development	Manufacturing	Transportation	Sales	Sum of the resources needed per strategic program
New product X					Σ
$\vdots$					Σ $\vdots$
Sum of the strategic resources needed per function	Σ	Σ	Σ	Σ	$\Sigma\Sigma$

Source: Richard F. Vancil, "Better Management of Corporate Development," Harvard Business Review (Sept.-Oct. 1972), p. 59

and each functional department should get adequate resources to carry out its strategic roles. These resources should not be made available to meet operating crises and day-to-day demands.

To recapitulate, a corporation engaged in a limited number of highly interrelated businesses adapts to its environment by choosing an appropriate organizational structure. Normally, the functional form is selected so that the corporation can develop a focus for pursuing an efficient way of competing. Management processes are also needed so that objectives can be modified and the necessary strategic programs can be delineated and executed. By choosing a proper combination of structure and process, an organization should be better able to cope strategically and prepare for its future.

THE DIVISIONALLY ORGANIZED FIRM

Many organizations find themselves at one time or another in situations where they face a highly heterogeneous environment. This often stems from attempts by the firm to diversify as it grows; it may also result from changes in the environment that present the firm with emerging opportunities to engage in several businesses rather than in one. The consequence of increased environmental complexity is an increased need for adaptation.

In a divisionalized structure, a firm attempts to adapt to its environment by developing relatively self-contained organizational entities around each of its businesses. Thus, although the chief executive of the functional organization is the only general manager in the firm, responsible for coordinating the various functional activities into an overall, consistent business strategy, in a divisionally organized firm there are several general managers, and of two different types. The chief executive is faced with managing the portfolio of businesses, and the division managers are charged with managing their own businesses.

The chief executive faces the task of achieving a balance among the firm's various businesses. He must focus on the generation and use of strategic resources—most notably, funds and human resources—and decide which of the firm's businesses should generate net funds and to which businesses these funds should go. He will also have to balance the firm's know-how base, as embodied in its management, which requires careful judgment in the development, evaluation, and assignment of key executives. He must also attempt to achieve an overall portfolio balance in the risk exposures—economic as well as political—that the different businesses face in their environments.

The second type of general manager is in charge of a self-contained business entity; these managers are frequently called division heads. They face tasks similar to those faced by the chief executive officer (CEO) of a functional organization; that is, they coordinate the division's functional activities into a particular business strategy. Thus, within each of the divisions, the focus continues to be one of specialization, as is the case with the functional organization.

A divisionalized structure (Figure 23-3) provides a firm with the ability to adapt to its environment at two different levels: At the business level, it allows the firm to address specific opportunities and requirements for each business, and at the corporate portfolio level, it helps the firm achieve a more explicit way of balancing its overall resource commitments and risk taking. A divisionalized structure may also be able to counteract the potentially negative effects of large, bureaucratic, and unfocused functional organizational entities that might otherwise develop when the firm grows.

The major potential drawbacks of this form, however, might include lost opportunities, or a weakening of the firm's cost position owing to duplication of effort caused by having several parallel organizational entities pursuing similar functional tasks. Within each division, too, there might be the familiar problems involved in adapting to environmental changes, as with a functional structure. To change drastically the balance between existing divisions may also be difficult; each division might have developed

FIGURE 23-3

Divisionalized Structure

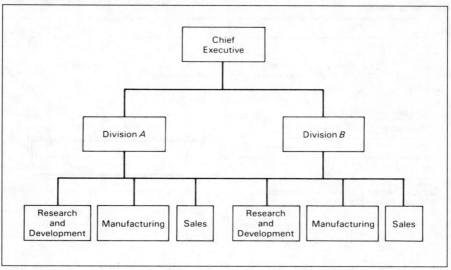

a vested interest in pursuing its business, and there might be resistance to redrawing the borders between the business charters of the divisions. Changing significantly the portfolio of businesses would make adaptation at the corporate level all the more difficult.

The management processes that reinforce the structure of a divisionally organized corporation must also support different business strategies as well as an overall corporate-wide portfolio strategy.

There is a need to articulate a business strategy for each of the businesses by delineating a business objective, strategic programs, and ways to implement the budget. The processes also need to help managers address the trade-off between using resources for the future repositioning and self-renewal of the business, and using them to meet operating pressures and achieve shorter-term, bottom-line results. Each business or division, then, requires management processes similar to those found in a functionally organized business.

There is an additional need, however, for a corporate-wide assessment of strategic resources to determine how much the corporation as a whole can afford to allocate for future growth, and where these strategic resources should be allocated among all of the firm's existing and potential businesses. The planning process should thus be extended to provide a corporate-wide, portfolio view in order to come up with a balanced set of business objectives. This should lead to a prudent overall balance among

FIGURE 23-4

An Interactive Process to Develop Both a Corporate-Wide Plan and a Business Plan

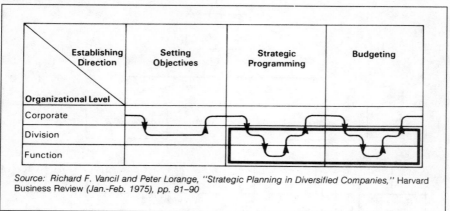

Source: Richard F. Vancil and Peter Lorange, "Strategic Planning in Diversified Companies," Harvard Business Review (Jan.-Feb. 1975), pp. 81–90

factors such as the generation of funds and their use, human resources and know-how, and exposure to economic or political risk. Objectives for all the businesses in the firm should be reconciled in terms of how they fit into the overall corporate-wide, portfolio point of view, and all strategic programs should compete for strategic resources.

To accomplish this sort of interaction, a divisionally organized firm must establish a top-down/bottom-up dialogue between the corporate level and each of the businesses within the corporation. The top-down signals should be based on a broad perception of the environment and should emphasize the firm's overall "architecture," the "fit" of each business within this overall portfolio, and the broad feasibility constraints on the corporate-wide allocation of strategic resources. The aim is to enhance the development of the overall portfolio. The bottom-up signals should describe the nature of the various business environments and identify opportunities for employing a particular business's strengths. Further, they should articulate realistic strategic programs, and include requests for the necessary strategic resources. These top-down and bottom-up interchanges are interrelated, contingent on each other, and mutually reinforcing. They require a process that is based on close cooperation and interaction.

Figure 23-4 illustrates an interactive top-down/bottom-up planning process that attempts both to develop business plans for each business and to reconcile these in a corporate-wide portfolio. The four cells at the bottom-right of Figure 23-4, encircled by a double line, represent the linking of strategic tasks to the various operating functions, as delineated in Figure 23-2.

A divisionalized organization, then, is in a strong position to adapt to its environment. Beyond the advantages stemming from its organizational structure, which pushes authority closer to each business area, it benefits from an accompanying elaboration of the strategic processes that attempts to have an impact on the allocation of strategic resources at several levels. This helps each business adapt to its situation, and it helps the corporation as a whole to balance its efforts to enter promising areas and to disengage from others. The strategic process facilitates the vigorous pursuit of business strategies among the firm's many businesses, and it also helps the corporation to pursue selected opportunities on a larger scale by channeling strategic resources into a few emerging business opportunities in a more proactive manner than otherwise might have been possible.

THE GEOGRAPHIC STRUCTURE

As a consequence of their success over time, many corporations end up with manufacturing facilities and markets scattered over large geographic areas. In discussing their structure and processes in this section, multinational corporations are used as an example, although the following considerations could apply to any geographically diverse corporation.

One type of multinational firm is a worldwide, product-organized corporation. It might manufacture cars, farm equipment, chemicals, or pharmaceuticals; characteristically, its manufacturing lines or products require heavy R&D or massive investment in manufacturing in order to turn out products at a reasonable cost. Such product types tend to be marketed worldwide, and they tend to be of uniform design and quality. This type of firm can be contrasted with a multinational that produces consumer-oriented products, such as foods, spirits, toiletries, or clothing. Here, a primary challenge is to adapt the products to the particular circumstances of each country. Standardizing the products on a worldwide basis would defy local preferences and requirements. This type of firm might be called a geographically organized corporation.

The worldwide, product-organized corporation has strong needs for cost-efficient development, manufacturing, and distribution of its products. Hence, it would typically adopt a divisional structure as its organizational form, based on its products. This type of firm, of course, must also adapt to local circumstances, perhaps by further fine-tuning its marketing and by modifying its products, even though such concerns might not tend to be equally important. Local country organizations typically are in place to take care of sales and distribution for each worldwide division.

Such a company might thus find itself with parallel sales/distribution organizations operating in a given country. At times, it might find it useful to consolidate some of these activities, so as to strengthen its position. This consolidation may take the relatively weak forms of shared office and support functions or of efforts to coordinate actions among governmental agencies and other external stakeholder groups, or it may appear as stronger forms of coordination such as joint marketing, distribution, and sales. The emergence of a second organizational dimension can be seen here: the seeds of a matrix structure. Although the worldwide, product-organized dimension is clearly the dominant one, a complementary geographic-area dimension might be "grown."

As with a normal divisional structure, a key task for the worldwide, business-divisionalized firm is to balance the portfolio of global businesses. Such a global portfolio strategy must take into account funds-flow characteristics as well as economic and political risk considerations stemming from its combinations of worldwide business activities. Assessing economic and political risk may be particularly difficult, in that each worldwide business strategy will be exposed to different risks in different countries. Consequently, although the basic characteristics of the management process will be similar to those of an ordinary divisionalized corporation—i.e., multi-level, with both business and portfolio dimensions—additional planning and control processes might also be established for each country in order to coordinate the various business strategies as they come to apply to particular countries.

The other type of multinational corporation, organized by geographic area, should have separate organizations in each country so it can adapt to local circumstances. Each country organization may, in fact, have its own divisions, and business strategies are built-up around local markets. The firm's corporate portfolio is determined largely by achieving a balance among its country divisions. Such an organization must focus on each local market and attempt to reach a balance among country exposures. For this, a country-based divisionalized structure is appropriate.

Here, there might also be opportunities for country organizations to coordinate aspects of their business operations, such as, for example, new business developments, approaches to manufacturing, or the sharing of process innovations. Thus, there might also be a need for worldwide coordination across particular products or processes.

The strengthening of the management processes should reflect this multidimensional challenge. To complement the hierarchical divisionalized process approach developed around the country division structure, a dual planning and control process might also be developed to strengthen the firm's ability to coordinate its production of global goods and to adapt its processes.

FIGURE 23-5
Matrix Organization Structure

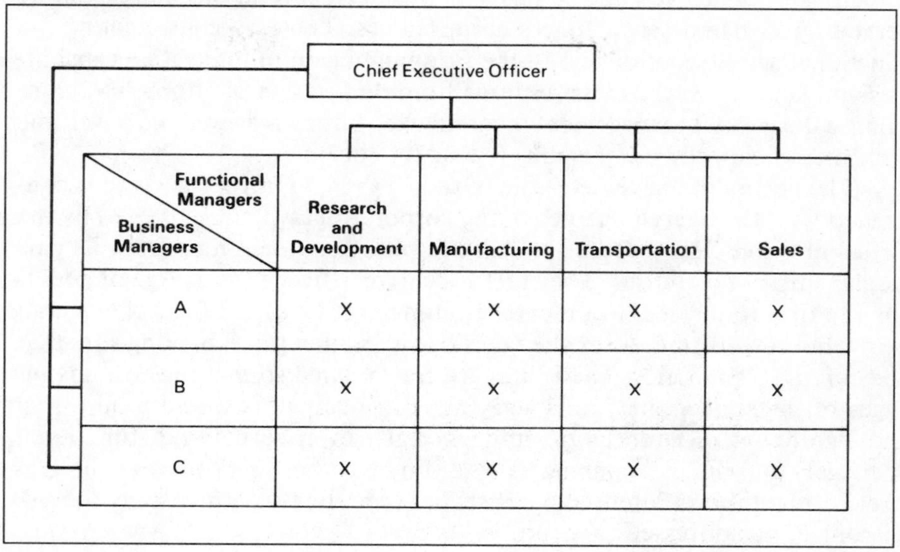

Business Managers \ Functional Managers	Research and Development	Manufacturing	Transportation	Sales
A	X	X	X	X
B	X	X	X	X
C	X	X	X	X

(Chief Executive Officer at top of chart)

THE MATRIX STRUCTURE

From the discussions of both the worldwide divisionalized structure and the geographic-area structure for multinational corporations, a so-called matrix organization can be suggested, one in which both a product and an area dimension can be more fully integrated into the organization's structure and processes, allowing considerations of adaptation and integration surrounding both dimensions to be dealt with more fully.

As discussed previously, one potential drawback with a divisionalized structure is the cost associated with the duplication of efforts among several organizational subunits within the firm, leading possibly to a loss of competitive edge. At least to some extent, the improvements in a firm's ability to adapt to changing circumstances provided by a division structure come as a trade-off against a lowering of the ability to achieve cost-efficient integration. The so-called matrix structure, illustrated in Figure 23-5, attempts in part to ameliorate this by emphasizing how to achieve both adaptive and integrative capabilities in a cost-beneficial manner by borrowing features from both the divisional and functional structures.

In a company with a matrix structure, each business is run by a business manager responsible for the general management task of setting and implementing the business's direction. The business manager's role in this respect is similar to that of a typical division manager; the business manager will not have full autonomy over a set of functional departments. Instead of reporting directly and exclusively to the business manager, several businesses will be served by a shared set of functional resources. Thus, by consolidating the functional activities of divisions, the firm might gain in integrative capabilities and keep down the costs resulting from duplication of efforts. By maintaining the general management focus on each business as well, however, the firm might still preserve the ability to adapt effectively.

The general management role of the CEO in a matrix structure is concerned with the overall balance of the corporation, which is affected by the firm's resource-flow patterns and risk implications stemming from its particular mix of businesses. The chief executive officer is in charge of adapting the firm to new environmental circumstances by modifying the overall portfolio. In addition, he or she takes on two added roles: making sure that the company's functional activities are coordinated so that the cost advantages of integrating the firm's activities can be achieved; and monitoring the significant differences of opinion that can arise between functional managers and business managers regarding whether to emphasize integration or adaptation. Potential conflicts between the two dimensions should, of course, be addressed early on.

This particular structural form, with its greater balance between the pressures of adaptation and integration at both the business level and the portfolio level, nonetheless does come with specific costs attached. Above all, these stem from the inevitable additional costs of communication, interaction, and fatigue from friction and ambiguity associated with the approach. The intricate pattern of structural interrelationships in the matrix structure also might create a de facto inertia against major shifts in strategic direction, and thus make it difficult to achieve adaptation in practice.

For a business manager in an organization with this structure, there will be heavy emphasis on negotiating with functional managers to persuade them to carry out the various tasks necessary to run each business. This might be achieved through extensive formal and informal meetings or one-to-one encounters. At times, it may be necessary to institute additional planning or control processes in order to achieve better coordination. Committees composed of business and functional representatives might be involved in this effort. Such processes help to delineate tasks in more detail, that is, who is to interact with whom, about what, and when. It should be stressed again that structural features alone do not automatically ensure appropriate strategic focus; an organization's structure needs to be complemented by appropriate management processes if it is to integrate its activities and adapt to changing circumstances successfully.

The nature of the planning process in an organization with a formal matrix structure (Figure 23-5) must address the challenge of providing the firm with the ability to deal with a hierarchy of strategies, much like the process used in a divisionally organized firm to develop both a corporate-wide plan and a business plan (Figure 23-4). However, in this case, instead of business divisions interacting with the corporate level, there will be a balance of business and functional elements providing the bottom-up inputs. All of the business managers should be deeply involved in the setting of objectives, so that they can attempt to set a meaningful strategic direction for their businesses. Environmental conditions in particular will be addressed at this stage, and the critical assumptions underlying the business strategy must be reassessed. The business managers should, however, consult with the functional managers so that they can realistically assess the organization's ability to actually implement particular strategies.

During the strategic programming stage, the business manager and the functional managers should decide how the different functional departments will coordinate their activities to carry out strategic programs for each business. The managers should interact extensively and come up with several preliminary solutions. The challenge facing each functional manager in this respect is the attempt to accommodate the strategic programming tasks from each business in such a way that the function's task still can be carried out with a reasonable degree of efficiency.

During the budgeting stage, this two-dimensional dialogue will continue; however, the functional departments will be even more centrally involved now, because they outline the detailed activity patterns for next year. The relative shift in involvement from the business to the functional dimension as the planning process moves along, in terms of having the initiative in delineating the bottom-up planning inputs as a basis for the interaction with the corporate portfolio level, is illustrated in Figure 23-6.

Although the matrix structure is conceptually very intriguing, there are several potential problems associated with making a planning process work within this complex kind of organizational structure. First, the cost of interaction may be considerable, both because of the time involved and because of the potential for disruptive conflicts. Managers may be forced to take extreme views, associating themselves with the one dimension they represent, when good strategies should be based on an eclectic synthesis. The process of reaching broad commitment to a strategy throughout the organization might easily get bogged down. Thus, by institutionalizing the functional and divisional dimensions, as is the case in a matrix structure, managers might, through their vested interests, limit the firm's ability to adopt to complex strategic changes.

THE "WEAK" MATRIX CONCEPT

An approach closely related to the matrix structure, but still a distinct design in its own right, is the "weak" matrix concept. This is based on the

FIGURE 23-6

Shifts Between the Business Manager's and Functional Manager's Relative Involvement in Providing Bottom-Up Inputs of the Planning Process

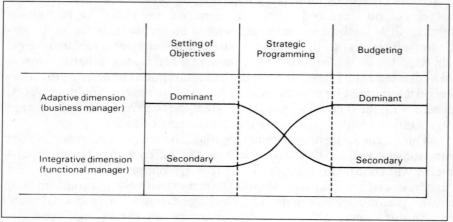

so-called dual strategic/operating structure. Like the matrix structure, this approach is appropriate for corporations that face both strong adaptive and integrative pressures. The matrix form might be an appropriate structural response for an organization to meet such strategic needs, but there are also strategic process options available that might strongly complement the matrix structure. Therefore, the weak matrix concept places less emphasis on the matrix structures, and more emphasis on developing matrix interrelationships through processes, by emphasizing how the same managers within the organization might wear two hats; that is, they develop strategies as members of business teams, which then provide the direction for them in their operating dimension roles.

The emergence of strategic business units (SBUs) signifies the rapidly gaining prominence of this approach. SBUs, or business elements, as they are referred to here, are the basic units of analysis a firm uses to create adaptive strategies to meet challenges from the environment. These units of analysis around which adaptive strategies are delineated are identified without taking the organization's formal organizational structure as the point of departure. They should be expected to change, since environmental conditions frequently change, although changes in such units of analysis may not necessarily have an impact on the formal organizational structure.

It is useful to think about business elements as specific products or services that go to particular markets. The first task in testing this initial definition of a business element is to see whether the product or service can be meaningfully described, including the identification of who the custom-

FIGURE 23-7

Delineation of Business Elements

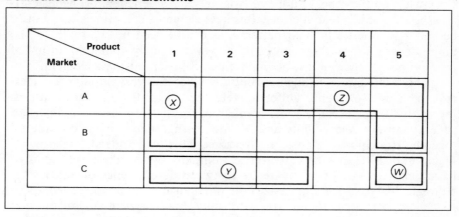

ers are. If so, a preliminary grid pattern of product/market cells should be obtainable, as shown in Figure 23-7. Other issues can then be raised in order to further fine-tune the business element definition. For example, one can seek to establish the rate of growth as well as the overall market potential for each particular product/market setting. One can specify who the firm's competitors are and what the firm's own competitive advantages are in comparison. A related issue is to explore whether there might be alternative ways for customers to satisfy their demand, i.e., whether there are available substitutes. If these questions can be answered in a reasonably ambiguous way, a firm can determine whether each product/market cell is internally homogeneous, i.e., whether it represents a distinctive strategic setting with its own business attractiveness and unambiguous competitive strength position. If these questions cannot be answered clearly, the initial, or "trial," product/market delineation may have been drawn too broadly, thereby creating a mix of rather unfocused business elements.

It may be impractical, however, for a firm to pursue entirely homogeneous business elements, because it may end up with too many planning units. It may be necessary, therefore, to carefully recombine units that, in fact, represent more or less similar competitive settings. As long as business attractiveness and competitive strength can be assessed in a relatively unambiguous way, the basic uniqueness of each strategic setting can be maintained, while cutting down on the degree of fragmentation. Figure 23-7 shows four such combinations of basic cells, or business elements.

It is important to recognize, of course, that imagination, intuition, and common sense have to play key roles when delineating business elements. A reasonable trade-off is necessary: On the one hand, the business elements should not be so small and so numerous that they are entirely impractical to work with; on the other hand, overly large, excessively heterogeneous entities should not be created either. Business elements sometimes turn out to be very asymmetric in their patterns, as can be seen in Figure 23-7. The major criterion should remain valid, however; namely, that a minimum of internal homogeneity must be maintained for each business element.

The term "strategic business unit" has become very popular for referring to business elements. Unfortunately, there is confusion over the meaning of this term, because some companies use it to represent a cluster of several closely related business elements that need to be considered together strategically for synergy reasons. This was, indeed, the original meaning of SBU at General Electric Company, where the term seems to have been coined. The term refers to two different types of entities for strategic analysis; one emphasizes the pursuance of an adaptive, competitive business strategy for a particular product/market segment, and another emphasizes how to achieve a coordinated strategy for a set of closely related product/market strategies, based on pursuing synergies. In this chapter, the terms "business element" and "business family," respectively, are used to differentiate between the two types of entities. Thus, the ambiguous term SBU, which does not make this distinction, can be avoided.

A business family thus consists of a set of closely interrelated business elements, identified in terms of two classes of synergies:

- *Market-derived synergies:* Two or more business elements serving the same or closely overlapping customers, or competing against the same or closely overlapping competitors, may find that their product lines or service offerings complement each other, particularly if conscientious efforts are made to achieve this through coordination of the business element strategies.

- *Internal synergies:* Two business elements may be integrated vertically, which might make it difficult to assess the competitive advantage of one in isolation from the other. Also, there may be technologically determined interrelationships, the use of a common sales force, or joint production. Business element strategies may be modified to make such integrative efforts more feasible.

Although business element strategies may be changed considerably in response to environmental circumstances, the business family level can be expected to be more stable, because there will be an "averaging" effect among the family's various business elements. There might be a considerable degree of strategic self-renewal within a business family, however, in that resources might get shifted from more mature business elements to new, high-potential business elements within the business family. Since the formal operating structure of the organization coincides (to a considerable extent, if not completely) with that of the business family, it might be relatively stable—which is important for organizational commitment—while still allowing the firm to adapt realistically at the business element level in response to environmental and competitive realities. Thus, executives can feel relatively confident that they will be transferred to new, high-growth business elements within the family after they have managed a more mature business element to the end of its life cycle. Without such a sense of security, management teams may be hesitant to manage mature businesses out of fear of self-liquidation.

This concept of delineating business elements and business families can be applied to a corporation organized along divisional lines, such as the one portrayed in Figure 23-3. For example, assume that the management of such a company has analyzed its product/market involvements and identified a dozen or so business elements. Furthermore, these business elements fall into a few clusters, or business families, owing to their interrelatedness. The four business elements indicated by X, Y, Z, and W in Figure 23-7 form one such business family (which coincides with Division A in Figure 23-3). Top management may wish to appoint a business element planning team for each of the four business elements. The chairperson of each team should be a senior manager, for example, a key functional manager. The members should be the best talents available, forming a representative cross-section of the firm's functions, but they may also come from central or division staffs.

A team of managers should also be established to cope with the business family level. The chairperson of this team should be the division manager, and the members should include the chairperson of each business element team. A few key staff executives, and possibly a few managers from other parts of the corporation, might be added to the team to make sure its views are sufficiently broad and eclectic.

Each business element team should prepare objectives and strategic programs for its respective business element. The team's output at each stage becomes the bottom-up ingredient of an interactive and iterative process, first with the business family team and then with the corporate level (similar to the one portrayed in Figure 23-4).

The bottom-up/top-down dialogue in the planning process regarding portfolio balance and overall resource allocation is thus carried out between the business families and the corporate portfolio level. This two-level portfolio approach may be seen as suboptimal, in that each family is allowed to delineate its "mini-portfolio" to take care of its self-renewal, and managers at the corporation level are left with developing a "portfolio of family residuals." However, the positive behavioral effects and political acceptance accompanying this approach might more than counterbalance the potential problems with resource allocation.

The strategic direction established for each business element and each business family by each team then becomes the basis for guiding the operating departments in carrying out their part in the implementation of the firm's strategies. Through a process analogous to the one portrayed in Figure 23-2, each operating department is given its assignments as part of the team for implementing the derived strategic program, as well as the necessary strategic resources, articulated through their strategic budget lines, to carry out their strategic tasks.

There are several important implications that should be pointed out about these emerging strategic and operating structures, which are illustrated in Figure 23-8. First, the strategic structure is not a structure in the sense that the term has been used previously in this chapter. Rather, it is an analytical dimension that the organization chooses to make use of when delineating its strategic direction. Thus, the same people wear two hats. One role is that of an employee performing a specific job assignment in the formal organizational structure; the other is that as a member of a business element team or business family team analyzing and determining strategic direction.

Second, this approach enhances the organization's integrative and adaptive capabilities. The operating organizational structure can be delineated in such a way that it lends itself to at least some degree of specialization, and it may remain relatively stable over time, so long as pressures to adapt do not have to be responded to by reorganizing the firm's structure. Thus, there should be organizational stability and efficiency; that is, the firm should be able to pursue experience-curve effects and take advantages of economies of scale.

The firm's adaptive capabilities, on the other hand, are provided for through the strategic structure, which can, and should, change frequently, in response to changes in the environment. Thus, adaptive strategies can be developed more freely on the basis of a realistic consideration of the environment, without being overly hampered by institutional considerations and vested interests. The strategic structure is, thus, intentionally, unstable, while the operating structure is intentionally stable.

Third, this combination of strategic and operating structures also enhances the organization's ability to adapt by intentionally focusing on promising new opportunities early, and in a systematic manner. Business element teams delineate strategies that allow them to answer the following type of questions affirmatively: Does a business element seem to possess sufficient future potential? Does the delineation of the business element seem right as the basis for identifying creative, imaginative competitive strategies; that is, can a good manager associate himself or herself with it? When answering these two questions, it is important to recognize that it is the potential rather than the actual size, that is important. All business elements, large or small, require management attention; unfortunately,

FIGURE 23-8

Strategic and Operating Structures

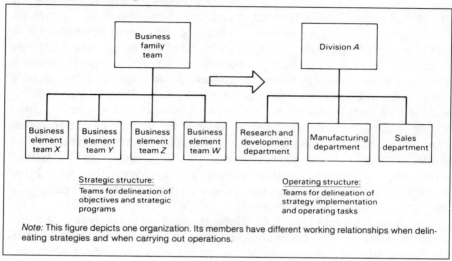

Note: This figure depicts one organization. Its members have different working relationships when delineating strategies and when carrying out operations.

management often ends up paying relatively too little attention to the small, emerging, and truly promising businesses, while too much emphasis goes to the larger, well-established ones.

Classic structural approaches might thus lead to a deemphasis on new business development and a perpetuation of the firm's present business involvements. One of the main purposes of a strategic structure, therefore, must be to delineate relevant business elements; i.e., those that are small but have potential, as well as those that are large. Executives should not protect their own kingdoms by setting up strategies around internally focused considerations. Instead, they should determine whether there is a basis for creating a truly innovative competitive strategy that is consistent with environmental realities. A noninstitutionalized strategic structure can achieve these aims more effectively.

Fourth, with this approach, the various strategies are actually carried out by the operating part of the organization, in conjunction with their day-to-day operating tasks. Thus, within each operating department, separate strategic budget lines should be created in addition to the operating budget for ordinary activities. There should also be a separate follow-up on the use of these resources, to prevent an operating department from borrowing the resources earmarked for carrying out the strategic tasks in order to meet some ad hoc operating crisis. It should be stressed that all implementational activities must be carried out by the operating organization; this again underscores that the strategic structure is not a structure in the ordinary sense, since no activities beyond the setting of strategic direction take place there.

To make clearer the notion of two dimensions in the budget—a strategic one as well as an operating one—it is useful to describe in some detail how each type might be defined. Failure to define clearly what constitutes strategic resources as opposed to operating resources may actually hamper the realistic implementation of strategy. The organization should appreciate that strategic resources are not "gifts" on top of the ordinary budget. When the dual strategic/operating budget concept is implemented, each unit in the organization develops a lean operating budget with no fat or frills, and then adds back the resources necessary to execute the strategic tasks. Without a clear definition of what is "strategic" and what is "operational," activities may be classified incorrectly. Units may be less than stringent in classifying activities, and they may feel tempted to move some operating activities into the strategic pool in order to relieve bottom-line pressure.

Strategic resources should be aimed at changing the direction of a particular business; that is, they should be used to carry out a change in business strategy. It follows that strategic resources are discretionary when seen in the context of current operations. In contrast, operating resources should be consistent with the expected operating activity level for a unit in the organization; they must take into account incremental changes from last year that affect this year's activity level target. Operational resources are used to achieve the best possible year-ahead results.

In practice, it is necessary to realize that strategic resources will normally be scarce, and that careful choices should be made to select priorities among a small set of strategic program activities. This focus on a few truly significant strategic activities may also make it easier for the organization to come address the difference between a strategic budget and an operating budget, and to manage the two types of activities together on a day-to-day basis within the various units in the organization.

Strategic resources can be classified into several types. The most important are the human resources needed to carry out strategic activities. People's skills can be difficult to assess, but it is essential that the best-suited people are assigned to the key tasks. This central aspect of resource allocation, unfortunately, is often not handled well in management processes. One way to help keep track of the allocation of human resources is to institute some broad accounting for the time-spending patterns of the most talented managers. Too often, it tends to be exactly these people who are drawn away from strategy implementation by various ad hoc "fire fighting" tasks.

Another class of strategic resources is discretionary finances allocated to enhance a given strategy. These may include investments in assets, such as plants or equipment, expenditures associated with R&D, such as product testing and introduction, market research, and process modification; and specific investments in working capital requirements stemming from inventory changes, changes in credit volume, or term changes. Such shifts in expenditures should be considered strategic resources when they are part of a specific effort to change strategic direction.

Even though all strategic resources can be classified into one of the above categories, it does not follow that all of these types of expenditures or investments are always strategic. For instance, expenditures for R&D may be incurred as a normal part of keeping an ongoing business moving. Similarly, investments may have to be made to modernize or to respond to ordinary increases in demand; such spending reflects business as usual, and not a change in strategy. This argument highlights the important point that when there is no clear and explicit distinction between strategic and operating resources, the bulk of a firm's investments may be nonstrategic; that is, they are plowed back into existing strategies in order to perpetuate them further. As a result, the existing businesses may become too capital-intensive because of over-investment, and they may gobble up such a large part of the firm's funds that too little is left for strategic self-renewal.

If an organization hopes to run smoothly and to get its members to accept the dual strategic/operating structure concept—in which everyone must wear two hats—the company will have to face the challenges of added job ambiguity. This calls for executives who appreciate that they have responsibility that is broader than their formal authority; they must have a broad attitude, and they must be skilled in resolving conflicts and adept at interpersonal relationships. It will be easier to get people to accept this setup if the strategic and operating structures are somewhat similar, so that the two structures can become associated as a common organizational identity. For example, the strategic and operating structures might come together at the division level/business family level, as shown in the Figure 23-8. In fact, the strategic structure and the operating structure almost always come together at the business family level, and these business families normally coincide with the division level of the operating organization.

A final management process for monitoring progress in strategy implementation is strategic control. This process is particularly important in strengthening an organization's ability to adapt. It helps a firm modify and improve strategies in between planning periods, as critical underlying assumptions change. For a corporation that must be able to adapt quickly and extensively to new circumstances (e.g., a firm active in new, rapidly changing businesses), the elaboration of a strategic control process to complement the management structure and the strategic processes discussed so far becomes a necessity.

Figure 23-9 suggests an overall, simplified picture of the strategic con-

FIGURE 23-9

The Control Process: Operating and Strategic

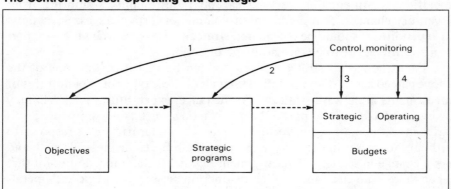

trol process and how it interlinks with the setting of strategic direction. It also indicates that the control process monitors both operating performance and strategic progress.

The strategic control processes shown in Figure 23-9 assess how well the critical assumptions underlying an objective are actually holding up (1). Changes in the assumptions may force the firm to revise that stated objective. The strategic control process should also include explicit follow-up on the progress of strategic programs (2), including an evaluation of the critical assumptions underlying the strategic programs. Also, the control process should exercise budgetary control over both the strategic budget (3) and the operating budget (4). The four dimensions of strategic control are indicated by the four solid arrows in Figure 23-9.

A key issue in strategic control, as it now has been more broadly defined, is that it must enable a firm to reconcile the trade-off between near-term and long-term performance in a more explicit manner. Thus, the control process should be able to monitor progress both in terms of an organization's ability to adapt (its effectiveness) and to integrate its activities (its efficiency). All the elements of performance measurement are interrelated, although they must be seen in context to give a meaningful picture of how an organization is progressing.

An organization's strategic focus, then, is greatly affected by its structure and accompanying management processes, whether it has a functional structure, a divisional structure, a geographic structure, or a weak or strong matrix structure. In many cases, a firm's structure is more important in simpler, more stable strategic settings, while the emphasis on processes increases when the firm faces more complex strategic settings. It would be futile to argue, however, whether a firm's structure or processes are most important, because they complement and reinforce each other. The challenge for an organization is, thus, to find a proper balance between structure and process and to achieve an overall consistency reflecting the strategic setting at hand.

INTERNAL TAILORING OF STRATEGIC PROCESSES AND STRUCTURE

Thus far, the discussion of organizational structures and management processes has been primarily from a corporate-wide perspective; however, within a firm, the various business elements face different competitive environments. Thus, they face different adaptive and integrative challenges. A new, rapidly growing business segment, for example, must be able to adapt to changing circumstances effectively, while its integrative capabilities are relatively less important. The contrary is true for a mature business element located in a more stable business niche where it enjoys a strong leadership position. For such a business element, (often called a "cash cow"), it is much more important that strong integrative capabilities be developed; adaptive capabilities in overabundance might be distractive, and, thus, dysfunctional. For the so-called star business element, located somewhere in between, a relatively balanced set of adaptive and integrative capabilities may be necessary.

A firm's strategic processes and aspects of its structure, then, must be modified to fit different internal organizational setups, that is, they must be tailored to fit diverse settings. In describing how this might be accomplished, examples of two business elements are used: a new business that needs to be able to adapt quickly and efficiently, and a more mature business that needs to effectively integrate its activities. The former might, for example, be a business element in a new, rapidly evolving segment of the electronics business; the latter could be a stable, mature entity in the food business.

To tailor a business element to its environment, the following aspects of the firm's strategic processes and structure must be addressed:

- The nature of the top-down/bottom-up interactive planning dialogue and review between the corporate headquarters and each business element (or business family)
- The choice of variables or focus to be emphasized in the planning process
- Managers' time-spending patterns
- The degree to which resources constrain decision making
- The flexibility of each business element's charter
- The control process
- The management incentive

The Top-Down/Bottom-Up Dialogue

For a new business element, the critical strategic issues involve articulating an objective, modifying strategic direction, and adjusting frequently strategic programs for implementing strategy. Strategy must be seen as fluid, for a variety of reasons; for example, the needs of the customer are still changing rapidly; the competition tends to try out new variations for capturing business; and changes in technology force frequent reexamination of the business concept. The planning and review dialogue conducted between corporate headquarters and the business element (or business family) should never lose sight of the fact that the business setting is fluid and that the rules of the game are not yet finalized. It is, thus, essential that the business element bring to the discussion a detailed knowledge of the business and a true feel for the situation. The substantive expertise of the business element team is essential, and its members must be skilled in entrepreneurship if the business is to succeed and is to be in a position to take advantage of the emerging opportunities that frequently appear. What the corporate level can contribute to the discussion is a pool of experience, seasoned judgment, the ability to add encouragement, and a sense of perspective. It is essential that the dialogue allows both sides to reason together —openly, informally, and frequently—in the attempt to reduce the distance between the corporate level and the business teams.

In the more mature business element, there are different requirements for the two management levels in their top-down/bottom-up dialogue. The business level must be geared to succeed within a much more clearly defined competitive arena; it contains, for example, firmly established customer preference patterns and less pressure to leapfrog from one technology to another. This calls for a tighter, more integrative emphasis on developing efficient strategies and maintaining costs at a competitive level. The challenge here is to take advantage of the greater maturity of the business by streamlining the internal activity patterns to achieve economies of scale, process efficiencies, and experience-curve effects. The dilemma, however, is to know how far to go along these lines without weakening the business's adaptive abilities excessively. There is always some need for adaptation in a business, and this must be recognized, even at the expense of a somewhat less focused integrative effort. The business level should bring a sensitivity for these issues to the discussion table.

From the corporate side, there are two important considerations. First, corporate headquarters must satisfy itself that the business is carrying out a sufficiently integrative strategy. It is normal for there to be a certain degree of resistance to moves to achieve integration; after all, measures such as trimming and standardization of product lines, plant rationalizations, and the combination of several sales and distribution forces into a more efficient one can be painful. Thus, the dialogue with the business element may involve directives from the top that set specific performance demands or apply more explicit pressure. Second, the corporate level must provide specialized staff advice on how to achieve the benefits of integration. There is often a body of knowledge and a pool of experience to draw on, in such cases, and the dialogue will tend to be dominated by this contribution of top-down substantive inputs to the strategies in question.

The management, then, needs to tailor its review style to the particular business element in question. In practice, however, upper managers are often content to review businesses in a more or less uniform manner, resorting to personal styles—developed over a lifetime career—that fail to distinguish among different settings.

Choice of Variables

For a new business that needs to be able to adapt to changing circumstances, the essential variables to be focused on differ from those of a mature business, with its need to achieve integration. This is the case both for the setting of objectives and for the strategic programming phase.

The key challenge in the setting of objectives for a new business is to establish a strategic window, i.e., to identify an attractive business niche and indicate how the organization can compete in this niche. To assess such a business niche, the business should focus on factors that might affect its growth potential, by performing a growth scenario analysis. To assess its own strength, the business needs to evaluate the comparative strength of its new products. A business should also assess the extent to which it can build distance between itself and its competitors.

For a mature business with an integrative need, the key variables are different. In assessing the business niche's future, such a business is much more concerned with analyzing its ability to get early warnings about cycles in demand and to assess factors that might cause the business to decline, such as the introduction of substitutions and demographic changes. Thus, the emphasis on discovering factors that might derail the business demand rather than on upward potential. Similarly, the firm's assessment of its competitive strength will differ; here, it will emphasize variables having to do with cost advantages related to process, plant technology, and other efficiency issues. The firm's strength is determined through its ability to maintain the strategic window, by developing further entry barriers based on economies of scale, process superiority, and modern plants.

At the strategic programming stage, a new business usually centers its strategy around the introduction of new products or entry into new markets. Thus, it must focus on variables that assess customer acceptance as well as the potential responses of competitors. The mature business's strategic program, on the other hand, is more concerned with how to improve

FIGURE 23-10

Process Tailoring of Basic Review Style and Choice of Key Variables for Business Elements With Adaptive and Integrative Needs

Tailoring Feature of Management Process / Type of Business Element	New Start-Up Business, with Predominantly Adaptive Needs	Established, Mature Business, with Predominantly Integrative Needs
Nature of top-down/ bottom-up dialogue	Open; bottom-up driven ("reason together")	Directive; top-down
Setting of objectives stage: choice of key variables	Growth; upward potential Product quality advantages	Stability; viability Process/cost advantages
Strategic programming stage: choice of key variables	Customer acceptance of product/market, entry moves, and competitor responses	Customer acceptance of price, promotional competition to defend position, and competitive responses

efficiency, and with how to keep or improve market share through price promotion and other means.

The differences in top-down/bottom-up management review style and in the key variables focused on by a new business and an established business can be described as shown in Figure 23-10. It helps make clear that the nature of the review process and the formats of the business plans should be tailored to a considerable extent, or, it they are not tailored, they should be slanted in such a way as to highlight the differences among the essential variables to be discussed in each setting.

Time-Spending Patterns

Executives spend different amounts of time on the different stages of a planning process: the setting of objectives, strategic programming, and budgeting. In a new, adaptive business, ample management time and energy must be spent on the front end of the process; managers must pursue the novel formulation of an objective and the creative activity of articulating accompanying strategic programs. In more mature, well-established business elements, on the other hand, the issue is not to spend time on reexamining the assumptions behind the business objectives, since they will have become relatively well understood and can be expected to change relatively little from before. Rather, time should be spent on articulating efficiency-oriented strategic programs and on developing the typically complex patterns necessary to integrate them into the budget. In this case, executives tend to spend more time on the back end of the process.

Resource Constraints on Planning and Decision Making

A new business element needs to allow for considerable flexibility in its patterns for spending resources, since there are often dramatic changes in the assumptions that underlie its strategies. Thus, it should not narrow down its options for pursuing its objectives too drastically or too quickly. Instead, it should develop contingency plans to build in a reasonable degree of flexibility.

A mature business element vs. on the other hand, become much more clear over time. As a result, the business can commit itself to them strongly and not worry as much about decision-making flexibility in the planning process.

The Flexibility of Each Business Element's Charter

A new, emerging business element should have a charter broad enough to allow it to develop gradually what might be the most useful definition of its boundaries. A charter that is too tightly and narrowly drawn might unnecessarily hamper creativity in forming a new business concept. For a mature business, on the other hand, the charter should be much more explicit to enable the business to focus on its relatively well-understood field, and to guard against distraction into exotic but probably less relevant, tangential opportunities.

The Control Process

The full-blown strategic control process is discussed toward the end of the section on the weak matrix concept, and is illustrated in Figure 23-9. The process can be tailored to particular business elements, however. A new business element must focus on controlling the assumptions underlying its objectives and the accompanying strategic programs. Clerical budgetary control, on the other hand, is probably not as important, except for monitoring the actual strategic budget lines.

For a mature business, the control needs are different. Here, tight budgetary control is essential if the business is to monitor efficiency levels effectively. This depends to a large extent on the successful coordination of different operating functions, a task for which the operating budget is indispensable. Control of the critical assumptions behind objectives and strategic programs, on the other hand, is normally less of a pressing issue. Strategic control is deemphasized even more by the fact that the strategic resource function of the overall budget tends to be much smaller for a business of this type than for a new, start-up business.

Management Incentives

In a new business, management incentives should focus more on the ability to implement the business strategic programs and to modify objectives and strategic programs in a proactive manner. In a mature business, the incentives should focus on rewarding classic responsibility—center performance.

From the discussions above on how to adjust strategic processes to enhance the adaptive or integrative focus of a business, it should be clear that tailoring a business's processes to its setting represents an important approach to fine-tuning a given company's ability to meet its differentiated needs. The discussion in this section has emphasized the need to see the choosing of management processes as a micro issue that complements the macro dominated views of structural design and process choice, presented earlier in the chapter.

CONCLUSION

The needs of an organization for support in coping with a multitude of strategic pressures stemming from its environment are fundamentally what dictate its choice of structure and process. A firm needs to be able to adapt to changing circumstances and to integrate its activities in order to compete effectively. It must pursue organizational self-renewal by shifting resources from mature businesses to emerging ones. Its top management should be cognizant of pressures it faces, and it should recognize that, in part, all challenges can be met by the adoption of an appropriate structure and processes. Top management, in particular, must attempt to assess the balance between the company's various sources of needs. Short-term demands for performance, for example, might create a tendency within some corporations to put too great an emphasis on the integrative dimension, particularly when determining the firm's structure.

Structure and process choices are highly interrelated. In fact, it is difficult to distinguish among the effects of different structures without considering them together with their accompanying processes at the same time. Management teams must guard against the tendency to see structures and processes as independent design alternatives. This would probably lead to less than optimal choices.

Even though structure and process are highly interrelated, there are still important differences among these complementary tools. Structural choices tend to be associated with more discrete or finite attempts by an organization to adjust to its environment; a change in structure signifies a major shift in an organization's potential ability to deal with its strategic challenges. Process choices, on the other hand, tend to bring about more incremental changes in the firm's ability to cope strategically. Management processes might thus be seen as a further fine-tuning or amplification of the basic structure.

Although in this chapter structure/process choices have been described as five separate options, in practice there might be a continuity of choices. Hybrids of the basic structural models might evolve; for example, a firm might end up with a matrix structure within one part of the organization, while the rest of the company remains divisionally organized. The firm's management processes also will contribute toward a continuous shift in its capabilities, since they are continually fine-tuned. Management needs to approach the task of developing a firm's abilities to adapt and integrate on a continuous basis, rather than addressing them only at certain intervals and then imposing dramatic shifts in structure and process. Major reorganizations should be undertaken only during exceptional circumstances, because the real costs to an organization of such interventions might indeed be greater than anticipated. Uprooting of management teams, disruption of communication channels, relocation of existing experience bases, managerial uncertainties, and diminishing of executive morale—all frequently associated with major changes in an organization's structure—may diminish the firm's ability to cope with its strategic challenges until the new organization is working. Such periods can be precarious. It is, therefore, a welcome alternative to see structure and process as one vehicle through which a steadier evolution can be achieved.

As an organization evolves in order to cope with more complex strategic challenges, and as it adopts a multidimensional structure and processes, there is a tendency to emphasize process considerations over structural ones. Management process considerations tend to be of continuous concern in complex organizations. To meet the diversity of needs faced by specific businesses within such a diversified firm, the management processes can be tailored to the particular settings of different businesses. Management processes thus offer a multiplicity of internal tailoring opportunities, all of which reinforce the basic structure chosen by the firm.

Decisions about structure and process should be seen as one of top management's normal ongoing tasks. By managing the organizational context within which strategic decisions are made, management can have a critical impact on the firm's strategic direction. If insufficient attention is paid to managing structure and process, on the other hand, it is unlikely that top management will be able to achieve its intended strategic results.

24

Organizing to Make Business Unit Strategies Work

RODERICK E. WHITE

School of Business Administration, The University of Western Ontario

---

INTRODUCTION

How do organizational choices affect business unit performance? How should large, multibusiness companies organize to implement business unit strategies? Well-formulated strategies may founder if they are not implemented properly. On the other hand, firms that are organized for effective implementation may successfully carry out even questionable business strategies. Ultimately, the performance of any business unit is a function not only of the strategy it chooses, but of how the firm organizes in order to implement the business unit's strategy.

Historically, strategy literature and strategy consultants have focused on industry and competitive position variables when explaining performance. These variables are important, but they do not tell the whole story. How a firm organizes to make important business decisions and to ensure that key tasks are accomplished also affects performance. Understanding the impact of organizational variables has an added attraction—these variables are manageable. If industry conditions depress performance, the only choice may be to exit the industry. However, if organizational conditions are impeding performance, changes in the conditions can be made fairly easily and often at a modest cost.

Inappropriate organizational relationships between a corporate office and its various business units can actually impede the accomplishment of an otherwise attractive strategy. This, in turn, destroys shareholder value and raises serious questions about the contribution of the corporate office. Business units that are caught up in these circumstances may do better if their relationships with the corporate offices are eliminated and they become independent entities. But this fate is not preordained. If corporate managers pay as much attention to organizational questions as they do to business strategy questions, business unit performance can be enhanced.

In large, multilevel/multibusiness companies, business unit strategy can be influenced by a variety of organizational attributes:

- Choice of key business unit personnel
- Internal organization of the unit
- Organizational influence from outside the business unit

To the extent that these factors are separable, the study presented in this chapter focuses on the last influence and how its effects on business unit performance differ depending on the unit's strategy. The chapter is based on a study of sixty-nine business units in twelve corporations.[1] Specifically, the study shows how differences in performance (sales growth and return on investment (ROI)) for business units with generic strategies of overall cost leadership and differentiation are associated with organizational differences.[2] The organizational characteristics examined deal with the broader organizational context of the multibusiness company rather than the internal organization of the business unit. Included are tightness of control and autonomy, frequency of reporting, and functional coordination.

CHOOSING A BUSINESS STRATEGY CONCEPT

Any attempt to categorize the complex phenomenon of business strategy into a limited number of strategy types requires simplification. It is neces-

---

[1] R.E. White, *Structural Context, Strategy and Performance.* Unpublished doctoral dissertation (Harvard University, 1981).

[2] M.E. Porter, *Competitive Strategy Techniques for Analyzing Industries and Competitors* (New York: The Free Press, 1980), ch. 2.

sary to concentrate on certain aspects of a business's strategic posture while ignoring others. The most popular business strategy typologies have been based on assessing the attractiveness of the industry or competitive environment, and the business's capabilities relative to other competitors. By arranging its portfolio of businesses in a matrix with industry attractiveness on one dimension and business position on the other, a multibusiness company could assign each business a strategic mission: divest/harvest, defend/maintain, or grow/build. This approach was first popularized by the Boston Consulting Group, with their industry growth/market share matrix.[3]

Because these schemes focus on the attractiveness of continued involvement in a business, given its relative competitive position and its industry environment, they do more to address the corporate strategy question (which business should we be in?) than the business strategy question (how should we compete in this business?). Organizing to address the business strategy question requires a corporation to apply a strategy concept consistent with this emphasis on how to compete in the business.

Market share and cash flow objectives based on build, hold, or harvest portfolio strategies do not provide useful guides for how corporate managers can effectively structure their formal relationships with their ongoing business units to address the business strategy question.[4] On the other hand, an understanding of a business unit's competitive strategy can provide corporate managers with some useful guidelines.

All business units end up generating or consuming cash and gaining, holding, or losing market share. It is important not to regard these variables as if they represent a strategy, but to see them as the results of strategic actions. A group vice-president of a large industrial company illustrated the difference when he said:

> Two of the divisions that report to me are in very sluggish industries. In one case, we have been able to develop more original strategies, we have the employees all fired up, and we're making a good return. But I have had to fight to keep the corporate planners from giving their view of the situation. In the other division, the view from the top that has permeated the unit is that it is a cash-generating division and should be squeezed. I feel we could do some original things there to improve our competitive position, but it's impossible to get anyone in the division very excited to try something new. Eventually, we'll probably sell or liquidate the division.[5]

---

[3] B.D. Henderson, *Perspectives on the Product Portfolio* (Boston: Boston Consulting Group, 1970).

[4] C.K. Bart, "Product Strategy and Formal Structure," *Strategic Management Journal,* vol. 7, no. 4 (July–Aug. 1986), pp. 293–312.

[5] R.G. Hamermesh and R.E. White, "Manage Beyond Portfolio Analysis," *Harvard Business Review* (Jan.–Feb. 1984), pp. 103–109.

GENERIC COMPETITIVE STRATEGIES

In his book *Competitive Strategy,* Michael Porter[6] argues that the creation of sustainable competitive advantage is the essence of strategy. Managers can achieve this advantage in two basic ways: by establishing an overall low-cost position, or by effectively differentiating the product and being able to charge a premium price. These approaches can result in a number of generic strategies. With a pure cost strategy, the business has a low-cost position and sells the product or service at a low price. Its key competitive advantage is its low-cost position. On the other hand, managers of businesses that use a pure differentiation strategy are able to command a premium price, but they also incur higher costs. Naturally the most desirable position—but the hardest to achieve—is to have both cost and differentiation advantages. For example, Caterpillar Tractor has a low-cost position, but it has also differentiated its product on the basis of reliability and after-sales service and parts-supply operations.

Numerous efforts have been made to generate strategic typologies (and to verify theoretical taxonomies).[7] Generally, the empirically derived strategic clusters found by these studies correspond to the theoretical strategy types. Even though the empirical results are often difficult to interpret because of the inherent complexity and multidimensionality of real-world strategies, these approaches tend to confirm the existence of Porter's theoretical taxonomy.

In studying business strategy/organization fit relationships, it makes sense to proceed by selecting a simple business strategy concept that incorporates a few critical dimensions, yet has strong theoretical underpinnings. Porter's generic business strategies fit these requirements. These generic strategies do not define all possible business strategies, but if Porter is correct, and they represent effective means to deal with competitive forces, this concept should be crucial to the organization of the business unit. As Porter argues, "Effectively implementing any of these generic strategies usually requires total commitment and supporting organizational arrangements that are diluted if there is more than one primary target.[8]

Porter's view is supported by evidence from companies that have recognized the importance of cost and differentiation as an organizing principle. For example:

---

[6] Porter, op. cit.

[7] G.G. Dess and D.S. Davis, "An Empirical Examination of Porter's (1980) Generic Strategies: An Exploratory Field Study and a Panel Technique," *Academy of Management Proceedings* (1982); C. Galbraith and D. Schendel, "An Empirical Analysis of Strategy Types," *Strategic Management Journal,* 4 (1983), pp. 158–173; and D.C. Hambrick, "High Profit Strategies in Mature Capital Goods Industries: A Contingency Approach," *Academy of Management Journal,* 26 (1983), pp. 687–707.

[8] Porter, op. cit.

[Union] Carbide restructured its operation in 1982 to reflect the sharply defined roles of its various businesses and the need to manage them accordingly.

By grouping high-volume petrochemicals operations together managers can focus on cost efficiency and aggressive marketing to maintain worldwide market leadership. And in the high technology end of the chemical business, where value is added by superior product performance and technical service, managers will have the R&D support and the entrepreneurial freedom they need. . . . [9]

The Dow Chemical Company has reported a similar reorganization worldwide. These examples suggest an important consideration when organizing within the context of a multibusiness company: Are the competitive premise and business strategy based on cost or on the differentiation of product performance and service?

LINKING BUSINESS STRATEGY AND ORGANIZATION

There has been considerable discussion about the central role that strategy should assume in organizational design. As White and Hamermesh[10] argued, "[I]t is through strategy that the firm interprets its environment and that strategy [should] guide the choice of organization structure." This interpretive view of strategy contends that the organization must cope with the demands of its chosen strategy rather than directly with its environment, although the choice of strategy should take into account environmental conditions. While arguing for a strategy-organization alignment, this perspective leaves unanswered the question of the appropriate strategy concept to employ when exploring this fit.

Formal study of the link between organizational characteristics and the generic business strategies of cost and differentiation is a relatively recent phenomenon. Porter prescribed organizational requirements for the pure strategies of overall cost leadership or differentiation. These tentative prescriptions formed the basis for a set of hypothesized effects of generic business unit strategy and organizational context on performance. But this area is still exploratory, and Porter's organizational prescriptions do not have a strong, independent theoretical base. However, adapting the uncertainty concept from the contingency theory does provide some theoretical insights into possible business strategy-organization-performance linkages.

Uncertainty is a powerful idea. The contingency theory has centered on the environment as the principal source of uncertainty. However, if an

---

[9] Union Carbide Corporation, Annual Report 1982, p. 9.

[10] R.E. White and R.G. Hamermesh, "Toward a Model of Business Unit Performance: An Integrative Approach," *Academy of Management Review* 6 (1981), pp. 213–223.

interpretive view of business strategy is accepted, then it is the uncertainty inherent in the business's chosen strategy with which the organization must cope. Because there are strong and complex links between strategy choice and environmental characteristics, it is to be expected that the uncertainty inherent in a business strategy may be strongly correlated with environmental uncertainty. In support of this premise, Hambrick's[11] evidence suggests that cost strategies are more effective in benign environments with stable prices, while differentiation strategies are more successful in relatively turbulent environments.

Cost-Strategy Variables: Activities by Type of Strategy

Pure cost leadership strategies focus on those business activities that allow the firm to achieve and maintain a low-cost position. The "competitive price" set by the marketplace is accepted. Conversely, a business with a pure differentiation strategy attempts to enhance the price component of the profit equation by offering customers something they perceive as unique and for which they are willing to pay a higher price. Differentiation usually requires the business to incur higher costs, but these incremental costs—if the strategy is successful—will be less than the incremental contribution attributable to the higher price. Some of the variables important to the two types of strategy are listed in Table 24-1.

TABLE 24-1
Important Business Activities by Generic Strategy

	Cost leadership	Differentiation
Factor inputs	Low-cost raw materials; labor productivity; capital to sustain necessary investment	Product technology; creativity/innovation
Processing	Efficient scale facilities; process engineering skills; minimal waste/high yields; employee productivity; logistics	Flexibility; quality
Product or service	Easily manufactured; capital intensity	Technical service; styling; uniqueness; options; quality/reliability; image; product variations
Allied services		Availability/delivery; financing; guarantees; new ideas for improved use; market research
Distribution	Efficient scale customers; simple product line; price discrimination	Credit; sales support; post-purchase service

Source: Adapted from Porter (1980), Levitt (1980), Hambrick (1983), and Hall (1980).

---

[11] Hambrick, op. cit.

The tasks associated with the cost-strategy variables focus mostly on a business's internal operations, with emphasis placed on the productive employment of capital and human resources. A cost strategy requires attention to operational details, a willingness to replace undepreciated yet obsolete equipment, the relentless substitution of capital for less efficient labor, and the minimization of overhead costs. Conversely, a differentiation strategy incorporates activities that rely principally on the business's environment. The product and allied services must be designed to meet unique customer needs; distribution and delivery systems must be tailored to the (changing) requirements of the market; and new technical features added to the product must anticipate and define customer needs.

Generic Business Strategies

As Porter recognized, but did not make explicit, differentiation and cost advantages are not mutually exclusive. These aspects of strategy are separately manifested in the business's cost and differentiation positions (see Figure 24-1). Porter originally described three generic strategies: differentiation, cost leadership, and focus. However, focus is the application of the first two strategies focused on an industry segment. Porter postulated no unique organizational requirements for a focus strategy. Furthermore, Dess and Davis[12] did not find "distinct strategic orientations on the part of managers" indicative of a focus strategy, although they did find such indications for differentiation and cost strategies. For these reasons, as well as sample size restrictions, and for the sake of simplicity, the study on which this chapter is based[13] was limited to a generic strategy concept that is based on the business unit's differentiated position (i.e., price) and cost position relative to the competition, resulting in two of the cells shown in Figure 24-1, pure cost and pure differentiation.

There is no reason to believe that successful differentiation necessarily precludes a business from having a low-cost position or vice versa. A com-

FIGURE 24-1

Generic Business Strategies

| | | Differentiation position | |
		Low	High
Cost position	Low	Pure cost	Cost and differentiation
	High	No competitive advantage	Pure differentiation

---

[12] Dess and Davis, op. cit.

[13] White, op. cit.

bined strategy is possible (at least in certain circumstances), as has been demonstrated by IBM in computers, Caterpillar in earthmoving equipment, Philip Morris in cigarettes, and IKEA in furniture. Thus cost and differentiation combined constitute a strategy concept used in this study and a cell in Figure 24-1. The final cell in Figure 24-1 represents no competitive advantage. For the sample of business units in this study, all four strategies are represented.

ORGANIZATIONAL CONTEXT

The sixty-nine business units in the study were divided into roughly equal groupings among the four business strategy cells defined in Figure 24-1, based on their relative cost and relative price position. The breakdown is shown in Table 24-2. The highest sales growth was achieved by those businesses that used a pure differentiation strategy. Not surprisingly, businesses reporting both cost and price advantages had the highest ROIs. Although achieving a combination of both cost and differentiation advantages is financially attractive, this strategy seems to involve conflicting organizational requirements. Initially, the discussion of strategy-organization fits will deal with the pure strategies of either cost leadership or differentiation.

The businesses in the study were all parts of multibusiness companies. The focus was on the organizational interface between these business units and the rest of the firm — the organizational context of the business unit. Of Porter's common organizational requirements, the following were employed: autonomy and tightness of control; frequency of reports and reviews; and functional coordination.

Autonomy

Cost reduction moves are generally viewed as being low-risk, or low-uncertainty. Uncertainty is less because cost reduction programs generally

TABLE 24-2

Performance of Business Units by Generic Strategy

	Average		
Generic strategy	Number of observations	Return on investment*	(Real) sales growth
Pure cost	15	28.6	3.9
Pure differentiation	16	22.1	10.9
Cost and differentiation	19	30.2	5.9
No competitive advantage	19	4.9	5.9
	69	21.0%	6.6%

*PIMS definitions of these variables, taking four-year averages, were employed (PIMS, 1977).

focus on internal processes that are familiar to the organization and its members. Differentiation strategies are more uncertain. Levitt argues that the simple cost-competitive product is the minimum necessary to participate in the game, stating, "To the potential buyer, a product is a complex cluster of value satisfactions."[14] Exploiting this buyer value complexity is the essence of a differentiation strategy. Complexity, however, has been recognized as a dimension of uncertainty. Furthermore, it seems reasonable to contend that differentiation generally involves less predictable factors such as innovation, customer preferences, and cooperation from distributors. Unpredictability also contributes to uncertainty.

A cost strategy is not necessarily easier to execute than a differentiation strategy. Within an established industry framework, a differentiation strategy presents more uncertainty. This contention has organizational implications for the multibusiness company. Research suggests that organizations cope with uncertainty through decentralization. Galbraith argues that increased uncertainty requires increased information processing by decision makers.[15] This demand can be addressed by decentralizing decision making; by allowing business units more autonomy.

As shown in Table 24-3, those businesses with low autonomy (more control and influence by the corporate office) have significantly higher ROI for business units with pure cost strategies. This relationship occurs with no apparent sacrifice in sales growth, even though, as suggested by the overall averages for the total sample, high autonomy is generally associated with higher sales growth. For those businesses with cost and differentiation or

TABLE 24-3

Business Unit Performance by Strategy and Autonomy

	Return on investment		(Real) sales growth	
Strategy	Low autonomy	High autonomy	Low autonomy	High autonomy
Pure cost	37.9 **	17.9	4.4	3.4
	n=8	n=7	n=8	n=7
Pure differentiation	20.9	23.0	6.7	14.1
	n=7	n=9	n=7	n=9
Cost and	31.6	29.5	0.6	8.4
differentiation	n=6	n=13	n=6	n=13
No competitive	9.7	−1.6	4.0	8.4
advantage	n=11	n=8	n=11	n=8
Overall	22.3	19.0	4.1	8.8

Note: Differences in cell means significant at the 2.5 percent level are indicated with a double asterisk (**); significance at the 5 percent level is indicated with a single asterisk (*).

[14] T. Levitt, "Marketing Success Through the Differentiation of Anything," *Harvard Business Review* (Jan.–Feb. 1980), pp. 83–91.

[15] J. Galbraith, *Designing Complex Organizations* (Reading, Mass.: Addison-Wesley, 1973).

pure differentiation strategies, the level of autonomy has no significant relationship with ROI.

Frequency of Reviews

Porter postulates that cost strategies benefit from "frequent detailed control reports." This argument may make more sense for operational reviews than for strategic reviews. However, in support of more frequent corporate-level reviews of business units with cost strategies is the contention that the feedback loop—the time between decisions, actions, and results—is shorter and the results more tangible than is the case with differentiation strategies. For example, the development of a unique brand image or a truly innovative product may take years. Because of these long lead times, frequent reviews may only serve to divert attention away from the implementation of differentiation strategies. On the other hand, if cost strategies have shorter feedback loops, they might benefit from more frequent reviews.

There are, however, counterarguments contending that organizations employ more cycles to deal with variability and unpredictability (equivocality).[16] If variability and unpredictability typify differentiation strategies, then more frequent reporting/review cycles could be beneficial. Furthermore, truly successful, enduring cost leadership may also involve long lead times. American management has been criticized for having a short-term, cost-cutting orientation while sacrificing the long-term, low-cost position. Arguments can be made on both sides of this particular strategy-organization question, and it needs to be resolved by empirical study.

As shown in Table 24-4, the ROI results for frequency of review are not significant for pure cost, pure differentiation or differentiation and cost strategies. That pure cost strategies benefit from more frequent reviews is *not* demonstrated. Although there is certainly a question of cause and effect, it is interesting that those businesses with no competitive advantage (high cost and low price) do, on average, have significantly higher ROI when subjected to more frequent reviews. Infrequent reviews are associated with higher than average sales growth for all strategies.

Functional Coordination

The functional integrity of business units within multibusiness companies can vary dramatically. Some business units are organized so as to incorporate all key functions. Others either share some key functions with sister business units or rely on centralized corporate services, such as research and development (R&D), for support. These choices result in different hier-

---

[16] K. Weick, *The Social Psychology of Organizing* (New York: Random House, 1979).

TABLE 24-4

Strategy Class Performance by Frequency of Review[1]

Strategy	Return on investment		(Real) sales growth	
	Frequent	Infrequent	Frequent	Infrequent
Pure cost	29.3 n=8	27.7 n=7	1.0 n=8	7.4 n=7
Pure differentiation	23.7 n=7	29.8 n=7	4.7 n=7	16.2 n=7
Cost and differentiation	22.2 n=4	32.3 n=15	3.2 n=4	6.7 n=15
No competitive advantage	11.1 ** n=13	−8.5 n=6	3.5 n=13	11.0 n=6
Overall	19.8	23.9	3.1	9.5

(1) Interval between frequent reviews is three months or less. Infrequent reviews occur at longer intervals, more than 3 months.

Note: Differences in cell means significant at the 2.5 percent level are indicated with a double asterisk (**); significance at the 5 percent level is indicated with a single asterisk (*).

archical arrangements that are capable of different degrees of functional coordination or integration.

Different strategies may require differences in functional coordination. Porter contends that differentiation strategies need "strong coordination amongst functions." Abell and Hammond also support this position by observing that "a company that differentiates itself from its competitors' functional activities . . . will reflect the 'theme' that distinguishes the company from its rivals."[17] It would seem that strong functional coordination, most easily achieved through the responsibility hierarchy, would be needed to develop and maintain these cross-functional themes.

When a cost strategy is employed, the relationships among functions, (R&D, marketing, sales, and production) are straightforward. The theme is simple: Production manufactures at low cost and the salespeople sell based on price. Because the product competes on its cost/price position, little coordination is required between production and sales activities. Indeed, it may be advantageous to have certain functions, such as production, report to a centralized unit. Such an arrangement may facilitate the exchange of cost-reducing ideas among plants serving different business units. Naturally, this advantage is greatest if manufacturing technology is related among the firm's different business units.

Shared or centralized functional responsibilities can also make it easier to share costly functions, such as a sales force, among a number of business

---

[17] D.F. Abell and J.S. Hammond, *Strategic Market Planning* (Englewood Cliffs, NJ: Prentice Hall, 1979).

units. This approach permits certain economies. When all of a business's products are handled by a sales force that competes on the same basis (i.e., price), it is easier for the salespeople to handle multiple lines and to represent different business units. The cost savings available are an especially attractive benefit for business units with low-cost strategies.

Equating self-contained responsibility for key functions with strong intra-business unit functional coordination, the results in Table 24-5 support the assertion that, for the pure differentiation strategy, business units with self-contained functional responsibility have, on the average, significantly higher sales growth. The results for ROI, while in the hypothesized direction, are not significant. However, business units that pursue pure cost strategies appear to have significantly higher ROI with shared rather than self-contained functional responsibility. This may occur partly because shared reporting relationships can facilitate the effective sharing of costly functions, thus enabling the minimization of costs.

CONCLUSION

In sum, strong relationships exist between the organizational and administrative structures associated with a business unit and its performance. A few relatively simple organizational characteristics are associated with different performance outcomes for business units with different generic competitive strategies. However, while this study has empirically demonstrated a business strategy-organization fit, it has done so only for the pure strategies. How businesses that achieve both advantageous cost and differentiation positions should be organized remains unresolved. In retrospect, given

TABLE 24-5

Strategy Class Performance by Functional Responsibility

| | Return on investment | | (Real) sales growth | |
Strategy	Shared	Self-contained	Shared	Self-contained
Pure cost	40.7 **	20.5	1.4	5.6
	n=6	n=9	n=6	n=9
Pure differentiation	12.3	25.3	-2.4 **	15.3
	n=4	n=12	n=4	n=12
Cost and	29.1	32.0	5.9	5.9
differentiation	n=12	n=7	n=12	n=7
No competitive	1.7	7.8	8.9	3.1
advantage	n=12	n=7	n=12	n=7
Overall	21.2	20.8	4.8	8.1

Note: Differences in cell means significant at the 2.5 percent level are indicated with a double asterisk (**); significance at the 5 percent level is indicated with a single asterisk (*).

what Porter says about the need for total organizational commitment, this finding is not surprising. The pure strategies may allow a more focused organizational effort directed toward either reducing costs or creating perceived uniqueness among customers. Achieving both of these outcomes simultaneously is a more complex organizational problem, one that is more difficult for organizations to solve, even though some companies appear to be able to do so, and more difficult for researchers to study.

It has been suggested that these excellent companies may be able to employ seemingly contradictory organizational arrangements simultaneously.[18] That is, while such companies are close to their customers (externally focused on opportunities to differentiate), they are at the same time internally oriented toward cost reduction. Alternatively, it may be that companies achieving both cost and price advantages give sequential, rather than simultaneous, attention to the different organizational requirements of these different business strategies.[19] Sequential attention to goals is one means by which organizations deal with apparently conflicting objectives. Both of these possibilities merit further study.

Study of the link between competitive strategy and certain organizational attributes needs to be extended. Organizational researchers must think more deeply about the exact nature of the relationship between business strategy and organizational attributes. Their assertions must then be empirically tested. Do the hypothesized links actually occur in practice? Such empirical examination requires a large data base, rich in strategic variables and replete with information about the organizations.

Given the limited size of the sample used and the complexity of the phenomenon, managers must apply the specific findings discussed herein with caution. More important than any of the individual relationships uncovered is the overall finding that the appropriate design of organizational contexts requires that top managers be sufficiently aware of the affairs of their business units to appreciate and understand the market conditions they face and the competitive strategies they are trying to implement. Taking this broader perspective, the research suggests that rather than focusing exclusively on portfolio management variables, corporate management needs to establish an appropriate organizational context for each of its business units. The character of each business's strategy should serve as a condition for the design of the firm's organizational context. In recent years, planners have zealously applied sophisticated strategic planning techniques to the problems of managing multibusiness companies. These techniques focus exclusively on indus-

---

[18] T. Peters and R. Waterman, Jr., *In Search of Excellence: Lessons From America's Best-Run Companies* (New York: Harper & Row, Publishers, 1982).

[19] R. Cryert and J. March, *A Behavioral Theory of the Firm* (Englewood Cliffs, NJ: Prentice-Hall, Inc., 1963).

try and competitive conditions as the determinants of business unit performance and on market share and cash flow objectives. The importance of these factors is not in dispute. However, some corporate executives have watched these variables exclusively and have ignored the important relationship between organizational context and business unit performance. In addition, executives can affect the context of their organization far more easily than they can competitive and environmental factors.

When managers design organizational contexts in light of these considerations, they can anticipate the impact of the contexts on business unit performance. Even the most sophisticated strategies can fail if corporate managers fail to pay sufficient attention to the organizational and administrative variables in the performance equation. And even questionable strategies can produce acceptable results if corporate executives organize to implement them appropriately.

25

Compensation Strategy: Matching Rewards to Risks

IRA KAY

The Hay Group

INTRODUCTION

Long-term incentives are like most forms of motivational pay: The theory is right on the mark, but the subsequent design and implementation often stray from the target. The result is that the long-term incentive does not achieve its primary objective—providing executives with real motivation for confronting organizational challenges and achieving corporate goals. These long-term incentives, extending beyond a year, also counterbalance the short-term focus of annual bonuses. For instance, by granting stock options, the company tries to instill a sense of "ownership" in the executive, encouraging long-term orientation and more aggressive management. By tying executive reward to the market value of a company stock, stock-based incentives attempt to motivate executives to perform in a way that will increase shareholder value.

Basic stock option programs are often criticized for providing executives with rewards but little risk, since they have no personal funds invested. This Chapter focuses on the challenge of the coming decade for businesses to fashion new executive compensation programs that redistribute reward—and risk—more equally among shareholders and executives. It examines the shortcomings of the current popular incentive programs and offers suggestions for restructuring bonuses and incentives to base executive compensation on more accurate measures of performance.

HISTORICAL PERSPECTIVE

In the sluggish, inflation-plagued 1970s, stock-based incentives did not have much appeal as a significant source of executive remuneration. Presented with a choice between awards in current cash or in long-range stock options, most executives opted for the cash. The market volatility that characterized the 1980s dramatically transformed the prevailing climate on Wall Street. A flurry of high-volume trading, stock manipulation, new securities (particularly, high-yield "junk" bonds), aggressive acquisitions, and bidding wars caused stock-based incentives suddenly to gain status as the key components of long-term executive compensation.

The result was a new and alarming disparity between the risk-reward profiles of executives and shareholders. Stock ownership in such an erratic market created the real possibility of conflict between executives' personal interests and the interests of shareholders at large. Shareholders began to question the strategic and financial decisions of their executive officers and interest grew in finding mechanisms that could ensure a proper balance between executives' personal financial incentives and their fiduciary responsibilities to shareholders.

PERFORMANCE-BASED PAY

Restoring the risk-reward balance within executive pay programs is in step with the continuing trend toward more performance-based compensation at all levels of the organization. The renewed emphasis on pay-for-performance has received considerable attention as it has been implemented in organizations such as Nucor Corporation and DuPont Company's Fibers Department. However, while pay-for-performance continues to gain con-

FIGURE 25-1

Long-Term Incentive Plans

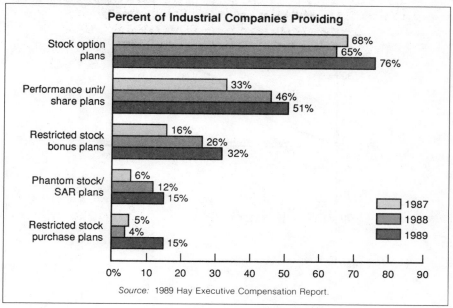

Source: 1989 Hay Executive Compensation Report.

verts and become a reality for managers and workers, it frequently remains only a concept at the executive and other levels.

On the surface, nearly every long-term executive compensation package appears to be performance-based. However, closer inspection reveals that much of the executive's "payoff" can be earned from traditional vehicles that are not closely tied to performance measures that ultimately link their interests to the shareholders.

Executive compensation packages have traditionally offered performance incentives, such as stock-based incentive plans, that are linked to the growth of the organization's earnings per share (EPS) or stock price. Figure 25-1 shows how the use of some of the various forms of these plans has grown in recent years. Traditional stock-based incentives tie a manager's awards to movement in company stock price, through one of three mechanisms: stock options, stock appreciation rights (SARs), and restricted stock options.

Stock Option Plans

Stock options—granting executives the right to purchase shares of their companies' stock at a fixed price for a fixed period of time—have been the

FIGURE 25-2

Executive Stock Option Risk-Reward Profile

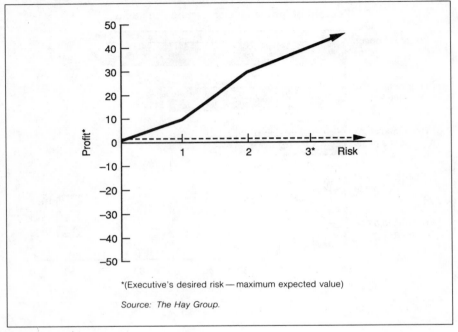

*(Executive's desired risk — maximum expected value)

Source: The Hay Group.

most prevalent of these incentives in recent years. These options are very attractive to the executive because they pose no downside risk and may offer lucrative payoffs that can quickly surpass or even dwarf the rewards earned through base salaries or cash bonuses.

Consider, for example, the hypothetical case of the chief executive officer (CEO) of a major defense conglomerate who holds stock options for 5,000 shares in addition to an annual salary of $200,000. This CEO's stock option entitles him to buy shares at any time within five years at the current market price of $50 per share. If, during those five years, the value of the company's stock has doubled to $100 per share, the executive could exercise his option to purchase the shares at $50. He would immediately resell them, resulting in a $250,000 gain, or $50,000 more than his annual salary. If, however, within that same five-year period the stock price has dropped by half its value to $25 per share, the executive would lose nothing, because he would simply choose not to exercise his option.

Figure 25-2 illustrates the risk-reward profile of an executive's stock option. "Risk-reward" is actually a misnomer, because there is no real risk in this case. The stock option presents unlimited potential for the executive

FIGURE 25-3

Regular Shareholder Risk-Reward Profile

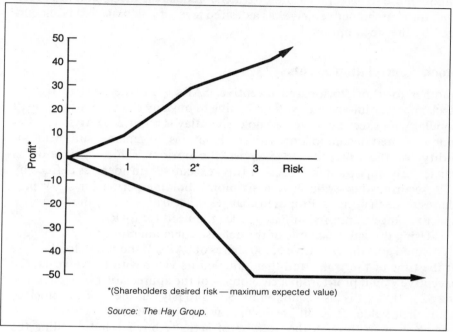

*(Shareholders desired risk — maximum expected value)

Source: The Hay Group.

as the stock's price climbs, while the risk is nonexistent, because the executive has invested no capital at the time of purchase, and the option is his to exercise or not. In short, the executive has everything to gain, and nothing to lose. Because stock options motivate executives to drive up the stock price, the executives are more likely to employ a riskier business strategy than the outside shareholder's risk profile warrants.

Figure 25-3 illustrates the risk-reward profile of the purchase of stock by an outside shareholder in the company. With increased risk created by the company's strategic and financial decisions, the shareholder's wealth may also increase. If the company's performance falls, however, and the fair market value of the stock price declines, the shareholder can lose a maximum of $50 per share, when the stock reaches zero—at which point the shareholder has nothing further to lose.

Clearly, certain restraints have always been imposed on executives to prevent excessive risk-taking. The very fact that executives report to board members who have fiduciary responsibilities to shareholders sends a message to executives that excessive risk-taking may jeopardize their base salaries and bonuses and even cost them their jobs. Although these factors inhibit executives from taking some risks, shareholders may prefer to impose more stringent measures, to further reduce the discrepancy between what the shareholder perceives as a desired level of risk and what is encouraged by the stock option.

Stock Appreciation Rights

Another form of stock-based incentive, SARs grant the right to receive stock appreciation in cash without having to buy any shares. SARs are very popular with executives because no cash outlay is required. SARs are commonly granted in conjunction with stock options, to generate sufficient liquidity for the executive to exercise the options. This motivation is particularly important for "Section 16B" executives (insiders, as defined by U.S. securities law) who have a six-month holding period for stock purchases through options. Proposed changes in securities law by the Securities and Exchange Commission may reduce the need for SARs.

Using the same example of the defense conglomerate CEO, this incentive would give the executive 5,000 shares of SARs. If the stock stood at $50 at the time of the grant, and then doubled its value within five years, the executive would profit from a cash bonus of the appreciation—again totaling $250,000. (It is also common for SARs to pay out the profit in stock of equivalent value.) The difference here would be that the executive would not have to go through the exercise of actually buying and reselling the stock; he would immediately receive the cash equivalent of the stock appreciation. In fact, approximately 70 percent of employees exercise and sell their stock options almost immediately. In this sense, there is no difference between an option and an SAR. However, the accounting treatment of the two vehicles is completely different. Options create no charge to reported earnings while SARs carry a potentially unlimited charge to earnings. This anomaly is currently being addressed by the Financial Accounting Standards Board (FASB).

Restricted Stock

A third mechanism—restricted stock—has become a very popular recruiting tool, and is the fastest-growing type of grant to executives. A recent study showed that below-average performing companies utilize restricted stock grants.[1] This correlation may be explained in two ways: (1) Low-performing companies grant restricted stocks to create value for executives because stock options are of limited upside value, or (2) restricted stock may be found to be a poor motivator for executives.

---

[1] "Incentive Pay That Doesn't Work," *Fortune* (June 28, 1989), p. –.

Restricted stock, which is an actual gift of company shares to the executive, is frequently used as a retention device. A company may use time, performance, or a combination of both, to trigger the lapse of restrictions. The rights to the stock are forfeited if the employee leaves the company before the termination of the specified period.

Restricted stock typically requires no cash outlay by the executive. Moreover, this type of stock is valuable even in a stagnant or declining market. The company benefits from a tax deduction when the restrictions lapse. Restricted stock is commonly used as a substitute for a hiring bonus for new executives, as a special award for key talent, or as a forced deferral portion of an annual incentive plan.

This form of incentive also features some unique flexibility. It may take the form of either actual shares of the company's stock, which entitle the executive to both voting and dividend rights, or "phantom shares," which are stock equivalents used to mirror real ownership. In the latter form, the executive receives cash equivalents of stock dividends, but is not entitled to voting rights.

Given the choice, most executives would probably prefer restricted stock to options or SARs, even though companies usually grant fewer shares of restricted stock than options. This alternative guarantees the most profit, with no chance for capital loss, because the executive profits with each point that the stock climbs. If the stock is worth $60 at the termination of the five-year period, the executive is awarded $60; if the stock doubles, he receives $100 per share. Even if the stock drops by half its value, the executive still receives $25 per share. Positive value is obtained from the shares until the stock price drops to zero. Figure 25-4 illustrates the significant upside potential of this incentive, as well as the lack of real risk.

Other Current Incentive Options

As executives have cashed in on these types of incentives and realized astronomical payoffs caused by the bull market's rapid acceleration of stock values, criticism has mounted. Critics charge the grants are nothing more than outright giveaways that fail to motivate executives to change their behavior and to act in the corporation's best interest. Significant improvement in the company's value, critics note, often reflects only the general bull market, which is partly caused by acquisitions that may increase revenues (and thereby increase executive base and bonus). Such acquisitions, however, also greatly increase debt and may even devalue the company's market worth over a long period. It may be counterproductive to hinge executive compensation so closely to such a measure without any downside risk to the executive to counterbalance the temptation to follow the market's siren songs.

FIGURE 25-4
Restricted Stock Potential

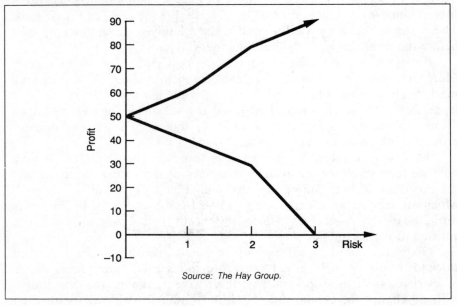

Source: The Hay Group.

To offset this disparity, interest has grown in methods that can increase an executive's motivation to ensure improved longer-term corporate performance. One such technique awards restricted stock grants or options in lieu of a significant portion of the cash bonus. The critical difference is the "hoped-for" behavior change incurred by executives risking part of their own personal balance sheets.

A precedent for this approach is long-standing. A decade ago, Chrysler CEO Lee Iacocca undertook such a risk and made headlines when he and his entire senior management staff forfeited a lucrative cash compensation package for a high-risk stock package. Iacocca's intent was to send a strong message to his employees—that he was willing to invest personally in the company's future. He structured an incentive program that was purely performance-based and that led to a critically needed boost in employee morale. The gamble resulted in a major win for the company by restoring economic stability, as well as an even higher personal payoff in stock value for Chrysler executives.

NEW INCENTIVE FRONTIERS

While these steps have been received positively among shareholders as arrangements that better align conflicting executive-shareholder interests, there is a school of thought that feels actual up-front investment by executives in company stock may be required to create a true alliance with shareholder interests.

Purchase Stock Options

One type of investment is the purchase stock option, through which the executive actually purchases a stock option at a reduced price (usually 10–20 percent of total value). The aim of a purchase option is to require the executive to invest personally in the company, while creating immediate ownership and offering significant upside potential. The purchase amount may be loaned to the executive at nominal interest rates or repaid from future bonuses. The size of the purchase option should be much larger than the regular grant. Valuation techniques can be used to estimate an equivalent value for a smaller "gift" of options versus the larger grant of purchase options. (The FASB is currently exploring ways to charge earnings for option value. If approved, the purchase option could help reduce this cost.)

Figure 25-5 depicts the potential for profit in a purchase option, which is similar to a regular option (except for the size of the grant). As the fair market value changes, the executive is at risk to lose his or her own investment—albeit a small portion of the market value. For example, using this mechanism, if a CEO actually purchased 5,000 shares at $5 per share, the total investment would be $25,000. If the stock then rose 10 points from its market value of $50, the profits would be $5 a share; a rise of 20 points would yield $15 per share. However, should the stock fall 10, 20, 30, or even 50 points, the loss would be contained at only $5 a share. It would, nevertheless, be a real loss. It is important to note that the executive pays $50 for each share, in addition to the $5 for the option itself.

While purchase options can potentially dilute EPS, shareholders are reassured by the knowledge that the executive's capital is also partly at risk. The purchase approach is also intended to motivate executives to utilize free cash flow in an optimum manner and to make more appropriate risk-adjusted acquisitions and divestitures. The company's dividend policy would also need to be adjusted to reflect the creation of shareholder value. In contrast to the riskless option, in which executives are more likely to reduce dividends to retain cash that could be used for acquisitions, in the purchase option vehicle, the dividend decision would be made in a more neutral environment. A potential solution involves paying dividends on the purchase option before the exercise.

Executives would also have a more balanced perspective on corporate financial restructuring, particularly the increase in debt. In a recent *Harvard Business Review* article[2] Michael Jensen questions the value of the

---

[2] Michael Jensen, "The Eclipse of the Public Corporation," *Harvard Business Review* (Oct./Nov. 1989), pp. 61–74.

FIGURE 25-5
Purchase Stock Option

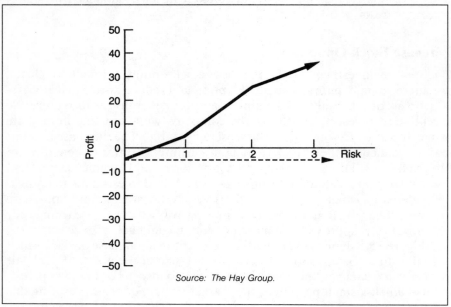

Source: The Hay Group.

public corporation structure (especially in low-growth, high cash-flow companies) and contends that replacement by leveraged buyouts may be superior. However, assuming significant debt in concurrence with risk-adjusted compensation programs could achieve the same goal.

Recently, an executive at a major food company opted to purchase a generous stock package with his own capital, forfeiting a cash bonus. The company's CEO waived a bonus of $1 million over a five-year period in return for stock options of an equivalent value on a current value basis. In this case, it was determined that for $200,000 per year, the executive could purchase $1 million of stock options with a ten-year term.

To be specific, if the CEO's total salary plus bonus for 1989 was $500,000, the new incentive program would entitle him to receive only $300,000 in cash. With the other $200,000, each year he would purchase options on 50,000 shares (assuming a market price of $20). In this arrangement, the CEO has put his own money at risk. If the market price of the company does not rise, he stands to lose $1 million. If the market price increases from $20 to $24, the executive will be no better off than had he received the $1 million in cash in lieu of the $5 million in options.

However, if the stock rises significantly, the CEO will be handsomely rewarded for his efforts. If the stock doubles to $40, for example, the CEO's

FIGURE 25-6
Purchase Restricted Stock

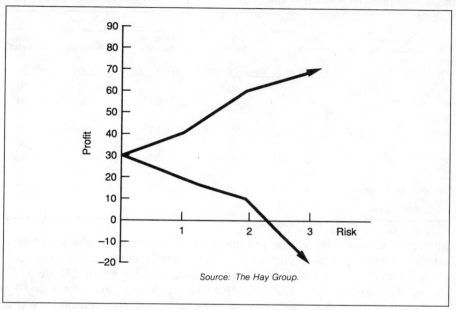

Source: *The Hay Group.*

$1 million investment will net him $4 million ($5 million in profit minus the $1 million cost.) This is clearly an example of an incentive program that makes the executive face the risk of losing a significant sum at the same time that it offers the reward of a big payoff, thereby motivating him to increase shareholder value.

Purchase of Restricted Stock

Another vehicle that can more closely link the investment interests of executives and outside shareholders is the purchase of restricted stock. With this mechanism, executives pay part of the fair market value of a restricted share. The same $50-per-share stock will now cost the CEO $20 per share. As the stock rises, the CEO will profit $10 for every ten-point increase. At a market price of $70, the executive profits $50 per share. Figure 25-6 shows that the restricted stock purchase also puts the executive's capital at risk, closely mirroring the risks of shareholders, but to a lesser degree.

A comparison of Figures 25-4 and 25-5 shows that with the stock option purchase, the executive's wealth does not increase until the market price increases to the current price plus the purchase price. With a restricted stock purchase, the executive's wealth is at risk only when the

TABLE 25-1

Stock Treatment Profitability Evaluation

			Profit			
Risk level	Fair market value/price (at sale or exercise)	Public shareholder (at $50 purchase price)	Employee stock option (at $50 strike)	Employee restricted stock (at $50 strike)	Purchase option (for $5)	Purchase restricted stock (for $20)
3	90	40	40	90	35	70
2	80	30	30	80	25	60
1	60	10	10	60	5	40
0	50	0	0	50	− 5	30
1	40	−10	0	40	− 5	20
2	30	−20	0	30	− 5	10
3	0	−50	0	0	− 5	−20
Figure comparison		2	3	4	5	6

Source: The Hay Group.

market value drops below the purchase point. Therefore, from the shareholder's point of view, a purchase option offers a more compelling reason for executives to focus on increasing shareholder value. (Table 25-1 provides a summary of values for the five stock programs discussed.)

Either form of purchase option, however, is clearly preferable to the giveaway options in terms of the incentives they provide to not let the company's market value slide. Under the traditional plans, if the stock price drops to $30 from an initial market value of $50, shareholders will lose $20 per share, and executives with stock options lose nothing; executives with restricted stock grants, in fact, will still be rewarded with $30 per share. However, with a purchased option, the executive will lose $5 per share, and with a restricted purchased option, the profit will be only $10 per share.

When taken to an extreme—even if the stock bottoms out at zero—the shareholder is no longer the only party whose wealth diminishes significantly. Executives' profits with conventional options and restricted options stay at zero, while purchased options cost them $5 per share, and restricted purchased options cost them $20 per share.

As shown in these examples, restricted purchases and purchase options introduce an element of executive risk to stock-based incentives. Another stimulus for creating shareholder value in long-term incentives is offering restricted stocks in tandem with a stock option—with the grant contingent upon the executive's holding any stock obtained through the option for a specific period. These devices are also aimed at strengthening the connection between a company's stock price and the executive's own interests.

NONEQUITY INCENTIVES AT THE DIVISION OR SUBSIDIARY LEVEL

While purchase options, restricted stock packages, and cash-based plans offer viable solutions for executives and CEOs of large corporations, these solutions are often not implemented at the division or subsidiary level. For example, an incentive program tied to stock market value may not pay off for a divisional executive whose performance is outstanding, because overall corporate results may have sagged due to forces beyond the division executive's control or to the influence of a general bear market. What can be done, then, to also motivate these key executives to contribute to the improvement of shareholder value?

"Phantom" Stock Programs

With some modification, the same principles used to fashion effective corporate executive incentive programs can be readjusted to focus on smaller groups or divisions. For example, traditional stock options can be issued to divisional executives through "phantom" performance stock programs. Through this approach, an independent assessment is made of the *unit's market value* and its executives are issued options on shares that reflect that value. After a specified period, the unit's value is reassessed and its executives are rewarded for positive improvements in the same fashion that corporate executives benefit from improvement in the parent's actual market value.

The value of the payout could be delivered partly or fully in corporate stock, serving as a reminder that the device is part of a larger entity. The advantage of these imaginary stock plans is that they are primarily tied to the performance of the division or subsidiary, and often take into account outside marketplace variables that would influence the performance of the division. This strategy is intended to restore the entrepreneurial spirit to these units, and to tie a greater percentage of the compensation earned by the unit executives directly to the unit's performance.

The variables used to measure performance are of key importance to non-equity-based incentives. Cash flow and earnings before interest and taxes are becoming more commonly used options. Simulated equity, evaluated by an investment banking appraisal, offers the advantage of discounted value of future cash flow—the most important link to shareholder value, according to numerous studies.

Performance Units

Performance units enable planners to set targets and quantitatively measure managers' achievements. Performance units are shares granted at no cost to the employee at the beginning of a specified period contingent upon specified company performance goals being attained during the period. The price of the company's stock at the end of a performance period (or other valuation criteria) determines the value of the payout. Performance units could also be purchased by the executive, preferably at a discount, for motivational purposes.

Divisional incentives using performance units as a measure of growth were implemented at one U.S. chemical company and proved to be a very effective method of evaluating the business's performance. The chemical company, formerly an independent business, was acquired by a major company owned by an even larger company. To determine whether there was a competitive need for long-term incentives at that level of the organization, the plan evaluated the smaller business as an autonomous unit.

At the time of the evaluation, compensation for existing divisional heads did not include any long-term incentive plans—there were no upside rewards for enacting long-term policy decisions that involved any professional or personal risk. The underlying message to executives was to play it safe, because there were no perceived rewards for their divisions' contributions to shareholder value.

The new incentive plan included recommendations to implement nonequity, stock-based incentives, linked to growth of specified performance shares that allowed the unit's executives to "buy into" the division and created a sense of ownership for divisional management.

The use of performance shares as a measure of nonequity compensation for this unit proved extremely effective in providing a direct tie between rewards and the achievement of performance objectives. The benefits of improved performance also enhanced the firm's overall strategy by reinforcing top management teamwork.

Moreover, by providing an incentive for executives to build the business through profitable volume, the parent's shareholders ultimately benefited from a more balanced risk-reward relationship, because the payout under such a plan was inherently linked to increased shareholder value.

"Alphabet" Stock

Finally, as an extreme, corporations could issue "Alphabet Stock," such as General Motors's GM-H or GM-E stock, which is publicly traded. Although subject to the ordinary pitfalls of minority stock, this alternative could be used to generate all of the recommended vehicles, including purchase options or restricted stock purchases.

Nonequity incentives can be a practical component of a compensation package and are especially applicable in diversified and large bureaucratic companies or in a family-owned business. Nonequity awards can offer an attractive solution where the intention is to reward nonfamily management, yet not dilute control and ownership. Acting as "golden handcuffs," nonequity incentives can be highly leveraged, and can focus unit executives' attention on key strategic/financial objectives.

Nonequity Programs on a Global Scale

Another example of a nonequity incentive plan, as it was applied to U.S. subsidiary executives, illustrates the potential for corporate and shareholder benefit on a global scale. A foreign company with a portfolio of several U.S. firms wanted to refocus annual and long-term incentives and link payout and performance more closely. Management also saw a need for a cost-efficient evaluation of its total compensation program, including base salary, annual incentives, long-term incentives, and benefits.

After reviewing management input and financial analyses from the firms it had acquired in the United States, a wide variation in annual incentive policies was found. Most long-term incentives were tied to each firm's results, a link that was deemed necessary to attract, motivate, and retain senior management within each unit. However, because of the extreme volatility in the foreign parent's profitability and the potential benefits from cooperation among the units, some degree of linkage to the parent company's financial performance was desirable.

The plan's objective for the subsidiaries was to focus each firm's executives on the growth of their own firms as well as on creating value for the parent shareholders. The plan's underlying principle was that reward should be based on the performance of the entity in which the executive could influence long-term results. The long-term incentive plan would seek to create wealth for the executive through the achievement of specified strategic objectives. Generating teamwork among the U.S. subsidiaries would be an important byproduct of the plan.

After thorough evaluation, the plan recommended awarding phantom shares to each firm. The shares would be paid out 50 percent in cash and 50 percent in parent company stock options (based on a valuation formula). Phantom shares offered the parent company an opportunity to commit executives to long-term sustained performance, without dilution of EPS. An additional benefit for the shareholders came from the ability to deduct the unit's cash layout as a compensation expense. Most important, the parent company maintained flexibility in designing share valuation formulas. The phantom shares required the payment to executives out of cash flow and the shares were taxed as ordinary income.

The stock options offered the parent company several valuable financial benefits. Although there was some shareholder dilution, there was no charge to earnings and the cost to the company was limited to the cost of holding the stock on which the options were granted. Like the phantom shares, the options offered the company a tax deduction and further served to align the long-term interest of the executives and shareholders.

The benefits to the executives from the stock option component included the psychological advantages of real share and common stock ownership. The executives were also provided with significant opportunities for capital accumulation. In addition, stock options represented a potential hedge against future tax reform and the possible reintroduction of capital gains. The only risk involved for the executives was the possible downward movement of stock price.

The parent company learned that to be effective, a long-term incentive plan of this type must limit eligibility to those key executives who are most accountable for establishing and achieving each firm's long-term strategy. Further, participation should be highly selective if the desired incentive and retention objectives are to be achieved. When allocating phantom shares, participant groups should be evaluated, based on job responsibility, to determine the levels of phantom share grants and the resulting long-term incentive award opportunity for each incumbent.

The phantom share's award, based on the firm's growth, should be determined by a formula tied to revenues and operating margin. Similarly, the growth in the value of each participant's share account should be based on revenues and operating margin.

As this example illustrates, the foundations of such a plan can offer promising benefits for both a foreign parent and its subsidiary firm. The combination of linking the subsidiary executives' pay to their own performance, as well as to the performance of the foreign parent, offers a creative solution to an often complicated relationship. There may be a need to educate the foreign parent about the use of this type of long-term incentive plan, as there may be no precedent for it in the parent's culture. Demonstrating the link between pay and performance, as well as the cost effectiveness of the plan, may be sufficient to enlighten the parent company about the plan's overall benefits.

DIAGNOSING INCENTIVE NEEDS

High executive turnover and recruiting difficulties may be initial signs of distress within an organization, but more subtle symptoms may also warrant a new executive compensation program. Internal problems, such as lack of teamwork or absence of long-term management perspective, can be addressed by a properly constructed incentive program. External signs, such as poor stock performance, takeover threats, unsuccessful divestiture/acquisition programs, or low market-to-book value, may also indicate a need for a more effective incentive program within the company.

TABLE 25-3

How to Choose the Right Vehicle

Factor	Issues	Vehicle of choice
Public vs. private company	Are reported earnings important?	Stock options (NQ or ISO)
Taxpayer status	Are significant tax deductions important?	• Stock options (NQ) • Restricted stock • Cash plans
Shareholder vs. other measures	Is creating shareholder value a top priority?	Stock options
Stock options — tax rates	Are capital gains taxed favorably relative to ordinary income?	Incentive stock options
Shares allocated to plans	Have 5 percent of shares been distributed to employees?	Cash plans
Earnings/stock price	Are earnings relatively volatile?	Full value plans; restricted stock
Strategic turnaround	Has recent performance been poor?	Cash plan with stock options
Current executive wealth	Are executives cash poor?	Stock options with recourse loan; cashless exercise (Reg. t)
Organizational level	Are many participants located at the divisional level?	Stock options and cash plan
Internal culture — deferred/actual	Does it need to be entrepreneurial?	Investment plans — stock options or phantom partnerships

New compensation alternatives, some of which have been outlined in this chapter, are designed to distribute the risks and rewards more evenly among executives and shareholders. A more complete list of alternatives, detailing the advantages and disadvantages of both, is shown in Table 25-2. The vehicles outlined can help create more balanced and productive incentive programs — plans that target management strategy for shareholder profit as well as executive reward. The type of vehicle used to implement these plans is of critical importance in achieving the desired goals. Depending on the organization, different accounting, organizational, and strategic factors determine the most effective vehicle. Table 25-3 lists the critical factors and issues in selecting the best mechanism for a particular organization.

Once the vehicle is chosen, the company needs to define the elements of the plan's architecture. Participation, performance measures and weights, payout ratios, and communication and administrative variables are key issues to be determined to ensure the plan's success. (See Table 25-4 for a detailed list of issues for consideration.)

TABLE 25-2

Compensation/Incentive Alternatives

Program	Description	Executive tax treatment
Purchase option	Executive pays for an option up front (possibly with company loan subject to performance-based forgiveness), increasing the risk/reward environment.	Upon exercise, the spread between market value and the exercise price, less the executive's upfront cost, is taxable income.
Premium option	Option granted with exercise price above current *fair market value*.	Option spread taxed as income in year of exercise.
Convertible debentures	Executive purchases a corporate debenture. Interest is paid at a rate that approximates the executive's cost of borrowing capital to purchase the note. The debenture is convertible into shares of the company's common stock. Later, based on what is then the fair market value of the stock, executive either takes delivery of the shares or redeems the note.	The executive realizes no taxable income when the debentures are purchased or at the time of conversion. Upon disposition of the stock, taxable income is realized. Interest is taxed as it is received.
Phantom partnerships with pretax "buy-in"	Executives invest pre-tax dollars in their company or division "as if" it were a partnership sharing in the profits, by using unfunded nonqualified deferred compensation.	No tax until the earlier of actual or constructive receipt of the deferred funds, or until receipt of an economic benefit.
Shareholder value unit	This is a hybrid vehicle. The executive receives one share of restricted stock. Each share of restricted stock has both a call option associated with it (exercisable at the current fair market value or at a premium) and a put option (whereby the executive will pay the company, on a dollar-for-dollar basis, for any decline in share value from the value at grant).	The executive is taxed on the fair market value of the restricted stock when it vests (unless a Section 83(b) election is made). If the call option is exercised, the executive is taxed on the spread between the exercise price and the fair market value. If the share price declines, the executive pays the company and nets the payment against the value of the restricted stock.
Elimination of SARs	The proposed SEC Section 16 rules will all but eliminate the need to grant or maintain existing SARs with their high earnings charge.	If SARS are cancelled and the executive does not receive anything in return, then there will be no tax consequences for the executive.
Junk-bond grants	The executive receives a grant of a company's high-yield securities at full value or at a discount, or purchases at a discount.	Grants. Executive realizes income in an amount equal to the fair market value of the bond. Purchased at discount. Executive realizes income equal to the spread between the purchase price and the fair market value. Interest is taxable when received.

TABLE 25-2 *(cont'd)*

Company tax treatment	Accounting	Pros	Cons
Like a "plain vanilla" option, the company receives a compensation deduction at the time and in the same amount that the executive recognizes taxable income.	No charge to earnings as long as the exercise price is equal to the fair market value at grant.	• Enhanced motivation to increase stock price	• Requires purchase by executive • Adds downside risk
Deduction for amount executive includes in income.	No earnings effect, at least today.	• Provides favorable tax and accounting treatment • Extra option price balances lower risk relative to shareholders	• Places executive more at risk • Executive has to accept downside risk
The company is entitled to an interest expense deduction as interest payments are made.	Unless compensation income is imputed to the executive (if amount paid is less than the fair market value), the only charge to earnings is the interest expense as interest is paid.	• Executive's downside risk is minimized • Offers flexibility, especially for spin-offs • Provides current interest income • Links executive and shareholder interests • Offers favorable accounting treatment	• Unpredictability of interest rates • IRS may impute income at time of grant • Limited value unless stock appreciates substantially • Complex
The company receives a compensation expense deduction at the time and in the same amount as the income recognized by the executive.	Charge to earnings for the deferrals by the executive.	• Allows pretax investment in the company • Links executive and shareholder interests	• Less favorable accounting than other stock programs • Complex
Payment to the company reduces the compensation deduction.	Possible variable accounting on restricted stock to track fair market value.	• Provides large upside potential • Links executive and shareholder interests	• Added risk to executive because share price may drop • Complex
There is no tax effect on the company upon cancellation of SARs.	Not clear, but previously accrued SAR expenses may possibly be recaptured.	• Unpopular feature with shareholders discontinued • Eliminates future and possible recapture of prior earnings charges	• Loss of a benefit for the executive
The company receives a compensation deduction equal to the income recognized by the executive upon grant or purchase, and also receives an interest expense deduction as payments are made.	A charge to earnings for the spread between the purchase price (if any) and the fair market value, plus interest expense as interest is paid.	• Links executive and company interests • Offers favorable tax and accounting treatment	• Executive risk is increased • Complexity in valuing

(continued)

TABLE 25-2 *(cont'd)*

Program	Description	Executive tax treatment
Employee LBO funds/ limited partnerships	Employees/executives invest in a fund or partnership that invests in their company's "deals" and acquisitions.	Taxable investment income to the extent of the share of income generated by the fund/partnership. Gains on sales are treated as capital gains.
Jumbo stock options	Selected (frequently high-potential) executives receive single large grants of stock options as opposed to smaller annual or periodic grants.	Like "plain vanilla" option, no tax upon grant. Upon exercise, the spread between market value and the exercise price is taxable income.
Dresser plan (restricted stock/stock options)	Restricted stock is granted in conjunction with exercise of stock options. Upon exercise of the option, for every five option shares exercised, one share of restricted stock is granted. The restricted stock vests if the related option shares are held for three years.	The option spread is taxed as income in the year of exercise. The executive is taxed on the future market value of the restricted stock when it vests (unless a Section 83(b) election is made).
Reload stock options	Upon a "stock for stock" option exercise or "cashless" exercise, an executive receives a new option at the current market price for the same number of shares that were traded in. Exercise of the reload option may be conditioned on not selling the shares received in the stock-for-stock exercise for a certain period of time (e.g., one year).	No taxable event at the time the reload option is granted. Upon exercise, the spread between the option price and the fair market value is taxable income. Currently the taxable event is deferred six months for "insiders" subject to insider shortswing trading rules. Under the SEC Section 16 proposals, the six-month deferral would be eliminated in most cases.
Revaluing underwater restricted stock	If the fair market value at vesting is less than the fair market value at grant, the restricted stock can be settled for cash and new restricted stock issued at the current market price.	There are no tax consequences to the executive unless a Section 83(b) election on the initial or revalued stock has been made.
Replacing underwater stock options	Old higher-priced underwater options are replaced with options at the current market price or are merely repriced.	Executive not taxed when the options are replaced or repriced. Upon exercise the spread between market value and the exercise price is taxed.

(continued)

TABLE 25-2 (cont'd)

Company tax treatment	Accounting	Pros	Cons
No compensation deduction.	No compensation charge to earnings.	• Provides executive shares in the ownership of acquisitions • Offers high motivation • Proves to be very popular w/ employees	• Risk associated with LBOs • Company has to share ownership of acquisitions
Like a "plain vanilla" option, the company receives a compensation deduction at the time and in the same amount that the executive recognizes taxable income.	No charge to earnings as long as the exercise price is equal to the fair market value at grant.	• Like regular option but with much stronger retention and higher potential, because base price frozen	• Shareholder perception of no downside risk to executive and inappropriate potential gain
The company receives a deduction in the amount and at the time the executive recognizes taxable income.	A charge to earnings equal to the fair market value of the restricted stock at grant.	• Encourages retention of stock • Links executive/shareholder interests • Offers large upside potential • Provides favorable tax/accounting treatment	• Shareholder perception of no downside risk to executive and no actual cash purchase
The company is entitled to a tax deduction for compensation expense at the time the executive exercises the reload option in the same amount as the executive recognizes taxable income.	No charge to earnings at any time.	• Provides the same potential future appreciation as cash exercises, without need to come up with cash • Encourages stock ownership, not sale • Gives executive a more valuable benefit vis à vis other companies	• Shareholder perception of further enhancing an already no-risk program
The company receives a deduction at the time and in the same amount that the executive recognizes taxable income.	The company recovers the prior earnings charge and a new charge is made based on the lower value.	• Increases executive benefit (purchase plans) • Offers favorable accounting treatment	• Negative shareholder perception
The company receives a deduction at the time and in the same amount that the executive recognizes taxable income.	No accounting charge as long as the option is not repriced or regranted more than once.	• Increases executive benefit • Offers favorable accounting treatment	• Negative shareholder perception

TABLE 25-4

Design Architecture

Issues	Questions
Participation	What positions/people truly influence long-term performance?
Vehicles	See separate sheet
Performance measures	What key measures relate directly to the strategic plan or shareholder value?
Performance weights	How should the different performance measures influence payouts?
Performance level (± from target)	How difficult is it to move beyond target?
Payout ratios	What does the competitive data show? How much is needed to change behavior here?
Staff vs. line	Should performance measures/weights/ratios/leverage differ?
Corporate vs. division	How should the architecture differ? Should the sum of the divisional performance measures add up to the corporate measure?
Timing	What should the timing be for measures/grants/plan earnings/payouts?
Payout form	Should payouts be in cash/stock?
Deferrals	Should additional deferrals be allowed?
Communication/administration	How should the plan be communicated? Who should administer it? What happens if you retire? Quit?
Shareholder/other approval	Is shareholder approval required? Compensation committee?

CONCLUSION

To provide real motivation for executive performance, long-term incentive programs need to be reevaluated to include incentives for sustained increases in shareholder value. By more closely aligning the investment interests of both executives and shareholders, newly structured incentive programs can improve opportunities for creating economic value and provide the longer-term orientation needed in today's economy.

26

Employee Involvement in Implementing Strategy

KEVIN D. CUTHBERT

CAROLYN L. MIDDLEBROOKS

Research for Management, Chicago, Illinois

INTRODUCTION

As organizations are faced with an ever-changing business environment, they are searching for more effective methods to implement their strategies and to develop or sustain competitive advantage. Many organizations are turning to a relatively untapped resource—their employees—in their strategy implementation efforts. These organizations are finding that employee involvement increases employee satisfaction and productivity and improves organization performance.

This chapter shows how and why organizations are using involvement initiatives in their strategy implementation efforts. Among other things, it defines "strategy" and "employee involvement" and presents a strategic planning process model that companies can use to effectively increase employee involvement in their strategy implementation efforts. It also discusses the approaches to employee involvement that leading companies such as Ford, Xerox, and Motorola have taken in their efforts to implement their strategies and improve organization performance.

OBSTACLES TO STRATEGY IMPLEMENTATION

Companies are having difficulty implementing their strategies and meeting their goals because of the increasing change, and the dramatic acceleration in the pace of change, in the business environment. Quite simply, organizations in almost every segment of industry are forced to do more with less because of changes in demographics, competition, the legal/regulatory environment, technology, and society in general.

The continuing shortage of entry level workers makes it increasingly difficult to staff and manage businesses. This, coupled with the need to offer more competitive, higher-quality products and services, has forced firms to focus increasingly on attracting, retaining, and motivating employees.

At the same time, increased foreign and domestic competition have led to cost cutting and downsizing, resulting in a lack of advancement opportunity for employees at all levels. With fewer, less-motivated employees, companies are finding it harder to achieve their strategic goals.

Interestingly, technology was supposed to be a major way that organizations could accomplish more with less. Although many companies have successfully implemented new technologies, at least as many have failed because they did not consider the implications of these innovations for the people using the new equipment or systems—their employees.

The rapid change and the resulting uncertainty in U.S. business have been accompanied by changes in the values of U.S. workers, leading to a changing "contract" between employer and employee. Companies used to offer lifetime employment to their employees, and in return employees gave their loyalty to the company. Now, continued employment is much more contingent on organization and individual performance, with companies increasingly requiring enhanced performance and specific skill sets. Not only are companies becoming more selective and demanding, but employees also are showing less commitment to their companies and more commitment to themselves, their lifestyles, and their families. These changing values have forced companies to take a more strategic approach to the ways they manage their employees.

ORGANIZATIONAL RESPONSE TO THE OBSTACLES— EMPLOYEE INVOLVEMENT

One way firms are responding to the myriad changes in the business environment is by increasing the level of involvement of employees in the day-to-day workings of the business. Organizations have found that increased employee involvement is an excellent method for achieving strategic goals and improving organization effectiveness.

Specifically, increased involvement helps alleviate the concerns caused by the decreasing number of entry level workers. By maximizing the potential of the work force, involvement initiatives allow organizations to accomplish more with fewer employees. Consequently, employee involvement is also being used to counteract the downsizing and cost cutting necessitated by increased competition and deregulation.

As the role of technology continues to grow, successful companies are also involving their employees more in the acquisition and implementation of new systems and equipment. This ensures the smoother integration of new technologies, since employees generally are more committed to, and better understand, the technology decisions made by the organization.

Overall, employee involvement provides opportunities for the work force to contribute more to the business operations. This better prepares employees for potential advancement, permits companies to select, reward, and promote those key contributors who excel in these expanded roles, and increases employee satisfaction and productivity and organization performance.

STRATEGY DEFINED AND DISTINGUISHED

Many organizations find it difficult to develop a strategy because they confuse strategy with other related concepts such as mission, vision, goals, and tactical plans. Strategy is primarily a method for implementing the organization's goals, which support its vision and mission. Tactical or operational plans are the ways in which a company implements its strategy. A company's strategy should guide the allocation of resources and functional actions. Strategy is doing the right things as opposed to doing things right, and it is a focus on effectiveness and not efficiency. Finally, a strategy should be realistic, should provide for reasonable returns, and should be flexible enough to provide for contingencies—its effective implementation creates a sustainable competitive advantage.

STRATEGY IMPLEMENTATION THROUGH EMPLOYEE INVOLVEMENT

Many organizations have found that a very effective way to implement their strategy is through the involvement of their employees. Employees who have control over their jobs and real influence or "say" in what they do to achieve their work goals feel more committed and are more motivated to carry out the organization's strategic direction.

In this section, employee involvement is defined and some of the benefits of employee involvement are discussed. The importance of taking a process approach to employee involvement in the implementation of a strategic plan is also addressed. Finally, a model is presented that an organization can use to design an employee involvement process and to align its various systems to fit its needs and strategies.

Employee Involvement Defined

Before discussing the benefits of employee involvement for strategy implementation, it is necessary to clarify what is meant by "employee involvement." Traditionally, it has been equated with specific techniques, ranging from employee meetings to quality circles, popular in the 1970s, to newly designed, high-involvement plants. Survey feedback, suggestion systems, task forces, quality of work-life committees, and self-managing work groups are also forms of employee involvement. Although these techniques are an aspect of employee involvement, organizations frequently fail to consider the various organizational systems that need to support an employee involvement process.

The level at which different types of decisions are made, the kinds of information that are available, the reward system that supports greater involvement, and the knowledge and skills provided also define employee involvement. Unless these types of systems are congruent with an employee involvement process, the process will ultimately not be effective.

Employee involvement also frequently involves a transformation of the organization's existing technologies, values and management styles, based on the need to modify the organization's culture. Thus, one of the keys to successful employee involvement efforts is managed change. An employee involvement process must continually adapt and change in response to the internal and external business environments.

This change-oriented, "systems" view of employee involvement is consistent with the evolving employee involvement processes in a number of successful organizations, such as Ford, Motorola, and Xerox. Ford began by forming employee/supervisor problem-solving groups. In order to make employee involvement a continuous process that affects management style and union-management relationships, Ford later expanded these efforts to include employee participation in planning, goal setting, communication, and decision making.[1]

Motorola began with an extensive gain sharing (group incentive) type of reward system. However, it soon became apparent that increased employee involvement was critical to achieving the goals set by the gain sharing plan. Motorola then developed the Participative Management Process to get employees involved in solving problems, setting goals, and making decisions that would help the company achieve its desired objectives. This employee involvement process is now an inherent part of Motorola's culture.

Xerox's approach has also evolved over time. Like Ford, it started with union-management committees and evolved to include Business Area Work Groups, employee problem-solving groups, self-managed work teams, and other organization-wide involvement efforts. Over time, Xerox recognized that a process approach to employee involvement, involving a variety of organizational systems, was critical to its success.

Two elements are common to all of these employee involvement efforts: (1) The organization systems are aligned to support the practice of employee involvement, and (2) the organizations use a long-term process approach that affects all levels of the organization and that changes to meet internal and external business conditions.

Benefits of Employee Involvement

Organizations implement their business strategies through employee involvement for a variety of reasons. One study reported that over 80 percent of responding organizations implement employee involvement primarily to improve productivity and quality.[2] Cost reduction and improvement in attitudes and morale are other frequently cited reasons. Finally, competitive pressures and reduced resistance to change were reported by over one third of the organizations as reasons for implementing employee involvement.

Another study[3] reported that over 80 percent of the 390 responding organizations believe that employee involvement is compatible with the increased competitive environment, pressure for improved performance,

[1] Paul A. Banas, "Employee involvement: A sustained labor/management initiative at the Ford Motor Company." In John P. Campbell, Richard J. Campbell and Associates, *Productivity in Organizations: New Perspectives From Industrial and Organizational Psychology* (San Francisco: Jossey-Bass Publishers, 1988).

[2] Carla O'Dell and Jerry McAdams, *People, Performance, and Pay* (Houston: American Productivity Center and Carla O'Dell, 1987).

[3] Edward E. Lawler, III, Gerald E. Ledford, Jr., and Susan Albers Mohrman, *Employee Involvement in America: A Study of Contemporary Practice* (Houston: American Productivity and Quality Center, 1989).

and the changing needs of the work force. Between 70 and 80 percent of the responding organizations indicated improvement in management decision making, organizational processes and procedures, and employee trust in management. However, employee involvement had the greatest impact on productivity, quality of products or services, customer service, and worker satisfaction.

With the increasing number of successful employee involvement efforts, organizations are even more aware of the competitive advantage that they can gain by using the knowledge and skills of employees to implement their financial, operational, and cultural strategies. Employee involvement increases the capability of employees to perform their jobs, gives employees more resources for planning and managing their careers, and enhances the value of employees to the organization. Involving employees in the decision-making process more effectively uses the knowledge and experience of the work force and adds value to the organization.

Need for a Process Approach

Although a large number of organizations are practicing employee involvement and are beginning to show significant benefits, the full potential of employee involvement efforts is not yet being realized. Information collected in the Research for Management data base over the last ten years suggests that even though employee perceptions of involvement have improved, many of these efforts are still ineffective.

The Research for Management data base represents the perceptions of over two million employees at all job levels in two thousand organizations in a variety of industries across sixteen countries. The extensiveness of this data base makes it a useful tool for tracking trends in employee involvement and other elements of organizational culture over time. National data over the past ten years indicate that employees feel they have significantly more opportunities for input (Figure 26-1) and more authority to carry out their responsibilities than they had in the past (Figure 26-2). However, their perceptions of the amount of authority they have to make decisions about how they do their jobs have not changed over the last decade (Figure 26-3). Employees, especially those at the lower levels of the organization, have also not perceived greater acceptance and adoption of their ideas (Figure 26-4).

A primary reason for these shortcomings is that many organizations approach employee involvement as a short-term program rather than as a long-term, integrated process. Employee involvement is not a "quick fix" that managers can implement and be done with. Above all else, it is critical to view employee involvement as a process and to design it accordingly.

There are critical differences between a program and a process orientation. In a process approach:

FIGURE 26-1

Perceptions of Encouragement of Employee Suggestions for Improvement

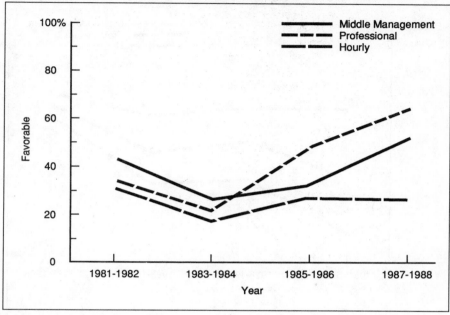

1. The time frame is generally longer.
2. The scope is more comprehensive.
3. The effort is ongoing and becomes an integral part of the organization's functioning.
4. The orientation is more strategic than tactical, because processes are driven by the organization's goals and strategies.
5. The process is not an end in itself but a way of doing business.

So the question is, how does an organization go about increasing or initiating employee involvement? Even more important, how does an organization ensure that these efforts will be sustained over the long term? The next section presents a process model that addresses these questions.

EMPLOYEE INVOLVEMENT: STRATEGIC PLANNING PROCESS MODEL

Employee involvement has the greatest impact when it is aligned with the strategic direction of the organization. The model shown in Figure 26-5 has been developed to ensure that (1) employee involvement is aligned with the

FIGURE 26-2
Perceptions of Having Adequate Authority to Carry Out Responsibilities

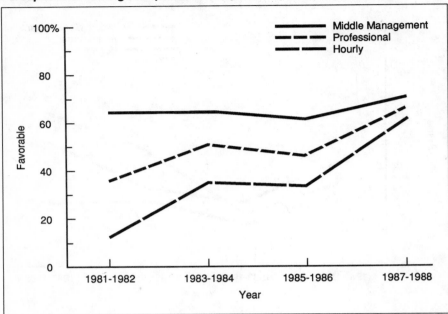

strategic needs of the organization, (2) organizations take a process approach to designing and implementing employee involvement, and (3) the potential of employee involvement efforts is maximized.

Assessment

Assessment is one of the primary precursors to strategy development. Traditionally, external assessments of an organization's competitors and customers and of industry dynamics are the foundation of a strategic plan. However, the need for an internal analysis of the organization's strengths and weaknesses is also being realized. One of management's primary responsibilities is to create a vision of where the organization is going. This involves a clear assessment of where the organization is today and where it wants to be in the future. Organizations are starting to realize and meet the need to manage their human resources strategically to make their visions a reality.

The internal assessment phase of the planning process can take many forms and serve a variety of purposes. It can be as informal as group interviews, focus groups, or individual interviews, or it can be formalized into a questionnaire administered to employees. Assessments identify areas needing improvement and create a felt need to change. Assessments can also determine the willingness and capabilities of an organization to change and

FIGURE 26-3

Perceptions of Amount of Authority to Make Decisions About How to Do One's Job

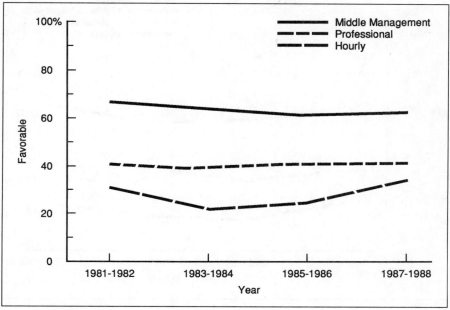

can establish baselines against which future improvement can be compared. Finally, an assessment determines the current financial, operational, and cultural state of the organization.

External Assessment. External assessments have traditionally included analysis of the structure of the pertinent market as well as of potential new entrants, product/service substitutes, and new relevant technologies. However, organizations also need to be aware of demographic, societal, technological, and regulatory trends that may affect the market for the company's products and services. More than a few organizations have suffered because they ignored the effects of these changes on their business.

A classic example is Tupperware's failure to recognize and respond to the increase in the number of women in the work force and in the number of dual income families. Both of these changes left potential customers with less time and inclination to attend traditional Tupperware parties. Because Tupperware was slow in adapting its sales and distribution strategy to account for these changes, it lost market share to companies such as Rubbermaid, which distributes similar products through retail channels.

Analysis of the appropriate industry and market segments is also cru-

FIGURE 26-4

Perceptions of Opportunities to Have One's Ideas Adopted and Put to Use

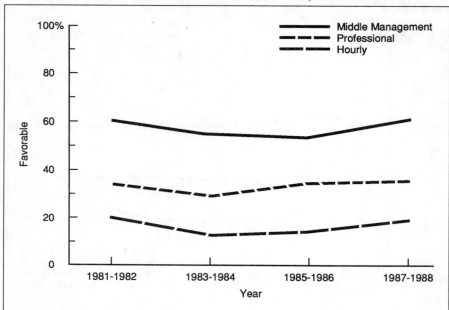

cial to the development of a sound strategy. The organization must evaluate the impact of competitors, suppliers, distributors, and customers on its business.

The key to evaluating and dealing with the impact of competitors is determining what their strengths and weaknesses are and incorporating this information into the development of an achievable strategy. Some important questions to answer about an organization's competitors are:

1. What is (are) their competitive advantage(s)?
   a. Are they the low-cost producer/distributor?
   b. Are they perceived as the high-quality producer?
   c. Do they develop products more quickly?
2. What is their image among consumers?
   a. How do they market their products/services?
   b. How much do they spend on advertising.
      i. What types of media do they use?
3. What is their relationship with suppliers and distributors?
4. In what segments do they compete?
   a. What segments might they be able/willing to penetrate?

FIGURE 26-5

Employee Involvement Strategic Planning Process

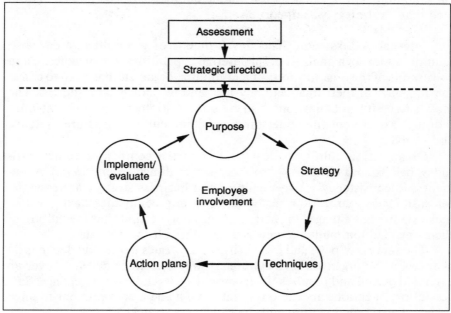

The organization must also assess its relationship with suppliers and distributors. A poor relationship with suppliers or distributors can be a source of tremendous advantage to competitors. The Stroh Brewery discovered this when Coors, as part of its entry into other geographic markets, listened and responded to the comments of distributors who were disgruntled by Stroh's apparent unwillingness to heed their comments about pricing, marketing, and distribution. Stroh's inattentiveness to its distributors made Coors' expansion easier and more successful.

Although the foregoing considerations are important to strategy development, nothing is more important than understanding the current and future needs of actual and potential customers. This includes the organization's current image among its customers and potential clients. In fact, many of the questions relative to competitors should also be asked and answered from the customer's perspective.

In the early 1980s, Saatchi & Saatchi, the once huge and growing communications and consulting organization, set out to become a "one stop shop for business consulting services." The Saatchi empire is now in a severe retrenchment phase back to its original advertising business. This is, at least in part, because businesses do not want, or are not structured, to use one organization for all their consulting needs. If Saatchi had asked its current and potential clients a few simple questions, it would have discovered that its strategy was ill-conceived.

Internal Assessment. The development of a sound strategy also requires a thorough analysis of the internal capabilities, competencies, and constraints of the organization. At a minimum, organizations need to assess the adequacy of their financial, physical, and technological resources. The most successful organizations also base their strategy development on a thorough assessment and understanding of their culture, structure, systems, and people.

Organization culture typically refers to the company's values, attitudes, beliefs, and customs—"the way we do things around here." Alignment and consistency between culture and business strategy are essential for sustained organization performance. Many companies have tried to make significant changes in their strategies only to find that the culture of their organization made the new strategy difficult to carry out.

The success of new, and even existing, strategies frequently depends on changes in the organization's culture. However, culture develops over an extended period and requires time, commitment, and effort to change. Successful organizations are the ones that have made a commitment to align their organizational culture and their business strategies.

Primarily because of foreign competition, the "Big Three" U.S. automakers have had to change their cultures to focus on issues such as quality and quicker product development. The new focus has required a drastic change in the values, attitudes, and beliefs of employees at all levels. Organizations that have adapted their strategy and culture to meet these new challenges, such as Ford, have seen the benefits in terms of improved performance.

The structure of an organization also has implications for strategy development. A highly centralized organization that is considering becoming more market-driven will have to decentralize its structure in order to be more responsive and adaptable to the marketplace. In order to compete with one another for consumer and commercial accounts, many electric and gas utilities have undergone this type of structural change, forcing decision making to lower levels, so they can be more responsive to changes in the marketplace.

The systems that make up an organization also need to be considered when developing a strategy. These include the communication, decision-making, and reward systems. For example, a management information system that is adequate under a product-driven strategy might be ineffective under a market-driven strategy. A centralized company that wants to become more market-driven must give people at lower levels the necessary data to make quality decisions related to the organization's strategic goals. Similarly, a compensation system that does not provide noticeably more incentive to excellent performers will derail any strategy that depends on enhanced individual or group performance.

Another important factor in strategy development is the extent to which the organization has the right people with the right skills. If a manufacturing organization wants to use a particular technique to improve quality, it must find people who know or have the capacity to learn, how to use it or develop such knowledge or capacity in its employees. Supervisors must also have the ability to manage such a process. Likewise, a company that wants to decentralize and/or encourage decision making at lower levels must assess the ability and potential of current managers and employees to take on these additional responsibilities.

The key to both the external and internal assessment processes is determining the organization's current and potential competencies. If an organization has thoroughly and rigorously assessed its capabilities, it should be relatively simple for it to develop a sound, achievable strategy. For instance, an organization whose assessment shows that it is highly structured and centralized, with a large number of authoritative, "old-line" managers, should probably not pursue a market-driven strategy in the short term. It can, however, plan ways to move in that direction by changing its structure, systems, and culture to accommodate the new strategy.

Strategic Direction

The strategic direction of an organization usually consists of its mission, vision, values, goals, and strategies. Understanding the strategic direction provides the information needed to establish an overall employee involvement process. It is critical that employee involvement not exist simply for its own sake. Employee involvement should be designed to achieve the strategic direction of the organization.

Organizations generally carry out the assessment and strategic direction phases of the model whether or not they use employee involvement to implement their strategies. These two phases are discussed here to emphasize the importance of using some type of assessment and of considering the organization's strategic direction to ensure that employee involvement is aligned with the organization's business strategies. The next five phases of the model, below the dotted line in Figure 26-5, are unique to the design and implementation of an employee involvement process.

Purpose

Defining the purpose and focus of a company's employee involvement efforts is essential to success. Many organizations set up employee involvement techniques without thinking through the types of decisions and problem-solving activities employees should be involved in, the type of information they need and, generally, where their efforts should be directed.

During the "purpose" stage of the planning process, management states what employee involvement is and why the organization believes it is important. The actual definition is not crucial as long as management is committed to employee involvement, thinks it through, and defines it in a way that makes sense for the organization. By working through this definition stage, managers gain a better understanding of the concept of employee involvement and learn specifically what they are trying to accomplish in their own company.

After defining employee involvement, the most important part of the "purpose" stage is determining the focus of the employee involvement process. The focus of employee involvement efforts should be derived from the primary focus of the organization's strategic direction. Quality, productivity, customer service, and innovation are some of the most common focus areas. For example, if quality is an organization's primary concern, employee involvement efforts should be directed toward solving problems and making decisions related to the quality of the organization's products and services.

The importance of linking employee involvement with the needs of the business cannot be overemphasized. Even if management is tempted to focus on multiple areas, a priority listing should be developed and communicated to employees. Establishing and clearly communicating the definition and focus provide employees with common terminology and a common direction. This common understanding by the work force of what the company is trying to accomplish and where it is heading is critical to making employee involvement a successful, ongoing effort.

The focus of employee involvement efforts should also change over time to meet the shifting needs of the business. For example, the initial focus of an employee involvement process may be on work environment issues. A few years later, with increased competition or changes in the external environment, the organization may find it needs to shift its employee involvement efforts to issues of cost reduction or productivity. This means employees would work with different types of information, solve different problems, and make different decisions.

In summary, management should determine the purpose of an employee involvement process by answering the following questions:

1. What do we mean by "employee involvement?" How should "employee involvement" be defined in this organization?

2. Why do we want employee involvement? How will it benefit the organization? What measurable results do we expect and in what time frame?

3. What should the focus of our employee involvement efforts be?

Strategy

After establishing the purpose of the employee involvement process, the next step is to develop a strategy to support it. The first step in developing this strategy is to determine how ready the organization is for different types of employee involvement. This readiness determination is one of the most frequently overlooked steps in establishing employee involvement processes. Information on the organization's readiness may be available from an earlier internal assessment. A number of operational, financial, and cultural dimensions of readiness should be considered, some of the most important being management commitment, support systems (e.g., compensation, communication), management and employee relations, management and employee skills and resources, and support personnel. By determining the organization's level of readiness and knowing its other strengths and weaknesses, management can begin to develop the employee involvement strategy. This is done by determining (1) the type of employee involvement the organization is currently implementing; (2) the practices the organization would like to implement in the future; and (3) how the organization intends to close the gap between the current and desired future conditions.

A classification of employee involvement types has been developed to assist organizations in developing their employee involvement strategies. Figuring out where the organization fits in this classification helps the organization determine what types of employee involvement it has now and what types it needs to effectively implement its business strategies. There are five basic types of involvement:

- Type 1: Authoritative/contractual
- Type 2: Limited/upward
- Type 3: Focused/parallel
- Type 4: Integrated/natural
- Type 5: Group authority/self-managed

Type 1 corresponds to the traditional contract between the employee and the organization, entailing nothing more than employees coming to work, doing the job, and being paid by the organization for doing this. Communication is limited or nonexistent, decision-making authority is solely at the management level, and training is limited to the skills needed to perform the job. Reinforcement and reward for participating or for managing in a participative manner do not exist.

Type 2 is characterized by one-way communication and limited involvement opportunities. Management may ask employees to provide input, through question and answer sessions or employee surveys, but it is generally not interested in soliciting or using recommendations for improvement. Management still retains decision-making authority, and rewards and training are not linked to employee involvement. The fact that employees perceive more opportunities for input but are still not seeing their ideas put to use—as shown in Figures 26-1 and 26-4 and the trend data discussed earlier—suggests that many organizations are still practicing Type 2 involvement.

Type 3 is characterized by focused opportunities for employees to participate in various problem-solving and decision-making activities. Management typically identifies an issue it would like employees to consider and make recommendations on. Communication tends to be both upward and downward, some decision-making authority is delegated to employees, and employees are generally rewarded for participating. Training in various problem-solving techniques or other technique-specific areas may also be provided.

Although more involvement is practiced in this type, the participation is still not completely integrated with the rest of the organization. Employees typically perform their jobs as usual and may be involved in some type of participation group as an add-on to their normal responsibilities.

For example, a large oil company used more than twenty employee task forces, orchestrated by an external consultant, to address various cultural and operational issues. Employees were assigned to these task forces, and after their recommendations were submitted, they returned to their normal day-to-day jobs. No process was in place to ensure that the employee involvement practices used in the task forces were integrated into the daily business operations; employee involvement was not the "way of doing business."

Employee involvement is not fully integrated into the systems, structures and practices of Type 1, 2, or 3 organizations, but in Types 4 and 5 it is well established.

Type 4 involvement requires the restructuring of the organization to facilitate greater involvement. Management is participative and uses employee involvement as an inherent part of daily operations. Type 4 generally pushes decision making down to the work group level. Natural work teams identify and solve problems on a daily basis. Employees may also be involved in implementing solutions and setting the direction of the work group or business unit. Communications are good laterally as well as upward and downward. The reward system is designed to reinforce participation, and employees and managers are trained in the various aspects of employee involvement.

Finally, Type 5 represents autonomous or self-managed forms of employee involvement. This type of involvement is rarely used throughout an organization. Instead, it is generally found in parts of larger companies. In Type 5 involvement, work teams are given complete authority for making decisions that are traditionally made by management. For example, they may be responsible for hiring and firing group members and determining pay raises. Most, if not all, decision-making authority is delegated to the group, communication is extensive, and training is critical. The reward system is also designed to support the autonomous structure.

It is important to understand that one type of employee involvement is not better or worse than another. The continuum and the readiness assessment are tools to help organizations develop their strategy by identifying the type of involvement they are currently practicing, the type they want to practice, and changes the organization may need to do to make its operations and practices better accommodate employee involvement and the company's strategic direction.

Techniques

Organizations often equate employee involvement with the use of a particular technique. Employee involvement is introduced in the form of quality circles or some other "technique du jour". However, the actual techniques used to promote employee involvement are only one part of a total employee involvement effort. For this reason, the techniques should not be chosen until after management has determined the purpose of employee involvement and the type of involvement it wants to achieve.

Survey feedback, suggestion systems, task forces, quality circles, and self-managed work teams are some of the more common techniques used in organizations. A detailed discussion of the different techniques is beyond the scope of this chapter and can be found elsewhere.[4] Here, it would be more useful to offer a few points to keep in mind about the use of employee involvement techniques in general.

First, employee involvement techniques can be used in different ways. For example, a suggestion system can be as simple as a box on the wall, with limited feedback to employees, or it can be an elaborate system involving feedback, training, implementation, and reward mechanisms. In practice, most organizations use a variety of employee involvement techniques to implement their strategy. Organizations such as Ford and Xerox initiated their processes using quality circles and then, over time, developed additional techniques and supporting systems as necessary.

Second, the techniques selected should support the objectives that the organization is trying to accomplish with its strategy. Employee involvement techniques are structured mechanisms that facilitate the involvement

---

[4] See John G. Belcher, Jr., *Productivity Plus: How Today's Best Run Companies Are Gaining the Competitive Edge* (Houston: Gulf Publishing Company, 1987), and Edward E. Lawler III, *High Involvement Management: Participative Strategies for Improving Organizational Performance* (San Francisco: Jossey-Bass Publishers, 1988).

of the work force. They are only the tactical side of employee involvement and are not ends in themselves.

Finally, techniques must be modified over time as the organization's strategy changes or as the techniques become inappropriate. For example, much of the failure attributed to quality circles is due not to inherent flaws in the technique, but to organizations' failure to modify the approach over time. Quality circles effectively introduce employees to basic problem-solving skills, but do not provide them with the necessary authority to carry out their recommendations. As business conditions and strategies change, the techniques need to be modified or new ones introduced to provide employees with the involvement opportunities that will most benefit the organization.

Xerox has done an excellent job of using and modifying employee involvement techniques over time. As management and union relationships improved over the years and the business strategy changed, Xerox evolved its approach from traditional quality circles to structured work groups to self-managing work groups, redesigned work units, and other, more advanced forms of involvement. As Xerox continues to implement its strategy to achieve greater competitive advantage, it plans to continually increase the involvement of its employees in setting the direction of the organization through more flexible organizational systems.

Action Plans

Once management has established the purpose of employee involvement, determined the desired state of employee involvement, and chosen the appropriate techniques, it is ready to develop an action plan. The action plan establishes the specific steps for implementing the employee involvement process. The plan also specifies who is responsible for specific aspects of the implementation, the time frame, and how the plan will be communicated and monitored.

It is most important to develop an integrated action plan. This means the action plan addresses the various organizational systems and issues that may affect the implementation of an employee involvement process. Steps addressing the direction, structures and systems, skills and knowledge, resources, accountabilities, and incentives need to be included to ensure a process approach to employee involvement. This lays the groundwork necessary for successful employee involvement and supports the need to take a long-term process approach.

Implementation and Evaluation

After the organization has developed and effectively communicated the action plan, it is ready to begin implementing the employee involvement process. Many organizations find it necessary to alter their performance management process to effectively hold people accountable for increasing employee involvement. Xerox adapted its performance and development objectives to include participative management skills. It also gave employees the opportunity to evaluate their supervisors, thus reinforcing these skills as part of the way business is conducted.

Evaluation of the process should begin soon after implementation and be carried out on an ongoing basis. Continual reassessment and modification make employee involvement an ongoing process and ensure its alignment with the organization's strategic requirements.

The organization evaluates the process primarily to determine whether it is achieving the employee involvement purpose it set for itself. To this end, it focuses on the extent to which the employee involvement techniques and related organizational systems are supporting involvement opportunities. Finally, it uses the evaluation to determine whether or not the original purpose still makes sense given any changes the organization may be experiencing. This stage completes one cycle of the model and leads back to reassessment of the purpose (Figure 26-5).

CRITICAL SUCCESS FACTORS

The model for designing an employee involvement process presented here is based on the experience of organizations, such as Motorola, Xerox, and Ford, that have used employee involvement to gain a competitive advantage in implementing their business strategies. In 1980, the year Ford began its employee involvement efforts, the company posted a loss of over $1.5 billion. In 1983, Ford recorded the largest turnaround from a loss position in U.S. corporate history, showing a profit of over $1.8 million. Although many factors were responsible for this improvement, one of the major contributors was the company's push toward greater employee involvement.[5]

Similarly, Xerox experienced a significant loss of market share in copier revenues from 1976 to 1982. Xerox's employee involvement efforts have helped it to regain some of that share and to increase profits in an era of intense foreign and domestic competition.

Motorola has also seen tremendous benefits from its Participative Management Process. In its semiconductor electroplating operation, employees cut the loss of gold from 40 percent to zero, resulting in a savings of nearly $3 million per year. At another facility, Motorola shipped 33 percent more volume of one device that it had six years earlier. This was accomplished even though the number of employees was substantially reduced.[6]

---

[5] Lindsay Li, "Ford's Better Idea," *Business Computer Systems, 3(6),* 38–52, June 1984.

[6] William J. Weisz, "Employee Involvement: How It Works at Motorola," *Personnel* (Feb. 1985.) pp. 29–33.

Companies like Ford, Motorola, and Xerox have demonstrated that a process-oriented, systems approach to increased employee involvement is an effective way to implement their strategies and gain tremendous competitive advantage. These companies have incorporated the two primary factors that are critical to the success of any employee involvement procedures: (1) taking a process, as opposed to a programmatic, approach to employee involvement, and (2) aligning the organization's systems with the employee involvement process to ensure effective implementation of the business strategy. Although these factors have been referred to throughout this chapter, their importance to the success of employee involvement merits additional discussion and illustration.

Process Approach to Employee Involvement

Taking a process approach allows the organization to instill feelings of ownership and of commitment to the process. Motorola, Ford, and Xerox all made concerted efforts to stimulate feelings of ownership and commitment to employee involvement at all levels of their organizations, largely through extensive communication of the overall objectives and goals of the process.

Ford and Motorola took the additional step of decentralizing the entire process to maximize the autonomy of local business units; the results were processes that looked and worked differently in different locations and increased commitment to the process at all levels. "Buy-in" and ownership in all three companies was also increased by the fact that managers and employees believed the process would make the organization more competitive.

A process approach also ensures that employee involvement is tied to the organization's business strategy. Xerox is probably the best example of an involvement process that mirrors the company's business strategy. After developing a long-term business plan, Xerox created a four-stage employee involvement strategy that paralleled its business strategy. Now in the third phase of its strategy, Xerox uses employee involvement through a process called Leadership Through Quality. Many other organizations, such as Ford and Motorola, also focus their involvement efforts on continuous quality improvement. In all of the quality approaches popular today, employee involvement is the organization's "way of doing business" instead of "just another program".

Finally, a process approach ensures that employee involvement is dynamic and changes with the needs of the organization. For almost all organizations, increased employee involvement requires a fundamental shift in organization culture, which cannot occur in a short period of time. Successful companies take a long-range view of employee involvement, setting achievable milestones over time. The process itself is continually assessed and revised as internal and external factors change. Motorola has been practicing employee involvement since the early 1970s; Ford and Xerox have been practicing it for over ten years. The key in all three organizations is that they committed to employee involvement over the long term and continue to enhance their processes along the way.

Alignment of Organizational Systems

The most successful organizations align their decision-making, communication, and reward systems with their employee involvement processes and make certain that their managers and employees possess the needed knowledge and skills to make the most of the involvement opportunities.

The extent to which decision making is pushed down to lower levels in the organization is the crux of successful employee involvement. For employee involvement to work, employees must be given the authority to make decisions and to solve problems that help the organization achieve its goals and strategies.

Organizations approach this challenge in a variety of ways. Some companies restructure and eliminate layers of management to give their employees the flexibility and authority they need to make decisions that affect their jobs. Other organizations institute various team structures to encourage employee problem-solving.

The communications/information systems are also essential to increased participation. Communications not only are important to the clarity of the objectives and expectations of an involvement process, but are also necessary to keep the process on track.

The key to Motorola's gain-sharing and employee involvement process is the constant flow of information about key performance indicators at the group level. This forces all employees of the group to focus on the profit and cost goals of the group. This focus has heightened awareness to the extent that some groups have decided to share the responsibilities of departing workers in order to keep costs down, rather than replace the employees.

Ford and Xerox use internal surveys extensively to elicit input about how to improve the involvement process. With this more structured form of upward communication, they have been able to adapt their processes and make them more effective over time.

Ford and Motorola also use steering committees as a vehicle for sharing, reviewing, and distributing information throughout the organization. These committees, composed of individuals from each major decision-making area, serve as a major forum for solving problems and improving the employee involvement process.

Information about the strategic direction of the organization must also be provided to employees so that they can make informed decisions. Employees at the middle and lower levels of the organization need to be informed about the organization's strategy, how it links with various division or business unit strategies, and how the strategy affects their jobs, if they are to contribute fully to the functioning of the organization.

Many organizations use a series of meetings and work sessions to cascade the organization's strategic direction to the lower levels of the organization. In one chemical company, the top thirty managers developed the organization's mission, vision, values, goals, and strategies through a series of meetings. Then they developed a leader's guide and video tape and distributed them to all managers in the organization. Managers used these tools to communicate the strategy to their employees. The employees participated in discussion sessions in which they gained a better understanding of how their jobs contributed to the organization as a whole.

The reward system is another crucial element of a successful employee involvement process. Motivation theory suggests that people will be motivated to the extent that they believe their effort will bring about some outcome they value. In other words, the work force will support employee involvement if it believes it will result in something of value. Therefore, organizations are experimenting with different reward systems. Some of the most common include gain sharing, pay for knowledge, and an all-salaried work force.

Motorola uses a complex gain-sharing system that pays groups of employees bonuses when they exceed specific, quantitative, predetermined goals. Although opinions of the motivational value of bonuses vary, this reward system is definitely perceived to lend credibility to the entire process. Xerox gears its systems more toward recognition, using various awards and ceremonies, among them a day-long event called "Teamwork," in which various teams set up booths to display their accomplishments. Not only does this provide recognition, it also allows teams to learn from one another about the effectiveness and feasibility of various techniques.

Finally, training is another important aspect of an employee involvement process. Both managers and employees may require training in such areas as problem solving, meeting management, and group dynamics. Clearly, if employees are expected to participate in problem-solving groups, use a suggestion system, or implement quality improvement techniques, they will need some guidance in these areas.

Even when all levels of the organization are committed to the process, many employees and especially many managers may not possess the requisite skills to make such a process successful. Moving toward greater participation demands a lot from employees, but it demands even more from managers.

Motorola, recognizing the importance of training after it had already initiated an employee involvement process, developed a multimillion dollar training center for all Motorola employees. A large percentage of the courses offered are directly related to its Participative Management Process.

CONCLUSION

Employee involvement facilitates the implementation of the organization's strategy through a variety of techniques and processes and, most importantly, through the alignment and support of the organization's systems. Many organizations, such as Xerox, Ford, and Motorola, believe that they could not have carried out their strategies and achieved their current levels of performance without the involvement of their employees. Undoubtedly, changing internal and external business conditions will continually require organizations to maximize the potential of their work forces through their increased involvement in daily business operations.

27

Growth Strategy in a Mature Industry: A Banking Model

DAVID M. ONDERSMA

THOMAS A. MOORE, JR.

First Michigan Bank Corporation

INTRODUCTION

First Michigan Bank Corporation (FMB) is a multibank holding company in West Michigan. It was founded in 1878 in Zeeland, Michigan, home to many people of Dutch origin. This Dutch influence provided the basis for the corporate culture. This chapter looks at FMB and examines how it has used its marketing strategy, its community banking strategy, and its people strategy to grow from its origins in 1878 to its present-day position as a $1.5 billion bank holding company and how it plans to be a survivor in the rapid shakeout occurring in the financial services industry.

FMB's mission statement reads in part: "to profitably serve as a leading and progressive financial corporation of high quality, offering services that are responsive to the needs of our customers . . . for the benefit of our stockholders, communities, and employees." The resolute belief in the positive aspects of people has provided the basis for FMB's participative management style and for its attention to the customer and the customer's needs and to the general work ethic of the West Michigan market, all of which have played a significant role in FMB's ability to meet its goals. It continues to achieve its strategic goals by practicing what might be referred to as a "homespun" management philosophy and by doing even the little things in new and better ways, without finding it necessary to make dazzling moves in order to gain attention.

PERFORMANCE FACTORS

FMB attributes its success, now and in the future, to its ability to differentiate itself by capitalizing on its main strengths:

- *Market strategy:* FMB's location offers a very prosperous banking marketplace that is growing at a rate faster than the state average. FMB will continue to focus its growth within the West Michigan area.

- *Community banking strategy:* FMB's organizational structure permits it to achieve its strategic objective of offering superior customer service through community banking in all of its markets. This higher-cost approach to providing banking services is offset by the consolidation and standardization of all functions not directly affecting the customer. FMB's continuing to offer community banking to the marketplace differentiates it from most of its bank holding company competitors.

- *People strategy:* Well managed and progressive, FMB is able to attract, develop, and retain highly capable, professional people at many organizational levels. The "service" attitude of FMB staff, acquired through training and job expectation, is fundamental to marketing strategy.

FMB's firm belief in serving the customer is one factor contributing to the distinct way in which it structures itself and brings its services to market. The strategy is to own and operate a group of community banks under the umbrella of a holding company. The affiliate banks remain individual and local in many respects. Each bank maintains its own character, name, president, board of directors, business plan, and focus on the community it serves. Each relies on the holding company for services that are transparent to the customer. The corporation acts as a conduit for services and capital resources where necessary.

At FMB's community banks, qualified staff at the local level make the decisions about extending credit and gathering deposits. Community banking involves a natural friendliness and courtesy, product knowledge, awareness of the customer, and ability to respond to the customer's needs. These are the keys to customer satisfaction. The strength of the community bank lies in the fact that it is local, and oriented to the needs of the community.

FMB adds value to its franchise by consolidating all functions that are transparent to the customer. FMB gains economies of scale through this sharing of common activities. This consolidation also ensures that the quality of these operations and services is consistent for the banks. The services that FMB consolidates are:

- Accounting
- Auditing
- Data processing
- Human resources
- Investments

- Marketing
- Operations
- Product development
- Shareholder services
- Wire transfer

MEASURING PERFORMANCE

In its 1990 Industry Survey,[1] Standard & Poor's comments that both profitability and financial condition need to be examined when analyzing a bank. Looking at profitability alone ignores management's perspective on risk.

Profitability and Financial Condition

FMB believes that profitability and success go hand in hand. The corporation has experienced excellent returns on assets and equity and has enjoyed a ten-year compound growth rate in deposits of 10.75 percent (see Table 27-1). As markets go through their cycles, quality has sustained FMB. Table 27-2 shows FMB's performance as measured against its goals.

TABLE 27-1

Financial Data

Year	Income	Per share	Return on assets	Return on equity
1985	$ 8,651,300	$1.50	0.96%	13.94%
1986	10,470,600	1.68	1.04	13.67
1987	11,700,700	1.87	1.07	13.83
1988	13,744,100	2.16	1.09	14.44
1989	16,313,777	2.51	1.12	15.02

Ten year compounded growth rates

Deposits	10.75%
Net income	11.72
Stockholders' equity	11.80
Cash dividends	7.61

Note: Figures have been adjusted for "pooled" acquisitions.

[1] Standard & Poor's *Industry Survey,* vol. 157, no. 36, sec. 1 (Sept. 7, 1989).

TABLE 27-2

FMB Performance Against Goals

Measurement	Goal	Actual (12/31/89)
Nonperforming loans/Total loans	0.50%	0.33%
Net charge-off/Average loans	0.35	0.26
Reserve for loan loss/Total loans	1.25	1.28
Interest sensitivity at one year	1.00	1.00
Loan/Deposit ratio	75.00%	76.90%
Equity/Assets	7.25	7.43

Market Share

Volumes have been written in an attempt to relate market share to profitability. However, market share is not a direct indicator of profitability. This is not to say that there is no relationship between the two. Most analysts would conclude that profitability is a result of a complex set of relationships, market share being one element. Market share, however, does provide management with a tool with which to assess shifts in customer preference within a defined market as well as to measure management's ability to maintain or increase its customer base.

Market share in the banking industry is traditionally measured as total deposits within a geographic area. The strategic plans of FMB banks identify the geographic boundaries of each market. Total deposits held at banks, savings and loan associations, and credit unions within that area are then considered to be the total market. A strong case can be made that this definition of market is much too narrow and that all consumer assets available for investment in that market should be included. This would include assets held under management, assets available for investment, mutual fund investments, and so forth. Unfortunately, data on all of these are not available, although measuring this type of market would undoubtedly indicate that all "traditional" financial institutions have been losing market share. Consequently, total deposits within a geographic area remains the best means of measurement.

FMB's market share within its major markets for the years 1983–1988 is presented in Table 27-3. These market share figures represent five years of market share growth in all of FMB's major markets. The three target markets with lower market share (Grand Rapids, Niles, and Big Rapids) provide opportunities for FMB. In each of these, market share has increased during this five-year period. The 14.3 percent total market share figure may seem small; however, this figure includes the sizeable ($4 billion) Grand Rapids market and FMB's small portion of that market. If the Grand Rapids market were excluded from the figures, FMB's total market share would approach the 25 percent mark as opposed to 14.3 percent.

TABLE 27-3
Market Share (as of 6/30/88)

Market	Share			
	1983	1987	1988	1989
Holland/Zeeland	22.6%	26.9%	28.8%	30.1%
Muskegon	12.9	14.4	15.2	17.0
Grand Rapids	1.3	2.4	2.6	2.8
Lowell	45.8	47.6	48.9	51.3
Greenville	26.6	30.4	32.5	33.1
Hart	41.0	41.5	44.8	46.0
Dowagiac	29.2	33.4	35.2	36.7
Niles	1.4	3.4	3.5	4.5
Reed City	38.5	38.9	40.5	38.3
Big Rapids	2.7	3.7	4.3	4.3
Manistee	39.6	38.4	38.6	40.6
Total	11.9%	13.9%	14.3%	14.9%

How has FMB attained its goals? As stated earlier, it has been the constant attention to differentiating itself in its strategic strengths: the West Michigan marketplace, the community banking approach to offering services, and its people and culture.

MARKET STRATEGY

FMB's market strategy is to offer community banking through a network of offices, not merely a chain of banks. Networking means the sharing of resources and the sharing of activities among the various units. It means a common quality, common service levels, common products, and a common FMB image throughout all of its markets. This is in contrast to a chain, in which all units are connected and dependent on one another but without shared activities.

This network philosophy has implications for its merger and acquisition strategy. Cultural traits are an important consideration in the analysis of potential acquisitions. For example, FMB expects all of its affiliates to share similar beliefs regarding the importance of customer service. It would be very difficult for an acquired company to assimilate into FMB's mode of operation if major cultural differences existed. When FMB acquires a bank, no major culture shock is expected because the corporation uses a selective process to find banks that want to remain community banks but that need support in non–customer related activities.

FMB manages its market growth through internal and external growth strategies. Internal growth refers to gaining new customers' deposits, cross-selling new services to existing customers, and expanding the delivery system with new branches or automated teller machines (ATMs). External growth is achieved through acquiring new banks.

Internal Growth

FMB has been able to generate growth in its existing markets near its goal of 12 percent annual growth. The objective is to continue to achieve this goal by providing exceptional service to its customers through up-to-date products, knowledgeable and helpful staff, and customer calling programs.

FMB also expands into new and attractive markets by branching out from its existing network of banks. Where bank branches have achieved high levels of market share and other attractive areas exist within a bank's market, the corporation encourages the bank to expand its services into those areas.

On occasion, FMB's community banking philosophy conflicts with its growth strategies. This occurs when FMB markets reach overlap conditions. To prevent competition for customers among FMB banks and confusion among customers, FMB has established corporate standards regarding product design, service charge structures, and quality of service. The issue of standardization sometimes appears to conflict with the concept of local decision making. In reality, there is no conflict; both seek to provide the greatest level of satisfaction to the customer regardless of bank location in West Michigan. FMB believes its customer should be able to access the same product and professional service at any FMB office. If one FMB bank offers a special type of savings account, the customer should be able to obtain the same account at all FMB banks.

In theory, the concept of identical products in all markets makes sense, but in practice, some problems are inherent. One bank may want to market a certain product and another may not, for any number of reasons, from cost limitations to customer preferences. This is a "conflict point" between the community banking strategy and the standardization/efficiency strategy. However, community banking and customer satisfaction are tied together. Community banking does not mean that a bank can pursue any direction in terms of product or pricing. FMB community banking means that banks have local decision-making authority as far as a particular customer's request is concerned, but all banks provide the same services. Although these strategies can be difficult to orchestrate, FMB's position is that careful management and resolution of these conflicts are a much more acceptable alternative than dismantling these strategies.

External Growth

FMB is positioned to take advantage of additional opportunities that exist in the economically prosperous West Michigan market area. It has chosen not to broaden its regional bases. At this time opportunities outside the West Michigan niche would involve higher cost in overhead and increased administrative time. FMB's uniqueness and strength in the prosperous West Michigan market would be lost.

FMB desires to grow externally, at a rate that will allow new affiliates time to become assimilated into the organization. Its goal is to achieve external growth through acquisition at a rate of approximately $300 million to $500 million in assets over a five-year period. In this way, FMB can avoid the problem of dilution of the culture, which often occurs with rapid external growth.

Another problem that FMB avoids that is also associated with rapid external growth is the operational difficulty of expansion that is not contiguous. FMB believes it is easier to extend its philosophy contiguously and, because of this, generally structures its merger and acquisition strategy accordingly. The company can tie together the expansion using its existing distribution system.

In addition to pure size, external growth provides FMB with a larger base with which to meet the loan demands of its customers. Some markets generate more loan activity than they can assume within their own bank. Having other banks that can assume those loans gives the originating bank the ability to meet the customers' needs. Some markets' loan demands are not as great and the banks are therefore not able to expand the more profitable lending portfolios. FMB's network allows these banks to continue to serve their markets and, in turn, serve the corporation by taking excess loan volume from other banks, thus improving the bank's (and the corporation's) profitability.

Future Growth Opportunities

FMB is positioning itself as a good alternative for the independent bank. Independent banks usually turn to a holding company for one of three reasons: lack of management succession, a major shareholder wanting to liquidate, or the need for "backroom" support. At some point, some of the West Michigan independent banks may need support in one of these areas. FMB is positioned to be their best alternative.

In addition, many banks remained independent because they believed this was the way to provide good, responsive service to their communities. Now, many are finding it difficult to remain independent because of increasing regulatory requirements and customer sophistication with respect to the vast array of investment vehicles available. FMB expects to be able to acquire a number of independent banks that want to maintain the community banking philosophy.

FMB always pays a fair price for each acquisition but it also limits its acquisition prices to a point where there will not be unrecoverable dilution.

Potential sellers must balance their expected price with the long-term return to the shareholder. It also believes that the long-term return will be enhanced through the community banking strategy. Holding companies that recover the dilution through the reduction of boards and presidents provide little value to the community. Selling banks must decide whether they are looking for the highest price or are interested in retaining their community position.

COMMUNITY BANKING STRATEGY

A multibank holding company can generally execute one of three organizational strategies:

1. Consolidation of all activities, transforming all banks into branches of one bank. This improves organization efficiency; however, it also removes from the local scene many of the decisions that affect the customer: credit approval, pricing, and so forth.
2. Continued autonomy of each bank. This is hard to justify when there are no apparent benefits to the holding company shareholder or to the bank customer.
3. An intermediate strategy. This is FMB's position. It consolidates all activities that are transparent to the customer (data processing, investments, and so forth) for cost efficiency and maintains local management and decision making at the bank level. This is FMB's community banking strategy.

The decision to be a "community bank" holding company was not a conscious one. This cornerstone strategy resulted from management's belief that community banking is the way customers want to be treated.

Before the late 1970s, all banks were basically the same because banks were governmentally regulated. Customer service was determined by customer geography and bank location: The branch that was closest to the customer served that customer. The late 1970s brought deregulation of interest rates and new money market accounts. Suddenly, there were investment decisions, rate decisions, product decisions, and service quality levels for banks to be concerned with. Although major bank holding companies have drifted away from community banking because they want to achieve as great an economy of scale as possible, FMB believes that the longer it can preserve the community bank structure and still control overhead, the better it will maintain its unique niche.

FMB's methodical and orderly approach to growth has permitted it to achieve efficient backroom consolidation and standardization. As each affiliate bank is brought in, a multiyear integration plan is developed for removing noncustomer activities from the affiliate and using FMB services.

FMB's centralization of noncustomer contact areas (investments, operations, and so forth) ensures that these areas provide not only efficiencies to the corporation but also professional and quality operations to the banks and to the FMB staff who serve the customers. FMB's structure and staffing allow assimilation of up to two banks in one year.

Acquisition Strategy

FMB's desires to expand its operations were limited by the branching laws that restricted FMB to within twenty miles of its main office and kept it outside of other incorporated areas where it wanted to provide banking services. Management's interest in the 1970s was in overcoming these constraints. It saw the advantage of the bank holding company laws, which came into place in 1971, as a way of going beyond what the branching laws dictated as a market area. Originally, FMB saw this as an opportunity to start new banks (FMB-Grand Rapids was formed in 1975). However, a great deal of effort and resources were required to build new banks, and FMB learned that it could accomplish its aims more easily through acquisitions. (FMB acquired the Community State Bank of Dowagiac in 1976.) Eventually, FMB's expansion strategy changed to reflect an acquisition rather than a new bank posture.

Recognizing the viability of the Grand Rapids market, FMB focused its growth objectives on this area and on smaller, profitable community banks. Its intent was and is to absorb new acquisitions slowly and deliberately.

In 1979 FMB acquired National Lumberman's Bank in Muskegon. The Lumberman's venture was close to a merger of equal sizes. Lumberman's was approximately $110 million and Zeeland was slightly over $200 million. This acquisition provided FMB with:

1. A size that made it a viable player among bank holding companies
2. The stimulus to develop an acquisition strategy
3. The beginning of the development of its community banking and consolidation strategies

The acquisition of Lumberman's involved a situation that came as a surprise. Even though FMB was acquiring Lumberman's, Lumberman's intended to be the survivor and ultimately take over FMB. This was Lumberman's viewpoint and the reasoning it used to persuade its board to agree to the acquisition.

What followed were some very difficult times for FMB. However, this experience created strong individuals in FMB corporate management and made them acutely aware of the need to take the lead in acquisition situations. FMB has had an easier time with acquisitions since this experience, and has not been placed in a position to compromise values.

Standardization

FMB controls its overhead by centralizing and standardizing all functions not affecting the customer. This strategy provides FMB with an additional benefit: The back-room services provided to the banks are uniformly of the highest quality.

FMB recognizes that in order to have the luxury and expense structure of bank managements and boards of directors, it must be able to maintain back-room efficiency and quality. It cannot afford to have an expansive and expensive structure and back-room inefficiencies.

The Lumberman's acquisition, discussed earlier, provided one of the impetuses for finding inefficiencies in the back room and for implementing the standardization process. Lumberman's had problems with its data processing system that made it apparent that changes had to be made, and the kinds of changes needed made clear the rationale for centralizing the function. As each successive opportunity presented itself, such as a position opening, FMB made a decision as to whether to consolidate the function or tasks or leave them with the bank.

FMB's community banking strategy is driven by a number of strong beliefs regarding customer expectations. The customer should not be able to differentiate among FMB banks because of different products or service characteristics. The customer should be able to see that the decision making is happening locally and should recognize a consistent level of service, but whether the customer is in one branch of the bank or another should not make any difference. Also, the customer should not hesitate to go into one FMB bank because the customer's account was opened at another FMB bank.

Officer Call Program

One of FMB's community bank strengths is its long-standing calling program, the Officer Call Program. It is FMB's way of staying close to the customer and there have been two keys to its success: organizational levels of calls and constant attention to the program.

FMB has made it a practice (and an expectation for officers of many different levels) to call on corporate officers. Accordingly, it is expected that more than one level of officer will call on more than one level of officer within every organization. Therefore, continuity is maintained as people move within either business.

The calling program is not new to FMB. It is part of the culture and the program is monitored and adjusted periodically to meet the needs of both bank employees and the customers. The calling program is one way FMB is recognized as being truly concerned about its customers.

It is also expected that this discipline will be a part of all banks within the holding company. However, there is sometimes apprehension on the part of acquired banks to enter into a calling program. The reasons are predictably consistent: The banker knows the customer fairly well and the demands placed on a bank officer at a smaller bank are usually quite varied and require time "on the floor." However, as these programs are slowly put into place, the acquired banks find that customers are receptive and the benefits of enhanced customer service are recognized rapidly.

Surveys have indicated that bank customers have the following desires:

- They would like their banker to call on them and ask what their needs are. They believe most bankers take customers for granted and assume too much about their business.
- They would like to have more of an ongoing relationship with their banker than they have at the present time.
- Some would like their banker to function as a type of management consultant. Care should be exercised here because the banker cannot be as close to the customer as is the customer's accountant or attorney. Because of the lending relationship, banks must stay at arm's length and remain aware of lender liability. Bankers cannot get so involved that they are advising the customer in making day-to-day decisions.
- Businesses would like assistance in their task of employee retention. Because of the low unemployment rate in the West Michigan area, companies are not able to retain employees as they would like. They would like the banker to help them in employee retention through such programs as direct deposit payroll. Businesses would like to tie their employees into their business and would like a banker to come in and help present their case to the employees.

FMB recognizes that it cannot be everything to its customers for both legal and practical reasons. However, it also realizes that customers want more than they are currently receiving from most banking relationships and it is attempting to respond to these needs.

PEOPLE STRATEGY

FMB has been able to attract, develop, and retain highly capable, professional people at many levels of the organization. Reasons for this include FMB's participative management style, which is a result of its planning principles, its high expectations of its employees, and its innovative style of developing products to serve the customers.

Planning Principles

FMB's strong planning principles have long been integral to its management style. Written long range plans are a relatively new addition to the planning process; however, formal, shorter-term financial plans such as budgets have been part of FMB's process for many years. Planning has been fostered by a participative management environment in which decisions are the result of strategic thinking.

In the late 1970s and early 1980s, it became apparent that FMB needed a written strategic plan that was corporately known and understood. Originally, the banks were not involved in the long-range planning process. Finally, there developed a need for a formal process by which objectives could be set forth and achieved at both the bank level and the corporate level.

This formal process has proven beneficial as FMB has grown. FMB units—nine banks, five support departments, and corporate administration—all have a different balance of people and backgrounds. All FMB units develop business unit plans to achieve business unit goals and corporate strategic goals. The units are held accountable for their objectives, goals, and strategic action steps. The formal corporate planning process provides the vehicle by which those business units can develop strategic plans and implement them.

Participative Management

FMB has been willing to pay more and therefore expect more, but work with less as far as the number of people is concerned. The corporation's participative management style has helped to encourage a high level of professionalism.

FMB decisions are always a very participative process. This is the result of having different people with different strengths in different areas. FMB achieved the right balance of people among the creative side, financial side, and banking side to be able to create better ideas and ways to implement them. The point to be made about participative management at FMB centers on FMB's belief in recognizing the positive aspects of all individuals. Participative management, like most management theories, is more applicable to some organizations than to others. The practice of participative management at FMB quickly became more than a slogan or an experiment. The practice of involving a broader cross-section of individuals in the decision-making process was very consistent with cultural norms and management philosophies and rapidly became a strategic strength of the organization. Today, that practice continues to be enhanced and remains a major strength of FMB.

The early vision for the corporation was to become a competitor of Old Kent (a major West Michigan bank holding company at that time). (See Table 27-4.) Even though FMB had assets of $100 million and Old Kent billions of dollars, FMB management consisted of far-sighted people, wise to consider FMB a viable competitor of Old Kent. This attitude came through loud and clear in terms of the type of people hired in the early 1970s. The bank holding company evolved through this participative management process.

High Expectations

An organization's total salary costs can be realized in several different ways. A company can pay less, expect less, and have more people generating the same volume, or it can pay more, expect more, and realize more productivity. FMB has thus implemented bonus programs and very good benefit programs. In return for these levels of compensation, FMB expects employees to follow a work ethic consistent with its Dutch heritage: high expectations, quality service, and commitment to the customer.

Products

FMB's philosophies also extend to the products it offers. FMB's objective is to develop products that meet the customer's needs and that provide advantages for the bank as well. Therefore, it uses interest margin rather than interest rate levels to determine whether it will be in a particular product market. FMB's recognition of the need to control the interest margin and not be vulnerable to the impact of fluctuating interest rates that could

TABLE 27-4

Top Ten Michigan Bank Holding Companies by Assets
(December 1988)

Rank	Holding company	Location	Assets (in millions)
1	NBD Bankcorp, Inc.	Detroit	$24,176
2	Michigan National Corp.	Farmington Hills	11,345
3	Comerica, Inc.	Detroit	11,143
4	First of American Bank Corp.	Kalamazoo	9,769
5	Manufacturers National Corp.	Detroit	9,311
6	Old Kent Financial Corp.	Grand Rapids	8,151
7	Security Bancorp, Inc.	Southgate	2,578
8	Citizens Banking Corp.	Flint	2,355
9	First Michigan Bank Corp.	Holland	1,288
10	Chemical Financial Corp.	Midland	1,128

Source: Sheshunoff & Co.

be either beneficial or detrimental has afforded it increased flexibility in developing products to offer its customers.

FMB's participative management style has led to the development of many new ideas and products. FMB entered the secondary market in mortgages because it believed that the long-term, fixed-rate portfolio was not going to be beneficial to its overall financial strength. This decision was made before it became known that there was going to be an interest-sensitivity game in the early 1980s. FMB's not building a significant fixed-rate portfolio has definitely proven advantageous.

FMB encourages its staff to be innovative and to find methods of meeting customer needs. Deregulation allowed the commercial banking industry to offer most deposit accounts without interest-rate or other restrictions. One lingering regulatory restriction prohibits banks from paying interest on business checking accounts. In order to meet the needs of its business account customers while also meeting regulatory requirements, FMB developed its Cash Investment Checking account (CIC). The CIC is a repurchase agreement sweep account where excess funds are moved from non-interest-bearing deposit accounts into an interest-bearing repurchase agreement daily. Because it is an overnight repurchase agreement, the CIC is a liability rather than a deposit of the bank. It is, therefore, not regulated and also not insured by the Federal Deposit Insurance Corporation. However, it is an account that is backed by bank-held securities and allows the bank to pay interest to its business customers on their excess funds. Overwhelmingly accepted by the customers, this account continues to attract nearly $100 million in funds for FMB.

The company uses creativity of FMB employees to come up with new ways to perform a job better, build volume and create customer satisfaction with new products. FMB moves into areas that do not have high up-front costs. Traditionally, the company has avoided ventures that involve high research and development (R&D) costs. Credit card activity is a good example. FMB investigated credit card operations in the 1970s and has never moved into that area. ATMs did not materialize until the market was ready to accept them. Rather than spending the money up front on R&D and experimentation, FMB prefers to focus its efforts on expanding product lines to meet customer needs.

CONCLUSION

FMB's excellent performance is the result of its constant attention to differentiating itself on its major strengths. It will continue to nurture its strengths of customer attention and quality service. In line with this, it has positioned itself to enter the arena of expanded financial services and expects to offer full brokerage services, investment advisory services, and mutual funds. It plans to approach this product expansion as a natural extension of existing product lines that fulfill customers' needs.

At the end of the 1980s, FMB initiated a comprehensive corporate-wide Sales Excellence program, which includes established goals and training modules for all bank employees. This strategy complements FMB's customer calling programs.

Complementing the sales effort is an expansive corporate-wide equipment upgrade to provide sales tools to all customer service representatives. This equipment represents a $2 million commitment to quality customer service, which also enhances quality throughout the organization.

FMB will continue to grow through its strategy of slow and deliberate acquisition and assimilation of independent banks that want to continue to practice community banking.

There is no question that the financial services industry is in a period of reorientation. Shakeouts are happening, strategy is changing, new players are appearing, industries are becoming services in a broader industry, and structure is changing. FMB's market strategy, community banking strategy, people strategy, and plans for growth should ensure its continued excellent performance against goals.

28

Job Competency Assessment

LYLE M. SPENCER, JR., PH.D.

President and CEO, McBer and Company
Partner and Technical Director, Human Resource Planning and Development
Practice Worldwide, Hay Management Consultants

NOTE: Portions of this chapter were presented at the Human Resource Planning Society Annual Conference, Naples, Florida, April 1, 1990.

INTRODUCTION

Firms implementing strategies in a rapidly changing environment must often identify the skills their employees will need to perform future jobs that do not currently exist.

Job competency assessment (JCA) is a research method developed by Harvard Professor David McClelland and colleagues at McBer and Company, a Boston human resources consulting firm, to identify characteristics that predict effective and superior job performance. Such skills can indicate an employee's probability for success in areas that will be important in the company's future.

This chapter describes the uses of JCA methods to support strategy implementation, including personnel specifications for future jobs, high-level single incumbent positions, and integrated human resource management information systems (IHRMIS).

COMPETENCY FACTORS

In every job, some employees perform better than others (that is, performance is normally distributed). Superior performers do their jobs differently and possess different characteristics, or competencies, than average performers. These differences are valuable, since superior performers (those whose performance is one standard deviation (SD) above the mean, or roughly one out of 10) produce between 19 and 120 percent more than average employees, as shown in Figure 28-1.

The more complex the job, the greater the value added by superior performers. In complex jobs, top performers are worth a minimum of 48 percent more salary than average job holders, because these superior performers do the work of 1.48 average workers. In sales and high-leverage jobs (e.g., executives responsible for investing hundreds of millions of dollars), the value added by the best performers is even greater. Studies by Schmidt, Hunter, and Judiesch[1] support the rule of thumb that top salespeople sell twice as much as average salespeople.

To improve performance, organizations should use their superior performers as their template or blueprint for employee selection and development. Competency-based selection and training can improve performance by as much as 0.67 standard deviation. Firms that do not explicitly base their selection and training programs on superior performance essentially select and train for mediocrity, i.e., the employees' current average level of performance.

---

[1] J.E. Hunter, F.L. Schmidt, & M.K. Judiesch, "Individual Differences in Output Variability as a Function of Job Complexity," 75 *Journal of Applied Psychology* 28–42 (1990).

FIGURE 28-1

What Superior Performance Is Worth

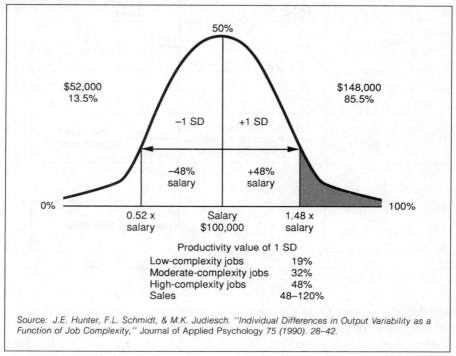

	Productivity value of 1 SD	
Low-complexity jobs		19%
Moderate-complexity jobs		32%
High-complexity jobs		48%
Sales		48–120%

Source: J.E. Hunter, F.L. Schmidt, & M.K. Judiesch. "Individual Differences in Output Variability as a Function of Job Complexity," Journal of Applied Psychology 75 (1990). 28–42.

"Competency" is defined as an underlying characteristic of an individual that can be shown to predict superior or effective performance in a job. Differentiating competencies distinguish superior from average performers. Threshold or essential competencies are required for minimally adequate or average performance. Threshold and differentiating competencies for a given job provide a template for personnel selection, succession planning, performance appraisal, and development.

Competencies can be personal characteristics, such as motives (e.g., producing a unique accomplishment); traits (e.g., stamina or endurance); self-concepts (e.g., attitudes or values, including team spirit vs. personal achievement); and knowledge and skills (e.g., active listening, electronic abilities). These personal characteristics predict skill behaviors such as goal setting, which in turn predict job performance. As Figure 28-2 illustrates, different competencies result in different job performances.

The type or level of a competency needed has practical implications for human resource planning. Core competencies, such as motives and traits, are hard to develop; therefore, it is most cost-effective to select candidates

FIGURE 28-2
Competency and Performance

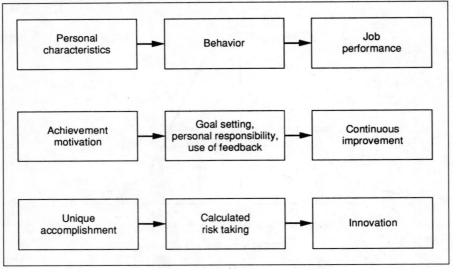

who already possess these characteristics. Peripheral knowledge and skill competencies are relatively easy to develop and training is the most cost-effective way to ensure these abilities. Self-concept, attitude, and value competencies can be changed, albeit with more time and difficulty; these attributes are most cost effectively addressed by training through develop-mental job assignments.

Competencies that differentiate superior from average performance and that are hard to develop are the most important for selection. Competencies more easily developed are less important for selection. Conversely, the more complex the job, the more important the competencies. Competency studies are the most cost-effective in staffing high-level technical, marketing, professional, and managerial positions.

USING JCA METHODS TO IMPLEMENT CORPORATE STRATEGY

JCA analysis for strategy implementation consists of the following preproject procedures:

- *Defining organization strategy:* Identifying goals and critical success factors for the firm, at present and over the next five to ten years, and developing strategic plans for how the firm will attain its goals. For example, Company X may see strategic business unit Y providing a significant amount of the firm's future growth, but this growth may be dependent on the firm's ability to attract, develop, and retain innovative technical managers with entrepreneurial skills.

- *Designing the organization structure:* Identifying how the firm will organize itself to carry out its plans. The emphasis must be on identifying critical jobs: the value-added "make or break" positions and the people who will make the biggest difference in whether the firm succeeds or fails—especially, those responsible for defining strategy and direction, those accountable for major strategic outcomes, those controlling critical resources (e.g., labor, capital, and technology), or those managing relationships with key markets or customers. Human resource management is most cost effective when it focuses on these jobs.

- *Designing the jobs:* Identifying the accountabilities and competencies necessary for critical jobs. Designing the organization's strategy and structure are usually done by reviewing a firm's business plans and interviewing its leadership; job design begins the JCA process. Figure 28-3 illustrates the relationship between the preproject planning steps.

COMPETENCY MODEL PROCESS

The preproject planning is designed to define those jobs that are critical to the firm's future and to delineate the competencies that will characterize superior performers in those jobs. The firm then can use this information to select and train those candidates who demonstrate the required competencies. A model of the competency-based selection process (see Figure 28-4) shows the following seven steps: selecting an expert panel, identifying the criterion sample, conducting behavioral event interviews (BEI), data analysis, validation, applications planning, and preparing the final report.

Expert Panels

A panel of knowledgeable human resource specialists, managers, and superior job incumbents should be appointed to target jobs or job families. The panel is responsible for determining the key accountabilities of the job (the most important duties, responsibilities, and product or service outcomes job incumbents produce), as well as the results measures for these accountabilities that can be used to identify superior performers in the job (as previously defined). Ideal criteria are "hard" outcome measures such as productivity data. In the absence of such criteria, ratings from supervisors, peers (where peers have an opportunity to observe one another's perfor-

FIGURE 28-3

Competency Planning Preproject Steps

Organizational Strategy	Organizational Structure	Job Design

Identify:
• Success criteria for firm
  — Current goals
  — Future goals over next
    5–10 years
• Plan: how firm will attain its
  goals
	Identify:
	• How firm will organize and
	  carry out its plan
	• Critical jobs in organization:
	  value-added "make-or-
	  break jobs," people who
	  will make the biggest
	  difference in whether the
	  firm succeeds or fails
	• Set direction: direct
	  involvement in strategy
	  formulation
	• Key to strategy
	  implementation
	  — Major accountability for
	    a major strategic
	    outcome
	  — Control critical resource
	    (capital, human
	    resources)
	  — Manage relationships
	    with key markets or
	    customers
	  — Possess key technical
	    know-how
	• Jobs hardest to fill
	  — Human resources most
	    effective when it
	    focuses on these jobs
		Identify on a continuing
		basis:
		• Accountabilities
		• Competency
		  Requirements

mance), subordinates (e.g., organizational climate survey), or customers can be used.

The expert panel can also establish the career paths that typically lead to the target job and the competencies employees need to perform the job at both the threshold and at a superior level, through the use of the job competency requirements inventory (JCRI), which assesses competencies required for threshold and superior performance in the job. Surveys such as the JCRI permit collection of sufficient data to do statistical analyses, and provide an inexpensive method of validating expert panel hypotheses about competencies needed for adequate and superior job performance.

The panel of experts also may respond as a group to questions posed by a computer-based expert system. These questions are keyed to an extensive data base of competencies identified by previous studies. The expert system

FIGURE 28-4

Competency Model Process

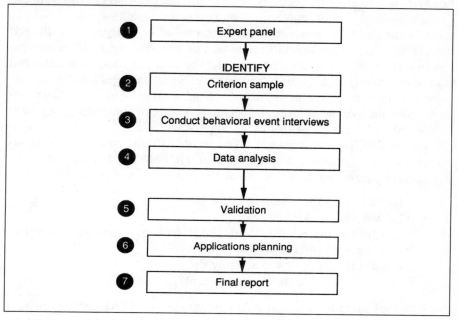

manages the analysis process and provides a detailed description of competencies required for adequate and superior performance in a job.

Thus, use of expert panels offers a number of benefits. Panels collect much valuable data quickly and efficiently. Participation in panel sessions educates panel members in human resources assessment methods and variables, and helps them develop a consensus and support for the panel findings.

Behavioral Event Interviews

A criterion sample of superior and average incumbents are interviewed using the BEI technique developed by McBer to assess competencies. The underlying principle of the BEI method is that the best predictor of what people will do is what they have done in the most similar critical experiences in their lives.

The criterion sample job incumbents who are consistently rated superior on a number of different performance criteria provide a template standard for comparison analyses with a sample of average performers. Ideally, each job study sample should include at least twenty subjects: twelve superior and eight average performers. A total number of twenty permits simple statistical tests of hypotheses about competencies. Smaller samples, such as six superior and three average performers, cannot be statistically validated but can provide valuable qualitative data on the expression of competencies in a given organization. For example, the data can show how influence is used effectively in a specific firm culture. Small samples should include more superior than average performers (e.g., a ratio of two superiors performers to one average performer) because the rule of competency research is "You always learn most from your superstars."

At the BEI, interviewees are asked to identify the most critical situations they have encountered in their jobs and to describe these situations in considerable narrative detail. Some of the questions might include:

- What led up to the situation?
- Who was involved?
- What did the interviewee think about, feel, and hope to accomplish in dealing with the situation?
- What did the interviewee actually do?
- What was the outcome of the incident?

The BEI includes Thematic Apperception Test (TAT) probes, which elicit data about the interviewee's personality and cognitive competencies (e.g. achievement motivation or convergent-thinking ability). Properly conducted, the BEI makes interview protocol data usable as a psychometric test. BEI protocols also provide a wealth of data for the identification of competencies and very specific descriptions of critical job behaviors in specific situations. Interviewees' career paths can be mapped and some estimate made of when, where, and how they acquired key competencies. An important by product of these interviews is the generation of numerous situation and problem narratives that can be used to develop highly relevant training materials (e.g., case studies, role playing, and simulations).

Advantages of the BEI method include:

- Empirical identification of competencies beyond or different from those generated by panels.
- Precision about what competencies are and how they are expressed in specific jobs and organizations (e.g. not only use of influence but examples of how influence is used to deal with a specific situation in a specific organization's political climate).
- Freedom from racial, gender, and cultural bias—indeed, the BEI assessment approach has been adopted by many organizations because it is predictively valid without being biased against minority

candidates (e.g., when used to admit non traditional students, such as minorities without academic qualifications, to college[2]).

Analysis and Development of Competency Models

Data from the expert panels, surveys, expert system, and BEIs are analyzed by content to identify those behaviors and personality characteristics that distinguish superior from average job incumbents, as well as those that are demonstrated by all incumbents adequately performing the job.

Competencies are scaled in just noticeably different (JND) intervals to permit precise definition of job competency requirements—and assessment of individuals—at any level in a job family.

For example, Figure 28-5 shows a scale for the achievement motivation competency. At lower levels, average employees are usually found to do their jobs well (level 1 on the achievement scale). Superior performers, in even low-level jobs, are usually found to take initiative to do their jobs better, to improve performance, for example, they do whatever their job is more efficiently, faster, with fewer resources (level 4 on the achievement scale).

At higher, managerial levels, average managers act to meet objectives and goals required of them, for example, not to exceed their department budgets (level 2 on the achievement scale). Superior senior managers act to improve their organizations—at the highest level, they take entrepreneurial risks and introduce innovative methods or procedures (levels 4–12 on the achievement scale).

Scales for assessing competencies are refined until jobs and people can be evaluated with acceptable inter-rater reliability. A detailed competency dictionary and assessment manual is prepared to train interviewers, assessment center raters, and managers to evaluate job competency requirements and employee competencies. This competency dictionary provides the competency model for the particular job.

Validating the Competency Model

The competency model can be validated by collecting BEI data on a second criterion sample and seeing if competencies identified in the first study distinguish superior from average performers in the second study. Another method of validating the competency model is constructing objective tests to measure the competencies and using test scores from a second criterion sample to test the model's criterion and/or predictive validity.

---

[2] A.U. Austin, C.J. Inouye, & W.S. Korn, *Evaluation of the CAEL Student Potential Program,* (Los Angeles: UCLA), August 1986.

FIGURE 28-5

Scaled Levels of Achievement Motivation—JND Intervals

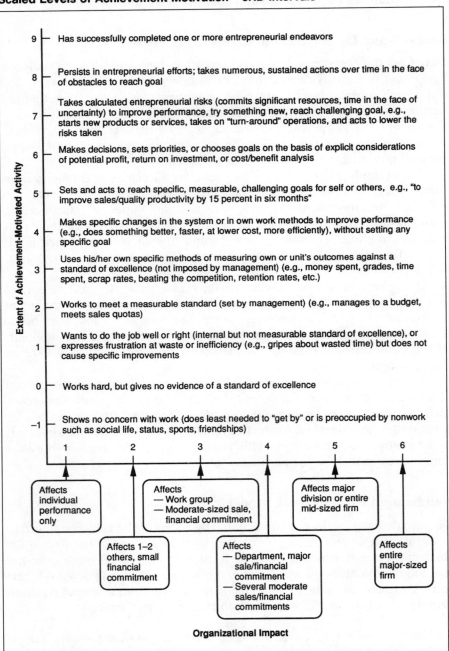

The results of the JCA process are one or more comprehensive competency models that include:

- *Purpose and content* of the job/job family: Tasks, responsibilities, and performance measures for the job rated as to level, frequency, and importance in a form that can be used to compare the target job's content with the content of other jobs

- *Career paths* for the target job: An estimate of when, where, and how key competencies for the job are developed

- *Competency requirements:* The skills and characteristics required for adequate and superior performance in the job

- *Assessment methods:* Ways to determine whether or not a candidate has the competencies needed to perform well in the target job (e.g., structured interview questions regarding past job experiences)

Human Resource Applications of Competency Model Data

Job competency analyses provide the basis for the design and implementation of many specific human resource functions: selection (recruitment and placement), performance appraisal, training and development, succession/human resource planning, retention and career pathing, and support activities such as organization and job design and development.

Recruitment and Selection. Competency-based recruiting systems usually focus on screening methods that can be used to select a small number of stong candidates from a large group of applicants quickly and efficiently. Assessing recruits involves special challenges such as screening many applicants in a short period of time (ninety-minute interviews) and eliminating those applicants who have just graduated from college and thus have little work experience on which to base judgments.

Competency-based recruiting systems, therefore, stress identification of a few (three to five) core competencies, which meet the following three criteria:

1. Competencies that applicants have already developed and demonstrated in their work lives to day (e.g., initiative).
2. Competencies that are likely to predict a candidates' long-run prospects for success and that are hard to develop through employer training or job experience (e.g., such master competencies as achievement motivation.
3. Competencies that can be reliably assessed using a short, targeted BEI. For example, if collaborative team leadership is a desired competency, interviewees might be asked to tell about a time when they were able to get a group to do a particular activity. Their responses would then be coded for consensus-building vs. adversarial behaviors.

Placement and Succession Planning. Competency-based placement and succession planning systems are best focused on identifying the top candidates for an organization's most important value-added jobs. Selection and placement systems should, therefore, stress careful identification of the most important competencies required by critical jobs and then use as many sources of information about candidates as possible to determine whether or not the candidate possesses the required competencies.

Assessment of candidates can involve a variety of methods: BEIs, tests, assessment center simulations, review of performance appraisal reports, and superior, peer, and subordinate ratings. Past job performance and BEI data are generally the most cost-effective selection tools.

Analysis of assessment data to make selection, placement, and succession planning decisions can be done either manually or by decision support computer systems, which compare all candidates' ratings on competencies found to be essential or desirable for superior job performance. Employees are recommended in rank order based on their total weighted scores on the competency criteria.

Application planning for competency-based placement or succession includes identification of needed competencies, given the candidate pool and selection system resources; identification of the most cost-effective candidate assessment methods; training of assessors in the BEI; and design of selection system data base including the candidate pool, administration and tracking systems, and follow-up evaluation of selectees to insure system effectiveness.

Career Pathing and Development. Competency-based career pathing and development programs are based on gaps between employees' competencies and the competency requirements of their present or future jobs, as defined by the competencies demonstrated by superior performers in these jobs.

For example, Figures 28-6 shows the competencies of a technical professional, JJ, in his first job (individual contributor) and his fourth job (manager of a technical facility). JJ can be seen to be a good match for his first job, which largely requires individual contributor competencies: achievement motivation, technical expertise, and cognitive skills. However, JJ is not a good match for his fourth job: His individual contributor skills exceed the managerial job's requirements, and JJ lacks the interpersonal and organization influence skills needed to succeed in upper management.

As shown in this figure, the competency requirements for a job define a template for development. Employees who are appraised as lacking in a specific competency can be directed to a specific development activity designed to teach them the missing competency to improve their perfor-

FIGURE 28-6

Competency Job-Person Match

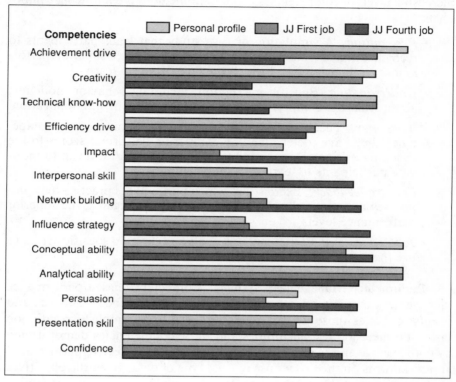

mance in their existing jobs, or to prepare them to advance to higher-level jobs in the future.

Competency development options include assessment center experiences (employees' self-knowledge about competencies needing development account for much of the training's effect), formal training courses, developmental job assignments/career pathing, mentor relationships, and the like.

Developmental decisions can be made manually (using if–then guidelines provided by the human resource staff), or by a computer-based expert system, which recommends development activities based on an assessment of the employee's competencies and the competency requirements of his present or future job. For example, if JJ is assessed as lacking in organizational influence skills, he might be offered a developmental assignment working as an aide to a senior manager known for his or her political astuteness.

A competency acquisition process (CAP) has been developed for increasing levels of competencies.[3] The CAP includes the following components:

- *Recognition.* A simulation or case study that leads participants to recognize one or more competencies that predict superior performance in their jobs, and which they may have to learn.

- *Understanding.* Specific instruction, including behavior modeling, about what the competency is and what it looks like in application.

- *Assessment:* Feedback to participants about how much of the competency they have (determined by comparing performer scores to the participants' scores), designed to create an actual/ideal gap to motivate participants to learn the competency.

- *Practice/feedback:* Exercises in which participants practice the competency and get feedback on how they perform against the superior performance level.

- *Job application:* Participants set goals and develop specific action to use the competency on their jobs.

Performance Management Systems. Competency-based performance management systems add to traditional job performance standards and results measures those job behaviors required to accomplish specific job tasks and meet job responsibilities and those competencies demonstrated by both average and superior performers in key jobs. Effective performance appraisal turns on the proper use of each type of data, given the objectives of the system and the degree of control the employee has over his performance on variables assessed.

Performance results data are usually used for decisions about rewards (e.g., merit bonuses based on sales or production quotas). If, however, an employee has little individual control over the final results (e.g., in a team production setting), rewards based solely on these results can demotivate superior people. In these cases, some portion of the reward should be based on job behaviors.

Job behavior data are usually used for decisions regarding skill development (e.g., if manager X is appraised as lacking group leadership skills, he or she might be advised to attend a leadership course to develop this skill). Skill-based compensation systems also explicitly tie rewards to skills developed. This is particularly appropriate when employees have little control over performance results.

---

[3] D.C. McClelland, "Toward a Theory of Motive Acquisition" *American Psychologist* 20, p. 321 ff. (1965), and L. Spencer, *Soft Skill Competencies,* (Edinburgh: Scottish Research Council on Education) 1983.

Competency appraisals are usually used for selection, placement, and succession planning decisions (e.g., whether manager *X* has the potential to be successful in a high-level job. If competencies can be developed, competency appraisal data should be used for developmental decisions.

FUTURE JOBS AND SINGLE INCUMBENT JOBS

Special challenges are posed by the need to determine the competency requirements for *future* jobs and *single incumbent* jobs. Competency assessment is an empirical procedure: Job competency requirements are determined by studying criterion samples of superior vs. average performers. Future and single incumbent jobs lack incumbents to sample because future jobs may not yet exist, and single incumbent positions offer at best a total of one employee (who may or may not be a superior performer).

Future Jobs

Several approaches for studying future jobs (in inverse order of desirability) are:

- Expert panel "guesstimates"
- Extrapolation from job elements with known competency correlates
- Sampling employees presently working in analogous jobs, either within the organization or in outside organizations

Expert Panels. Experts first list the accountabilities, results measures, and competencies of the most similar current job(s) in the organization, and then identify accountabilities and competencies likely to be required by the *future* job(s). Experts can even construct critical incident scenarios for future jobs (i.e. hypothesizing about situations a person in the future job might face, and identifying competencies needed to deal with these situations effectively).

Extrapolation From Known Job Elements. Future jobs will often include job elements or accountabilities for which the competencies have previously been identified. Competency models for a future job can be assembled from these elements. For example, a U.S. telecommunications firm needed a competency model for senior marketing representatives capable of getting European government and community officials' approval for telecommunication equipment to be sold in the European common market beginning in 1992. This firm had no overseas personnel or experience, and hence, no superior or average performers to study.

An analysis of this future technical ambassador job indicated that it combined elements of diplomatic and high-tech sales jobs for which competency models existed. Identified competencies for the technical ambassador job included cross-cultural interpersonal sensitivity, overseas adjustment (adaptability, preference for novelty, resistance to stress caused by the annoyances of living overseas), and speed of learning (foreign) political networks from the diplomatic model; and achievement motivation and consultative selling skills from high-tech sales models.

Analysis of Analogous Present Jobs. The most reliable way to determine the requirements of future jobs is to study superior performers presently in similar jobs and to use labor economics studies to extrapolate how many people will be employed in these jobs (and that need the requisite competencies) in the future.

For example, knowledge engineers (persons who interview experts in fields such as medicine or petroleum exploration and translate their expertise into artificial intelligence, expert system computer programs) now represent fewer than 1 percent of employees in electronic data processing (EDP) but are expected to hold 20 percent of EDP jobs after the year 2000. A competency study might show superior knowledge engineers have both higher-level cognitive competencies such as pattern recognition, conceptualization, and analytic thinking and the interpersonal interviewing skills needed to establish rapport with subject matter experts. These findings suggest selection and training criteria for EDP personnel to be hired and developed over the next decade.

While the behavioral indicators for competencies may change, the underlying competencies do not. Competency models are both stable and dynamic because despite changes in the way tasks are carried out, the core motivational, interpersonal, and cognitive competencies that predict success remain the same over time.

Single Incumbent Jobs

Competencies for single incumbent jobs can be determined by triangulating data from key people who interact with the person in the job. For example, the position of vice-president of human resources for a major hospital chain was empty—the previous incumbent had been fired. Competencies for this job were identified by conducting BEIs with the previous incumbent's superiors (the hospital's chief executive officer and directors), peers (other functional and operating vice presidents), key subordinates, and customers (union leaders and prominent members of the community who dealt with human resource issues at the hospital). Respondents were asked to identify critical incidents in which they felt previous vice-presidents of human resources had been particularly effective or ineffective. If respondents could not think of incidents involving a previous job incumbent, they were asked for incidents involving any health care vice-president of human resources they knew to be particularly effective or ineffective.

When asked for an example of effective performance, the chief executive officer said that at a very tense meeting with the nursing staff, who were about to go out on strike, the previous human resources vice-president told a joke, which lessened the tension. When asked for examples of ineffective performance, the CEO said that the previous vice-president once gave an absolutely disastrous presentation at a top-management "vision for the future" retreat.

> Everyone was supposed to present where he or she though we should be going in the next 10 years, based on labor force demographics, economic, technological, industry, and market trends.

> The previous incumbent was the kind of person who lives in the "now" and never looked far ahead. He had his staff write a speech for him, but he did not bother to read the speech before trying to give it. He embarrassed himself and everyone else. Then, when he got negative feedback, his response was to go back and punish his *staff* for writing a lousy speech.

The CEO recounted another embarrassing incident in which the daughter of one of the directors sent in an application for a job. The human resources department lost the application and when the applicant called a number of times, no one returned her phone calls.

When asked for critical incidents involving any health care human resources vice-president he had seen as particularly effective, the CEO said that the best one he knew was the head of a university health system who thought ahead and had done some innovative staffing. When the university hospital couldn't get nurses at a reasonable salary, this vice-president recruited from foreign medical and nursing schools, where he could get first-rate people who were eager for a chance to come to the United States.

It is not hard to identify competencies important to this CEO from his critical incidents comments—he obviously values strategic thinking, concern for impact, presentation skills, customer service orientation, quality concern, innovativeness, and political influence skills.

The competencies organizations most often seek in future top executives are strategic vision; the ability to change the organization quickly if conditions, such as technological breakthroughs or market fluctuations, warrant; and the ability to manage relationships both with those inside the company and with customers, suppliers, government agencies, and public interest groups.

For middle management and professionals, organizations value flexibility in the face of changing conditions; the ability to work effectively anywhere in the world; concern with continuous improvement to gain a competitive advantage; customer service orientation; and teamwork.

Support staff are valued for their ability to learn and use paraprofessional skills. An interesting trend is firms' increasing interest in competency models for recruiting, selecting, training, and retaining clerical and administrative personnel. Motivation for this may be the increased use of support staff to handle work previously done by professionals and the increased amount of client contact with the support staff.

INTEGRATED HUMAN RESOURCE MANAGEMENT INFORMATION SYSTEMS

A major trend in human resource strategic planning is the development of competency-based IHRMIS.[4] An IHRMIS is a comprehensive set of personnel functions and programs that share a common information system and architecture or language and are organized to complement and reinforce one another. This integration of IHRMISs and programs contrasts with the typical personnel department in which functions do not share a common language or complement one another, for example, personnel selection decisions are made on one set of criteria, performance is appraised on a second set of criteria, and the training function teaches a third set of skills.

Functions of the IHRMIS

The nucleus of an IHRMIS is a set of core data about (1) job elements, such as purpose and content, performance standards and measures, measurement points for setting compensation, and competency requirements, and (2) employee competencies (see Figure 28-7).
A fully developed IHRMIS can track, and with artificial intelligence assist and even automate, many basic human resource management functions, including:

1. Charting the company's organization—The IHRMIS can devise and update an organizational chart that presents information about both the jobs (e.g., job descriptions) and the incumbents (e.g., performance appraisal data).
2. Conduct job analysis—The system can identify the competency requirements and compensation points for a job, using questionnaire responses from managers or human resource specialists.

---

[4] R. Page, "Job Analysis and HR Planning" in W. Casio, *Human Resource Planning, Employment and Placement* (Washington, DC: BNA Books), 1989.

FIGURE 28-7

Integrated Uses of Job Information

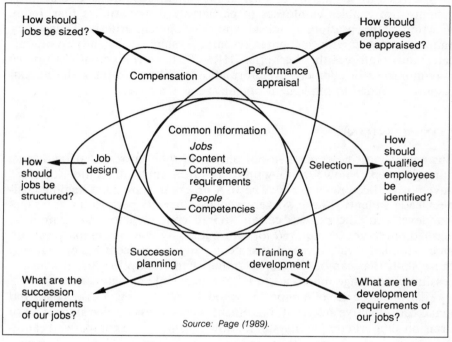

Source: Page (1989).

3. Assess employees' competencies using on-screen tests, instruments, and assessment scores, the ratings given by managers and other supervisors, and performance appraisal data.
4. Match jobs and candidates—Identify which candidates competencies best match the job competency requirements.
5. Plan development—Provide training or career paths for individuals, based on the gaps between the person 's competencies and either his current job, or a future job for which he or she might be considered.

Benefits of an IHRMIS

The three major benefits of an IHRMIS are cost savings/increased productivity, enhanced management, and employee participation and reinforcement. A common IHRMIS reduces the extent to which separate human resource functions develop and maintain duplicate (and often competing) databases, training and administrative overhead.

The IHRMIS clearly communicates the language of human resources management and, enables line managers, with the assistance of artificial intelligence, to undertake more human resource management functions themselves without having to rely on the human resources. Use of these systems also enables employees to participate in the studies that define selection, compensation, appraisal, and development criteria. Thus, every employee contact with the human resources system consistently communicates and reinforces these criteria. IHRMISs have the potential to make maximum use of competency information to plan and track the human resources needed to implement organizations strategies.

CONCLUSION

Businesses must be concerned not only with their current staffing needs, but must prepare now for filling future positions that will require skills that have not yet been determined. The JCA program is aimed at helping business leaders identify those workers who are currently performing at a superior level and who possess certain inbred competencies that cannot be learned but might be required for future jobs. By selecting employees with an eye to their future career paths, a company can concentrate on teaching those skills that can be developed rather than attempting (usually unsuccessfully) to change inbred attitudes and personal characteristics.

Through the use of competency models, managers can assess data and make cost effective selection, placement, and succession decisions. Use of decision support computer systems allows businesses to compare all candidates' ratings and identify those candidates who possess the needed competencies for the target job.

The use of an IHRMIS further enhances the way a firm uses its human resources department by establishing a uniform information system of criteria for completing such functions as personnel selection, performance evaluation, and appraisal of training programs.

29

Management Culture

DENIS H. DETZEL

Vice-President, The May Group

INTRODUCTION

Managers are constantly bombarded with news about changes in their operating environments. The popular and business media are full of stories
about dramatic changes in the speed of technological change, the growing
international nature of competition, and the changing composition of
employee demographics. Managers do not have to wait to read about these
changes to know that operating environments are indeed different from just
a few years ago; they see these changes in their daily activities.

While this chapter supports the belief that businesses are increasingly
confronted with new, more demanding challenges, it also argues that effec-

tive managers must better understand specifically what these changes are in their environment. After summarizing a number of the major changes facing U.S. businesses, the chapter examines, in greater empirical detail, significant findings about specific organizational trends of direct consequence to effective management in the business environment of today and the future.

THE STRATEGIC MARKETPLACE: RADICAL CHANGE

During the last decade, radical changes in strategic market conditions brought about a revitalizing revolution in American business. Domestic industry is being driven by changes in American demography, economics, the legal and regulatory climate, technology, social trends and values, and executive vision.

Demography

From a demographic standpoint, the majority population in the United States has become older, better educated, and more demanding regarding the quality of products and services that are consumed. The younger members of the majority population are increasingly demystifying "business reasons" for nonperformance through wholesale enrollment in business curricula and increased expertise in solving business problems.

Domestic minority populations are predictably gaining in political power and are beginning to demand (through political channels) expanded levels of business service and increased participation in the business process.

Worldwide, new market opportunities are appearing at breathtaking rates. The falling away of walls, barbed wire fences, and iron curtains is creating access to vast markets that redefine "pent-up demand." Similarly, newly participating countries offer significant opportunities as sites of production and their populations are affecting the domestic labor force through immigration.

Economics

The overall U.S. economy has grown more slowly, if perhaps more steadily, since the last recession. This slow growth has helped create a more competitive business environment, forcing organizations to vie more effectively for more limited and more highly valued consumer dollars.

Internationally, the increased need for more competitive domestic business activity combined with the willingness of traditional "debtor nations" to more effectively participate in business processes has created increased consumer and production opportunities in formerly ignored areas. Nogales and Nuevo Laredo, Mexico, are rapidly growing American business communities.

The Legal and Regulatory Environment

The American legal and regulatory climate has been moving steadily toward a more competitive national and international marketplace. Past protectionist or monopolistic principles are being eroded throughout most U.S. private industry sectors.

Internationally, political pressure and economic necessity have made traditional foreign markets more receptive to American products and services as well as to American-owned production facilities. Despite continuing problems with the trade balance, American exports have increased dramatically since 1985.

Technology

Fed in part by the international race for dominance in space and defense, the technological marketplace continues to change at an exponential rate. Paper continues to give ground to the computer; communications from car, plane, home, or the street corner by voice or fax are becoming commonplace; robotics is altering labor, materials are becoming more durable; transportation and shipping options have increased.

Technological change has significantly changed the mission and structure of industry sectors such as manufacturing, health care, telecommunications, and trucking. In addition to raising the expected standards for product quality and service delivery, technological innovation has dramatically changed the knowledge and skill requirements necessary for effective participation in the labor force.

Social Trends and Values

World social trends and values are changing radically. There is more emphasis on the here and now and less patience for the slow and steady climb to success. Noncapitalist systems appear to be breaking down because of their inability to deliver basic goods (e.g., toothpaste) to their political constituencies.

Similarly, values are shifting away from the group toward the self. The era of narcissism may only be beginning. Older, more highly educated and self-oriented consumers will not permit concerns regarding "the nationalist economy" to prevent them from gaining access to the goods and services they "require."

Political Initiatives

As mentioned earlier, U.S. and international industries have undergone revolutionary change in response to dramatic changes in market demand. The domestic and international responses to these changes appear to begin with "deregulation"—the removal of legal and regulatory protections and constraints that restrict consumer choice and lower quality and service standards while they directly or indirectly dramatically increase cost.

Deregulation has taken a variety of forms, including (1) local consumer initiatives designed to control cost or eliminate monopolies (e.g., telecommunications, gas and electric utilities); (2) state and then federal legislative initiatives (e.g., trucking, airlines, health care); and (3) international trade agreements (e.g., manufacturing).

The immediate consequences of these "political" initiatives are (1) bankruptcies and business failures; (2) mergers and acquisitions; (3) international entries into the domestic marketplace; (4) layoffs and terminations; and (5) the structural realignment of the remaining competitors. "Structural realignment" refers to organization and geographic changes that result in a shortened distance between the marketplace and top management and improved quality and (paradoxically) reduced cost. (See Figure 28-1.)

ORGANIZATION RESPONSE: THE PATTERN OF CHANGE

During the last decade, the pattern of change (illustrated in Figure 29-1) has affected virtually all U.S. industries and organizations. Figure 29-2 presents a model of the progression of change through selected industry sectors.

Although virtually all industries are regulated by their government hosts, some industry sectors are more highly regulated than others. The point being made here is that increases and decreases in regulation appear to promote specific directional changes in the missions, strategies, organi-

FIGURE 29-1

The Pattern of Change

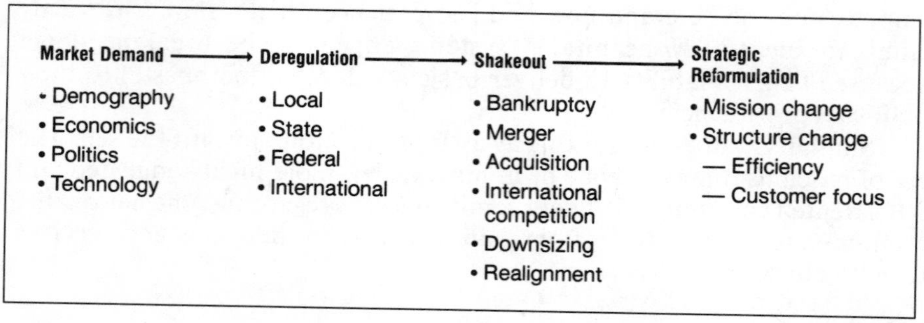

Market Demand ⟶	Deregulation ⟶	Shakeout ⟶	Strategic Reformulation
• Demography	• Local	• Bankruptcy	• Mission change
• Economics	• State	• Merger	• Structure change
• Politics	• Federal	• Acquisition	— Efficiency
• Technology	• International	• International competition	— Customer focus
		• Downsizing	
		• Realignment	

FIGURE 29-2

Market Forces: Organization Response

Regulation →	Affected Industries	→ Mission →	Strategy →	Strategy Implementation →	Market Results
Less	Retailing	Change from	Change from	Planning	Higher-quality,
	Manufacturing	public	standardized	Decision	lower-cost
	Hospitality	service to	to	making	consumer
	Agriculture	competitive	Efficiency	Organization	options
	Telecommunications	enterprise(s)	Quality	integration	
	Banking and		Customer	Leadership	
	financial services		service	style	
	Health care			Performance	
	Insurance			orientation	
	Railroads			Organization	
	Airlines			vitality	
	Government			Management	
	services			development	
More				Corporate identity	

zation systems, and market results of affected organizations. Therefore, it should hold that the recipients of government services would have fewer, higher-cost, lower-quality, and less effective products and services available to them than those who receive products and services from less highly regulated business sectors. Whether or not the theory of free enterprise and free enterprise's relationship to the body politic work, superpowers and their populations both seem to be moving in its direction.

The continuation (or the reversal) of the trends illustrated in Figure 29-2 depends in part on the ability of free enterprise theory implementers to design organization systems that maximize economic output and service to the consumer and provide the populations they serve with access to desirable employment opportunities. High-quality, low-cost products and services and a strong national economy are of little consequence to a population denied access to the products and services or for whom the investment in terms of the work experience is simply not worth the reward.

Each year the Hay Group (an international consulting firm specializing in the design and implementation of organization systems) conducts an Environmental Scan to determine the direction of systems changes within foreign and domestic business organizations. The scan is conducted by collecting qualitative information from its consultants researching secondary sources (i.e., literature reviews), and conducting in-depth interviews with selected clients.

Hay's 1989–1990 Environmental Scan notes specific trends in the design and implementation of organization in the following areas:

1. Organization and job design
2. Staffing
3. Selection
4. Training
5. Benefits
6. Compensation

The trends in these areas provide some insight into how organizations are regrouping to meet the demands of a new and more competitive (deregulated) marketplace. These trends are discussed in the following sections.

Organization

Organizations are breaking down into smaller, more autonomous business units. In the strategic context of meeting increased market demands and improving organization performance, the reasons cited for this trend include:

- Increasing the strategic business units' (SBUs') responsiveness to their specific competitive environments
- Increasing cost consciousness
- Improving the organization's ability to gain employee identification and commitment
- Increasing the organization's ability to effectively measure and manage subunit contributions

Some examples of this trend cited by the Hay Group are:

- A large conservative oil company breaking down into eight SBUs
- Three domestic regional insurance companies developing operating SBUs for investments, development, and new products
- An international food distribution company reorganizing its "international" unit into country-specific SBUs
- A regional manufacturer (auto parts supplier) granting operating SBU status to its plants and distributing headquarters staff accordingly

Job Design

Project-oriented, cross-functional teams of managers and professionals are being increasingly used to examine issues and make decisions that were formerly reserved for top management or functional (departmental) unit heads. The reasons cited for this trend include:

- Providing improved cross-functional communications and so more flexibility and business responsiveness
- Providing opportunities for new job challenges in the face of reduced promotional opportunities

- Providing an instant network for new employees
- Reducing the need for additional levels of management

Some examples of this trend cited by the Hay Group are:

- A midwestern utility whose CEO and direct reports delegate many decisions to the over forty-one cross-functional teams of managers and employees
- A regional insurance company reorganizing to divert operating decisions to a cross-functional team of officers and managers
- Ten manufacturing plants being managed by cross-functional groups of hourly employees
- An international hotel corporation where all decisions within its operating units are made by local on-site executive teams
- A general trend toward the concept of "office of" the chief operating officer, staffed by a team of cross-functional unit heads

Job design in these organizations has changed radically from the traditional set of approved and directed behaviors within a functional unit to the charge to "do whatever you find it takes to achieve our corporate objectives." This shift requires that all potentially contributing individuals be (1) thoroughly informed regarding corporate direction; (2) oriented to the approved value framework of the organization; and (3) systematically selected and trained to understand the organization consequences of their individual and group decisions. Like the chief executive officer (CEO), they must be reasonably able to act for the good of the whole rather than just for their own good.

As with the fewer levels of management above them, hourly employees are being organized to work as units or teams. This trend at the "floor level" of the organization is being driven by: (1) new, more complex and increasingly interrelated technologies and organization designs that demand a higher level of skill and general awareness on the part of the hourly worker; (2) the need to provide disciplined, on-going, cost-effective and closely monitored on the job training for current and new hourly employees as new technology is introduced into the work setting; and (3) the need to provide fair and equitable access to skills, knowledge, upward mobility, and reward for hourly workers.

Examples of this trend toward smaller, and frequently more autonomous, teams at the floor level include:

- An international food-processing organization with twenty-three processing plants in the United States. For forty years, all of the plants operated with the inherited segmented hourly job classification system. Now the sixteen hourly job classifications on the plant floor have been reduced to three. A "model" plant has been opened with one plant-floor hourly job classification containing three progressive levels and requiring the systematic accumulation of skills, experience, and problem-solving capabilities to move from one level to the next. Most supervisory responsibilities have been delegated to organized shift teams or to the "shift council," which reports directly to the plant manager. Shift supervisors have been replaced by shift trainers whose primary responsibility is to manage the systematic growth of team members in knowledge and skill acquisition. The trainer reports to the teams.

- An international fiberglas insulation manufacturer using a team/team council approach to its new plant organization. The company has replaced plant staff functions in the areas of shipping, purchasing, employee relations, quality control, and scheduling, with rotating employee groups reporting to the plant manager and headquarters staff personnel.

- An international restaurant company testing the concept of distributing management "paperwork" functions to its hourly employees. Its aims are to reduce the need for two levels of management and to expand the pool of trained and experienced personnel who can readily move into management ranks.

It is important to note that in each of these organizations, (1) organization changes are beginning in new facilities with new sophisticated technologies; (2) new "floor" personnel are carefully screened for the desire and capability to acquire multiple skills; (3) new facilities contain "tried and proven" financial statistical methods to monitor performance, quality, and customer service; (4) management has a history and tradition of "egalitarianism"; (5) a progressive record of equal employment opportunity exists; and (6) results to date indicate the economic superiority of the methods employed.

Staff Levels

Increasingly, organizations are making employment contingent on business conditions. Competitive cost pressures no longer permit organizations to absorb the cost of maximum staffing levels during times of decreased revenue producing activities.

Industries that have reasonably predictable cycles in their revenue producing activities, such as hospitality, food service, health care, and agriculture, have long been making employment contingent on business conditions. However, not all other industries, or at least their individual business units, have similarly predictable cycles. In these cases, methods of staffing and organization designed to take "normal business cycles" into account are being developed. The following are indicators of the growth of cyclical and part-time employment methods:

- There has been a nationwide increase in the number and size of professional part-time employment services. In addition to traditional part-time employment agencies for hourly workers, more nurses, medical technologists, lawyers, engineers, analysts, programmers, architects, accountants, and marketing, advertising, and human resources professionals are being employed by firms that offer their services to the marketplace at a premium rate that falls well below the cost of maintaining these services internally on a "permanent" basis. Companies using these professional services note that the cost of acculturation may be more than offset by the decreased labor cost of term employment as well as by the new ideas introduced into the environment by temporary personnel who have not "learned" that a particular concept is "not accepted here.
- A regional health care network of twenty-two hospitals and extended care facilities reports that 38 percent of its registered nurses are "temporary." This percentage has doubled (from 19 percent) since 1985.
- A growing auto parts manufacturer has a part-time hourly work force of 42 percent. This is up from less than 10 percent in 1985.
- An international food-processing organization maintains a part-time hourly plant work force of 48 percent in the United States. The percentage of part-timers was less than 8 percent in 1985.
- An international restaurant organization that employs more than 500,000 people in the United States annually reports its system-wide part-time employment as 95 percent. (This percentage is *down* slightly over the past ten years owing in part to increasingly fierce competition in the firm's smaller traditional labor markets.)

New users cite these reasons for subscribing to the part-time labor concept: (1) decreased annual labor cost; (2) new ideas introduced from diversified organization experiences; (3) a preference among many of their hourly workers for a "more flexible" hourly labor experience; and (4) their ability to make better, more careful full-time employment decisions as the primary reasons for their growing use of the part-time labor concept.

Staffing Selection

Concurrent with the growth in the use of part-time labor, organizations are making significant changes in their criteria for entry into the full-time work force and for upward mobility within it. Although linear technical skills will remain an important factor in entry and upward mobility in the labor force, interpersonal and decision-making skills are acquiring increasing importance at all levels within the organization.

Hay Group clients report that the ascendance of interpersonal and decision-making skills is generated by: (1) rapid changes in technology that quickly make fixed or linear technical skill sets obsolete; (2) new, team-oriented organization concepts that require interpersonal and decision-making capabilities at all levels and within most functions in the organization; (3) higher expectations of increasingly scarce qualified workers at all levels; and (4) a heightened awareness of available avenues for redress of grievances.

Indicators of this trend include spectacular growth in the use of consulting services for measuring these qualities in prospective candidates, and the internal use of more sophisticated tools and techniques required to accurately predict whether or not potentially costly investments in training or career development are worthwhile.

The following are a few examples of this trend.

- The new CEO of a regional property and casualty company retains the services of a clinical psychologist to: (1) assess whether the CEO has the "critical competencies" he believes are required to successfully implement his strategy; (2) assess the CEO's direct reports to determine their capabilities in the "competency areas" that the CEO requires to support his initiatives; and (3) provide recommendations regarding career development and individual development.
- A gas utility has hired a clinical psychologist to assess selected members of its hourly work force and develop career path plans leading to supervisory roles and beyond. Interpersonal and decision-making skills are considered very key factors.
- An international oil company has hired a clinical psychologist, who reports directly to the CEO, to assess the competencies of the organization's entire management work force against capabilities believed to be required for effective competition in the next decade. Interpersonal and decision-making skills and ability to learn and apply new styles and methods are considered key factors.

Training

The increasing scarcity of truly qualified and adaptable workers at all levels of the organization has brought about the need for lifelong learning and cross-training programs. Companies that hire at midcareer or from established professional or hourly part-time labor pools may not need to provide as much technical training, but they are using training as a way of quickly transmitting the organization mission, strategy, values, and culture.

Corporate universities, such as those developed by McDonald's and Holiday Inn, are becoming a regular part of many organization environments. A public utility in Ohio, an insurance company in Wisconsin, and a telecommunications company in California are among more than twenty-two Hay Group clients who have developed "world class" training facilities since 1985. Within newly developed facilities, the curriculum still contains technical skill components, but a growing part of corporate students' time is dedicated to (1) the study of the corporate mission and values, (2) the key strategic components that are presumed to give the organization competitive advantage, and (3) the models of management behavior that the organization perceives as valuable to its success. Even McDonald's highly regarded Hamburger University, which offers courses accredited by some colleges and universities, has shifted the emphasis of its curriculum markedly from technical skills to interpersonal and decision-making skills. Although Hamburger University continues to play a role in determining career development and expansion opportunities for managers and licensees, its primary role is to acculturate or "McDonaldize."

Organizations are also making large training investments to (1) teach their employees to effectively differentiate between employees and to deal productively with the employees affected by that differentiation; (2) teach employees (especially current line managers) how to train others; (3) teach employees with diverse backgrounds how to succeed in strong, unified, and frequently inhospitable organization cultures; and (4) teach employees how to understand and work with people with different values and styles.

Although it is not yet identifiable as a trend, some business organizations are beginning to extend their training efforts outside the organization through participation in training and education programs in the community. More than fifty business organizations in Chicago, for example, offer industry education in such areas as insurance, banking, hospitality, and health care as curriculum components within the Chicago public schools. The nonprofit Cosmopolitan Chamber of Commerce, whose membership includes many large Chicago area companies and more than 200 small minority owned companies, offers business education courses to potential minority entrepreneurs and employees through the Chamber's Free School of Business Management.

Reaching out to the parents of children in the relatively few existing corporate, employee, externally operated corporate child-care programs, many organizations are attempting to identify, select, and develop a high-potential employee population; teach appropriate interpersonal and decision-making skills; and inculcate corporate values.

Benefits

The new and more competitive strategic marketplace, changing labor force demographics, and corporate attempts to deal with the challenges posed are also promoting rapid change in the general area of reward.

Hay clients report, for example, that they expect to offer core benefits to all (including part-time) employees. Legislation requiring this is expected, and a concurrent shift away from richer benefits programs may permit it to occur. Many have long perceived the need for universal core benefits to facilitate the entry of the persistently underemployed and unemployed into the work force, and serious studies of this are currently under way among the traditional and new large-scale employers of low-skilled part-time personnel.

This direction in benefits will be accompanied by continued reductions in expensive benefits (perquisites, on "perks") for higher-level executives; increased "participation" or contribution by all employees in benefits above a core or floor level; and continuing movement toward a flexible benefits concept.

Although many of the benefits trends indicated here are generated by cost considerations, there is also a strong interest in shifting the resulting "savings" over a larger employee base. New additions to many corporate benefits portfolios are corporate wellness and employee assistance programs, along with corporate policies, equipment, and facilities designed to improve worker health and safety. Increasingly, organizations are offering corporate exercise facilities, no-smoking work environments, confidential drug and alcohol referral and treatment, new CRT screens, family counseling, and other services as ways to reduce total benefits cost and retain personnel.

Compensation

Perhaps the most effective tool for motivating change within the new organization environment is pay.

Performance-contingent compensation is appearing in virtually all business sectors. The most frequently cited reasons for the shift from fixed to contingent compensation are: (1) increased competition; (2) shrinking profit margins; (3) rising costs; (4) pressure to increase productivity; (5) the need to link costs to affordability; (6) the related need to justify compensation increases; (7) a general movement to revitalize corporate structures; (8) a need to reemphasize performance orientation; and (9) a need to recognize and encourage a new type of (performance-oriented) talent.

A final factor influencing the shift from fixed or incremental compensation arrangements to contingent compensation programs is the abject failure of most corporate merit systems to realize their promise. Although the reasons for the failure of merit systems are legion, those most frequently cited are: (1) an automatic addition to fixed cost; (2) insufficient funds for effective motivation; (3) inept administration; and (4) their being laid on top of an already inappropriate compensation mix.

Table 29-1 illustrates the general direction of contingent compensation practices that have traditionally been the sole domain of upper level management personnel. Table 29-2 indicates the diversity and "initially projected growth" of emerging contingent compensation arrangements. During the record period of Japanese modeling (1986–1989), numerous compensation experts and firms were quite optimistic regarding the use of

TABLE 29-1

Traditional Contingent Compensation Practices

Compensation practice	Organizations using	Organizations considering
Individual incentive	55%	12%
Long-term incentives	39	3
"Cash" profit sharing	35	10

Source: Hay Contingent Compensation Survey

contingent compensation arrangement. The data in Table 29-2, however, seem to suggest a more conservative movement toward its use. Most Hay clients with "emerging" contingent compensation arrangements (i.e., gain-sharing, unit incentives) have installed this method within the past five years. As a result, the long-term effectiveness of the method has not yet been proven. Although initial reports are positive, increased experience with these programs will be required before the number of those considering their use can be expected to grow significantly.

It is noteworthy that most "emerging" contingent compensation arrangements are applied at all levels within an organization and are designed to encourage group (team) behavior as well as individual initiative.

THE NEED FOR INFORMATION TO MANAGE ORGANIZATION CHANGE

To determine the need for and the effectiveness of change, a growing number of business organizations are using quantitative research methods. This research usually takes the form of quality, customer service, and management and employee information, usually collected through

TABLE 29-2

Emerging Contingent Compensation Practices

Compensation practice	Organizations using	Organizations considering
Gainsharing	14%	16%
Unit incentives	20	11
Key contributor	47	4
Base salary offshoots		
Lump-sum merit	28	16
Two-tier structure	14	2
Pay for know-how/skill	14	11

Source: Hay Contingent Compensation Survey

organization surveys. Some more sophisticated organizations like Hyatt Hotels, McDonald's Corporation, and Avis Rent-A-Car systematically examine the relationship among the three measures. The theory is a simple one: If a viable market perceives the organization as effectively changing to meet its needs, and if the organization's best employees perceive that the organization is providing them with the tools (including information, systems, and processes) required for effectively meeting market demand, it is likely that the organization's economic performance is superior.

There are at least three reasonably available methods to measure whether or not the kinds of changes discussed earlier are required or desirable within an organization to accommodate new market realities. These measures are (1) financial performance, (2) market data, and (3) executive and employee perceptions of organization effectiveness.

Performance

The most direct measure of the need for change is the organization's financial performance. An organization that is performing poorly can generally be said to be in need of constructive change, with the primary questions being what to change and how best to change it. However, an organization that is performing well may also be in need of change. The reason for performance differences may be directly related to the amount of internal change that is occurring. That is, an organization may be performing well because rapid change is always occurring.

Market

Market information can provide an effective signal that customer behavior is likely to change. Market factors that indicate the need for new business concepts or strategic approaches include the entry of new products or services into the marketplace; the disappearance of mature products and services (e.g., the drive-in theater); major demographic shifts (e.g., the aging of the population); increased competition; regulatory changes; and technological changes.

Employee Perception

Performance and market information, however, are not the only information required to secure competitive advantage. During the past twenty years the Hay Group has been evolving a comprehensive technology to measure employee perceptions of organization effectiveness. Referred to as the "Organization Effectiveness Survey," the process focuses the organization's attention on nine fundamental dimensions normally presumed to be associated with effectiveness. The nine Hay culture dimensions are:

1. *Planning systems:* The extent to which the organization relies on formal and complete planning systems and has established clear courses of action. Have plans and goals been well formulated? Have the strategy and the plans and goals been communicated to appropriate management down the line?

2. *Decision making/organization:* The degree to which decisions are systematically formulated, implemented, and reviewed. Are information systems providing the information needed for decision making? How centralized is the decision-making process? Are the organizational structure and the staffing levels appropriate in light of the strategy?

3. *Organization integration:* The degree of cooperation and communication among units in the organization.

4. *Leadership style:* The pattern of encouragement and support for initiative taking and openness. How much freedom do managers have? Are managers encouraged to take risks, or does top management send out a "play it safe" message? How are conflicts aired and resolved?

5. *Performance orientation:* The amount of emphasis placed on individual accountability for clearly defined results. Are the managers held accountable for achieving these results?

6. *Organization vitality:* The dynamic nature of an organization as reflected by its responsiveness to change in its business environment, the development of pacesetting programs, and the creation of venturesome goals. Is this a fast-paced, market-responsive organization, or is it conservative and slow-paced?

7. *Management compensation:* The extent to which the compensation system is seen as being internally equitable, externally competitive, and tied to performance.

8. *Management development:* The level of emphasis on training, career-path planning, and promotion from within the organization.

9. *Corporate identity:* The manner in which the corporate image is defined and expressed within the organization, and the extent to which managers identify with the organization.

Although initially the Hay Group collected only management perceptions on these dimensions, the changes in organizations in the late 1980s made the Organization Culture Survey generally applicable to employees at all levels. The Hay management culture data base contains the responses of more than 2 million managers and employees in more than 2,000 organizations.

FIGURE 29-3

Organization Effectiveness Survey Results

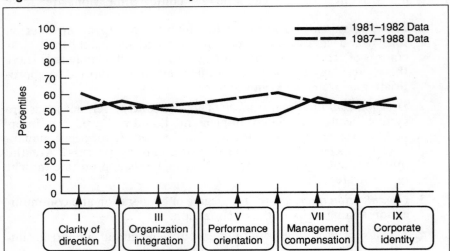

PATTERNS IN PERCEPTION: 1981–1982 VS. 1987–1988

To determine the perceived impacts, if any, of the organization changes indicated above data collected in the period 1981–1982 were compared against data collected during the period 1987–1988. To arrive at the relative profiles, the 1981–1982 samples were percentiled within the total database (1981–1989).

Although this approach contains several complex methodological problems that cannot be effectively addressed here, it can be argued that the data present a fair representation of the internal perceptions of the work forces sampled in 1981–1982 and in 1987–1988. During this interval, most of the organization changes discussed earlier were thoroughly discussed in organization literature and some had been introduced into the sampled business organizations. Thus, it can be argued that the samples represent a reasonable comparison of employee perceptions affected by the described interventions at the time that the samples were drawn.

The culture profiles resulting from the survey are shown in Figure 29-3. Overall, the data suggest that clarity of direction, leadership style, performance orientation, and organization vitality have improved. Perceptions of organization integration and management development, have remained about the same. Perceptions of decision making, management compensation, and corporate identity have become slightly more negative.

Individual item analysis reveals that with regard to clarity of direction, the 1987–1988 sample

- Is clearer about the organization's goals
- Perceives the organization's planning process as more formal and complete and oriented toward a longer term
- Sees the organization's planning process as more likely to produce defined plans to meet its goals

The Hay Group's experience in working with organizations that regularly conduct organization effectiveness surveys reveals that these kinds of changes in perception are likely to occur when

- More individuals actively participate in the organization's planning process.
- The organization more effectively communicates its plans and its progress against them throughout the organization.
- Pay is perceived to be related to goal attainment.

From these data it may be inferred that some of the trends discussed in the "Environmental Scan" sections (e.g., contingent compensation) are having a favorable impact on employee perceptions of clarity of direction. The most likely related trends would be: a flatter organization with fewer communication barriers, enhanced communication of corporate goals, and a greater sense of team purpose among employees.

Within the leadership style dimension, perceptions of freedom to take independent action, encouragement for taking reasonable risks, encouragement for open discussion of conflicts, encouragement for innovative action, and encouragement for constructive criticism have improved.

These changes are most normally related to changes in organization and job design that encourage individuals to leave their cubicles and participate in a free exchange of ideas. More directly these changes occur when organization leaders signal that constructive conflict is preferable to a stagnant peace.

Results in the area of performance orientation indicate that employees in the 1987–1988 sample perceive

- More clarity regarding the end results that are expected of them in their jobs
- Increased accountability for their end results
- More clarity regarding how their performance is judged
- Increased demands for higher levels of performance
- That their organization's goals are more challenging

These results are usually achieved when organization management consistently signals that job security is performance related. The dismissal of nonperformers and the rewarding of effective performers are the most direct signals that management sends. It is reasonable to infer that employees in 1987–1988 are more aware of the need to perform effectively than were the employees in the 1981–1982 sample.

Consistent with results within the performance orientation dimension, employees in the 1987–1988 sample perceive

- Their organization's goals as decidedly more venturesome (less cautious)
- Organization decision making as more innovative and timely
- Their organizations as pacesetters (rather than followers) relative to the competition
- A significantly improved organization vitality reflected by an enhanced pace of activities and sense of urgency

These results are predictably associated with more productive organizations—organizations that are endeavoring to do more with less. The need for downsizing that hit American organizations during the 1980s and its flattening effect on organization structure as well as contingent compensation may have had a significant impact on the overall vitality of business organizations.

Although overall perceptions of management compensation changed only slightly between the years 1981–1982 and 1987–1988, an individual item analysis reveals that employees in 1987–1988

- Are less satisfied with their noncash benefits
- Have less understanding of their benefits program
- Have less understanding of how their salaries are administered

This would seem to indicate that many of the changes in benefits programs indicated above have not been well received in many organizations. It may be that while some of these trends (e.g., increased employee contributions and reduced benefits packages) have been quickly implemented, other compensating trends (e.g., flexible benefits, core benefits for part-time employees) are taking longer to materialize. It is interesting to consider whether or not these changes will voluntarily occur or if legislation or labor organization will be required to promote them.

Although little overall change appears to have occurred within the management development dimension (see Figure 29-3), an item analysis reveals that 1987–1988 managers

- Are decidedly more optimistic regarding their promotional opportunities

- Are far more favorable regarding promotion based on capability
- See their organizations as less effective at developing people from within
- See their organizations as more likely to go outside to buy the talent they require

Although these findings are indicative of reasonable progress with regard to performance recognition and reward, they do not speak well of corporate training, internal development, or career-path planning initiatives during the 1982–1988 interval.

Although there has been little overall change on the Hay Group's image of the organization dimension, item analysis indicates three critical shifts.

1. Management morale has *improved* considerably;
2. Managers perceive that their organizations are *less* well regarded by the general public; and
3. Managers perceive that their organizations are *less* well regarded by rank and file employees.

These summary indicators (supported by other indicators from the Hay Employee Survey data base) suggest that by 1987–1988, many organizations had introduced significant changes affecting management personnel, but that these changes had not yet "trickled down" to rank and file employee groups. If this hypothesis is valid, it suggests that (1) U.S. business organizations may not have been changing appreciably to deal effectively with the needs of their rank and file employees; (2) much untapped potential remains at the bottom of organizations; and (3) the direction of change at least as it stood in 1987–1988 may be setting the stage for a reverse swing of the political pendulum.

CONCLUSION: THE NEED FOR ORGANIZATION CHANGE

The U.S. and international marketplaces are changing radically. U.S. business organizations are being challenged by the need to respond effectively to the opportunities presented. New strategic directions are being developed and pursued aided by popular support and radical change in domestic and international political initiatives.

Information from the Hay Group's Environmental Scan suggests that leadership organizations are implementing their strategic directions aided by significant changes in their organization's internal systems and processes. More and more effective models for organization problem solving are being effectively applied than ever before.

Data from the Hay Group's Organization Effectiveness Survey seem to indicate that these changes are having a positive effect on employee perceptions of clarity of direction, leadership style, performance orientation, and organization vitality. In other words, the new directions in organization change seem to be improving the organization's ability to meet new challenges and implement new strategic directions.

A discouraging insight contributed by the data seems to be that the positive impacts of organization change appears to be more clearly perceived at the top of business organizations. Rank and file employees may be sharing the costs of creating more competitive and flexible business organizations, but they may not be proportionately sharing in the tangible and intangible rewards. While it is reasonable for it to take some time for productive changes in selection, benefits, contingent compensation, organization job design, and the like to "trickle down" to lower-level employee groups, it seems urgent that these changes occur before U.S. business organizations lose the political support required to make them happen. Until "trickle-down" occurs, most of the promise of effective organization change may remain unrealized.

Much more could be said about how organizations are changing internal human resource management systems to accommodate new organization realities. A significant corporate trend not dealt with here involves the shift from passive, one-way communications to two-way, interactive communications. This shift and others mirror the sentiments of many observers who are calling for less management and more hands-on leadership.

It is also noteworthy that while these human resource systems can be separated out for purposes of explanation, these new directions almost always constitute part of an organic whole. For example, one might reasonably expect to find that an organization that uses interactive communications, gain sharing, and flexible benefits also has an employee assistance program and a corporate exercise facility. This may be because most of these new trends constitute a wholistic CEO vision of what an organization needs to be in order to survive, prosper, and grow amid new realities. It is interesting to consider whether or not individual changes adapted on an ad hoc basis bear the same chance of success as systematically planned comprehensive change.

Index

[Chapter numbers are boldface and are followed by a colon; lightface numbers after the colon refer to pages within the chapter.]

Forecasting *(cont'd)*
  producing forecasts
    existing products, **11:**7–10
    new products, **11:**13–14
  promotional usage of product
    existing products, **11:**6
    new products, **11:**12–13
  prophetic approach, **11:**16
  qualitative predictive models,
    11:14–16
  quantitative predictive models,
    11:16–24
  scenario approach, **8:**8–9
  surveys on new products, **10:**6–7
  time series methods, **8:**4, **11:**16–23
  unified approach, benefits, **11:**3
Foreign Corrupt Practices Act, **9:**13
Foreign countries
  See also Global strategy;
    International trade;
    Multinational corporations
  emergence of companies as
    significant force, **9:**4
  specialization by business
    community in, **9:**24
  state-owned companies, **9:**4–5
Frequency of reviews, corporate-level
  reviews of multibusiness company
  units, **24:**10
Functional organizational structure,
  23:6–9
  multibusiness company's choice of
    strategy, effect on, **24:**11–12

G

Gaining market share. *See* Market
  share, strategy to increase
Gainsharing, **26:**21–22
Gap between current and desired
  positions, **8:**10–12
Generally accepted accounting
  principles, **7:**5–6, 10, 17
Generic competitive strategies, **24:**4–5
Geographic organizational structure,
  23:13–14
Giveaways of products, effect on
  forecasting, **11:**6, 12–13
Global strategy, **Ch. 22**
  See also International trade;
    Multinational corporations

current awareness of competition
  and customers, **22:**3
customer service, location of facility,
  22:9
developing global perspective, **22:**4
distribution channels, **22:**8–11
flexibility needed, **22:**2–6
global sourcing, **22:**10
information-based partnerships,
  22:6–9
integration needed, **22:**4–7
  external, **22:**6–7
  internal, **22:**4–6
leadership needed, **22:**6
location of manufacturing and
  distribution facilities, **22:**9–10
logistics management, **9:**13–14,
  12:7–8
materials management, **22:**11
network planning issues, **22:**9–10
new products, **22:**10
operational redesign, **22:**5
organizational structure suited to,
  23:13–14
post-merger synergy, **22:**10
reengineering needed, **22:**4–7
technology's effect on, **9:**23–24, **22:**5
transportation issues, **22:**9, 11–13
U.S.-Canada trade agreement,
  ramifications, **22:**10
Golden handcuffs
  non-equity incentives as, **25:**14–15
  restricted stock as, **25:**7
Government action
  See also Political strategy;
    Regulatory policies of
    government
  competitive implications for
    business, **20:**9–11
  divestiture due to, **12:**34
  educating managers about, **20:**6–9
  multinational corporations, relations
    with foreign governments,
    9:14–15
  participation in, **20:**11–13
Grass-roots political action, **20:**12
Growth. *See* Market share, strategy to
  increase
Guarantee of employment for
  managers after acquisition, **15:**9
Gullibility causing mistake in strategy,
  4:10